MW01620727

Principles of Perfection

Principles of Perfection

Hyrum L. Andrus

Volume II

Foundations of the Millennial Kingdom of Christ

Deseret Book Company
Salt Lake City, Utah

First printing, 1970
Revised pagination and typography, 1999

Library of Congress Cataloging Card Number: 68-56891

ISBN 1-57345-463-X

Printed in the United States of America 18961-4610

10 9 8 7 6 5 4 3 2 1

To Helen Mae

. . . I give unto you a commandment, to teach these things freely unto your children, saying:

That by reason of transgression cometh the fall, which fall bringeth death, and inasmuch as ye were born into the world by water, and blood, and the spirit, which I have made, and so became of dust a living soul, even so ye must be born again into the kingdom of heaven, of water, and of the Spirit, and be cleansed by blood, even the blood of mine Only Begotten, that ye may be sanctified from all sin, and enjoy the words of eternal life in this world, and eternal life in the world to come, even immortal glory;

For by the water ye keep the commandment; by the Spirit ye are justified, and by the blood ye are sanctified;

Therefore it is given to abide in you; the record of heaven; the Comforter; the peaceable things of immortal glory; the truth of all things; that which quickeneth all things, which maketh alive all things; that which knoweth all things, and hath all power according to wisdom, mercy, truth, justice, and judgment.

And now, behold, I say unto you: This is the plan of salvation unto all men, through the blood of mine Only Begotten, who shall come in the meridian of time.—THE REVELATION OF THE GOSPEL TO ADAM.

Contents

KEY TO ABBREVIATIONS USED IN NOTES

The Bible, Book of Mormon, and Pearl of Great Price references are made by name of book, chapter, and verse. Thus—Genesis 4:3, Mosiah 2:9, or Moses 3:7.

The Doctrine and Covenants references are made by the abbreviation D&C followed by the section and verse. Thus—D&C 93:36.

Names of books in The Book of Mormon:

1 Nephi	Alma
2 Nephi	Helaman
Jacob	3 Nephi
Enos	4 Nephi
Jarom	Mormon
Omni	Ether
Words of Mormon	Moroni
Mosiah	

Names of units in The Pearl of Great Price:

Moses	Smith 2
Abraham	Articles of Faith
Smith 1	

Preface

Principles of Perfection, the second volume in a series of four on the thought and teachings of the Prophet Joseph Smith,[1] is an analysis of the program of the gospel of Jesus Christ which was restored to earth through the latter-day Seer. Joseph Smith taught that the primary purpose of the plan of life and salvation is to bring man into a meaningful spiritual union with the Son of God so that he can be taught and renewed spiritually by the Master, through the Holy Spirit. The Prophet held that only within this divine union can man develop to his full potential as an eternal being and be glorified in Christ as Jesus is glorified in the Father.

It follows that the value of a theological analysis of the gospel is that it may show man, through the systematic treatment of the principles, laws, and ordinances of the plan of life and salvation, how to achieve the primary purpose of that divine plan. Such a study may also help man to understand why he must achieve the spiritual union with Christ which the gospel makes possible, and what benefits he may expect to receive by subordinating his life in truth to Christ.

Since the gospel is an expanding system of eternal truth and power with continuous revelation as the essence of the divine program, no man can write the *Summa Theologiae* (the sum of theology) of the plan of life and salvation. By revelation, the Lord instructed the Saints: "Teach ye diligently and my grace shall attend you, *that you may be instructed more perfectly in theory, in principle, in doctrine, in the law of the gospel, in all things that pertain unto the kingdom of God, that are expedient for you to understand.*"[2] There are various levels of insight into divine truth, and an analysis of the gospel such as is found in this book is but a treatment of the expanding plan on a given plane—not the last or complete word on the subject. The Prophet wrote: "The things of God are of deep import; and time, and experience, and careful and ponderous and solemn thoughts can only find them out."[3]

In this study, I have tried to present Joseph Smith's thought in the depth and breadth that evidence makes possible. In areas where his teachings are not fully reported or made clear, I have qualified my conclusions accordingly. Though others have read parts of the manuscript and have offered helpful suggestions, I alone am responsible for the views expressed in this book and for the conclusions that have been drawn from the evidence available. This is not an authoritative work setting forth the doctrines of The Church of Jesus Christ of Latter-day Saints, but a study based on more than twenty years of research, analysis, and teaching on the subject.

I give special thanks to my wife, Helen Mae, for her intelligent assistance over the years and for her help in preparing this manuscript for publication. Paul Toscano, my student assistant at Brigham Young University, made some helpful suggestions in the arrangement of materials in the early chapters. I am also indebted to the following men for reading parts of the manuscript and offering advice and counsel: Dr. Ellis T. Rasmussen, Chairman of the Department of Ancient Scripture at Brigham Young University; Dr. Richard L. Anderson, Professor of Religious Instruction at Brigham Young University; and A. Bent Peterson, past President of the Manti Temple. I express appreciation to Don E. Norton, Jr., Assistant Coordinator of Freshman English at Brigham Young University, for his valuable assistance in reading the manuscript and checking its style and grammar. Finally, I give special thanks to George Bickerstaff for his careful work in the final preparation of the manuscript for publication.

Hyrum L. Andrus, DSS
Professor of Religious Instruction
Brigham Young University
June 1, 1970

Notes

1. Volume I is entitled *God, Man, And The Universe.*
2. D&C 88:78.
3. HC, III, p. 295. See footnote 1, chapter 1, to identify this source.

1

The Gospel and Its Objectives

. . . this is the gospel, the glad tidings, which the voice out of the heavens bore record unto us—

That he came into the world, even Jesus, to be crucified for the world, and to bear the sins of the world, and to sanctify the world, and to cleanse it from all unrighteousness;

That through him all might be saved whom the Father had put into his power and made by him;

Who glorifies the Father, and saves all the works of his hands, except those sons of perdition who deny the Son after the Father has revealed him.—JOSEPH SMITH.

That which distinguished Joseph Smith from other prominent men of his age was the claim that through him the gospel of Jesus Christ had been restored to earth in its purity and in its fulness. In 1823, the angel Moroni informed the young prophet that "the time was at hand for the Gospel in all its fullness to be preached in power, unto all nations *that a people might be prepared for the Millennial reign.*"[1] The divine program was to be a new principle for regenerating man which was not then known in the modern world. "The great designs of God in relation to the salvation of the human family, are very little understood by the professedly wise and intelligent generation in which we live," Joseph Smith explained.[2] He was sent as a prophet of God to make clear its message and program. "I never design to communicate any ideas but what are simple," the Prophet declared; "for to this end I am sent."[3]

Basic Concepts Of The Gospel

Central Place of Christ in the Gospel

The gospel of Jesus Christ is often defined as the good news, or glad tidings, of salvation. This it is. Joseph Smith wrote: "Now, what do we hear in the gospel which we have received? A voice of gladness! A voice of mercy from heaven; and a voice of truth out of the earth."[4] But the Prophet more specifically stressed "that it was one thing to proclaim good tidings, and another to tell what these good tidings were."[5]

The glad tidings which the gospel proclaims concern Jesus Christ and that which He did to bring about the salvation of man from his fallen state. Joseph Smith therefore declared that the fundamental principle of the gospel "is the testimony of the apostles and prophets concerning Jesus Christ, that He died, was buried, and rose again the third day, and ascended into heaven." Of this central principle the latter-day Seer said: "All other things which pertain to our religion are only appendages to it."[6]

Being the central figure in the divine plan of life and salvation, Christ is honored by having that plan named after Him. He is the light and the life of the world, for He is the source of the divine powers of truth, light, life, and godliness which man receives from the Father. The plan of salvation, therefore, is called the gospel of Jesus Christ. But the truth and power which Jesus gives to man originate with the Father, Elohim, and Christ came to earth to do the will of the Man of Holiness. The gospel is the Father's plan of salvation for man.[7]

As Jesus ministered to the Nephites after His resurrection, special attention was given to the primary message of the gospel. As He descended from heaven, the voice of the Father declared: "Behold my Beloved Son, in whom I am well pleased, in whom I have glorified my name—hear ye him."[8] Christ then stretched forth His hand and said:

> . . . I am Jesus Christ, whom the prophets testified shall come into the world.

> And behold, I am the light and the life of the world; and I have drunk out of that bitter cup which the Father hath given me, and have glorified the Father in taking upon me the sins of the world, in the which I have suffered the will of the Father in all things from the beginning.[9]

That there might be no mistake concerning His identity and the nature of the mission which He performed in making the atonement, Jesus then said: "Arise and come forth unto me, that ye may thrust your hands into my side, and also that ye may feel the prints of the nails in my hands and in my feet, that ye may know that I am the God of Israel, and the God of the whole earth, and have been slain for the sins of the world."[10]

Thus the testimony of Jesus was given to the Nephites with unimpeachable evidence to support the central truths of the divine plan of life and salvation. Christ later elaborated upon the foundations of the gospel, saying:

> . . . I have given unto you my gospel, and this is the gospel which I have given unto you—that I came into the world to do the will of the Father, because my Father sent me.
>
> And my Father sent me that I might be lifted up upon the cross; and after that I had been lifted up upon the cross, that I might draw all men unto me, that as I have been lifted up by men even so should men be lifted up by the Father, to stand before me, to be judged of their works, whether they be good or whether they be evil—
>
> And for this cause have I been lifted up; therefore, according to the power of the Father I will draw all men unto me, that they may be judged according to their works.[11]

The message of Christ as given in the above declarations and others which are found in the scriptures may be categorized into the following statements concerning Him:

1. He is the Son of God—the Only Begotten Son of the Father, the Man of Holiness.
2. He is the Messiah, the Anointed One, whom the prophets testified would come into the world.
3. He is the light and the life of the world in that the glory of the Father is first extended to Him and given through Him to others.

4. He came to earth to acquire a physical body as part of the divine plan for His own eternal progression and that of others.

5. He came to do the will of the Father—to be the light and the life of the world, to establish the way of salvation, and to drink of the bitter cup which the Father gave Him.

6. He came to descend below all things in His mortal experience and in His atonement, that He might comprehend all things and thereby know intelligently how to succor His people and lead them from spiritual darkness and death unto light.

7. He came that He might be lifted up upon the cross, to satisfy the demands of divine justice in relation to Adam's transgression and the sins of all men.

8. He came to break the bands of physical death on earth.

9. He came to overcome the world's spiritual death.

10. He came to acquire the fulness of the Father's glory and to develop that glory in others according to their willingness to receive it.

11. He came to gain the right and the power to lift all men up in the resurrection and to judge them at the last day.

By fulfilling His divine mission on earth, Jesus became man's redeemer, his mediator with the Father, his judge, and his advocate before the Man of Holiness. The proclamation of these glorious truths constitutes the foundation of the gospel message.

Man's Obligations and Promises in the Gospel

Like a coin, the gospel of Jesus Christ may be said to have two sides and two separate but related inscriptions. On one side is inscribed the glad tidings concerning the Son of God and that which He did to establish the program of salvation in the world. On the other side is inscribed that which fallen man must do in order to be reconciled to God and to partake of the mercy, truth, and power of the great Redeemer unto eternal life.

Having proclaimed that part of the gospel which related directly to His mission, Jesus explained to the Nephites what man must do to fulfill his obligations in the plan of life and salvation. "No unclean thing can enter into his [the Father's] kingdom," Christ observed; "therefore nothing entereth into his rest save it be those who have washed their garments in my blood, because of their faith, and the repentance of all their sins, and their faithfulness unto the end." Of the way man must come unto Jesus to accomplish these objectives, the Master said: "Now this is the commandment: Repent, all ye ends of the earth, and come unto me and be baptized in my name, that ye may be sanctified by the reception of the Holy Ghost, that ye may stand spotless before me at the last day." Concluding, Jesus stressed: "Verily, verily, I say unto you, this is my gospel."[12]

In another statement to the Nephites, Jesus said:

> . . . this is my doctrine, [that] . . . whoso believeth in me, and is baptized, the same shall be saved; and they are they who shall inherit the kingdom of God; . . . and whoso believeth in me believeth in the Father also; and unto him will the Father bear record of me, for he will visit him with fire and with the Holy Ghost.[13]

This is the message which was revealed to the world in modern times through the Book of Mormon as a new witness for Christ. Concerning the way that leads to eternal life, Nephi said:

> . . . the gate by which ye should enter is repentance and baptism by water; and then cometh a remission of your sins by fire and by the Holy Ghost. *And then are ye in this straight and narrow path which leads to eternal life;* yea, ye have entered in by the gate; ye have done according to the commandments of the Father and the Son; and ye have received the Holy Ghost, which witnesses of the Father and the Son, unto the fulfilling of the promise which he hath made, that if ye entered in by the way ye should receive.[14]

Jacob, the brother of Nephi, explained:

> . . . he [God] commandeth all men that they must repent, and be baptized in his name, having perfect faith in the Holy One of Israel, or they cannot be saved in the kingdom of God.
>
> And if they will not repent and believe in his name, and be baptized in his name, and endure to the end, they must be damned; for the Lord God, the Holy One of Israel, has spoken it.[15]

Revelations given to Joseph Smith define the basic program of the gospel in similar terms. One said in January of 1831: "And this is my gospel—repentance and baptism by water, and then cometh the baptism of fire and the Holy Ghost, even the Comforter, which showeth all things, and teacheth the peaceable things of the kingdom."[16] Another revelation instructed:

> . . . open your mouths and they shall be filled, saying: Repent . . . and be baptized, every one of you, for a remission of your sins; yea, be baptized even by water, and then cometh the baptism of fire and of the Holy Ghost.
>
> Behold, verily, verily, I say unto you, this is my gospel; and remember that they shall have faith in me or they can in nowise be saved; and upon this rock I will build my church. . . .[17]

The basic message of the gospel as it pertains to man's responsibility in the divine plan of life and salvation may be categorized into the following points:

1. Man must exercise living faith in Jesus Christ as the Son of God and the Savior of the world.
2. He must repent of all sin.
3. Man must be baptized in water to obtain a remission of personal sins.
4. He must receive the baptism of fire and the Holy Ghost, which is given as a gift of God to those who come unto God in the right way.

By complying with these requirements, man can enter the straight and narrow path which leads to eternal life. By continuing in that path in obedience to the higher principles and ordinances of the gospel, he can finally enter into the presence of God crowned with glory and power.

First Principles and Ordinances of the Gospel

In referring to that phase of the divine plan of life and salvation which pertains to man and his obligations, Joseph Smith said: "The first principles of the Gospel are faith, repentance, baptism for the remission of sins, with the promise of the Holy Ghost."[18] These principles are also the first ordinances, or channels of divine mercy and power, in the plan of salvation. In identifying them as such and in stating their relationship to the atonement of Christ, the Prophet wrote:

> We believe that through the atonement of Christ all mankind may be saved by obedience to the laws and ordinances of the Gospel. We believe that these *ordinances* are 1st, Faith in the Lord Jesus Christ; 2d, Repentance; 3d, Baptism by immersion for the remission of sins; 4th, Laying on of hands for the gift of the Holy Ghost.[19]

Since these principles are also the initial ordinances of the gospel, it is proper to designate them as "the first principles and ordinances of the Gospel," as does the current version of the Articles of Faith.[20]

Necessity of All the Principles and Ordinances

Each principle and ordinance of the gospel is a necessary step in acquiring the grace and power of Jesus Christ. Each step is designed to prepare and guide those who express genuine faith into full spiritual union with God. The principles of the gospel constitute the essential truths within the divine plan, while the ordinances of the gospel are the designated rites or ceremonies which act as channels through which the mercy and power of God are extended to man. The laws of the gospel set forth the standard of conduct that teaches the exactness of Christ, and they reveal the need for man's nature to be changed so that he can attain to the righteousness of God. All who exercise living faith in Christ and apply the principles of the gospel in their lives are given, through the ordinances of the gospel, strength, power, and enlightenment by the

Holy Spirit to enable them to obey the laws of God. In turn, obedience to the laws of the gospel brings a greater manifestation of divine truth and power into the life of man, which results in a more perfect union with Christ.

It follows that it would be futile for man to believe in only one principle or to receive only one ordinance of the gospel without eventually receiving and applying them all. Joseph Smith therefore considered baptism of water and the baptism of fire, or the Holy Ghost, as being "necessarily and inseparably connected."[21] He said:

> You might as well baptize a bag of sand as a man, if not done in view of the remission of sins and getting of the Holy Ghost. Baptism by water is but half a baptism, and is good for nothing without the other half—that is, the baptism of the Holy Ghost.[22]

Speaking of the interrelationship of all the first principles and ordinances of the gospel, the Prophet said:

> We discover, in order to be benefited by the doctrine of repentance, we must believe in obtaining the remission of sins. And in order to obtain the remission of sins, we must believe in the doctrine of baptism in the name of the Lord Jesus Christ. And if we believe in baptism for the remission of sins, we may expect a fulfillment of the promise of the Holy Ghost, for the promise extends to all whom the Lord our God shall call.[23]

The above program is but the foundation of the gospel upon which man must build. After having complied with the first principles and ordinances of the gospel and having thereby established his life upon the gifts, powers, and blessings of the Holy Ghost, man must continue in the program of the gospel and meet the challenge which Jesus made to the Nephites when He said: "Whoso repenteth and is baptized in my name shall be filled; and if he endureth to the end, behold, him will I hold guiltless before my Father at that day when I shall stand to judge the world."[24]

Gospel of Reconciliation

Joseph Smith referred to the plan of life and salvation as "the Gospel of reconciliation."[25] First, by the infinite atonement which He made, Jesus reconciled the demands of eternal law for the sins of all men; He paid the full debt of justice for Adam and all his descendants to the latest generation. Second, having reconciled the demands of divine law, Christ requires all men to be reconciled to Him as their Redeemer. Herein the two major phases of the gospel plan are expressed. In his Inspired Revision of the Bible, the Prophet corrected the biblical rendering of the Apostle Paul's statement on the gospel of reconciliation to read:

> . . . if any man live in Christ, he is a new creature; old things are passed away; behold, all things are become new,
>
> And receiveth all the things of God, *who hath reconciled us to himself by Jesus Christ, and hath given to us the ministry of reconciliation:*
>
> To wit, *that God is in Christ, reconciling the world unto himself,* not imputing their trespasses unto them; and *hath committed unto us the word of reconciliation.*
>
> Now then we are ambassadors for Christ, as though God did beseech you by us; *we pray you in Christ's stead, be ye reconciled to God.*
>
> For he hath made him to be sin for us, who knew no sin; that we might be made the righteousness of God in him.[26]

The task of reconciling himself to Christ requires preparation on the part of man and is not to be achieved in a moment. Having spoken of the final place which man may attain through the gospel, Joseph Smith said: "But we consider that this is a station to which no man ever arrived in a moment: he must have been instructed in the government and laws of that kingdom by proper degrees, until his mind is capable in some measure of comprehending the propriety, justice, equality, and consistency of the same."[27] Only when man is able to understand and fully apply God's perfect law of liberty and truth in his life can the gospel of reconciliation fulfill its final purpose.

Doctrines of Resurrection and Eternal Judgment

Having reconciled the demands of eternal law and having provided man with the divine program by which it is possible for him to be reconciled to God, Jesus then designs to raise all men from the grave and judge them according to the way they respond to the message of truth and life. These actions will complete the program of the gospel for man. Joseph F. Smith, nephew of the Prophet and a President of the Church, said: "If there is one principle of the gospel of Jesus Christ that goes directly to the very foundation of justice and righteousness, it is that great and glorious and God-like principle that every man will have to render an account for that which he does, and every man will be rewarded for his works, whether they be good or evil."[28]

Since the actions of resurrection and judgment are basic in the plan of life and salvation, Joseph Smith stated that "the Doctrine of the Resurrection of the Dead and the Eternal Judgment are necessary to preach among the first principles of the Gospel of Jesus Christ."[29] The Prophet explained "that the doctrine of eternal judgment was perfectly understood by the [ancient] Apostles."[30] Because the message of man's accountability to God in the resurrection is inseparably associated with the proclamation of the gospel, the Quorum of the Twelve instructed the Elders: "Preach the first principles of the doctrine of Christ—faith in the Lord Jesus Christ, repentance toward God, baptism in the name of Jesus Christ for the remission of sins, laying on of hands for the gift of the Holy Ghost, *the resurrection of the dead, and eternal judgment.*"[31]

Christ made the atonement in order to bring about the resurrection and judgment of all men. "He suffereth this that the resurrection might pass upon all men," Jacob declared, "that all might stand before him at the great and judgment day."[32] Having explained that as He had been "lifted up by men," even so will all men be "lifted up by the Father" to stand before Him to be judged, Jesus said to the Nephites:

> . . . for this cause have I been lifted up; therefore, according

to the power of the Father I will draw all men unto me, that they may be judged according to their works.

And it shall come to pass, that whoso repenteth and is baptized in my name shall be filled; and if he endureth to the end, behold, him will I hold guiltless before my Father at that day when I shall stand to judge the world.

And he that endureth not unto the end, the same is he that is also hewn down and cast into the fire, from whence they can no more return [to the presence of God], because of the justice of the Father.

And this is the word which he hath given unto the children of men.[33]

As Jesus said, this is the word, or the gospel, which God has declared unto men.

The doctrines of resurrection and eternal judgment were basic elements in the message of the gospel which the Nephite prophets taught. Having explained that mercy is given to the penitent through the atonement of Jesus Christ, Alma continued: " . . . and the atonement bringeth to pass the resurrection of the dead; and the resurrection of the dead bringeth back men into the presence of God; and thus they are restored into his presence, to be judged according to their works, according to the law and justice."[34]

The actions of resurrection and judgment occur for all men, whether they are wicked or righteous. In confirming the teachings of Amulek to the people of Ammonihah, Alma said:

. . . Amulek hath spoken plainly concerning death, and being raised from this mortality to a state of immortality, and being brought before the bar of God, to be judged according to our works.

Then if our hearts have been hardened, yea, if we have hardened our hearts against the word, insomuch that it has not been found in us, then will our state be awful, for then we shall be condemned.

For our words will condemn us, yea, all our works will condemn us; we shall not be found spotless; and our thoughts will also condemn us; and in this awful state we shall not dare to look up to our God; and we would fain be glad if we could command the rocks and the mountains to fall upon us to hide us from his presence.

But this cannot be; we must come forth and stand before him in his glory, and in his power, and in his might, majesty, and dominion, and acknowledge to our everlasting shame that all his judgments are just; that he is just in all his works, and that he is merciful unto the children of men, and that he has all power to save every man that believeth on his name and bringeth forth fruit meet for repentance.[35]

The Gospel A Plan Of Mercy, Truth, And Power

The Gospel the Power of God unto Salvation

"The Apostle [Paul] says the gospel is the power of God unto salvation unto them that believe," Joseph Smith observed; "and also informs us that life and immortality were brought to light through the gospel."[36] Having cited Paul's definition of the gospel, Sidney Rigdon explained:

> It is God's scheme of saving men, and this scheme is made known in the New Testament, which scheme of things (or gospel) consists in putting men in possession of the power of God; for it is God's *power* to save men. And how is it God's power unto salvation? Answer, by putting those who receive it into possession of the power of God.[37]

Other leading men among the Saints stressed this view of the gospel. Lorenzo Snow reasoned: "It would be simply foolish indeed to expect the Latter-day Saints in these last days to comply with the celestial law that proceeds from God, and with his designs to elevate the people into his presence, except they were sustained by a supernatural power." The manifestation of divine power is necessary, Elder Snow continued, that men might be prepared to endure the trials and afflictions required "to prepare them more fully for celestial glory; so that they should walk not in darkness, but in the light and power of God, and be raised above the things of the world, and be superior to the things around them; so that they might walk independently beneath the celestial world, and in the sight of God and heaven, as free men, pursuing that course that should be marked out to them by the Holy Ghost; that course by which they could elevate themselves to knowledge and power, and thus prepare themselves to receive the glory that God proposes to confer upon them."[38]

When man reconciles himself to God through the gospel, the Holy Spirit comes to him in comfort, in enlightenment, in strength, and in power. Joseph Smith observed that those saints who faithfully apply the principles and ordinances of the gospel in their lives may expect to have the Holy Ghost as their "constant companion";[39] and by walking in the light and power of the Spirit, they may finally "grow up" in Christ and "receive a fulness of the Holy Ghost."[40] In voicing this objective, Brigham Young said: "I want to see men and women breathe the Holy Ghost in every breath of their lives, living constantly in the light of God's countenance."[41]

The Gospel a Program of Human Regeneration

The gospel is a divine program by which man can be regenerated and made a "new creature"[42] in Christ. Jesus spoke of His disciples as those who were following Him in "the regeneration" which leads to immortal glory.[43] This regeneration is necessary because, by the transgression of Adam, mortal man is in a fallen state.[44] Unless he is transformed by the living power of Christ, he cannot inherit the kingdom of heaven.[45]

It takes divine truth and power to regenerate man so that he is able to enter into the presence of God. Moroni declared that God works "by power, according to the faith of the children of men, the same today and tomorrow and forever."[46] Only in this way can man rise out of spiritual darkness and death into the light and life of God's glory. "That which is of God is light," a revelation explained; "and he that receiveth light, and continueth in God, receiveth more light; and that light groweth brighter and brighter until the perfect day."[47] Another revelation stated that if the Spirit "be in you it shall abound." It then added: "And if your eye be single to my glory, your whole bodies shall be filled with light, and there shall be no darkness in you." By following this path, man can enter eventually into the presence of God. The revelation concluded: "Therefore, sanctify yourselves that your minds become single to God, and the days will come that you shall see him; for he will unveil his face unto you."[48]

To such extent did Nephi and Moroni view the gospel as being an enlightening and transforming power, they declared that those who obey the requirements of the divine program will be able to "speak with a new tongue, yea, even with the tongue of angels."[49] By means of this divine, regenerating power, the Nephites were made alive in Christ."[50] Joseph Smith considered this renewal a literal and tangible transformation. He wrote by revelation that the Saints could be "sanctified by the Spirit unto the renewing of their bodies."[51] He and others also spoke of the Spirit as having actual physical effects upon the body that could be observed outwardly by others.[52]

The Gospel a Plan to Redeem Man from the Fall

As a divine plan for regenerating man spiritually, the gospel is designed to redeem him from his fallen state in mortality. The plan of life and salvation should therefore be seen in light of the doctrines which have been set forth in earlier chapters of this work[53]—the doctrine of God, the state of life in the creation, the fall of Adam, the nature of man in mortality, and the atonement of Jesus Christ. Joseph Smith set the basic program of the gospel in this context when he wrote by revelation:

> . . . there is a God in heaven, who is infinite and eternal, from everlasting to everlasting the same unchangeable God, the framer of heaven and earth, and all things which are in them;
>
> And . . . he created man, male and female, after his own image and in his own likeness, created he them;
>
> And gave unto them commandments that they should love

and serve him, the only living and true God, and that he should be the only being whom they should worship.

But by the transgression of these holy laws man became sensual and devilish, and became fallen man.

Wherefore, the Almighty God gave his Only Begotten Son, as it is written in those scriptures which have been given of him.

He suffered temptations but gave no heed unto them.

He was crucified, died, and rose again the third day;

And ascended into heaven, to sit down on the right hand of the Father, to reign with almighty power according to the will of the Father;

That as many as would believe and be baptized in his holy name, and endure in faith to the end, should be saved—

Not only those who believed after he came in the meridian of time, in the flesh, but all those from the beginning, even as many as were before he came, who believed in the words of the holy prophets, who spake as they were inspired by the gift of the Holy Ghost, who truly testified of him in all things, *should have eternal life,*

As well as those who should come after, *who should believe in the gifts and callings of God by the Holy Ghost,* which beareth record of the Father and of the Son;

Which Father, Son, and Holy Ghost is one God, infinite and eternal, without end. Amen.

And we know that all men must repent and believe on the name of Jesus Christ, and worship the Father in his name, and endure in faith on his name to the end, or they cannot be saved in the kingdom of God.[54]

Preparatory Gospel Compared with Everlasting Gospel

The divine plan of the gospel can be divided into two general divisions: (1) the preparatory gospel and (2) the fulness of the everlasting gospel. The preparatory gospel is the initial phase of the divine plan, and it is designed to "prepare the way for a greater revelation of God."[55] A revelation explained that the preparatory gospel as taught by John the Baptist in New Testament times consisted of "the gospel of repentance and of baptism, and the remission of sins, and the law of carnal commandments."[56] The fulness of the everlasting gospel, on the other hand, is the higher program of salvation which is concerned with developing in man the divine truths, powers, gifts, and blessings of the Holy Spirit until he is able to partake of the divine nature, or glory, of God and make his calling and election sure to a fulness of glory in the resurrection. When President Martin Van Buren asked Joseph Smith how the Latter-day Saints were different in their religious system from other faiths, the Prophet explained that they "differed in mode of baptism, and the gift of the Holy Ghost." "All other considerations," he assumed, "were contained in the gift of the Holy Ghost."[57] The earthly program of this higher phase of the plan of life and salvation is consummated when man receives the fulness of the sealing power of the priesthood.

The preparatory gospel is administered by the authority of the Aaronic Priesthood. When Joseph Smith and Oliver Cowdery received this priesthood, they were told that the work which they could perform by its authority was "a preparatory work, or a going before." Their office and authority "did not extend to the laying on of hands for the giving of the Holy Ghost." That was "a greater work."[58]

The everlasting gospel is administered by the authority of the Melchizedek Priesthood. Of the higher priesthood a revelation said: "This greater priesthood administereth the gospel and holdeth the key to the mysteries of the kingdom, even the key of the knowledge of God."[59] That knowledge includes more than theological concepts. It consists, essentially, of the personal revelation of God to man through the power of the Holy Ghost, and the knowledge which man can acquire by coming into the presence of God and being made like Him. The above revelation continues:

> Therefore, in the ordinances thereof [of the Melchizedek Priesthood], the power of godliness is manifest.
>
> And without the ordinances thereof, and the authority of the priesthood, the power of godliness is not manifest unto men in the flesh;
>
> For without this [the power of godliness] no man can see the face of God, even the Father, and live.[60]

The term "preparatory gospel" implies that when this phase of the plan of salvation is completed it may then be terminated. That which prepares man for a higher program is fulfilled and consummated when he is established fully on the greater law.[61] This may have been what John the Baptist meant when he said, as he conferred the Aaronic Priesthood upon Joseph Smith and Oliver Cowdery: " . . . and this shall never be taken again from the earth, *until* the sons of Levi do offer again an offering unto the Lord in righteousness."[62] The statement implies that when the designated sacrifice is made, the functions of the Aaronic Priesthood which the angel specified may be discontinued in the earth.

Joseph Smith indicated that one aspect of the sacrifice by the sons of Levi[63]—that sacrifice which is to be accomplished by service in the priesthood—can be made by the Saints administering the ordinances of the gospel to others.[64] When the preparatory gospel has been given to all who will receive it, who are appointed to come to the earth, its functions may then be discontinued. There will be no need to preach repentance or administer baptism to those who dwell on the resurrected and celestialized earth; nor will the ministry of angels, a function related to the preparatory gospel, be required for those who dwell in the presence of God.

By contrast, the everlasting gospel is designed to bring man into a spiritual union with God which will never cease. Unlike the preparatory gospel, there will be no point, either in time or in eternity, when the program of the everlasting gospel will be fulfilled or consummated. Jesus declared to the brother of Jared: "In me shall all mankind have light [i.e., glory], *and that eternally,* even they who shall believe on my name."[65] The faithful will continue to receive light and truth, or glory, through Christ forever.[66]

Objectives And Purposes Of The Gospel

Man's Ultimate Goal in the Gospel

Joseph Smith taught that before man can successfully apply the gospel in his life, he must understand the ultimate objective to which the plan of life and salvation leads. He wrote by revelation that the Saints should look to the "end of their salvation."[67] In expressing the great objective of the gospel, the Prophet said: "It is the first principle of the gospel [i.e., the initial proposition upon which the divine plan rests] to know for a certainty the character of God, and *to know that we may converse with Him as one man converses with another.*"[68] On another occasion, he spoke of the gospel as "the plan of redemption, a power of atonement, a scheme of salvation, *having as its great objects, the bringing of men back into the presence of the King of heaven, crowning them in the celestial glory, and making them heirs with the Son to that inheritance which is incorruptible, undefiled, and which fadeth not away.*"[69] Because this is man's goal in the gospel, a revelation admonished the Saints to "seek the face of the Lord always."[70] "How indescribably glorious are these things to mankind," the latter-day Seer exclaimed! "Of a truth they may be considered tidings of great joy to all people; and tidings, too, that ought to fill the earth and cheer the heart of every one when sounded in his ear."[71]

The How and What of True Worship

Joseph Smith taught that by true worship man can acquire the attributes and powers of God through the Holy Spirit until he is able to receive a fulness of the Father's glory in the resurrection. The Prophet explained: "As the Son partakes of the fullness of the Father through the Spirit, so the saints are, by the same Spirit, to be partakers of the same fullness, to enjoy the same glory."[72] This, essentially, is the purpose of true worship. In expressing vital insight into the nature of God's glory, a revelation stated:

> I give unto you these sayings *that you may understand and know how to worship, and know what you worship,* that you may come unto the Father in my [Christ's] name, and in due time receive of his fulness.
>
> For if you keep my commandments you shall receive of his fulness, and be glorified in me as I am in the Father; therefore, I say unto you, you shall receive grace for grace.[73]

The several points in this statement enable man to see clearly the nature and purpose of true worship. First, man must recognize that God is a personal being of glory and power.

Second, man must approach the Father, Elohim, in the name of His Son, Jesus Christ.[74] This is the only name which is given under heaven whereby salvation can come unto man.[75] In Christ are centered the glory and power of the Father which are to be given to man.[76]

Third, man's purpose in true worship is to obtain divine truth and power until, in due time, he receives a fulness of the Father's glory. Jesus is the great prototype. He did not possess the fulness of the Father's glory at first.[77] But by obedience to the will of the Father, He finally obtained a fulness.[78] True worship is designed to make man like Christ in possessing the glory and power of the Man of Holiness.

Fourth, man must keep the commandments of Christ in order to receive a fulness of glory. Of the relationship of obedience to the glorification of man, the revelation says: "He that keepeth his [God's] commandments receiveth truth and light, until he is glorified in truth and knoweth all things."[79]

Fifth, though it is the truth and power of the Father, Elohim, which man receives in true worship, these things are given to him through Christ; and man must be glorified in Christ, as Jesus is glorified in the Father. For this reason Christ made the atonement, "that he might be in all and through all things, the light of truth."[80] The glorification of man in Christ, as He is glorified in the Father, is the consummation of the Master's purpose regarding those who obey His law of redemption.[81]

Finally, man must receive "grace for grace" in acquiring the glory of God; he must receive grace from God by giving grace to others.[82] Service in doing the will of God is the key to the spiritual development of man. Man can truly worship only by serving his fellow men in the way marked out by the law of God. By receiving grace for grace, Jesus finally acquired a fulness of the glory of the Father.[83] Man must do the same. A basic difference between Christ and man is that man is in need of a remission of personal sins, while Jesus was not. But when man receives a remission of sins through the preparatory gospel, he is in a situation similar to that of Jesus, in His acquisition of the glory of God. Man must then give grace to others, in doing the will of God, until he develops from grace to grace and finally receives a fulness of the glory of the Father. Wilford Woodruff explained:

> The revelations of Jesus Christ teach us that the Saviour was born in the flesh; and the Father said that He did not give him a fulness [of glory] at first, but [He] continued from grace to grace until he had received a fulness, and was called the Son of God because he did not receive a fulness at first. *We in like manner should seek with all our souls to grow in grace, light, and truth, that in due time we may receive a fulness.*[84]

An incident in the life of Moses illustrates the central purpose of the gospel and of true worship. Having beheld Christ in the glory and power of the Father, Moses was later tempted by Satan, who came unto him saying: "Moses, son of man, worship me." But Moses responded:

> Who art thou? For behold, I am a son of God, in the similitude of his Only Begotten; and *where is thy glory, that I should worship thee?* . . .
>
> For behold, I could not look upon God, except his glory should come upon me, and I were strengthened before him. But I can look upon thee in the natural man. Is it not so, surely?
>
> Blessed be the name of my God, for his Spirit hath not altogether withdrawn from me, or else where is thy glory, for it is darkness unto me?[85]

When Lucifer persisted and again commanded Moses to worship him, the ancient lawgiver called upon the Lord for strength and declared: "Depart from me, Satan, for this one God only will I worship, *which is the God of glory.*"[86] One who is aware of his true relationship to God will only worship a being of glory and power, for only in this way can he acquire the divine nature of God.

Worshiping God in Spirit and in Truth

Because the truth and light of God's glory are communicated to man through the Holy Spirit, man must worship God in Spirit and in truth. True worship is not a mechanical procedure; nor is it merely a mental process. As recorded in Joseph Smith's Inspired Revision of the Bible, Jesus said to the woman of Samaria:

> . . . the hour cometh, and now is, when the true worshippers shall worship the Father in Spirit and in truth; for the Father seeketh such to worship him.
>
> For unto such hath God promised his Spirit. And they who worship him, must worship in Spirit and in truth.[87]

The Hope of Glory

In true worship, man should exercise a living and intelligent hope for the glory of Christ, or for the glory which the Man of Holiness has given to His Only Begotten Son, for by true worship man is made a partaker of that glory and power. Joseph Smith's Inspired Revision of the Bible gives the Apostle John's testimony of Jesus as follows:

> . . . in the beginning was the word, even the Son, who is made flesh, and sent unto us by the will of the Father. *And as many as believe on his name shall receive of his fulness. And of his fulness have all we received, even immortality and eternal life, through his grace.* For the law [of carnal commandments] was given through Moses, but *life and truth* came through Jesus Christ.[88]

Jesus exemplified the desire that man should have of attaining the glory of God. "I have glorified thee on earth," He prayed to His Father. "And now, O Father, glorify thou me with thine own self with the glory which I had with thee before the world was."[89]

Jesus also wanted His disciples to be glorified so that they could be united with Him in the great system of celestial truth and power over which the Father presides.[90] Through the program of the gospel, they were to be glorified in Him as He is glorified in the Father. He therefore continued in His prayer to the Father:

> Neither pray I for these alone, but for them also which shall believe on me through their word;
> That they all may be one; *as thou, Father, art in me, and I in thee,* that they also may be *one in us:* that the world may believe that thou hast sent me.
> And *the glory which thou gavest me I have given them; that they may be one, even as we are one:*
> *I in them, and thou in me,* that they may be made perfect in one; and that the world may know that thou hast sent me, and hast loved them, as thou hast loved me.[91]

The union for which Jesus prayed was more than a union of heart and purpose. It was celestial union which could be achieved only by developing the divine powers of truth and light of His Father's glory in His disciples. They were to be one, He observed, "as thou, Father, art *in me,* and *I in thee.*" Of the way this was to be done, Jesus said: "And *the glory which thou gavest me* I have given them; *that* they may be one, even as we are one: *I in them,* and *thou in me,* that they may be made perfect in one."[92]

In discussing this subject, Joseph Smith observed that "salvation consists in the glory, authority, majesty, power and dominion which Jehovah possesses."[93] That which God does, he stressed, is designed to "end in the greatest amount of good and glory to those who become the recipients of his laws and ordinances."[94] Having quoted the above statement of Jesus, the Prophet commented:

> What language can be plainer than this? The Savior surely intended to be understood by his disciples. . . . He says, And the glory which thou gavest me, I have given them, that they may be one, even as we are one. As much as to say, that *unless they have the glory which the Father had given him, they could not be one with them:* For he says he had given them the glory that the Father had given him, that they might be one; or in other words, to make them one.[95]

When Jesus ministered to the Nephites, He expressed a similar desire. First, He endowed the disciples whom He chose with glory to the extent that "they were encircled about as if it were by fire," and "they were as white as the countenance and also the garments of Jesus." Then Christ thanked the Father for purifying them, and He prayed that all who would believe their words would also be purified by divine power. Finally, the Master said: "Father, I pray not for the world, but for those whom thou hast given me out of the world, because of their faith, that they may be purified in me, *that I may be in them as thou, Father, art in me, that we may be one, that I may be glorified in them.*"[96]

Because the ultimate purpose of the gospel is to glorify those who come unto Christ, the Nephite prophets taught that man must "come to a knowledge of the glory of God";[97] and having obtained this knowledge, man must exercise "a hope" therein.[98] This was General Mormon's desire in behalf of his son Moroni.[99] Jacob admonished his brethren to be reconciled unto the Father through Christ and thereby obtain "a good hope of glory in him."[100] Aaron taught the Lamanites "that the sting of death should be swallowed up in the hopes of glory."[101] And Alma testified: "I know that he [God] will raise me up at the last day, to dwell with him in glory."[102]

The restored gospel was given to men for the same purpose: that they might be "made partakers" of the glory of God.[103] A revelation in February, 1832, explained in some detail the doctrine of glorification as it relates to the final destiny of all classes of men.[104] An earlier revelation stated that the Lamanites must come to the knowledge of their fathers, that they might learn to "rely upon the merits of Jesus Christ, and be glorified through faith in his name."[105]

The hope of glory was expected to sustain the Saints in all their earthly trials. "Even if they [the world] do unto you as they have done unto me, blessed are ye," Christ explained in a revelation, "for you shall dwell with me in glory."[106] To a member of the Church who mourned the loss of a loved one, the Prophet said in comfort: "You shall soon have the company of your companion in a world of glory."[107] Nevertheless, the powers of spiritual darkness and death weigh heavily upon man in mortality. "Notwithstanding all this glory," Joseph Smith therefore observed in a funeral address, "we for a moment lose sight of it, and mourn the loss, but we do not mourn as those without hope."[108] He held that to fail to qualify for the glory of God after death is a greater catastrophe than physical death. "We have a knowledge that those we bury here God will bring up again, clothed upon and quickened by the Spirit of the great God," he declared; "and what mattereth it whether we lay them down, or we lay [sic] down with them when we can keep them no longer?"[109] "The great misery of departed spirits in the world of spirits, where they go after death," the Prophet stressed, "is to know that they come short of the glory that others enjoy and that they might have enjoyed themselves, and they are their own accusers."[110]

Because he considered the glorification of man to be a final result of the program of the gospel, Joseph Smith admonished the Saints to live by every word that comes from God, "lest they come short of the glory that is reserved for the faithful."[111] He warned: "I say to all those who are disposed to set up stakes for the Almighty, You will come short of the glory of God."[112] Like the Apostle Paul, the latter-day Seer taught that the hope of true Christians is to be glorified in Christ, and that any suffering the Saints might be called upon to endure would not be worthy to be compared with the glory which would be revealed in them. With earnest expectation, they should "rejoice in hope of the glory of God";[113] and they should wait patiently for the manifestation of glory which is given to the sons of God, by which they are delivered from the bondage of their fallen spiritual state into the glorious liberty, light, and life of the children of God.[114] Having exemplified this hope and given their lives to witness their testimony of the restored gospel, it was said of the Prophet and his brother Hyrum: "They lived for glory; they died for glory; and glory is their eternal reward."[115]

Summary

The restored gospel has its center in the atoning mission of Jesus Christ. For this reason the proclamation of the testimony that Jesus was indeed the Son of God is the basic message of the gospel. For man to embrace the gospel, he must exercise living faith in Christ, repent of his sins, and be baptized by a legal administrator. He must then receive the gift of the Holy Ghost by the laying on of authorized hands, which gives him a right to the manifestations of the Holy Ghost in all their divine expressions. This is the basic program of the gospel. But in addition, there are higher ordinances within the plan of life and salvation, and the challenge is given to man to endure to the end and make his calling and election sure to celestial glory. Finally, man must overcome all things by faith; and having been raised from the grave in the resurrection, he must be judged by Christ as being worthy to receive eternal life.

Essentially the gospel is a system of divine mercy, truth, and power. The forgiveness of personal sins is given to man through the preparatory gospel; and in the gift of the Holy Ghost, man is given access to divine truth and power. All the principles and ordinances within the divine plan are designed to bring man to the point of faith and spiritual excellence which will enable him to enter the presence of God and be endowed with celestial glory. This means that man is organized with the capacity to acquire the attributes and powers of God, and a major purpose of the gospel is to glorify man in Christ, as Jesus has been glorified in the Father. To this end, man must worship God in Spirit and in truth; he must acquire a hope for the glory of God; and he must act upon that hope until he attains eternal life, which is to possess the living attributes and powers of celestial glory in the resurrection.[116]

Notes

1. *History of the Church,* ed. B. H. Roberts (Salt Lake City, 1946, IV, p. 537. (Italics by the writer.) Hereafter this source will be abbreviated HC, followed by the volume and page number. As in Volume I of this study, all italics have been added by the writer unless otherwise indicated.

2. *Ibid.,* p. 595.

3. *Ibid.,* V, p. 529.

4. D&C 128:19.

5. HC, II, p. 364.

6. *Ibid.,* III, p. 30.

7. See Volume I of this study, the section in chapter eleven entitled "Procedures of the Grand Council of the Gods." See also Moses 4:2; 2 Nephi 31:10; 3 Nephi 11:11.

8. 3 Nephi 11:7.

9. 3 Nephi 11:10–11.

10. 3 Nephi 11:14.

11. 3 Nephi 27:13–15.

12. 3 Nephi 27:19–20.

13. 3 Nephi 11:32–35.

14. 2 Nephi 31:17–18.

15. 2 Nephi 9:23–24.

16. D&C 39:6.

17. D&C 33:10–13. See HC, V, p. 344, where Joseph Smith stressed the message of the gospel which the Elders were to preach.

18. HC, VI, p. 57.

19. *Times and Seasons,* II (March 1, 1842), p. 709. This publication was the official church organ of the Latter-day Saints between 1839 and 1846. Hereafter this source will be abbreviated TS, followed by the volume, date, and page number.

20. See HC, IV, p. 541, as edited by B. H. Roberts. See also *ibid.,* II, pp. 255–256, where Joseph Smith discusses the first principles and ordinances of the gospel.

21. *Ibid.,* VI, p. 316.

22. *Ibid.,* V, p. 499.

23. *Ibid.,* II, p. 256.

24. 3 Nephi 27:16. To Nephi at an earlier time, the Lord also made this challenge an integral part of the gospel program. See 2 Nephi 31:15–16 in light of the verses that precede and follow these verses.

25. HC, IV, p. 425.

26. I. R., 2 Corinthians 5:17–21.

27. HC, II, p. 8.

28. *The Improvement Era,* XXI, p. 104.

29. HC, III, p. 379. Again the Prophet said: "The doctrine of eternal judgments belongs to the first principles of the Gospel in these last days."—*Ibid.,* VI, p. 364.

30. *Ibid.,* IV, p. 359. See also *ibid.,* VI, p. 58.

31. *Ibid.,* III, p. 396.

32. 2 Nephi 9:22.

33. 3 Nephi 27:14–18.

34. Alma 42:23.
35. Alma 12:12–15.
36. TS, III (September 1, 1842), p. 904. For the statements by the Apostle Paul to which the Prophet refers, see Romans 1:16; 2 Timothy 1:10.
37. *Latter Day Saints' Messenger And Advocate,* Kirtland, Ohio, II (March, 1836), p. 273. (Italics in the original.) This was the official church organ of the Latter-day Saints between 1834 and 1837. Hereafter this source will be abbreviated MA, followed by the volume, date, and page number.
38. *Journal of Discourses,* XX, pp. 363–364. This work is a collection of discourses delivered by leading authorities of the Church between 1851 and 1886. Most of these men were taught by the Prophet. Hereafter this source will be abbreviated JD, followed by the volume and page number.
39. D&C 121:46.
40. D&C 109:15.
41. JD, IX, pp. 288–289.
42. Mosiah 27:25–26.
43. Matthew 19:28.
44. See Volume I of this study, the section in chapter seventeen entitled "Human Life Must Be Transformed by the Power of Christ."
45. Mosiah 27:26.
46. Moroni 10:7.
47. D&C 50:24.
48. D&C 88:66–68.
49. 2 Nephi 31:14; 32:2; Mormon 9:24.
50. 2 Nephi 25:25.
51. D&C 84:33.
52. HC, III, p. 380; JD, XI, p. 10; XII, p. 270.
53. See Volume I of this work.
54. D&C 20:17–29.
55. HC, VI, p. 250.
56. D&C 84:27. Since the time Christ made his atoning sacrifice and thus fulfilled the law of carnal commandments which God gave to Israel through Moses, the preparatory gospel has not included that law in its program. The law of carnal commandments was considered to be a schoolmaster to bring the Israelites to Christ. See Galatians 3:24.
57. HC, IV, p. 42.
58. *Ibid.,* I, p. 39; VI, pp. 249–250.
59. D&C 84:19.
60. D&C 84:20–22. For other statements indicating that man must be a recipient of divine power in order to see God, see D&C 67:10–12; Moses 1:1–11.
61. This cannot take place while man is in mortality. In his Inspired Revision of the Bible, Joseph Smith corrected a statement by the Apostle Paul to indicate that man does not leave the initial principles and ordinances of the gospel behind as he goes on to perfection. See I. R., Hebrews 6:1; also HC, VI, p. 58. But when man is finally perfected, the preparatory gospel will have fulfilled its purposes. Its functions can then be discontinued or taken from the earth.
62. D&C 13; Smith 2:69.
63. There are two kinds of sons of Levi: (1) those who are literal sons of

Levi in the flesh and (2) those who become sons of Moses and of Aaron, who were of the tribe of Levi (see Exodus 4:16; 6:18, 20; Numbers 26:59), by receiving the priesthood and by being regenerated by means of its divine powers (see D&C 84:32–34). There are also two kinds of sacrifice by the sons of Levi: (1) a blood sacrifice which will be made for purposes of restoration, in the temple when the New Jerusalem is built (see HC, IV, pp. 210–212); and (2) a sacrifice of service in extending the blessings of the gospel to others (see D&C 128:24).

64. D&C 128:24.

65. Ether 3:14. See chapter six, the section entitled "Nature of the Gift."

66. This point will be discussed in volume IV of this work.

67. D&C 46:7.

68. HC, VI, p. 305.

69. *Ibid.,* II, p. 5.

70. D&C 101:38.

71. HC, II, p. 6.

72. *Lectures on Faith,* No. 5. These lectures were published as part of the original edition of the Doctrine and Covenants, at Kirtland, Ohio, in 1835, and were designated as theological lectures "on the doctrine of the Church Of The Latter Day Saints." Joseph Smith was not their sole author, but they were written by a committee over which he presided. This committee was appointed in a meeting of the High Council at Kirtland, September 24, 1834, the minutes of which state:

> The council then proceeded to appoint a committee to arrange the items of the doctrine of Jesus Christ, for the government of the Church of Latter-day Saints, which Church was organized and commenced its rise on the 6th of April, 1830. These items are to be taken from the Bible, Book of Mormon, and the revelations which have been given to the Church up to this date, or that shall be given until such arrangements are made.
>
> Councilor Samuel H. Smith nominated President Joseph Smith, Jun., Oliver Cowdery, Sidney Rigdon, and Frederick G. Williams to compose said committee, which was seconded by Councilor Hyrum Smith. The Councilors then gave their vote in the affirmative, which was also agreed to by the whole conference.—HC, II, p. 165. See also p. 180.

It is not known specifically which member, or members, of the committee put the *Lectures on Faith* in their written form. But there can be no doubt that the theological ideas which they contain came from Joseph Smith. All the major ideas within them can be found in his revelations and teachings before 1834.

73. D&C 93:19–20.

74. See Moses 1:17; 5:8; Moroni 4:2; D&C 20:29. See also Moses 1:21; 6:52; D&C 14:8; 18:18, 23, 40; 42:3; 50:31; 88:64.

75. Moses 6:52; 2 Nephi 25:20; D&C 18:21–25.

76. For a discussion of this subject, see chapters eight and nine of Volume I of this study.

77. D&C 93:12.

78. D&C 93:12–13, 16.

79. D&C 93:28.

80. D&C 88:6.

81. See 3 Nephi 19:28–29.

82. D&C 93:20. See Volume I of this study, the section in chapter eight entitled "Service the Pathway to Eternal Life."

83. D&C 93:12.

84. JD, V, p. 50.

85. Moses 1:13–15.

86. Moses 1:19–20.

87. I. R., John 4:24–26.

88. I. R., John 1:16–18.

89. John 17:4–5.

90. The relationship of the Father and the Son in glory has been discussed in Volume I of this study, in the section in chapter eight entitled "The Relationship in Glory of the Father and the Son."

91. John 17:20–23.

92. *Ibid.*

93. *Lectures on Faith,* No. 7.

94. HC, V, p. 135.

95. *Lectures on Faith,* No. 7. Again the Prophet said: "Jesus prayed that those that the Father had given him out of the world might be made one *in them,* as they were one."—HC, V, p. 426. See also D&C 50:43.

96. 3 Nephi 19:14, 25, 28–29.

97. Mosiah 4:1.

98. Jacob 4:4.

99. Moroni 9:25.

100. Jacob 4:11.

101. Alma 22:14.

102. Alma 36:28.

103. D&C 133:57.

104. D&C 76.

105. D&C 3:20.

106. D&C 6:30.

107. HC, V, pp. 360–363.

108. *Ibid.,* IV, p. 554.

109. *Ibid.,* V, pp. 360–363.

110. *Ibid.,* p. 425.

111. *Ibid.,* p. 404.

112. *Ibid.,* p. 554.

113. Romans 5:2.

114. See Romans 8:16–21.

115. D&C 135:6.

116. See D&C 88:3–4; Moses 6:59.

2

The Spiritual Power of the Restored Gospel

> *. . . our gospel came not unto you in word only, but also in power, and in the Holy Ghost, and in much assurance.*
> —PAUL.

The gospel of Jesus Christ as given to the world through Joseph Smith was not only a challenging and meaningful theological system but also a body of related principles and ordinances through which man could acquire spiritual truth and power from God. The promise of divine truth and power was inseparably associated with the message of the gospel. The restored gospel called for the renewal and regeneration of man in Christ; and when living faith in the Master was expressed, that faith was accompanied by the manifestation of enlightening spiritual powers and gifts which stirred the heart of man and transformed his life.

Expressions Of Gospel Power

Unique Spiritual Powers of Restored Gospel

The spiritual powers of the restored gospel had no equivalent in the contemporary world. This Joseph Smith pointed out editorially.[1] Several of his associates made similar explanations. Brigham Young observed that but few men understood the nature of those spiritual powers.[2] John Taylor agreed: "There is a feeling and Spirit resting upon the Saints that is not known nor experienced among any other people," he declared, while maintaining that "all the kings, potentates, and powers" in the world were "entirely ignorant" of the new spiritual forces.[3] Lorenzo Snow stated: "This gift of the Holy Ghost is a different principle from anything that we see manifest in the sectarian world."[4] So obvious was this fact, George Q. Cannon asserted, that if men would honestly inquire into the matter and judge the new spiritual powers that were manifested through the restored gospel by their tangible operations and effects they would be constrained to acknowledge the presence of something different from anything else known in the world.[5]

The Holy Spirit as a substance of life, or a living substance, which gives man divine attributes and powers that lead to eternal life, has been discussed earlier in this study.[6] Since the Spirit endows man with new attributes and powers of life, Joseph Smith could point out that there is "nothing unnatural" in its influence upon man. Consequently there can be "nothing indecorous" in the actions of those who partake of this divine power of truth and life.[7] Instead, man is given increased powers and attributes of life through the Spirit. To the man of faith, the influence of this divine substance is much like that of sunlight upon the vegetable kingdom; it is a natural but phenomenal power which stimulates spiritual growth and leads man upward to God, the giver of life. The Prophet referred to the Spirit as a powerful agent capable of greatly "expanding the mind, enlightening the understanding, and storing the intellect with present knowledge."[8] So potent is its influence, Brigham Young explained, that "it swallows up the organization which pertains to this world," opening the vision of man's mind so that "all things are made new."[9] John Taylor observed: "When the Spirit that dwells in the bosom of the Almighty dwells in ours, and an intercourse is open between heaven and us, we are then placed in a position to understand that which it would be impossible to comprehend upon any natural principle known to us."[10]

There can be little doubt that the spiritual powers of the restored gospel greatly influenced the lives of the Saints. Orson Pratt said: "The gift of the Holy Ghost . . . gave me a testimony concerning the truth of this work that no man can ever take from me."[11] He declared that the gift and power of the Holy Ghost "is the greatest evidence any man or woman can have concerning the kingdom of God."[12] Brigham Young was equally emphatic. "The eye, the ear, the hand, all the senses may be deceived, but the Spirit of God cannot be deceived," he observed; "and when inspired with that Spirit, the whole man is filled with knowledge, he can see with a spiritual eye, and he knows that which is beyond the power of man to controvert."[13] For this reason Charles W. Penrose declared that his testimony of the restored gospel did not depend upon Joseph Smith, Brigham Young, or any other man. Having "bowed in obedience" to the gospel, he explained, "I received a testimony for myself of its truthfulness, and that testimony has never departed from me."[14] Here, observed John Taylor, "is a secret that the world does not comprehend."[15] Upon this "peculiarity," George Q. Cannon asserted, the new system was being built. "Legions of witnesses" could testify unanimously that "by the outpouring of the Holy Ghost upon them" God had given them a knowledge of the truthfulness of the latter-day work "as strong as the knowledge that they themselves live[d]."[16]

Spiritual Powers Attest to Book of Mormon

Joseph Smith claimed that the Book of Mormon was brought forth by the gift and power of God to be a tangible witness of the new dispensation, containing "the fulness of the gospel of Jesus Christ to the Gentiles and to the Jews also."[17] Because of the clarity of the gospel principles which it contains, the Prophet declared "that the Book of Mormon was the most correct of any book on earth, and the keystone of our religion, and a man would get nearer to God by abiding by its precepts, than by any other book."[18]

The Spirit of God is inseparably associated with the word of God;[19] and since the Book of Mormon claimed to be the word of God, it was given to the world with the admonition that man should test its authenticity with a spiritual criterion. Before concluding the record of the Nephites, Moroni, the last surviving prophet of that ancient culture, wrote to those who would read that record in the latter days: "When ye shall receive these things, I would exhort you that ye would ask God, the Eternal Father, in the name of Christ, if these things are not true; and if ye shall ask with a sincere heart, with real intent, having faith in Christ, he will manifest the truth of it unto you, by the power of the Holy Ghost."[20]

Upon this basis the Book of Mormon, as a new witness for Christ and His gospel, was to be judged. "Wherever that book is candidly perused," Parley P. Pratt affirmed, "the Spirit will bear record of its truth."[21] On this assumption, missionaries delivered their message to William and Emeline Anderson, "with the admonition to pray to God who would reveal whether the doctrine was true or false."[22] And when Luman Shurtliff inquired regarding the divine origin of the Nephite scripture, he was told: "Ask God and he will show you."[23]

Having presented the claim of the new scripture to the world for a number of years, Orson Pratt and Charles W. Penrose each declared that by this divinely established means "scores of thousands have proved the divinity of this work."[24] For example, Wilford Woodruff reported that as he read the Book of Mormon "the Spirit bore witness that the record which it contained was true."[25] Parley P. Pratt observed: "The Spirit of the Lord came upon me, while I read, and enlightened my mind, convinced my judgment, and rivetted the truth upon my understanding, so that I knew that the book was true, just as well as a man knows the daylight from the dark night."[26] Brigham Young also affirmed: "I knew it was true, as well as I knew that I could see with my eyes, or feel by the touch of my fingers, or be sensible of the demonstration of any sense."[27] While not yet a member of the Church, William W. Phelps wrote from Canandaigua, New York, to an acquaintance in Ohio: "I had ten hours discourse with a man from your state, named Sidney Rigdon, a convert to its [the Book of Mormon's] doctrines, and he declared it was true, and he knew it by the power of the Holy Ghost."[28] After embracing the faith, Phelps said of that volume: "Who can . . . estimate the worth of such a book? He only who is directed by the Holy Ghost in all things."[29]

In addition to providing a testimony of the new dispensation of the gospel, the spiritual powers associated with the Book of Mormon enlightened the minds of men to see the message of salvation as it was given in both ancient and modern times. "By that book," William W. Phelps wrote, "I found a key to the holy prophets; and by that book began to unfold the mysteries of God, and I was glad."[30] Joseph Holbrook, another early convert, also expressed the point that the Nephite scripture was "a key to the Bible"; and by the light it shed upon the prophetic and doctrinal themes of the Jewish record, the Bible became "a new book, having the seals broken, [with] light and life and salvation on its pages."[31] Having read the Book of Mormon, Sarah De Armon Pea was so "astonished at its contents that," said she, "it left an impression upon my mind not to be forgotten"[32] And of its impact generally, Elder Phelps observed: "When the Book of Mormon came forth, those who received it, and embraced its truths, saw new light upon the scriptures, and a true beauty in holiness; and they began to have confidence in the promises of God; faith in prayer; faith in miracles, and a holy anxiety to share in the glory that should follow, after much tribulation."[33]

The Saints and Gift of the Holy Ghost

In addition to the initial enlightening witness of the Holy Spirit which was given to those who read the Book of Mormon and inquired of God in faith concerning its divine claims, Bishop Edward Partridge reported that those who accepted the restored gospel "have this further testimony: they receive the gift of the Holy Ghost."[34] According to Oliver Cowdery, the promise that this would be the case was given to Joseph Smith by the angel Moroni in 1823.[35] This promise was reaffirmed in the Book of Mormon[36] and in several revelations given to the Prophet;[37] and thereby the reception of the Holy Ghost was made a fundamental proposition upon which the new dispensation was founded. Lorenzo Snow observed: "I noticed that Joseph Smith assumed a position which no false prophet would dare, *viz:* that he had received the visitation of three angels: Peter, James and John, who . . . authorized him to preach the gospel, administer its ordinances, and promise the Holy Ghost which would impart a knowledge of his authority, and divine mission, and his right to organize the church of God on the earth."[38]

Because man's acceptance of the new dispensation rested upon a spiritual foundation, John Taylor declared that the claims of the restored gospel were "susceptible of proof." Just as a farmer might know if a certain seed were good by planting it and properly cultivating the plant that developed from it, so could a person know if the new covenant's law of spiritual regeneration were true by complying with its requirements. It would admit to "as strong evidence as anything in nature."[39]

There is ample proof that spiritual manifestations accompanied the proclamation of the restored gospel. John Murdock, who was baptized November 5, 1830, wrote: "The Spirit of the Lord sensibly attended the ministration, and I came out of the water rejoicing and singing praises to God and the Lamb."[40] When he and about thirty others were confirmed members of the Church and received the gift of the Holy Ghost by the laying on of hands, he testified: "I knew for a certainty that the Spirit rested upon me as it had never done before, and others said that they had glorious visions and saw the Lord."[41] John Corrill visited Kirtland, Ohio, about that time and found the new converts enjoying "the gift and power of the Holy Ghost." Shortly thereafter, while he was still unwilling to believe, he went again to Kirtland and "watched every movement with a jealous eye." He later wrote:

> I attended several meetings, one of which was the laying on of hands for the gift of the Holy Ghost, which, I thought, would give me a good opportunity to detect their hypocrisy. The meeting lasted all night, and such a meeting I never attended before. They administered the sacrament, and laid on hands [for the gift of the Holy Ghost]. . . . I watched closely and examined carefully, every movement of the meeting, and after exhausting all my powers to find the deception, I was obliged to acknowledge, in my own mind, that the meeting had been inspired by some supernatural agency.[42]

The Saints and Gifts of the Holy Ghost

Having received the gift of the Holy Ghost, the Saints were entitled to receive its supernatural endowments—the gifts of the Holy Ghost. Concerning those who would embrace the restored gospel, the angel Moroni said to Joseph Smith in 1823: " . . . with signs and with wonders, with gifts and with healings, with the manifestations of the power of God, and with the Holy Ghost shall the hearts of the faithful be comforted."[43]

Joseph Smith made reference to the spiritual endowments which accompanied the latter-day work when he observed that the first missionaries "began to preach as the Spirit gave them utterance, and though weak, yet were they strengthened by the power of God." Of the impact of these spiritual powers upon the early converts, he then said: "They saw visions and prophesied, devils were cast out, and the sick healed by the laying on of hands."[44] The spiritual powers which were manifested at the first conference of the

Church, in June, 1830, were typical of those that were identified with the work as the new dispensation was ushered in. The Prophet wrote of that conference:

> Much exhortation and instruction was given, and the Holy Ghost was poured out upon us in a miraculous manner—many of our number prophesied, whilst others had the heavens opened to their view, and were so overcome that we had to lay them on beds or other convenient places; among the rest was Brother Newel Knight, who had to be placed on a bed, being unable to help himself. By his own account of the transaction, he could not understand why we should lay him on the bed, as he felt no sense of weakness. He felt his heart filled with love, with glory, and pleasure unspeakable, and could discern all that was going on in the room; when all of a sudden a vision of the future burst upon him. He saw there represented the great work which through my instrumentality was yet to be accomplished. He saw heaven open, and beheld the Lord Jesus Christ, seated at the right hand of the majesty on high, and had it made plain to his understanding that the time would come when he would be admitted into His presence to enjoy His society for ever and ever. When their bodily strength was restored to these brethren, they shouted hosannas to God and the Lamb, and rehearsed the glorious things which they had seen and felt, whilst they were yet in the Spirit.[45]

The Saints boldly testified that signs and gifts truly followed those who received the restored gospel. Writing to his children from Adams county, Illinois, David Foote repudiated popular religious emotionalism and contended that "there is something in the religion of Jesus which is sound; it cannot be moved by every wind of doctrine." Continuing, he explained: "It is that which gives a man an assurance that he is doing the will of God; his mind will expand, the mysteries of the kingdom will open to his view, and if he continues to travel on in this way he will attain to the ministering of angels and all the gifts of God mentioned in scripture."[46] On this subject, Edward Partridge wrote to his old friends in Painesville, Ohio:

> I assure you that the signs do follow in this, the church of Christ, who receive the book of Mormon as the fulness of the gospel of Christ. In many instances the sick have been healed by the laying on of the elders' hands, and also devils cast out. Many

speak with new tongues, or in other languages; some speak in a number of different languages shortly after they receive the gift; others are confined to one or two—These are not idle assertions; I know that these things are so. Some have the gift of interpretation and some have not, as yet. But say you these gifts are strange things! Well strange as they may appear, they are the gift of the Holy Ghost.[47]

Speaking in tongues was one of the more interesting (but for church members in general, less useful) gifts of the Holy Ghost. John Corrill stated that he witnessed the expression of this gift among the Saints at Kirtland, Ohio, in the fall of 1830:

I heard them prophesy and speak in tongues unknown to me. Persons in the room who took no part with them, declared, from the knowledge they had of the Indian languages, that the tongues spoken were regular Indian dialects, which I was also informed, on inquiry, the persons who spoke had never learned.[48]

Another similar report was given by Vilate Kimball. In 1831, five Latter-day Saint missionaries began to proselyte in the town of Victor, about five miles from Mendon, Monroe county, New York, where Brigham Young and Heber C. Kimball lived. The two men went to hear them; and Vilate Kimball, the wife of Heber, said: "At their meetings Brigham and Heber saw the manifestations of the Spirit and heard the gift of speaking and singing in tongues." Desiring to learn more of the new faith, they then went with their wives and others to Columbia, Bradford county, Pennsylvania, in January, 1832, a distance of about 125 miles, where a branch of the Church had been established. Vilate wrote: "They stayed with the church about six days, saw the power of God manifested and heard the gift of tongues, and then returned rejoicing, bearing testimony to the people by the way."[49]

The Saints in the Columbia branch may have enjoyed the gift of tongues before the above visit, for Brigham Young later wrote that these early converts "were the first in the Church who received the gift of tongues."[50] Having been baptized and ordained April 14, 1832, Elder Young said:

> A few weeks after my baptism I was at brother Kimball's house one morning, and while family prayer was being offered up, brother Alpheus Gifford commenced speaking in tongues. Soon the Spirit came on me, and I spoke in tongues, and we thought only of the day of Pentecost, when the Apostles were clothed upon with cloven tongues of fire.[51]

That fall Brigham Young, Heber C. Kimball, and others went to Kirtland, Ohio, to see the Prophet. As they visited branches of the Church along the way, Brigham Young spoke in tongues at the meetings.[52] Upon meeting the Prophet at Kirtland, Elder Young again spoke in tongues while in prayer. He later reported:

> As soon as we arose from our knees the brethren flocked around him [Joseph Smith], and asked his opinion concerning the gift of tongues that was upon me. He told them it was the pure Adamic language. Some said to him they expected he would condemn the gift brother Brigham had, but he said, "No, it is of God, and the time will come when brother Brigham Young will preside over this Church." The latter part of this conversation was in my absence.[53]

In his report of this meeting, the Prophet said: "Brother Brigham Young and John P. Greene spoke in tongues, which was the first time I had heard this gift among the brethren; others also spoke, and I received the gift myself."[54]

Thereafter the gift of speaking in tongues became general among the Saints in Ohio. The Prophet wrote of a conference held January 22, 1833:

> The gifts which follow them that believe and obey the Gospel, as tokens that the Lord is ever the same in His dealings with the humble lovers and followers of truth, began to be poured out among us, as in ancient days;—for as we . . . were assembled in conference, on the 22nd day of January, I spoke to the conference in another tongue, and was followed in the same gift by Brother Zebedee Coltrin, and he by Brother William Smith, after which the Lord poured out His Spirit in a miraculous manner, until all the Elders spake in tongues, and several

members, both male and female, exercised the same gift. Great and glorious were the divine manifestations of the Holy Spirit. Praises were sung to God and the Lamb; speaking and praying, all in tongues, occupied the conference until a late hour at night, so rejoiced were we at the return of these long absent blessings.[55]

During the period the Saints resided at Kirtland, the spiritual gifts were manifested to a great degree. Eliza R. Snow wrote: "There we had the gift of prophecy—the gift of tongues—the interpretation of tongues—visions and marvelous dreams were related—the singing of heavenly choirs was heard, and wonderful manifestations of the healing power, through the administration of the Elders, were witnessed."[56] Of the meetings in Kirtland in which the Saints gathered to fast and pray, she said:

> These, called fast-meetings, were hallowed and interesting beyond the power of language to describe. Many, many were the pentecostal seasons of the outpouring of the Spirit of God on those days, manifesting the gifts of the gospel and the power of healing, prophesying, speaking in tongues, the interpretation of tongues, etc. I have there seen the lame man, on being administered to, throw aside his crutches and walk home perfectly healed; and not only were the lame made to walk, but the blind to see, the deaf to hear, the dumb to speak, and evil spirits to depart.[57]

Prescindia Huntington related that her family was visited at Kirtland by a skeptical cousin who wanted to go to a fast meeting to hear someone speak or sing in tongues. She expected to "have a hearty laugh" as a result of the experience. Prescindia recalled:

> Accordingly we went with our cousin to the meeting, during which a Brother McCarter rose and sang a song of Zion in tongues; I arose and sang simultaneously with him the same tune and words, beginning and ending each verse in perfect unison, without varying a word. It was just as though we had sung it together a thousand times.
>
> After we came out of meeting, our cousin observed, "Instead of laughing, I never felt so solemn in my life."[58]

The gifts and blessings of the Spirit were also given to the Saints in other areas of the Church. Writing of conditions in Jackson county, Missouri, in the winter of 1831–32, Parley P. Pratt said: "We enjoyed many happy seasons in our prayer and other meetings, and the Spirit of the Lord was poured out upon us, and even on the little children, insomuch that many of eight, ten or twelve years of age spoke, and prayed, and prophesied in our meetings and in our family worship."[59]

"In June, 1833," John Whitmer recorded, "we received the gift of tongues in Zion [Missouri]."[60] Among those who lived in Missouri at this time was Mary Elizabeth Rollins, who records the expression of this gift by the Saints on several occasions.[61]

The gifts of the Spirit were not restricted to members in the main bodies of the Church, but those who received the gospel in outlying areas were also given these intelligent endowments. Having baptized eight people at Henderson, Jefferson county, New York, in March, 1833, David W. Patten said: "When hands were laid upon them, the Holy Ghost fell on them, and they spoke with tongues and prophesied."[62] Orson Pratt spoke in tongues in the city of New York while ordaining Wandle Mace to the office of Elder.[63]

Joseph Smith and Sidney Rigdon were preaching in the vicinity of Mount Pleasant, Brant county, Ontario, Canada, in October, 1833. On the evening of Monday the 28th, members of the family of Freeman A. Nickerson were seated with some friends around the wide old-fashioned fireplace in the parlor listening to the Prophet's words. "I would be so glad if some one who had been baptized could receive the gift of tongues as the ancient Saints did and speak to us," Moses Nickerson said.

The Prophet replied: "If one of you will rise up and open your mouth, it shall be filled, and you shall speak in tongues."

Everyone then turned as if by a common instinct to Lydia Bailey and said with one voice, "Sister Lydia, rise up."

And then the great glory of God was manifested to this

weak but trusting girl. She was enveloped as with a flame, and, unable longer to retain her seat, she arose and her mouth was filled with the praises of God and His glory. The spirit of tongues was upon her, and she was clothed in a shining light, so bright that all present saw it with great distinctness above the light of the fire and the candles.[64]

Among the gifts of the Holy Spirit, that of healing was significantly manifested in behalf of those who believed in the restored gospel. Ezra Booth, a minister of another faith in northeast Ohio of "much more than ordinary culture and with strong natural abilities," went with others to see the Prophet in 1831. One of the visiting group, a Mrs. Johnson, had been afflicted for some time with an injured arm and was not able to lift her hand above her head. During the interview, the conversation turned to the supernatural gifts which were given to the Saints in New Testament times. At length someone said: "Here is Mrs. Johnson with a lame arm; has God given any power to men now on earth to cure her?" Shortly thereafter, according to A. S. Hayden, the Campbellite historian, the Prophet arose and, taking Mrs. Johnson by the hand, said in the most solemn and impressive manner: "Woman, in the name of the Lord Jesus Christ I command thee to be whole." And while the company looked on in awe, he left the room as the woman rejoiced in the natural strength and vigor that she again possessed in her limb.[65]

Incidents of this kind could be multiplied at length, but a few cases will suffice to illustrate the manifestations of the power of the restored gospel among the Saints. In his journal for the spring of 1831, Jared Carter wrote:

> About this time we witnessed some display of the power of God in a miraculous manner in the Church in Thompson, [Ohio]. One case I will mention which happened in my own family under the instrumentality of Joseph the Seer. My youngest child was distressingly sick at the time Joseph came to visit my house, and I told him that I had faith that the babe might be healed; he then spoke in the name of the Lord and said that it should be to me according to my faith; the child was healed immediately. On the same day, one of our sisters was healed from blindness by his instrumentality.[66]

After returning from a mission to the East in the fall of 1832, Elder Carter reported that since he had been identified with the latter-day work he had witnessed "many marvelous manifestations of the power of God, in more than eighty instances." One instance of healing took place in the state of New York. Having been requested to visit a woman whose breast was infected with cancer which had eaten and disfigured it in a most painful manner, and which "was threatening the very dissolution of her body," Elder Carter reported:

> I administered to her and prayed my Heavenly Father in the name of Christ to heal her. A few moments later she told me that all pain had left her, and she also told me that a peaceful happy feeling rested upon her, and a pleasant sensation around the afflicted part. I visited her again a few days later, when she informed me that she had been entirely healed, and that all there was left of the cancer was a little scar which was fast healing up.[67]

Benjamin F. Johnson wrote of another incident of healing which occurred in his father's family under the instrumentality of Elder Carter, in the year 1834:

> In the course of the summer Elder Jared Carter, a man then of mighty faith, came with other elders to our house, and seeing sister Nancy upon her crutches commanded her in the name of Jesus Christ of Nazareth to leave her crutches and walk, which she at once did, and never again did she use them, although for years she had borne no weight upon her broken joint. We all knew it to be the power of God, and almost felt to shout Hosanna! to think our beloved sister was again sound in limb and able to walk.[68]

While in New England in the spring and summer of 1833, Orson Pratt recorded in his journal several instances of healing under his administration, one of a woman who had been afflicted for about ten years.[69] Erastus Snow visited another woman, in Boston, who had been "pronounced incurable" by a council of physicians. He wrote:

> We anointed her with holy oil, laid our hands upon her and prayed and rebuked the disease; and it departed. This being in the evening. She arose next morning and dressed herself, walked

the house and the next day was out of doors, much to the surprise of her physicians and joy of her family.[70]

Before leaving on a mission to England in 1837, Willard Richards and others were instrumental in healing two children, one a suckling child that "lay at the point of death." Elder Richards reported:

> I took it in my arms and presented it before the Elders who laid their hands upon it. While in my arms we healed it in the name of Jesus Christ. I then returned it whole to its mother. The other child was also healed; and the parents praised God for his goodness.[71]

Philo Dibble was critically wounded in an encounter with a mob which drove the Saints from Jackson County, Missouri, in 1833. An ounce ball and two buck shot entered his body to the right of his navel, causing him to bleed internally until his body was filled with blood. When he finally received medical attention two days later, the physician, who was a veteran of the Black Hawk War, said he had seen a great many wounded men but never one in this condition who had recovered. Thereupon he pronounced Dibble a dead man. The wounded man later said:

> After the surgeon had left me, Brother Newel Knight came to see me, and sat down on the side of my bed. He laid his right hand on my head, but never spoke. I felt the Spirit resting upon me at the crown of my head before his hand touched me, and I knew immediately that I was going to be healed. It seemed to form like a ring under the skin, and around the first bullet hole, also the second and third. Then a ring formed on each shoulder and on each hip and followed down to the ends of my fingers and toes and left me. I immediately arose and discharged three quarts of blood or more, with some pieces of my clothes that had been driven into my body by the bullets. I then dressed myself and . . . from that time not a drop of blood came from me; and I never afterwards felt the slightest pain or inconvenience from my wound, except that I was somewhat weak from the loss of blood.
>
> The next day I walked around the field, and the day following I mounted a horse and rode eight miles, and went three miles on foot.[72]

The spring of 1839 was a trying time for the Saints, but the 22nd July was remembered by them as a day when the power of healing was manifested to a phenomenal degree through the Prophet. Thousands of Latter-day Saints had been driven from the state of Missouri in the winter of 1838-39, and many of them had gathered to Commerce, Illinois, (later named Nauvoo) where a new gathering place had been designated. Many were seriously ill from exhaustion, the exposures they had suffered in being driven from Missouri, and the poor living conditions under which they were endeavoring to build a city on the swampy banks of the Mississippi River. Scores of people were living in wagons, in tents, and on the ground; and the Prophet had given up his log cabin to the sick and moved his family into a tent, while he ministered day and night to the needs of the afflicted.[73]

On the 22nd of July, Joseph arose and, reflecting upon the situation of the Saints, he called upon the Lord in mighty prayer in their behalf. The Spirit rested upon him in a powerful manner, and he went forth healing all who were in his house and yard. Accompanied by Sidney Rigdon and several members of the Quorum of the Twelve, "he went through among the sick lying on the bank of the river, and he commanded them in a loud voice, in the name of Jesus Christ, to come up and be made whole, and they were all healed." The Prophet then crossed the river to Montrose, Iowa.[74] The first home he entered was that of Brigham Young, who later wrote: "He . . . commanded me in the name of Jesus Christ to arise and be made whole. I arose and was healed."[75] From there the group went to the house of Elijah Fordham. Wilford Woodruff, who was present[76] and whose account agrees with the statements of others who were witnesses, later said:

> Brother Fordham had been dying for an hour, and we expected each minute would be his last. I felt the power of God that was overwhelming His Prophet. When we entered the house, Brother Joseph walked up to Brother Fordham, and took him by the right hand; in his left hand he held his hat. He saw

that Brother Fordham's eyes were glazed, and that he was speechless and unconscious. After taking hold of his hand, he looked down into the dying man's face and said: "Brother Fordham, do you not know me?" At first he made no reply, but we could all see the effect of the Spirit of God resting upon him. He again said: "Elijah, do you know me?" With a low whisper, Brother Fordham answered, "Yes!" The Prophet then said, "Have you not faith to be healed?" The answer, which was a little plainer than before, was: "I am afraid it is too late. If you had come sooner, I think it might have been." He had the appearance of a man waking from sleep. It was the sleep of death. Joseph then said: "Do you not believe that Jesus is the Christ?" "I do, Brother Joseph," was the response. Then the Prophet of God spoke with a loud voice, as in the majesty of the Godhead: "Elijah, I command you, in the name of Jesus of Nazareth, to arise and be made whole!" The words of the Prophet were not like the words of man, but like the voice of God. It seemed to me that the house shook from its foundation. Elijah Fordham leaped from his bed like a man raised from the dead. A healthy color came to his face, and life was manifest in every act. His feet were done up in Indian meal poultices. He kicked them off his feet, scattered the contents, and then called for his clothes and put them on. He asked for a bowl of bread and milk, and ate it; then put on his hat and followed us into the street to visit the others who were sick.[77]

The company next went to the home of Joseph B. Noble, who also lay very sick in his bed. Brigham Young reported: "He was healed in the same manner."[78] Wilford Woodruff related:

As soon as we left Brother Fordham's house, we went into the house of Joseph B. Noble, who was very low and dangerously sick. When we entered the house, Brother Joseph took him by the hand, and commanded him, in the name of Jesus Christ, to arise and be made whole. He did arise and was immediately healed.[79]

When Joseph Smith and those who accompanied him from Nauvoo were about to re-cross the Mississippi to their homes, a man who was not a member of the Church requested the Prophet to go and heal his twin children about five months of age, who were "both lying sick nigh unto death." Joseph turned to Wilford Woodruff and said:

"You go with the man and heal his children." The Prophet then gave Elder Woodruff a red silk handkerchief from his pocket and instructed him to wipe their faces with it when he administered to them, and they would be healed. "I went with the man and did as the Prophet commanded me," Elder Woodruff related, "and the children were healed."[80]

Spiritual Powers As Aids In Spreading The Gospel

The restored gospel challenged men to express living faith in God, with honest hearts, and believe "in the power of Jesus Christ."[81] Though the doctrines of the new dispensation appealed to many, the fact that dynamic, intelligent powers were associated with the work caused others to join with the Saints; and the spiritual blessings which were given to those who believed created in them a desire to spread the gospel abroad. Of the effect of the manifestations of the Spirit during the first conference of the Church, Joseph Smith said:

> Such scenes as these were calculated to inspire our hearts with joy unspeakable, and fill us with awe and reverence for that Almighty Being, by whose grace we had been called to be instruments in bringing about, for the children of men, the enjoyment of such glorious blessings as were now at this time poured out upon us. To find ourselves engaged in the very same order of things as observed by the holy Apostles of old; to realize the importance and solemnity of such proceedings; and to witness and feel with our own natural senses, the like blessings of the Holy Ghost, and the goodness and condescension of a merciful God unto such as obey the everlasting Gospel of our Lord Jesus Christ, combined to create within us sensations of rapturous gratitude, and inspire us with fresh zeal and energy in the cause of truth.[82]

Though spiritual gifts properly follow rather than precede the expression of faith in Christ, to the observer they may supply the evidence that is required to stimulate faith.[83] Here the incentive to believe comes as a gift to the responsive soul, made possible by those who have previously expressed saving faith. E. D. Howe, a bitter critic of the Prophet and his work, observed sarcastically: "Hundreds were soon convinced of the truth of the whole [message of the restored gospel] by hearing of and seeing the manner in which the 'tongues' were performed, although the trick would seem more susceptible to discovery than any previous one."[84]

Though the unbeliever was free to assign the origin of the spiritual manifestations which the Saints claimed to enjoy to some clever device or to the action of an unperceived natural agent, Joseph Smith challenged the world to believe; and he promised, as did the emissaries of the Christian message in New Testament times, that signs would follow those who expressed living faith. "I am God, and mine arm is not shortened," a revelation through the Prophet stated, "and I will show miracles, signs and wonders unto all those who believe on my name."[85] The restored gospel was to "be preached unto every creature, with signs following them that believe."[86] While proselyting in Michigan Territory, the Prophet therefore declared: "If you will obey the Gospel with honest hearts, I promise you, in the name of the Lord, that the gifts as promised by our Savior will follow you, and by this you may prove me to be a true servant of God."[87] Of the realization of this promise, Edward Stevenson said:

> I am, with others, a witness that these gifts did follow many in the branch of the Church which was raised up in Pontiac. Among them was Deacon Samuel Bent of the Presbyterian Church, who was the first one baptized (and who afterwards became President of the High Council in Nauvoo, Illinois). His daughter, Mary, was the first one who spoke in tongues in his branch. Besides Mary Curtis, Joseph Wood, Elijah Fordham and others also enjoyed that gift. We felt that we were blessed above kings, rulers, and potentates of the earth, and truly we were a happy branch of the Church of Jesus Christ of Latter-day Saints. Our souls were full of joyous thanksgiving, and our songs of gladness rejoiced the heart by day, dispelled the gloom of night and welcomed the coming morn.[88]

The Prophet's associates took a similar position in their proselyting efforts. Orson Pratt continually "preached upon the subject of more revelations and miracles and the New Covenant."[89] Ambrose Palmer wrote from New Portage, Medina county, Ohio, that when Sidney Rigdon preached in that area in April, 1833, he "opened the scriptures to our understanding in that clear light in which we had never before understood them, even by showing us the fruits which the Gospel produced in former ages, as also the gifts that were in the Church—such as visions, revelation, the ministering of angels, the gift of the Holy Spirit, and prophecy—and that these were again restored to the world and found in the Mormon Church."[90]

When Luther Barney, who had previously been converted to the restored gospel, reasoned with his father's family and friends in western Illinois "upon the gifts and blessings of the Gospel enjoyed by the former-day Saints," he contended "that it was the privilege of the church now to enjoy the same gifts and blessings, and if the church was not in possession of that power it was not the true church and was not acknowledged of God as His church." As the people searched the scriptures, they became "convinced of these things" and were baptized; and in a short time there was a branch of about thirty members in that area.[91]

In his report of the progress of the work in New York City in 1837, Parley P. Pratt also testified of the spiritual basis upon which the restored gospel was presented:

> It has been with much exertion that the truth has taken root in this city, but at length the Spirit of the Lord is beginning to manifest itself in mighty power and showing that He is able to do His own work. On last Sunday we, while preaching at the house of a good old Cornelius [See Acts 10], who had not yet obeyed the Gospel, but was seeking and believing, while I yet spake he was carried away in a vision and saw the two sticks representing the two books [the Bible and the Book of Mormon] and the light and glory of God shining around them; to this he arose and testified in the power of the Spirit and immediately spake in tongues and interpreted the same, speaking of the two records and the remnant of Joseph and how they would soon come to the knowledge of the truth; and nearly all present

believed and glorified God, and several are intending to obey the ordinance. The gift of healing is also beginning to be enjoyed here in some degree, and we are now preaching daily.[92]

The above incidents are representative of the basic methods of conversion which many missionaries employed in spreading abroad the program of the restored gospel. When John F. Boynton and Evan M. Greene were requested to bless an afflicted woman with a painful stomach disorder, they "commanded the disease in the name of Jesus to depart from her." Continued Elder Greene:

> Then I prayed that the cloud of darkness might be broken, and I exhorted and contended for the gifts of the Church. Then, for the first time in this place, the Lord poured out his Spirit in mighty power and gave the gift of tongues unto the public, and we had a glorious time. Some were convinced of the power of God.[93]

Shortly thereafter when another expression of these gifts occurred, two people who were present requested to be baptized.[94]

Similar manifestations with like results accompanied other missionaries in that vicinity.[95] And from Columbiana county, Ohio, Lorenzo D. Barnes later wrote that as the Saints and others in that area met to fast and pray,

> The Spirit of the Lord came down in power, and seldom have the Saints in the last days witnessed a more glorious time. It was a little Pentecost indeed: some spake in tongues, and some prophesied, some interpreted, and some cried out as in former times: Brethren what shall we do to be saved? Five went forward immediately and were baptized in the name of Jesus Christ for a remission of sins.[96]

In Willsboro, Essex county, New York, there lived a woman who had been lame and unable to walk for some time. When she began to believe the testimony of Jared Carter concerning the restored gospel, she remarked that her physical condition would prevent her from being baptized. Elder Carter thereupon assured her that if she would obey the gospel the Lord would give her power to walk. She having made this promise, he reported: "I then took her by the hand and commanded her in the name of Jesus to walk, and the God of Heaven gave her power to do so."[97]

In his journal, Orson Pratt recorded several incidents of healing in which the person thereafter embraced the gospel. While proselyting in New England, in 1833, he visited a family where there was a young woman who "had been sick about 12 weeks, and vomited much blood; and it was supposed by many that she could not live many days." She desired Elder Pratt to "pray for her that she might be healed, at the same time covenanting before God to obey the gospel." He said: "Therefore I prayed for and laid my hands upon her in the name of Jesus Christ, and she was immediately healed." Three days later she was baptized.[98]

The following Sunday Elder Pratt wrote:

> I was invited to tarry through the night with Mr. Kelsey whose wife lay sick of a disease with which she had been afflicted 5 or 6 years. She covenanted to obey the gospel if the Lord would heal her. I prayed for and laid my hands upon her in the name of Jesus, and she began to recover and a few days after was baptized.[99]

In a letter to his daughter written from Pittsburgh, Pennsylvania, July 10, 1843, Heber C. Kimball reported the healing of an English woman in Cincinnati, Ohio, who immediately went through the neighborhood "telling the people what had been done." Shortly thereafter Elder Kimball was awakened at night by a man whose daughter was ill. The modern apostle wrote: "I laid hands upon her and she was healed and went to sleep. She was well in the morning, and they were all believing." Before leaving Cincinnati, Elder Kimball baptized the man and his daughter.[100]

David W. Patten possessed the gift of healing to a remarkable degree and often employed it in a way that would encourage people to consider the merits of the restored gospel. While a missionary in the East, he reported:

When we found any sick, I preached to them faith in the ordinances of the gospel; and where the truth found place in their hearts, I commanded them in the name of the Lord Jesus Christ to arise from their beds of sickness and be made whole. In many instances the people came after me to lay hands on their sick, because of this gift which the Lord had bestowed upon me, and almost daily the sick were healed under my hands. A woman who had an infirmity for nearly twenty years was instantly healed.[101]

Wilford Woodruff and Abraham O. Smoot observed the labors of Elder Patten and later said that they never knew of an instance in which his humble petition for the sick was not answered.[102] Of Elder Patten's visit to the afflicted wife of Ezra Strong while on the above mission, his biographer wrote: "After the usual testimony and questions respecting her faith in the gospel, David rubbed and anointed her eyes, when immediately she was restored to sight; and so thoroughly was she healed that she prepared dinner for the household."[103] Concerning this period of his ministry, Elder Patten again said:

The Lord did work with me wonderfully, in signs and wonders following them that believed in the fulness of the Gospel of Jesus Christ, insomuch that the deaf were made to hear, the blind to see, and the lame were made whole. Fevers, palsies, crooked and withered limbs were healed by the power of God, that was manifested through His servants.[104]

Summary

The restored gospel was much more than a system of theology; it was a formula of enlightening and regenerating spiritual power by which those who embraced the plan of life and salvation were given the revelations and visions of God, and the supernatural gifts which were part of the Christian system in New Testament times—visions, healings, the gift of tongues, prophecy, etc. Man was challenged to believe in Christ, to obey the saving ordinances, and to apply the principles of the gospel in his life as a means of acquiring divine truth and power. He could then know of the truthfulness of the program by the intelligent manifestations of the Spirit unto himself, while those who did not believe were left to doubt and to question in spiritual darkness. This was the real issue of the message and program which was given to the world through Joseph Smith. The fact that the proclamation of the restored gospel was accompanied by the manifestation of spiritual gifts did much to spread its message abroad and to establish the truth of the new dispensation in the hearts of those who believed.

Notes

1. HC, IV, pp. 571–581; V, pp. 26–32.
2. See JD, VII, pp. 54ff.
3. *Ibid.,* V, pp. 189–190; XIX, p. 150; XXIII, pp. 51–52.
4. *Ibid.,* XX, p. 330.
5. *Ibid.,* XI, p. 333; XIV, p. 52.
6. See Volume I of this study, the section in chapter six entitled "Spirit and Life"; also Volume I, the sections in chapter eight entitled "Eternal Life" and "Birth the Gateway to Life."
7. HC, IV, pp. 576, 580.
8. *Ibid.,* III, p. 380. For a similar statement by John Taylor, see JD, XX, p. 330.
9. JD, I, pp. 90–91.
10. *Ibid.,* XI, pp. 22–23. For a similar statement by Charles W. Penrose, see *ibid.,* XXV, pp 40–41.
11. *Ibid.,* VII, p. 178.
12. *Ibid.,* p. 179.
13. *Ibid.,* XVI, p. 46; See also XIII, p. 336.
14. *Ibid.,* XX, p. 295.
15. *Ibid.,* XXIII, pp. 51–52.
16. *Ibid.,* XXV, p. 25. For other statements by Elder Cannon, see *ibid.,* XXIII, pp. 201, 215. John Taylor called for a show of hands by members of a large congregation who could so testify, and "a perfect forest of hands was held up."—*Ibid.,* XXV, p. 183. Wilford Woodruff declared that it was upon this basis that the barren deserts of the West were colonized by saints coming from many lands. "If the Lord Almighty had not backed up the testimony of the Elders of Israel as He had done [by giving the people the Holy Ghost]," he contended, "Utah today would have been as when we found it 36 years ago."—*Ibid.,* XXIV, pp. 241–242.
17. D&C 20:9.
18. HC, IV, p. 461.
19. See Volume I of this study, the section in chapter ten entitled "The Light, Life, and Power of the Gospel."
20. Moroni 10:4.
21. JD, V, pp. 195–196.

22. *Eventful Narratives, The Thirteenth Book of the Faith-Promoting Series* (Salt Lake City, 1887), p. 69.

23. "Biographical Sketch of the Life of Luman Andros Shurtliff, 1807–1864," p. 18.

24. JD, XXI, pp. 133–134, 139–140, 143. Again from Elder Pratt:

> There are . . . scores of thousands who know as well as they know they have an existence, that the Book of Mormon is a divine record; that the Bible is a divine record; that the revelations given through the Prophet Joseph Smith, published in the Doctrine and Covenants, are divine; they know it. Would they be willing to suffer martyrdom? I think they would.—*Ibid.,* p. 174.

25. Matthias F. Cowley, *Wilford Woodruff* (Salt lake City, 1909), p. 34.

26. JD, V. p. 194.

27. *Ibid.,* III, p. 91.

28. Letter to Eber D. Howe, January 15, 1831, in E. D. Howe, *History of Mormonism* (Painesville, Ohio, 1840).

29. MA, I (September, 1835), p. 178.

30. *Ibid.*

31. "The Life of Joseph Holbrook, 1806–1871," by himself, p. 22; typewritten copy in the Brigham Young University Library.

32. The journal of Sarah De Armon Pea Rich, typewritten copy in the Brigham Young University Library, p. 17. She later married Charles C. Rich, who became a prominent elder in the Church.

33. Letter of William W. Phelps to Oliver Cowdery, MA, I (February, 1834), p. 66.

34. MA, I (January, 1835), p. 59.

35. MA, II (October, 1835), p. 199.

36. For example, 1 Nephi 10:17; 13:37; 2 Nephi 31:13; Alma 9:21; 3 Nephi 9:20; 11:35; 12:1–2; 27:20; Mormon 7:10; Ether 12:14; Moroni 8:26.

37. For example, D&C 14:8; 18:18; 19:31; 20:41, 43; 33:15; 35:5–6; 68:25; 84:64; 121:26, 46.

38. *Juvenile Instructor,* XXII, pp. 22–23. For the restoration of the Melchizedek Priesthood and apostleship, see Volume I of this study, the section in chapter four entitled "The Melchizedek Priesthood Restored." Again Lorenzo Snow declared:

> Where in all the world can you find a class of ministers that dare take the position our elders do? Where is the man or the set of men that can be found that dare to present themselves before the world and say that they have been authorized by God to administer certain ordinances from God? Any one announcing a doctrine of this kind would soon be found out if he were an imposter—he would place himself in a very dangerous position, and would soon be discovered if he held no such authority. Our elders, however, dare take this position. We have taken this position for nearly fifty years.—JD, XX, p. 331.

Wilford Woodruff made a similar statement in reference to the ministration of Peter, James, and John to Joseph Smith and Oliver Cowdery: "These angels told Joseph Smith to . . . preach the gospel as taught by Jesus Christ and the Apostles, and the Lord would back up their testimony; that when they laid hands upon those who had been baptized for the remission of sins, and who had received their testimony, they should receive the Holy Ghost."—*Ibid.*, XXIV, pp. 241–242.

39. JD, XXIII, pp. 51–52.

40. *Journal History,* under date.

41. *Ibid.*, November 7, 1830. See also the journal of John Murdock, Church Historian's Library, Salt Lake City, Utah, pp. 12–13.

42. John Corrill, *A Brief History of the Church of Christ of Latter Day Saints* (St. Louis, 1839), pp. 8–9.

43. MA, II (October, 1835), p. 199.

44. HC, IV, p. 538.

45. *Ibid.*, I, pp. 84–85.

46. *Journal History,* May 14, 1839.

47. MA, I (January, 1835), p. 60.

48. Corrill, *op. cit.*, pp. 8–9.

49. Edward W. Tullidge, *Women of Mormondom* (New York, 1877), p. 105.

50. MS, XXV (July 4, 1863), p. 424.

51. *Ibid.*, (July 11, 1863), p. 439.

52. *Ibid.*

53. *Ibid.*

54. HC, I, pp. 296–297.

55. *Ibid.*, pp. 322–323. They assembled again on the next day and enjoyed "much speaking, singing, praying, and praising God, all in tongues."—*Ibid.*, p. 323. Zebedee Coltrin, who was among the above group, wrote in his journal that he heard Joseph Smith speak and sing in tongues. See the journal of Zebedee Coltrin, Church Historian's Library, Salt Lake City, Utah, p. 50.

56. Eliza R. Snow Smith, *Biography and Family Record of Lorenzo Snow* (Salt Lake City, 1884), p. 11.

57. Tullidge, *op. cit.*, p. 100. Again Eliza R. Snow said of the Kirtland period: "Many times have I witnessed manifestations of the power of God, in the precious gifts of the gospel,—such as speaking in tongues, the interpretation of tongues, prophesying, healing the sick, causing the lame to walk, the blind to see, the deaf to hear, and the dumb to speak."—*Ibid.*, p. 65.

58. *Ibid.*, pp. 208–209.

59. *Autobiography of Parley P. Pratt,* (3rd ed.; Salt Lake City, 1938), pp. 76–77.

60. *The Book of John Whitmer,* chapter 10; original in the Church Historian's Library, Salt Lake City, Utah.

61. See the diary of Mary Elizabeth Rollins Lightner, typewritten copy, Brigham Young University Library, pp. 5–6.

62. *Journal History,* March 25, 1833.

63. See the journal of Wandle Mace, 1809–1890, typewritten manuscript in Brigham Young University Library, p. 21.

64. Related by Lydia Bailey, later the wife of Newel Knight, *Journal History,* October 29, 1833. In his private journal, the Prophet wrote on that date: "One of the sisters received the gift of tongues, which made the Saints rejoice exceedingly. May God increase the gifts among them for his Son's sake."—*Ibid.* See also HC, I, p. 422.

65. A. S. Hayden, *Early History of the Disciples' Church in the Western Reserve* (1876), pp. 250–251. Hayden referred to this incident as a "well-attested fact."

66. *Journal History,* June 8, 1831.

67. *Ibid.,* October 19, 1832.

68. Benjamin F. Johnson, *My Life's Review* (Independence, Mo., 1947), pp. 17–18.

69. See the journal of Orson Pratt, June 15, 23; July 3, 4,; and August 7, 1833. Original in the Church Historian's Library, Salt Lake City, Utah.

70. The journal of Erastus Snow, October 18, 1842.

71. *Journal History,* June 12, 1837.

72. *Ibid.,* November 4, 1833.

73. *Ibid.,* July 22, 1839. In reporting these incidents Wandle Mace said: "At this time all were sick, no one was able to walk about except a negro called Black Jack and myself."—The journal of Wandle Mace, 1809–1890, typewritten copy in Brigham Young University Library, p. 42.

74. As reported later by Wilford Woodruff, *Journal History,* July 22, 1839. Brigham Young said:

> Joseph arose from his bed of sickness, and the power of God rested upon him: he commenced in his own house and dooryard, commanding the sick in the name of Jesus Christ to arise and be made whole, and they were healed according to his word; he then continued to travel from house to house, and from tent to tent upon the bank of the river, healing the sick as he went, until he arrived at the upper stone house, where he crossed the river in a boat, accompanied by several of the quorum of the Twelve, and landed in Montrose.—*Journal History,* under date.

See also journal of Wandle Mace, *op. cit.*

75. *Journal History, op. cit.* Brigham Young states that he then followed the Prophet on his healing mission. In reporting this phase of the Prophet's mission, Wilford Woodruff said:

> The first house they went into was President Brigham Young's. He was sick on his bed at the time. The Prophet went into his house and healed him, and they all came out together.—*Journal History, op. cit.*

76. After the company left the home of Brigham Young, Wilford Woodruff said:

> As they were passing by my door, Brother Joseph said: "Brother Woodruff, follow me." These were the only words spoken by any of the company from the time they left Brother Brigham's house till we crossed the public square, and entered Brother Fordham's house.—*Ibid.*

77. *Ibid.* Of this incident, Brigham Young said:

> Elijah Fordham . . . was supposed to be dying by his family and friends. Joseph stepped to his bedside, took him by the hand and commanded him in the name of Jesus Christ to arise from his bed, and be made whole: his voice was as the voice of God. Bro. Fordham instantly leaped from his bed, called for his clothing and followed us into the street.—*Ibid.*

In his report, Wandle Mace said:

> They went next to the house of Elijah Fordham who was sick nigh unto death. He was unable to speak and seemingly unconscious. Joseph took his hand and held it some time in silence. A change came over brother Fordham, and he regained consciousness. Bro. Joseph then asked him if he knew him. He faintly answered, "Yes." He then asked him if he wished to live. He replied "Yes," but feared it was too late. Still holding his hand, Joseph stood a few moments, and then with a loud voice said, "Brother

Fordham, I command you in the name of Jesus Christ to arise and be made whole."

He immediately arose from his bed, and shook from his feet the onion poultices which were on them, and with assistance put on his clothes, and walked with the company of brethren a few rods to the house of Joseph Bates Noble, who was laying very sick.—The journal of Wandle Mace, *op. cit.*

Still another report, made some years later, was given by William Farrington Cahoon, who said of the Prophet:

I have seen the sick healed under his administrations in many instances. I have seen cripples healed immediately, and leap for joy after being administered to. I was present and well remember a case of healing at Montrose, Iowa. One day about two o'clock in the afternoon, I was down at Brother Fordham's to see if he was still alive, (he being very low,) and as I was going home I saw Brother Joseph, the Prophet, coming up from the river. He went immediately to the house of Brother Fordham, opened the door and went in. I then, with two or three of the brethren, went back to Fordham's immediately. The Prophet went to Brother Fordham's bedside and said, "Are you very sick Brother Fordham?" But he could not speak; he made a little motion with his head. The Prophet then laid his hands upon the sick man's head, and said, "Brother Fordham, in the name of the Son of God, and the Holy Priesthood which I hold, be thou made well from this very moment."

In a few minutes the Prophet said, "Brother Fordham, get up, put on your clothes, and go with me to visit some more sick people. And all saw the Prophet and Brother Fordham, going off to another house together. I am willing to testify to this before God, and angels, and all men at any time.—*The Juvenile Instructor,* XXVII (August, 1892), p. 492.

78. *Journal History, op. cit.*

79. *Ibid.*

80. *Ibid.*

81. D&C 11:10.

82. HC, I, pp. 85–86.

83. This is not to say that all who witnessed the gifts and manifestations of the Spirit believed. While proselyting in Ohio, George A. Smith had a discussion with a Mr. William Rood, who finally acknowledged that the doctrines set forth by the Saints "were strictly scriptural" and that "the Church was organized precisely according to the true pattern" revealed in the New Testament. But he raised the issue that the new system might be "a form without the power" and stated that "if he could see one sick person healed he would then be satisfied the work was of God." Replied Elder Smith: "You would then query." "No," said the investigator. "I pledge myself that I will receive it and spend my life to spread it abroad."

A short time thereafter Elder Smith was called to bless a child in that neighborhood that had been given up in its illness as being beyond recovery. Upon his arrival, he knelt down and laid his hands upon the unconscious infant and "rebuked its disease in the name of Jesus Christ, and then hurried off to fulfill an appointment." A few days later the Elder met Mr. Rood, who informed him that a miraculous thing had occurred as a result of his administration. Said Rood: "I hid myself behind the curtain that you might not know that I was there, and I know that the child was healed, for you had not passed the gate until he got up and called for food, and then was dressed and within an hour afterwards went to his grandmother's, a mile distant, and has continued sound ever since." Elder Smith then inquired if he was ready to embrace the faith as he had promised. The hesitant witness replied: "I know it is as notable a miracle as any recorded in the New Testament. Now if I only knew the devil did not perform it, I would receive the work." Elder Smith concluded: "I have never since desired that any unbeliever should see miracles to convince him of the truth."—Journal of George A. Smith, following the entry made on date of July 4, 1836.

84. E. D. Howe, *op. cit.,* pp. 132–133.

85. D&C 35:8.

86. D&C 58:64. See also D&C 63:10–11; 68:10; 84:65; 124:98.

87. *Journal History,* October 16, 1834.

88. *Ibid.*

89. See, for example, the journal of Orson Pratt under the dates of June 11, 12, 13, 22, 30, July 1, 6, 7, 10, 12, 13, 16, 18, 20, August 8, 15, September 1, 4, 1833.

90. *Journal History,* January 28, 1835.

91. "History of Lewis Barney," by himself, typewritten copy in the Brigham Young University Library, p. 18.

92. *Journal History,* October 3, 1837. Under date of February 19, 1840, Heber C. Kimball wrote from New York City to his wife, Vilate, in Nauvoo, Illinois:

> Brother Orson Pratt and myself were called upon to visit a very sick woman; she could not turn herself in bed. We anointed her with oil in the name of the Lord, and she was healed and made whole. She did not belong to the Church, nor her husband; but in two days after she and her husband were baptized and fourteen others.—Helen Mar Whitney, "Early Reminiscences," *Woman's Exponent,* X (February 1, 1882), p. 130.

93. *Journal History,* January 15, 1833.

94. *Ibid.*

95. See *Ibid.*

96. *Ibid.,* October 8, 1837.

97. *Ibid.,* October 19, 1832.

98. The journal of Orson Pratt, June 15, 18, 1833.

99. *Ibid.,* June 23, 1833. Having recorded other incidents of healing under his administration, Elder Pratt wrote on date of August 7, 1833: "The 7th, prayed for and laid my hands upon a young woman who was sick, and the Lord healed her; and a few days after she was baptized."—*Ibid.,* under date.

100. *Woman's Exponent,* XI (August 1, 1882), p. 40.

101. *Journal History,* November 9, 1832. See also Lycurgus A. Wilson, *Life of David W. Patten* (Salt Lake City, 1904), p. 14.

102. Wilson, *op. cit.,* p. 7.

103. *Ibid.,* p. 16.

104. *Ibid.*

3

The Requisites for Faith in God

Faith comes by hearing the word of God, through the testimony of the servants of God; that testimony is always attended by the Spirit of prophecy and revelation. —JOSEPH SMITH.

Joseph Smith taught that since the beginning of the world, preparations have been made by the Lord to induce man to reach up to God and acquire the living powers and attributes of the Spirit to enlighten his mind and transform his fallen nature. These preparations are concerned with the methods by which faith in Jesus Christ can be engendered and matured within the human soul. Thereby the hope of immortal glory can be awakened in man, and he can be induced to begin the upward climb into the presence of God.

Testimony The Basis Of Faith

Testimony and Teaching the Gospel

"Whenever salvation has been administered," Joseph Smith explained, "it has been by testimony."[1] The Prophet taught that "faith comes by hearing the word of God, through the testimony of the servants of God." But testimony is not sustained by man alone; it "is always attended by the Spirit of prophecy and revelation."[2] Nephi wrote: "When a man speaketh by the Holy Ghost, the power of the Holy Ghost carrieth it *unto* the hearts of the children of men."[3] Those who hear and respond to such testimony by inquiring of God with true desire concerning its truth have their minds enlightened by the Spirit so that they can see the kingdom of God. "I know that His [God's] Spirit will bear testimony to all who seek diligently after knowledge from Him," Joseph Smith declared.[4] In this way, they can determine whether or not they wish to enter into the kingdom of God and partake of its divine truths and powers eternally.

There is a technical point of some significance in Nephi's statement above. He did not say that the Holy Spirit would carry the divine message "into" the heart of man, but "unto" the heart of man. The Holy Ghost would bring the message of truth, as it were, to the door of man's heart, but it would not establish the truth therein except by the individual's consent. There apparently is a divine restriction placed upon the Spirit by which the freedom of the individual is held inviolate. It is given to each person to accept or reject the message of truth, with its accompanying power. Though testimony may be given and though the Holy Ghost may carry it *unto* the heart of man, each heart must open by its own volition to receive that which is extended. A man whose heart is not right before God may reject the divine witness by shutting out the enlightening power of the Spirit. He may resist the Spirit; and by the expression of his agency, he may prevent the Holy Ghost from revealing its enlightening truth and power in his life. Consequently, he must be left to doubt the message of salvation and even to fight against God. But when man opens his heart to God, the hope which he expresses makes it possible for the Spirit to enter into his heart with its several divine manifestations and powers.

Upon this basis salvation is given to man. By the enlightening power of the Spirit which accompanies the message of life, responsive souls can be awakened to ponder the word and inquire of God concerning its truth and its meaning in their lives. All who do so in hope and humility, with honest hearts,[5] are given the revelations of the Holy Spirit personally, by which they may acquire faith and come to know the truth of God's work in their day. This was why Joseph Smith was commanded to show the gold plates containing the record of the Nephites only to special witnesses, who then gave their testimony to the world.[6] A revelation described the way the message of the gospel within the Book of Mormon would be given to the world:

> . . . the testimony of three witnesses will I send forth of my word. And behold, whosoever believeth on my words, them will I visit with the manifestation of my Spirit; and they shall be born of me, even of water and of the Spirit.[7]

Role of Testimony

To illustrate these points, the Prophet explained the way in which faith in God was first implanted in the heart of man on earth. Though Adam transgressed the law of Eden and fell from the presence of God, the latter-day Seer emphasized that "his transgression did not deprive him of the previous knowledge with which he was endowed relative to the existence and glory of his Creator." "Neither did God cease to manifest his will unto him."[8] The Lord said: "I, the Lord God, gave unto Adam and unto his seed, that they should not die as to the temporal death, until I, the Lord God, should send forth angels to declare unto them repentance and redemption, through faith on the name of mine Only Begotten Son."[9] "Adam, thus being made acquainted with God," Joseph Smith continued, "communicated the knowledge which he had unto his posterity; and it was through this means that the thought was first suggested to their minds that there was a God, *which laid the foundation for the exercise of their faith,* through which they could obtain a knowledge of his character and also of his glory."[10]

Having been given evidence of the existence of God through the testimony of their father, the children of Adam "were dependent upon the exercise of their own faith for a knowledge of his character, perfections, and attributes." Only those who acted with hope upon the testimony which they received through Adam were given a personal witness from God concerning His existence and the plan of salvation. Those who received a knowledge of God testified, in turn, of that knowledge to others. In this way, the plan of salvation was perpetuated. In discussing "upon what foundation the testimony was based which excited the inquiry and diligent search of the ancient saints to seek after and obtain a knowledge of the glory of God," Joseph Smith concluded: "It was the credence they gave to the testimony of their fathers, this testimony having aroused their minds to inquire after the knowledge of God."[11]

Alma explained the above points to the people of Ammonihah. Having spoken of the judgments of God upon man as a result of Adam's transgression in Eden, he continued:

> . . . after God had appointed that these things should come unto man, behold, then he saw that it was expedient that man should know concerning the things whereof he had appointed unto them [for their salvation];
>
> Therefore he sent angels to converse with them, who caused men to behold of his glory.
>
> And they began from that time forth to call on his name; therefore God conversed with men, and made known unto them the plan of redemption, which had been prepared from the foundation of the world; and this he made known unto them according to their faith and repentance and their holy works.[12]

Faith stimulated by evidence and acquired through the manifestations of the Spirit perpetuates testimony. To establish faith in the world after the fall of Adam, God sent angels to converse with man, and they caused man in his fallen state to behold the glory of God. Thus the knowledge of God which Adam possessed before the fall was reaffirmed to man in mortality, giving him a hope of the glory of God. With this hope, the Lord gave man the plan of salvation; and to the degree that man expressed faith, God revealed Himself unto him.

In the generations which followed Adam, God continued to manifest Himself to men according to these principles so that, by their faith, they could lay hold upon the gifts and blessings of the gospel. Mormon wrote:

> God . . . sent angels to minister unto the children of men, to make manifest concerning the coming of Christ; and in Christ there should come every good thing.
>
> And God also declared unto prophets, by his own mouth, that Christ should come.
>
> And behold, there were divers ways that he did manifest things unto the children of men, which were good; and all things which are good cometh of Christ; otherwise men were fallen, and there could no good thing come unto them.
>
> Wherefore, *by the ministering of angels, and by every word which proceeded forth out of the mouth of God, men began to exercise faith in Christ;* and thus by faith, they did lay hold upon every good thing; and thus it was until the coming of Christ.
>
> And after that he came men also were saved by faith in his name; and by faith, they become the sons of God. And as sure as Christ liveth he spake these words unto our fathers, saying: Whatsoever thing ye shall ask the Father in my name, which is good, in faith believing that ye shall receive, behold, it shall be done unto you.[13]

Having made this general explanation, Mormon spoke specifically of the ministry of angels and their function in establishing a basis for man to exercise faith in God:

> . . . they are subject unto him [Christ], to minister according to the word of his command, showing themselves unto them of strong faith and a firm mind in every form of godliness.
>
> And the office of their ministry is to call men unto repentance, and to fulfill and to do the work of the covenants of the Father, which he hath made unto the children of men, *to prepare the way among the children of men, by declaring the word of Christ unto the chosen vessels of the Lord, that they may bear testimony of him.*
>
> And by so doing, *the Lord God prepareth the way that the residue of men may have faith in Christ, that the Holy Ghost may have place in their hearts,* according to the power thereof.[14]

The following points should be noted in Mormon's explanation: First, in establishing the program of salvation in the world, God raises up chosen oracles who are men of strong faith and a firm mind in every form of godliness.

Second, God declares His word to these chosen men, by the ministry of angels. Third, the chosen oracles are then required to bear testimony of Christ, giving others the evidence which will stimulate in them a hope for God's mercy and glory.[15] (Their testimony is accompanied by the enlightening power of the Holy Ghost.) Fourth, testimony stimulates inquiry in others. Fifth, by inquiring of God with an honest desire to know concerning the truth of the divine message, others can receive for themselves a witness of its truth by the power of the Holy Ghost. In this way the Father brings to pass His purposes among men in their probationary state. Man's actual faith is proved, and salvation is given only to those who humbly respond to the Holy Spirit and follow its enlightening influence until they attain the presence of God.

The divine process is continued when those who receive a witness of the truth bear testimony in turn to others. In a revelation given through the Prophet to David Whitmer, Christ said: "It shall come to pass, that if you shall ask the Father in my name, in faith believing, you shall receive the Holy Ghost, which giveth utterance, *that you may stand as a witness of the things of which you shall both hear and see,* and also that you may declare repentance unto this generation."[16]

Foundations Of Living Faith

Idea that God Exists

Joseph Smith explained that certain knowledge or ideas "are necessary in order that any rational and intelligent being may exercise faith in God unto life and salvation." First, man must possess the idea that God actually exists. Of the basis of faith among the ancient saints and prophets, the latter-day Seer said: "It was by reason of the knowledge of his [God's] existence that there was a foundation laid for the exercise of faith in him." "Faith," he concluded, "could not center in a Being of whose existence we have no idea, because the idea of his existence in the first instance is essential to the exercise of faith in him."[17]

As stated previously, the knowledge that God actually exists was given to Adam when he dwelt in the presence of God; and after the fall, Adam retained that knowledge and taught it to his children. "From this we see that the whole human family in the early ages of their existence, in all their branches, had this knowledge disseminated among them," Joseph Smith explained; "so that the existence of God became an object of faith in the early ages of the world."[18] God then supplemented this early knowledge by revealing Himself to men of faith in later generations. In this way and through the ministry of angels, the knowledge that God actually exists was established and has been perpetuated in the world as a necessary basis for engendering faith in Him.

Correct Idea of Character of God

The second thing[19] a rational and intelligent being must know to exercise true faith in God is "a correct idea of his character." Man is indebted to God for the revelations He has given concerning His character, the Prophet maintained, for, without these revelations, "no man by searching could find out God."[20] "Without correct ideas of his character," man could not acquire sufficient power with God to exercise faith unto eternal life. Joseph Smith therefore concluded: "Correct ideas of his character lay a foundation, as far as his character is concerned, for the exercise of faith, so as to enjoy the fullness of the blessing of the Gospel of Jesus Christ even that of eternal glory."[21]

Having examined the subject of God's character from the testimony of ancient and modern scripture, the Prophet concluded the following respecting the character of God: (1) "that he was God before the world was created, and the same God that he was after it was created"; (2) "that he is merciful and gracious, slow to anger, abundant in goodness, and that he was so from everlasting, and will be to everlasting"; (3) "that he changes not, neither is there variableness with him"; (4) "that he is a God of truth and cannot lie"; (5) "that he is no respecter of persons: but in every nation he that fears God and works righteousness is accepted of him"; and (6) "that he is love."[22] In discussing the importance of these points of God's character as a basis for man to exercise faith in deity, Joseph Smith said:

> An acquaintance with these attributes in the divine character, is essentially necessary, in order that the faith of any rational being can center in him for life and salvation. For if he did not, in the first instance, believe him to be God, that is, the Creator and upholder of all things, he could not *center* his faith in him for life and salvation, for fear there should be a greater than he, who would thwart all his plans, and he, like the gods of the heathen, would be unable to fulfill his promises; but seeing he is God over all, from everlasting to everlasting, the creator and upholder of all things, no such fear can exist in the minds of those who put their trust in him, so that in this respect their faith can be without wavering.[23]

Of the need for man to understand that God is gracious and slow to anger in order to exercise faith in Him, the Prophet said:

> Unless he was merciful, and gracious, slow to anger, long suffering, and full of goodness, such is the weakness of human nature, and so great the frailties and imperfections of men, that unless they believed that these excellencies existed in the divine character, the faith necessary to salvation could not exist; for doubt would take the place of faith, and those who know their weakness and liability to sin, would be in constant doubt of salvation, if it were not for the idea which they have of the excellency of the character of God, that he is slow to anger, and long suffering, and of a forgiving disposition, and does forgive iniquity, transgression and sin. An idea of these facts does away [with] doubt, and makes faith exceedingly strong.[24]

Concerning the need for man to be assured that God does not change, the latter-day Seer said:

> It is equally as necessary that men should have the idea that he is a God who changes not, in order to have faith in him, as it is to have the idea that he is gracious and long suffering. For without the idea of unchangeableness in the character of the

Deity, doubt would take the place of faith. But with the idea that he changes not, faith lays hold upon the excellencies of his character with unshaken confidence, believing he is the same yesterday, to-day and forever, and that his course is one eternal round.[25]

Regarding the acquisition of faith in God, Joseph Smith stressed the importance of the knowledge that He is truthful:

> The idea that he is a God of truth and cannot lie, is equally as necessary to the exercise of faith in him, as the idea of his unchangeableness. For without the idea that he was a God of truth and could not lie, the confidence necessary to be placed in his word in order to the exercise of faith in him could not exist. But having the idea that he is not man, that he cannot lie, it gives power to the minds of men to exercise faith in him.[26]

About the need for man to understand that God is no respecter of persons in order to exercise faith in him, the Prophet said:

> It is also necessary that men should have an idea that he is no respecter of persons; for with the idea of all the other excellencies in his character, and this one wanting, men could not exercise faith in him, because if he were a respecter of persons, they could not tell what their privileges were, nor how far they were authorized to exercise faith in him, or whether they were authorized to do it at all, but all must be confusion; but no sooner are the minds of men made acquainted with the truth on this point, that he is no respecter of persons, than they see that they have authority by faith to lay hold on eternal life, the richest boon of heaven, because God is no respecter of persons, and that every man in every nation has an equal privilege.[27]

Finally, the latter-day Seer spoke of man's need to realize that God is a being of love:

> Lastly, but not less important to the exercise of faith in God, is the idea that he is love; for with all the other excellencies in his character, without this one to influence them, they could not have such powerful dominion over the minds of men; but when the idea is planted in the mind that he is love, who cannot see the just ground that men of every nation, kindred and tongue, have to exercise faith in God so as to obtain eternal life?[28]

Joseph Smith held that the foregoing description of the character of God is that which is given in the Lord's revelations to both the former-day saints and the Latter-day Saints. And here, he concluded, "there is a sure foundation for the exercise of faith in him among every people, nation, and kindred, from age to age, and from generation to generation." Men in every dispensation have had essentially the same basis upon which to exercise faith in God, "because the same character" respecting God has been revealed to men in all ages whenever the plan of life and salvation has been sent forth from heaven.[29]

Correct Idea of Attributes of God

After making the above points, Joseph Smith proceeded "to show the connection there is between correct ideas of the attributes of God, and the exercise of faith in him unto eternal life." To begin, he said: "Let us here observe, that the real design which the God of heaven had in view in making the human family acquainted with his attributes, was, that they, through the ideas of the existence of his attributes, might be enabled to exercise faith in him, and through the exercise of faith in him, might obtain eternal life; for without the idea of the existence of his attributes which belong to God, the minds of men could not have power to exercise faith in him so as to lay hold upon eternal life." He therefore concluded that "the divine communications made to men in the first instance were designed to establish in their minds the ideas necessary to enable them to exercise faith in God, and through this means to be partakers of his glory."[30]

The Prophet listed the major attributes of God as knowledge, faith or power, justice, judgment, mercy, and truth, and then analyzed them separately as a basis upon which man can build faith in God. Of the first of these attributes, he said: "Without the knowledge of all things, God would not be able to save any portion of his creatures; for it is by reason of the knowledge which he has of all things, from the beginning to the end, that enables him to give that understanding to his creatures by which they are made partakers of eternal life; and if it were not for the idea existing in the minds of men that God had all knowledge it would be impossible for them to exercise faith in him."[31]

Of the need for man to understand that God possesses the attribute of faith or power, the Prophet said:

> Unless God had power over all things, and was able by his power to control all things, and thereby deliver his creatures who put their trust in him from the power of all beings that might seek their destruction, whether in heaven, or earth, or in hell, men could not be saved. But with the idea of the existence of this attribute planted in the mind, men feel as though they had nothing to fear who put their trust in God, believing that he has power to save all who come to him to the very uttermost.[32]

Besides possessing the idea that God is a being of knowledge and power, man must understand that He is just and equitable in all that He does. The Prophet explained: "Without the idea of the existence of the attribute justice in the Deity, men could not have confidence sufficiently to place themselves under his guidance and direction; for they would be filled with fear and doubt, lest the Judge of all the earth would not do right; and thus fear, or doubt, existing in the mind, would preclude the possibility of the exercise of faith in him for life and salvation." But when man possesses the idea that God is just, there is no room for doubt in his heart. Consequently, "the mind is enabled to cast itself upon the Almighty without doubt, and with [the] most unshaken confidence, believing that the Judge of all the earth will do right."[33]

The idea of the attribute of judgment in God is equally important as a basis for man to exercise faith in Him. Joseph Smith said of man's need to possess an understanding of this attribute of God:

> Without the idea of the existence of this attribute in the Deity, it would be impossible for men to exercise faith in him for life and salvation, seeing that it is through the exercise of this attribute that the faithful in Christ Jesus are delivered out of the

hands of those who seek their destruction; for if God were not to come out in swift judgment against the workers of iniquity and the powers of darkness, his saints could not be saved; for it is by judgment that the Lord delivers his saints out of the hands of all their enemies, and those who reject the gospel of our Lord Jesus Christ. But no sooner is the idea of the existence of this attribute planted in the minds of men than it gives power to the mind for the exercise of faith and confidence in God, and they are enabled, by faith, to lay hold on the promises which are set before them, and wade through all the tribulations and afflictions to which they are subjected by reason of the persecution from those who know not God, and obey not the gospel of our Lord Jesus Christ: believing that in due time the Lord will come out in swift judgment against their enemies, and they shall be cut off from before him, and that in his own due time he will bear them off conquerors, and more than conquerors, in all things.[34]

There is no place in Joseph Smith's thought for the view that the faithful will forever be thwarted in their righteous aspirations. Individual dignity and righteous self-realization are dominant themes within the restored gospel. But these objectives must be attained by the proper exercise of faith in God; and to this end the righteous must possess the idea that judgment is an attribute of deity—that God will come out in judgment against iniquity and oppression, and that righteousness and human dignity will finally prevail. For this reason, Alma quoted in his discourse on faith the prophet Zenos, who exclaimed to God: "Thou hast also heard me when I have been cast out and have been despised by mine enemies; yea, thou didst hear my cries, and wast angry with mine enemies, and thou didst visit them in thine anger with speedy destruction."[35]

In order for man to exercise faith in God unto salvation, it is also important for him to understand that God possesses the attribute of mercy. The latter-day Seer observed:

Without the idea of the existence of this attribute in the Deity, the spirits of the saints would faint in the midst of the tribulations, afflictions and persecutions which they have to endure for righteousness' sake; but when the idea of the existence of this attribute is once established in the mind it gives life and energy to the spirits of the saints: believing that the mercy of God will be poured out upon them in the midst of their afflictions, and that he will compassionate them in their sufferings; and that the mercy of God will lay hold of them and secure them in the arms of his love, so that they will receive a full reward for all their sufferings.[36]

Last, and very important to the exercise of faith, is the idea that God is a being of truth. The Prophet said of man's need to understand this attribute:

Without the idea of the existence of this attribute the mind of man could have nothing upon which it could rest with certainty: all would be confusion and doubt; but with the idea of the existence of this attribute in the Deity, in the mind, all the teachings, instructions, promises and blessings become realities, and the mind is enabled to lay hold of them with certainty and confidence: believing that these things, and all that the Lord has said, shall be fulfilled in their time; and that all the cursings, denunciations and judgments, pronounced upon the heads of the unrighteous will also be executed in the due time of the Lord: and by reason of the truth and veracity of him, the mind beholds its deliverance and salvation as being certain.[37]

Finally Joseph Smith summarized the relationship that exists between a correct idea of the several attributes of God and the exercise of faith in Him unto eternal life:

Let the mind once reflect sincerely and candidly upon the ideas of the existence of the before mentioned attributes in the Deity, and it will be seen, that as far as his attributes are concerned, there is a sure foundation laid for the exercise of faith in him for life and salvation. For in as much as God possesses the attribute knowledge he can make all things known to his saints necessary for their salvation; and as he possesses the attribute power he is able thereby to deliver them from the power of all enemies; and seeing also, that justice is an attribute of the Deity, he will deal with them upon the principle of righteousness and equity, and a just reward will be granted unto them for all their afflictions and sufferings for the truth's sake. And as judgment is an attribute of the Deity also, his saints can have the most unshaken confidence that they will, in due time, obtain a perfect deliverance out of the hands of all their enemies, and a complete victory over all those who have sought their hurt and

> destruction. And as mercy is also an attribute of the Deity, his saints can have confidence that it will be exercised toward them; and through the exercise of that attribute toward them, comfort and consolation will be administered unto them abundantly, amid all their afflictions and tribulations. And lastly, realizing that truth is an attribute of the Deity, the mind is led to rejoice amid all its trials and temptations, in hope of that glory which is to be brought at the revelation of Jesus Christ, and in view of that crown which is to be placed upon the heads of the saints in the day when the Lord shall distribute rewards unto them, and in prospect of that eternal weight of glory which the Lord has promised to bestow upon them when he shall bring them into the midst of his throne to dwell in his presence eternally.
>
> In view, then, of the existence of these attributes, the faith of the saints can become exceedingly strong: abounding in righteousness unto the praise and glory of God, and can exert its mighty influence in searching after wisdom and understanding, until it has obtained a knowledge of all things that pertain to life and salvation.
>
> Such, then, is the foundation, which is laid through the revelation of the attributes of God, for the exercise of faith in him for life and salvation.[38]

Like the revelation of the character of God, the foregoing attributes are those which the Lord has manifested to man in all ages of time, whenever He has spoken from heaven. Since it is by the revelation of these attributes that a foundation is laid for the exercise of faith in God unto life and salvation, Joseph Smith concluded his discussion of this subject by stressing "that all men have had, and will have, an equal privilege" to acquire faith unto eternal life.[39]

Correct Idea of Perfections of God

Having shown the importance of having a correct idea of God's character and attributes before man can exercise faith in Him, Joseph Smith then treated man's need to possess an undertanding of the perfections of God[40] and to be assured that man, too, can acquire the character and attributes of God in their perfection by receiving the blessings and powers of the Holy Spirit and by maturing in them until he is given eternal life.

The several attributes of God in their perfection are integral parts of His glory and power. They constitute essential elements of the divine intelligence that centers in Him and which is manifested throughout universal space by means of the Holy Spirit. By strict obedience to the will of the Father, Christ attained a fulness of the perfections of the Father; and through Christ man may also acquire the glory of God. To this end, Joseph Smith emphasized that man must understand that the Father's glory dwells within Christ in its fulness; and that by growing in the blessings and endowments of the Holy Spirit man may also come to possess the same mind, glory, and power which Christ possesses. Thereby man may be "transformed into the same [divine] image or likeness, even the express image of him who fills all in all; being filled with the fullness of his glory, and become one in him, even as the Father, Son and Holy Spirit are one." Joseph Smith explained further:

> The saints have a sure foundation laid for the exercise of faith unto life and salvation, through the atonement and mediation of Jesus Christ; by whose blood they have a forgiveness of sins, and also a sure reward laid up for them in heaven, *even that of partaking of the fullness of the Father and the Son through the Spirit. As the Son partakes of the fullness of the Father through the Spirit, so the saints are, by the same Spirit, to be partakers of the same fullness, to enjoy the same glory;* for as the Father and the Son are one, so, in like manner, the saints are to be one in them. Through the love of the Father, the mediation of Jesus Christ, and the gift of the Holy Spirit, they are to be heirs of God, and joint heirs with Jesus Christ.[41]

Since the endowment of man with the glory and power of the Father is a major objective of the plan of life and salvation, man must have an assurance that he can achieve this goal if he is to be able to exercise faith unto eternal life. He may acquire this assurance by studying the promises of God[42] and by relying upon the promise that if he receives the Holy Spirit through the gospel and continues to mature in his spiritual union with Christ he will be endowed with a fulness of glory in the resurrection, according to the promise of God.[43] If the Spirit is real in man's life on earth, the glory of God in its fulness will be equally real in his life in the resurrection.

Knowledge that Man's Course is Divinely Approved

If man is to continue to exercise faith in God unto salvation the Prophet taught that he must have "an actual knowledge that the course of life which he is pursuing is according to his [God's] will."[44] He explained:

This knowledge supplies an important place in revealed religion; for it was by reason of it that the ancients were enabled to endure as seeing him who is invisible. An actual knowledge to any person that the course of life which he pursues is according to the will of God, is essentially necessary to enable him to have that confidence in God, without which no person can obtain eternal life. It was this that enabled the ancient saints to endure all their afflictions and persecutions, and to take joyfully the spoiling of their goods, knowing, (not believing merely,) that they had a more enduring substance. Heb. 10:34.

Having the assurance that they were pursuing a course which was agreeable to the will of God, they were enabled to take not only the spoiling of their goods and the wasting of their substance joyfully, but also to suffer death in its most horrid forms; knowing, (not merely believing,) that when this earthly house of their tabernacle was dissolved, they had a building of God, a house not made with hands, eternal in the heavens. Second Cor. 5:1.

Such was and always will be the situation of the saints of God, that unless they have an actual knowledge that the course that they are pursuing is according to the will of God, they will grow weary in their minds and faint; for such has been and always will be the opposition in the hearts of unbelievers and those that know not God, against the pure and unadulterated religion of heaven, (the only thing which ensures eternal life,) that they will persecute, to the uttermost, all that worship God according to his revelations, receive the truth in the love of it, and submit themselves to be guided and directed by his will, and drive them to such extremities that nothing short of an actual knowledge of their being the favorites of heaven, and of their having embraced that order of things which God has established for the redemption of man, will enable them to exercise that confidence in him necessary for them to overcome the world, and obtain that crown of glory which is laid up for them that fear God.[45]

As man exercises faith in God, the Lord reveals truth and light to him. With these the man of faith walks continually in spiritual union with God. Being in the path of life and salvation, he is aware of that fact by the revelation of the Holy Spirit; and such knowledge becomes, in turn, a means by which he can act with greater faith in God. It also sustains him against trials and tribulations. "For a man to lay down his all, his character and reputation, his honor, and applause, his good name among men, his houses, his lands, his brothers and sisters, his wife and children, and even his own life also—counting all things but filth and dross for the excellency of the knowledge of Jesus Christ—requires more than mere belief or supposition that he is doing the will of God," the Prophet stressed; "but actual knowledge, realizing that, when the sufferings are ended, he will enter into eternal rest, and be a partaker of the glory of God." With such knowledge, so that he "most assuredly knows that he is doing the will of God, his confidence can be equally strong that he will be a partaker of the glory of God."[46]

Need to Sacrifice All Things

Faith, as will be discussed in the next chapter, is not mere belief, but is synonymous with power—the power of the soul to operate in the realm of the Holy Spirit. To acquire faith unto eternal life, man must be willing to give all he possesses to obtain the divine gift. To this end sacrifice is necessary. "A religion that does not require the sacrifice of all things never has power sufficient to produce the faith necessary unto life and salvation," Joseph Smith declared; "for, from the first existence of man, the faith necessary unto the enjoyment of life and salvation never could be obtained without the sacrifice of all earthly things."[47] Continuing, he declared:

> It was through this sacrifice, and this only, that God has

> ordained that men should enjoy eternal life. . . . When a man has offered in sacrifice all that he has for the truth's sake, not even withholding his life, and believing before God that he has been called to make this sacrifice because he seeks to do his will, he does know, most assuredly, that God does and will accept his sacrifice and offering, and that he has not, nor will not seek his face in vain. *Under these circumstances, then, he can obtain the faith necessary for him to lay hold on eternal life.*[48]

From a careful reading of the Prophet's statement it is apparent that he does not mean that man must actually give his life as a martyr to the cause of truth in order to obtain faith unto eternal life, but that he must manifest a willingness to sacrifice all he possesses, including his life should it be necessary, to sustain the kingdom of God upon the earth. This sacrifice is primarily one of mind or of attitude. But it must be genuine and without reservation. To attain salvation, man must place all he possesses as a sacrifice upon the altar of his heart. The danger of worldly wealth or power is that man often sets his heart upon that which is temporal at the exclusion of that which is eternal. When he does this, faith in God wanes and doubt begins to prevail in his mind, and the gift of eternal life is lost. By revelation the Lord said: "Whoso is not willing to lay down his life for my sake is not my disciple."[49] Again: "I have decreed in my heart, saith the Lord, that I will prove you in all things, whether you will abide in my covenant, even unto death, that you may be found worthy. For if ye will not abide in my covenant ye are not worthy of me."[50]

Only by complying with the principle of sacrifice can man acquire the knowledge that his course in life is divinely approved. Having stated this principle, the Prophet concluded:

> Those, then, who make the sacrifice will have the testimony that their course is pleasing in the sight of God; and those who have this testimony will have faith to lay hold on eternal life, and will be enabled, through faith, to endure unto the end, and receive the crown that is laid up for them that love the appearing of our Lord Jesus Christ. But those who do not make the sacrifice cannot enjoy this faith, because men are dependent

upon this sacrifice in order to obtain this faith: therefore, they cannot lay hold upon eternal life, because the revelations of God do not guarantee unto them the authority so to do, and without this guarantee faith could not exist.

All the saints of whom we have account, in all the revelations of God which are extant, obtained the knowledge which they had of their acceptance in his sight through the sacrifice which they offered unto him; and through the knowledge thus obtained, their faith became sufficiently strong to lay hold upon the promise of eternal life, and to endure as seeing him who is invisible; and were enabled, through faith, to combat the powers of darkness, contend against the wiles of the adversary, overcome the world, and obtain the end of their faith, even the salvation of their souls.

But those who have not made this sacrifice to God do not know that the course which they pursue is well pleasing in his sight; for whatever may be their belief or their opinion, it is a matter of doubt and uncertainty in their mind; and where doubt and uncertainty are there faith is not, nor can it be.[51]

Summary

Joseph Smith taught that there must be a proper foundation laid if man is to exercise faith in God. The hope of immortal glory must be awakened in man, and he must be stimulated to reach up to God for the divine truth and power necessary for his return to the presence of God. For this reason, salvation can be administered only by testimony.

For testimony to be given, chosen oracles must be raised up to whom God ministers, by His own voice and by messengers sent from His presence. The chosen oracles must then testify to others of that which they know to be true, and their testimony must be accompanied by the power of the Holy Ghost, which stimulates additional inquiry in others. When those who hear such testimony inquire of God with an honest heart and a true desire concerning the truth of the divine message, they are given a witness of its truth by the power of the Holy Ghost. In this way, man is proven in his desire for righteousness, and salvation is given only to those who respond to the Holy

Spirit and develop its divine blessings in their lives until they attain the presence of God.

As a basis upon which the above program can best function, some general requisites must exist, if man is to acquire faith unto salvation: First, man must possess the idea that God actually exists. Second, he must have a correct idea of the character of God. Third, he must have a true concept of the attributes of God—knowledge, faith or power, justice, judgment, mercy, and truth. Fourth, he must have a correct understanding of the perfections of God. Fifth, he must know by the Spirit of revelation that the course which he is pursuing in life is according to the will of God. Finally, man must live a consecrated life; that is, he must hold all else as secondary to Jesus Christ and the establishment of His kingdom in the earth, and he must genuinely feel disposed to sacrifice all things, his own life not excluded, to sustain the testimony of Christ and the program of His kingdom in the earth. Only then can man's faith become perfect unto salvation.

Notes

1. HC, III, pp. 389–390.
2. *Ibid.,* p. 379.
3. 2 Nephi 33:1.
4. HC, I, p. 442.
5. See D&C 8:1; 11:10.
6. See Volume I of this study, the section in chapter four entitled "Witnesses to the Ancient Record."
7. D&C 5:15–16.
8. *Lectures on Faith,* No. 2.
9. D&C 29:42.
10. *Lectures on Faith,* No. 2.
11. *Ibid.*
12. Alma 12:28–30.
13. Moroni 7:22–26.
14. Moroni 7:30–32.
15. For example, a revelation declared that the Book of Mormon was "confirmed to others [besides the Prophet] by the ministering of angels, and is declared unto the world by them."—D&C 20:10.
16. D&C 14:8.
17. *Lectures on Faith,* No. 3.
18. *Ibid.,* No. 2.
19. Joseph Smith placed this requisite and the two that follow under one

general heading in his *Lectures,* but for the purpose of better organization in this work the writer has placed each of these requisites under separate headings.

20. *Lectures on Faith,* No. 3.
21. *Ibid.,* No. 4.
22. *Ibid.,* No. 3.
23. *Ibid.* (Italics in the original.)
24. *Ibid.*
25. *Ibid.*
26. *Ibid.*
27. *Ibid.*
28. *Ibid.*
29. *Ibid.*
30. *Ibid.,* No. 4.
31. *Ibid.*
32. *Ibid.*
33. *Ibid.*
34. *Ibid.*
35. Alma 33:10.
36. *Lectures on Faith,* No. 4.
37. *Ibid.*
38. *Ibid.*
39. *Ibid.*
40. For a discussion of the perfections of God, see Volume I of this study, the section in chapter five entitled "The Perfection of Deity."
41. *Lectures on Faith,* No. 5.
42. See, for example, D&C 93:19–20, 28; 3 Nephi 19:29.
43. *Ibid.*
44. *Lectures on Faith,* No. 3.
45. *Ibid.,* No. 6.
46. *Ibid.*
47. *Ibid.*
48. *Ibid.*
49. D&C 103:28.
50. D&C 98:14–15.
51. *Lectures on Faith,* No. 6. On the subject of sacrifice, Brigham Young said:

> Suppose we were called to leave what we have now, should we call it a sacrifice? Shame on the man who would so call it; for it is the very means of adding to him knowledge, understanding, power, and glory, and prepares him to receive crowns, kingdoms, thrones, and principalities, and to be crowned in glory with the Gods of eternity. Short of this, we can never receive that which we are looking for.—JD, II, p. 7.

4

Faith in the Lord Jesus Christ

> *I would show unto the world that faith is things which are hoped for and not seen; wherefore, dispute not because ye see not, for ye receive no witness until after the trial of your faith.*—Moroni.

Joseph Smith taught that not merely faith, but faith in the Lord Jesus Christ, is the first principle of the restored gospel.[1] Faith in Christ is a living and moving principle. It is power, or the power of the human soul to act in the realm of the Holy Spirit. As such, it is based upon the assurance that there is a higher order of life than that which is experienced by the natural man on earth and which man may attain through the mercy and power of the great Redeemer. Through the proper expression of desire and hope, man can achieve spiritual union with Christ who is a glorified being and develop the ability to act in and through the Spirit so that he receives the blessings and powers of the Spirit. To the degree that man can do this he has living faith in Jesus Christ; and by the expression of faith, he can acquire the divine truth and power by which he may be sanctified and enter eventually into the presence of God.

Doctrine Of Faith In Jesus Christ

Evidence a Basis for Faith in Christ

Faith in the Lord Jesus Christ is based upon the evidence which man has of Him and of His divine mission. It follows that the extent to which man may develop faith in the great Redeemer depends in some measure upon the persuasiveness of the evidence which he possesses, and upon his ability and willingness to accept that evidence. A revelation observed that the latter-day dispensation of the gospel—in which man is given new evidence and assurance of the divine mission of Christ—was revealed so that faith "might increase in the earth."[2] Orson Pratt wrote of the role of evidence in developing faith in man:

> As evidence precedes faith, the latter should be weak or strong in proportion to the weakness or strength of the evidence. Where the evidence is accompanied by circumstances of a doubtful nature; or where it relates to things which are, in some degree, improbable in themselves; or where there is an opposing evidence of nearly the same influence or weight; or where there is only circumstantial evidence—faith should be weak. On the other hand, where the evidences are direct; where they relate to events or things, not improbable; where they are accompanied by favourable circumstances of a confirmatory nature; where no evidence, or any influence or weight, are in opposition—faith should be strong. The weakness or strength of faith will, therefore, in all cases, be in proportion to the weakness or strength of the impressions, produced upon the mind by evidence.[3]

Roles of External and Internal Evidence

When evidence concerning the existence of God is presented to an open and inquiring mind, it stimulates in man a desire for righteousness and a living hope in Christ. There are both external and internal evidences, and each plays a role in developing faith in man. External evidence is that evidence which man can perceive by means of the physical senses. By contrast, internal evidence is given to man through the Holy Spirit as it enlightens his mind and gives him an assurance of the things of God. Man can perceive this kind of evidence only as he responds by the expression of desire to the enlightening influence of the Holy Spirit.

External evidence can lead man to believe in God. But belief is merely the forerunner of faith. Alma exhorted some people to develop faith by first believing in the word of God.[4] In the act of believing, man accepts the conclusions of evidence. Because of evidence, he may believe that the sun will continue to rise and set, the tide continue to ebb and flow, and the seasons continue to come and go. By giving serious consideration to the evidence that there is a Supreme Being, he may also begin to believe in God.[5]

But man may believe in God and still lack faith. External evidence alone cannot produce saving faith in the heart of man, nor can it alone bring him into a meaningful spiritual union with Christ. It is primarily by means of the internal evidence which man is given through the Holy Spirit that he achieves living faith in God. True faith is more than man's submission to reasonable arguments which support given doctrines, concepts, or conclusions. It is more than reason grown courageous enough to span the dark abyss between the known and the unknown. Faith is true belief strengthened and enhanced by the Holy Spirit which man receives when he reaches up to God with desire and hope; it is the power which man acquires when his soul is illuminated and his mind is sustained in its actions by the enlightening influence of the Holy Spirit. External evidence may stimulate man to believe, but only when he obtains divine truth, light, and power through the Holy Spirit by expressing desire and hope in Christ can man possess true faith. Only then can he acquire the divine truth and power by which the human soul is regenerated, the sick healed, the elements controlled, and the dead raised to life. If man had the faith of a grain of mustard seed—the ability to assimilate and use the divine powers which are available to him by faith as does a mustard seed in its sphere of life—he could move a mountain through the power of the Spirit or cast a sycamine tree into the depths of the sea.[6] "The brother of Jared said unto the mountain Zerin, Remove," the Book of Mormon reports, "and it was removed."[7] This was not done by mere belief, but by faith.

The relationship between belief and faith was made clear in a revelation which instructed the Saints: "*As all have not faith,* seek ye diligently and teach one another words of wisdom; seek learning, even by study and also by faith."[8] Many to whom this revelation referred had joined the Church. But not all of them possessed faith. Faith is something to be obtained by those who believe,[9] and it is something to be exercised.[10] Unless it is continually sustained, the faith of the believer may fail.[11] The righteous must be upheld by the prayer of faith.[12] The Lord instructed the Saints (in the revelation quoted above) to study diligently from the best books, which included those of holy writ, that their belief might mature into faith. To acquire knowledge by study is to do so primarily by mental processes. Thereby man may strengthen his belief. But to acquire knowledge by faith, man must bring his whole soul into such union with God that the Holy Spirit becomes a channel of revelation and of power unto him. The task of maturing belief into living faith can be man's greatest challenge and his most noble and rewarding endeavor.

Several associates of the Prophet expressed the view that the greatest evidence of God which man can receive (short of seeing the Lord in His glory) is that evidence which is given to him through the Holy Spirit as he begins to exercise a living hope in Christ.[13] By this evidence, primarily, true faith can be matured within man. Having referred to the illumination of the mind by the Spirit giving evidence of God, Alma reasoned: "Now behold, would not this increase your faith? I say unto you, Yea."[14] Because the Holy Spirit accompanies the teaching of the gospel, Joseph Smith concluded: "Faith comes not by signs [i.e., external evidence], but by hearing the word of God."[15]

In a letter to James Arlington Bennet, the Prophet stressed the importance of that evidence which is given to man by the enlightening influence of the Holy Spirit. He declared:

> The world at large is ever ready to credit the writings of Homer, Hesiod, Plutarch, Socrates, Pythagoras, Virgil, Josephus, Mahomet, and an hundred others; but where, tell me, where, have they left a line—a simple method of solving the truth of the plan of eternal life? Says the Savior, "If any man will do his [the Father's] will, he shall know of the doctrine, whether it be of God, or whether I speak of myself." *Here, then, is a method of solving the divinity of men by the divinity within yourself, that as far exceeds the calculations of numbers as the sun exceeds a candle.* Would to God that all men understood it and were willing to be governed by it.[16]

The Relationship of Desire, Hope, and Faith

Man must express desire and hope before he can acquire saving faith in Christ. In expressing desire, man wishes or longs for something which he would like to possess. But desire is only the beginning of faith. Man must then exercise hope, which is an expression of the soul that goes beyond desire. In expressing hope, man desires the thing which he would like to possess and has confidence or assurance that he can obtain it. Hope therefore adds these elements to desire; it is desire accompanied by confidence or assurance.

A desire for the things of God may begin with the realization which is born of man's mortal experience that his finite powers alone are not sufficient to enable him to attain the righteousness, peace, joy, and power for which his soul hungers. Desire is also stimulated in man by the presentation of evidence concerning God and by the influence of testimony accompanied by the enlightening power of the Holy Spirit. Alma therefore began a discourse on faith by admonishing the people: "If ye will awake and arouse your faculties . . . and exercise a particle of faith, *even if ye can no more than desire to believe, let this desire work in you, even until ye believe in a manner that ye can give place for a portion of my words.*"[17]

As man expresses a desire for the truth, power, and righteousness of Jesus Christ, he is given the enlightening manifestations of the Holy Spirit which develop an assurance in him of the things of God. Hope springs up in his heart. He begins to learn of the reality of the Spirit and to acquire confidence in the things of God.

When man begins to act in and through the Spirit, the hope which he possesses matures into living faith, which, as stated above, is the power of the human soul to operate in the realm of the Spirit and to utilize the blessings and powers of that divine agent to achieve righteous objectives.

Man's desire must mature into hope if he is to acquire faith. "How is it that ye can attain unto faith," Mormon inquired, "save ye shall have hope?"[18] Such hope must be expressed intelligently toward the right ends. "What is it that ye shall hope for?" the Nephite general continued. "Behold I say unto you that ye shall hope through the atonement of Christ and the power of his resurrection to be raised unto eternal life, and this because of your faith in him according to the promise."[19] In an inspired prayer, Moroni said: "Thou hast said that thou hast prepared a house for man, yea, even among the mansions of thy Father, in which man might have a more excellent hope; *wherefore man must hope, or he cannot receive an inheritance in the place which thou hast prepared.*"[20]

Because hope is an extension of desire, it, too, is based upon evidence and testimony. For this reason Alma inquired concerning those who believed in the message of salvation before his day: "What grounds had they to hope for salvation?"[21] In other words, upon what evidence was their hope based? The evidence which stimulates true hope is that which is given to man by the Holy Spirit. Jacob therefore observed: "We search the prophets, and we have many revelations and the spirit of prophecy; and *having all these witnesses we obtain a hope, and our faith becometh unshaken.*"[22]

Enos is an example of one who expressed the element of hope and thereby acquired some of the blessings that lead to salvation. Being the son of Jacob, a Nephite prophet, he was taught "in the nurture and admonition of the Lord." Enos wrote of his experience: "The words which I had often heard my father speak concerning eternal life, and the joy of the saints, sunk deep into my heart." "My soul hungered," he continued, "and I kneeled down before my Maker, and I cried unto him in mighty prayer and supplication for mine own soul; and all the day long did I cry unto him; yea, and when the night came I did still raise my voice high that it reached the heavens." Finally, Enos reported: "There came a voice unto me, saying: Enos, thy sins are forgiven thee, and thou shalt be blessed."[23]

Here all the ingredients of true faith were expressed: evidence of God which Enos had received from his father; a willingness to accept and to act upon that evidence; a desire for righteousness; and a hope expressed as an inner hunger of soul and as a confidence or assurance that sustained him in his upward reach to God. When in this way Enos brought his soul into a living spiritual union with God, he had sufficient faith to commune with the Lord through the Holy Spirit.

Hope not only must precede faith, but it is also the product of faith. The blessings that follow the expression of faith give man a greater hope for the things of God. Ether taught that hope "cometh of faith,"[24] and Moroni observed that those who have faith "have hope."[25] Speaking of the law of Moses which gave the Nephites evidence to strengthen their faith in the coming of Christ, Mormon explained: "And thus, *they did retain a hope through faith,* unto eternal salvation."[26] The Nephite historian reasoned: "Wherefore if a man have faith he must needs have hope; for without faith there cannot be any hope."[27] By faith in Christ and obedience to the gospel, man is given "the Holy Ghost," he wrote, "which Comforter filleth with hope."[28]

On the other hand, the hope which faith produces enables man to obtain greater faith, thus making the acquisition of hope and faith a cyclical process that leads to eternal life.

Alma's Explanation Of Faith

The finest explanation of how faith can be developed in man that can be found anywhere in sacred literature was given by Alma. Beginning his address, he said: "There are many who do say: If thou wilt show unto us a sign from heaven, then we shall know of a surety; then we shall believe." But he inquired, "Is this faith?" "Behold, I say unto you, Nay; for if a man knoweth a thing he hath no cause to believe, for he knoweth it." "Faith," he then explained, "is not to have a perfect knowledge of things; therefore *if ye have faith ye hope for things which are not seen, which are true.*"[29]

To act in faith, man must reach up to God in hope, desiring that which he has not yet seen but which is true. This same principle of hope applies in the search for scientific knowledge. Nuclear physicists probed into the realm of the unknown in an effort to release the power of the atom. Before they discovered the process of nuclear fission, they acted without a perfect knowledge, hoping for things which they had not seen but which were true. Having assembled the proper data and arranged the necessary equipment, they acted by faith; and their faith led to knowledge as the unknown was revealed in the release of atomic power.[30]

This is the process man must apply on a higher, spiritual plane in order to bring the Holy Spirit into his life and thereby be able to exercise faith. He must begin by studying the law of God to acquire a knowledge of the principles of eternal truth. He must also begin to harmonize his life with the requirements of heaven. He must then probe by the expression of genuine desire into the realm of spiritual truth and power. To the degree that man inquires of God with true desire, the Lord reveals Himself by the manifestation of His Holy Spirit. There is a release of divine truth and power, which gives man a hope or an assurance of the things of God. But unlike a nuclear reaction, this transforming response takes place within man, and it results in the illumination of his mind to the knowledge of God. In this way, man begins to acquire faith unto salvation.

Man's growth in faith can be a real, though it may be a gradual, process. For this reason Alma compared the development of faith and its divine fruits in the life of man to a seed that is planted in the soil and, by proper nurturing and cultivation, develops into a mature tree that bears delicious fruit. He said:

> . . . as I said concerning faith—that it was not a perfect knowledge—even so it is with my words. Ye cannot know of their surety at first, unto perfection, any more than faith is a perfect knowledge.
>
> But behold, if ye will awake and arouse your faculties, even to an experiment upon my words, and exercise a particle of faith, yea, even if ye can no more than desire to believe, let this desire work in you, even until ye believe in a manner that ye can give place for a portion of my words.
>
> Now, we will compare the word unto a seed. Now, if ye give place, that a seed may be planted in your heart, behold, if it be a true seed, or a good seed, if ye do not cast it out by your unbelief, that ye will resist the Spirit of the Lord, behold, it will begin to swell within your breasts; and when you feel these swelling motions, ye will begin to say within yourselves—It must needs be that the word is good, for it beginneth to enlarge my soul; yea, it beginneth to enlighten my understanding, yea, it beginneth to be delicious to me.[31]

On the assurance that the Holy Spirit accompanies the teaching of the word of God, Alma challenged his listeners to open their hearts so that they could begin to experience the enlightening influence of the Spirit. In this way they could begin spiritually to see the kingdom of God. Alma began at the very lowest rung on the ladder of faith by suggesting that they awake from spiritual darkness and arouse their faculties of mind and soul to an experiment in the expression of faith. They were to desire, even if it were no more than in the least degree, to know if the word of God was true as he testified. By their encouraging that desire to work in them, thereby inviting the Spirit to be with them, the power of the living word of God would begin to cause a swelling motion within their hearts—enlarging their souls, enlightening their minds, and manifesting to them the love of God and the joy of His redemption. These would be the evidences by which they could know that they were being spiritually renewed in accordance to the divine plan of life and salvation.

"Now behold, would not this increase your faith?" Alma inquired. He replied: "I say unto you, Yea."[32] To try the experiment with real intent, even on a limited scale, would give man the internal evidence to increase his faith—to act by and in the Spirit. And it would give him greater assurance in repeating the experiment on a larger scale. To the degree that man would apply himself in the experiment, his faith would also lead to knowledge. In stressing this point, the Nephite prophet declared:

> . . . is your knowledge perfect? Yea, your knowledge is perfect in that thing [that is, insofar as faith has brought a revelation of truth], and your faith is dormant; and this because ye know, for ye know that the word hath swelled your souls, and ye also know that it hath sprouted up, that your understanding doth begin to be enlightened, and your mind doth begin to expand.
>
> O then, is not this real? I say unto you, Yea, because it is light; and whatsoever is light, is good, because it is discernible, therefore ye must know that it is good.[33]

Though man would acquire knowledge to the degree he applied faith, Alma cautioned that in his initial expression of faith man would not grow "up to a perfect knowledge."[34] "Neither must ye lay aside your faith," he explained, "for ye have only exercised your faith to plant the seed that ye might try the experiment to know if the seed was good."[35] Having planted the seed, man must then nourish the tree in the proper way. Alma said:

> And behold, as the tree beginneth to grow, ye will say: Let us nourish it with great care, that it may get root, that it may grow up, and bring forth fruit unto us. And now behold, if ye nourish it with much care it will get root, and grow up, and bring forth fruit.
>
> But if ye neglect the tree, and take no thought for its nourishment, behold it will not get any root; and when the heat of the sun cometh and scorcheth it, because it hath no root it withers away, and ye pluck it up and cast it out.
>
> Now, this is not because the seed was not good, neither is it because the fruit thereof would not be desirable; but it is because your ground is barren, and ye will not nourish the tree, therefore ye cannot have the fruit thereof.
>
> And thus, if ye will not nourish the word, looking forward with an eye of faith to the fruit thereof, ye can never pluck of the fruit of the tree of life.[36]

But of those who would nourish the word so that they could reap the rewards of their faith, Alma said:

> . . . if ye will nourish the word, yea, nourish the tree as it beginneth to grow, by your faith with great diligence, and with patience, looking forward to the fruit thereof, it shall take root; and behold it shall be a tree springing up unto everlasting life.
>
> And because of your diligence and your faith and your patience with the word in nourishing it, that it may take root in you, behold, by and by ye shall pluck the fruit thereof, which is most precious, which is sweet above all that is sweet, and which is white above all that is white, yea, and pure above all that is pure; and ye shall feast upon this fruit even until ye are filled, that ye hunger not, neither shall ye thirst.[37]

The growth which Alma desired the people to experience was spiritual in nature—a development in the living powers and attributes of the Holy Spirit. Only in this way could they express true faith; and by maturing in these divine powers and attributes they could acquire eternal life—the glory of the celestial kingdom.

As Alma concluded his discourse, the people came forward inquiring "how they should plant the seed, or the word of which he had spoken, which he said must be planted in their hearts; or in what manner they should begin to exercise their faith."[38] This was a crucial question. In response, Alma instructed them to lift up their souls to

God in worship—in the wilderness, in their fields, in their homes, in their closets, and in their congregations. But this was not all. "Begin to believe in the Son of God," he stressed, "that he will come to redeem his people, and that he shall suffer and die to atone for their sins; and that he shall rise again from the dead, which shall bring to pass the resurrection, that all men shall stand before him, to be judged at the last and judgment day, according to their works."[39] These were the essential principles and doctrines which man would have to plant in his heart before he could be regenerated by the living word of God and partake of the blessing of eternal life. Alma concluded:

> And now, my brethren, I desire that ye shall plant this word in your hearts, and as it beginneth to swell even so nourish it by your faith. And behold, it will become a tree, springing up in you unto everlasting life. And then may God grant unto you that your burdens may be light, through the joy of his Son. And even all this can ye do if ye will.[40]

Characteristics Of Faith

Faith the Assurance of Things Man Hopes For

In discussing the subject of faith, Joseph Smith began simply and directly: "faith itself—what it is."[41] He continued:

> The author of the epistle to the Hebrews, in the eleventh chapter of that epistle and first verse, gives the following definition of the word faith:
>
> "Now faith is the substance (assurance) of things hoped for, the evidence of things not seen."
>
> From this we learn that faith is the assurance which men have of the existence of things which they have not seen.[42]

As a principle within the plan of life and salvation, faith in the Lord Jesus Christ is the assurance which man can possess that the great Redeemer lives as a divine and glorified being commissioned by the Father to bring man from his fallen spiritual state into the presence of God. It is also the assurance that the plan of salvation is of divine origin and that it actually works as a system of redemption and power. These assurances are given to man as he brings his life into tune with the Holy Spirit.

Man can possess assurance in either temporal or spiritual things. In the temporal sphere, a farmer may plant and cultivate his crop; and, though he cannot know at first the final results of his labor, he can possess an assurance of things which he does not then see. This assurance comes by evidence which is gained from the experience of previous years and by observing his crop grow and mature. In spiritual matters, faith in the Lord Jesus Christ is the assurance which is born of the Holy Spirit that there is a higher order of life from which Adam fell, and to which man may return. "Whoso believeth in God might *with surety* hope for a better world," the prophet Ether explained, "yea, even a place at the right hand of God, which hope cometh of faith."[43] In possessing this divine assurance, the man of faith understands that spiritual truth and power characterize that higher order of life, and that to exercise faith in Jesus Christ is to obtain the saving truth and power and apply them in his life as the means of returning to the presence of God.

Faith in Christ a Principle of Action

There is no such thing as inactive faith. Man does not have faith unless it is a principle of action in his life. Joseph Smith spoke of faith as "the principle of action in all intelligent beings."[44] This is true in both the spiritual and temporal spheres of life. The Prophet explained:

> Were [members of] this class to go back and reflect upon the history of their lives, from the period of their first recollection, and ask themselves what principle excited them to action, or what gave them energy and activity in all their lawful avocations, callings, and pursuits, what would be the answer? Would it not be that it was the assurance which they had of the existence of things which they had not seen as yet? Was it not the hope which you had, in consequence of your belief in the existence of unseen things, which stimulated you to action and

exertion in order to obtain them? Are you not dependent on your faith, or belief, for the acquisition of all knowledge, wisdom, and intelligence? Would you exert yourselves to obtain wisdom and intelligence, unless you did believe that you could obtain them? Would you have ever sown, if you had not believed that you would reap? Would you have ever planted, if you had not believed that you would gather? Would you have ever asked, unless you had believed that you would receive? Would you have ever sought, unless you had believed that you would have found? Or would you have ever knocked, unless you had believed that it would have been opened unto you? In a word, is there anything that you would have done, either physical or mental, if you had not previously believed? Are not all your exertions of every kind, dependent on your faith? Your food, your raiment, your lodgings, are they not all by reason of your faith? Reflect, and ask yourselves if these things are not so. Turn your thoughts on your own minds, and see if faith is not the moving cause of all action in yourselves; and, if the moving cause in you, is it not in all other intelligent beings?[45]

Faith in Christ a Principle of Power

"Faith is not only the principle of action, but of power also, in all intelligent beings," the Prophet declared, "whether in heaven or on earth." He taught that "the principle of power which existed in the bosom of God, by which the worlds were framed, was faith; and . . . it is by reason of this principle of power existing in the Deity, that all created things exist; so that all things in heaven, on earth, or under the earth exist by reason of faith as it existed in Him."[46] It may therefore be concluded that faith is the power which God possesses as a glorified being to express His will in creative activities and to sustain that which He has created, a power based upon the assurance which He has that the righteous application of truth will exalt Him and others in the scale of organized existence.

When man's faith is centered in Christ, it becomes a principle of power, and here it differs from mere belief in God. Man may accept a principle as true and sustain it as something in which he believes, but he cannot possess saving faith unless, or until, his action upon that principle results in a release of divine power in his life or through his administration. When man begins to act by and through the Holy Spirit, true faith is born within him as a principle of power. He then has an actual assurance of the things of God, and he is able to act in the same divine sphere of truth and power as that in which God acts.

The expression of saving faith requires mental and spiritual, more than physical, exertion. Because God is a divine being who acts by and through the agency of His glory, His Holy Spirit is His word,[47] which is His power.[48] For this reason, the Lord said of the many worlds which He has organized: "By *the word of my power* have I created them."[49] Joseph Smith explained: "God spake, chaos heard, and worlds came into order by reason of the faith there was in Him."[50] He also declared that when a man works by faith he works by mental exertion instead of physical force. "It is by words, instead of exerting his physical powers, with which every being works when he works by faith."[51] To illustrate this point, the Prophet said:

> Joshua spake, and the great lights which God had created stood still. Elijah commanded, and the heavens were stayed for the space of three years and six months, so that it did not rain: he again commanded and the heavens gave forth rain. All this was done by faith. And the Savior says, "If you have faith as a grain of mustard seed, say to this mountain, 'Remove,' and it will remove; or say to that sycamine tree, 'Be ye plucked up, and planted in the midst of the sea,' and it shall obey you." Faith, then, works by words; and with these its mightiest works have been, and will be, performed.[52]

Learning to act by faith in spiritual matters is the means of gaining salvation in the presence of God. If faith is a "principle of power, it must be so in man as well as in the Deity," Joseph Smith stressed. "This is the testimony of all the sacred writers, and the lesson which they have been endeavoring to teach to man."[53] Continuing, the Prophet explained:

> Moroni, while abridging and compiling the record of his fathers, has given us the following account of faith as the principle of power. He says . . . that it was the faith of Alma and

Amulek which caused the walls of the prison to be rent . . . ; it was the faith of Nephi and Lehi which caused a change to be wrought upon the hearts of the Lamanites, when they were immersed with the Holy Spirit and with fire . . . ; and it was by faith the mountain Zerin was removed when the brother of Jared spake in the name of the Lord. . . .

In addition to this we are told in Hebrews xi. 32, 33, 34, 35, that Gideon, Barak, Samson, Jephthah, David, Samuel, and the prophets, through faith subdued Kingdoms, wrought righteousness, obtained promises, stopped the mouths of lions, quenched the violence of fire, escaped the edge of the sword; out of weakness were made strong, waxed valiant in fight, turned to flight the armies of the aliens, and that women received their dead raised to life again, &c., &c.[54]

If man is to grow in faith as a principle of divine power, he must begin by exerting the faith which he has in Christ to surmount the immediate obstacles that confront him on the path to eternal life. At first he may not have power to move a mountain or pluck up a sycamine tree. But by applying the faith which he has to meet the challenges which confront him and by taking advantage of the opportunities for service open to him in the gospel, man can obtain faith to do greater things until eventually he has power to do all things which are expedient to and consistent with divine wisdom and truth. To this end he must acquire the truth of God and become familiar with the operations of the Holy Spirit until he can utilize the power of the Spirit in righteousness to do all things in the name of Jesus Christ. Moroni therefore promised: "Behold, I say unto you that whoso believeth in Christ, doubting nothing, whatsoever he shall ask the Father in the name of Christ it shall be granted him; and this promise is unto all, even unto the ends of the earth."[55] This is the standard promise given in the scriptures to those who exercise faith in the Lord Jesus Christ.[56] Only by acquiring such faith can man attain celestial glory and utilize celestial power in the resurrection.

Independent and Dependent Faith

There is an important distinction between the faith of God and the faith of man.

"The principle of faith dwells independently" in God, Joseph Smith taught, because "God is the only supreme governor and independent being in whom all fulness and perfection dwell, . . . and . . . in [whom] . . . every good gift and every good principle dwell." To the question, "How do you prove that God has faith in himself independently?" the Prophet replied: "Because he is omnipotent, omnipresent, and omniscient; without beginning of days or end of life, and in him all fulness dwells."[57] A being who possesses all power, who is everywhere present, and who knows all things is not dependent upon any other being. Such a being can have faith in Himself independently. Faith, the latter-day Seer reasoned, is a "principle or attribute"; and if it were taken "from the Deity, . . . he would cease to exist."[58] Conversely, if every good gift, attribute, and principle dwells in God, then faith must dwell in Him in its fulness.

Though God possesses truth and life and power on an independent principle, man in his fallen temporal state is dependent upon the Lord for the divine powers which quicken the life within him and for the higher spiritual powers by which he may rise out of his fallen state and achieve a state of glory. If man is to acquire divine truth and power to rise out of his fallen spiritual state, he must obtain them from God, by exercising faith in the Supreme Intelligence. For this reason Joseph Smith wrote that God is "the object in whom the faith of all other rational and accountable beings center for life and salvation."[59] But by reconciling himself to Jesus Christ through obedience to the law of God, man's faith can become a productive principle that yields the mercy of Christ and the fruits, gifts, graces, and powers of the Holy Spirit by which man can become like God.

Man may also have a degree of faith in his own finite capacity to achieve worthwhile objectives. And in the exercise of such faith, he may do many things by his independent initiative through the life and agency which Christ has given unto him. But man's faith in his own finite power and ability cannot by itself bring him to eternal salvation.

The ideal relationship is for man to couple proper faith in his own finite capacity with a superior faith in Jesus Christ. Having achieved a divine spiritual union with the great Creator and Redeemer, man may then apply faith in himself to the extent that his finite judgment and ability provide a valid base upon which to act while drawing from God the truth that is required to give him a divine orientation for his labors and the necessary intelligence and power to accomplish them. In this way, man may become a co-worker with God in his progress in the eternal scheme of life. Man's faith in Christ and in himself are then dedicated to one grand and eternal purpose.

Effects Of Faith

Faith Produces Fruits

Before man can acquire true and intelligent faith in God he must begin on the assumption that there are certain results which follow the application of faith. As a principle of action and of power in all intelligent beings in heaven and on earth, faith produces various fruits. To such extent is this true that faith and its fruits are inseparable. If a man possesses faith or power, he will enjoy its fruits; and if he does not possess the fruits of faith, he does not have faith.

The products of God's faith in His own creative capacity are innumerable. According to Joseph Smith, they include "the whole visible creation." He said:

> No world has yet been framed that was not framed by faith, neither has there been an intelligent being on any of God's creations who did not get there by reason of faith as it existed in himself or in some other being; nor has there been a change or a revolution in any of the creations of God, but it has been

effected by faith; neither will there be a change or a revolution, unless it is effected in the same way, in any of the vast creations of the Almighty, for it is by faith that the Deity works.[60]

The same principle must apply to man on earth. "No man since the world was had faith without having something along with it," Joseph Smith declared in a statement in which he stressed that a man who has none of the divine fruits of faith "has no faith."[61] "It is by faith that miracles are wrought," Mormon declared; "and it is by faith that angels appear and minister unto men; wherefore, if these things have ceased wo be unto the children of men, for it is because of unbelief, and all is vain."[62] In speaking of Christ's promise to those who would believe the gospel,[63] the Prophet said: "To show how the believers are to be known from the unbelievers, he continues and says: And these signs shall follow them that believe: in my name shall they cast out devils: they shall speak with new tongues: they shall take up serpents: and if they drink any deadly thing it shall not hurt them: they shall lay hands on the sick and they shall recover."[64]

The fruits of saving faith consist of any and all things which God manifests to man through the Holy Spirit. Those who attain a living spiritual union with Christ do so by faith; and all that they receive as a product of that union may be classified in a broad and general sense as the fruits of faith. This includes the knowledge they are given of the things of God, the mercy they receive in the remission of their sins, and the manifestations of the Holy Spirit in its several and varied endowments. Those who have had faith in past ages have possessed power through the Spirit to do many marvelous things. Hence, Joseph Smith wrote, "the ancients quenched the violence of fire, escaped the edge of the sword, women received their dead, etc."[65]

"Where faith is," the Prophet declared, "there will the knowledge of God be also, with all things which pertain thereto—revelations, visions, and dreams, as well as every necessary thing, in order that the possessors of faith may be perfected, and obtain salvation." With the above fruits, the latter-day Seer listed faith's "train of attendants" as "apostles, prophets, evangelists, pastors, teachers, gifts, wisdom, knowledge, miracles, healings, tongues, interpretation of tongues, etc." "These," he concluded, "are the effects of faith, and always have attended, and always will, attend it."[66]

Faith Leads to Knowledge

Faith in the Lord Jesus Christ is a principle of revelation which leads man to the knowledge of God. As man acts with true desire and hope upon the evidence of divine things, the Holy Spirit begins to enlighten his mind. In this way, God reveals Himself to the man of faith, and faith leads man to knowledge.

The Book of Mormon stresses that man must exercise faith in God if he wishes to acquire divine truth. As Moroni abridged the record of the Jaredites, he recorded that Ether, the last great prophet of that ancient civilization, prophesied "great and marvelous things unto the people, which they did not believe, because they saw them not." Moroni then declared: "And now I, Moroni, would speak somewhat concerning these things; I would show unto the world that *faith is things which are hoped for and not seen;* wherefore, dispute not because ye see not, for ye receive no witness until after the trial of your faith."[67] To illustrate his point, Moroni observed that it was by faith that Christ showed Himself unto the Nephites after His resurrection. "Wherefore," he concluded, "it must needs be that some had faith in him, for he showed himself not unto the world."[68]

Not only did Jesus show Himself in resurrected form unto the Nephites as a result of their faith, but Moroni explained: "There were many whose faith was so exceedingly strong, even before Christ came, who could not be kept from within the veil, but truly saw with their eyes the things which they had beheld with an eye of faith, and they were glad."[69] In these instances, the faith which leads to knowledge was brought to a perfect fruition, as the faithful were raised spiritually from their fallen state to stand in the presence of God. The brother of Jared was a case in point. Because of his faith, "the Lord could not withhold anything from his sight," Moroni observed; "wherefore he showed him all things, for he could no longer be kept without the veil."[70]

Faith Leads to Salvation

Only by the exercise of faith can man acquire the living attributes and powers of God's glory which constitute eternal life. "The knowledge *which tends to life* disappears without faith," Joseph Smith explained, "but returns when faith returns."[71] For this reason he explained that when men in past ages sought after God in faith, "the inquiry frequently terminated, indeed always terminated when rightly pursued, in the most glorious discoveries and eternal certainty."[72]

In stressing the point that the path of faith leads man back into the presence of God, Joseph Smith explained that by faith the ancient saints sought after a knowledge of God's "character, perfections and attributes" until they became acquainted with Him, communed with Him in His glory, partook of His power, and stood in His presence.[73] The Prophet explained:

> Let us here observe that after any portion of the human family are made acquainted with the important fact that there is a God who has created and does uphold all things, the extent of their knowledge respecting his character and glory will depend upon their diligence and faithfulness in seeking after him, until, like Enoch, the brother of Jared, and Moses, they shall obtain faith in God and power with him to behold him face to face.[74]

Again, he inquired:

> How do men obtain a [personal] knowledge of the glory of God, his perfections and attributes? By devoting themselves to his service, through prayer and supplication incessantly strengthening their faith in him, until, like Enoch, the brother

of Jared, and Moses, they obtain a manifestation of God to themselves.[75]

To insure that others would understand the ultimate objective that man may achieve by the exercise of faith, the Prophet inquired: "What situation must a person be in in order to be saved? or what is the difference between a saved man and one who is not saved?" He then explained:

> From what we have before seen of the heavenly worlds, they must be persons who can work by faith and who are able, by faith, to be ministering spirits to them who shall be heirs of salvation; and they must have faith to enable them to act in the presence of the Lord, otherwise they cannot be saved. And what constitutes the real difference between a saved person and one not saved is—the difference in the degree of their faith—one's faith has become perfect enough to lay hold upon eternal life, and the other's has not.[76]

But to possess eternal life, man must do more than return to the presence of God; he must acquire the divine gifts, fruits, endowments, and powers of the Spirit until he becomes like Christ—a glorified and exalted being. "When men begin to live by faith they begin to draw near to God," said Joseph Smith; "and when faith is perfected they are like him."[77] To stress this point, the Prophet queried: "Where shall we find a prototype into whose likeness we may be assimilated, in order that we may be made partakers of life and salvation?" By answering this question properly, he reasoned, man can "ascertain without much difficulty what all others must be in order to be saved." The Prophet found his answer in Christ. All will agree in this," he said of the Son of God, "that he is the prototype or standard of salvation; or, in other words, that he is a saved being." Basing his statement upon the assumption that to be saved is to be made like Christ, the latter-day Seer declared: "Salvation consists in the glory, authority, majesty, power and dominion which Jehovah possesses and in nothing else." Having discussed this point in light of Christ's teachings, the Prophet concluded:

> These teachings of the Savior most clearly show unto us the nature of salvation; and what he proposed unto the human family when he proposed to save them—That he proposed to make them like unto himself; and he was like the Father, the great prototype of all saved beings: And for any portion of the human family to be assimilated into their likeness [made like them] is to be saved; and to be unlike them is to be destroyed: and on this hinge turns the door of salvation.[78]

To be like Christ, and therefore to be like the Father, man must be glorified in Christ as Jesus has been glorified in the Man of Holiness. This is the great design of the plan of life and salvation. Joseph Smith taught that for this reason the gospel is established in the world.

Summary

There is a difference between faith and belief. Belief is a mere mental or intellectual assent or acceptance of a particular principle or assumption. On the other hand, faith is the power to act in and through the Holy Spirit in a true expression of belief in God. As the first principle of revealed religion, faith is the basis of all right action. It is based upon evidence, particularly that evidence of God which is given to man when his mind is enlightened by the Holy Spirit.

The faith which leads to salvation must center in Jesus Christ. God is an independent being, and faith dwells independently in God in its fulness. But man as a dependent being must center his faith in Jesus Christ if he is to acquire divine mercy and power unto salvation. Faith is the assurance of things for which man hopes, and it is preceded by the expression of desire. In the acquisition of faith, evidence stimulates desire, desire brings forth hope, and hope matures into faith, which is a principle of action and of power. Alma compared the acquisition of faith to a seed which man must plant in his heart and cultivate as he would a tree until it grows up within him as a principle of spiritual truth and power which leads to eternal life.

As a principle of action and of power, faith produces

divine fruits of a miraculous nature. These are the natural effects of faith. Faith also leads to knowledge until, by the application of faith, man is able to penetrate the veil and stand in the presence of God. Faith therefore leads man to salvation.

Notes

1. Articles of Faith, No. 4.
2. D&C 1:21.
3. Orson Pratt, *The True Faith* (Liverpool, England, 1856), p. 3. There are exceptions to this general statement. Elder Pratt noted:

> It is often the case, that the judgment becomes so weak and beclouded, that the evidences, however great, and clear, and lucid, and demonstrative, produce no sensible impression upon the mind. Hence, faith does not always exist in impaired or vitiated minds with a strength proportioned to the degree or force of evidence.—*Ibid.*

4. Alma 32:27.
5. Latter-day Saint thought distinguishes between true and false belief. True belief results from authentic evidence, accurate perception, and sound thinking. False belief, on the other hand, is the product of false evidence, faulty perception, or immature thinking. Man's challenge is to examine carefully the evidence of God and to perceive cautiously and logically, with true and righteous desires, the meaning of that evidence. Only in this way can he acquire faith.
6. Matthew 17:20; Luke 17:6. See also Matthew 21:21; Mark 11:23.
7. Ether 12:30.
8. D&C 88:118.
9. See D&C 17:3–7.
10. See D&C 5:24, 28; 44:2; 104:80.
11. See D&C 35:19; 61:18.
12. See D&C 43:12.
13. JD, I, pp. 90–91; VII, pp. 178–179; XI, pp. 22–23; XIII, p. 336; XVI, p. 46; XXV, pp. 40–41.
14. Alma 32:29.
15. HC, III, p. 379.
16. *Ibid.*, VI, p. 77. In the *History of the Church,* the name of the recipient of the Prophet's letter is spelled "Bennett," but his signature on letters now preserved in the Church Historian's Library is spelled "Bennet."
17. Alma 32:27.
18. Moroni 7:40.
19. Moroni 7:41.
20. Ether 12:32. See also Alma 13:29.
21. Alma 5:10.
22. Jacob 4:6.
23. Enos 1:1–5. To raise one's voice high unto heaven as did Enos need not mean to shout verbally, but to commune spiritually with God by the energy of one's soul.
24. Ether 12:4.

25. Ether 12:8–9.
26. Alma 25:16.
27. Moroni 7:42.
28. Moroni 8:25–26.
29. Alma 32:17–18, 21.
30. The view that the great scientific discoveries of modern times are produced by the influence of the Spirit will be discussed in volume III of this study.
31. Alma 32:26–28.
32. Alma 32:29.
33. Alma 32:34–35.
34. Alma 32:29.
35. Alma 32:35–36.
36. Alma 32:37–40.
37. Alma 32:41–43.
38. Alma 33:1.
39. Alma 33:22.
40. Alma 33:23.
41. *Lectures of Faith,* No. 1.
42. *Ibid.* By this the Prophet meant that faith "is the assurance which we have of the existence of unseen things."—*Ibid.* In his Inspired Revision of the Bible, he corrected the passage in Hebrews to read: "Now faith is the *assurance* of things hoped for, the evidence of things not seen."—I. R., Hebrews 11:1.
43. Ether 12:4.
44. *Lectures on Faith,* No. 1.
45. *Ibid.*
46. *Ibid.*
47. D&C 84:45; 88:66.
48. D&C 88:5–13; 93:16–17.
49. Moses 1:32. See also Moses 2:1–3, 5.
50. *Lectures on Faith,* No. 1.
51. *Ibid.,* No. 7.
52. *Ibid.*
53. *Ibid.,* No. 1.
54. *Ibid.* For Moroni's treatment of faith as a principle of power, see Ether 12:13–15 in relation to Alma 14:26–29; 17:29–39; Helaman 5:20–52.
55. Mormon 9:21. See also verse 28.
56. See 3 Nephi 18:20; D&C 4:7; 6:5, 11, 14, 15; 7:1; 8:1, 9, 11; 9:7, 8; 11:5; 12:5; 14:5, 8; 18:18; 19:38; 29:6, 34; 35:9; 42:3, 56, 61, 62, 68; 46:7, 28, 30; 49:26; 50:31; 66:9; 75:27; 88:63–65, 83; 101:27; 103:31, 35; 132:40; Matthew 7:7, 8; Luke 18:1; James 1:5.
57. *Lectures on Faith,* No. 2.
58. *Ibid.,* No. 1. The question may be asked, if faith is the assurance of things which are unseen (see Hebrews 11:1; Alma 32:21), how does God have faith if he sees and understands the future? The power which God possesses to see the future and to order it according to his divine will is a product of his faith, not a nullification of the attribute of faith which centers in him in its fulness. Without faith God could not see the future; and without faith, he could not exert power in truth to order that which is to come according to his will.

59. *Ibid.,* No. 2.
60. *Ibid.,* No. 7.
61. HC, V, p. 218.
62. Moroni 7:37.
63. Mark 16:17–18.
64. TS, III (September 1, 1842), pp. 902–903. See also HC, IV, p. 603.
65. HC, V, p. 218.
66. *Lectures on Faith,* No. 7.
67. Ether 12:5–6.
68. Ether 12:7. See 3 Nephi 11.
69. Ether 12:19.
70. Ether 12:21. See Ether 3:4–20.
71. *Lectures on Faith,* No. 7.
72. *Ibid.,* No. 2.
73. *Ibid.*
74. *Ibid.*
75. *Ibid.*
76. *Ibid.,* No. 7.
77. *Ibid.*
78. *Ibid.*

5

The Preparatory Gospel

> *The preparatory gospel . . . is the gospel of repentance and of baptism, and the remission of sins.*—REVELATION TO JOSEPH SMITH.

Joseph Smith taught that the Saints would never leave the first principles and ordinances of the gospel behind as they traveled the road to perfection in the kingdom of God.[1] Nevertheless, part of the plan of life and salvation is designated as the preparatory gospel. The purpose of this phase of the gospel plan is "to prepare the way for a greater revelation of God."[2] It does not function independent of the higher principles and ordinances of the gospel, but in conjunction with them.

Place Of Faith In Preparatory Gospel

Faith the First Principle of the Gospel

Faith in the Lord Jesus Christ is not designated specifically as part of the preparatory gospel,[3] yet Joseph Smith declared that it is the first principle in the over-all program of life and salvation[4] and "the foundation of all righteousness."[5] For these reasons, it is the basis of the preparatory gospel.

Faith the First Ordinance of the Gospel

As the first principle of the gospel, faith in the Lord Jesus Christ is also the initial ordinance in the plan of life and salvation.[6] An ordinance is a religious rite or ceremony which, among other things, is a channel through which divine mercy and power are given to man. In this sense, faith in Jesus Christ qualifies as an ordinance: First, it is a channel through which divine power is given to man.[7] Second, it is the basis of the over-all program by which the full blessings of salvation are given to man. In confirming the fact that the gifts and signs of the Spirit follow those who express true faith, the Lord said in a revelation to Joseph Smith:

> . . . I am God, and mine arm is not shortened; and I will show miracles, signs, and wonders, unto all those who believe on my name.
>
> And whoso shall ask it in my name in faith, they shall cast out devils; they shall heal the sick; they shall cause the blind to receive their sight, and the deaf to hear, and the dumb to speak, and the lame to walk.[8]

The Book of Mormon holds that before man can express true faith he must perform a divinely prescribed ritual or sacrifice. This sacrifice, however, is to be performed within man—within the privacy of his own heart—rather than outwardly where it may be viewed by others. To the Nephites, Jesus instructed: "Ye shall offer for a sacrifice unto me a broken heart and a contrite spirit."[9] This sacrifice Christ substituted in place of the outward rite of blood sacrifice which the law of Moses required, and He made it clear that it is the initial ritual that man must perform in order to embrace the gospel.[10] The Nephites who offered this sacrifice and complied with its related principles and outward ordinances in the plan of salvation were promised that they would be baptized "with fire and with the Holy Ghost.[11] In this way, faith in Christ was to be to them a channel to divine mercy and power.

Man's sacrifice of a broken heart and a contrite spirit is symbolic of the sacrifice which Jesus made when, with humility, sorrow, and a broken heart, He fulfilled His atoning mission on earth. In like manner, man must offer as a sacrifice a broken heart and a contrite spirit as he is brought to see the nature of his fallen state and the gravity of his sins, and as he realizes his need for the mercy and power of Christ to cleanse him from sin and enable him to return to the presence of God and be made like Him. Lehi therefore declared of the mission of the Messiah: "Behold, he offereth himself a sacrifice for sin, to answer the ends of the law, *unto all those who have a broken heart and a contrite spirit;* and unto none else can the ends of the law be answered."[12]

Repentance Toward God

Meaning of Repentance

When coupled with faith in the Lord Jesus Christ, the principle of repentance becomes the second ordinance of the gospel.[13] As a ministering angel, John the Baptist conferred "the keys . . . of the gospel of repentance" upon Joseph Smith and Oliver Cowdery, on May 15, 1829,[14] which gave them and those whom they commissioned authority to call men to repentance and to have their message binding upon the world.

To repent is to turn, often with sorrow, contrition, regret, or remorse, from a past course of action to one that is based upon rectitude and truth. A revelation to Joseph Smith said of repentance: "By this ye may know if a man repenteth of his sins—behold, he will confess them and forsake them."[15]

In its true form within the plan of the gospel, repentance is not a negative or an abstract principle, but a positive and spiritual one. Several revelations implied that the purpose of repentance was to "bring souls" to Christ.[16] A person who begins to believe in Christ not only seeks to repent of error, but, more specifically, he repents *toward* God. The Twelve in the Prophet's day classified among the first principles of the doctrine of Christ the principle of "repentance towards God."[17] Joseph Smith reaffirmed the biblical doctrine that true repentance is based upon the atonement of Jesus Christ.[18] Therein man takes Christ as his standard; and by faith in the Savior, he conforms his life to the pattern which was set by Jesus. Man also begins to utilize the truth and power of the gospel in a positive way in his effort to become like the Son of God. To do this, he must get the spirit of repentance, which is that spirit that comes as a result of a broken heart—the spirit of sorrow and contrition for sin. It is also the spirit of desire and hope for the righteousness of God. Those who express the spirit of repentance by looking with hope to Christ are given divine power to strengthen them in the battle against sin and the weaknesses of the flesh, and to cleanse them from the effects of sin in their lives.[19] The faith which they then acquire leads to repentance.

Necessity of Repentance

It is not the design of God to save man *in* his sins, but to save him *from* his sins.[20] Helaman explained that there are "conditions of repentance" which bring men "unto the power of the Redeemer, unto the salvation of their souls."[21]

According to Joseph Smith, God declared to Adam in the early ages of the world why man must repent. "All men, everywhere, must repent," the Lord explained; "or they can in nowise inherit the kingdom of God, *for no unclean thing can dwell there, or dwell in his presence;* for . . . Man of Holiness is his name, and the name of his Only Begotten is the Son of Man [of Holiness]."[22] Joseph Smith made the same point when he wrote by revelation: "We know that all men must repent . . . or they cannot be saved in the kingdom of God."[23] To the Saints he explained:

> If you wish to go where God is, you must be like God, or possess the principles which God possesses. . . .
>
> Is not God good? Then you be good; if He is faithful, then you be faithful.[24]

In a revelation to the Prophet, God declared: "I the Lord cannot look upon sin with the least degree of allowance; nevertheless, he that repents and does the commandments of the Lord shall be forgiven."[25] As a divine being perfect in righteousness, God cannot sanction the least variation from the path of virtue and truth. Nevertheless, man has been placed in a fallen state so that he might receive a physical body and be proved in the endowments of the flesh; and since man possesses a corrupt body in mortality through which sin is conceived in his heart,[26] repentance must be granted to him, if he is to be saved in the kingdom of God. Alma therefore described mortality as a probationary state which is given to man that he might repent.[27] Amulek explained:

> . . . behold, this life is the time for men to prepare to meet God; . . . therefore, I beseech of you that ye do not procrastinate the day of your repentance until the end. . . .
>
> Ye cannot say, when ye are brought to that awful crisis, that I will repent, that I will return to God. Nay, ye cannot say this; for that same spirit which doth possess your bodies at the time that ye go out of this life, that same spirit will have power to possess your body in that eternal world.
>
> For behold, if ye have procrastinated the day of your repentance even until death, behold, ye have become subjected to the spirit of the devil, and he doth seal you his.[28]

The Prophet also advised against procrastinating repentance. "Repentance is a thing that cannot be trifled with every day," he declared. "Daily transgression and daily repentance is not that which is pleasing in the sight of God."[29] Again he said:

> We should take warning and not wait for the death-bed to repent, as we see the infant taken away by death, so may the youth, and middle-aged . . . be suddenly called into eternity. Let this, then, prove as a warning to all not to procrastinate repentance, or wait till a death-bed, for it is the will of God that man should repent and serve Him in health, and in the strength and power of his mind, in order to secure his blessing, and not wait until he is called to die.[30]

Repentance a Divine Process

True repentance is a divine, rather than a mere human, process. This is true of each phase of the over-all gospel program. First, there can be no genuine recognition of error by man unless Christ's standard of truth and righteousness has been clearly set forth. Without a standard, morality becomes a relative thing to be determined by the judgment or whim of each individual, or by the group with which he associates.

Second, there can be no remorse capable of effecting the kind of genuine sorrow for sin which works repentance without the knowledge of divine law and justice.

Third, man cannot be induced to reach up and acquire the goodness of God unless he realizes that in mortality he is in a fallen state and that he must rely upon Christ for mercy, truth, and power.

Fourth, only when man clearly understands his fallen nature and state in mortality, and understands the blessings of life and glory which are promised to those who obey the gospel, can he fully resolve to come to the fountain of all truth and righteousness.

Fifth, being under the bondage of sin, man cannot by himself restore that which he has lost by sin. If he is to be free from the baneful effects of sin, he must reconcile himself to Christ.

Finally, fallen man is severed from the presence of God, and his physical body is corrupted by the fall of Adam. Unless he is renewed spiritually and is sanctified by the power of the Holy Ghost, he cannot permanently refrain from sin.

For these reasons, the natural man in mortality cannot by his own efforts attain the righteousness of God. Repentance must of necessity follow the expression of faith in the Lord Jesus Christ as a basic principle within the divine plan by which man can partake of the mercy, the enlightening truth, and the transforming power of God.

Repentance a Gift of God

In many ways, repentance is a gift of God: First, God gave man a divine gift in the standard of righteousness exemplified by Jesus.

Second, Christ paid the debt of divine justice for man's sins so that man could repent and be forgiven. A revelation declared: "Behold, the Lord your Redeemer suffered death in the flesh; wherefore he suffered the pain of all men, *that all men might repent* and come unto him."[31] Without the atonement, repentance would be impossible, and it could have no ultimate value to man. Unmitigated divine justice would still consign him to a state of spiritual darkness.

Third, repentance is a gift of God in that the Spirit of God strives with man to bring him to a state of righteousness until such time as man may turn away from God and harden his heart against the divine influence.[32] When man responds to the uplifting influence of the Holy Spirit and seeks to come unto Christ, the Lord gives him strength and power to repent. Joseph Smith taught that by faith those who are weak may be made strong.[33] The Book of Mormon stresses the same point. Of those who would rely upon His grace, Christ said to Moroni: "I [will] make weak things become strong unto them."[34]

Finally, repentance is a divine gift in the blessing of forgiveness that results from the act of repentance when it is done in conjunction with the program of the gospel.

Scriptural R's Of Repentance

Recognition of Christ

The divine process of repentance can be outlined by listing the major steps within it under six R's. The first R in the divine program might stand for Recognition of Jesus Christ. The Master is the center of all righteousness for man, the beginning point in his quest for the truth and righteousness of God. In teaching a group of people who had assembled on the hill Onidah the beginning point in achieving salvation, Alma said of man's need to recognize Christ and of His place in the divine plan of life and salvation:

> . . . begin to believe in the Son of God, that he will come to redeem his people, and that he shall suffer and die to atone for their sins; and that he shall rise again from the dead, which shall bring to pass the resurrection, that all men shall stand before him, to be judged at the last and judgment day, according to their works.[35]

To recognize Christ, man must accept the declaration of Nephi: "As the Lord God liveth, there is none other name given under heaven save it be this Jesus Christ, . . . whereby man can be saved."[36] A revelation to Joseph Smith also stressed: "Behold, Jesus Christ is the name given of the Father, and there is none other name given whereby man can be saved."[37] For this reason Nephi wrote: "My soul delighteth in proving unto my people that save Christ should come all men must perish."[38]

To recognize Christ, man must also accept and sustain His Church on earth—the Church of Jesus Christ. To the Nephites, Jesus said: "Whatsoever ye shall do, ye shall do it in my name; therefore ye shall call the church in my name, . . . [for] how be it my church save it be called in my name?" In His explanation to the Nephites, Jesus set forth the essential requisites for His church. "If it be called in my name then it is my church," He observed, "if it so be that they [the members] are built upon my gospel."[39] Here is a simple, but intelligent, declaration that cuts across jarring creeds and contending opinions and goes directly to the heart of the issue. Simply stated, Christ's church must (1) be called by His name and (2) be built upon His gospel. In expressing a third criterion by which man may recognize His church, Jesus said: "If it so be that the church is built upon my gospel then will the Father show forth his own works in it."[40] To recognize Christ, man must accept these plain and logical conclusions.

Remorse for Sin

Remorse for sin is the second R in the divine process of repentance. Recognition of Christ carries with it the obligation to look to Him as the one who exemplified to perfection obedience to the law of God. To the Saints, the Lord instructed: "Look unto me in every thought."[41] When man looks seriously to Christ, he begins to see the need for repentance in his own life. And as he measures his own conduct in life against the Master's example of obedience to the law of the Father, man is made aware of his mortal weaknesses and his inability, alone, to conform to the perfect standard of conduct which the law of God ultimately requires of those who are given salvation in the kingdom of God. Recognition of these facts should produce remorse for sin in the heart of a conscientious person. For this reason, Alma declared that the knowledge of God's just law brings "remorse of conscience unto man."[42]

Alma's own experience illustrates the remorse that can come to the sinner who is brought to recognize Christ. Having been brought, in a dramatic way, to realize the truth of the gospel after he had openly opposed the church of God, Alma said of his feelings:

> . . . I was racked with eternal torment, for my soul was harrowed up to the greatest degree and racked with all my sins.
>
> Yea, I did remember all my sins and iniquities, for which I was tormented with the pains of hell. . . .
>
> And now, for three days and for three nights was I racked, even with the pains of a damned soul.[43]

Reliance upon Christ

Remorse of conscience can stimulate man to reach up to Christ, in humility and in hope, for divine mercy and for power to overcome the flesh and the world. In logical sequence, the next R in the scriptural process of repentance stands for Reliance upon Jesus Christ. It is at this stage of the program that remorse for sin can have a constructive purpose in the experience of man, as is well illustrated in the conversion of Alma. In the midst of his torment, Alma finally remembered that he had heard his father "prophesy unto the people concerning the coming of one Jesus Christ, a Son of God, to atone for the sins of the world." He said:

> . . . as my mind caught hold upon this thought, I cried within my heart: O Jesus, thou Son of God, have mercy on me, who am in the gall of bitterness, and am encircled about by the everlasting chains of death.
>
> And now, behold, when I thought this, I could remember my pains no more; yea, I was harrowed up by the memory of my sins no more.
>
> And oh, what joy, and what marvelous light I did behold; yea, my soul was filled with joy as exceeding as was my pain!
>
> Yea, I say unto you, . . . that there could be nothing so exquisite and so bitter as were my pains. Yea, and again I say unto you, . . . that on the other hand, there can be nothing so exquisite and sweet as was my joy.[44]

Since Jesus paid the debt of sin for all men, and is the light and the life of the world, He is the only source of mercy or power by which man may be redeemed to the presence of God. To rely upon Christ, man must place his hope and trust in the Savior, believing implicitly that He will do all that He has promised to do for the salvation of man. Lehi explained: "Wherefore, all mankind were in a lost and in a fallen state, and ever would be save they should rely on this Redeemer."[45] Nephi also observed that man can come unto salvation only by "relying *wholly* upon the merits of him who is mighty to save."[46] This was the position which was taken by the Nephite church. Of those who identified themselves with the Church of Jesus Christ among the Nephites, Moroni said: "Their names were taken, that they might be remembered and nourished by the good word of God, to keep them in the right way, to keep them continually watchful unto prayer, *relying alone upon the merits of Christ,* who was the author and the finisher of their faith."[47] In relying upon Christ, man begins to form that relationship by which he can be sanctified in

Christ, perfected in Him, and finally glorified in the God of this earth.[48]

Resolution to Come unto Christ

With reliance, there must be Resolution to come unto Christ, which is the fourth R in the divine process of repentance. Christ's invitation to the sinner is "Come, follow me."[49] Because the resolution to do this is an indispensable factor in the divine plan, Moroni wrote of those who were given the benefits of the gospel among the Nephites: "And none were received unto baptism save they took upon them the name of Christ, having a determination to serve him to the end."[50] The same resolution was required of those who received the gospel through Joseph Smith. Before baptism, they were required to manifest a willingness "to take upon them the name of Jesus Christ, having a determination to serve him to the end."[51] In warning men to flee from modern spiritual Babylon, the Lord said: " . . . he that goeth, let him not look back lest sudden destruction shall come upon him."[52]

Reconciliation to Christ

The fifth R stands for Reconciliation to Jesus Christ. The need for reconciliation is based upon the fact that except for the merciful intervention of the great Redeemer, fallen man would be estranged from God and would remain so throughout eternity. But in making His infinite atonement, Jesus reconciled the demands of divine law for Adam and his posterity. In this way, He became the Savior of the world. Man's obligation in the divine plan of salvation is to reconcile himself to Christ, by repentance and obedience to the gospel. Only in this way can man receive the mercy and power of God unto salvation. The Nephite prophet Jacob advised: "Wherefore, my beloved brethren, reconcile yourselves to the will of God, and not to the will of the devil and the flesh; and remember, after ye are reconciled unto God, that it is only in and through the grace of God that ye are saved."[53]

The works of righteousness which man may perform on earth, including the works of repentance, neither remit his sins nor save him. *Only as they are a means of reconciling him to Christ* do works of righteousness become effective in helping man on his path to salvation. It is the Son of God who remits sin by the power of His atonement. In recognition of this fact, Nephi said: "We labor diligently to write, to persuade our children, and also our brethren, to believe in Christ, and to be reconciled to God; for we know that it is by grace that we are saved, after all we can do."[54] Having stated that he had charity for both Jew and Gentile, Nephi again declared: "But behold, for none of these can I hope except they shall be reconciled unto Christ, and enter into the narrow gate, and walk in the straight path which leads to life, and continue in the path until the end of the day of probation."[55]

Before man can be reconciled to Christ, he must be reconciled to his fellow man for any injustice he may have done. After warning His disciples on the Western hemisphere against being angry with a brother, Jesus instructed the Nephites: "Therefore, if ye shall come unto me, or shall desire to come unto me, and rememberest that thy brother hath ought against thee—Go thy way unto thy brother, and *first be reconciled to thy brother,* and then come unto me with full purpose of heart, and I will receive you."[56]

To reconcile himself to his fellow men, one must confess his transgressions and make restitution as far as it is possible. In cases of continued abuse, when the offended person has not retaliated, the offender may be required to restore fourfold before the law of God is satisfied.[57]

Finally, before man can be reconciled to Christ, he must enter by baptism into a covenant relationship with the Master. Not only is repentance a necessary prelude to baptism, but within the gospel program baptism is the consummation of repentance and the official act by which man is reconciled to Jesus. Mormon declared that "the first fruits of repentance is baptism."[58] Here the interrelationship of the principles and ordinances of the gospel may be seen.

Renewal of Man in Christ

The final R in the process of repentance stands for the Renewal of man in Christ. When man truly repents, God enters with mercy and transforming power into his quest for righteousness: the conditional benefits of the atonement are extended to him;[59] he receives the Spirit of Christ unto the remission of his sins;[60] and, by the power of the Spirit which is given to him in the gospel, he is changed from the carnal and fallen state which prevails on earth to a righteous state of spiritual life in Christ. When the people to whom Alma taught the gospel repented, God "changed their hearts" and "awakened them out of a deep sleep" so that the bands of spiritual death were broken, and "their souls were illuminated by the light of the everlasting word."[61] In this way, also, the Lamanites whom Ammon converted were renewed and transformed so "that they had no more desire to do evil."[62] Mormon observed: " . . . and they became a righteous people."[63] As new creatures in Christ, they could refrain from wilful sin and grow up spiritually in the Master.

Illustration Of Scriptural R's Of Repentance

An illustration of the divine process of repentance can be seen in the experience of the Nephite people under King Benjamin. Before anointing his son Mosiah to rule in his place, King Benjamin called his people together and taught them the message an angel had given him concerning the great plan by which fallen man could be renewed spiritually in Christ.[64] Because man must begin to repent by *recognizing* Christ as the God of the earth, King Benjamin admonished his people:

> Believe in God; believe that he is, and that he created all things, both in heaven and in earth; believe that he has all wisdom, and all power, both in heaven and in earth; believe that

> man doth not comprehend all the things which the Lord can comprehend.
>
> And again, believe that ye must repent of your sins and forsake them, and humble yourselves before God; and ask in sincerity of heart that he would forgive you. . . .[65]

As a result of King Benjamin's teaching and admonitions, the people felt great *remorse* of conscience for their sins. The "fear of the Lord" came upon them, and they "viewed themselves in their own carnal state, even less than the dust of the earth."[66] They realized that without Christ they were nothing. They therefore *relied* upon Christ as they cried out: "O have mercy, and apply the atoning blood of Christ that we may receive forgiveness of our sins, and our hearts may be purified; for we believe in Jesus Christ, the Son of God, who created heaven and earth, and all things, who shall come down among the children of men."[67]

Not only did the people express their reliance upon Christ, but they *resolved* to come unto Him, for King Benjamin had stressed: "And now, if you believe all these things see that you do them."[68]

By their willingness to come unto Christ, the people were *reconciled* to Him, and their reconciliation was evidenced by the spiritual blessings which they received. The record states: "It came to pass that . . . the Spirit of the Lord came upon them, and they were filled with joy, having received a remission of their sins, and having peace of conscience, because of the exceeding faith which they had in Jesus Christ."[69] Finally, their repentance was accompanied by a *renewal* of their lives in Christ. When King Benjamin inquired if they believed the words which he had spoken to them, they cried out: "Yea, we believe all the words which thou hast spoken unto us; and also, we know of their surety and truth, because of the Spirit of the Lord Omnipotent, which has wrought a mighty change in us, or in our hearts, that we have no more disposition to do evil, but to do good continually."[70]

Baptism

Nature of Baptism

Baptism as the third principle and the first outward ordinance of the gospel follows as a logical concomitant of true repentance. When man begins to exercise living faith in Jesus Christ, the desire to be baptized springs up in his heart as a result of his contrition of soul and his desire for spiritual union with the Master. For this reason, Mormon, after designating baptism as "the first fruits of repentance," declared: "And baptism cometh by faith unto the fulfilling of the commandments."[71] Having exercised faith in Christ and repented of his sins, the penitent soul is required by divine commandment to enter into a covenant with Jesus that he will follow the Lord and give evidence of his spiritual renewal by an outward ordinance, as a sign or symbol of his new profession. This symbol, which is designed in the plan of redemption to represent a cleansing of man from sin, is baptism in water.

"Baptism," the Prophet explained, "is a sign to God, to angels, and to heaven that we do the will of God."[72] In baptism, man covenants that he will seek with all his heart to observe the laws of God and to serve Him until the end of his mortal probation.[73] Thus Alma admonished the people of Gideon: "Come and go forth, and show unto God that ye are willing to repent of your sins and enter into a covenant with him to keep his commandments, and witness it unto him this day by going into the waters of baptism."[74] Of the specific obligations man takes upon himself in baptism, the elder Alma said to a group he had been instrumental in converting to the gospel:

> Behold, here are the waters of Mormon . . . and now, as ye are desirous to come into the fold of God, and to be called his people, and are willing to bear one another's burdens, that they may be light;
>
> Yea, and are willing to mourn with those that mourn; yea, and comfort those that stand in need of comfort, and to stand as witnesses of God at all times and in all things, and in all

places that ye may be in, even until death, that ye may be redeemed of God, and be numbered with those of the first resurrection, that ye may have eternal life—

Now I say unto you, if this be the desire of your hearts, what have you against being baptized in the name of the Lord, as a witness before him that ye have entered into a covenant with him, that ye will serve him and keep his commandments, that he may pour out his Spirit more abundantly upon you?[75]

Mode of Baptism

The true mode of baptism is another point of doctrine that was made clear in the new dispensation. Joseph Smith explained: "The gospel requires baptism by immersion for the remission of sins, which is the meaning of the word in the original language—namely, to bury or immerse."[76] He said: "Let us understand that the word *baptise* is derived from the Greek verb *baptiso,* and means to immerse or overwhelm, and that sprinkle is from the Greek verb *rantiso,* and means to scatter on by particles."[77]

Several latter-day scriptures teach that baptism must be performed by immersion. A revelation to the Prophet states that to receive celestial glory in the resurrection, man must be baptized after the manner of Christ's "burial, being buried in the water in his name, and this according to the commandment which he has given."[78] Another revelation which discloses early events in the history of the world states that in being baptized, Adam was carried by the Spirit "down into the water, and was laid under the water, and was brought forth out of the water."[79] When Nephi, the grandson of Helaman, was baptized in accordance with the instructions of the resurrected Christ, he "went down into the water and was baptized," after which "he came up out of the water."[80] In like manner, Alma, Helam, and others "were buried in the water, . . . and came forth out of the water."[81]

The specific procedure of baptism is twice set forth in modern revelation. One explanation is found in Christ's instructions to the Nephites at the time He ministered to them after His resurrection.[82] The other is in a major revelation to Joseph Smith, which sets forth the doctrine and practices of the Church in this dispensation. This statement, which gives the same procedure as the first, explains:

> Baptism is to be administered in the following manner unto all those who repent—
>
> The person who is called of God and has authority from Jesus Christ to baptize, shall go down into the water with the person who has presented himself or herself for baptism, and shall say, calling him or her by name: Having been commissioned of Jesus Christ, I baptize you in the name of the Father, and of the Son, and of the Holy Ghost. Amen.
>
> Then shall he immerse him or her in the water, and come forth again out of the water.[83]

Symbolism of Baptism

The Prophet wrote by revelation that all things in life "have their likeness, . . . that they may accord one with another."[84] Baptism is symbolic of the central events in the divine plan of life and salvation. This holy ordinance by which man enters that stage of life which leads to eternal life is made symbolic of the birth process by which he acquires a physical body in this mortal sphere.[85] The renewal of innocence which accompanies baptism is also symbolic both of the innocence of Christ and the innocence of man in his infant mortal state.

In addition, baptism is symbolic of Christ's death, burial, and resurrection. As Jesus voluntarily submitted His body to the cross, so must those who follow Him crucify the natural man by true repentance and thus die according to the man of sin. Like the Son of God who submitted His body to the silent tomb, each one who crucifies the old man must be buried with Jesus by baptism into death.[86] Enveloped in water, with the normal life functions of his body momentarily suspended, man is in a state which is symbolic of the sealed tomb, and his body is made like the lifeless tabernacle of the Master. Then, like the Son of Man who was raised up from the dead by the glory of the Father[87] to enjoy the full spiritual powers of celestial or eternal life, man must come forth from the watery grave of baptism to walk in the newness of life which the gospel makes possible. Man's emergence from the baptismal tomb is symbolic of Christ's triumphant rise from the dead; and the renewal of spiritual life within the man of faith is symbolic of the glory which Jesus received in the resurrection. As the Father extended His glory to raise up the Son of God from the tomb, so does Christ give His Holy Spirit to raise up spiritually those who are baptized in His holy name and to place them upon the path which leads to eternal life or glory. Jesus went from earth life to the full presence of the Man of Holiness by passing through the tomb. So may man enter into a newness of life by passing through the watery grave of baptism to the spiritual realm of life that leads to immortal glory.

Age for Baptism

Those who are born into the Church should be baptized when they are eight years of age. A revelation instructed parents in Zion and her stakes to teach their children the first principles and ordinances of the gospel early in life, then added: "And their children shall be baptized for the remission of their sins when eight years old, and receive the laying on the hands [for the gift of the Holy Ghost]."[88]

Need For Baptism

Baptism an Essential to Salvation

"Upon looking over the sacred pages of the Bible, searching into the prophets and sayings of the apostles," Joseph Smith observed, "we find no subject so nearly connected with salvation as that of *baptism.*" Continued the latter-day Seer:

> As it is well known that various opinions govern a large portion of the sectarian world as to this important ordinance of the

gospel, it may not be amiss to introduce the commissions and commandments of Jesus Christ Himself on the subject.—He said to the Twelve, or rather eleven at the time: Go ye therefore, and teach all nations, *baptising* them in the name of the Father, and of the Son, and of the Holy Ghost; teaching them to observe all things whatsoever I have commanded you: Thus it is recorded by Matthew. In Mark we have these important words: Go ye into *all the world,* and preach the gospel to every creature. He that believeth and is *baptised* shall be saved, and he that believeth not shall be *damned.* And to show how the believers are to be known from the *unbelievers,* he continues and says: And these signs shall follow them that believe: in my name shall they cast out devils: they shall speak with new tongues: they shall take up serpents: and if they drink any deadly thing it shall not hurt them: they shall lay hands on the sick and they shall recover. And in Luke we find the finishing clause like this,—that it was necessary that Christ should die and rise the third day—that remission of sins should be preached in his name among all nations, beginning at Jerusalem. *And ye are witnesses of these things.*[89]

Jesus had also said to Nicodemus, a member of the Jewish Sanhedrin: "Verily, verily, I say unto thee, Except a man be born of water and of the Spirit, he cannot enter into the kingdom of God."[90] Having quoted this declaration, Joseph Smith commented:

This strong and positive answer of Jesus, as to water baptism, settles the question: If God is the same yesterday, today, and forever; it is no wonder He is so positive in the great declaration: He that believes and is *baptised* shall be *saved,* and he that believes not shall be damned! There was no other name given under heaven, nor no other ordinance admitted, whereby men could be saved: No wonder the Apostle said, being *"buried* with him in *baptism,"* ye shall rise from the dead [in the likeness of His glorified body]! No wonder Paul had to arise and be baptised and wash away his sins: No wonder the angel told good old Cornelius that he must send for Peter to learn how to be saved: Peter could baptize, the angels could not, so long as there were legal officers in the flesh holding the keys of the kingdom, or the authority of the priesthood.[91]

The view that man's salvation depends upon his obedience to the requirements of baptism is taught repeatedly in modern scriptures. By revelation to Joseph Smith, the

Lord said: "As many as repent and are baptized in my name, which is Jesus Christ, and endure to the end, the same shall be saved."[92] Of the doctrine of Christ, the Nephite prophet Jacob said: "He commandeth all men that they must repent, and be baptized in his name, having perfect faith in the Holy One of Israel, or they cannot be saved in the kingdom of God."[93] Mormon also quoted Jesus as saying: "Repent all ye ends of the earth, and come unto me, and be baptized in my name, and have faith in me, that ye may be saved."[94] As Jesus ministered to the Nephites after His resurrection, He said in unequivocal terms:

> . . . whoso believeth in me, and is baptized, the same shall be saved; and they are they who shall inherit the kingdom of God.
>
> And whoso believeth not in me, and is not baptized, shall be damned.
>
> Verily, verily, I say unto you, that this is my doctrine, and I bear record of it from the Father. . . .[95]

The Nephite scripture makes the Savior's baptism at the hands of John a point of special significance in showing the need for man to be baptized. Though Christ did not have any sins to be washed away in baptism and though He was conceived in the flesh with the glory of the Father within Him, He nevertheless subscribed to the ordinance of baptism in order "to fulfill all righteousness"[96]—to show others the gate into the kingdom of God and to honor the established way. Only in this way could He say to others, "Come, follow me!" Centuries before this exemplary act occurred, Nephi foretold the baptism of the Savior and explained how righteousness would thereby be fulfilled:

> . . . I would ask of you, my beloved brethren, wherein the Lamb of God did fulfil all righteousness in being baptized by water?
>
> Know ye not that he was holy? But notwithstanding he being holy, he showeth unto the children of men that, according to the flesh he humbleth himself before the Father, and

witnesseth unto the Father that he would be obedient unto him in keeping his commandments.

Wherefore, after he was baptized with water the Holy Ghost descended upon him in the form of a dove.

And again, it showeth unto the children of men the straightness of the path, and the narrowness of the gate, by which they should enter, he having set the example before them.

And he said unto the children of men: Follow thou me. Wherefore, my beloved brethren, can we follow Jesus save we shall be willing to keep the commandments of the Father?

And the Father said: Repent ye, repent ye, and be baptized in the name of my Beloved Son.[97]

Joseph Smith also cited the Lord's baptism as evidence that man must be baptized. Having referred to Christ's request to John, "*Now let me be baptized:* for no man can enter the kingdom without obeying this ordinance: *for thus it becometh us to fulfil ALL RIGHTEOUSNESS,*" the Prophet remarked: "Surely, then, if it became John and Jesus Christ, the Savior, to fulfill *all righteousness to be baptized*—so surely, then, it will become every other person that seeks the kingdom of heaven to go and do likewise; for he is the door, and if any person climbs up any other way, the same is a thief and a robber!"[98]

Requirement of Divine Authority to Baptize

In order for baptism to be efficacious the officiator must have authority from God to perform this holy ordinance. "There is no salvation between the two lids of the Bible without a legal administrator," Joseph Smith explained.[99] This view is expressed in the Book of Mormon. When Alma baptized in the waters of Mormon, he stated that he had "authority from the Almighty God" to do so.[100] And when Jesus ministered to the Nephites, ushering in a new dispensation of the gospel, He said to those whom He had chosen to conduct the affairs of His kingdom: "I give unto you power that ye shall baptize this people when I am again ascended into heaven."[101] In performing this sacred ordinance, the officiator therefore states specifically that he has been commissioned, or given authority, of Jesus Christ to baptize the candidate.[102]

Of the need for divine authority to officiate in the things of God, Brigham Young explained:

> When people are filled with understanding to discern and comprehend the principles by which the worlds were made, and by which they are governed and controlled, they realize that there is a vast difference between the man who assumes his authority and the one who is appointed by his master to go and transact business. Suppose that a number of individuals having no appointment, credentials, or authority, should come from any foreign country to the capital of our nation, and pretend to be ministers of the government from whence they came, what attention would be paid to them by our Government? None, officially; though they would probably be treated kindly, and as gentlemen, if they behaved themselves. But when a minister from the English or any other European court comes with his appointment, credentials, recommends, &c., the President of the United States, the Congress, and officers of state are ready to receive him with the respect due to his position. So it is in the kingdom of God.[103]

Those who perform the ordinance of baptism must be ordained ministers of Jesus Christ acting in the authority of the Aaronic Priesthood and under the direction of the living prophet who holds the keys of this holy function on earth. This priesthood, with its keys and powers, was restored to the earth in the new dispensation by John the Baptist. As a heavenly messenger, he ordained Joseph Smith and Oliver Cowdery, stating: "Upon you my fellow servants, in the name of Messiah I confer the Priesthood of Aaron, which hods the keys of . . . baptism by immersion for the remission of sins."[104]

Purposes Of Baptism

Man Accepts Name of Christ

Baptism serves several basic purposes. Latter-day scriptures accord with the Bible in declaring that in baptism the faithful "put on Christ."[105] Nephi taught that the divine plan of salvation requires man to take upon himself "the name of Christ, by baptism." This man must do by following Jesus "down into the water, according to his word."[106] Joseph Smith also wrote by revelation that those who are "willing to take upon themselves the name of Jesus Christ, having a determination to serve him to the end," were to "be received by baptism" into Christ's church.[107]

This requirement is made of all who desire to obtain eternal life in the kingdom of God. When the Nephites inquired of the Lord by what name they should be called, they were informed:

> Have they not read the scriptures, which say ye must take upon you the name of Christ, which is my name? For by this name shall ye be called at the last day; and whoso taketh upon him my name, and endureth to the end, the same shall be saved at the last day.[108]

A revelation in modern times also explained:

> Behold, Jesus Christ is the name which is given of the Father, and there is none other name given whereby man can be saved;
>
> Wherefore, all men must take upon them the name which is given of the Father, for in that name shall they be called at the last day;
>
> Wherefore, if they know not the name by which they are called, they cannot have place in the kingdom of my Father.[109]

In taking upon themselves the name of Jesus Christ in the covenant of baptism, the obedient enter as sons and daughters into the divine family of the Son of Man. Having observed that his people who had made such a covenant were "called the children of Christ," King Benjamin explained:

> . . . therefore, ye are born of him and have become his sons and his daughters.
>
> And under this head ye are made free, and there is no other head whereby ye can be made free. There is no other name given whereby salvation cometh; therefore, I would that ye should take upon you the name of Christ, all you that have

entered into the covenant with God that ye should be obedient unto the end of your lives.

And it shall come to pass that whosoever doeth this shall be found at the right hand of God, for he shall know the name by which he is called; for he shall be called by the name of Christ.

And now it shall come to pass, that whosoever shall not take upon him the name of Christ must be called by some other name; therefore, he findeth himself on the left hand of God.[110]

Man Enters Path to Eternal Life

By accepting Christ in baptism (which must be followed by the baptism of the Holy Spirit), man enters the path that leads ultimately to eternal life. Many years before the earthly ministry of Jesus, Nephi was shown in vision the baptism of the Messiah, so that the people on the Western hemisphere would know the path which leads to salvation. "The gate by which ye should enter," the ancient seer then explained, "is repentance and baptism by water; and then cometh a remission of your sins by fire and by the Holy Ghost; and *then are ye in this straight and narrow path which leads to eternal life.*"[111] A revelation to Joseph Smith also designates baptism as the "gate" to the path that leads to salvation.[112] The Prophet spoke of the ultimate blessing to be achieved by baptism when he said: "A man may be saved, after the judgment, in the terrestrial kingdom, or in the telestial kingdom, but he can never see the celestial kingdom of God, without being born of water and of the Spirit."[113]

Man Receives Remission of Sins

By baptism, man is given access to the mercy of Christ unto the remission of his sins. Baptism therefore is a cleansing ordinance designed to wash away man's transgressions. When Nephi, the grandson of Helaman, baptized his people, the record states that "there was a great remission of sins."[114] Nephi also ordained assistants in the ministry, so that those who came to them might be baptized "as a witness and a testimony before God, and unto the people, that they had repented and received a remission of their sins."[115]

Mormon bore strong testimony to the efficacy of baptism as a means of washing away man's sins.[116] "Baptism is unto repentance," he wrote, "to the fulfilling the commandments unto the remission of sins."[117] This is also the testimony of many revelations given through Joseph Smith.[118] The Elders were commanded to teach the people: "Repent and be baptized in the name of Jesus Christ, according to the holy commandment, for the remission of sins."[119]

Man Enters Christ's Church

Having taken upon himself the name of Christ in baptism, the penitent believer may then be confirmed a member of Christ's church "by the laying on of the hands of the elders."[120] For this reason, Moroni reported that after those who accepted Christ among the Nephites "had been received unto baptism, and were wrought upon and cleansed by the power of the Holy Ghost, they were numbered among the people of the church of Christ."[121]

Man Receives Gift of the Holy Ghost

Finally, a major reason for baptism is that the Holy Ghost will not dwell in an unjustified person—in one to whom the atonement has not been extended to pay the debt of his personal sins. Only by being legally acquitted of his sins through baptism can man be given the Holy Ghost as a permanent gift. Joseph Smith observed: "Baptism is a holy ordinance preparatory to the reception of the Holy Ghost; it is the channel and key by which the Holy Ghost will be administered."[122] By being baptized in water, man has "the promise of the gift of the Holy Ghost," he declared, " . . . and in no other way is the gift of the Holy Ghost obtained."[123] Again, he explained:

> On the day of the Pentecost, when there was a marvelous display of the gifts [of the Holy Spirit], according to the promise [which Christ gave, as recorded] in Mark, many were pricked in

the heart, and said unto Peter, and to the rest of the Apostles, Men and brethren what shall we do? Peter said unto them: Repent, and be *baptised* every one of you in the name of Jesus Christ, for the remission of sins, and ye shall receive the gift of the Holy Ghost, etc.—Here one of the witnesses [of Christ] says in so many words, repent and be *baptised.* And we are of the opinion that Peter having been taught by the Lord, and commissioned by the Lord, and endowed by the Lord, would be about as correct a counselor, or ambassador as we or they could inquire of to know the *right way* to enter into the kingdom.

Again, Luke in his record of the Acts of the Apostles, says: And it came to pass, that while Apollos was at Corinth, Paul having passed through the upper coasts, came to Ephesus; and finding certain disciples, he said unto them, Have ye received the Holy Ghost since ye believed? And they said unto him, We have not so much as heard whether there be any Holy Ghost. And he said unto them, Unto what then were ye baptised? And they said: unto John's baptism. Then said Paul, John verily baptised with the baptism of repentance, saying unto the people, that they should believe on him which should come after him, that is on Christ Jesus. When they heard this, they were baptised in the name of the Lord Jesus.—And when Paul had laid his hands upon them, the Holy Ghost came on them; and they spake with tongues, and prophesied.

From the above witnesses we are informed that *baptism* was the essential point on which they could receive the gift of the Holy Ghost. It seems from the reasoning above that some sectarian Jew had been baptising like John, but had forgotten to inform them that there was one to follow by the name of Jesus Christ, to baptise with fire and the Holy Ghost:—which showed these converts that their first baptism was illegal, and when they heard this they were gladly baptised, and after hands were laid on them, they received the gifts [of the Spirit], according to promise, and spake with *tongues and prophesied.*[124]

Infant Baptism

Since little children are alive in Christ through the power of the atonement, they need not be baptized until they arrive at the age of accountability. The Prophet explained:

The doctrine of baptizing children, or sprinkling them, or they must welter in hell, is a doctrine not true, not supported in

Holy Writ, and is not consistent with the character of God. All children are redeemed by the blood of Jesus Christ, and the moment that children leave this world, they are taken to the bosom of Abraham.[125]

Again he said:

"Do you believe in the baptism of infants?" asks the Presbyterian. No. "Why?" Because it is nowhere written in the Bible. Circumcision is not baptism, neither was baptism instituted in the place of circumcision. Baptism is for remission of sins. Children have no sins. Jesus blessed them and said, "Do what you have seen me do." Children are all made alive in Christ, and those of riper years through faith and repentance.[126]

In a revelation to Mormon, the Lord was more emphatic. "Listen to the words of Christ, your Redeemer, your Lord and your God," He declared. "Behold, I came into the world not to call the righteous but sinners to repentance; the whole need no physician, but they that are sick; wherefore, little children are whole, for they are not capable of committing sin; wherefore the curse of Adam is taken from them in me, that it hath no power over them; and the law of circumcision is done away in me."[127]

On the strength of this revelation, the Nephite prophet declared that "it is solemn mockery before God" to baptize little children.[128] He declared:

Behold, baptism is unto repentance to the fulfilling the commandments unto the remission of sins.

But little children are alive in Christ, even from the foundation of the world; if not so, God is a partial God, and also a changeable God, and a respecter of persons; for how many little children have died without baptism!

Wherefore, if little children could not be saved without baptism, these must have gone to an endless hell.

Behold I say unto you, that he that supposeth that little children need baptism is in the gall of bitterness and in the bonds of iniquity, for he hath neither faith, hope, nor charity; wherefore, should he be cut off while in the thought, he must go down to hell.

For awful is the wickedness to suppose that God saveth one child because of baptism, and the other must perish because he hath no baptism. . . .

Little children cannot repent; wherefore, it is awful wickedness to deny the pure mercies of God unto them, for they are all alive in him because of his mercy.

And he that saith that little children need baptism denieth the mercies of Christ, and setteth at naught the atonement of him and the power of his redemption.[129]

Summary

The preparatory gospel through which man can come unto Jesus Christ and receive a remission of his personal sins is designed to bring each true believer to receive a greater revelation of God. In this divine program, repentance follows faith in the Son of God as the second principle and ordinance of the gospel. When correctly applied, repentance enables man to achieve a meaningful spiritual union with Christ, and for this reason it is a principle of life and power. Fallen man must repent toward God, not merely in order to conform his life to the standard of conduct which the law of God requires, but as a means of obtaining divine mercy, truth, and power by which he can become a new creature in Christ. Repentance, therefore, is a gift of God, both in the program of repentance which God has given to man and in the results which follow the application of that program. True repentance is a divine, rather than a mere human, process. To comply with this divine program, man must (1) recognize Christ, (2) express remorse for sin, (3) rely upon the Son of God, (4) resolve to come unto Jesus, (5) be reconciled to the Redeemer, and (6) be renewed by the truth and power of God. Only in this way can repentance be a meaningful and lasting experience which leads man into the presence of God.

In the plan of life and salvation, baptism is the first fruits of repentance. Thereby men enter into a sacred covenant with Christ that they will bear one another's burdens, comfort those who stand in need of comfort, and stand as witnesses of God before the world. Being administered by immersion by one who has authority from God, baptism is symbolic of physical birth and of the death, burial, and resurrection of the Son of God. Without baptism there can be no salvation, for only in this way can man take upon himself the name of Christ and enter the path which leads to eternal life. By complying with this requirement, man receives a remission of sins and prepares himself to enter the Church of Jesus Christ and receive the gift of the Holy Ghost. In this way, man is prepared for the greater revelation of God by which he can be sanctified and enter, eventually, into the presence of God.

Notes

1. See HC, VI, p.58; I. R., Hebrews 6:1. As indicated in chapter one, there are some functions of the preparatory gospel, such as repentance and baptism, that may be discontinued among the Saints after they achieve perfection.
2. *Ibid.,* p. 250.
3. See D&C 84:26–27.
4. HC, VI, p. 57.
5. *Lectures on Faith,* No. 1.
6. See chapter one, the section entitled "First Principles and Ordinances of the Gospel."
7. See chapter four, the section entitled "Effects Of Faith."
8. D&C 35:8–9. See also Mark 16:17–18.
9. 3 Nephi 9:20.
10. See Helaman 8:15; 3 Nephi 9:20; 12:19; Ether 4:15; Moroni 6:2.
11. 3 Nephi 9:20.
12. 2 Nephi 2:7.
13. See chapter one, the section entitled "First Principles and Ordinances of the Gospel," where Joseph Smith refers to repentance as an ordinance of the gospel.
14. HC, I, p. 39; D&C 13.
15. D&C 58:43.
16. D&C 3:20; 15:6; 16:6.
17. HC, III, p. 396.
18. *Ibid.,* II, pp. 255–256. See Luke 24:46–47.
19. 3 Nephi 9:20. This assumes that by true repentance they accept Christ in the way which He has prescribed.
20. Alma 11:34–37.
21. Helaman 5:10–11.
22. Moses 6:57.
23. D&C 20:29.
24. HC, IV, p. 588.
25. D&C 1:31–32. See also Alma 45:16.
26. See Moses 6:55.
27. See Alma 12:24; 34:32; 42:4.
28. Alma 34:32–35.

29. HC, III, p. 379.
30. *Ibid.,* IV, p. 554.
31. D&C 18:11. See Volume I of this study, the section in chapter sixteen entitled "Conditional Benefits Of The Atonement."
32. See Mosiah 2:36; 2 Nephi 26:11; Ether 2:15; Genesis 6:3; Moses 8:17; D&C 1:33.
33. *Lectures on Faith,* No. 1.
34. Ether 12:27. Nephi wrote: "If it so be that the children of men keep the commandments of God he doth nourish them, and strengthen them, and provide means whereby they can accomplish the thing which he has commanded them."—1 Nephi 17:3.
35. Alma 33:22.
36. 2 Nephi 25:20. See also Acts 4:12; 2 Nephi 11:6–7.
37. D&C 18:23.
38. 2 Nephi 11:6.
39. 3 Nephi 27:7–9.
40. 3 Nephi 27:10.
41. D&C 6:36.
42. Alma 42:18.
43. Alma 36:12–13, 16.
44. Alma 36:18–21.
45. 1 Nephi 10:6.
46. 2 Nephi 31:19.
47. Moroni 6:4.
48. See Moroni 10:32–33; D&C 93:19–20.
49. 2 Nephi 31:10–12; D&C 38:22; 56:2; 100:2; 112:14.
50. Moroni 6:3.
51. D&C 20:37.
52. D&C 133:15.
53. 2 Nephi 10:24.
54. 2 Nephi 25:23.
55. 2 Nephi 33:9.
56. 3 Nephi 12:23–24.
57. See D&C 98:39–47. See also Exodus 22:1–5; 2 Samuel 12:6; Luke 19:8–9.
58. Moroni 8:25.
59. See Volume I of this study, the section in chapter sixteen entitled "Conditional Benefits Of The Atonement."
60. See D&C 20:37.
61. See Alma 5:7–15.
62. Alma 19:33. See also Mosiah 5:2, for a report of like effects upon the people of King Benjamin.
63. Alma 19:35.
64. See Mosiah 2:18–19; 5:7.
65. Mosiah 4:9–10.
66. Mosiah 4:1–2.
67. Mosiah 4:2.
68. Mosiah 4:10.
69. Mosiah 4:3.
70. Mosiah 5:2.

71. Moroni 8:25.
72. HC, IV, p. 555.
73. Mosiah 18:13.
74. Alma 7:15.
75. Mosiah 18:8–10.
76. HC, V, p. 499.
77. TS, III (September 1, 1842), p. 903. (Italics in the original.)
78. D&C 76:51.
79. Moses 6:64.
80. 3 Nephi 19:11–12.
81. Mosiah 18:12–16.
82. See 3 Nephi 11:22–27.
83. D&C 20:72–74.
84. D&C 128:13.
85. See Moses 6:59.
86. See D&C 76:51; Romans 6:3–6.
87. Romans 6:4.
88. D&C 68:25–27.
89. TS, III (September 1, 1842), pp. 903–904. (Italics in the original.)
90. John 3:5.
91. TS, *loc. cit.*, p. 905. (Italics in the original.)
92. D&C 18:22. See also D&C 112:29.
93. 2 Nephi 9:23.
94. Moroni 7:34. See also Ether 4:18.
95. 3 Nephi 11:33–35.
96. Matthew 3:13–15.
97. 2 Nephi 31:6–11.
98. TS, *op. cit.*, p. 905. (Italics in the original.)
99. Discourse by Joseph Smith, July 23, 1843, manuscript report in Church Historian's Library, Salt Lake City, Utah.
100. Mosiah 18:13.
101. 3 Nephi 11:21–22.
102. 3 Nephi 11:25. See D&C 20:73 for a statement of the baptismal prayer in this dispensation.
103. JD, VIII, p. 194.
104. HC, I, p. 39. For the account of the restoration of the Aaronic Priesthood, see Volume I, the section in chapter four entitled "The Aaronic Priesthood Restored."
105. Galatians 3:27.
106. 2 Nephi 31:13.
107. D&C 20:37.
108. 3 Nephi 27:5–6.
109. D&C 18:23–25.
110. Mosiah 5:7–10.
111. 2 Nephi 31:17–18.
112. D&C 22.
113. HC, I, p. 283.
114. 3 Nephi 1:23.
115. 3 Nephi 7:24–26.
116. 3 Nephi 30:2.

117. Moroni 8:11.
118. See D&C 19:31; 55:2; 68:27; 76:51, 52; 84:27, 74.
119. D&C 49:13. See also D&C 33:11.
120. D&C 20:41, 43, 68.
121. Moroni 6:4.
122. HC, III, p. 379.
123. *Ibid.,* IV, p. 555. See also D&C 84:74.
124. TS, III (September 1, 1842), p. 904. (Italics in the original.) For the account of the day of Pentecost and Paul's ministry at Ephesus, see Acts 2 and 19, respectively.
125. HC, IV, p. 554.
126. *Ibid.,* V, p. 499.
127. Moroni 8:8.
128. Moroni 8:9.
129. Moroni 8:11–15, 19–20.

6

The Everlasting Gospel

> *The gospel of Jesus Christ . . . consists of eternal principles, unfolding light and intelligence, and is adapted to the nature of man as a mortal and immortal being—principles that . . . lead to life everlasting.*—JOHN TAYLOR.

Modern revelation given through Joseph Smith implies that the everlasting gospel is a divine program by which man can achieve a living spiritual union with Christ and mature in divine truth and light as it is given to him through the Holy Ghost until he receives a fulness of God's glory in the resurrection. The preparatory gospel is designed to bring man to Christ and to justify him through the atonement of the Son of God. But the everlasting gospel is concerned, primarily, with how the Holy Spirit is given to enlighten man's mind, to sanctify him from all sin, and to act through the Holy Priesthood to seal him to eternal life in the resurrection. Only the basic principles and doctrines of the everlasting gospel will be treated in this chapter. Other aspects of this phase of the plan of life and salvation will be considered in later chapters.

Gift Of The Holy Ghost

Nature of the Gift

After baptism in water, the major ordinance by which man is placed on the path which leads to eternal life is the laying on of authorized hands for the bestowal of the gift of the Holy Ghost. This act, Joseph F. Smith explained, "confers upon a man the right to receive at any time, when he is worthy of it and desires it, the power and light of truth of the Holy Ghost."[1] So vital and important is this gift to man and so far-reaching in its effects that the Prophet referred to it as "the unspeakable gift of the Holy Ghost."[2] By the divine truth and power which man may receive through the gift of the Holy Ghost, the spiritual renewal which begins when he starts to express living faith in Jesus Christ can continue until man is given access to Christ's glory directly in those manifestations which are related to the second Comforter.

As early as 1823, Joseph Smith was told that the gift of the Holy Ghost would be given to those who accepted the restored gospel. In speaking of the gold plates from which the Book of Mormon was to be translated, the angel Moroni said: "When they are interpreted the Lord will give the holy priesthood to some, and they shall begin to proclaim this gospel and baptize by water, and after that they shall have power to give the Holy Ghost by the laying on of their hands."[3]

Joseph Smith said of this divine gift:

> We believe in the gift of the Holy Ghost being enjoyed now, as much as it was in the Apostles' days; we believe that it [the gift of the Holy Ghost] is necessary to make and to organize the Priesthood, that no man can be called to fill any office in the ministry without it; we also believe in prophecy, in tongues, in visions, and in revelations, in gifts, and in healings; and that these things cannot be enjoyed without the gift of the Holy Ghost. We believe that the holy men of old spake as they were moved by the Holy Ghost, and that holy men in these days speak by the same principle; we believe in its being a comforter and a witness bearer, that it brings things past to our remembrance, leads us into all truth, and shows us of things to come; we believe that "no man can know that Jesus is the Christ, but by the Holy Ghost." We believe in it [the gift of the Holy Ghost] in all its fullness, and power, and greatness, and glory; but whilst we do this, we believe in it rationally, consistently, and scripturally, and not according to the wild vagaries, foolish notions and traditions of men.[4]

From this statement it is evident that the gift of the Holy Ghost is the spiritual foundation of the Church of Jesus Christ. Through this divine channel the Saints were expected to draw spiritual truth and power from God to establish their lives in righteousness and to build up the kingdom of God upon the earth.

It is not intended that all divine manifestations which pertain to the plan of life and salvation should be given to man through the gift of the Holy Ghost. When the mission of the Holy Ghost is viewed in light of the total program of the gospel, His functions are seen to be of an intermediary nature. The ultimate purpose of the gospel is to glorify man in Christ, as Jesus has been glorified in the Father.[5] This the Holy Ghost cannot do.[6] His mission is to take the truth and power which the Man of Holiness has given to Christ and bestow them on man,[7] until man is sufficiently prepared to receive the personal ministry of Christ as a second Comforter and be glorified directly by and in the Master.

In performing His divine mission, the Holy Ghost bears witness to man of the things of God:[8] He testifies of the Father and the Son[9] and gives enlightening assurance to the humble that Christ rose from the dead and that the Master will raise all men from the grave to be judged by Him.[10] Thereby, "man can *know* that Jesus is the Lord."[11] By means of His divine power of truth and light, the holy Comforter also brings things past to the remembrance of man and shows him that which is to come,[12] while sealing the conviction of divine truth upon the human heart and mind.[13] Concerning the functions of the Spirit, a Nephite historian said: "There are many among us who have many revelations, for they are not all stiffnecked; and as many as are not stiffnecked and have faith have communion with the Holy Spirit, which maketh manifest unto the children of men, according to their faith."[14] His statement accords with a revelation which was given through the Prophet which declares that the Holy Ghost "manifesteth all things which are expedient unto the children of men."[15]

The function of the Holy Ghost in developing the living attributes of the Spirit within man was well stated by Parley P. Pratt. Having first explained that man was created in the image of God and possessed every organ, attribute, sense, sympathy, affection, etc., that is possessed by God Himself, Elder Pratt explained:

> These are possessed by man, in his rudimental state, in a subordinate sense of the word. Or, in other words, these attributes are in embryo; and are to be gradually developed. They resemble a bud—a germ, which gradually develops into bloom, and then, by progress, produces the mature fruit, after its own kind.
>
> The gift of the Holy Spirit adapts itself to all these organs or attributes. It quickens all the intellectual faculties, increases, enlarges, expands, and purifies all the natural passions and affections; and adapts them, by the gift of wisdom, to their lawful use. It inspires, develops, cultivates and matures all the fine-toned sympathies, joys, tastes, kindred feelings and affections of our nature. It inspires virtue, kindness, goodness, tenderness, gentleness and charity. It develops beauty of person, form and features. It tends to health, vigor, animation and social feeling. It develops and invigorates all the faculties of the physical and intellectual man. It strengthens and gives tone to the nerves. In short, it is, as it were, marrow to the bone, joy to the heart, light to the eyes, music to the ears, and life to the whole being.[16]

Authority Required to Confer the Gift

The angel Moroni's promise to Joseph Smith in 1823, cited in the preceding section, indicates that man must be commissioned with divine authority in order to possess the right and power to confer the gift of the Holy Ghost. Jesus "laid his hands" upon the disciples whom He chose among the Nephites and "gave them power to give the Holy Ghost." Thereafter, "on as many as they laid their hands, fell the Holy Ghost."[17]

The fact that divine authority is necessary in order to confer the gift of the Holy Ghost was made clear when the foundations of the new dispensation of the gospel were established. When John the Baptist bestowed the Aaronic Priesthood upon Joseph Smith and Oliver Cowdery, which gave them authority to baptize, he informed them that this priesthood "had not the power of laying on hands for the gift of the Holy Ghost"; the higher authority would be given to them thereafter.[18] This promise was fulfilled when Peter, James, and John conferred the Holy Melchizedek Priesthood upon the Prophet and his associate. A revelation said of this priesthood: "The power and authority of the higher, or Melchizedek Priesthood, is to hold the keys of all the spiritual blessings of the church."[19] Through this priesthood and its ordinances, including the laying on of hands for the gift of the Holy Ghost, the "power of godliness"—the divine power which is given to man by the Holy Ghost—is manifest. "And without the ordinances thereof, and the authority of the priesthood," another revelation explained, "the power of godliness is not manifest unto men in the flesh."[20]

Laying on of Hands

In explaining how the gift of the Holy Ghost is given to man, Joseph Smith said: "The scriptural way of attaining the gift of the Holy Ghost is by baptism, and by the laying on of hands."[21] He added: "In no other way is the gift of the Holy Ghost obtained."[22] Jesus said to the Twelve whom He chose on the Western hemisphere: "Ye shall call on the Father in my name, in mighty prayer; and after ye have done this ye shall have power that to him upon whom ye shall lay your hands, ye shall give the Holy Ghost; and in my name shall ye give it, for thus do mine apostles [at Jerusalem]."[23]

The Lord's statement that His apostles at Jerusalem conferred the gift of the Holy Ghost by the laying on of their hands reveals the accord that exists between the New Testament and the Nephite scripture on this doctrine and practice. When Philip (who had been ordained by the apostles at Jerusalem to a lesser order of the priesthood that concerned temporal functions and carried with it the authority to baptize[24]) converted the people of Samaria to Christ and baptized them, he immediately sent for Peter and John. When the apostles arrived, they prayed for the people, "that they might receive the Holy Ghost." In reporting these actions, the record clarifies: "For as yet he [the Holy Ghost] was fallen upon none of them: *only* they were baptized in the name of the Lord Jesus." Baptism in water was not sufficient; they had *only* been baptized. The record continues by relating the action of the apostles: "Then laid they their hands on them and they received the Holy Ghost." When Simon, a sorcerer who was standing nearby, "saw that through the laying on of the apostles' hands the Holy Ghost was given, he offered them money, saying, Give me also this power, that on whomsoever I lay hands, he may receive the Holy Ghost." But Peter rebuked him, stating: "Thy money perish with thee, because thou hast thought that the gift of God may be purchased with money."[25]

When the apostle Paul baptized some believers at Ephesus, the biblical record reports how he introduced them into the way of salvation, stating: "And when Paul had laid his hands upon them, the Holy Ghost came on them; and they spake with tongues, and prophesied."[26] Paul also referred to this sacred ordinance in his admonition to Timothy not to neglect the gift of God that had been given to him by the laying on of hands.[27] And among the "principles of the doctrine of Christ," the writer of the epistle to the Hebrews listed the "laying on of hands."[28]

The practice of conferring the gift of the Holy Ghost by the laying on of hands was restored to earth in the new dispensation. A revelation given at the time the Church was organized stated that those who had been baptized were to be confirmed "by the laying on of hands for the baptism of fire and the Holy Ghost, according to the scriptures." Other revelations also instructed: "On as many as ye shall baptize with water, ye shall lay your hands, and they shall receive the gift of the Holy Ghost."[29] Having cited biblical sources to show that this gift is given by the laying on of hands, Joseph Smith stated:

> Now where is the man who is authorized to put his finger

on the spot and say, Thus far shalt thou go [in accepting the doctrines of Christ] and no farther: there is no man. Therefore let us receive the whole, or none. . . . I consider these to be some of the leading items of the gospel, as taught by Christ and his apostles, and as received by those whom they taught. I wish you would look at these, carefully and closely, and you will readily perceive that the difference between me and the other religious teachers, is in the Bible.[30]

Righteousness and the Reception of the Holy Ghost

Because the gift of the Holy Ghost is bestowed by the laying on of hands, it does not follow that the act of conferring this divine gift is but a mechanical process. Instead Joseph Smith declared: "The Gift of the Holy Ghost by the laying on of hands, cannot be received through the medium of any other principle than the principle of righteousness, for if the proposals are not complied with, it is of no use, but withdraws."[31] Thus Lehi received the Holy Ghost "by faith on the Son of God."[32] Parley P. Pratt explained:

> An agent filled with this heavenly spirit cannot impart of the same to another, unless that other is justified, washed, cleansed from all his impurities of heart, affections, habits or practices, by the blood of atonement which is generally applied in connection with the baptism of remission.
>
> A man who continues in his sins, and who has no living faith in the Son of God, cannot receive the gift of the Holy Ghost through the ministration of any person, however holy he may be. The impure spirit will repulse the pure element, upon the natural laws of sympathetic affinity, or of attraction and repulsion.[33]

A Requirement for Salvation

Having explained that man must "receive the ordinance of the laying on of the hands of him who is ordained and sealed unto this power" in order to receive the gift of the Holy Ghost, Joseph Smith said: "This is according to the Holy Scriptures, and the Book of Mormon; and the only way that man can enter into the celestial kingdom."[34] Again he stressed that this was "according to the order of God," then added: "I know that all men will be damned if they do not come in the way which He hath opened, and this is the way marked out by the word of the Lord."[35] As evidence that this divine gift must be received by man as a vital part of the gospel program, the Prophet cited Peter's instructions on the day of Pentecost.[36] Christ's chief apostle promised the gift of the Holy Ghost to those who would comply with the divine requirement to be baptized, and declared: "For this promise is unto you, and to your children, and to all that are afar off, even as many as the Lord your God shall call."[37] No person who received baptism by an authorized agent was to be exempt or excluded in any age of time.

The need for man to receive the gift of the Holy Ghost in order to attain salvation is also stressed in the Nephite scripture. Mormon wrote: "If it so be that ye believe in Christ, and are baptized, first with water, then with fire and with the Holy Ghost, following the example of our Savior, according to that which he hath commanded us, it shall be well with you in the day of judgment."[38] Jesus was even more emphatic in His instructions to the Nephites. Having promised that those who would be baptized according to His instructions would be visited by the Father "with fire and with the Holy Ghost," Christ declared:

> Verily, verily, I say unto you, that this is my doctrine, and whoso buildeth upon this buildeth upon my rock, and the gates of hell shall not prevail against them.
>
> And whoso shall declare more or less than this, and establish it for my doctrine, the same cometh of evil, and is not built upon my rock; but he buildeth upon a sandy foundation, and the gates of hell stand open to receive such when the floods come and the winds beat upon them.[39]

Revelations to Joseph Smith stress the same doctrine. "Verily, verily I say unto you," a revelation declared, "they who believe not on your words, and are not baptized in water in my name, for the remission of their sins, that they may receive the Holy Ghost, shall be damned, and shall not come into my Father's kingdom where my Father and I am."[40]

Sign Of The Dove

When Jesus was baptized by John, Matthew states that the forerunner to the Messiah "saw the Spirit of God descending like a dove, and lighting upon him."[41] Mark and John make similar statements,[42] and Luke wrote that "the Holy Ghost descended in a bodily shape like a dove upon him."[43] The latter statement in particular has caused some to conclude that the Holy Ghost actually took the body of a dove on this occasion. But in speaking of the baptism of Christ, Joseph Smith referred to the Holy Ghost descending '"in the form of a dove, or rather in the *sign* of the dove, in witness of that administration," then explained:

> The sign of the dove was instituted before the creation of the world, a witness for the Holy Ghost, and the devil cannot come in the sign of a dove. The Holy Ghost is a personage, and is in the form of a personage. It does not confine itself to the *form* of the dove, but in *sign* of the dove. The Holy Ghost cannot be transformed into a dove; but the sign of a dove was given to John to signify the truth of the deed, as the dove is an emblem or token of truth and innocence.[44]

Baptism Of Fire And Of The Holy Ghost

The mission of the Holy Ghost is to manifest the Spirit or glory of Christ to man with all its divine blessings and endowments. "He shall receive of *mine,*" Jesus said of the third great personage in the Godhead, "and shall shew it unto you."[45] This is the baptism of the Holy Ghost, which is sometimes called the baptism of fire, or the baptism of the Holy Ghost and of fire, which both ancient and modern scriptures promise to the obedient after baptism in water. Fire is a symbol of the glory of God.[46] To receive the baptism of fire is to be enveloped in the heavenly element and cleansed by its divine action. If baptism in water is immersion in the earthly element, so must the baptism of the Spirit be an immersion in the divine substance called the Spirit or glory of God. It is by the action of the Spirit that those who are baptized in water are sanctified from all sin and prepared to stand spotless in the presence of God.

The baptism of fire is the "portion of the celestial glory" (that is, of the everlasting fire or burnings of God) with which man must be quickened as a preparation to "receive of the same, even a fulness," in the resurrection.[47] For this reason the Prophet wrote of the faithful: " . . . that through the power and manifestations of the Spirit, while in the flesh, they may be able to bear his [God's] presence in the world of glory."[48] Unless man receives the power and manifestations of the Spirit, he will not be prepared to dwell in the glory and power of God in the resurrection.

Modern scriptures speak repeatedly of the baptism of fire and the Holy Ghost as being an indispensable part of the gospel plan of salvation. A revelation to Joseph Smith indicates that when Adam was immersed by baptism in water and then enveloped in the power of the Holy Spirit, he heard a voice out of heaven say: "Thou art baptized with fire, and with the Holy Ghost."[49] Nephi taught: "By following your Lord and your Savior down into the water, according to his word, behold, then shall ye receive the Holy Ghost; yea, then cometh the baptism of fire and of the Holy Ghost."[50] Mormon taught the same doctrine.[51] To the Nephites, Jesus said: "Verily, verily, I say unto you, that this is my doctrine, and I bear record of it from the Father; and whoso believeth in me believeth in the Father also; and unto him will the Father bear record of me, for he will visit him with fire and with the Holy Ghost."[52] Having given His disciples power to baptize, Christ promised: " . . . and after that ye are baptized with water, behold, I will baptize you with fire and with the Holy Ghost."[53]

To Joseph Smith, the Lord spoke of His gospel as consisting of repentance, baptism, and "the baptism of fire and the Holy Ghost."[54] He also instructed those who were sent to teach the restored gospel: "Yea, open your mouths, . . . saying: Repent . . . and be baptized, everyone of you, for a remission of your sins; yea, be baptized even in water, and then cometh the baptism of fire and of the Holy Ghost."[55]

An example illustrating what the baptism of the Holy Ghost and of fire can mean to man is given in the Book of Mormon. Sometime prior to Christ's appearance upon the Western hemisphere after His resurrection, two faithful missionaries named Nephi and Lehi, while laboring among the Lamanites, were thrown into prison. But when the Lamanites came to the prison to kill their captives, they found that Nephi and Lehi were "encircled about as if by fire insomuch that they [the Lamanites] durst not lay their hands upon them." "Nevertheless," the record states, "Nephi and Lehi were not burned; and they were as standing in the midst of fire and were not burned."[56] Nephi and Lehi then preached the gospel unto them. And as the Lamanites beheld this marvelous manifestation of God's glory, they began to exercise faith in the Lord. They were then endowed with powers of the Spirit similar to those which Nephi and Lehi received. The record states:

> . . . behold, they . . . were encircled about, yea every soul, by a pillar of fire.
>
> And Nephi and Lehi were in the midst of them; yea, they were encircled about; yea, they were as if in the midst of a flaming fire, yet it did harm them not, neither did it take hold upon the walls of the prison; and they were filled with that joy which is unspeakable and full of glory.
>
> And behold, the Holy Spirit of God did come down from heaven, and did enter into their hearts, and they were filled as with fire, and they could speak forth marvelous words.[57]

When Jesus ministered to the Nephites, He cited the above incident as illustrating the degree to which man may be endowed with the Spirit or glory of God by means of the gospel. To the Nephites, He said:

> . . . ye shall offer for a sacrifice unto me a broken heart and a contrite spirit. And whoso cometh unto me with a broken

heart and a contrite spirit, him will I baptize with fire and with the Holy Ghost, *even as the Lamanites, because of their faith in me at the time of their conversion, were baptized with fire and with the Holy Ghost . . .*[58]

Many Nephites realized the fulfillment of Christ's promise. The day after the Lord's initial visit to them, the twelve disciples whom Jesus chose to minister His gospel to the Nephites met together with a multitude of interested persons. Having prayed to the Father that He would give them the Holy Ghost, they were baptized. The record then states:

> . . . the Holy Ghost did fall upon them, and they were filled with the Holy Ghost and with fire,
>
> And behold, they were encircled about as if it were by fire; and it came down from heaven, and the multitude did witness it, and did bear record.[59]

While the disciples were enveloped in the heavenly element, Jesus again appeared unto the Nephites. And as He blessed the Twelve whom He had chosen, "the light of his countenance did shine upon them, and behold they were as white as the countenance and also the garments of Jesus; and behold the whiteness thereof did exceed all the whiteness, yea, even there could be nothing upon earth so white as the whiteness thereof."[60]

To be endowed with the glorious powers of the Holy Ghost, man must express intelligent faith in Jesus Christ and obey the divine plan of life and salvation. "So great faith have I never seen among all the Jews," Christ observed to the Nephites; "wherefore I could not show unto them so great miracles, because of their unbelief."[61]

The gospel message Joseph Smith was called to give to the world also contained the promise that those who would believe and be baptized would receive the baptism of fire. The reception of the Holy Ghost was to Heber C. Kimball a literal immersion in the heavenly element. Of it he said:

> Under the ordinances of baptism and the laying on of hands, I received the Holy Ghost, as the disciples did in ancient

days, which was like a consuming fire. I felt as though I sat at the feet of Jesus, and was clothed in my right mind, although the people called me crazy.

I continued in this way for many months, and it seemed as though my body would consume away; at the same time the scriptures were unfolded to my mind in such a wonderful manner that it appeared to me, at times, as if I had formerly been familiar with them.[62]

Concerning the baptism of fire and the Holy Ghost which Lorenzo Snow received, he wrote:

In June, 1836, previous to accepting these ordinances [of the gospel], I became convinced in my investigations of the principles taught by the Latter-day Saints, which I proved by comparison to be the same as those mentioned in the New Testament, taught by Christ and his Apostles, that obedience to them would impart miraculous powers, manifestations and revelations. With sanguine expectation of this result, I received baptism and the ordinance of laying on of hands by one who professed to have divine authority; and having thus yielded obedience I was in constant expectation of the fulfillment of the promise of the reception of the Holy Ghost.

This manifestation did not immediately follow my baptism as I expected. But, although the time was deferred, when I did receive it its realization was more perfect, tangible and miraculous than even my strongest hopes had led me to anticipate. One day while engaged in my studies, some two or three weeks after I was baptized, I began to reflect upon the fact that I had not obtained a *knowledge* of the truth of the work—that I had not realized the fulfillment of the promise: "He that doeth my will shall know of the doctrine"; and I began to feel very uneasy.

I laid aside my books, left the house and wandered around through the fields under the oppressive influence of a gloomy, disconsolate spirit, while an indescribable cloud of darkness seemed to envelop me. I had been accustomed, at the close of the day, to retire for secret prayer to a grove, a short distance from my lodgings, but at this time I felt no inclination to do so.

The spirit of prayer had departed, and the heavens seemed like brass over my head. At length, realizing that the usual time had come for secret prayer, I concluded I would not forego my evening service, and, as a matter of formality, knelt as I was in the habit of doing, and in my accustomed retired place, but not feeling as I was wont to feel.

I had no sooner opened my lips in an effort to pray than I heard a sound, just above my head, like the rustling of silken robes, and immediately the Spirit of God descended upon me completely enveloping my whole person, filling me from the crown of my head to the soles of my feet, and O the joy and happiness I felt! No language can describe the instantaneous transition from a dense cloud of mental and spiritual darkness into a refulgence of light and knowledge, as it was at that time imparted to my understanding. I then received a perfect knowledge that God lives, that Jesus Christ is the Son of God, and of the restoration of the Holy Priesthood, and of the fulness of the gospel.

It was a complete baptism—a tangible immersion in the heavenly principle or element, the Holy Ghost; and even more real and physical in its effects upon every part of my system than the immersion of water, dispelling forever, so long as reason and memory last, all possibility of doubt or fear in relation to the fact handed down to us historically, that the "Babe of Bethlehem" is truly the Son of God; also the fact that he is now being revealed to the children of men, and communicating knowledge, the same as in the apostolic times. I was perfectly satisfied, as well I might be, for my expectations were more than realized, I think I may safely say, in an infinite degree.

I cannot tell how long I remained in the full flow of this blissful enjoyment and divine enlightenment, but it was several minutes before the celestial element, which filled and surrounded me, began gradually to withdraw. On arising from my kneeling posture, with my heart swelling with gratitude to God beyond the power of expression, I felt—I knew that he had conferred on me what only an omnipotent Being can confer—that which is of greater value than all the wealth and honors worlds can bestow. That night, as I retired to rest, the same wonderful manifestations were repeated, and continued to be for several successive nights. The sweet remembrance of those glorious experiences, from that time to the present, bring them fresh before me, imparting an inspiring influence which pervades my whole being, and I trust will to the close of my earthly existence.[63]

The Holy Ghost And Gift Of The Holy Ghost

Joseph Smith stated that "a man may receive the Holy Ghost, and it may descend upon him and not tarry with him."[64] This means that there "is a difference between the Holy Ghost and the gift of the Holy Ghost."[65] To illustrate this point, the Prophet cited the example of Cornelius, the righteous gentile who was converted to the gospel in New Testament times, and said:

> Cornelius received the Holy Ghost before he was baptized, which was the convincing power of God unto him of the truth of the Gospel, but he could not receive the gift of the Holy Ghost until after he was baptized. Had he not taken this sign or ordinance upon him, the Holy Ghost which convinced him of the truth of God, would have left him. Until he obeyed these ordinances and received the gift of the Holy Ghost, by the laying on of hands, according to the order of God, he could not have healed the sick or commanded an evil spirit to come out of a man, and it obey him; for the spirits might say unto him, as they did to the sons of Sceva: "Paul we know and Jesus we know, but who are ye?"[66]

Three points which the Prophet makes in this statement should be stressed: First, the power of the Holy Ghost may be given to man before baptism to convince him of the truth of the gospel; but this does not assure that he will retain the influence of the Holy Ghost in his life as a permanent gift. Instead, the divine Witness or Testator will eventually withdraw his power and influence if man does not obey the gospel. It is therefore possible for man to experience to some degree the truth, light, and power of God's kingdom before baptism so that he may determine for himself whether or not he will embrace the divine plan by which he may enjoy the blessings of the Comforter as a permanent gift to aid him in his spiritual development toward eternal life.

Second, the gift of the Holy Ghost is not given to man unless he is obedient to the ordinances of the gospel. "There are certain key words and signs belonging to the Priesthood which must be observed in order to obtain the blessing," the Prophet stated. He explained:

> What if we should attempt to get the gift of the Holy Ghost through any other means except the signs or ways which God hath appointed—would we obtain it? Certainly not; all other means would fail. The Lord says do so and so, and I will bless you. . . .
>
> The sign of Peter was to repent and be baptized for the

remission of sins, with the promise of the gift of the Holy Ghost; and in no other way is the gift of the Holy Ghost obtained.[67]

Finally, the difference between man being a recipient of the Holy Ghost in its initial manifestations and in receiving the Holy Ghost as a permanent gift lies in the claim he has upon the spiritual power which is manifested through the third personage in the Godhead. In its preliminary expressions before baptism, the power of the Holy Ghost is given to man essentially as a result of his faith and righteous desires. But in receiving the gift of the Holy Ghost by the laying on of hands following baptism, he has a legal claim by covenant to the manifestations of the holy Comforter, and the right to use the divine truth and power of the Holy Ghost in performing righteous works upon the earth within the scope of his life's activities and his jurisdiction within the gospel program.

The Prophet's explanation reconciles the view that the Holy Ghost may be given to enlighten man before baptism (and may at that time even bestow its supernatural gifts upon him) with the scriptural testimony that it is only by receiving the ordinances of the gospel that man may obtain the gift of the Holy Ghost.

Several expressions of this basic point are found in Latter-day Saint literature. In concluding the history of the Nephites, Moroni sealed up the ancient record with the promise that those who would read its latter-day translation and sincerely ask the Father in the name of Christ if it was a true record would have its truth revealed unto them "by the power of the Holy Ghost."[68] The manifestation of the Holy Ghost in this instance was expected to be given to the individual before baptism.

Another example of spiritual powers being given to men who have not yet received the gospel is found in the promise of the Father that He would pour out the Holy Ghost through Christ upon the gentiles,[69] including the early American colonists who lived before the gospel was restored through Joseph Smith in the latter-day dispensation. Nephi was shown in vision that by the enlightening influences of "the Spirit of the Lord" the American colonists would "prosper and obtain the land for their inheritance."[70] To the Nephites, Jesus declared that the gentiles in this land would "be set up as a free people by the power of the Father,"[71] and that by the influence of the Holy Ghost they would become "mighty above all."[72]

The divine spiritual power which the gentiles who would settle the Western hemisphere were to receive, according to the Book of Mormon, was obviously something more than the basic quickening Spirit or Light which is given to enlighten every man who comes into the world.[73] This conclusion finds support in the fact that many people who became converts to the restored gospel, when the latter-day dispensation was introduced through Joseph Smith, had been recipients of the supernatural gifts and powers of the Holy Ghost before they heard of the Prophet or were baptized.[74]

Cornelius was no exception to the general rule in the manner of his conversion,[75] except in the degree to which the Holy Ghost was manifested to him before baptism. But even on this issue, the spiritual endowment which he and his associates received was less than that which was given before baptism to the Lamanites who were converted by Nephi and Lehi, for "they were encircled about . . . by a pillar of fire." Of the Lamanites, the record declares: "Behold, the Holy Spirit of God did come down from heaven, and did enter into their hearts, and they were filled as if with fire, and they could speak forth marvelous words."[76]

God, then, may give the Holy Ghost to man according to his faith, independent of the outward ordinances of the gospel. But when man is brought to a knowledge of the gospel, he is required by the law of heaven to embrace its prescribed ordinances. To be a recipient of the preliminary manifestations of the Holy Ghost, without receiving the permanent gift of the Holy Ghost, is not sufficient to prepare man to receive the full endowments of celestial glory in the resurrection.

Purposes Of Gift Of The Holy Ghost

Channel of Divine Truth

The gift of the Holy Ghost is the basic channel within the program of the gospel through which the truth and power of God are given to man. God does not need to communicate His truth to man by speaking and having His voice conveyed by sound waves to the ear of the recipient. Being a corporeal being, He can do this, but He is not limited to such means of communication. As a glorified personage, that pure substance called the Holy Spirit centers in Him as an integral part of His organization. Having a great capacity to receive and convey intelligence, the Holy Spirit partakes of the truth of God and manifests it to others. For this reason, the voice of the Lord is said to be Spirit—the Spirit of truth, or the Spirit of revelation.[77]

The mission of the Holy Ghost, as the third personage in the Godhead, is to reveal divine truth and light, by means of that pure substance called the Holy Spirit, to those who enter into the stage of life which leads to celestial glory.[78] "No man can receive the Holy Ghost without receiving revelations," the Prophet observed. "The Holy Ghost is a revelator."[79] In revealing the gospel to Adam, the Lord promised him that through the gift of the Holy Ghost he could ask "all things" in the name of Christ and that whatsoever he asked would be given unto him.[80] With like emphasis, Noah taught the people of his day that by receiving the gift of the Holy Ghost they could "have all things made manifest."[81] Concerning the function of the Holy Ghost in revealing the truth of God to man in all ages of time, Nephi said:

> . . . the Holy Ghost . . . is the gift of God unto all those who diligently seek him, as well in times of old as in the time that he should manifest himself unto the children of men.
>
> For he is the same yesterday, to-day, and forever; and the way is prepared for all men from the foundation of the world, if it so be that they repent and come unto him.

For he that diligently seeketh shall find; and the mysteries of God shall be unfolded unto them, by the power of the Holy Ghost, as well in these times as in times of old, and as well in times of old as in times to come; wherefore, the course of the Lord is one eternal round.[82]

Because of the gift of the Holy Ghost, the gospel is a principle of revelation and of continuing knowledge to man rather than a mere system of theology or a social order.

Source of Regenerating Power

To the man of faith, the gift of the Holy Ghost is a source of divine power by which important transformations can be effected in his life. Thereby he can put off the man which is natural, or conditioned, to the world's fallen and carnal state and become "a saint through the atonement of Christ the Lord."[83] The process of renewing man spiritually is not complete when he begins to express faith in the Son of God and to repent of his sins. The full change is effected only in those who receive the gift of the Holy Ghost and apply its power to this end.

The transformations that take place by the power of the Holy Ghost can actually renew man's body.[84] But there is more need for the Holy Ghost to transform physically those who are not the literal seed of Israel than those who are descendants of the house of Israel in the flesh. Joseph Smith explained:

The Holy Ghost . . . is more powerful in expanding the mind, enlightening the understanding, and storing the intellect with present knowledge, of a man who is of the literal seed of Abraham, than one that is a Gentile, though it may not have half as much visible effect upon the body; for as the Holy Ghost falls upon one of the literal seed of Abraham, it is calm and serene; and his whole soul and body are only exercised by the pure spirit of intelligence; while the effect of the Holy Ghost upon a Gentile, is to purge out the old blood, and make him actually of the seed of Abraham. That man that has none of the blood of Abraham (naturally) must have a new creation by the Holy Ghost. In such a case, there may be more of a powerful effect upon the body, and visible to the eye, than upon an

Israelite, while the Israelite at first might be far before the Gentile in pure intelligence.[85]

It is only through being regenerated by the power of the Holy Ghost that man can be sanctified from the effects of sin. This is a major objective of the gospel.[86] Jesus taught the Nephites that unless they were "sanctified by the reception of the Holy Ghost" they could not "stand spotless" before Him at the last day.[87]

Source of Spiritual Gifts

Those who receive the gift of the Holy Ghost by the laying on of hands have a right, by covenant, to the supernatural endowments which are called the gifts of the Holy Ghost. "There are many gifts," a revelation explained as it spoke of the gifts which are given to the Church, "and to every man is given a gift by the Spirit of God."[88] It follows that those who receive the gospel "should believe in the gifts and callings of God by the Holy Ghost,"[89] for only by exercising the gifts and powers of the Spirit can man do the kind of good that leads others to celestial salvation. "If there be one among you that doeth good," Moroni stressed, "he shall work by the power and gifts of God."[90]

Summary

The everlasting gospel is a divine program by which man may attain a living spiritual union with Jesus Christ and mature in that union until he acquires a fulness of the glory of God in the resurrection. This program is centered, primarily, in the manifestations of the Holy Spirit to man. The basic channel through which these divine powers are given is the gift of the Holy Ghost, which is conferred by the laying on of hands by those who bear the Holy Priesthood. This gift gives man the right to receive, by continued faith and worthiness, the truth, power, and gifts of Jesus Christ, as they are given through the third personage of the Godhead. Without the gift of the Holy Ghost, man cannot attain salvation in the celestial kingdom of God. Through this divine gift, he may receive the baptism of fire which Jesus came to give to His true disciples.

There is a difference between the Holy Ghost and the gift of the Holy Ghost. Man may be given some of the blessings of the Holy Ghost before baptism, but he cannot receive the right to the full blessings and endowments of the Holy Ghost as a permanent gift unless he complies with the prescribed ordinances through which that gift is given. The purpose of the gift of the Holy Ghost is to mature man spiritually and to elevate him from his fallen spiritual state on earth to the point that he can enter the presence of God and be glorified directly by and in Jesus Christ. To this end, the holy Comforter enlightens man's mind to the things of God, strengthens him in his battle with the flesh and the world, comforts him in the trials of life, and sanctifies him from all sin. In this way, a true believer can put off the natural man and become a saint through the power and atonement of Jesus Christ. He can also partake of the gifts of the Spirit unto eternal life.

Notes

1. *Improvement Era,* XII (March, 1909), p. 389.
2. D&C 121:26.
3. MA, II (October, 1835), p. 199.
4. TS III (June 15, 1842), p. 823; HC, V, p. 27. See also MA, I (December, 1834), p. 37. Again the Prophet said: "No man can preach the gospel without the Holy Ghost."—HC, II, p. 477.
5. See chapter one, the section entitled "The Hope of Glory." See also D&C 93:19–20; 3 Nephi 19:29.
6. Since only resurrected beings can be endowed with a fulness of the Father's glory, it may be concluded that the Holy Ghost does not possess the glory of the Father in its eternal fulness. For this reason the Holy Ghost cannot fully glorify resurrected man. Nor is it intended that he should. The scriptures state that man is to be glorified in Christ. But by means of the Holy Ghost man can be brought to the point of receiving the second Comforter and communing directly with Christ, and he can then be glorified directly by and in the Master.
7. For a treatment of the mission of the Holy Ghost, see Volume I of this study, the section in chapter nine entitled "The Holy Ghost Speaks for Christ—the Father and the Son"; and the section in chapter ten entitled "The Power of the Holy Ghost."
8. HC, V, p. 27.

9. 3 Nephi 11:32; Ether 5:4; Moses 5:9.

10. HC, II, p. 19.

11. *Ibid.,* IV, pp. 602–603. (Italics in the original.)

12. *Ibid.,*V, p. 27.

13. *Ibid.,* VI, pp. 302–303; 2 Nephi 33:1. Charles W. Penrose spoke of the Holy Ghost as a "power given unto us as an abiding witness, to be a light to our feet and a lamp to our path; as a restraint against sin, to guide us into all truth, to open the vision of the mind, to bring things past to our remembrance, and to make manifest things to come."—JD, XXIII, p. 350.

14. Jarom 4.

15. D&C 18:18. See also Moses 6:52; Moses 8:24.

16. Pratt, *Key to Theology,* pp. 101–103. Some redundant terms have been deleted from this statement in the later editions of this work. The writer has to a degree followed the later editions.

17. 3 Nephi 18:36–37; Moroni 2.

18. HC, I, p. 39. See also *ibid.,* VI, p. 250.

19. D&C 107:18.

20. D&C 84:20–21.

21. HC, IV, p. 579. Again the Prophet said: We believe that the Holy Ghost is imparted by the laying on of hands of those in authority."—*Ibid.,* V, p. 27.

22. *Ibid.,* IV, p. 555.

23. Moroni 2:2.

24. Acts 6:1–6.

25. Acts 8:5–20.

26. Acts 19:1–6.

27. Timothy 1:6.

28. Hebrews 6:1–2. See HC, IV, p. 359, where Joseph Smith uses this quotation to identify the first principles and ordinances of the gospel.

29. D&C 20:41, 43, 68; 39:23. See also D&C 24:9; 33:15; 35:6; 49:14; 52:10. The Prophet pointed out that "the doctrine of laying on of hands for the gift of Holy Ghost was discarded" by the churches of his day.—HC, IV, p. 359.

30. TS, I (February, 1840), p. 55.

31. HC, III, p. 379.

32. 1 Nephi 10:17.

33. Pratt, *op. cit.,* p. 99.

34. HC, I, pp. 314–315. See also p. 283.

35. *Ibid.,* IV, p. 555.

36. See *ibid.,* V, p. 499. See also *ibid.,* II, pp. 256–257.

37. Acts 2:38–39.

38. Mormon 7:10.

39. 3 Nephi 11:39–40.

40. D&C 84:74.

41. Matthew 3:16.

42. Mark 1:10; John 1:32.

43. Luke 3:22.

44. HC, V, pp. 260–261. (Italics in the original.)

45. John 16:14–15. See also Volume I of this study, the section in chapter

nine entitled "The Holy Ghost Speaks for Christ—the Father and the Son"; and also the section in chapter ten entitled "The Power of the Holy Ghost."

46. See Volume I of this study, the section in chapter five entitled "God Dwells in Everlasting Burnings."

47. D&C 88:29.

48. D&C 76:118.

49. Moses 6:66.

50. 2 Nephi 31:13.

51. See Mormon 7:10.

52. 3 Nephi 11:35.

53. 3 Nephi 12:1.

54. D&C 39:6.

55. D&C 33:11.

56. Helaman 5:13.

57. Helaman 5:43–45. It is apparent from the record that these Lamanites had not been baptized before they received this divine endowment. For an explanation of this point, see the section in this chapter entitled "The Holy Ghost And Gift Of The Holy Ghost."

58. 3 Nephi 9:20.

59. 3 Nephi 19:13–14. On the day of Christ's initial visit to the Nephites, the Book of Mormon states:

> . . . he spake unto the multitude, and said unto them: Behold your little ones [children].
>
> And as they looked to behold they cast their eyes towards heaven, and they saw the heavens open, and they saw angels descending out of heaven as it were in the midst of fire; and they came down and encircled those little ones about, and they were encircled about with fire; and the angels did minister unto them.—3 Nephi 17:23–24.

60. 3 Nephi 19:25.

61. 3 Nephi 19:35.

62. Orson F. Whitney, *Life of Heber C. Kimball* (Salt Lake City, Utah, 1945), pp. 22–23.

63. *Juvenile Instructor,* XXII, pp. 22–23. (Italics in the original.)

64. D&C 130:23.

65. HC, IV, p. 555.

66. *Ibid.* For a discussion of this point in relation to man's birth into the kingdom of God, see the section in chapter seven entitled "Birth to Enter the Kingdom of God."

67. *Ibid.* For Peter's statement, see Acts 2:38–39.

68. Moroni 10:3–4.

69. See 3 Nephi 20:27. The fact that the Holy Ghost would impart power to the gentiles does not necessarily imply that the Spirit would cause them to scatter the people of Israel.

70. 1 Nephi 13:12–19.

71. 3 Nephi 21:4.

72. 3 Nephi 20:27. The influence of this divine spiritual power in the rise of Western civilization to a position of power in the earth will be treated in some detail in volume III of this series.

73. For a discussion of the role of the Light of Christ in the program of life and salvation, see chapter ten in volume I of this study.

74. Volume III of this study will give documentary evidence to support this statement.

75. See Acts 10.

76. Helaman 5:43–45. See also the discussion of this incident in the preceding section of this chapter.

77. See D&C 18:33–36; 84:45; 88:66. Jesus said " . . . the words that I speak unto you, they are spirit, and they are life."—John 6:63.

78. See Volume I of this study, the section in chapter ten entitled "The Light, Life, and Power of the Gospel."

79. HC, VI, p. 58.

80. Moses 6:52.

81. Moses 8:24.

82. 1 Nephi 10:17–19.

83. Mosiah 3:19. For a discussion of the natural man, see Volume I of this study, the section in chapter seventeen entitled "The Natural Man."

84. See D&C 84:33.

85. HC, III, p. 380. Brigham Young stated:

> When a person of real gentile blood, through honesty of heart, submits to the gospel and is baptized and receives the laying on of hands from a man duly authorized, you might naturally suppose, from the contortions of the muscles, that such a person had a fit, for the power of the Holy Ghost falls upon and renovates that rebellious blood and stirs it up, and perhaps the person thus administered to falls prostrate on the floor. I have seen this, and it is in consequence of the power of the Holy Ghost operating upon the power of the enemy within the individual.—JD, XII, p. 270.

For a similar statement by George A. Smith, see *Ibid.,* XI, p. 10.

86. See Moses 6:59. See also Alma 13:12; Moroni 6:4.

87. 3 Nephi 27:20.

88. D&C 46:11.

89. D&C 20:27.

90. Moroni 10:25.

7

Becoming Sons and Daughters of Christ

Beloved, now are we the sons of God, and it doth not yet appear what we shall be: but we know that, when he shall appear, we shall be like him.—JOHN THE APOSTLE.

Joseph Smith taught that the program of the gospel which is made possible by the atonement of Christ is concerned with two basic propositions: First, mortal man is in a fallen state, which is a corrupt and carnal state, and for this reason he must be transformed spiritually by the influence of divine truth and power and become a new creature in Christ. Otherwise he cannot inherit the kingdom of God.[1] Second, the "kingdom of Jehovah" is a patriarchal structure[2] over which Jesus Christ presides, under the direction of the exalted Man of Holiness. Those who accept the gospel and are transformed by the action of the Spirit by being born into the kingdom of God become the sons and daughters of Jesus Christ. This transformation is not merely figurative or symbolic, but real and literal.[3] The Prophet referred to those who accept the plan of life and salvation as "the begotten sons of Jesus through the gospel."[4] A revelation said:

Hearken and listen to the voice of him who is from all eternity to all eternity, the Great I AM, *even Jesus Christ*—

> The light and the life of the world; a light which shineth in darkness and the darkness comprehendeth it not;
>
> The same which came in the meridian of time unto mine own, and mine own received me not;
>
> *But to as many as received me, gave I power to become my sons; and even so will I give unto as many as will receive me, power to become my sons.*[5]

By continuing to acquire the living attributes and powers of the Holy Spirit, the Saints may grow up to be like Christ in that they may acquire the powers and attributes of eternal life which He possesses.[6]

Doctrine Of Birth Into Kingdom Of God

Christ's Atonement the Basis of Rebirth

Because Jesus opened the way into that stage of life in which the faithful become His sons and daughters, the atonement is the foundation of the divine program of birth into the kingdom of God. By revelation, the Lord declared: "I am Jesus Christ, the Son of God, who was crucified for the sins of the world, even as many as will believe on my name, *that they may become the sons of God.*"[7] To Orson, Pratt, the Master explained:

> My son Orson, hearken and hear and behold what I, the Lord God, shall say unto you, even Jesus Christ your Redeemer. . . .
>
> *Who so loved the world that he gave his own life, that as many as would believe might become the sons of God.* Wherefore you are *my son.*[8]

This point is mentioned in several revelations which were given through the Prophet Joseph Smith.[9]

Necessity of Obedience

Man must obey the gospel in order to become a son of Christ. A revelation explained: "Verily I say unto you, all those who receive my gospel are sons and daughters in my kingdom."[10] This point was stressed by Abinadi in his commentary on Christ, the suffering servant, prophesied of in Isaiah 53. Isaiah foretold: "When thou shalt make his soul an offering for sin, he shall see his seed."[11] Having quoted this prophetic declaration concerning Christ, Abinadi explained that those who had given heed to the words of the prophets "and believed that the Lord would redeem his people, and have looked forward to that day for a remission of their sins, . . . are his seed." They are "heirs of the kingdom of God," the Nephite prophet explained. "For these are they whose sins he has borne; these are they for whom he has died, to redeem them from their transgressions." "And now," he concluded, "are they not his seed?"[12]

Purpose of Rebirth

The doctrine that man can become a son of Christ must be seen in the context of the three basic stages of life in the over-all plan of life that began with spirit birth and will be consummated when the righteous are crowned with celestial glory in the resurrection. As stated earlier in this study, these basic stages of life are (1) spirit life, (2) physical life, and (3) eternal life.[13]

Family relationships exist in each of these basic stages of life. Because Jesus received spirit life, physical life, and the divine attributes and powers of eternal life directly from the exalted Man of Holiness, He is the Son of His Father in all three basic stages of life.[14] Man, on the other hand, is a son of the Father, Elohim, in spirit life and a son of a mortal being in physical life. By obeying the gospel, man can also become a son of Jesus Christ in the divine attributes and powers of the Spirit which constitute eternal life.[15]

The Holy Spirit which man receives in the gospel is a living substance and actually gives him new attributes and powers of life. Jesus said: "He that heareth my words, and believeth on him that sent me, is passed from death *unto life.*"[16] Again: "If thou wilt enter *into life,* keep the commandments."[17] The Book of Mormon reaffirms these divine declarations. It declares that, through Christ, man enters into "the way that *leads to life.*"[18] Great joy is given to him as he receives "the light of Christ *unto life.*"[19] By walking "in the straight path *which leads to life,*"[20] he has the promise of coming forth in "the resurrection of *everlasting life,*" as contrasted to "the resurrection of *damnation.*"[21] To receive the resurrection of life is to be endowed at that time with the full powers and attributes of life, or the Spirit, which constitute the glory of God. This means that in some respects the waters of baptism are as much a womb as is the womb of a mortal mother, and that a baptismal font might be likened to a delivery room in a community hospital. In the baptism of water and the Spirit, man literally enters into a new stage of life. Daniel H. Wells therefore exclaimed:

> I know that the Spirit of the Lord gives life, and that men grow younger when they come into this kingdom and live their religion. I know that the feelings of the righteous are enlivened, their flesh and blood are quickened, and they become a glorious people; they receive and enjoy the Spirit of the Lord.[22]

The living attributes and powers which the faithful receive through the Holy Spirit are the attributes and powers of deity. Jesus was called "the Son of God, because he received not of the fulness [of divine attributes and powers] at the first,"[23] but was subordinate to His Father in obtaining them. By acquiring them in their fulness, Christ was given all power in heaven and on earth.[24] He then possessed the full attributes and powers of the Father—the fulness of the Godhead. The acquisition of these divine attributes and powers by man leads him to a similar goal. Joseph Smith taught that in this way man may become a son of God—a member of the divine family of Jesus Christ. Having grown up spiritually in the gospel, he can become ultimately a being of glory and power similar to Christ, possessing the full attributes and powers of deity. This is what it means to become a son of God.

The purpose of birth into the kingdom of God can be seen from another vantage point. Before Adam fell, he was a physical-spiritual being.[25] The living powers of the Spirit, or glory, of God were organized to some degree within him. But the fall of Adam cut man off from the glory of God; he died, in a literal sense, a spiritual death. By the fall, man's spirit is also made subject to his physical body in that it must express itself through the body which is in a fallen state and subject to mortal corruption. By being born into the kingdom of God, man can begin to come alive again spiritually. He can begin to acquire those divine and living spiritual powers which were taken away by the fall of Adam, and in this way man can begin again to act by and through the Spirit of God.[26]

This means that by birth into the kingdom of God, man can be transformed spiritually from his fallen carnal state in mortality to a higher state of life in which he is made a new creature in Christ. This transformation must come to all who are born into earth's mortal state and live to the age where they are accountable to God for their actions, if they are to attain celestial salvation. To Alma, the son of Alma, the Lord declared: "Marvel not that all mankind, yea, men and women, all nations, kindreds, tongues and people, must be born again; yea, born of God, *changed from their carnal and fallen state, to a state of righteousness,* being redeemed of God, becoming his sons and daughters; and thus *they become new creatures;* and unless they do this they can in nowise inherit the kingdom of God."[27]

This statement does not say that men are necessarily carnal and sensual in their desires and actions before they are transformed by the influence of the Holy Spirit. But all men, having been conceived physically in a state of mortal corruption, which is a carnal and fallen state, must put off the natural man—the man which is natural to this fallen state—by receiving the enlightening and regenerating power of the Holy Spirit.[28] This is the path which leads man upward to God out of mortal corruption and spiritual darkness. Thereby every faithful individual can and should overcome the world. "Whosoever is born of God doth not continue in sin," the Apostle John wrote, as recorded in Joseph Smith's Inspired Revision of the Bible, "for the Spirit of God remaineth in him; and he cannot continue in sin, because he is born of God."[29] In being truly born again, man is transformed spiritually into a new state of life, a "state of righteousness,"[30] and it is inconsistent for him to be in this state of divine truth and light and life and to continue in sin.

The above statement from the Prophet's Inspired Revision of the Bible implies that the transformation or rebirth may not always be immediate or rapid, and it may be consummated only as an individual masters sin and is sanctified from the effects of sin. Nevertheless, the renewal of man by the aid of the Spirit is actual and literal, and it may be accomplished to the degree he achieves spiritual union with Christ through the gospel. Heber C. Kimball spoke of this regeneration as "an improvement, or an advancement in the things of God"—a "change and renovation of the soul by the Spirit and grace of God." This, he explained, "is called the new birth." Continuing, he said:

> Titus is somewhat more explicit upon the subject. He says, "But after that the kindness and love of God our Savior toward man appeared, not by works of righteousness which we have done, but according to his mercy he saved us, by the washing of regeneration, and the renewing of the Holy Ghost; which he shed on us abundantly, through Jesus Christ our Savior; that being justified by his grace, we should be made heirs according to the hope of eternal life." And our Savior speaking to Nicodemus, says, "Verily I say unto thee, except a man be born again, he cannot see the kingdom of God." In another place Jesus says:—"Verily I say unto you, that ye which followed me in the regeneration, when the Son of Man shall sit on the throne of his glory, ye also shall sit upon twelve thrones, judging the twelve tribes of Israel."[31]

The fact that those who are born again pass in an actual and meaningful sense from a state of spiritual darkness and death into a new and divine state of life from which they need not die in this world nor in the world to come assumes that within man there are latent and dormant factors which can be awakened and developed by the Holy Spirit to make possible the renewal of life within him. When Adam was taught the plan of life and salvation and received it in faith, the Holy Spirit "descended upon him, and thus he was born of the Spirit, and became *quickened in the inner man.*"[32] In this way he was made alive in Christ and experienced the "newness of life" which the gospel makes possible.[33]

Joseph Smith made it clear that the message of the gospel since the earliest ages of the world has been that man must be born into the kingdom of God in order to attain celestial salvation as a son of Christ. When Adam complied with the divine plan, he was given the manifestations of the Holy Spirit. He then heard a voice out of heaven say: "Thou art baptized with fire, and with the Holy Ghost. . . . Behold, thou art one in me, a son of God; and *thus may all become my sons.*"[34] Having declared this doctrine to the people of his day, the patriarch Enoch observed: "Behold, our father Adam taught these things, and *many have believed and become the sons of God,* and many have believed not, and have perished in their sins, and are looking forth with fear, in torment, for the fiery indignation of the wrath of God to be poured out upon them."[35]

Because those who were born again in ancient times were given the attributes and powers of deity through the agency of the Holy Spirit,[36] they were called the "sons of God," or the "children of God."[37] A revelation stated, for example: "Noah and his sons hearkened unto the Lord, and gave heed, and they were called the sons of God."[38] But those who did not accept the message of life were designated "sons of men."[39] They did not enter into that stage of life in which they could receive the attributes and powers of deity, but were merely given in physical birth the attributes and powers of man in his fallen temporal state.

The doctrine that man must be born again is expressed repeatedly in the Book of Mormon. General Mormon wrote that by faith, men in all ages of time "become the sons of God."[40] The Lord informed Alma the younger that this requirement is made of all men, if they are to be saved.[41] This was the nature of the gospel and its divine message which Alma proclaimed. "This is the order after which I am called," he explained, "yea, to preach unto you my beloved brethren, yea, and every one that dwelleth in the land, . . . that they must repent and be born again."[42] He therefore declared the need of all men to be born again and stressed: "The Spirit saith if ye are not born again ye cannot inherit the kingdom of heaven."[43] Finally, in the Nephite culture, as in earlier times, those who embraced the gospel were called the "sons of God," or the "children of God."[44]

Although the scriptures speak of those who obey the gospel as being sons and daughters of God, only those who acquire a fulness of the Father's glory in the resurrection are to be given that distinction finally. These, a revelation designates as *"gods,* even the *sons of God."*[45] Both terms are applied to the same individuals. To be a son of God in the resurrection, therefore, is to be a god, and vice versa. On the other hand, those who do not acquire a fulness of the Father's glory in the resurrection may attain a "saved condition"; but from that time forth they "are not gods, but are ministering servants, to minister for those who are worthy of a far more, and an exceeding, and an eternal weight of glory."[46] A servant is not a son, nor does a servant enjoy the rights and prerogatives of a son. A son also grows up to become like his father in every essential respect, which is not true of those who become ministering angels in the resurrection.[47] Consequently, those who are sons of God in the resurrection become gods in their own right. This is the glorious objective which the gospel enables man to achieve in eternity.

Necessity of Divine Power in Rebirth

As stated in the introduction of this chapter, before true believers can become sons and daughters of God they must be made partakers of divine truth and power. Before man can become like the Father and the Son, he must partake of their divine nature, or glory. It is not merely a matter of accepting some prescribed beliefs and complying with some established ordinances. More than this, man must acquire the truth, light, life, and power of God. For this reason the gospel is defined appropriately as the "power of God unto salvation."[48]

The Latter-day Saint belief is the same as that which New Testament writers expressed. Speaking of Jesus, the Apostle John said: " . . . as many as received him, *to them gave he power to become the sons of God,* even to them that believed on his name: which were born, not of blood, nor of the will of the flesh, nor of the will of man, but of God."[49] The Apostle Paul also wrote: " . . . as many as are led by the Spirit of God, they are the sons of God."[50] Of such he said: "And because ye are sons, God hath sent forth the Spirit of his Son into your hearts, crying, Abba, Father. Wherefore thou art no more a servant, but a son; and if a son, then an heir of God through Christ."[51]

By revelation to Joseph Smith, Christ confirmed this doctrine. "I came unto mine own, and mine own received me not," He said of His earthly ministry; "but unto as many as received me *gave I power* to do many miracles, and *to become the sons of God;* and even unto them that believed on my name *gave I power* to obtain eternal life."[52]

Modern revelation also states that the same promise is given to man through the restoration of the gospel in modern times. "Verily, verily, I say unto you," Christ declared, "that as many as receive me, to them will I *give power* to become the sons of God, even to them that believe on my name."[53]

Enoch's Explanation Of Rebirth

By revelation, Joseph Smith was given Enoch's explanation of the process of birth into the kingdom of God in which the ancient patriarch quoted the word of God to Adam on the subject. Enoch first instructed the people concerning man's mortal state and of his need to be born again. He said:

> Because that Adam fell, we are; and by his fall came death; and we are made partakers of misery and woe.
>
> Behold Satan hath come among the children of men, and tempteth them to worship him; and men have become carnal, sensual, and devilish, and are shut out from the presence of God.[54]

This is one of the clearest and most concise statements concerning the nature of man in mortality found in sacred literature. Its essential points are worthy of review: (1) because Adam fell, we are; (2) by the fall came death; (3) in his fallen mortal state man is subject to misery and woe; (4) Satan tempts mortal man to worship him; (5) by giving heed to Satan, man becomes carnal, sensual, and devilish; and (6) for the above reasons, man is shut out from the presence of God—no longer privileged to enjoy God's glory and power.[55]

Having made the above observations concerning the nature of fallen man, Enoch cited the Lord's declaration to Adam of the first principles and ordinances of the gospel as the way by which he and his posterity could be redeemed. Upon hearing God's statement, Adam inquired: "Why is it that men must repent and be baptized in water?"[56] The Lord then began His explanation of the plan of salvation by first stating the nature of fallen man and the issues that confront him in mortality. "I have forgiven thee thy transgression in the Garden of Eden," He said. Consequently the saying went abroad among the people "that the Son of God hath atoned for original guilt, wherein the sins of the parents cannot be answered upon the heads of the children, for they are whole from the foundation of the world."[57]

Though Adam's children were absolved, by the promised atonement, from the legal consequences of their father's transgression in the Garden of Eden, God nevertheless declared to Adam that his children were "conceived in sin." For this reason, the Lord continued, "when they begin to grow up, sin conceiveth in their hearts, and they taste the bitter, that they may know to prize the good."[58] Here is a basic fact pertaining to the nature of man in his mortal state: though man is absolved from the responsibility of Adam's transgression, the forces of mortal sin and corruption are planted in his physical body at conception. When man's physical body begins to develop, sin therefore conceives in his heart as a result of the influence of these adverse forces, and he tastes the bitter that he may know to prize that which is good.

This, according to Enoch's explanation, is the basis of man's moral and spiritual agency in mortality.[59] "It is given unto them [men] to know good from evil," the Lord observed; "wherefore they are agents unto themselves."[60] In order for fallen man to have such agency, so that he could choose either eternal life or eternal damnation, the way had to be opened for him to return to the presence of God. The Lord therefore explained: "I have given unto you another law and commandment"—that is, an addition to that law which God gave to Adam in the Garden of Eden and which Adam transgressed in order to bring about the mortal state on earth. The new law and commandment pertained to the plan of life and salvation. God said: "Wherefore teach it unto your children, that all men, everywhere, must repent, or they can in nowise inherit the kingdom of God, for no unclean thing can dwell there, or dwell in his presence; for . . . Man of Holiness is his name, and the name of his Only Begotten is the Son of Man, even Jesus Christ, a righteous Judge, who shall come in the meridian of time."[61]

God is a pure and holy being of infinite glory and power; and before man can return to the presence of God, he must be made like the Man of Holiness. To this end, man must be born into the kingdom of God. "Therefore I give unto you a commandment, to teach these things freely unto your children," the Lord instructed Adam, "saying: That by reason of transgression cometh the fall, which fall bringeth death, and inasmuch as ye were born into the world by water, and blood, and the spirit, which I have made, and so became of dust a living soul, even so ye must be born again into the kingdom of heaven, of water, and of the Spirit, and be cleansed by blood, even the blood of mine Only Begotten."[62]

Birth into the kingdom of God is symbolic of mortal birth, in that man is born into this mortal world by water, blood, and the organized spirit which God made in the pre-earth state; and so he becomes of dust a living soul. Birth into the kingdom of God requires the action of similar elements. Man must be immersed in water, in baptism, and come forth, even as he was enveloped in water within his mother's womb and came forth in mortal birth. The blood of Christ which was shed in the atonement must be applied to make possible man's birth into the kingdom of God; it corresponds to the blood which accompanies mortal birth. Finally, to be born into the kingdom of God, man must be quickened by that living substance which is called the Holy Spirit and thereby enter into the newness of life (the new stage of life) which the gospel makes possible. This quickening action is symbolic of the life which man's organized spirit gives to his physical body.

Having stated that birth into the kingdom of God is symbolic of mortal birth, the Lord explained that the new birth is necessary so "that [1] ye might be sanctified from all sin, and [2] enjoy the words of eternal life in this world, and [3] eternal life in the world to come, even immortal glory."[63]

According to Enoch's explanation of the Lord's statement to Adam, birth into the kingdom of God is the way ordained of God for man to be sanctified from all sin. Only in this way can he receive a forgiveness of sins and acquire the enlightening, renewing, and sanctifying power of the Holy Spirit to cleanse him from the effects of sin and transform him from his fallen mortal state to that state of righteousness which leads to celestial glory.

Birth into the kingdom of God gives man the right to

enjoy the words of eternal life in this world. He cannot enjoy eternal life (the full endowments of celestial glory) in this fallen sphere, but merely the words of eternal life. These are the living words of God—the revelations of the Holy Spirit. To Joseph Smith, the Lord explained: "For the word of the Lord is truth, and whatsoever is truth is light, and whatsoever is light is Spirit, even the Spirit of Jesus Christ."[64] The word of God, therefore, is truth, or light, or Spirit, or the Spirit of Jesus Christ. By birth into the kingdom of God, man may enjoy the living words of God, or the revelations of God's Holy Spirit which teach him of eternal life and give him a foretaste of the light and power of that future glorified state. It is on this basis that man may stand in hope of the glory of God. The essence of his faith is that he looks forward with an assurance founded in the manifestations of the Spirit unto himself that the time will come when the full truth, light, and power of God's glory will be extended to him to give him eternal life.

Enoch quoted the Lord as stating to Adam that the final result which man may achieve by being born into the kingdom of God is to be endowed with immortal glory in the presence of God in the resurrection, and in this way acquire eternal life. He will then be glorified in Christ, as Jesus has been glorified in the Father, and know the Father and the Son on their exalted plane of celestial life.

Birth into the kingdom of God, like physical birth, is an indispensable requirement in the over-all plan of life by which man can become an exalted being like the Man of Holiness. Just as there is no other way ordained of God for man to obtain a body of flesh and bones except by physical birth, neither is there another way for man to acquire the divine attributes and powers that lead to eternal life except through birth into the kingdom of God. Having explained man's need to be born again, God said to Adam: "Therefore *it is given to abide in you* the record of heaven; the Comforter; the peaceable things of immortal glory; the truth of all things; that which quickeneth all things, which maketh alive all things; that which knoweth all things, and hath all power according to wisdom, mercy, truth, justice, and judgment." "This," the Lord concluded with emphasis, "is the plan of salvation unto all men, through the blood of mine Only Begotten."[65]

Each term or expression in the above statement refers to a specific manifestation of the Holy Spirit in the life of man. The "record of heaven" is the Holy Ghost in His function of recording truth and bringing it to man's memory. When Adam was baptized with fire and the Holy Ghost, a voice out of heaven said unto him: "This is the record of the Father, and the Son, from henceforth and forever."[66] The "Comforter" is also the Holy Ghost, in the function of giving comfort and assurance to the faithful. The "peaceable things of immortal glory"—the peaceable attributes of divine intelligence or glory—consist of the fruits of the Holy Spirit: love, peace, joy, longsuffering, gentleness, meekness, etc.[67] The "truth of all things" has reference to that divine substance, or Spirit, which is designated scripturally as the Spirit of Truth.[68] That which "quickeneth all things" is the glory of God—that divine Light which emanates from the presence of God to fill the immensity of space. Being in and through all things, it "maketh alive all things." It also "knoweth all things, and hath all power according to wisdom, mercy, truth, justice, and judgment."[69] The Holy Spirit, in all these expressions of its divine truth and power, begins to abide in man when he is born into the kingdom of God.

Process Of Birth Into Kingdom Of God

Birth to See the Kingdom of God

Joseph Smith taught that birth into the kingdom of God is a two-step process. First, man must be born to see that kingdom. According to an explanation which the Prophet made, Jesus spoke of this initial step in the divine process when He conversed with Nicodemus, a ruler of the Jews. Having been attracted to the Master by the outward evidences of His divine power, Nicodemus said: "Rabbi, we know that thou art a teacher come from God: for no man can do these miracles that thou doest, except God be with him."[70] Outward evidences of divine truth and power have their place in the plan of salvation, for they stimulate man to investigate those divine forces that produce the outward results which Nicodemus observed. But the transformation which the gospel makes possible takes place within man; and until it occurs, he must remain in the spiritual darkness of the world. Jesus therefore directed the attention of His prominent visitor to the divine spiritual forces to which man must respond if he is to see the kingdom of God. "Verily, verily, I say unto thee," He declared in unequivocal terms, "Except a man be born again [or born from above, as the marginal note reads], he cannot see the kingdom of God."[71]

This initial phase of the divine birth consists of the illumination of man's mind by the spiritual powers which attend the preaching of the gospel. Thereby he can see the kingdom of God and its divine program of life and salvation. The Prophet explained:

> The birth here spoken of . . . was not the gift of the Holy Ghost, which was promised after baptism, but was a portion of the Spirit which attended the preaching of the Gospel by the Elders of the Church. The people wondered why they had not previously understood the plain declarations of scripture, as explained by the Elders, as they had read them hundreds of times. When they read the Bible it was a new book to them. This was being born again to *see* the Kingdom of God. They were not in it, but could see it from the outside, which they could not do until the Spirit of the Lord took the veil from before their eyes. It was a change of heart but not of state; they were converted, but were yet in their sins.[72]

Alma discussed man's birth to see the kingdom of God as he spoke to a group of people on the hill Onidah. Of the enlightenment of mind that comes to those who plant the word of God in their hearts and respond with true desire to the message of salvation, he said:

. . . ye . . . know that . . . your understanding doth begin to be enlightened, and your mind doth begin to expand.

O then, is not this real? I say unto you, Yea, because it is light; and whatsoever is light, is good, because it is discernible, therefore ye must know that it is good.[73]

Birth to Enter the Kingdom of God

The fact that man may be enlightened by the Holy Spirit to see the kingdom of God and as a result have a change of heart does not mean that he is then a member of that kingdom. "It is one thing to see the kingdom of God, and another to enter it," the Prophet declared. "We must have a change of heart to see the kingdom of God, and subscribe [to] the articles of adoption to enter therein."[74] The articles of adoption are the prescribed ordinances—the first principles and ordinances of the gospel—by which true believers become sons and daughters of Jesus Christ. To support his explanation of this last step in the divine birth process, Joseph Smith cited another injunction of Jesus to Nicodemus. "Verily, verily, I say unto thee, Except a man be born of *water* and of the *Spirit,* he cannot *enter* into the kingdom of God."[75] To be born of water and of the Spirit, the Prophet concluded, means "to be immersed in water for the remission of sins and receive the gift of the Holy Ghost thereafter, . . . by the laying on of hands of one having authority given him of God."[76] In this way, those who have been born to see the kingdom of God may enter it and obtain by covenant a legal claim to the mercy, truth, and power of Jesus Christ.

Joseph Smith also discussed the situation of those who are born to see the kingdom of God but thereafter refuse to enter it. This is the case with many who hear the gospel and are enlightened by the Spirit to see the kingdom, but who, because of fear, pride, love of the world, etc., do not comply with the saving ordinances of the plan of life. "Cornelius [the righteous gentile of New Testament times] received the Holy Ghost before he was baptized, which was the convincing power of God unto him of the truth of the Gospel," the Prophet explained, "but he could not receive the permanent gift of the Holy Ghost until after he was baptized." Continuing, he stressed: "Had he not taken this sign or ordinance upon him, the Holy Ghost which convinced him of the truth of God would have left him."[77] In this event, the initial faith which Cornelius expressed and the enlightenment by the Spirit which he received, and by which he was brought to see the kingdom of God, would have availed him nothing.

Strictness of Law of Rebirth

The law by which man is born into the kingdom of God is as strict in its requirements as that law by which he is born into the physical, mortal sphere of life. It is set by divine decree and cannot be altered by man, if he is to receive the desired blessings. Joseph Smith taught that the whole plan of life is based upon eternal truth and law and their immutable requirements. The organization of spheres throughout the vast domain of God and the organization of those beings who reside upon them is carried out "agreeable to the most perfect order and harmony," he declared. "Their limits and bounds were fixed irrevocably, and voluntarily subscribed to in their heavenly estate by themselves." The same policy was observed in placing our first parents upon this earth. They, too, were made strictly amenable to divine law and its requirements, which they willingly accepted. Since this is the way God deals with others and since He has said that man must be born of water and of the Spirit in order to enter into the kingdom of God, the Prophet emphasized that reason and consistency show "the importance of embracing and subscribing to principles of eternal truth by all men upon the earth that expect eternal life."[78] Again he explained:

> God has set many signs on the earth, as well as in the heavens; for instance, the oak of the forest, the fruit of the tree, the herb of the field, all bear a sign that seed hath been planted there; for it is a decree of the Lord that every tree, plant, and herb bearing seed should bring forth of its kind, and cannot

come forth after any other law or principle. Upon the same principle do I contend that baptism is a sign ordained of God, for the believer in Christ to take upon himself in order to enter into the Kingdom of God, "for except ye are born of water and of the Spirit ye cannot enter into the Kingdom of God," said the Savior. It is a sign and a commandment which God has set for man to enter into His kingdom. Those who seek to enter in any other way will seek in vain; for God will not receive them, neither will the angels acknowledge their works as accepted, for they have not obeyed the ordinances, nor attended to the signs which God ordained for the salvation of man, to prepare him for, and give him a title to, a celestial glory.[79]

Role of the Spirit and of Ordinances

Joseph Smith pointed out that the process by which man is born into the kingdom of God does not place total reliance upon the ordinances of the gospel as the means of transforming man into the new stage of life which the gospel makes possible. Neither is it consistent to suppose that a mere change of heart is sufficient to introduce man into the way of eternal life. Instead, the latter-day Seer observed: "Being born again comes *by* the Spirit of God *through* ordinances."[80]

In this terse statement, Joseph Smith came to grips with a basic issue that has divided the Christian world for centuries. Man is not born into the kingdom of God by the action of the Holy Spirit independent of the ordinances of the gospel; nor is he born again merely by subscribing to the outward ordinances of admission. Birth into the kingdom of God, with the spiritual and moral transformation that accompanies it, cannot take place independent of man's response to the word of God, either spoken or written. That word is Spirit, which is life.[81] But God has appointed ordinances through which the Spirit in its more intelligent endowments is given to man as a permanent gift. The Holy Spirit and the ordinances of the gospel therefore both play important roles in the divine plan of birth into the kingdom of God. The mind of the man of faith must first be enlightened by the Spirit or word of God so that he can see the kingdom of God. He must then enter into the kingdom by subscribing to the ordinances of admission. Only then can the process of birth into the kingdom of God be properly consummated by man receiving the baptism of fire and the Holy Ghost.

Examples Of Birth Into Kingdom Of God

Alma and His People

Several accounts of conversion in the Book of Mormon illustrate the divine process of birth into the kingdom of God and the transformation that can occur in human life through the power of the gospel. The conversion of the people whom Alma the elder baptized at the waters of Mormon is a good example. Alma was converted by the preaching of the prophet Abinadi. "Did he not speak the words of God, and my father Alma believed them?" Alma the younger inquired. "And according to his faith there was a mighty change wrought in his heart."[82] The elder Alma then proclaimed to others the message of regenerating truth and power. Of the transformation which then occurred, the younger Alma said: "A mighty change was also wrought in their hearts, and they humbled themselves and put their trust in the true and living God."[83] Continuing, he explained:

> Behold, he [God] changed their hearts; yea, he awakened them out of a deep sleep, and they awoke unto God. Behold, they were in the midst of [spiritual] darkness; nevertheless, their souls were illuminated by the light of the everlasting word; yea, they were encircled about by the bands of [spiritual] death, and the chains of hell, and an everlasting destruction did await them.
>
> And now I ask of you, my brethren, . . . were the bands of [spiritual] death broken, and the chains of hell which encircled them about, were they loosed? I say unto you, Yea, they were loosed, and their souls did expand, and they did sing redeeming love. And I say unto you that they are saved.[84]

Membership alone in the Church of Jesus Christ is not sufficient to give man salvation. Man's compliance with the outward ordinances of the gospel and with the established social order is merely a means to an end. As Alma the younger recited the history of his father to the members of the Nephite church at Zarahemla, whose fathers Alma the elder had been instrumental in converting, he therefore inquired:

> . . . behold, I ask of you, my brethren of the church, have ye spiritually been born of God? Have ye received his image in your countenances? Have ye experienced this mighty change in your hearts?
>
> Do ye exercise faith in the redemption of him who created you? Do you look forward with an eye of faith, and view this mortal body raised in immortality, and this corruption raised in incorruption, to stand before God to be judged according to the deeds which have been done in the mortal body? . . .
>
> And now behold, I say unto you, my brethren, if ye have experienced a change of heart, and if ye have felt to sing the song of redeeming love, I would ask, can ye feel so now?
>
> Have ye walked, keeping yourselves blameless before God? Could ye say, if ye were called to die at this time, within yourselves, that ye have been sufficiently humble? That your garments have been cleansed and made white through the blood of Christ, who will come to redeem his people from their sins?
>
> Behold, are ye stripped of pride? I say unto you, if ye are not ye are not prepared to meet God. Behold ye must prepare quickly; for the kingdom of heaven is soon at hand, and such an one hath not eternal life.[85]

King Lamoni and His People

Among the examples of the transforming power of the gospel in the life of man are those of Lamoni, a Lamanite king, and his father. Having gone to teach the gospel to the Lamanites and having gained an audience with King Lamoni, Ammon, a son of the Nephite king Mosiah, taught him of the creation of the world and of Adam, and told him of all "things concerning the fall of man . . . and . . . the coming of Christ." Upon hearing these things, King Lamoni cried: "O Lord, have mercy; according to thy abundant mercy which thou hast had upon the people of Nephi, have upon me, and my people."[86]

King Lamoni having cried with great faith unto God, the power of God came upon him and he fell to the earth as if he were dead; and his servants carried him to his wife, and he was laid upon a bed. For two days and nights his wife and family mourned over him, greatly lamenting his loss. When they were about to lay him in a sepulchre, the queen sent for Ammon and asked him if he thought the king were dead. "Some say that he is not dead," she explained, "but others say that he is dead and that he stinketh, and that he ought to be placed in the sepulchre." "But as for myself," she concluded, "to me he doth not stink."[87] The record then states: "Now, this is what Ammon desired, for he knew that *king Lamoni was under the power of God;* he knew that the dark veil of unbelief was being cast away from his mind, and *the light which did light up his mind, which was the light of the glory of God, which was a marvelous light of his goodness—yea, this light had infused such joy into his soul, the cloud of darkness having been dispelled, and that the light of everlasting life was lit up in his soul, yea, he knew that this had overcome his natural frame, and he was carried away in God*—therefore, what the queen desired of him was his only desire."[88]

When Ammon saw the king, he knew that he was not dead; and having assured the queen, he promised her that King Lamoni would rise again on the morrow. Whereupon she expressed belief in Ammon's promise and watched over the bed of her husband until he arose at the designated time. As King Lamoni stood upon his feet, he exclaimed to his wife: "Blessed be the name of God, and blessed art thou. For as sure as thou livest, behold, I have seen my Redeemer; and he shall come forth, and be born of a woman, and he shall redeem all mankind who believe on his name." Continuing, the record states: "Now, when he had said these words, his heart was swollen within him, and he sunk again with joy; and the queen also sunk down, being overpowered by the Spirit."[89]

"Ammon seeing the Spirit of the Lord poured out according to his prayers upon the Lamanites, . . . fell upon his knees" in prayer. "And he was also overpowered with joy; and thus they all three had sunk to the earth." At this point, the servants of the king "also began to cry unto God, for the fear of the Lord had come upon them." "And it came to pass that they did call on the name of the Lord, in their might," the account states, "even until they had all fallen to the earth, save it were one of the Lamanitish women, whose name was Abish, she having been converted unto the Lord for many years, on account of a remarkable vision of her father." She ran from house to house "making known unto the people what had happened among them, [in the hope] that by beholding this scene it would cause them to believe in the power of God."[90]

When many people came together at the house of the king, "they began to marvel . . . among themselves what could be the cause of this great power, or what all these things could mean." But when contention arose among them, the woman servant who had summoned them took the queen by the hand, that perhaps she might raise her from the ground. At the servant's touch the queen arose and cried with a loud voice, "O blessed Jesus, who has saved me from an awful hell! O blessed God, have mercy on this people!" With other expressions of joy, she took her husband by the hand, and he arose and began to speak to the people. Ammon and the servants of the king also arose and spoke to the multitude. "And they did all declare unto the people the selfsame thing—that *their hearts had been changed; that they had no more desire to do evil.*" The report concludes: "And it came to pass that there were many that did believe in their words; and *as many as did believe were baptized;* and they became a righteous people, and they did establish a church among them."[91]

King Lamoni's Father and His People

By Lamoni's conversion, the gospel was introduced to his father, who was king over all of the Lamanites. The record describes how Aaron, the brother of Ammon, explained the plan of life and salvation to him:

> . . . Aaron did expound unto him the scriptures from the creation of Adam, laying the fall of man before him, and their carnal state and also the plan of redemption, which was prepared from the foundation of the world, through Christ, for all whosoever would believe on his name.
>
> And since man had fallen he could not merit anything of himself; but the sufferings and death of Christ atone for their sins, through faith and repentance, and so forth; and that he breaketh the bands of death, that the grave shall have no victory, and that the sting of death should be swallowed up in the hopes of glory. . . . [92]

Here is a clear declaration of man's present fallen, carnal, or mortal state and of his need to rely wholly upon the merits of Jesus Christ in order to attain salvation. These facts give meaning to the plan of redemption; and for those who come to an understanding of that divine plan, the sting of death is "swallowed up in the hopes of glory."[93] This was true of the Lamanite king. After Aaron expounded these things unto him, he exclaimed:

> What shall I do that I may have this eternal life of which thou hast spoken? Yea, what shall I do that I may be born of God, having this wicked spirit rooted out of my breast, and receive his Spirit, that I may be filled with joy, that I may not be cast off at the last day?[94]

Aaron admonished the king to call upon the Lord in faith, promising him that in this way he would "receive the hope" which he expressed. When the king did so, his natural strength was overcome by the power of God and "he was struck as if he were dead."[95] In the events that followed, all the members of the king's household were converted. A proclamation was then sent throughout the land giving support and protection to the Nephite missionaries, and by their labors "thousands were brought to the knowledge of the Lord."[96] In concluding his account of this great conversion, Mormon wrote: "As sure as the Lord liveth, so sure as many as believed, or as many as were brought to the knowledge of the truth, through the preaching of Ammon and his brethren, according to the spirit of revelation and of prophecy, and the power of God working miracles in them—yea, I say unto you, as the Lord liveth, as many of the Lamanites as believed in their preaching, and were converted unto the Lord, never did fall away."[97]

Summary

To attain celestial salvation, man must be transformed from his fallen and carnal state in mortality by being born into the kingdom of God. Thereby he may become a son of Jesus Christ in the living attributes and powers of the Spirit which lead to eternal life. The atonement of Christ is the basis of this divine plan of rebirth, and to become a son of God man must obey the gospel. In this way, he may become a recipient of new and divine attributes and powers of life. But to be accorded the distinction of being a son of God in the resurrection, man must continue on the path of life and salvation until he is endowed with a fulness of the glory of God.

Ancient prophets, including the patriarch Enoch, taught the doctrine of rebirth. Enoch cited the word of God to Adam to the effect that man must be born into the kingdom of heaven in order to be sanctified from all sin, enjoy the words of eternal life in this life, and acquire eternal life in the world to come, even immortal glory. According to Joseph Smith, the principles of rebirth are strict and exact, and unless man obeys them in the way which has been ordained of God he cannot acquire eternal life. He must first be born to see the kingdom of God. Then he must be born of water and of the Spirit to enter the kingdom. This process has been taught by prophets in all ages of time. It does not place total reliance upon either the action of the Spirit or the role of ordinances, but upon both. Being born again comes by the Spirit of God through ordinances. In this way the power of God is manifested to make man a son of God. Examples of rebirth in the Book of Mormon evidence the renewal that takes place when man sincerely accepts and applies the plan of life and salvation.

Notes

1. See Volume I of this study, the sections in chapter seventeen entitled "The Natural Man" and "Man's Dependence Upon Christ."
2. See HC, VI, p. 252, in light of the Prophet's discourse in which this reference is found.
3. Mosiah 3:19; 5:7; 27:25–26. Christ is the God of the earth because the glory of the Man of Holiness dwells in Him and is manifest through Him. It is in this sense that those who receive Christ's gospel become the sons and daughters of God.
4. TS, III (September 1, 1842), pp. 904–905.
5. D&C 39:1–4.
6. The Prophet referred to the Saints as developing in "every good quality that adorns the children of the blessed Jesus."—HC, II, p. 229.
7. D&C 35:2.
8. D&C 34:1, 3.
9. See D&C 11:30; 35:2; 42:52; 45:8; 50:41; 76:24, 58; 93:22.
10. D&C 25:1.
11. Isaiah 53:10.
12. Mosiah 15:11–12.
13. See Volume I of this study, the section in chapter eight entitled "The Way Of Life." Each organized being does not necessarily enter into all of these stages of life or receive the full endowments that pertain to them, for there are many who fail to comply with all the requirements of the plan of life and salvation.
14. See Volume I of this study, the section in chapter eight entitled "Christ the Son of God in Eternal Life."
15. See D&C 25:1; 34:1–3; 39:1–4; John 1:12; 1 John 3:1–2.
16. John 5:24. See also John 6:63.
17. Matthew 19:17.
18. 3 Nephi 14:14; 27:33.
19. Alma 28:14.
20. 2 Nephi 33:9.
21. Mosiah 16:11; 3 Nephi 26:5. See also John 5:29, where Jesus speaks of the "resurrection *of life,*" as opposed to the "resurrection of *damnation.*"
22. JD, XXIII, p. 350.
23. D&C 93:14.
24. D&C 93:16–17.
25. See Volume I of this study, the section in chapter twelve entitled "God's Objectives In The Creation."
26. See, for example, D&C 46:28–33.
27. Mosiah 27:25–26.
28. See again Mosiah 3:19.
29. I. R., 1 John 3:9.
30. Mosiah 27:25–26.
31. JD, X, p. 77, citing Titus 3:5; John 3:5; Matthew 19:28.

32. Moses 6:64–65.
33. Mosiah 27:25–26; Romans 6:4.
34. Moses 6:66, 68.
35. Moses 7:1.
36. See Moses 6:59, 61.
37. Moses 6:8; 8:13.
38. Moses 8:13.
39. Moses 5:52; 6:15; 8:14–15.
40. Moroni 7:26.
41. Mosiah 27:25–26.
42. Alma 5:49.
43. Alma 7:14.
44. Alma 6:6; 30:42; 3 Nephi 9:17; 12:9; 4 Nephi 1:39; Moroni 7:48.
45. D&C 76:58.
46. D&C 132:16–17.
47. This subject, as it pertains to man's final destiny in eternity, will be discussed in Volume IV of this study.
48. Romans 1:16. For a statement by the Prophet on this point, see TS, III (September 1, 1842), p. 904.
49. John 1:12–13.
50. Romans 8:14.
51. Galatians 4:6–7.
52. D&C 45:8.
53. D&C 11:30. See also D&C 39:3–4.
54. Moses 6:48–49.
55. For a discussion of these points, see Volume I of this study, chapters fourteen and seventeen entitled "The Fall Of Man" and "The Nature And Challenge Of Mortal Man."
56. Moses 6:53.
57. Moses 6:53–54.
58. Moses 6:55. For a discussion of this subject, see Volume I of this study, the section in chapter seventeen entitled "The Nature Of Man's Physical Being."
59. See Volume I of this study, the section in chapter sixteen entitled "Spiritual and Moral Freedom Given by the Atonement."
60. Moses 6:56.
61. Moses 6:57.
62. Moses 6:58–59.
63. Moses 6:59.
64. D&C 84:45. See also D&C 18:34–36; 88:66–67.
65. Moses 6:61–62.
66. Moses 6:66.
67. God's glory is His Holy Spirit. The peaceable things of immortal glory, therefore, are the peaceable things of the Spirit, or the fruits of the Spirit.
68. See, for example, D&C 93:26.
69. Moses 6:61. See this statement in light of D&C 88:6–13, 40–41, 49–50, 66–68.
70. John 3:2.
71. John 3:3 and the accompanying marginal note.
72. *Juvenile Instructor,* XXVII (February 1, 1892), pp. 93–94.

73. Alma 32: 34–35.
74. HC, VI, p. 58. For a treatment of the divine law of adoption, see Orson Pratt, *Orson Pratt's Works* (Salt Lake City, 1945), chapter 2. This work was first published serially in Liverpool, England, between 1848 and 1851.
75. John 3:5.
76. *Juvenile Instructor, loc. cit.*
77. HC, IV, p. 555. See Acts 10 for the conversion of Cornelius.
78. HC, VI, p. 51.
79. *Ibid.*, IV, p. 554.
80. *Ibid.*, III, p. 392.
81. See D&C 84:45; John 6:63.
82. Alma 5:11–12.
83. Alma 5:13.
84. Alma 5:7–9.
85. Alma 5:14–15, 26–28.
86. Alma 18:36–41.
87. Alma 18:43; 19:1–5.
88. Alma 19:6–7.
89. Alma 19:12–13.
90. Alma 19:14–17.
91. Alma 19:24–35.
92. Alma 22:13–14.
93. Alma 22:14.
94. Alma 22:15.
95. Alma 22:16–18.
96. Alma 23:5.
97. Alma 23:6.

8

The Doctrines of Justification and Sanctification

> *We know that justification through the grace of our Lord and Savior Jesus Christ is just and true;*
>
> *And we know also, that sanctification through the grace of our Lord and Savior Jesus Christ is just and true, to all those who love and serve God with all their mights, minds, and strength.*—JOSEPH SMITH.

Joseph Smith taught that in the program of the gospel man is justified and sanctified through the grace and power of Jesus Christ. Justification is concerned, essentially, with acquitting man legally from the demands of broken law; it is accomplished primarily through the program of the preparatory gospel. The teachings which show man how to obtain and retain a remission of personal sins through Christ constitute the doctrine of justification. Sanctification is concerned with cleansing man from the effects of sin and making him pure and holy before God; it is accomplished through the atonement and by the aid of the Holy Spirit which Christ gives to man in the gift of the Holy Ghost. The teachings which show man how to be sanctified from the effects of sin constitute the doctrine of sanctification.

Doctrine Of Justification

Justification Defined

The word "justification" comes from the word "justify," which means to show to be just or to vindicate one in his actions—to exonerate him or to declare him guiltless or blameless. It also means to make a person just or right in the eyes of the law. In the plan of the gospel, the word "justify" means to regard and treat man as a just person on the basis that the benefits of Christ's atonement have been extended to him. Justification, therefore, is a state of being justified—either of being vindicated or acquitted in regard to one's actions, or of being forgiven of one's sins. One who is justified either has never transgressed the law of God, or he is in a condition in which the penalties which divine justice prescribes for his transgressions have been paid. If he has not sinned, he is vindicated by his righteousness. If he has transgressed, he can be justified either by paying the debt of sin himself[1] or by being reconciled to Christ through the atonement, which will absolve him from the demands of eternal law. In the latter event, justification is made possible by the gracious act of Jesus Christ.

Justification by Law

Theoretically, it is possible for man to be justified by law—to meet the challenge of earth's trials and temptations without transgressing any of the laws of God. This no man has done. Lehi could therefore declare: "By the law no flesh is justified; or, by the law men are cut off."[2]

There was one exception. Jesus lived on earth and "did no sin."[3] For this reason He could say of His freedom from the claims of the Adversary: "The prince of darkness, who is of this world, cometh, but hath no power over me."[4]

Justification by Grace

There are many expressions of the doctrine of justification by grace in the plan of life and salvation. Grace is unearned (not necessarily unmerited) divine assistance—a gift for which man does not pay an equivalent price or value. As indicated earlier in this study, some expressions of God's grace are given to man unconditionally or without regard to his personal conduct or actions.[5] To begin, Christ cushions the power of the first spiritual death so that life on earth is not subject completely to its power. By paying the debt of divine justice for Adam's transgression, Jesus is able to extend the Light of Christ to quicken life on earth[6] without disregarding the demands of justice. Otherwise no life could have existed on this temporal sphere after the fall of Adam. Mortal life, therefore, is a gift of God. It is made possible by the extension of Christ's grace to man and to other forms of life, and for this reason it is an expression of the doctrine of justification by grace.

By the power of the atonement, all children are "alive in Christ."[7] They are innocent in that the transgression of Adam cannot legally condemn them;[8] Satan is checked in his power to tempt them until they begin to be accountable before God;[9] and they are not held accountable to the law of God until they are eight years of age.[10] These benefits are given to children by the grace of Jesus Christ, and they are expressions of the doctrine of justification by grace. People who live on earth without the law of God are also justified unconditionally by the grace of Jesus Christ.[11]

Man's spiritual and moral agency on earth—his opportunity to choose either liberty and eternal life or captivity and spiritual death—is also given as an expression of the grace of Christ, and for this reason it has its basis in the doctrine of justification by grace. Except for the fact that Jesus freely paid the debt of sin and extends His mercy and power to hold in abeyance the demands of divine justice, man would have no alternative to spiritual death and darkness. And without spiritual truth and light, moral excellence would be but an illusive ideal which would fade as a hope within man as the forces of mortal corruption gained ascendancy over his desire to do good. Lehi therefore declared that because men are redeemed from the fall by the power of Christ's atonement, "they have become free forever, knowing good from evil; to act for themselves and not to be acted upon, save it be by the punishment of the law at the great and last day, according to the commandments which God hath given."[12]

The resurrection of all men and the redemption of all men from the power of the first spiritual death, wherein they are brought back into the presence of God to be judged for their deeds in the flesh, are also made possible by the grace and power of Jesus Christ; and they are expressions of the doctrine of justification by grace.[13] Here also the demands of justice are paid unconditionally, and these actions are performed in behalf of man without regard for his personal merits or goodness.

Though some expressions of Christ's grace are given unconditionally to all men, others are extended only on a conditional basis, as man complies with the requirements of the gospel. One expression of grace which man must merit is that which is given to justify him before the bar of God for his personal sins, when he is offered the plan of life and salvation and is made responsible to its requirements. In the plan of the gospel, the justification of a believing individual results from the action of both Christ and man. In effecting the atonement, Jesus satisfied the demands of divine law; He paid the debt of sin for all men. But before man can obtain the benefits of the atonement and receive forgiveness for his sins, he must reconcile himself to the Redeemer by exercising living faith in Jesus Christ, repenting of his sins, and being baptized according to the Lord's commandment. The Son of God then extends the benefits of His atonement to man to justify him before the eternal bar of the Father. For this reason the Prophet wrote by revelation: "We know that justification *through the grace of our Lord and Savior Jesus Christ* is just and true."[14]

This is a fundamental doctrine of the Book of Mormon. Lehi exclaimed: "How great the importance to make these things known unto the inhabitants of the earth, that they may know that *there is no flesh that can dwell in the presence of God, save it be through the merits, and mercy, and grace of the Holy Messiah.*[15] His son Nephi therefore explained:

> . . . we labor diligently to write, to persuade our children, and also our brethren, to believe in Christ, and to be reconciled to God, for we know that *it is by grace that we are saved, after all we can do. . . .*
>
> We talk of Christ, we rejoice in Christ, we preach of Christ, we prophesy of Christ, and we write according to our prophecies, *that our children may know to what source they may look for a remission of their sins.*[16]

Joseph Smith taught that when man accepts the gospel he enters into a *state of grace* in which he has access to the mercy and power of Christ unto salvation.[17] Because the atonement frees him from the demands which divine justice would otherwise impose upon him for his sins, the man of faith may then receive the blessings, gifts, and powers of Christ's Holy Spirit to enable him to mature in the path of truth and light which leads to eternal life. So long as he does not transgress the law of God to the extent that he falls from grace,[18] he may continue to receive these benefits until he is finally perfected in Christ.

A person who is baptized and thereafter transgresses the law may receive some divine reprimand but still not fall completely from grace. Christ controls the extension of His mercy to man, and He is free to handle each person as his case requires. Nevertheless, Jesus is merciful and sympathetic to the weaknesses of man; and so long as man expresses a genuine desire to attain the righteousness of God and is striving conscientiously toward that goal, the Lord extends the blessings of the atonement to free man from the obligations of divine justice and to aid him to grow in the knowledge and power of the Spirit until he overcomes the world.

Justification by Faith

Faith in the Lord Jesus Christ is the primary principle and power by which man in his lost and fallen mortal state can reconcile himself to God. When viewed in this light, the doctrine of justification by faith is seen to have an important place in the divine plan of life and salvation. Modern revelation is in accord with the Apostle Paul, who wrote:

> Therefore *being justified by faith,* we have peace with God *through our Lord Jesus Christ:*
>
> By whom also *we have access by faith into this grace* wherein we stand, and rejoice in hope of the glory of God.[19]

Justification by Righteous Works

Man can only obtain and thereafter retain a condition of justification through Christ by doing the righteous works which the gospel requires. The initial works by which man achieves justification consist of obedience to the program of the preparatory gospel. Thereafter man must dedicate his life to the service of God and man in order to continue in a state of justification through the grace of the Master.[20]

It should be stressed that without the grace of Christ, man's works would avail him nothing in his quest for salvation. The righteous works of man are not unto justification, but unto reconciliation through the grace of Jesus Christ; and then, man's righteous works must flow as an outward expression of the hope and faith of an enlightened and grateful heart. Works of themselves do not save man. But by hope and faith, coupled with obedience to the ordinances of the gospel and the righteous works of service, man is reconciled to God. Man's righteous works merely register the presence and strength of reconciling qualities within him.[21]

Justification by the Holy Spirit

Joseph Smith implied that there is a difference between the *condition* of justification and the *process* by which justification is achieved in the gospel. The condition of justification is the state of being justified through the atonement of Jesus Christ, while the process of justification is that program by which fallen man may attain the state of justification. The Holy Spirit plays an important role in leading man to obtain the benefits of the atonement so that he can be brought to a condition of justification. In the sense that this is true, the Lord declared to Adam: "By the Spirit ye are justified."[22]

The doctrine of justification by the Spirit may be divided into four major areas of discussion: First, as an active agent in the process by which man may attain a condition of justification, the Holy Spirit reaches down and invites man to raise his soul to God.[23] The Lord loves man before man in his fallen state learns to reciprocate God's pure love, or is capable of doing so in obedience to the requirements of heaven. If man expresses a true desire for righteousness and an initial hope in Christ as a result of the uplifting influence of the Spirit of God, he is given strength and encouragement by the Spirit to comply with the principles, ordinances, and laws of the gospel. In this way, the Spirit justifies man, or leads him to be a justified man.

Second, when man yields to the uplifting power of the Holy Spirit so that this divine agent has a meaningful influence in his life, he is free *conditionally* from the demands of divine justice. Joseph Smith wrote by revelation that when men of faith manifest "by their works that they have *received the Spirit of Christ unto the remission of their sins* [i.e., unto justification]," they may be baptized.[24] Technically, this statement indicates that the remission of sins is given to man before baptism, and man's sins are remitted when the Spirit begins to have a significant influence in his life. The Holy Ghost cannot dwell in man before he receives a remission of sins,[25] because it will not abide in an unjustified person—one to whom the benefits of the atonement have not been extended to remit his sins.[26] The mercy of Christ must reach down and absolve man from his sins when he begins to express a desire for the righteousness of God and a living hope in Christ. Otherwise the demands of divine justice will prevent him from receiving the gifts and graces of the Spirit which are necessary to bring him to Christ. It follows that man must be justified on a conditional basis by the action of the Spirit before baptism. He must then be baptized *to make official and binding by covenant that which God has previously granted to him on a temporary or contingent basis by the action of the Spirit.* It is in this sense that baptism is for the remission of sins; and in this way, man is justified by the Spirit.

Receiving a remission of sins before baptism is in accord with the doctrine that the Holy Ghost may be given to a man before he receives the laying on of hands.[27] At times the Spirit may even manifest its supernatural gifts and powers to the unbaptized.[28] But should man fail to heed the injunction to be baptized after being enlightened by the Spirit to see the kingdom of God, the preliminary blessings of the Spirit which he has enjoyed will be withdrawn. Apparently the same principle applies when man's sins are remitted on a conditional basis before baptism. Should the Spirit withdraw after absolving man from the demands of divine justice, he would be left in his sins.

These provisions reflect the mercy and justice of God. They are of particular importance when the outward ordinances of the gospel are not immediately available to those who express living faith in Christ, or when there is no authority on earth to perform those saving ordinances. In such cases, God is not bound to execute the demands of justice against those who have not been baptized, and He may even extend the power and gifts of the Holy Ghost in some degree to such individuals as a result of their faith. It was apparently by such provisions that earlier generations of gentiles in America were blessed "unto the pouring out of the Holy Ghost" upon them.[29] There were also many converts of the restored gospel who received the enlightening manifestations of the Holy Ghost before they were baptized, and they felt an inner peace which evidenced the extension of Christ's mercy unto them.[30]

The third aspect of the doctrine of justification by the Spirit derives from the fact that the Holy Ghost must ratify all ordinances of the gospel before they are accepted officially in heaven. In this action, the Holy Ghost acts as a Spirit of promise, and for this reason He is called at times the Holy Spirit of promise.[31] Each ordinance of the gospel carries with it stipulated blessings and promises; and in ratifying an ordinance, the Holy Ghost confirms its associated blessings to the individual. The Father sheds forth the Holy Spirit of promise upon all those who embrace the gospel and are just and true.[32] Since the Holy Ghost ratifies all ordinances of the gospel, including that of baptism for the remission of sins, it may be said that man is justified by the Spirit at the time the Spirit acts to ratify the ordinance of baptism.

Finally, in the program of the gospel the full and complete acquittal of man from sin is made possible only by the action of the Holy Spirit upon him. Only as man is renewed and changed from his fallen state to a state of righteousness can he fully receive a forgiveness of sins, for until he is thus transformed he must continue to some extent in the ways of the world, which are the ways of spiritual darkness and sin. Although man is justified when he achieves that kind of a spiritual union with Christ which leads him to obey the gospel, he is then in a conditional state of justification where the atonement must act continually to shield him from the demands of eternal law. This is also true in some degree after he has been baptized and until he is fully sanctified and perfected in Christ. Man cannot be completely acquitted until he has overcome all things and can live in perfect accord with the laws of God. This he cannot do until he has been thoroughly cleansed, or sanctified, by the power of the Holy Spirit, and until he has matured sufficiently in the divine attributes and powers of the Spirit to overcome the world. Justification in the final or ultimate sense therefore depends upon the work of the Holy Spirit. For this reason, Nephi declared that man is given a remission of sins "by fire and by the Holy Ghost,"[33] or, as a revelation to the Prophet said, "*by baptism* and *by fire,* yea, even the Holy Ghost."[34]

Retaining a Remission of Sins

The divine doctrine of justification may be divided into two programs: (1) the program by which man may initially *obtain* a remission of sins, and (2) the program by which he may thereafter *retain* a remission of sins. It is one thing to obtain a remission of sins as man obeys the ordinances of the gospel. But to receive an official acquittal of sins by baptism does not mean that he is then perfect, or that he will thereafter obey the law of God to perfection. It is therefore necessary for one who is baptized to be able to retain a remission of sins from day to day as he grows in grace and in the knowledge of the truth.

Man's need to retain a remission of sins after accepting the gospel comes from the weakness of his mortal nature in this fallen state. The plan of life and salvation is designed so that man must rely continually in faith upon Jesus Christ until he is perfected in Christ,[35] and glorified in Christ.[36] "I give unto men weakness that they may be humble," the Lord explained, "and *my grace* is sufficient for all men that humble themselves before me."[37] Having lamented the weakness of his flesh, Nephi thus qualified: "Nevertheless, I know in whom I have trusted. My God hath been my support."[38]

In order for one who has embraced the gospel to retain a remission of his sins as he struggles upward against the power of the fall and the influence of the world, he must exemplify Christ in his dedication to divine truth. As he applies the blessings of the gospel in his life, he must live outside of himself in love and service to others. The Prophet stated: "To be *justified before God* we must love one another: we must overcome evil; we must visit the fatherless and the widow in their affliction, and we must keep ourselves unspotted from the world."[39] In a more elaborate statement, King Benjamin explained to his people the requirements associated with this phase of the gospel, after they had taken upon themselves the name of Christ. He said:

> . . . as ye have come to the knowledge of the glory of God, or if ye have known of his goodness and have tasted of his love, and have received a remission of your sins, which causeth such exceeding great joy in your souls, even so I would that ye should remember, and always retain in remembrance, the greatness of God, and your own nothingness, and his goodness and long-suffering towards you, unworthy creatures, and humble yourselves even in the depths of humility, calling on the name of the Lord daily, and standing steadfastly in the faith. . . .
>
> And behold, I say unto you that if ye do this ye shall always rejoice, and be filled with the love of God, *and always retain a remission of your sins; and ye shall grow in the knowledge of the glory of him that created you, or in the knowledge of that which is just and true.*
>
> And ye will not have a mind to injure one another, but to live peaceably, and to render to every man according to that which is his due.
>
> And ye will not suffer your children that they go hungry, or naked; neither will ye suffer that they transgress the laws of God, and fight and quarrel one with another, and serve the devil, who is the master of sin. . . .
>
> But ye will teach them to walk in the ways of truth and soberness; ye will teach them to love one another, and to serve one another.
>
> And also, ye yourselves will succor those that stand in need of your succor; ye will administer of your substance unto him that standeth in need; and ye will not suffer that the beggar putteth up his petition to you in vain, and turn him out to perish. . . .
>
> And now, for the sake of these things which I have spoken unto you—that is, *for the sake of retaining a remission of your sins from day to day, that ye may walk guiltless before God*—I would that ye should impart of your substance to the poor, every man according to that which he hath, such as feeding the hungry, clothing the naked, visiting the sick and administering to their relief, both spiritually and temporally, according to their wants.[40]

The Wayward Believer

Revelations to Joseph Smith indicate that special action should be taken to justify before the bar of God those who accept the gospel and later commit grievous sin. The Saints are to confess their sins to those whom they offend and to the Lord.[41] But when a person commits a sin that jeopardizes his standing in the Church, that sin should also be confessed before the proper official, or officials, of the Church. As a common "judge in Israel," the bishop is appointed to "sit in judgment upon transgressors."[42] Other presiding officials are also charged with this responsibility.[43] Having explored the details of a given transgression, the appropriate officials may determine if the offending person should retain his standing in the Church, or if his repentance justifies the law being waived in his case. In making the necessary adjustment, a bishop cannot tell him his sins are forgiven, unless he is specifically directed to do so by the Spirit of revelation. Instead, the justification of the offending person through the extension of Christ's mercy unto him should be evidenced by the return of the fruits and blessings of the Holy Spirit in his life. Because the Holy Ghost does not dwell in an unjustified person, the presence of the holy Comforter will indicate when the person is again in a state of justification before the Lord.

Doctrine Of Sanctification

Sanctification Defined

Joseph Smith taught that in being sanctified, man is not only forgiven of sin but cleansed from the effects of it so that he is made a pure and holy being. The English word "sanctify" comes from the French word *sanctifier,* which means to make holy, which in turn derives from the Latin root *sanctus,* which means holy. It is one thing to forgive man of his sins and thereby acquit him of personal responsibility to divine law, but it is quite another thing to purge and renovate his soul from the effects of those sins and from the influences of this fallen mortal state. The latter tasks are those which are involved in the work of sanctification. Orson Pratt explained:

> After you have been immersed . . . in the water [of baptism], and been cleansed and received a remission of your sins, you also have the promise of baptism of fire and of the Holy Ghost, by which you are . . . sanctified from all your evil affections, and you feel to love God and that which is just and true, and to hate that which is sinful and evil. Why? Because of this sanctifying, purifying principle that comes upon you, by the baptism of fire and the Holy Ghost.[44]

Orson Hyde defined the state of sanctification as follows:

> . . . it means a purification of, or a putting away from, us, as individuals and as a community, everything that is evil, or that is not in accordance with the mind and will of our heavenly Father.
>
> Sanctification has also an eye to our own preservation for usefulness—for executing, carrying forward, and perpetuating the work of the Most High God.[45]

Of the state of sanctification, Brigham Young said:

> . . . it consists in overcoming every sin and bringing all into subjection to the law of Christ. God has placed in us a pure spirit; when this reigns predominant, without let or hindrance, and triumphs over the flesh and rules and governs and controls as the Lord controls the heavens and the earth, this I call the blessing of sanctification.[46]

In the sense that sanctification means a cleansing of man from sin, all who repent, either in this world or in the spirit world hereafter, will be sanctified and endowed with a degree of glory in the resurrection. A revelation explained that Christ made His atonement "to sanctify the world, and to cleanse it from all unrighteousness, . . . except those sons of perdition who deny the Son after the Father has revealed him."[47] But in a more positive sense, sanctification means more than to be cleansed from the effects of sin. It denotes possession of the powers and attributes of God—a condition of being matured in the divine nature of God. Only those who qualify for celestial redemption will be sanctified in this sense. Brigham Young explained that "when we sanctify ourselves to enter into the presence of the Father and of the Son, we will be filled with the same patience that he is filled with."[48]

Man's Challenge to Be Sanctified

Brigham Young explained that man has been placed on earth "to be sanctified, that every thought, and desire and feeling may be brought into subjection to the will of God."[49] This is true particularly of those who have embraced the gospel. "We are gathered together to sanctify these bodies," he explained, "to deal, act, transact and do everything we do in the love of God."[50]

By sanctification, man may be cleansed and purified from (1) the effects of the fallen and corrupt nature that exists upon the earth as a result of Adam's transgression and the subsequent sins of man, and (2) the effects of his personal sins. Regarding the first issue, it is by being sanctified that man is changed from his "carnal and fallen state, to a state of righteousness." By the action of the Spirit he puts off the natural man, or the man that is natural to the order of life that prevails on this fallen sphere, and becomes a new creature in Christ.[51] This transformation is necessary regardless of man's personal righteousness or purity. It is a factor separate and apart from the second issue mentioned above. Because Jesus was born of a mortal woman in this temporal state, He had to be sanctified from the effects of this fallen state, even though He had no personal sins. Speaking of His disciples, He said: "For their sakes *I sanctify myself,* that they also might be sanctified through the truth."[52] Many elements that made up Christ's physical body were mortal elements; and the nature He received from His mother was a mortal nature. He, too, found it necessary to put off the natural man by the action of divine power.

To the degree that man transgresses the laws of God,

the task of becoming sanctified is made more difficult, for by sin he loses virtue and becomes contaminated by the baneful influences which are in the world. In addition to being transformed from the fallen mortal state, which is a corrupt state,[53] he must be cleansed from the effects of his personal sins and have built back into him the substance of virtue and power which he lost by transgression. This can only be done by the action of the Holy Spirit, which is a substance of virtue and truth. By its influence, man can partake of the virtue of Christ and be endowed with the attributes and powers of God. In this way, sinful man can be cleansed and renewed by the gospel, to become a new creature in Christ.

But when man is contaminated by sin and enveloped in the spiritual darkness which follows transgression, it is often hard for him to see how to extricate himself. And even when he is brought to see the way of life and truth, he may find it difficult to follow. The fact that he has lost virtue in some form may evidence a weakness of character that makes it hard for him to apply the principles by which he can regain innocence and acquire spiritual strength. Nevertheless, the pangs of guilt and remorse of conscience which the sinner feels may awaken in him a desire for righteousness which he had not previously possessed. With a new determination to do right, coupled with the mercy and power which God extends to aid those who truly desire to come unto Him, a wayward person can be renewed to a state of purity and power in Christ.

In facing the challenge of sanctification, man should, according to Brigham Young, keep in mind that "the power of God is greater than the power of the wicked one; and unless the Saints sin against light and knowledge, and wilfully neglect their plain and well understood duties, and the Spirit of God is grieved and it ceases to strive with them, *the Spirit is sure to prevail over the flesh, and ultimately succeed in sanctifying the tabernacle for a residence in the presence of God.*"[54] This fact should give the Saints great consolation and a hope of ultimate victory by complying with the program of the gospel.

Nevertheless, man in mortality cannot be sanctified completely from the effects of sin and of this fallen state. "Some suppose that they can in the flesh be sanctified body and spirit and become so pure that they will never again feel the effects of the power of the adversary of truth," Brigham Young observed. He explained: "Were it possible for a person to attain to this degree of perfection in the flesh, he could not die neither remain in a world where sin predominates."[55] So long as man has a mortal body, there are corrupt elements within his system which, like centrifugal forces pulling a revolving object away from its center, tend to alienate man from God, so that the struggle of man's mortal probation continues until death. For this reason the Lord said, as He warned the Saints of the possibility of falling from grace: "Yea, and even let those who are sanctified take heed also."[56] But as man becomes sanctified, he gains the mastery over the flesh and the world; and he may retain that mastery by the continual exercise of his will and of his reliance on Christ, except possibly in instances of slight or inadvertent departures from the path of strict rectitude which arise out of the weaknesses of human nature on earth.[57] Brigham Young continued: "If we live our religion it will enable us to so overcome sin that it will not reign in our mortal bodies but will become subject to us, and the world and its fulness will become our servant instead of our master."[58]

Sanctification by the Blood of Christ

The atonement is the foundation of the divine plan by which man may be sanctified,[59] and Jesus "wrought out this perfect atonement through the shedding of his own blood."[60] It may be said, therefore, that man is sanctified by the blood of Jesus Christ.

Several scriptures refer to the doctrine of sanctification in this light. God explained to Adam that to enter the kingdom of heaven, his children had to be "cleansed by . . . the blood" of His Only Begotten Son, and in this way they could be "sanctified from all sin." God stressed: "By the blood ye are sanctified."[61] Jesus taught the Nephites that only those who "washed their garments" in His blood could be saved.[62] Nephi and Moroni made similar statements.[63] Of the faithful in ancient days, Alma said: "They . . . were sanctified, and their garments were washed white through the blood of the Lamb."[64] And the Lord warned the wicked in these last days: "My blood shall not cleanse them if they hear me not."[65]

Sanctification by the Spirit

Though the shedding of Christ's blood in the atonement is the foundation of the divine program by which man may be sanctified, the active agent in the process of sanctification is the power of the Holy Ghost. Having referred to some in ancient times whose "garments were washed white through the blood of the Lamb," Alma explained: "Now they, after being *sanctified by the Holy Ghost,* having their garments made white, being pure and spotless before God, could not look upon sin save it were with abhorrence."[66]

Alma again expressed this view when he spoke of those who embraced the gospel in his day as "having been sanctified by the Holy Spirit."[67] Jesus taught the Nephites to receive the gospel that they might "be sanctified by the reception of the Holy Ghost" and thereby "stand spotless" before Him at the last day.[68] Moroni wrote of those who received the message of redemption in his day: "After they had been received unto baptism, and were *wrought upon and cleansed by the power of the Holy Ghost,* they were numbered among the people of the church of Christ."[69] And in modern times a revelation to Joseph Smith spoke of the faithful as being "sanctified by the Spirit unto the renewing of their bodies."[70]

To the Father, Jesus prayed in behalf of His disciples: "Sanctify them through thy truth: thy word is truth."[71] This is the living word, which is truth, or light, or Spirit—

the Spirit of Jesus Christ.[72] Divine truth given to man through the Holy Spirit has an enlightening and sanctifying influence in his life. Of this divine substance, which is called the glory of God—intelligence, or, in other words, light and truth—and which is the Spirit of truth, a revelation said: "Light and truth forsake that evil one [the Adversary]."[73] "That which is of God is light," another revelation said, as it explained the manifestations of the Spirit of truth to the Saints; "and he that receiveth light, and continueth in God, receiveth more light; and that light groweth brighter and brighter until the perfect day."[74] A sanctified person is filled with the light of the Spirit which abounds within him.[75] These explanations were made so that the Saints might "know the truth," that they might "chase darkness" from among them, and, by becoming sanctified, that they might return, eventually, to the presence of God.[76]

Justification Compared with Sanctification

The doctrine of justification is identified with the preparatory gospel,[77] by which man is made ready to receive "a greater revelation of God."[78] Since justification is essentially a preparatory action and state, it alone cannot bring man to the ultimate goal of salvation. Unless the work of justification is associated with the cleansing, renewing, and maturing powers of the Holy Spirit—powers that go beyond the enlightening influences by which a man of faith may be born to see the kingdom of God—it is useless in the final analysis. Man cannot be redeemed from his fallen state to celestial glory by the program of justification alone.

Orson Pratt, in explaining the relationship between the divine program by which man may receive a remission of personal sins and the means by which he can be sanctified from the effects of sin, stated:

> The Holy Spirit dwells not in unholy temples; that is, it dwells not there, to sanctify, teach, and comfort the mind, but merely has an existence in such temples, to carry on the

common operations of nature. To receive the Holy Spirit, so as to have the mind benefited, requires a preparation both of the body and mind. The body and mind of a natural man [i.e., a man who is conditioned to the world and its fallen state], have both been defiled by sin; consequently, both are unholy, impure, and altogether unprepared for the indwelling of the holy Comforter. Now there is but one way for them to be properly prepared for the residence of this pure Spirit. This one way is of divine origin, and consists of three important steps; . . . namely, Faith, Repentance, and Water Baptism. By these three steps, taken sincerely and properly, the sinner is forgiven of all past sins, and both mind and body are prepared for the Baptism of fire and the Holy Ghost.

Water Baptism is only a preparatory cleansing of the believing penitent; it is only a condition of a cleansing from sin [i.e., a condition of justification]; whereas, the Baptism of fire and the Holy Ghost cleanses more thoroughly, by renewing the inner man, and by purifying the affections, desires, and thoughts which have long been habituated in the impure ways of sin. Without the aid of the Holy Ghost, a person who has long been accustomed to love sin, and whose affections and desires have long run with delight in the degraded channel of vice, would have but very little power to change his mind, at once, from its habituated course, and to walk in newness of life. Though his sins may have been cleansed away, yet so great is the force of habit, that he would, without being renewed by the Holy Ghost, be easily overcome, and contaminated again with sin. Hence, it is infinitely important that the affections and desires should be, in a measure, changed and renewed, so as to cause him to hate that which he before loved, and to love that which he before hated. To thus renew the mind of man is the work of the Holy Ghost.[79]

Sanctification by Grace

Sanctification, like justification, comes by the grace of God. Having written by revelation sanctioning the doctrine of justification by grace, Joseph Smith declared: "We know also, that sanctification *through the grace of our Lord and Savior Jesus Christ* is just and true, to all those who love and serve God with all their mights, minds, and strength."[80] Man cannot sanctify himself. He is powerless by his own means to transform himself from his fallen and carnal state on earth to that state of righteousness which leads to eternal life. He cannot endow himself with the divine intelligence and power which are required to achieve full spiritual union with God. Nor does he earn that which he receives from Christ. A fallen being has little with which to purchase the divine endowments by which his renewal to a state of glory is made possible.

The basic means of receiving sanctifying truth and power is through the gift of the Holy Ghost. As indicated, this is a *gift.* But sanctification is a process, not a state to be achieved immediately upon reception of this gift. Having entered by faith and obedience into a state of grace, man must mature in the blessings and gifts of the Holy Spirit until he is glorified in Christ at the time of his resurrection. "Ye are little children and ye cannot bear all things now," a revelation explained to the Saints; "ye must *grow in grace* and in the knowledge of the truth."[81] King Benjamin expressed the same point as he spoke to his people of their need to continue in the path of eternal life. "If ye do this," he declared, "ye shall always rejoice, and be filled with the love of God, and always retain a remission of your sins; and ye shall grow in the knowledge of the glory of him that created you, or in the knowledge of that which is just and true."[82]

Because man must grow in the gifts and blessings of God after he receives the gospel, a revelation promised an early convert "grace and assurance" within the divine plan of life and salvation if he would continue faithful.[83] Joseph Smith referred with approval to the declaration of the Apostle Peter that "grace and peace" are multiplied—given more abundantly or in manifold proportions—to the saints "through the knowledge of God, and of Jesus our Lord."[84] Concerning the means by which the Saints could acquire such knowledge, a revelation said: "Teach ye diligently and *my grace shall attend you,* that you may be instructed more perfectly in theory, in principle, in doctrine, in the laws of the gospel, in all things that pertain unto the kingdom of God, that are expedient for you to understand."[85] Because he understood the relationship between man's efforts and the grace of God in the salvation of those who accept the gospel, Jacob explained, when some Nephites acquired power by faith to do great miracles: "Nevertheless, the Lord God showeth us our weaknesses that we may know that *it is by his grace, and his great condescension unto the children of men,* that we have power to do these things."[86] By continuing "from grace to grace," Jesus acquired a fulness of the Father's glory,[87] and man must do the same.[88] In the words of the Prophet, man must go "from one small degree to another, and from a small capacity to a great one; *from grace to grace,* from exaltation to exaltation," until he has attained to the resurrection of the dead and is "able to dwell in everlasting burnings, and to sit in glory, as do those who sit enthroned in everlasting power."[89]

Moroni completed the account of the Nephites and their religious teachings with the admonition that man must recognize and acquire the grace of God if he is to obtain salvation. Before sealing up the ancient record, he declared:

> . . . I would exhort you that ye would come unto Christ, *and lay hold upon every good gift,* and touch not the evil gift, nor the unclean thing. . . .
>
> Yea, come unto Christ, and be perfected in him, and deny yourselves of all ungodliness; and if ye shall deny yourselves of all ungodliness and love God with all your might, mind and strength, *then is his grace sufficient for you, that by his grace ye may be perfect in Christ; and if by the grace of God ye are perfect in Christ, ye can in nowise deny the power of God.*
>
> And again, *if ye by the grace of God are perfect in Christ, and deny not his power, then are ye sanctified in Christ by the grace of God,* through the shedding of the blood of Christ, which is in the covenant of the Father unto the remission of your sins, that ye become holy, without spot.[90]

Sanctification by Works of Righteousness

Though man is sanctified by the grace of God, the Prophet wrote by revelation that grace to this end is given only to those who "love and serve God with all their mights, minds, and strength."[91] This means that if man is to be sanctified he must commit his life and interests completely to Christ. He may be sanctified only by service *in doing the will of God.* A revelation declared that those who magnify their "calling" are "sanctified by the Spirit unto the renewing of their bodies."[92]

In the sense that man must serve God in righteousness in order to receive the sanctifying powers of the Spirit, it may be said that he is sanctified by his works. Having declared that if man's eye is "single" to the glory of God his whole body will be filled with the light of the Spirit, a revelation admonished the Saints: "Therefore, *sanctify yourselves* that your minds become single to God."[93] Another revelation explained that for man to obtain the powers and attributes of God's glory he must receive "grace *for* grace."[94] This means that he can receive grace (i.e., the divine truth, powers, and attributes of the Spirit) from God only as he gives grace to others.

Sanctification comes to those who reconcile themselves to Christ. It is the Lord's purpose to sanctify man through the gospel,[95] and in Him is centered the power to do so. But to be sanctified, man must perform, in faith and love, the works of reconciliation and service which the law of God requires. To the degree that man does these things, he may be sanctified. Mormon wrote of a group of Nephite saints: "They did fast and pray oft, and did wax stronger and stronger in their humility, and firmer and firmer in the faith of Christ, unto the filling their souls with joy and consolation, yea, even to the purifying and the sanctification of their hearts, which sanctification cometh because of their yielding their hearts unto God."[96] Having obeyed the gospel, man is sanctified in degree commensurate with his yielding his heart to God.

God's Methods of Sanctifying Man

A revelation to Joseph Smith indicates that God uses various methods in His effort to sanctify man so that man can be endowed with celestial glory in the resurrection. But man must respond to the uplifting hand of God and yield obedience to the law of God. "They who are not sanctified through the law which I have given unto you, even the law of Christ," the revelation declares, "must inherit another kingdom, even that of a terrestrial kingdom, or that of a telestial kingdom."[97] The revelation then explains:

> . . . that which is governed by law is also preserved by law and perfected and sanctified by the same.
>
> That which breaketh a law, and abideth not by law, but seeketh to become a law unto itself, and willeth to abide in sin, cannot be sanctified by law, neither by mercy, justice, nor judgment. Therefore, they must remain filthy still.[98]

God first extends His law to man, and by obeying that law man may receive a remission of his sins and the power of the Holy Spirit by which he may be sanctified. Obedience to law thus leads man to a state of sanctification; and without obedience man cannot be sanctified. Basing his statement on the testimony of scripture, Brigham Young declared: "The people must be sanctified by law, they must live according to that law; and they must be justified, purified, and sanctified in order to get into the kingdom of heaven, that is, the highest glory."[99]

Since fallen man does not obey the law of God to perfection, the Lord next extends mercy to those who seek for His righteousness, so that by mercy they may receive the blessings of the Holy Spirit and be sanctified. By being sanctified by the Spirit, man may then more fully keep the law of God. In referring to the way the gifts of the Holy Spirit are received, a revelation said: "Verily I say unto you, they are given for the benefit of those who love me and keep all my commandments, *and him that seeketh so to do.*"[100] Not totally by law, but by mercy also, the blessings of the Spirit are given to man.

Third, if man rejects mercy, God has no alternative but to exercise justice upon him to bring him to an awareness of his responsibility to divine law. But in executing divine justice, God stands ready to extend mercy and power to repentant man, to sanctify him from sin and redeem him to a state of righteousness.

God's dealings with the people who perished in the flood in the days of Noah is an example of this policy. The Lord explained to the patriarch Enoch that Christ would pay the debt of their sins if they would repent when the message of redemption was given to them in the spirit world, after the crucifixion, but until that time they would be in torment. Enoch was then shown that after the resurrection of Christ "as many of the spirits as were in prison came forth, and stood on the right hand of God."[101] But when God is required to exercise justice in order to bring man to repentance, man's waywardness may evidence a lack of dedication to truth and righteousness on his part. When this is the case, man cannot be sanctified to the point that he can receive the full glory and power of celestial existence. Those who perished in the flood are, in general, redeemed only to a terrestrial state of glory in the resurrection.[102]

Finally, the word "judgment" is used in the above statement to portray a method by which God seeks to sanctify man. Judgment denotes a more harsh and exacting action against a wayward person than does justice. Justice may be tempered with mercy, but judgment is more demanding and enduring in its prescribed penalties. In referring to the doctrine of eternal judgment, Joseph Smith explained that it is possible for man to sin against truth and light to the extent that he cannot receive mercy even though he should repent. In such cases, man himself must pay the debt of justice for his sins, unmitigated by mercy, before he can be forgiven and sanctified to the degree that he can attain a kingdom of glory in the resurrection.

Murderers in an enlightened Christian society are in this class. "If the ministers of religion had a proper understanding of the doctrine of eternal judgment, they would not be found attending the man who forfeited his life to the injured laws of his country, by shedding innocent blood," the Prophet explained; "for such characters cannot be forgiven, until they have paid the last farthing." Murderers are outside of the pale of mercy. "The prayers of all the ministers in the world can never close the gates of hell against a murderer,"[103] the latter-day Seer concluded.

Neither is mercy extended to the man who falls from the sanctified state in which he has made sure his calling and election to celestial glory. He must suffer the judgments of God unmitigated by mercy before he can inherit the blessings that have been sealed upon his head. He cannot receive final sanctification and glorification except by judgment.[104]

At times the sanctifying process requires that the Saints "be chastened and tried, even as Abraham, who was commanded to offer up his only son." The Lord explained: "For all those who will not endure chastening, but deny me, cannot be sanctified."[105] Another revelation declared of the latter-day program:

> Zion shall be redeemed, although she is chastened for a little season. . . .
>
> Therefore, let your hearts be comforted; for all things shall work together for good to them that walk uprightly, and to the sanctification of the church.
>
> For I will raise up unto myself a pure people, that will serve me in righteousness.[106]

To become fully sanctified, the Saints are required to apply every aspect of the law of God in their lives so that they can be reconciled in every way to Christ and receive the full powers of the Holy Spirit. Not only must their hearts be dedicated to God, but the institutions of society among them must be patterned after the law of heaven. Only then can the Spirit and power of the gospel be revealed in their fulness among the people of God. Having given the Saints some instructions concerning the divine order which they are to establish and uphold, a revelation said:

And thus ye shall become instructed in the law of my church, and be sanctified by that which ye have received. . . .

That inasmuch as ye do this, glory shall be added to the kingdom which ye have received. Inasmuch as ye do it not, it shall be taken, even that which ye have received.[107]

Thus God and man work together in the divine process of sanctifying man, and for this reason the Saints were admonished:

Prepare ye, prepare ye, O my people; sanctify yourselves; gather ye together, O ye people of my church. . . .

Go ye out from Babylon. Be ye clean that bear the vessels of the Lord.

Call your solemn assemblies, and speak often one to another. And let every man call upon the name of the Lord.[108]

Sacrament of the Lord's Supper

The sacrament of the Lord's supper is an essential part of the divine program by which man can be justified and sanctified before God. As He introduced this sacred rite among the Nephites, Jesus instructed: "Behold there shall one be ordained among you, and to him will I give power that he shall break bread and bless it and give it unto the people of my church, unto all those who shall believe and be baptized in my name." "This shall ye do in remembrance of my body, which I have shown unto you," He continued. "And it shall be a testimony unto the Father that ye do always remember me." Finally, He promised: "And if ye do always remember me *ye shall have my Spirit to be with you.*"[109] This Spirit is the power of the Holy Ghost which Christ gives to man in the gospel in order to sanctify him before God.[110]

The sacramental prayer which Jesus gave the Nephites to bless the bread incorporates the above ideas into this sacred ritual. It states:

O God, the Eternal Father, we ask thee in the name of thy Son, Jesus Christ, to bless and sanctify this bread to the souls of all those who partake of it; that they may eat in remembrance of the body of thy Son, and witness unto thee, O God, the

> Eternal Father, that they are willing to take upon them the name of thy Son, and always remember him, and keep his commandments which he hath given them, that they may always have his Spirit to be with them. Amen.[111]

Having administered this part of the sacrament to the Nephites, Jesus commanded His disciples to take wine and drink, and to give it to the multitude. He then said: "This is fulfilling my commandments, and this doth witness unto the Father that ye are willing to do that which I have commanded you." Continuing, He instructed: "This shall ye always do to those who repent and are baptized in my name; and ye shall do it in remembrance of my blood, which I have shed for you, that ye may witness unto the Father that ye do always remember me." He then promised again: "And if ye do always remember me *ye shall have my Spirit to be with you.*"[112]

The sacramental prayer which Jesus gave the Nephites to bless the wine, like that which He gave to bless the bread, incorporates the above ideas into this sacred ritual. It states:

> O God, the Eternal Father, we ask thee, in the name of thy Son, Jesus Christ, to bless and sanctify this wine to the souls of all those who drink of it, that they may do it in remembrance of the blood of thy Son, which was shed for them; that they may witness unto thee, O God, the Eternal Father, that they do always remember him, that they may have his Spirit to be with them. Amen.[113]

The mere act of partaking of the sacrament does not bring the results which Jesus promised, for He stated specifically that if those who were baptized would always "remember" Him[114] and partake of the sacred emblems worthily they would have His Spirit—the power of the Holy Ghost—to be with them. Though the outward ritual was to be observed, the blessings of the Holy Spirit were to be given only to those who lived in true remembrance of Christ. By being continually in a state of justification through the power of His atonement, they could partake day by day of the blessings of His Holy Spirit.

Later when Jesus again administered the sacrament to the Nephites, He expressed in Hebraic symbolism the spiritual blessings which were to be given to those who partook of the sacrament worthily. "He that eateth this bread eateth of my body *to his soul,*" He explained; "and he that drinketh of this wine drinketh of my blood *to his soul;* and his soul shall *never hunger nor thirst, but shall be filled.*"[115]

The sacrament of the Lord's supper and the first principles and ordinances of the gospel constitute the basic program of the gospel of Jesus Christ. Having administered the sacrament to the Nephites, Jesus explained: "And if ye do always do these things blessed are ye, for ye are built upon my rock."[116] The record then states that "when the multitude had all eaten and drunk, behold, they were filled with the Spirit."[117]

Final Purpose of Sanctification

The final purpose of the gospel is to sanctify man so that he can be crowned with celestial glory in the resurrection. Having endowed His disciples on the Western hemisphere with some of His glory, which was to them a sanctifying agent, Jesus prayed: "Father, I thank thee that thou hast purified those whom I have chosen, because of their faith, and I pray for them, and also for them who shall believe on their words, that they may be purified in me, through faith on their words, even as they are purified in me."[118] The end-purpose of their sanctification, Jesus then observed, was that He might "be glorified in them."[119]

The same objective was set for the Saints in the latter days. A revelation declared: "Sanctify yourselves and ye shall be endowed with power."[120] Of the final goal to be achieved, another revelation said: "Unto him that repenteth and sanctifieth himself before the Lord shall be given eternal life."[121] Only by being sanctified can man abide in the presence of God. Having admonished the Saints to sanctify themselves so that their minds were "single to God," the Prophet wrote by revelation: "The days will come that you shall see him; for he will unveil his face unto you."[122]

Evidences Of A Sanctified Life

Several characteristics distinguish a sanctified man: First, he has spiritually been born of God. There has been a mighty change wrought in his heart, for he is quickened by the Spirit in the inner man, and he is continuing to travel the path which leads to eternal life or glory.[123] Second, his eye is single to the glory of God; he yields his heart to the Lord.[124] Third, he feels continually a nearness of the Holy Spirit and enjoys its sacred fruits, gifts, and blessings in his life.[125] Fourth, by means of the Spirit, he loves and serves God with all his heart, might, mind, and strength, living outside himself in genuine interest for the welfare of his fellow men.[126] Finally, he has lost the desire for sin, and he cannot look upon that which is perverse except with abhorrence.[127] He has achieved such union spiritually with God that he views things as God sees them, and the light and truth of the Spirit dictate his every action. Brigham Young explained: "When through the Gospel, the spirit in man has so subdued the flesh that he can live without willful transgression, the Spirit of God unites with his spirit, they become congenial companions, and the mind and will of the Creator is thus transmitted to the creature."[128]

Since the elements of mortal corruption still exist in some measure in a sanctified person's mortal body and exert a baneful influence upon him, his whole being which is made sensitive to impure influences by the refining power of the Spirit may feel keenly the corruption of the flesh. With Nephi he may mourn: "O wretched man that I am! Yea, my heart sorroweth because of my flesh."[129] Nevertheless, Brigham Young explained, he takes "a firmer hold on the enduring substance behind the veil, drawing from the depths of that eternal Fountain of Light sparkling gems of intelligence which surround [him] . . . with a halo of immortal wisdom."[130] In patience, he possesses his soul, and he waits earnestly for his corrupt mortal body to be raised to an incorrupt state endowed with a fulness of the Spirit which he has come to know and to esteem above all else on earth.

Summary

The programs of justification and sanctification are prominent features in the plan of the gospel. Justification is concerned, primarily, with the legal acquittal of man from the demands of broken law, and sanctification has to do with the purification of man from the effects of sin and the fallen mortal state. There are several aspects of the doctrine of justification: justification by law, justification by grace, justification by faith, justification by man's righteous works, and justification by the Holy Spirit. By abiding continually in Christ, man can retain a remission of his sins from day to day—live day by day in a state of justification. But one who commits serious transgressions of the law of God after receiving the gospel must have his acts judged by a bishop or another appropriate official of the Church to see if he is worthy by repentance to retain his standing among the Saints. Having repented of his sins and made the required adjustment with the Church, the offending person may know that the Lord has forgiven him by the return of the blessings and manifestations of the Spirit.

Man is sanctified by the power of the Holy Ghost, by being transformed from his fallen state to a state of righteousness and being cleansed from the effects of sin. As with justification, there are several aspects of the doctrine of sanctification: sanctification by the blood of Christ, sanctification by the Spirit, sanctification by grace, and sanctification by man's righteous works. Having given man the law by which he can be sanctified, God extends mercy to man to enable him to become sanctified. The Lord may also administer justice and judgment upon man, if they are necessary, to bring man to realize his responsibility to divine law that he may be sanctified. When man responds to the law of God and begins to become sanctified, he is given the manifestations of the Holy Spirit in greater abundance, making the sanctifying process in some respects a cyclical one. The sacrament of the Lord's supper plays a significant role in the programs of justification and sanctification. When man is sanctified, he is a new creature in Christ, having been purified by the power of the Holy Ghost and endowed with its enlightening and enlivening powers.

Notes

1. There may be a question whether or not a person can pay for all his sins; but those who are thrust down to hell do so, at least, in part. See D&C 19:16–18.
2. 2 Nephi 2:5.
3. D&C 45:4.
4. I. R., John 14:30.
5. See Volume I of this study, the section in chapter sixteen entitled "Universal Results Of The Power Of Atonement."
6. See D&C 33:16; 88:6–13.
7. Mosiah 3:16; Moroni 8:8, 12.
8. D&C 93:38; Moses 6:53–54.
9. D&C 29:47.
10. D&C 68:25–27; I. R., Genesis 17:11.
11. See Volume I of this study, the section in chapter sixteen entitled "People Without Law not Subject to Divine Justice."
12. 2 Nephi 2:26.
13. See Volume I of this study, the sections in chapter sixteen entitled "Resurrection Given to all Men by Atonement" and "Redemption from First Spiritual Death Given to All by Atonement."
14. D&C 20:30.
15. 2 Nephi 2:8.
16. 2 Nephi 25:23, 26.
17. D&C 20:4, 30–32; 50:40; 76:94; 93:20; 109:10, 44.
18. See D&C 20:30–32; 50:40; HC, VI, pp. 252–253.
19. Romans 5:1–2. In his Inspired Revision of the Bible, Joseph Smith revised several passages in this chapter, but he did not change these verses.
20. See Mosiah 4:12, 26; Alma 42:13–14. There are exceptions to this rule in cases where man is not physically capable of giving such service.
21. This is the point the Apostle James made when he wrote: "Shew me thy faith without thy works, and I will shew thee my faith by my works."—James 2:18.
22. Moses 6:60.
23. See Volume I of this study, the section in chapter ten entitled "Christ's Holy Spirit Leads Man Upward to God."
24. D&C 20:37.

25. For evidence that the Holy Ghost does dwell in man before baptism, see the section in chapter six entitled "The Holy Ghost And Gift Of The Holy Ghost," and the sections in chapter seven entitled "Birth to See the Kingdom of God" and "Birth to Enter the Kingdom of God."

26. It is sometimes said erroneously that the Holy Ghost will not dwell in an unclean tabernacle. The unsanctified body is an unclean body; and in order for man to be sanctified, the Holy Ghost must dwell in him before he is sanctified. But the Holy Ghost will not dwell in an *unjustified* person. The atonement must first act to absolve man from the legal demands of divine justice.

27. See the section in chapter six entitled "The Holy Ghost And Gift Of The Holy Ghost."

28. See, for example, Acts 10:44–48; Helaman 5:42–45.

29. 3 Nephi 20:27. See also 1 Nephi 13:12–19; 3 Nephi 21:4.

30. Such manifestations will be discussed in volume III of this work.

31. See, for example, D&C 88:3.

32. See D&C 76:53.

33. 2 Nephi 31:17.

34. D&C 19:31.

35. See Moroni 10:32–33.

36. D&C 93:19–20.

37. Ether 12:27.

38. 2 Nephi 4:19–20. See Volume I of this study, the section in chapter seventeen entitled "Man's Dependence Upon Christ."

39. HC, II, p. 229.

40. Mosiah 4:11–16, 26. See also Alma 4:14.

41. See D&C 42:88–93; 59:12.

42. D&C 107:72. See also D&C 58:17–18; 64:40; 72:17.

43. The discussion of these and related matters as they are to be handled by the High Council will be found in volume III of this work.

44. JD, XVI, p. 319.

45. JD, I, p. 71.

46. *Ibid.,* X, p. 173.

47. D&C 76:41, 43.

48. JD, XI, p. 291.

49. *Ibid.,* p. 289.

50. *Ibid.,* p. 290.

51. Mosiah 3:19; 27:25–26.

52. John 17:19.

53. See Volume I of this study, the section in chapter seventeen entitled "Man's Physical Body Corrupted by the Fall."

54. JD, XI, p. 237.

55. *Ibid.,* X, p. 173.

56. D&C 20:34.

57. Nephi illustrates this point in 2 Nephi 4:17–19, 27.

58. JD, X, p. 173.

59. See Volume I of this study, the section in chapter sixteen entitled "By the Atonement the Faithful are Sanctified."

60. D&C 76:69.

61. Moses 6:59–60.

62. 3 Nephi 27:19.

63. 1 Nephi 12:10; Ether 13:11.
64. Alma 13:11.
65. D&C 29:17.
66. Alma 13:11–12.
67. Alma 5:54.
68. 3 Nephi 27:20.
69. Moroni 6:4.
70. D&C 84:33.
71. John 17:17.
72. D&C 84:43–45. See also John 6:63.
73. D&C 93:36–37.
74. D&C 50:24.
75. D&C 88:66–68.
76. D&C 50:25; 88:66–68.
77. See again D&C 84:26–27, for a statement on the preparatory gospel.
78. HC, VI, p. 250.
79. Orson Pratt, *The Holy Spirit* (Liverpool, 1856), pp. 56–57. President Brigham Young, with his counselors and a majority of the Twelve, officially condemned this article as containing some elements of false doctrine, but said: "The last half of the tract entitled 'The Holy Spirit' contains excellent and conclusive arguments, and is all that could be wished."—*Deseret News,* XIV (August 23, 1856), pp. 372–373. This quote is taken from that part of the document which they praised.
80. D&C 20:31.
81. D&C 50:40.
82. Mosiah 4:12.
83. D&C 106:8.
84. HC, V, pp. 387–390; 401–403, citing 2 Peter 1:2.
85. D&C 88:78.
86. Jacob 4:7.
87. D&C 93:13, 16.
88. D&C 93:20.
89. HC, VI, p. 306.
90. Moroni 10:30, 32–33.
91. D&C 20:31. See also Moroni 10:32.
92. D&C 84:33.
93. D&C 88:67–68.
94. See D&C 93:19–20, in light of verses 12–13.
95. D&C 76:41.
96. Helaman 3:35.
97. D&C 88:21. The various kingdoms of glory in the resurrection will be discussed in volume IV of this study.
98. D&C 88:34–35.
99. JD, XIII, p. 283.
100. D&C 46:9.
101. Moses 7:39, 57.
102. D&C 76:73.
103. HC, IV, p. 359.
104. See D&C 132:26; Hebrews 10:26–29; 1 Corinthians 5:5.

105. D&C 101:4–5. In the divine patriarchal order, Abraham had but one son as heir in the flesh.

106. D&C 100:13, 15–16.

107. D&C 43:9–10. The nature of the social, economic, and political institutions of the kingdom of God will be discussed in volume III of this study.

108. D&C 133:4–6.

109. 3 Nephi 18:5–7.

110. For a discussion on this subject, see Volume I of this study, the section in chapter ten entitled "The Power of the Holy Ghost."

111. Moroni 4:3; D&C 20:77.

112. 3 Nephi 18:8–11.

113. Moroni 5:2; D&C 20:79. When Joseph Smith went to procure wine for a sacrament meeting in which he planned to confirm his wife and the wife of Newel Knight members of the Church, he was met by a heavenly messenger, who said:

> Listen to the voice of Jesus Christ, your Lord, your God, and your Redeemer, whose word is quick and powerful.
>
> For, behold, I say unto you, that it mattereth not what ye shall eat or what ye shall drink when ye partake of the sacrament, if it so be that ye do it with an eye single to my glory—remembering unto the Father my body which was laid down for you, and my blood which was shed for the remission of your sins.
>
> Wherefore, a commandment I give unto you, that ye shall not purchase wine neither strong drink of your enemies;
>
> Wherefore, you shall partake of none except it is made new among you; yea, in this my Father's kingdom which shall be built up on the earth.—D&C 27:1–4.

On the basis of this revelation, the Church later changed the practice of using wine in the sacrament to using water.

114. 3 Nephi 18:7, 11; Moroni 4:3; 5:2.

115. 3 Nephi 20:8.

116. 3 Nephi 18:12.

117. 3 Nephi 20:9.

118. 3 Nephi 19:28.

119. 3 Nephi 19:29.

120. D&C 43:16.

121. D&C 133:62.

122. D&C 88:68.

123. Mosiah 27:24–28; Alma 5:6–14; D&C 5:16; Moses 6:59–62.

124. D&C 88:66–68; Helaman 3:35.

125. Mosiah 18:10, 13; Alma 34:17–27; D&C 20:77–79.

126. Mosiah 18:8–10.

127. Alma 13:11–12; HC, II, p. 8.

128. JD, IX, pp. 287–288.

129. 2 Nephi 4:17.

130. JD, IX, p. 288.

9

The Spiritual Life of the Gospel

I am come that they might have life, and that they might have it more abundantly.—JESUS.

Revelations to Joseph Smith stress repeatedly that Jesus is the *light* and the *life* of the world,"[1] and that the gospel is a divine program that leads man literally into a new stage of life.[2] Since Christ's Holy Spirit is a substance of life, or a living substance, which develops divine attributes and powers of eternal life in man,[3] the Prophet's Inspired Revision of the Bible declares that in Jesus "was the gospel, and *the gospel was the life.*" Again it states: *"Life* and truth came through Jesus Christ." For this reason it declares that "the gospel was *after the power of an endless life.*"[4] Knowing this, Nephi sought to bring his people to "that life which is in Christ."[5] It is the purpose of this chapter to discuss the divine attributes and powers of life which are given to man in the gospel and without which he does not possess the gospel.

Manifestations Of Gospel Life To Man

Union of Man with Christ in Spirit

One of the major "items of command and promise" which the ancient apostles were given to deliver to the world was that the gospel consisted of divine "power."[6]

Because the gospel was a means by which man could acquire living power, the Savior's parable of the vine was a fit illustration of the union true believers have with Christ.[7] Joseph Smith sanctioned this fact[8] and in many ways illustrated its application among the Saints. "I am the true vine, and my Father is the husbandman," Christ declared. "Every branch in me that beareth not fruit he taketh away: and every branch that beareth fruit, he purgeth it, that it may bring forth more fruit."[9]

The Prophet taught that man's union with Christ should be a living thing, productive of living fruits and gifts. The man of faith acts in and through and by the Spirit in all that he does, and the Spirit becomes a principle of life and of power within him. "He that asketh in Spirit shall receive in Spirit," a revelation declared as it spoke of the sacred gifts of the Holy Ghost.[10] In this way, the Saints were to grow up in Christ until they acquired eternal life in the resurrection. Brigham Young advised: "Seek unto the Lord for his Spirit, without any cessation in your efforts, until his Spirit dwells within you like eternal burnings. Let the candle of the Lord be lighted up within you."[11]

Diversity in Manifestations of the Spirit

The divine powers and attributes of life which are given to man by the Holy Spirit are manifested in many ways, depending upon the will of God and the constitution of the individual. A revelation to Joseph Smith reaffirmed the testimony of biblical writers that there are diversities of gifts, but the same Spirit; differences of administration, but the same Lord; and diversities of operation, but the same God who worketh all in all.[12] Concerning the Holy Spirit, George Q. Cannon said: "Some men possess it to a greater extent than others." He also observed: "Some have the gift in one direction and they are capable of receiving communication from God in a direction that others are not." This is because "their minds are better prepared to receive revelation upon a given subject than the minds of others."[13] To some, the Holy Spirit may come as a vivid power that is manifested in soul-stirring reality, but the Prophet declared that to others it is "calm and serene" in its effects so that the recipient's "whole soul and body are only exercised by the pure spirit of intelligence."[14]

The several manifestations of the Spirit produce some common effects in man. They all bring him to the true knowledge of Christ, and they effect a spiritual union between man and God. In this way, they quicken man and make him alive in Christ, and the recipient begins to partake of the living attributes and powers of eternal life.

By developing in the blessings of the Spirit, man may grow up in Christ to "receive a fulness of the Holy Ghost."[15] When he achieves this objective, man is given all the living gifts, powers, attributes, and blessings of the Spirit. Of the growth of the individual in the Spirit, Brigham Young said: "The Spirit that is within him will continue to increase until it becomes like a fountain of living water; until it is like the tree of life; until it is one continued source of intelligence and instruction to that individual."[16]

Spirit of Revelation

The Spirit of revelation is one of the primary expressions of spiritual life and light within those who receive the gospel. So important is it that the Prophet declared: "Salvation cannot come without revelation; it is vain for anyone to minister without it."[17] The Lord defined the Spirit of revelation when He said:

> . . . I will tell you in your mind and in your heart, by the Holy Ghost, which shall come upon you and which shall dwell in your heart.
>
> Now, behold, this is the spirit of revelation; behold, this is the spirit by which Moses brought the children of Israel through the Red Sea on dry ground.[18]

The Prophet once defined the Spirit of revelation as

"pure intelligence flowing" into man, giving him "sudden strokes of ideas" which, when they concerned the future, would "come to pass."[19] Of his own experience with the Spirit of revelation, he wrote: "Thus saith the still small voice, which whispereth through and pierceth all things, and often times it maketh my bones to quake while it maketh manifest, saying. . . ."[20] He then recorded the divine communication.

An illustration of one of the ways the Spirit of revelation is expressed to man is found in the experience of Enos, a Nephite prophet. Having sought the Lord diligently in prayer, he said: "While I was thus struggling in the spirit, behold, *the voice of the Lord came into my mind* . . . saying. . . ."[21] Apparently this was not an audible voice in the ordinary sense of meaning, but it came to him as a manifestation of the Spirit that took the form of words in his mind.

Some prominent characteristics of the Spirit's influence are noted in the scriptures and in the experiences of the Saints. First, the Spirit of revelation as a living and intelligent power causes a burning in the bosom and a feeling of rightness within man. Having admonished Oliver Cowdery to study a problem or issue about which he desired a divine manifestation, a revelation said:

> . . . then you must ask me if it be right, and if it is right I will cause that your bosom shall burn within you; therefore, you shall feel that it is right.
>
> But if it be not right you shall have no such feelings, but you shall have a stupor of thought that shall cause you to forget the thing which is wrong; therefore, you cannot write that which is sacred save it be given you from me.[22]

In reporting the influence of the Holy Spirit upon some brethren in the Kirtland Temple, Joseph Smith spoke of the inner burning which it causes. "The quorum of the Seventy enjoyed a great flow of the Holy Spirit," he remarked. "Many arose and spoke, testifying that they were filled with the Holy Ghost, *which was like fire in their bones,* so that they could not hold their peace, but were constrained to cry hosanna to God and the Lamb, and glory in the highest."[23]

Second, the Spirit of God has an enlightening influence upon man's mind. "That which doth not edify is not of God, and is darkness," a revelation explained. "That which is of God is light; and he that receiveth light, and continueth in God, receiveth more light; and that light groweth brighter and brighter until the perfect day."[24]

Third, the Spirit of revelation prompts man to deal justly and honestly with his fellow men. A revelation admonished Hyrum Smith: "Put your trust in that Spirit which leadeth to do good—yea, to do justly, to walk humbly, to judge righteously; and this is my Spirit."[25]

Finally, a feeling of joy is inseparably associated with the manifestation of the Spirit of revelation in man. The above revelation continued: "Verily, verily, I say unto you, I will impart unto you of my Spirit, which shall enlighten your mind, which shall fill your soul with joy."[26] When the people of King Benjamin desired to enter into a covenant with Christ, the Nephite scripture therefore states: " . . . the Spirit of the Lord came upon them, and they were filled with joy."[27]

Wilford Woodruff reported that Joseph Smith taught his associates "to obtain the Holy Spirit, get acquainted with it and its operations, and listen to the whisperings of that Spirit and obey its voice, and it soon would become a principle of revelation" unto them.[28] The Prophet said of the Spirit of revelation and of man's need to develop in the principle of revelation as a means of obtaining salvation:

> A person may profit by noticing the first intimation of the spirit of revelation; for instance, when you feel pure intelligence flowing into you, it may give you sudden strokes of ideas, so that by noticing it, you may find it fulfilled the same day or soon; (i.e.) those things that were presented unto your minds by the Spirit of God, will come to pass; *and thus by learning the Spirit of God and understanding it, you may grow into the principle of revelation, until you become perfect in Christ Jesus.*[29]

By growing in the Spirit of revelation man is finally

perfected in Christ. The central truth which pertains to life is that truth which relates to the Master; and the best method man can apply to acquire truth is to learn by faith through the revelations of the Spirit. This approach to truth is far above the process of mere intellectual analysis, and its results are infinitely greater. "I assure the Saints that truth . . . can and may be known *through the revelations of God in the way of His ordinances, and in answer to prayer,"* the Prophet declared. "Could you gaze into heaven five minutes, you would know more than you would by reading all that ever was written on the subject."[30]

A revelation explained that the design of true worship is to develop in man the divine substance of truth and light, or intelligence, which is called glory, until man receives a fulness and is glorified in Christ as Christ is glorified in His Father.[31] This is merely another way of saying that man must grow in the Spirit of revelation until he achieves a fulness of the truth and light of the Father's glory. Having referred to Jesus as the Spirit of truth because He is the center of this intelligent, living substance for man, the revelation then said of Christ's acquisition of the glory and power of the Man of Holiness and of the possibility of man acquiring a fulness:

> He [Christ] received a fulness of truth, yea, even of all truth.
>
> And no man receiveth a fulness unless he keepeth his commandments.
>
> He that keepeth his commandments *receiveth truth and light, until he is glorified in truth and knoweth all things.*[32]

In a statement that in some respects is a commentary on this revelation, Joseph Smith taught the same basic doctrine. Having declared that the Father and the Son are exalted beings of Spirit, glory, and power, the Prophet spoke of this divine substance: " . . . which Spirit is shed forth upon all who believe on his [Christ's] name and keep his commandments; and all those who keep his commandments shall grow up from grace to grace, and become heirs of the heavenly kingdom, and joint heirs with Jesus Christ; possessing the same [divine] mind, being transformed into the same [divine] image or likeness, even the express image of him who fills all in all; being filled with the fullness of his glory, and becoming one in him, even as the Father, Son and Holy Spirit are one."[33] Continuing, the latter-day Seer explained: "As the Son partakes of the fullness of the Father through the Spirit, so the saints are, by the same Spirit, to be partakers of the same fullness, to enjoy the same glory; for as the Father and the Son are one, so, in like manner, the saints are to be one in them."[34]

Because of the nature of His divine operations, the Holy Ghost is referred to in revelations to Joseph Smith as "enlightening" man's mind and as imparting truth unto man "line upon line, precept upon precept."[35] "Unto him that keepeth my commandments I will give the mysteries of my kingdom," the Lord promised, "and the same shall be in him a well of *living water springing up unto everlasting life.*"[36] For this reason the Prophet could assure the Saints: "God shall give unto you knowledge by his Holy Spirit, yea, by the unspeakable gift of the Holy Ghost, that has not been revealed since the world was until now."[37] Of the faithful, a revelation declared in greater detail:

> . . . to them will I reveal all mysteries, yea, all the hidden mysteries of my kingdom from days of old, and for ages to come, will I make known unto them the good pleasure of my will concerning all things pertaining to my kingdom.
>
> Yea, even the wonders of eternity shall they know, and things to come will I show them, even the things of many generations.
>
> And their wisdom shall be great, and their understanding reach to heaven; and before them the wisdom of the wise shall perish, and the understanding of the prudent shall come to naught.
>
> *For by my Spirit will I enlighten them, and by my power will I make known unto them the secrets of my will—yea, even those things which eye has not seen, nor ear heard, nor yet entered into the heart of man.*[38]

Because the Spirit of revelation is a basic expression of divine truth and power in the life of man, the Saints could testify of the enlightening influences which came into their lives as they embraced the plan of life and salvation. Charles W. Penrose spoke for many others when he said:

> When hands were laid upon me by the servants of God, and I received the gift of the Holy Ghost, I . . . found that my mind was opened, that I had greater light; that something had come upon me by which I could see clearly the things of God; and when I read the scriptures new light dawned upon them. I was brought up to believe in the Bible. I had read it when a child, and committed a great deal of it to memory; and when I received this gift from the Almighty through the laying on of hands, it brought those things that were past to my remembrance; they stood up clearly and in bold relief before me, and I could comprehend something concerning God. I could feel that I was in communion with Him. When I prayed I could realize that my words were heard, that God hearkened and answered. When I prayed for knowledge and understanding concerning the things of God, they were manifested to me. It brought to me that which is called in the scriptures, "the peace of God that passeth all understanding." The joy, the peace, the satisfaction that it brought to me could not be described in words. I knew that my Redeemer lived; I knew that I was born again; I knew the Holy Spirit was working in my heart. Truths were manifested to me that I had never heard of or read of, but which I afterwards heard preached by the servants of the Lord; all this was testimony to me that I had received the truth. I make mention of this because I know this to be the experience of others.[39]

Since the purpose and essence of true worship is for man to obtain divine truth and light by revelation from God, Jesus admonished the Nephites: "Ye must always pray unto the Father in my name; and whatsoever ye shall ask the Father in my name, which is right, believing that ye shall receive, behold it shall be given unto you."[40] This is a standard promise given to all who receive the gospel. Moroni declared: "Behold, I say unto you that whoso believeth in Christ, doubting nothing, whatsoever he shall ask the Father in the name of Christ it shall be granted him; and this promise is unto all, even unto the ends of the earth."[41] In modern times the Lord reconfirmed this promise by stating to the Saints:

> Draw near unto me and I will draw near unto you; seek me

diligently and ye shall find me; ask, and ye shall receive; knock, and it shall be opened unto you.

Whatsoever ye ask the Father in my name it shall be given unto you, that is expedient for you;

And if ye ask anything that is not expedient for you, it shall turn unto your condemnation.[42]

Fruits of the Spirit

As man becomes a recipient of the living spiritual powers of the gospel, the fruits of the Spirit—love, joy, peace, long-suffering, gentleness, goodness, meekness, temperance, patience, etc.[43]—are developed in him and become essential expressions of his character. So important are the fruits of the Spirit that unless man acquires them he cannot become like God or dwell in the presence of God.[44] Man must mature in the living attributes of the Spirit in order to acquire eternal life—the glory of the celestial kingdom.[45] A revelation to Joseph Smith referred to these divine attributes as "the peaceable things of immortal glory."[46] Because God's glory is the manifestation of His divine attributes, the Lord equated His glory with His "goodness."[47]

Possibly the greatest attribute of God which man may acquire through the influence of the Holy Spirit is charity, which the Book of Mormon defines as the pure love of Christ.[48] Mormon wrote: "Wherefore, my beloved brethren, if ye have not charity, ye are nothing, for charity never faileth. Wherefore, cleave unto charity, which is the greatest of all, for all things must fail—but charity is the pure love of Christ, and it endureth forever; and whoso is found possessed of it at the last day, it shall be well for him."[49] Concerning the importance of charity to salvation, Moroni observed in a prayer to Christ: "Except men shall have charity they cannot inherit that place which thou hast prepared in the mansions of thy Father."[50]

Charity is a composite of several traits, attributes, and qualities of character. Mormon observed that "if a man be meek and lowly in heart, and confess by the power of the

Holy Ghost that Jesus is the Christ, he must needs have charity." These things are essential components of charity. Like the Apostle Paul, Mormon then wrote in greater detail: "And charity suffereth long, and is kind, and envieth not, and is not puffed up, seeketh not her own, is not easily provoked, thinketh no evil, and rejoiceth not in iniquity but rejoiceth in the truth, beareth all things, believeth all things, hopeth all things, endureth all things."[51] Man must have all the traits and qualities which this statement prescribes, in the degree of maturity which the gospel makes possible, if he is to possess charity. The pure love of Christ is the culmination of all the fruits, endowments, and blessings of the Spirit.

The Nephite prophets stressed that charity is not a man-made quality in those who possess it, but an endowment of the Holy Spirit, bestowed in some measure upon those who are born into the kingdom of God and thereafter increased in man by the influence of the Holy Ghost, as he grows in grace and in the knowledge of God. The fact that charity is bestowed upon man by God is graphically portrayed in Lehi's dream of the human family groping through the mist of mortal darkness toward the tree of life, the fruit of which is desirable to make man happy. Lehi also beheld a rod of iron, symbolizing the word of God, that led along the narrow path to the tree, aiding man in his quest of the fruit. The tree with its precious fruit was also symbolic. Nephi said of it: "It is *the love of God, which sheddeth itself abroad in the hearts of the children of men;* wherefore, it is the most desirable above all things . . . and the most joyous to the soul."[52] Lehi referred again to the divine origin of this pure love when he testified of God: "I have beheld his glory, and am encircled about eternally in the arms of his love."[53]

Other Book of Mormon prophets testified that man could acquire this pure and perfect love—this divine attribute of eternal life—only from Christ, through the manifestations of the Holy Spirit. Mormon wrote that "the visitation of the Holy Ghost . . . filleth [man] with hope and perfect love."[54] King Benjamin stated that only by yielding "to the enticings of the Holy Spirit" could man put off the natural man that pertains to this fallen temporal state and be "full of love."[55] Because charity was a sacred endowment which man received from God and without which he could not become like Christ, Mormon admonished: "Wherefore, my beloved brethren, pray unto the Father with *all the energy of heart, that ye may be filled with this love, which he hath bestowed upon all who are true followers of his Son,* Jesus Christ; *that ye may become the sons of God;* that when he shall appear we shall be like him."[56] Unless man prays for pure love with "all the energy" of his heart, it is not enough. He cannot become a son of God unless he acquires charity through the blessings and power of the Holy Ghost.

The love of God cannot mature in man without accompanying human effort. Mormon stressed that pure love must endure in man "by diligence unto prayer, until the end shall come, when all the Saints shall dwell with God."[57] Besides indicating that pure love comes to man from God, Lehi's dream illustrates the true relationship which exists between the righteous desires and works of man and the gifts and graces of God.[58] By expressing hope and living faith, man can follow the rod of iron, which symbolizes the word of God, along the narrow path of truth and holiness to the tree of life. As he partakes of the fruit of the tree, which symbolizes the love of God, man finds that the benefits of the sacred endowments exceed in value the effort which he has expended to obtain them. Though man's righteous desires and efforts are necessary, he is nevertheless a recipient of grace in attaining the fruits of the Spirit. And he cannot receive grace unless he exerts his will toward righteousness and applies himself to serve and love others. Only then will the Holy Spirit dwell in him and mature the love of God in him. Alma therefore admonished the people of his day to seek the Lord in faith, that they might "be led by the Holy Spirit, becoming humble, meek, submissive, patient, full of love and all long-suffering."[59]

The Prophet expressed similar views on the fruits of the Spirit. "There is a love *from God* that should be exercised toward those of our faith, who walk uprightly, *which is peculiar to itself,"* he wrote from a dungeon cell, "but it is without prejudice; it also gives scope to the mind, which enables us to conduct ourselves with greater liberality towards all that are not of our faith, than what they exercise towards one another."[60] On another occasion, he explained: "A man filled with the love of God, is not content with blessing his family alone, but ranges through the whole world, anxious to bless the whole human race."[61]

Though pure love comes from God, Joseph Smith held that man must strive to cultivate it in his life. "If we would secure and cultivate the love of others, we must love others, even our enemies as well as our friends," he declared.[62] "It is a time-honored adage that love begets love," he said. "Let us pour forth love—show forth our kindness unto all mankind, and the Lord will reward us with everlasting increase."[63] While commenting upon the need for charity, the latter-day Seer advised: "As you increase in innocence and virtue, as you increase in goodness, let your hearts expand, let them be enlarged towards others; you must be long-suffering, and bear with the faults and errors of mankind."[64] "Charity, which is love, covereth a multitude of sins," he observed, " . . . but the prettiest thing is to have no faults at all."[65]

Works of Righteousness

It is apparent from what the Prophet taught that the Holy Spirit prompts man to perform works of righteousness. As a person achieves a meaningful spiritual union with Christ and partakes of the fruits of the Spirit, his whole soul begins to be filled with the desire to serve God and his fellow men. The works of righteousness which man performs register the degree to which he has achieved a living spiritual union with Christ through the gospel.

"See that ye have faith, hope, and charity," Alma admonished, "and *then ye will always abound in good works.*"[66] This doctrine is consistent with that which the Apostle James expressed. Though he spoke of the works of righteousness, he did not suggest that of themselves they constituted the way to salvation. Instead, he placed primary emphasis upon that kind of faith which manifests itself in good works. "Shew me thy *faith* without thy works," he declared, "and I will shew thee my faith by my works."[67]

Latter-day revelations express a similar view. It has been shown earlier in this study that by service in which He did the will of His Father, Christ obtained the divine attributes and powers of eternal life, and that man must do the same.[68] Therefore, the fact that a person serves God and his fellow men in the way which is marked out by the will of God is evidence that the gospel has a meaningful place in his life. Works of righteousness are products of the spiritual life of the gospel.

Gifts of the Holy Spirit

Joseph Smith taught that through the gift of the Holy Ghost man could receive those intelligent, supernatural endowments which are called the gifts of the Holy Spirit.[69] These gifts are given to man according to his faith, subject to the will of heaven. Joseph Smith therefore expressed his belief in "the spiritual gifts according to the will of God."[70]

Concerning spiritual gifts, Orson Pratt said: "Whenever the Holy Ghost takes up its residence in a person, it not only cleanses, sanctifies, and purifies him in proportion as he yields himself to its influence, but also imparts to him some gift, intended for the benefit of himself and others." These gifts, Elder Pratt observed, are "very numerous." Having identified a score or more gifts, he said: "All these, and many too numerous to mention, are the gifts of God to the Church, through the operation and power of the Holy Ghost, shed forth upon the members thereof."[71]

There are two particular places in modern scripture in

which some of the major endowments, or gifts, of the Holy Ghost are delineated. A statement combining all these gifts is as follows:

> To some it is given by the Holy Ghost to know that Jesus Christ is the Son of God, and that he was crucified for the sins of the world.
>
> To others it is given to believe on their words, that they also might have eternal life if they continue faithful.
>
> And again, to some it is given by the Holy Ghost to know the differences of administration, as it will be pleasing unto the same Lord, according as the Lord will, suiting his mercies according to the conditions of the children of men.
>
> And again, it is given by the Holy Ghost to some to know the diversities of operations, whether they be of God, that the manifestations of the Spirit may be given to every man to profit withal.
>
> And again, verily I say unto you, to some is given, by the Spirit of God, that they may teach the word of wisdom; and to another, that he may teach the word of knowledge by the same Spirit, that all may be taught to be wise and to have knowledge;
>
> And to another, exceeding great faith;
>
> And to another, it is given to have faith to be healed;
>
> And to others it is given to have faith to heal.
>
> And again, to some is given the working of miracles;
>
> And to another, that he may prophesy concerning all things;
>
> And again, to another, the beholding of angels and ministering spirits;
>
> And to others the discerning of spirits.
>
> And again, it is given to some to speak with tongues;
>
> And to another, the interpretation of languages and of divers kinds of tongues.
>
> And all these gifts come from God, for the benefit of the children of God.
>
> And unto the bishop of the church, and unto such as God shall appoint and ordain to watch over the church and to be elders unto the church, are to have it given unto them to discern all those gifts lest there shall be any among you professing and yet be not of God; . . . that unto some it may be given to have all those gifts, that there may be a head, in order that every member may be profited thereby.[72]

Knowledge through the Spirit is given both on a dependent and an independent principle. One who has the gift of knowing that Jesus is the Christ has arrived at that state of faith and spiritual maturity of receiving knowledge through the Spirit independent of earthly agencies. He knows by the gift and power of the Holy Ghost that Jesus is the Son of God. By the power of the Spirit he may also have seen through the veil so that he knows by his own experience and is not dependent upon another's for the knowledge and assurance which he has of God. Lehi said, for example, of his son Jacob: "Thou hast beheld in thy youth his [Christ's] glory; wherefore, thou art blessed even as they unto whom he shall minister in the flesh."[73] This is the kind of knowledge which all great prophets and spiritual leaders have possessed. In this dispensation, Joseph Smith and Sidney Rigdon testified of Christ: "After the many testimonies which have been given of him, this is the testimony, last of all, which we give of him: That he lives! For we saw him, even on the right hand of God; and we heard the voice bearing record that he is the Only Begotten of the Father."[74]

In the above list, the second gift, or that of believing on another's word, is a dependent gift. This is the initial gift which most people who receive the gospel through an earthly agent must exercise—the gift of believing in the words and testimony of another. Since this is a preliminary gift and those who receive it must acquire other gifts in order to attain a fulness of celestial glory, the Lord promised that those who possess this initial gift may obtain eternal life "if they continue faithful."[75]

The next two gifts listed above are administrative gifts—gifts of the Spirit that pertain particularly (though not exclusively) to those who are called to administer the affairs of the Church. That they might aid in the spiritual development of the Saints, presiding officers of the Church may know by the Holy Ghost the differences of administration, that is how the Spirit is given to the members in their several individual conditions and degrees of progress. The Spirit adapts itself to the needs and circumstances of man; and before presiding officers can know how to aid in the spiritual development of the

Saints, they must know the differences of administration of the Spirit. Those who preside may also have the power of discerning different spiritual manifestations to determine if they come from God, so that the manifestations of the Spirit may profit every man within the system and lead him to eternal life, and so that false spiritual influences may be detected and driven out from among the Saints. "The gift of discerning spirits will be given to the Presiding Elder," Joseph Smith remarked. "Pray for him that he may have this gift."[76]

Instructional gifts are given to the Saints through the Holy Ghost, such as the gift of teaching the word of knowledge and the gift of teaching the word of wisdom. Those who possess these gifts enjoy the Spirit of revelation to a marked degree, as a means of acquiring both the knowledge which they impart to others and the power of true and right discernment. They also have the spirit of teaching by the Holy Ghost. Otherwise the precious truths which they acquire by the aid of the Spirit cannot be communicated fully and adequately to others in the wisdom and discretion which should characterize a true teacher of the gospel.

Another gift which is designed primarily to aid in teaching the gospel is the gift of tongues. "The ultimate design of tongues," Joseph Smith declared, "is to speak to foreigners."[77] Again he explained: "Tongues were given for the purpose of preaching among those whose language is not understood, as on the day of Pentecost, etc., and it is not necessary for tongues to be taught to the Church particularly, for any man that has the Holy Ghost, can speak of the things of God in his own tongue as well as to speak in another; for faith comes not by signs, but by hearing the word of God."[78]

Nevertheless, the gift of tongues may be manifested within the Church when all present have a common language so that the Saints may learn of its operation and acquire confidence in it. But here the Prophet cautioned:

> If you have a matter to reveal, let it be in your own tongue;

do not indulge too much in the exercise of the gift of tongues, or the devil will take advantage of the innocent and unwary. You may speak in tongues for your own comfort, but I lay this down for a rule, that if anything is taught by the gift of tongues, it is not to be received for doctrine.[79]

"The gift of tongues is the smallest gift perhaps of the whole, and yet it is one that is the most sought after," the latter-day Seer observed. "Be not so curious about tongues," he cautioned; "do not speak in tongues except there be an interpreter present."[80] On the latter point, he again said:

Speak not in the gift of tongues without understanding it, or without interpretation. . . . Let no one speak in tongues unless he interpret, except by the consent of the one who is placed to preside; then he may discern or interpret, or another may.[81]

The caution which Joseph Smith gave concerning the gift of tongues he extended in a general way to all the gifts of the Spirit. "The gifts of God are all useful in their place," he said, "but when they are applied to that which God does not intend, they prove an injury, a snare and a curse instead of a blessing."[82]

"All have not every gift given unto them," a revelation stated; "for there are many gifts, and to every man is given a gift by the Spirit of God."[83] Joseph Smith explained:

Paul says, "To one is given the gift of tongues, to another the gift of prophecy, and to another the gift of healing;" and again: "Do all prophesy? do all speak with tongues? do all interpret?" evidently showing that all did not possess these several gifts; but that one received one gift, and another received another gift—all did not prophesy, all did not speak in tongues, all did not work miracles; but all did receive the gift of the Holy Ghost; sometimes they spake in tongues and prophesied in the Apostles' days, and sometimes they did not. The same is the case with us also in our administrations.[84]

Having observed that "there are different ways that these gifts are administered," Moroni said: "They are given by the manifestations of the Spirit of God unto men, to profit them."[85] A revelation to Joseph Smith also stated that spiritual gifts are given "that all may be benefited that seek or that ask of me, that ask not for a sign that they may consume it upon their lusts."[86]

The divine intent is for each member of the Church, or body of Christ, to develop that which he has received so that he will grow spiritually in the divine nature of God and that others can be benefited by the use of his gift. One to whom God has given the gift of prophecy may then by its expression bless not only himself but others as well. The same is true of those who receive the gifts of wisdom, of knowledge, of healing, or any other endowment of the Spirit. As expressions of the grace of Christ unto true believers, the gifts of the Holy Ghost are to be used to bless all who will come unto God.

Not all gifts of the Holy Ghost are expressed visibly; nor are they immediately manifested when a person receives the gift of the Holy Ghost by the laying on of hands. Having cited the Apostle Paul's statement on the gifts of the Spirit,[87] Joseph Smith said:

> There are several gifts mentioned here, yet which of them all could be known by an observer at the imposition of hands? The word of wisdom, and the word of knowledge, are as much gifts as any other, yet if a person possessed both of these gifts, or received them by the imposition of hands, who would know it? Another might receive the gift of faith, and they would be as ignorant of it. Or suppose a man had the gift of healing or power to work miracles, that would not then be known; it would require time and circumstances to call these gifts into operation. Suppose a man had the discerning of spirits, who would be the wiser of it? Or if he had the interpretation of tongues, unless someone spoke in an unknown tongue, he of course would have to be silent; there are only two gifts that could be made visible—the gift of tongues and the gift of prophecy. These are things that are the most talked about, and yet if a person spoke in an unknown tongue, according to Paul's testimony, he would be a barbarian to those present. They would say that it was gibberish; and if he prophesied they would call it nonsense. . . .
>
> The greatest, the best, and the most useful gifts would be known nothing about by an observer.[88]

Gifts of the Holy Ghost are not conferred merely by

the laying on of hands; they must be sought after by prayer and faith. Having quoted the Apostle Paul on the gifts of the Spirit, Joseph Smith reasoned:

> It is very evident from these Scriptures that many of them [the early Christians] had not spiritual gifts, for if they had spiritual gifts where was the necessity of Paul telling them to follow after them, and it is as evident that they did not all receive those gifts by the imposition of the hands; for they as a Church had been baptized and confirmed by the laying on of hands—and yet to a Church of this kind, under the immediate inspection and superintendency of the Apostles, it was necessary for Paul to say, "Follow after charity, and desire spiritual gifts, but rather that ye may prophesy," evidently showing that those gifts were in the Church, but not enjoyed by all in their outward manifestations.[89]

A revelation admonished the Saints to ask "in Spirit," that they might receive the gifts of the Holy Ghost; and the divine promise was: "He that asketh in Spirit shall receive in Spirit." Continuing, the revelation explained: "He that asketh in the Spirit asketh according to the will of God; wherefore it is done even as he asketh." But this was not all, for it stated: "And ye must practice virtue and holiness before me continually."[90]

Joseph Smith taught that the gifts of the Spirit which a person possesses register the degree of his faith. "A man who has none of the gifts has no faith; and he deceives himself, if he supposes he has," the Prophet explained. "Faith has been wanting, not only among the heathen, but in professed Christendom also, so that tongues, healings, prophecy, and prophets and apostles, and all the gifts and blessings have been wanting."[91] Orson Pratt stressed: "A person who is without a spiritual gift has not the Spirit of God dwelling in him, in a sufficient degree, to save him; he cannot be called a Saint, or a child of God; for all Saints who constitute the Church of Christ, are baptized into the same Spirit; and each one, without any exception, is made a partaker of some spiritual gift."[92]

The Book of Mormon stresses that the gifts of the Spirit are the natural products of the gospel in man; and if they are lacking, the power of redemption is not manifested in his life. Moroni wrote of spiritual gifts: "He that denieth these things knoweth not the gospel of Christ; yea, he has not read the scriptures; if so, he does not understand them." Spiritual gifts cease, the Nephite prophet stressed, only when men "dwindle in unbelief, and depart from the right way, and know not the God in whom they should trust."[93] Again he declared:

> . . . now I speak unto all the ends of the earth—that if the day cometh that the power and gifts of God shall be done away among you, it shall be because of unbelief.
>
> And wo be unto the children of men if this be the case; for there shall be none that doeth good among you, no not one. For if there be one among you that doeth good, he shall work by the power and gifts of God.
>
> And wo unto them who shall do these things away and die, for they die in their sins, and they cannot be saved in the kingdom of God; and I speak it according to the words of Christ; and I lie not.[94]

Mormon also emphasized that if a man rejects the gifts of the Spirit he must die in his sins, because he will not have access to Christ's atonement unto the remission of them. "No man can be saved, according to the words of Christ, save they shall have faith in his name," he declared; "wherefore, if these things [the gifts of the Spirit, which are natural products of saving faith] have ceased, then has faith ceased also; and awful is the state of man, for *they are as though there had been no redemption made.*"[95]

The emphatic declarations found in the Book of Mormon indicate that God works "by power, according to the faith of the children of men, the same today, and tomorrow, and forever."[96] This is the only way the divine nature of God can be developed in man, for God's glory is His power which is in and through all things; and to be matured in man, it must be manifested in him with its supernatural gifts. Otherwise there can be no redemption to eternal life. Joseph Smith stressed this point when an inquirer asked: "May I not repent and be baptized, and not pay any attention to dreams, visions, and other gifts and graces of the Spirit?" In reply the Prophet likened these divine endowments of the Spirit to the food required to sustain the physical body and cause it to grow, concluding that in like manner the spiritual gifts are necessary in order to develop and mature the divine nature of God within man.[97]

Though it was intended that every person should receive and exercise at least one spiritual gift, there was to be room in the Church for those with little capacity to express the kind of faith that is required to obtain the greater gifts of the Spirit, but who sought to do the will of God in their lives. Reference has been made to the initial gift which man must exercise to enter the kingdom of God—the gift to believe on the testimony of another person.[98] There was to be a place in the Church for all who would receive the blessings of the Spirit down to and including this initial gift. Having explained that all who had faith to be healed could be healed—the blind, the deaf, the lame, etc.—a revelation added: "And they who have not faith to do these things, but believe in me, have power to become my sons; and inasmuch as they break not my laws thou shalt bear their infirmities."[99] These infirmities were not physical only, but spiritual. Of the physical care such ailing members were to receive, the revelation said: "Whosoever among you are sick, and have not faith to be healed, but believe, shall be nourished with all tenderness, with herbs and mild food."[100] Acting on these and related principles, the High Council in Missouri corrected Lyman Wight for teaching "that medicine administered to the sick is of the devil; for the sick in the Church ought to live by faith."[101]

The fact that the gifts of the Spirit are given by the Holy Ghost to those who ask in Spirit precludes the possibility that the world in general can comprehend and appreciate them. For this reason, and because of the world's unworthiness, spiritual gifts were not, as a general rule, to be displayed before unbelievers. A revelation cautioned: "Remember that that which cometh from above is sacred, and must be spoken with care, and by constraint of the Spirit; and in this there is no condemnation."[102] Having discussed the lack of understanding in the world, Joseph Smith said of the personal and sacred nature of spiritual gifts and manifestations:

> . . . we shall finally have to come to the same conclusion that Paul did—"No man knows the things of God but by the Spirit of God;" for with the great revelations of Paul when he was caught up into the third heaven and saw things that were not lawful to utter, no man was apprised of it until he mentioned it himself fourteen years after; and when John had the curtains of heaven withdrawn, and by vision looked through the dark vista of future ages, and contemplated events that should transpire throughout every subsequent period of time, until the final winding up scene—while he gazed upon the glories of the eternal world, saw an innumerable company of angels and heard the voice of God—it was in the Spirit, on the Lord's day, unnoticed and unobserved by the world.
>
> The manifestations of the gift of the Holy Ghost, the ministering of angels, or the development of the power, majesty or glory of God were very seldom manifested publicly, and that generally to the people of God, as to the Israelites. . . .[103]

The kingdom of God cannot be recognized in all instances by the outward display of divine gifts and powers. The Prophet explained:

> There is a difference between the kingdom of God and the fruits and blessings that flow from the kingdom; because there were more miracles, gifts, visions, healings, tongues, &c., in the days of Jesus Christ and His apostles, and on the day of Pentecost, than under John's administration, it does not prove by any means that John [the Baptist] had not the kingdom of God, any more than it would that a woman had not a milkpan because she had not a pan of milk, for while the pan might be compared to the kingdom, the milk might be compared to the blessings of the kingdom.[104]

Summary

Joseph Smith taught that the living and intelligent manifestations of the Holy Spirit are many and varied in the lives of those who obey the gospel with full purpose of heart. In one of its basic expressions, the Spirit is a source of revelation to man—the channel through which man may receive the truth and light that leads to glorification in the presence of God. It follows, therefore, that if man is to attain eternal life he must grow in the principle of revelation until he becomes perfect in Christ.

The Spirit also develops its divine fruits—the attributes of deity—in man. One of the most precious endowments of the Spirit is that pure love which is called charity. By regenerating man spiritually and by filling him with the pure love of God, the Spirit also enables man to live outside of himself in service and genuine interest toward others, so that works of righteousness are also products of the spiritual life of the gospel.

Another major function of the Holy Spirit is to bestow upon man those supernatural endowments called gifts of the Holy Ghost. Each member of the Church should possess one or more gifts of the Holy Ghost. By exercising the gifts which he has and by acquiring other spiritual gifts, man can mature in the powers and blessings of the Spirit toward eternal life. Not all gifts, however, are outwardly or visibly manifested. Having embraced the gospel, man must grow in grace until, eventually, he acquires the fulness of the Spirit in the resurrection and is glorified in Christ, as Christ is glorified in the Father. This is the plan of life which the gospel opens to man.

Notes

1. See, for example, D&C 10:70; 11:28; 12:9; 34:2; 39:2; 45:7.

2. See the section in chapter seven entitled "Purpose of Rebirth." Of the gospel, John Taylor said: "It is the principle that brings life and immortality to light."—JD, XXI, p. 94.

3. See Volume I of this study, the sections in chapter eight entitled "Eternal Life" and "Christ As Our God."

4. I. R., John 1:4, 17–18.

5. 2 Nephi 25:27.

6. MA, I (December, 1834), p. 38. The writer stated: "Let the reader compare Matthew 28:19, 20, with Mark 16:15, 16, 17, 18—Luke 24:45, 46, 47, 48, with the second chapter of the acts of the apostles and he will be enabled to see and understand the apostolic commission without either priest or commentator."—*Ibid.*

7. See John 15.
8. HC, IV, p. 478.
9. John 15:1–2.
10. D&C 46:28.
11. JD, VII, p. 138.
12. D&C 46:11, 16. See, for example, 1 Corinthians 12:4–6.
13. JD, XXI, pp. 75–76.
14. HC, III, p. 380. See also JD, XI, p. 10; XII, p. 270.
15. D&C 109:15. The Prophet prayed on behalf of a man and his wife who desired to do right: "'May they have the light of eternal truth continually springing up in them like a well of living water; may . . . their faith increase from day to day until they shall have power to lay hold on the blessings of God and the gifts of the Spirit until they are satisfied."—HC, VI, p. 265.
16. JD, III, p. 192.
17. HC, III, p. 389.
18. D&C 8:2–3.
19. HC, III, p. 381.
20. D&C 85:6.
21. Enos 1:10.
22. D&C 9:8–9.
23. HC, II, p. 392.
24. D&C 50:23–24.
25. D&C 11:12. For a further treatment of this subject, see Volume I of this study, the section in chapter ten entitled "Christ's Holy Spirit Leads Man Upward to God."
26. D&C 11:13–14.
27. Mosiah 4:3.
28. Wilford Woodruff, *Leaves From My Journal* (Salt Lake City, 1881), pp. 86–87.
29. HC, III, p. 381.
30. *Ibid.,* VI, pp. 50–51.
31. See D&C 93:19–20 in conjunction with verses 11 through 17.
32. D&C 93:26–28.
33. *Lectures on Faith,* No. 5. Though in this lecture the Prophet does not speak specifically of that divine personage who is called the Holy Spirit, it is excellent on the purpose of the gospel.
34. *Ibid.*
35. D&C 11:12–13; 98:12.
36. D&C 63:23.
37. D&C 121:26.
38. D&C 76:7–10.
39. JD, XXIII, p. 351.
40. 3 Nephi 18:19–20.
41. Mormon 9:21. Continuing, Moroni admonished: "Be wise in the days of your probation; strip yourselves of all uncleanness; ask not, that ye may consume it on your lusts, but ask with a firmness unshaken, that ye will yield to no temptation, but that ye will serve the true and living God."—Mormon 9:28.
42. D&C 88:63–65.
43. See Galatians 5:22.

44. 2 Nephi 26:30; Alma 7:24; Ether 12:28–37; Moroni 7:44–47; 10:20–21.

45. D&C 88:3–4.

46. Moses 6:61.

47. Exodus 33:18–23.

48. See Ether 12:34; Moroni 7:47.

49. Moroni 7:46–47.

50. Ether 12:34.

51. Moroni 8:44–45.

52. 1 Nephi 11:22–23.

53. 2 Nephi 1:15.

54. Moroni 8:25.

55. Mosiah 3:19.

56. Moroni 7:48.

57. Moroni 8:25.

58. See 1 Nephi 8; 11:22–25.

59. Alma 13:28.

60. HC, III, p. 304. He observed: "It is one evidence that men are unacquainted with the principles of godliness to behold the contraction of affectionate feelings and lack of charity in the world."—*Ibid.,* V, p. 24.

61. *Ibid.,* IV, p. 227.

62. *Ibid.,* V, p. 498.

63. *Ibid.,* p. 517.

64. *Ibid.,* IV, p. 606.

65. *Ibid.,* V, p. 517.

66. Alma 7:14. See also Mosiah 5:15; Ether 12:4.

67. James 2:18.

68. D&C 93:12–13, 19–20. See Volume I of this study, the section in chapter eight entitled "Service the Pathway to Eternal Life."

69. HC, V, pp. 27–28.

70. *Ibid.,* III, p. 30.

71. *Masterful Discourses of Orson Pratt,* ed. N. B. Lundwall (Salt Lake City, nd), pp. 539–540.

72. D&C 46:13–27; Moroni 10:9–17. The writer has combined the statements in these two sources in making the above list.

73. 2 Nephi 2:4.

74. D&C 76:22–23.

75. D&C 46:14.

76. HC, III, p. 392.

77. *Ibid.,* V, p. 31.

78. *Ibid.,* III, p. 379. See also *ibid.,* IV, pp. 485–486.

79. *Ibid.,* IV, p. 607.

80. *Ibid.,* V, pp. 30–31. Writing to the brethren in Missouri, the Prophet said:

> As to the gift of tongues, all we can say is, that in this place we have received it as the ancients did: we wish you, however, to be careful, lest in this you be deceived. Guard against evils which may arise from any accounts given by women, or otherwise; be careful in all things lest any root of bitterness spring up among you, and thereby many be defiled. Satan will

no doubt trouble you about the gift of tongues, unless you are careful; you cannot watch him too closely, nor pray too much.—*Ibid.,* I, p. 369.

81. *Ibid.,* III, p. 392.
82. *Ibid.,* V, pp. 31–32.
83. D&C 46:11.
84. HC, V, p. 28.
85. Moroni 10:8.
86. D&C 46:8–9. "To some is given one [gift], and to some another," the revelation declared, "that all may be profited thereby."—D&C 46:12.
87. See 1 Corinthians 12:4–11.
88. HC, V, pp. 29–30.
89. *Ibid.,* p. 28.
90. D&C 46:28, 30, 33.
91. HC, V, p. 218.
92. *Masterful Discourses of Orson Pratt,* pp. 539–540.
93. Mormon 9:7–8, 20.
94. Moroni 10:24–26.
95. Moroni 7:38.
96. Moroni 10:7.
97. HC, V, pp. 218–219.
98. See again D&C 46:14.
99. D&C 42:48–52.
100. D&C 42:43.
101. *Journal History,* August 21, 1834.
102. D&C 63:64.
103. HC, V, pp. 30–31.
104. *Ibid.,* p. 258.

10

The Law of the Gospel

> *My beloved brethren, after ye have gotten into this straight and narrow path, I would ask if all is done? Behold, I say unto you, Nay; for ye have not come thus far save it were by the word of Christ with unshaken faith in him, relying wholly upon the merits of him who is mighty to save.*
>
> *Wherefore, ye must press forward with a steadfastness in Christ, having a perfect brightness of hope, and a love of God and of all men.*—NEPHI.

Joseph Smith taught the Saints that the gospel is not only a means of receiving divine truth and power, but a program of right action and conduct. As he spoke of this phase of the plan of life and salvation, the Prophet cited the admonition of Peter to add to one's faith "virtue, knowledge, temperence, patience, godliness, [and] brotherly kindness." "If these things be in you, and abound," he quoted the ancient apostle, "they make you that ye shall neither be barren nor unfruitful in the knowledge of our Lord Jesus Christ."[1] Only by growing in the knowledge of Christ, as that knowledge is given to man through the Spirit and as he applies the above admonition, can man be saved.

Sermon On The Mount

Gospel Context of the Sermon

Latter-day revelation makes it plain that Christ's teachings in the Sermon on the Mount are set in the context of the gospel; and they reveal the standard of conduct which is required of those who embrace the plan of life and salvation. When Jesus delivered the Sermon on the Mount to the Nephites, He gave important clarifications to this effect. By revelation, Joseph Smith also made revisions in Matthew's account of that classic statement which give significant insight into the meaning of this greatest of all gospel sermons.

Before Jesus delivered the Sermon on the Mount to the Nephites, He taught them that the basic program of the gospel is the "rock" upon which all things must be built in His church.[2] According to Joseph Smith's Inspired Revision of the Bible, Christ also prefaced His sermon to the Jews with a statement of the basic program of the gospel.[3] When the Lord's discourse is seen in this context, two things are apparent: first, the teachings in the sermon are designed to aid those who receive the gospel to develop the attributes and powers of the Holy Spirit in their lives;[4] second, the full standard and ideal of Christian conduct which is set forth in that sermon can be achieved successfully only when man is strengthened and uplifted in his righteous desires by the enlightening and sanctifying power of the Spirit as it is given to him through the gospel. Not only did Jesus teach that man should be perfect as the Father is perfect,[5] but He opened up the channels of divine truth and power by which that standard of perfection can be made possible.[6] Though the Sermon on the Mount contains many universal truths which may serve as ideals for all men, it is clear from its gospel context that it pertains primarily to those who accept Christ in baptism. More than mere ideals, the teachings in this sermon must become a practical standard of conduct for those who embrace the gospel, if they are to attain salvation. "Verily I say unto you," Jesus said to the Nephites, "that except ye shall keep my commandments, which I have commanded you at this time, ye shall in no case enter into the kingdom of heaven."[7]

Place of Beatitudes in the Gospel

Both the Nephite version of the beatitudes and Joseph Smith's Inspired Revision of Matthew's account contain preliminary statements, or beatitudes, which the account in the New Testament does not give. These preliminary beatitudes are the foundation of all the other beatitudes, and they make clear the gospel context in which the remaining beatitudes were meant to be understood. Having taught the Nephites the gospel,[8] Jesus said concerning His ordained disciples, or Apostles:

> *Blessed are ye if ye shall give heed unto the words of these twelve* whom I have chosen from among you to minister unto you, and to be your servants; and unto them I have given power that they may baptize you with water; and after that ye are baptized with water, behold, I will baptize you with fire and with the Holy Ghost; therefore *blessed are ye if ye shall believe in me and be baptized,* after that ye have seen me and know that I am.
>
> And again, more *blessed are they who shall believe in your words because that ye shall testify that ye have seen me,* and that ye know that I am. Yea, *blessed are they who shall believe in your words, and come down into the depths of humility and be baptized,* for they shall be visited with fire and with the Holy Ghost, and shall receive a remission of their sins.[9]

After these introductory beatitudes, Christ's sermon to the Nephites seems to be worded in such a way that each subsequent beatitude becomes an extension of these initial beatitudes, thereby showing the several qualities which man may acquire by applying the gospel in his life.

In the first subordinate beatitude which Jesus gave, He said: "*Yea,* blessed are the poor in spirit *who come unto me,* for theirs is the kingdom of heaven."[10] The introductory term "yea" is a transitional word which ties this beatitude to Christ's previous statement regarding the blessedness of those who are baptized and receive the Holy Ghost, thus expanding the meaning of that prior statement to mean that they who receive the gospel and utilize its divine truth and power to become poor in spirit (poor in the spirit of the world or of the unregenerated man) shall inherit the kingdom of heaven by coming unto Him. The stipulation that man must come unto Jesus confirms the assertion that he must embrace the gospel as the Master explained it to the Nephites if he is to attain the kingdom of heaven. Being poor in the spirit of the world then leads to being rich in the spirit and power of the gospel. Brigham Young explained that the poor in spirit are those who divest themselves of the characteristics of the world—pride, arrogance, vanity, etc.—so that they feel their dependence upon Christ and realize that only in and through Him can they acquire that which leads to strength and salvation. He said:

> Jesus had no other meaning than simply, blessed are they who have the light of revelation to understand the providences of God, and to know Him and themselves.
>
> The rich that He and other writers have referred to . . . are those who trust in the riches of this world, and forget their God. . . .
>
> The Lord loves those who trust in Him, *who feel their dependence upon Him, and feel and understand their own weakness and inability, who are thankful for their organization, and have full confidence in the providences of the Lord, trusting in His mercy and goodness to bring them off conquerors.*[11]

In the second subordinate beatitude, Jesus said: "*And again,* blessed are all they that mourn, for they shall be comforted."[12] The introductory expression "and again" ties this beatitude to the previous statements of the Master and thereby establishes its proper gospel framework. Given this context, the beatitude assumes that little comfort can be extended to the natural man who mourns without an enlightened hope in Christ. But in referring to those who have received the gospel and are brought to mourn, Jesus declared that they shall be comforted. This is one of the functions of the Holy Ghost which man receives in the gospel; and for this reason the Holy Ghost is called the Comforter. At the funeral services of Lorenzo D. Barnes, the Prophet exclaimed: "Hosanna, hosanna, hosanna to Almighty God, that rays of light begin to burst forth upon us."[13] Though the Saints are not immune from sorrow in this world, they may be sustained above its baneful influences by the enlightening powers of the Spirit in their lives. Sorrow may then be swallowed up in a hope that is made real by the comforting assurances of the Spirit. Meanwhile, sorrow, mourning, and disappointment teach the faithful who live in spiritual union with Christ the need for continual reliance upon Him; experiences which bring sorrow can be the means of perfecting the bond of spiritual union between the faithful and God, and can develop in them the attributes of patience and trust.

In the third subordinate beatitude, Jesus declared: "*And* blessed are the meek, for they shall inherit the earth."[14] The coordinate conjunction "and" again seems to tie this beatitude to the previous declarations of the Savior so that it establishes the framework in which the beatitude is to be understood. It then becomes apparent that a meek person is one who has tamed his unruly impulses, conquered his worldly aspirations and pride, and subdued the corruption in his flesh by utilizing the transforming power of the gospel in his life. When Joseph Smith was in Springfield, Illinois, on one occasion, some people expressed the opinion that he was not a very meek prophet. The latter-day Seer reported:

> I told them: "I am meek and lowly in heart," and will personify Jesus for a moment, to illustrate the principle, and cried out with a loud voice, "Woe unto you, ye doctors; woe unto you, ye lawyers; woe unto you, ye scribes, Pharisees, and hypocrites!" But you cannot find the place where I ever went that I found fault with their food, their drink, their house, their lodgings; no, never; and this is what is meant by the meekness and lowliness of Jesus.[15]

A meek person is free from the haughtiness, pride, and arrogance of the world; he possesses a gentle and long-suffering disposition, and is submissive and compliant to the will of God. Many revelations admonished the Saints to develop this quality in their lives.[16] True meekness brings a spiritual quality to man which is a principle of peace and power within him. "Walk in the meekness of my Spirit," a revelation admonished, "and you shall have peace in me."[17] The meek have power to possess the earth. Nephi observed that God continually raises up righteous nations and destroys the nations of the wicked.[18] But more than this, those who receive and apply the gospel in their lives have the promise that they will inherit the earth when it is made into a glorified celestial sphere in the resurrection. "After it hath filled the measure of its creation, it shall be crowned with glory, even with the presence of God the Father," a revelation said of the earth; "that bodies who are of the celestial kingdom may possess it forever and ever; for, for this intent was it made and created, and for this intent are they sanctified."[19] Only the meek will have power to inherit the earth in that future day.[20]

On the Western hemisphere and in Joseph Smith's Inspired Revision of Matthew's account, Jesus expressed the fourth subordinate beatitude as follows: "*And* blessed are all they who do hunger and thirst after righteousness, for they shall be filled *with the Holy Ghost.*"[21] Again the coordinate conjunction "and" seems to bind this beatitude to all that goes before it; and the promise that those Saints who hunger and thirst after righteousness shall be filled with the Holy Ghost assumes that their desire to attain the righteousness of God is accompanied by obedience to the ordinances of the gospel. Only by combining righteous desires with acceptance of God's holy ordinances can man be filled with the Holy Ghost. In expressing a similar point, a revelation said: "He that prayeth, whose spirit is contrite, the same is accepted of me, if he obey mine ordinances."[22] To be filled in this manner with the Holy Ghost is the only way the desires of the righteous can be satisfied, for it is through the manifestations of the Spirit that all things pertaining to life and godliness are to be given unto them.

In expressing the fifth subordinate beatitude, Jesus

said: "*And* blessed are the merciful, for they shall obtain mercy."[23] By binding this beatitude to His previous statements, Jesus implied that mercy is also a quality that can be developed within man through the influence of the gospel. Mercy is akin to love and springs as a by-product of that parent attribute which is matured in man through the Holy Spirit.[24] In declaring that the merciful shall find mercy, Jesus expressed the great principle of retribution that man will be judged by the same standard by which he judges others. Joseph Smith said of the subject of mercy:

> Suppose that Jesus Christ and holy angels should object to us on frivolous things, what would become of us? We must be merciful to one another, and overlook small things. . . .
>
> Christ was condemned by the self-righteous Jews because He took sinners into His society; He took them upon the principle that they repented of their sins. . . . Nothing is so much calculated to lead people to forsake sin as to take them by the hand, and watch over them with tenderness. When persons manifest the least kindness and love to me, O what power it has over my mind, while the opposite course has a tendency to harrow up all the harsh feelings and depress the human mind.
>
> It is one evidence that men are unacquainted with the principles of godliness to behold the contraction of affectionate feelings and lack of charity in the world. The power and glory of godliness is spread out on a broad principle to throw out the mantle of charity. God does not look on sin with allowance, but when men have sinned, there must be allowance made for them.
>
> All the religious world is boasting of righteousness: it is the doctrine of the devil to retard the human mind, and hinder our progress, by filling us with self-righteousness. The nearer we get to our heavenly Father, the more we are disposed to look with compassion on perishing souls; we feel that we want to take them upon our shoulders, and cast their sins behind our backs. My talk is intended for all. . . . If you would have God have mercy on you, have mercy on one another.[25]

The sixth subordinate beatitude Jesus gave as follows: "*And* blessed are all the pure in heart, for they shall see God."[26] The word in italics implies that Christ again placed this beatitude in its gospel context, and He indicates that only by utilizing the sanctifying power of the Holy Ghost can man become pure in heart. One may be *honest in heart* before he embraces the gospel, but it requires the manifestations of the Spirit to make him *pure in heart* to the degree which is required by the law of God in the plan of salvation. Since the great purpose of the gospel is to sanctify man so that he can return to the presence of God and behold His face,[27] those who utilize the Holy Spirit to purify themselves from all sin may expect to realize the promise associated with this beatitude.

In stating the next beatitude, Jesus said: "*And* blessed are all the peacemakers, for they shall be called the children of God."[28] This beatitude, like the former ones, was to be understood in the context of the gospel. Christ is the Prince of Peace.[29] But the peace which He gives to the Saints is not given in the way the world seeks to establish peace. The peace to which Christ referred comes only through the Holy Ghost. Men in the world may endeavor to alleviate stress and strain between individuals and nations in worthwhile ways, but there are no true peacemakers in the sense that Jesus designated them except those who teach the true gospel of Christ and administer its saving ordinances to men. Thereby the power of the Holy Ghost, with its divine fruits and blessings, is given to man, and by partaking of "the peaceable things of immortal glory"[30] through the Spirit, man can achieve that kind of peace which is found only in Christ. True peacemakers are those who become the children of God—those who have been born into the kingdom of God and who publish the gospel to others. Having referred to those who are the children of Christ in the gospel, Abinadi said: " . . . these are they who have published peace, who have brought good tidings of good, who have published salvation; and said unto Zion: Thy God reigneth!"[31]

The Lord's declaration that all peacemakers shall be called the children of God may also imply that those who truly seek for peace will necessarily develop the peaceable fruits and attributes of the Spirit in their lives. As man responds to the Spirit, he is led unto Christ; and if those who truly seek for peace continue to cultivate the blessings of the Spirit in their lives, they will be brought unto God, even the Father, and learn of the covenant by which they can become sons and daughters of Jesus Christ.[32] Either on earth or in the world to come, true peacemakers will become the children of God.

Though Matthew's report of the Sermon on the Mount merely states in the final beatitude that they are blessed who are persecuted for righteousness sake, the Nephite version of this beatitude and Joseph Smith's Inspired Revision of Matthew's account indicate that Christ is the center of all righteousness. To His disciples on the Western hemisphere, Jesus said: "*And* blessed are all they who are persecuted *for my name's sake,* for theirs is the kingdom of heaven."[33] Taken in its designated context, this statement assumes that the attributes of righteousness which are enumerated in all the preceding beatitudes come to man from Christ by man's obedience to His gospel. By taking upon themselves the name of Jesus Christ and by receiving the enlightening and regenerating powers of His Holy Spirit, those who accept the gospel are made partakers of His righteousness. For this reason they are persecuted. The abuse and ridicule which they receive from the world bear witness that they are not of the world. And as the reward of their continued faithfulness, they shall be given the kingdom of heaven. This is a fitting benediction to the list of beatitudes. In reiterating this beatitude, Jesus added: "For ye shall have great joy and be exceeding glad, for great shall be your reward in heaven; for so persecuted they the prophets who were before you."[34]

On the assumption that His disciples would receive the gospel and develop the fruits, gifts, and blessings of the Holy Spirit in their lives, Jesus said:

> Verily, verily, I say unto you, I give unto you to be the salt of the earth; but if the salt shall lose its savor wherewith shall the earth be salted? The salt shall be thenceforth good for nothing, but to be cast out and to be trodden under foot of men.
>
> Verily, verily, I say unto you, I give unto you to be the light of this people. A city that is set on a hill cannot be hid.
>
> Behold, do men light a candle and put it under a bushel?

Nay, but on a candlestick, and it giveth light to all that are in the house;

Therefore let your light so shine before this people, that they may see your good works and glorify your Father who is in heaven.[35]

Law of the Gospel Contrasted to Law of Moses

Jesus next turned His attention to the law of Moses and contrasted the requirements of that law to the standard of conduct which is set forth in the law of the gospel. The preparatory gospel which Moses gave Israel did not include the gift of the Holy Ghost.[36] But in giving His disciples the Holy Ghost, Jesus revealed a higher standard of personal conduct to them. He first spoke of the law of the gospel concerning anger:

> Ye have heard that it hath been said by them of old time, and it is also written before you, that thou shalt not kill, and whosoever shall kill shall be in danger of the judgment of God;
>
> But I say unto you, that whosoever is angry with his brother shall be in danger of his judgment. And whosoever shall say to his brother, Raca, shall be in danger of the council; and whosoever shall say, Thou fool, shall be in danger of hell fire.
>
> Therefore, if ye shall come unto me, or shall desire to come unto me, and rememberest that thy brother hath aught against thee—
>
> Go thy way unto thy brother, and first be reconciled to thy brother, and then come unto me with full purpose of heart, and I will receive you.[37]

The law of Moses with its injunction against killing sought merely to control man's outward acts. But, by following the law of the gospel, man could sanctify his feelings and emotions by the power of the Spirit and thus avoid anger and reproachful speech.

Jesus next spoke of the gospel law governing the reconciliation of man to his fellow man. In the event a disciple was at fault so that his adversary had claim upon him, Jesus admonished him to admit it quickly and turn from the course of error lest judgment come upon him. The Master said:

> Agree with thine adversary quickly while thou art in the way with him, lest at any time he shall get thee, and thou shalt be cast into prison.
>
> Verily, verily, I say unto thee, thou shalt by no means come out hence until thou hast paid the uttermost senine. And while ye are in prison can ye pay even one senine? Verily, verily, I say unto you, Nay.[38]

Continuing, Jesus referred to the law of the gospel as it applies to virtuous thought. Having stated that the old law forbade adultery, He said: "But I say unto you, that whosoever looketh on a woman to lust after her, hath committed adultery already in his heart." The law of Christ requires man to become pure in heart through the sanctifying influence of the Holy Spirit. The Lord therefore instructed: "Behold, I give unto you a commandment, that ye suffer none of these things to enter into your heart; for it is better that ye should deny yourselves of these things, wherein ye will take up your cross, than that ye should be cast into hell."[39] According to the Prophet's Inspired Revision of Matthew, Jesus explained: "For a man to take up his cross, is to deny himself all ungodliness, and every worldly lust, and keep my commandments."[40]

The Nephite account of this statement, unlike that of Matthew, does not imply that a person should actually pluck out an offending eye or cut off an unruly hand rather than use the member of his body to commit transgression.[41] The reason for this omission may be that the Nephites did not need the added emphasis that Christ's Jewish disciples did. In the Western hemisphere, the kingdom of God was established and its righteous influence extended throughout the land. But in Palestine, Christ's disciples were confronted with the apostate standards and practices of the Jewish system and the carnality of the Roman world. However, Joseph Smith's Inspired Revision of the Bible, after repeating the above injunction concerning adultery which Jesus gave to the Nephites, clarifies Matthew's report by stating:

> Wherefore, if thy right eye offend thee, pluck it out and cast it from thee: for it is profitable for thee that one of thy members

should perish, and not that thy whole body should be cast into hell.

Or if thy right hand offend thee, cut it off and cast it from thee; for it is profitable for thee that one of thy members should perish, and not that thy whole body should be cast into hell.

And now *this I speak, a parable concerning your sins;* wherefore, cast them from you, that ye may not be hewn down and cast into the fire.[42]

By giving the above injunction as a parable, Jesus stressed the seriousness of transgressions of a sexual nature without really stating that man should dismember his body. Sexual sin constitutes a perversion of the most sacred and far-reaching physical endowment which God has given to man. By the prostitution of this endowment, a saint may forfeit his claim to eternal life. A revelation to Joseph Smith declared: "He that looketh upon a woman to lust after her shall deny the faith, and shall not have the Spirit; and if he repents not he shall be cast out."[43] Because of the seriousness of this kind of transgression, Jesus commanded the Nephites to cast such things away from them, that they might not be brought down to hell.

Jesus next spoke of divorce. Moses permitted a man to put away his wife if he gave her "a writing of divorcement."[44] But the Lord declared: "I say unto you, that whosoever shall put away his wife, saving for the cause of fornication, causeth her to commit adultery; and whoso shall marry her who is divorced committeth adultery."[45] Christ's law governing divorce has its basis in the sanctity of the sexual relationship and in the provision that marriage should continue for time and all eternity.[46] When Jesus expressed this statement on divorce, His disciples said: "If the case of the man be so with a wife, it is not good to marry." But Christ replied: "All cannot receive this saying; it is not for them save to whom it is given."[47] It seemed to apply, therefore, only to those who received the Lord's law of marriage.

If those who were united in the new and everlasting covenant of marriage truly lived the gospel so that they were guided by the light and inspiration of the Holy Spirit as they entered into that sacred relationship, and if they applied the gospel in their lives thereafter, the union would endure forever. When marriage was viewed in this light, man had no right to put away his wife by the provision of God's law, unless she committed fornication.[48] Otherwise the union was indissoluble with respect to man's right to put away his wife by divorce.[49] If he disregarded the binding power of God's law and put away his wife unjustifiably, he would cause her to commit adultery if she married again. The man who married her without a proper cancellation of the former contract would also commit adultery.

Jesus then directed His attention to the gospel law of personal integrity in keeping one's word. In showing the distinction between the law given by Moses and the law of the gospel, He said:

> And again it is written, thou shalt not forswear thyself, but shall perform unto the Lord thine oaths;
>
> But verily, verily, I say unto you, swear not at all; neither by heaven, for it is God's throne;
>
> Nor by the earth, for it is his footstool;
>
> Neither shalt thou swear by the head, because thou canst not make one hair black or white;
>
> But let your communication be Yea, yea; Nay, nay; for whatsoever cometh of more than these is evil.[50]

In the Mosaic dispensation, the taking of oaths was approved as a means of attesting to the truth of a statement or to one's determination to keep a pledge.[51] Oaths were often made in the name of the Lord; and when expressed by the righteous, they could be relied upon with absolute assurance. For example, Nephi, his life in grave danger, sought to persuade Laban's servant, Zoram, to go with him into the desert. "I spake unto him, even with an oath," he reported, "that he need not fear." When Zoram "made an oath" in turn, promising his support, Nephi's fears ceased concerning him.[52]

But Jesus revealed a higher standard of truthfulness and personal integrity. In this standard, simplicity and straight-forwardness in speech were to characterize those who received the gospel. *Yea* was to mean *Yea,* and *Nay* was to mean *Nay.* No oath was to be required; and man's word was to be as true and accurate as though he had spoken it with a sacred oath.

Jesus next set forth the law of the gospel on patience and forebearance. In the system of justice which Moses established, an offended person could require by the process of law an eye for an eye and a tooth for a tooth, or its equivalent in value, of one who injured him. This was a law of just and equitable retribution. But of the law of the gospel, Jesus said to the Nephites:

> . . . I say unto you, that ye shall not resist evil, but whosoever shall smite thee on thy right cheek, turn to him the other also;
>
> And if any man will sue thee at the law and take away thy coat, let him have thy cloak also;
>
> And whosoever shall compel thee to go a mile, go with him twain.
>
> Give to him that asketh thee, and from him that would borrow of thee turn thou not away.[53]

The true intent of Christ's statement is expressed in Joseph Smith's revision of Luke's report of this saying:

> . . . unto him who smiteth thee on the cheek, offer also the other; or, in other words, it is better to offer the other, than to revile again. And him who taketh away thy cloak, forbid not to take thy coat also.
>
> For it is better that thou suffer thine enemy to take these things, than to contend with him. Verily I say unto you, Your heavenly Father who seeth in secret, shall bring that wicked one into judgment.[54]

The law of the gospel requires that man suffer personal abuse rather than retaliate. To the Nephites, Jesus declared: "He that hath the spirit of contention is not of me, but is of the devil, who is the father of contention, and he stirreth up the hearts of men to contend with anger, one with another."[55] Christ's doctrine is that "such things should be done away."[56] Nevertheless, one who embraces the gospel should view himself as a person of dignity and value, too mature in character to engage in petty strife, but not a walking mat for corrupt and thoughtless individuals to trample upon with impunity. The Lord explained in modern times how a true Christian should conduct himself when he suffers abuse:

> Now, I speak unto you concerning your families—if men will smite you, or your families, once, and ye bear it patiently and revile not against them, neither seek revenge, ye shall be rewarded;
>
> But if ye bear it not patiently, it shall be accounted unto you as being meted out as a just measure unto you.
>
> And again, if your enemy shall smite you the second time, and you revile not against your enemy, and bear it patiently, your reward shall be an hundred-fold.
>
> And again, if he shall smite you the third time, and ye bear it patiently, your reward shall be doubled unto you four-fold;
>
> And these three testimonies shall stand against your enemy if he repent not, and shall not be blotted out.
>
> And now, verily I say unto you, if that enemy shall escape my vengeance, that he be not brought into judgment before me, then ye shall see to it that ye warn him in my name, that he come no more upon you, neither upon your family, even your children's children unto the third and fourth generation.
>
> And then, if he shall come upon you or your children, or your children's children unto the third and fourth generation, I have delivered thine enemy into thine hands;
>
> And then if thou wilt spare him, thou shalt be rewarded for thy righteousness; and also thy children and thy children's children unto the third and fourth generation.
>
> Nevertheless, thine enemy is in thine hands; and if thou rewardest him according to his works thou art justified; if he has sought thy life, and thy life is endangered by him, thine enemy is in thine hands and thou art justified.
>
> Behold, this is the law I gave unto my servant Nephi, and thy fathers, Joseph, and Jacob, and Isaac, and Abraham, and all mine ancient prophets and apostles.[57]

This revelation also makes it clear that the requirement to forgive seventy times seven applies only when an offender asks forgiveness and makes proper restitution for his injurious deeds. The revelation states:

> . . . verily I say unto you, if after thine enemy has come upon thee the first time, he repent and come unto thee praying

thy forgiveness, thou shalt forgive him, and shalt hold it no more as a testimony against thine enemy—

And so on unto the second and third time; and as oft as thine enemy repenteth of the trespass wherewith he has trespassed against thee, thou shalt forgive him, *until seventy times seven.*

And if he trespass against thee and repent not the first time, nevertheless thou shalt forgive him.

And if he trespass against thee the second time, and repent not, nevertheless thou shalt forgive him.

And if he trespass against thee the third time, and repent not, thou shalt also forgive him.

But if he trespass against thee the fourth time thou shalt not forgive him, but shalt bring these testimonies before the Lord; and they shall not be blotted out until he repent and reward thee four-fold in all things wherewith he has trespassed against thee.

And if he do this, thou shalt forgive him with all thine heart; and if he do not this, I the Lord, will avenge thee of thine enemy an hundred-fold;

And upon his children, and upon his children's children of all them that hate me, unto the third and fourth generation.

But if the children shall repent, or the children's children, and turn to the Lord their God, with all their hearts and with all their might, mind, and strength, and restore four-fold for all their trespasses wherewith they have trespassed, or wherewith their fathers have trespassed, or their father's fathers, then thine indignation shall be turned away;

And vengeance shall no more come upon them, saith the Lord thy God, and their trespasses shall never be brought any more as a testimony before the Lord against them.[58]

Finally, Jesus stated the law of love which the gospel requires and which the power of the Holy Ghost makes possible as it fills a man with the sacred fruits of the Spirit. The Master declared:

. . . it is written also, that thou shalt love thy neighbor and hate thine enemy;

But behold I say unto you, love your enemies, bless them that curse you, do good to them that hate you, and pray for them who despitefully use you and persecute you;

That ye may be the children of your Father who is in heaven; for he maketh his sun to rise on the evil and on the good.[59]

Only when man is filled with the love of God through the Holy Spirit can he act toward those who do him evil with the patience and compassion with which God acts.[60] Such action is evidence that man is indeed reconciled to God through the gospel.

"Those things which were of old time, which were under the law in me are all fulfilled," Jesus stressed as He concluded this phase of His great sermon on the law of the gospel. "Old things are done away, and *all things have become new.*"[61] Not only was there a new law, but under the new program man could become a new creature in Christ. Concerning the goal of perfection which man can achieve in eternity by acquiring the divine attributes and powers of the Spirit in this new stage of life, Jesus said: "Therefore I would that ye should be perfect even as I, or your Father who is in heaven is perfect."[62]

It is noteworthy that Jesus included Himself with His Father as a standard of the perfection to which the gospel leads, while in His sermon to the Jews He cited only His Father as an example of that standard.[63] Perfection is not merely to obey perfectly the law of God, for in the divine plan of life obedience is but a means to an end. The end is to be endowed with the full attributes and powers of the Father's glory.[64] Though Jesus kept the law of His Father to perfection during His earthly mission and in this respect was a true example which man can follow,[65] it was not until He was resurrected that He acquired a fulness of His Father's glory and became perfect like the Father. He was not perfect in that sense when He gave the Sermon on the Mount to His Jewish disciples. This is the goal which Christ gave to those who obey the gospel.

Outward and Inward Man of Righteousness

Obedience to the law of the gospel brings spiritual growth and development, and for this reason obedience produces its own reward. One who receives the divine attributes and powers of life which come from obeying the law of the gospel needs no outward recognition, but may be content to enjoy the peace and truth and power which he feels within. Nevertheless, he has the promise that God will reward him openly.

Jesus, as He spoke of various requirements of the law of the gospel, stressed these points and warned His disciples against the outward show of righteousness. Of the giving of alms, He said:

> Verily, verily, I say that I would that ye should do alms unto the poor; but take heed that ye do not your alms before men to be seen of them; otherwise ye have no reward of your Father who is in heaven.
>
> Therefore, when ye shall do your alms do not sound a trumpet before you, as will hypocrites do in the synagogues and in the streets, that they may have glory of men. Verily I say unto you, they have their reward.
>
> But when thou doest alms let not thy left hand know what thy right hand doeth;
>
> That thine alms may be in secret; and thy Father who seeth in secret, himself shall reward thee openly.[66]

Joseph Smith gave a similar admonition when he said: "Let not any man publish his own righteousness, for others can see that for him; sooner let him confess his sins, and then he will be forgiven, and he will bring forth more fruit."[67]

Prayer is another important feature of the gospel program that can become ritualistic, spiritually drab, or vain. Jesus instructed:

> . . . when thou prayest thou shalt not do as the hypocrites, for they love to pray, standing in the synagogues and in the corners of the streets, that they may be seen of men. Verily I say unto you, they have their reward.
>
> But thou, when thou prayest, enter into thy closet, and when thou hast shut thy door, pray to thy Father who is in secret; and thy Father, who seeth in secret, shall reward thee openly.[68]

Prayer should be simple and direct communion with God, not artificial or unnatural. "When ye pray, use not vain repetitions, as the heathen," Jesus stated, "for they think that they shall be heard for their much speaking."

Having affirmed that the Father knows what man has need of before he prays, so that there is no need to repeat the petition at length or with unnatural expression, Christ gave an illustration of the true simplicity of prayer in what has since become known as the Lord's prayer. The Nephite version of this prayer states:

> Our Father who art in heaven, hallowed be thy name.
> Thy will be done on earth as it is in heaven.
> And forgive us our debts, as we forgive our debtors.
> And lead us not into temptation, but deliver us from evil.
> For thine is the kingdom, and the power, and the glory, forever. Amen.[69]

The fact that this prayer omits two phrases which are found in the prayer which Jesus gave to His disciples in Palestine perhaps illustrates the point that in prayer man should not use vain and meaningless phrases. The two omitted phrases are: "Thy kingdom come" and "Give us this day our daily bread." With Christ's ministry among the Nephites, His kingdom was fully established on the Western hemisphere—spiritually, socially, economically, and politically. There followed an era of prosperity unequalled in Nephite history.[70] It may be suggested that it was not necessary for the Nephites to pray for the coming of God's kingdom, for it was in their midst. Nor presumably did they need to ask the Lord to bless them with nourishment for their bodies when He had given them an economic system through which there would be great prosperity in material things and an equal opportunity for every man to acquire the things of the earth.

Joseph Smith taught and illustrated this concept of prayer. When a man who had been an exhorter in another faith before embracing the restored gospel was asked to bless the food, he did so with great glowing terms and high-sounding phrases. "Brother Joshua," the Prophet admonished at the close of the blessing, "don't let me ever hear you ask another such blessing."[71] When Joseph sat down to eat a scanty meal of corn bread at another time, he prayed: "Lord, we thank Thee for this johnny cake, and ask Thee to send us something better. Amen." Before the bread was eaten, a man brought him some flour and a ham. After thanking the man for his gift, the Prophet said to his wife: "I knew the Lord would answer my prayer."[72] In recording his impression of a prayer which the latter-day Seer uttered publicly, Daniel Tyler said: "There was no ostentation, no raising of the voice as by enthusiasm, but a plain conversational tone, as a man would address a present friend." Yet Elder Tyler observed: "That prayer, I say, to my humble mind, partook of the learning and eloquence of heaven. . . . It was the crowning . . . of all the prayers I ever heard."[73]

The Prophet taught that in true prayer man must commune spiritually with God; otherwise he merely expresses words but does not pray. "He that asketh *in the Spirit* asketh according to the will of God," a revelation explained; "wherefore it is done even as he asketh." The revelation instructed: "Ye must give thanks unto God *in the Spirit* for whatsoever blessing ye are blessed with."[74] To obtain the Spirit in prayer, man must express faith and be contrite in heart. "The Spirit shall be given unto you by the prayer of faith," a revelation observed.[75] Again: "Pray always, and I will pour out my Spirit upon you, and great shall be your blessings."[76] "Ye receive the Spirit through prayer," still another revelation stated; "wherefore, without this there remaineth condemnation."[77]

True prayer is whole-soul communion with God. The Saints were instructed to pray always[78] and to do all things with much prayer, faith, and thanksgiving.[79] Amulek set a high, but appropriate, standard of prayer when he admonished:

> God grant unto you, my brethren, that ye may begin to exercise your faith . . . to call upon his holy name, that he would have mercy upon you;
>
> Yea, cry unto him for mercy; for he is mighty to save.
>
> Yea, humble yourselves, and continue in prayer unto him.
>
> Cry unto him when ye are in your fields, yea, over all your flocks.

> Cry unto him in your houses, yea, over all your household, both morning, mid-day, and evening.
>
> Yea, cry unto him against the devil, who is an enemy to all righteousness.
>
> Cry unto him over the crops of your fields, that ye may prosper in them.
>
> Cry over the flocks of your fields, that they may increase.
>
> But this is not all; ye must pour out your souls in your closets, and your secret places, and in your wilderness.
>
> Yea, and when you do not cry unto the Lord, let your hearts be full, drawn out in prayer unto him continually for your welfare, and also for the welfare of those who are around you.[80]

This kind of prayer is more than mere supplication for needed blessings and the expression of thanks for divine favor. It is a means of strengthening man and maturing him spiritually. For these reasons the Saints are instructed: "Pray always, that you may come off conqueror."[81] Again: "Pray always, that ye may not faint."[82] Prayer keeps man from falling "into temptation,"[83] where the wicked one has power in him.[84]

To pray with humility and contrition of heart, man must possess the spirit of forgiveness for those who have transgressed against him. True humility is always accompanied by the spirit of forgiveness in man. This is an important feature of the concept of prayer which Jesus taught. "If ye forgive men their trespasses your heavenly Father will also forgive you," He stressed after giving them the Lord's prayer; "but if ye forgive not men their trespasses neither will your Father forgive your trespasses."[85]

The Prophet expressed this principle by charging the Saints not to follow the example of the adversary in accusing the brethren, and said:

> If you do not accuse each other, God will not accuse you. If you have no accuser you will enter heaven, and if you will follow the revelations and instructions which God gives you through me, I will take you into heaven as my back load. If you will not accuse me, I will not accuse you. If you will throw a cloak of charity over my sins, I will over yours—for charity covereth a multitude of sins.[86]

In His sermon to the Nephites, Jesus next turned His

attention to the true practice of fasting, which is part of the law of the gospel, and said:

> Moreover, when ye fast be not as the hypocrites, of a sad countenance, for they disfigure their faces that they may appear unto men to fast. Verily I say unto you, they have their reward.
>
> But thou, when thou fastest, anoint thy head, and wash thy face;
>
> That thou appear not unto men to fast, but unto thy Father, who is in secret; and thy Father, who seeth in secret, shall reward thee openly.[87]

Fasting is closely associated with prayer. When the sons of Mosiah went to proclaim the gospel to the Lamanites, "they fasted much and prayed much that the Lord would grant unto them a portion of his Spirit to go with them, and abide with them."[88] Alma later met them, after they had performed a notable work among the Lamanites, and wrote that "they had waxed strong in the knowledge of the truth; for they were men of a sound understanding and they had searched the scriptures diligently, that they might know the word of God." "But this is not all," he stressed; "they had given themselves to much prayer, and fasting; therefore they had the spirit of prophecy, and the spirit of revelation, and when they taught, they taught with power and authority of God."[89]

Fasting was an important practice among the Nephite saints. The people of Nephi "did fast much, and they did worship God with exceeding great joy."[90] Mormon gave a similar report at a later period.[91] And of their practice after the time of Christ, Moroni said: "The church did meet together oft, to fast and to pray, and to speak one with another concerning the welfare of their souls."[92]

A similar practice was established among the Latter-day Saints. They were advised to "continue in prayer and fasting from this time forth."[93] Having indicated that in true fasting man's joy is made full, a revelation said: "Verily, this is fasting and prayer, or in other words, rejoicing and prayer."[94] By fasting and prayer, man may acquire a true spiritual union with Christ, and such union brings joy and rejoicing to the human heart. That they might realize these blessings more fully in their lives the Saints were instructed to build "a house of prayer, a house of fasting, a house of faith, a house of learning, a house of glory, a house of order, a house of God."[95]

The law of the gospel requires that man's eye be single to the glory of God. Man's central hope in Christ—that which should be his ultimate desire and to which all else is subordinate in the plan of life and salvation—should be to acquire a fulness of the Father's glory.[96] "The light of the body is the eye," Jesus declared as He spoke of this central hope in the gospel; "if therefore thine eye be *single to the glory of God,* thy whole body shall be full of light."[97] In the full statement of this requirement which He made to the Nephites, the Lord said:

> Lay not up for yourselves treasures upon earth, where moth and rust doth corrupt, and thieves break through and steal;
>
> But lay up for yourselves treasures in heaven, where neither moth nor rust doth corrupt, and where thieves do not break through nor steal.
>
> For where your treasure is, there will your heart be also.
>
> The light of the body is the eye; if, therefore, thine eye be single, thy whole body shall be full of light.
>
> But if thine eye be evil, thy whole body shall be full of darkness. If, therefore, the light that is in thee be darkness, how great is that darkness!
>
> No man can serve two masters; for either he will hate the one and love the other, or else he will hold to the one and despise the other. Ye cannot serve God and Mammon.[98]

Admonitions and Instructions on Law of the Gospel

Having set forth the law and standard of the gospel to the Nephites, Jesus concluded His sermon by giving them appropriate admonitions and instructions on the law of the gospel. He first spoke of their agency in judging the issues of life and admonished:

> Verily, verily, I say unto you, Judge not, that ye be not judged.
>
> For with what judgment ye judge, ye shall be judged; and with what measure ye mete, it shall be measured to you again.

And why beholdest thou the mote that is in thy brother's eye, but considerest not the beam that is in thine own eye?

Or how wilt thou say to thy brother: Let me pull the mote out of thine eye—and behold, a beam is in thine own eye?

Thou hypocrite, first cast the beam out of thine own eye; and then shalt thou see clearly to cast the mote out of thy brother's eye.[99]

Inherent in the injunction that man should not trust in the arm of flesh[100] is the fact that he should not rely upon mere finite powers of reason and analysis to determine the truth of a principle or the propriety of a given action. Things are not always what they appear to be to the physical senses. "The devil has great power to deceive," Joseph Smith cautioned; "he will so transform things as to make one gape at those who are doing the will of God."[101] The life of a saint should be centered in the enlightening power of the Holy Spirit which, as a Spirit of discernment, enables him "to judge righteously."[102] Mormon admonished: "And now, my brethren, seeing that ye know the light by which ye may judge, which light is the light of Christ, see that ye do not judge wrongfully; for with that same judgment which ye judge ye shall also be judged."[103] Modern scriptures imply that in expressing views and opinions, and in rendering judgments, man should first be sure that his eye is single to the glory of God, for only when his body is filled with the light of the Spirit can he judge righteously. For this reason, the Lord admonished the Nephites to reserve judgment and first cast out the beam from their own eyes. Man's final reward in eternity will depend largely upon the judgments he has rendered in this life, not only because of the law of retribution but because his judgments will evidence the degree to which his life has been in tune with the Holy Spirit.

Jesus next instructed His disciples: "Give not that which is holy unto the dogs, neither cast ye your pearls before swine, lest they trample them under their feet, and turn again and rend you."[104] Man is on earth to be proved in all things and to develop in the attributes and powers of the Holy Spirit by obeying the plan of life and salvation, not merely to satisfy his curiosity to know the mysteries of God. An understanding of the mysteries is given as a result of man's faith, not as a means of building faith; nor is it given to the unworthy. Alma explained: "It is given unto many to know the mysteries of God; nevertheless they are laid under a strict command that they shall not impart only according to the portion of his word which he doth grant unto the children of men, according to the heed and diligence which they give unto him."[105]

This does not mean that man should not seek to know the mysteries of God, but that he should come unto God in the right way in order to receive them. Having given the above admonition, Jesus then declared:

> Ask, and it shall be given unto you; seek, and ye shall find; knock, and it shall be opened unto you.
>
> For every one that asketh, receiveth; and he that seeketh, findeth; and to him that knocketh, it shall be opened.
>
> Or what man is there of you, who, if his son ask bread, will give him a stone?
>
> Or if he ask a fish, will he give him a serpent?
>
> If ye then, being evil, know how to give good gifts unto your children, how much more shall your Father who is in heaven give good things to them that ask him?[106]

To gain a knowledge of divine truth, man must obey the law by which he can receive personal revelation from God. In addition to receiving the ordinances of the gospel, that law requires that man ask of God and that he love and respect his fellow men. As an extension of His promise that the Father would give good things to those who would seek them in the right way, Jesus said: "Therefore, all things whatsoever ye would that men should do to you, do ye even so to them, for this is the law and the prophets."[107] Upon this great principle of individual dignity, justice, and brotherhood the gospel rests in all ages of time. "Enter ye in at the strait gate," the Master stressed; "for wide is the gate, and broad is the way, which leadeth to destruction, and many there be who go in thereat; because strait is the gate, and narrow is the way, *which leadeth unto life,* and few there be that find it."[108] The gospel is not merely a code of conduct, but a way of receiving divine attributes and powers of life.

Following these admonitions, Jesus expressed two major warnings. The first concerned those who would come representing themselves as ministers of God without legal claim to that office. Of such, He said:

> Beware of false prophets, who come to you in sheep's clothing, but inwardly they are ravening wolves.
>
> Ye shall know them by their fruits. Do men gather grapes of thorns, or figs of thistles?
>
> Even so every good tree bringeth forth good fruit; but a corrupt tree bringeth forth evil fruit.
>
> A good tree cannot bring forth evil fruit, neither a corrupt tree bring forth good fruit.
>
> Every tree that bringeth not forth good fruit is hewn down, and cast into the fire.
>
> Wherefore, by their fruits ye shall know them.[109]

A true minister of Christ must be called of God in the proper way, and he must "work by the power and gifts of God."[110] These are the criteria by which a true minister may be identified. Is he called of God in the right way? Does he do the works of Christ? And are the powers, gifts, and fruits which Jesus possessed manifested in his labors?

A true minister of God must have the basic qualifications of a prophet; and in his sphere of action, he must be a prophet to his people. Joseph Smith often cited the statement of the angel to John on the Isle of Patmos that the testimony of Jesus constitutes the spirit of prophecy,[111] which indicates that if a man has a testimony from the Holy Ghost that Jesus is the Son of God, he has the basic qualifications of a true prophet of God. The latter-day Seer explained:

> According to John, *the testimony of Jesus is the spirit of prophecy;* therefore, if I profess to be a witness or teacher, and have not the spirit of prophecy, which is the testimony of Jesus, I must be a false witness; but if I be a true teacher and witness, I must possess the spirit of prophecy, and that constitutes a prophet; and *any man who says he is a teacher or preacher of righteousness, and denies the spirit of prophecy, is a liar, and the truth is not in him; and by this key false teachers and imposters may be detected.*[112]

In His second warning, Jesus stressed man's need of accepting the message of life and salvation and of acting upon it in the right way. The Master explained:

> Not every one that saith unto me, Lord, Lord, shall enter into the kingdom of heaven; but he that doeth the will of my Father who is in heaven.
>
> Many will say to me in that day: Lord, Lord, have we not prophesied in thy name, and in thy name have cast out devils, and in thy name done many wonderful works?
>
> And then will I profess unto them: I never knew you; depart from me, ye that work iniquity.
>
> Therefore, whoso heareth these sayings of mine and doeth them, I will liken him unto a wise man, who built his house upon a rock—
>
> And the rain descended, and the floods came, and the winds blew, and beat upon that house, and it fell not, for it was founded upon a rock.
>
> And every one that heareth these sayings of mine and doeth them not shall be likened unto a foolish man, who built his house upon the sand—
>
> And the rain descended, and the floods came, and the winds blew, and beat upon that house; and it fell, and great was the fall of it.[113]

The Lord's Day

The Saints were instructed to commemorate the Lord's Day as a means of assisting them to keep more fully the law of the gospel. A revelation given to the Church through the Prophet on that day, Sunday, August 7, 1831, set forth the law of God on this subject.[114] The revelation said:

> . . . that thou mayest more fully keep thyself unspotted from the world, thou shalt go to the house of prayer and offer up thy sacraments upon my holy day;
>
> For verily this is a day appointed unto you to rest from your labors, and to pay thy devotions unto the Most High;
>
> Nevertheless thy vows shall be offered up in righteousness on all days and at all times;
>
> But remember that on this, the Lord's day, thou shalt offer thine oblations and thy sacraments unto the Most High, confessing thy sins unto thy brethren, and before the Lord.

And on this day thou shalt do none other thing, only let thy food be prepared with singleness of heart that thy fasting may be perfect, or, in other words, that thy joy may be full.

Verily, this is fasting and prayer, or in other words, rejoicing and prayer.

And . . . ye [shall] do these things with thanksgiving, with cheerful hearts and countenances, not with much laughter, for this is sin, but with a glad heart and a cheerful countenance.[115]

The Lord's Day is a day for the Saints to cease their labors of the week and pay their devotions to the Most High. It is the Christian Sabbath,[116] and as such it is "given unto man for a day of rest; and also that man should glorify God."[117] Sunday is a day of rest with respect to both aspects of the term, for the word "rest" means not only to cease from one's daily labors but to achieve a state of spiritual union with God. Spiritually the term "rest" means to enter into the presence of God and partake of His glory.[118] As a day of rest, the Sabbath is symbolic of the state when the faithful enter into the full glory, or rest, of the Lord.[119] By achieving true spiritual union with God through the gospel and by maturing in that divine relationship through the proper observance of the Lord's Day, the Saints can anticipate and approximate the great objective of the gospel, which is to bring man to enter into the Lord's rest, or into the fulness of His glory.[120]

The law of the Lord's Day is positive rather than negative in its requirements. The emphasis is upon those things which the Saints are to do to make the Lord's Day truly a day of spiritual rest. Thereby they can be filled with joy and gladness, and have cheerful countenances.[121] Because the gospel is a divine program of *life* and salvation, the Saints can experience in the observance of the Sabbath the joy of redemption[122] and of spiritual light.[123] To realize these blessings, they must avoid such things as loud and boisterous laughter, light-mindedness, light and vain speech, and evil speaking of others and of the Lord's servants.[124] These requirements are part of the law of the gospel.

Word Of Wisdom

Latter-day revelations indicate that man must give proper care to his physical body if he is to develop spiritually to a significant degree. Physical well-being is essential to mental vigor;[125] and both physical health and mental vigor have an influence upon the spiritual life of man. Joseph Smith received a revelation, popularly designated as the Word of Wisdom, which expressed important principles and teachings concerning man's temporal well-being that play a vital role in the plan of life and salvation. The Word of Wisdom, therefore, is part of the law of the gospel.

Joseph Smith reaffirmed the biblical doctrine that "man is the tabernacle of God, even temples,"[126] and that the Spirit of God dwells in man.[127] Both temporal and spiritual blessings thus follow obedience to the Word of Wisdom. This revelation set "forth the order and will of God in the temporal salvation of all saints in the last days," and the law therein contained was given "for a principle with promise, adapted to the weakest of all saints, who are or can be called saints."[128]

The Word of Wisdom first warned the Saints of temptations which they would meet in the last days, then advised against harmful substances commonly taken into the body:

> Behold, verily, thus saith the Lord unto you: In consequence of evils and designs which do and will exist in the hearts of conspiring men in the last days, I have warned you, and forewarn you, by giving unto you this word of wisdom by revelation—
>
> That inasmuch as any man drinketh wine or strong drink among you, behold it is not good, neither meet in the sight of your Father, only in assembling yourselves together to offer up your sacraments before him.
>
> And behold, this should be wine, yea, pure wine of the grape of the vine, of your own make.
>
> And, again, strong drinks [i.e., alcoholic drinks] are not for the belly, but for the washing of your bodies.
>
> And again, tobacco is not for the body, neither for the belly, and is not good for man, but is an herb for bruises and all sick cattle, to be used with judgment and skill.

And again, hot drinks [i.e., tea, coffee, etc.] are not for the body or belly.[129]

After stating some of the things which the Saints were not to partake of, the revelation mentioned many things which could appropriately be used:

. . . all wholesome herbs God hath ordained for the constitution, nature, and use of man—

Every herb in the season thereof, and every fruit in the season thereof; all these to be used with prudence and thanksgiving.

Yea, flesh also of beasts and of the fowls of the air, I, the Lord, have ordained for the use of man with thanksgiving; nevertheless they are to be used sparingly;

And it is pleasing unto me that they should not be used, only in times of winter, or of cold, or famine.

All grain is ordained for the use of man and of beasts, to be the staff of life, not only for man but for the beasts of the field, and the fowls of heaven, and all wild animals that run or creep on the earth;

And these hath God made for the use of man only in times of famine and excess of hunger.

All grain is good for the food of man; as also the fruit of the vine; that which yieldeth fruit, whether in the ground or above the ground—

Nevertheless, wheat for man, and corn for the ox, and oats for the horse, and rye for the fowls and for swine, and for all beasts of the field, and barley for all useful animals, and for mild drinks, as also other grain.[130]

By obedience to the Word of Wisdom, the Saints are promised both physical and spiritual blessings. Of the first, the revelation said: "All saints who remember to keep and do these sayings, walking in obedience to the commandments, shall receive health in their navel and marrow to their bones; . . . and shall run and not be weary, and shall walk and not faint."[131] Spiritually, the Saints are promised "wisdom and great treasures of knowledge, even hidden treasures."[132] These blessings are those which the faithful receive when their bodies are fit dwelling places for the Holy Ghost.

Summary

The Prophet made it clear that for man to develop in the divine truth, power, gifts, and blessings of the Holy Spirit after entering the path which leads to life and salvation,he must obey the law of the gospel. The classic statement of this law is in Christ's Sermon on the Mount. The Nephite record, in particular, places this great statement in its proper gospel context. Having taught His disciples on the Western hemisphere the basic program of the gospel upon which man must establish his life in order to receive celestial salvation, Jesus gave them the beatitudes as eight subordinate statements which specify the ways by which those who accept the gospel and apply its divine truth and power in their lives may expect to be blessed, or may become blessed. Christ then contrasted the law of the gospel with the law of Moses and indicated that by receiving the manifestations of the Holy Ghost and continuing in this path, man can eventually become perfect in all the divine attributes and powers of the Father and the Son. Since these divine attributes and powers have the effect of transforming man and renewing him to a state of righteousness, Jesus next spoke of the outward as contrasted to the inward man of righteousness, while stating the law and the standard of the regenerated man. Finally, the Master issued appropriate admonitions and instructions to those who heard His message. Only by hearing those sayings and actually doing them can man build his life upon the rock of Christ and acquire salvation. The Lord's Day and the Word of Wisdom also play significant roles in this divine program of human development.

Notes

1. HC, V, p. 402, citing 2 Peter 1.
2. See 3 Nephi 11:20–41.
3. See I. R., Matthew 5:1–4.
4. See, for example, 3 Nephi 12:6.
5. 3 Nephi 12:48.
6. Man cannot achieve the full standard of perfection until the resurrection.

7. 3 Nephi 12:20.
8. See 3 Nephi 11.
9. 3 Nephi 12:1–2.
10. 3 Nephi 12:3; I. R., Matthew 5:5.
11. JD, X, p. 299.
12. 3 Nephi 14:4; I. R., Matthew 5:6.
13. HC, V, p. 362.
14. 3 Nephi 12:5; I. R., Matthew 5:7.
15. HC, V, p. 218.
16. See, for example, D&C 19:23, 41; 25:5, 14; 32:1, 9; 52:16; 58:41; 63:57; 84:106; 100:7; 118:3; 121:41.
17. D&C 19:23.
18. 1 Nephi 17:36–38. The Jaredites and Nephites are examples of the operation of the principle expressed in this statement.
19. D&C 88:19–20.
20. When God gave Abraham a land of inheritance, the latter inquired:

> . . . Lord God how wilt thou give me this land for an everlasting inheritance?
>
> And the Lord said, Though thou wast dead, yet am I not able to give it thee?
>
> And if thou shalt die, yet thou shalt possess it, for the day cometh, that the Son of Man shall live; but how can he live if he be not dead? he must first be quickened.
>
> And it came to pass, that Abram looked forth and saw the days of the Son of Man, and was glad, and his soul found rest, and he believed in the Lord.—I. R., Genesis 15:9–12.

21. 3 Nephi 12:6; I. R., Matthew 5:8.
22. D&C 52:15.
23. 3 Nephi 12:7; I. R., Matthew 5:9.
24. See Moroni 7:48; 8:26.
25. HC, V, pp. 23–24.
26. 3 Nephi 12:8; I. R., Matthew 5:10.
27. See the section in chapter one entitled "Man's Ultimate Goal in the Gospel."
28. 3 Nephi 12:9; I. R., Matthew 5:11.
29. Isaiah 9:6.
30. Moses 6:61.
31. Mosiah 15:14.
32. See D&C 84:45–48.
33. 3 Nephi 12:10; I. R., Matthew 5:12.
34. 3 Nephi 12:12. See also I. R., Matthew 5:14.
35. 3 Nephi 12:13–16. See also I. R., Matthew 5:15–18.
36. D&C 84:19–27.
37. 3 Nephi 12:21–24. See also I. R., Matthew 5:23–26.
38. 3 Nephi 12:25–26. See also I. R., Matthew 5:27–28. For a statement on the value of a senine, see Alma 11:5ff.
39. 3 Nephi 12:27–30. See also I. R., Matthew 5:29–31.
40. I. R., Matthew 16:26.
41. The statement in Matthew seems to be a strong figure of speech rather than an actual injunction that man should dismember his body.

42. I. R., Matthew 5:32–34.
43. D&C 42:23. See also D&C 63:16.
44. 3 Nephi 12:31. See Leviticus 21:7, 14; Deuteronomy 24:1–4.
45. 3 Nephi 12:32. See also Matthew 19:9; Mark 10:2–12.
46. See D&C 132.
47. I. R., Matthew 19:10–11.
48. The term "fornication" comes from the Greek *porneia* and is used in sacred literature as a general word for sexual immorality or harlotry, including not only on the part of the unmarried (Genesis 38:24; Deuteronomy 22:20–21), but also of the married (Hosea 2:2–4, Septuagint). Jacob warned the people of Nephi (not merely the unmarried) "against fornication and lasciviousness, and every kind of sin."—Jacob 3:12. See also I Corinthians 5:1; 7:2. There is also a spiritual sense in which Christ's church or people can commit fornication against him. This use of the term seems to be derived from the concept of the divine law of marriage. The Lord views Himself as being in a marriage relationship with His people. He is the husband and His church is the wife. See Isaiah 50:1; 54:1, 5; Jeremiah 3:14; Matthew 9:15; 25:1–13; D&C 33:17; 65:3; 88:92; 133:10, 19. By instituting idolatry, Jehoram, a king of Judah, "caused the inhabitants of Jerusalem to commit fornication, and compelled Judah thereto."—2 Chronicles 21:4–11. When the Nephites began to depart from God, their prophet charged: "Ye are ripening, because of your murders and your fornication and wickedness, for everlasting destruction."—Helaman 9:26. By departing from the true gospel, apostate Christianity "has made all nations drink of the wine of the wrath of her fornication."—D&C 35:11; 88:94, 105. When viewed in light of these statements, the sin of fornication by married women seems to include any kind of serious sexual transgression.
49. See D&C 132:44 for the provision by which, under the law of God, a faithful woman can be taken lawfully from an unworthy husband and given to another in marriage.
50. 3 Nephi 12:33–37.
51. See, for example, Numbers 30:2.
52. 1 Nephi 4:33, 37.
53. 3 Nephi 12:38–42. Joseph Smith's Inspired Revision of the Bible gives this statement in Matthew with some variations. The distinctive passages are:

> And if any man will sue thee at the law, and take away thy coat, let him have it; and if he sue thee again, let him have thy cloak also.
>
> And whosoever shall compel thee to go a mile, go with him a mile; and whosoever shall compel thee to go with him twain, thou shalt go with him twain.—I. R., Matthew 5:42–43.

54. I. R., Luke 6:29–30.
55. 3 Nephi 11:29.
56. 3 Nephi 11:30.
57. D&C 98:23–32.
58. D&C 98:39–48.
59. 3 Nephi 12:43–45.
60. See HC, III, p. 304.
61. 3 Nephi 12:46–47.
62. 3 Nephi 12:48.
63. Matthew 5:48.

64. D&C 93:19–20.

65. In light of this point, see Luke 6:40.

66. 3 Nephi 13:1–4. The Prophet's Inspired Revision of Matthew states: "But when thou doest alms, let it be unto thee as thy left hand not knowing what thy right hand doeth."—I. R., Matthew 6:3.

67. HC, IV, p. 479.

68. 3 Nephi 13:5–6.

69. 3 Nephi 13:7–13. Joseph Smith's Inspired Revision of Matthew has these distinctive passages in the Lord's prayer:

> And forgive us our trespasses, as we forgive those who trespass against us.
>
> And suffer us not to be led into temptation, but deliver us from evil. —I. R., Matthew 6:13–14.

70. See 4 Nephi.

71. *Juvenile Instructor,* XXVII, p. 129.

72. *Ibid.,* p. 172.

73. *Ibid.,* p. 129.

74. D&C 46:30, 32.

75. D&C 42:14.

76. D&C 19:38.

77. D&C 63:64.

78. See D&C 10:5; 19:38; 20:33; 32:4; 88:126; 90:24; 93:49.

79. D&C 26:2; 28:13; 46:7; 90:24.

80. Alma 34:17–27. The Saints were instructed to pray both publicly and privately, and to establish a house of prayer in which they could offer up their oblations and their sacraments unto the Most High. See D&C 19:28; 20:47, 51; 23:6; 59:9, 12; 81:3; 109:8, 16.

81. D&C 10:5.

82. D&C 88:126. See also D&C 101:81.

83. D&C 20:33. See also D&C 31:12; 61:39.

84. D&C 93:49.

85. 3 Nephi 13:14–15.

86. HC, IV, p. 445.

87. 3 Nephi 13:16–18.

88. Alma 17:9.

89. Alma 17:2–3.

90. Alma 45:1.

91. Helaman 3:35.

92. Moroni 6:5.

93. D&C 88:76.

94. D&C 59:13–14.

95. D&C 88:119. See also D&C 95:16; 109:16.

96. D&C 93:19–20. See again the section in chapter one entitled "The Hope of Glory."

97. I. R., Matthew 6:22. See also D&C 88:67.

98. 3 Nephi 13:19–24. Two references from Joseph Smith's Inspired Revision of the gospel by Luke should be noted in conjunction with the above statement: "If thy whole body therefore is full of light, having no part dark, the whole shall be full of light, as when the bright shining of a candle lighteneth a room and doth give the light in all the room."—I. R., Luke 11:37.

"This he spake unto his disciples, saying, Sell that ye have and give alms; provide not for yourselves bags which wax old, but rather provide a treasure in the heavens, that faileth not; where no thief approacheth, neither moth corrupteth."—I. R., Luke 12:36.

In the Lord's sermon to the Nephites, the remaining instructions which are recorded in 3 Nephi 13 were given specifically to the Twelve and pertain to their service in the ministry. For this reason they are not discussed here.

99. 3 Nephi 14:1–5. In Joseph Smith's Inspired Revision of Matthew, Jesus indicates that this phase of the law of the gospel was to be used in preaching repentance to the world. It states:

> Now these are the words which Jesus taught his disciples that they should say unto the people.
>
> Judge not unrighteously, that ye be not judged; but judge righteous judgment.
>
> For with what judgment ye shall judge, ye shall be judged; and with what measure ye mete, it shall be measured to you again.
>
> And again, ye shall say unto them, Why is it that thou beholdest the mote that is in thy brother's eye, but considerest not the beam that is in thine own eye?
>
> Or how wilt thou say to thy brother, Let me pull out the mote out of thine eye; and canst not behold a beam in thine own eye?
>
> And Jesus said unto his disciples, Beholdest thou the Scribes, and the Pharisees, and the Priests, and the Levites? They teach in their synagogues, but do not observe the law, nor the commandments; and all have gone out of the way, and are under sin.
>
> Go thou and say unto them, Why teach ye men the law and the commandments, when ye yourselves are the children of corruption?
>
> Say unto them, Ye hypocrites, first cast out the beam out of thine own eye; and then shalt thou see clearly to cast out the mote out of thy brother's eye.
>
> Go ye into the world, saying unto all, Repent, for the kingdom of heaven has come nigh unto you.—I. R., Matthew 7:1–9.

100. See Volume I of this study, the section in chapter seventeen entitled "Man Should Not Trust in the Arm of Flesh."

101. HC, IV, p. 605.

102. D&C 11:12.

103. Moroni 7:14–18. See Volume I of this study, the section in chapter ten entitled "Christ's Holy Spirit Leads Man Upward to God."

104. 3 Nephi 14:6. Continuing the view that this phase of the law of the gospel was to be used in preaching repentance to the world, Jesus said to His disciples in Palestine, as recorded in Joseph Smith's Inspired Revision of the Bible:

> . . . the mysteries of the kingdom ye shall keep within yourselves; for it is not meet to give that which is holy unto the dogs; neither cast ye your pearls unto swine, lest they trample them under their feet.
>
> For the world cannot receive that which ye, yourselves, are not able to bear; wherefore ye shall not give your pearls unto them, lest they turn again and rend you.—I. R., Matthew 7:10–11.

105. Alma 12:9. See also D&C 63:64.

106. 3 Nephi 14:7–11. Though Jesus warned His Jewish disciples not to

reveal the mysteries of the kingdom unto the world, He instructed them concerning those who had not embraced the gospel:

> Say unto them, Ask of God; ask, and it shall be given you; seek, and ye shall find; knock, and it shall be opened unto you.
>
> For every one that asketh, receiveth; and he that seeketh, findeth; and unto him that knocketh, it shall be opened.
>
> And then said his disciples unto him, they will say unto us, We ourselves are righteous, and need not that any man should teach us. God, we know, heard Moses and some of the prophets; but us he will not hear.
>
> And they will say, We have the law for our salvation, and that is sufficient for us.
>
> Then Jesus answered, and said unto his disciples, thus shall ye say unto them.
>
> What man among you, having a son, and he shall be standing out, and shall say, Father, open thy house that I may come in and sup with thee, will not say, Come in, my son; for mine is thine, and thine is mine?
>
> Or what man is there among you, who, if his son ask bread, will give him a stone?
>
> Or if he ask a fish, will he give him a serpent?
>
> If ye then, being evil, know how to give good gifts unto your children, how much more shall your Father who is in heaven give good things to them that ask him?—I. R., Matthew 7:12–20.

107. 3 Nephi 14:12.

108. 3 Nephi 14:13–14. Consistent with the approach taken in Joseph Smith's Inspired Revision of the Bible, Jesus instructed His disciples to say to those to whom they preached the gospel: "Repent, therefore, and enter ye in at the strait gate. . . ."—I. R., Matthew 7:22.

109. 3 Nephi 14:15–20.

110. Moroni 10:24–25.

111. Revelation 19:10.

112. HC, V, pp. 215–216. See also *ibid.*, III, p. 28; V, pp. 231–232, 427.

113. 3 Nephi 14:21–27. In the Prophet's Inspired Revision of the Bible, this statement is set more fully in context with the doctrine of eternal judgment, which is a fundamental principle of the gospel. "Verily I say unto you, it is not every one that saith unto me, Lord, Lord, that shall enter into the kingdom of heaven; but he that doeth the will of my Father who is in heaven," Jesus explained. "For the day cometh, that all men shall come before me to judgment, to be judged according to their works."—I. R., Matthew 7:30–31. In that day, the Master declared that He would say to those who keep not his sayings: "Ye never knew me; depart from me ye that work iniquity."—I. R., Matthew 7:33. On the other hand, Jesus promised the Nephites, as He concluded His sermon: "Therefore, whoso remembereth these sayings of mine and doeth them, him will I raise up at the last day."—3 Nephi 15:1.

114. In New Testament times following the crucifixion of Christ, the Lord's Day was the day especially associated with the Lord Jesus Christ—Sunday, or resurrection day. It is mentioned by this name in Revelation 1:10. Sunday, the first day of the week, was devoted by the apostles as a time for meeting and performing spiritual activities—administering the sacrament, communing with God, receiving instructions and admonitions in spiritual things, giving religious offerings, and occupying time in holy thought and

prayer. On this day, Christ arose from the grave, and during that day He appeared to His disciples and apostles on five different occasions. Also after eight days, on the first day of the next week, He appeared to the eleven apostles. At Pentecost, which some scholars contend fell that year on the first day of the week, the apostles and disciples "were all united with one accord in one place" when they had spiritual gifts conferred upon them and began to give these blessings to others by preaching the gospel and administering its ordinances to those who believed. See Acts 2. Later, when the practice of the early Church had assumed a settled form, Paul preached to the saints at Troas "upon the first day of the week, when the disciples came together to break bread."—Acts 20:7. To the Corinthians, Paul instructed: " . . . upon the first day of the week . . . lay up . . . in store."—1 Corinthians 16:2. The collection of religious offerings on that day seems to have been a standard practice, for Paul wrote: "Now concerning the collection for the saints, as I have given order to the churches of Galatia, even so do ye."—1 Corinthians 16:1. After citing these references and others, the *New Smith's Bible Dictionary,* p. 216, adds: "And all these passages have remarkable confirmation in the fact that this day is noted in similar manner, being associated with the Lord's resurrection, by extrabiblical usage; also it is never questioned, but is accepted as equally apostolic with baptism, ordination, etc.; and according to principal writers in the centuries after John's death, it existed as part and parcel of apostolic, and so of scriptural, Christianity."

115. D&C 59:9–15.

116. See D&C 68:29, where it is referred to as the Sabbath.

117. I. R., Mark 2:26.

118. See D&C 84:24.

119. See Volume I of this study, the section in chapter thirteen entitled "The Seventh Day One of Rest."

120. D&C 19:9; 121:32.

121. See D&C 59:15; 61:36; 68:6; 78:18; 112:4; 123:17; 128:19–20.

122. Moses 5:11; 2 Nephi 2:25.

123. D&C 11:12–13.

124. D&C 20:54; 42:27; 43:34; 84:61; 88:121; 98:11; 100:7; 121:16; 124:116; 136:21, 23.

125. Here a revelation declared: "Cease to be idle; cease to be unclean; . . . cease to sleep longer than is needful; retire to thy bed early, that ye may not be weary; arise early, that your bodies and your minds may be invigorated."—D&C 88:124.

126. D&C 93:35. See 1 Corinthians 6:19.

127. D&C 88:50. See 1 Corinthians 6:19.

128. D&C 89:2–3.

129. D&C 89:4–9. For evidence that strong drinks are alcoholic drinks, see D&C 27:3. For evidence that hot drinks were defined in Joseph Smith's day as tea, coffee, etc., see TS, III (June 1, 1842), pp. 799–800.

130. D&C 89:10–17.

131. D&C 89:18, 20.

132. D&C 89:19.

11

The Temple Program Inaugurated

> *Verily I say unto you, that your . . . baptisms for the dead, and your solemn assemblies, and your memorials for your sacrifices by the sons of Levi, and for your oracles in your most holy places wherein you receive conversations, and your statutes and judgments, for the beginning of the revelations and foundation of Zion, and for the glory, honor, and endowment of all her municipals, are ordained by the ordinance of my holy house, which my people are always commanded to build unto my holy name.*—REVELATION TO JOSEPH SMITH.

Joseph Smith taught that the initial ordinances of the gospel can be administered in any suitable place, but, except on rare occasions, the higher ordinances of the plan of life and salvation can be performed only in holy sanctuaries known as temples. When the people of God are able to build a temple, they are required to do so in order that they may receive these sacred rites and ordinances. But if they are unable to erect such a structure, exceptions can be made. "The rich can only get them in the Temple," the Prophet said of the higher ordinances, "the poor may get them on the mountain top as did Moses."[1]

Need For Temples

Necessity of Temples in Gospel Program

By derivation and accepted usage, the term "temple" literally interpreted refers to a place which is considered to be distinctly holy. The Latin *Templum,* and its Hebrew equivalent *Beth Elohim,* specified the "abode of God." An edifice dedicated as a temple therefore is considered literally the house of the Lord. It is a meeting place, or a point of contact, between heaven and earth. It is a place where God can "come" and reveal His ordinances unto His people, and where they can "receive conversations."[2]

A revelation made it clear that God's people in all ages of time were commanded to build temples whenever they were prepared to receive the higher ordinances of the gospel. "For this cause I commanded Moses that he should build a tabernacle, that they should bear it with them in the wilderness," the Lord explained as a case in point, "and to build a house in the land of promise, that those ordinances might be revealed which had been hid from before the world was." For this reason God's "people are always commanded" to build a temple to His name.[3]

Among the first things Nephi did when his people became a distinct group on the Western hemisphere was to build a temple.[4] Thereafter frequent mention is made of temples as important edifices and as centers of Nephite worship.[5]

Revelations to the Prophet early in this dispensation indicated that there would be temples erected in modern times for the benefit of the Saints. In July, 1831, a revelation officially designated the site for a great temple to be built at Independence, Jackson county, Missouri.[6] Several months earlier another revelation stated that if the Saints proved themselves worthy, the Lord would make a personal appearance in that consecrated building when it was completed.[7] In December, 1832, still another revelation directed the immediate construction of a temple at Kirtland, Ohio.[8] It was while the Saints were building the Kirtland Temple at Kirtland, Ohio, and the Nauvoo Temple at Nauvoo, Illinois, that the purpose of such sanctuaries was explained by the Prophet, and that the higher ordinances of the gospel which were to be performed in the house of the Lord were administered.

Joseph Smith said of the purpose of the temple: "The main object was to build unto the Lord a house whereby He could reveal unto His people the ordinances of His house and the glories of His kingdom, and teach the people the way of salvation; for there are certain ordinances and principles that, when they are taught and practiced, must be done in a place or house built for that purpose."[9] Again he explained:

> It was the design of the councils of heaven before the world was, that the principles and laws of the priesthood should be predicated upon the gathering of the people in every age of the world. . . .
>
> It is for the same purpose that God gathers together His people in the last days, to build unto the Lord a house to prepare them for the ordinances and endowments. . . . [10]

Temple and the Fulness of the Priesthood

The ultimate objective of the gospel is to raise every man spiritually to the point of receiving a fulness of the priesthood and glory of God. This is a factor of utmost importance. "God hath not revealed anything to Joseph," the latter-day Seer observed, "but what He will make known unto the Twelve, and even the least Saint may know all things as fast as he is able to bear them."[11] In referring to the destiny of those who rise to their full potential in the resurrection, a revelation stated: "The saints shall be filled with his [God's] glory, and receive their inheritance and be made equal with him."[12] Of God's blessings upon the faithful in eternity, another revelation said: "He makes them equal in power, and in might, and in dominion."[13]

Joseph Smith taught that the family unit as it is organized and sealed in the temple—not the social order of the gospel or a particular office or position in the Church—is the basis of exaltation and glory for man. The Saints were to receive a fulness of priesthood and glory within the divine patriarchal order,[14] not by occupying a given office in the priesthood or holding a designated position in the Church. To receive a fulness, a man had to have the Melchizedek Priesthood conferred upon him and, as an elder in that priesthood, receive all the rites and ordinances of the temple. The Prophet explained: "If a man gets a fulness of the priesthood of God he has to get it in the same way that Jesus Christ obtained it, and that was by keeping all the commandments and obeying all the ordinances of the house of the Lord."[15] Again he declared:

> The question is frequently asked "Can we not be saved without going through with all those ordinances, &c.?" I would answer, No, not the *fulness of salvation.* Jesus said, "There are many mansions in my Father's house, and I will go and prepare a place for you." *House* here named should have been translated kingdom; and any person *who is exalted* to the highest mansion has to abide a celestial law, and *the whole law too.*[16]

It is one thing for a man to receive keys and offices in the priesthood, or in the Church with its assigned task of perfecting the Saints through the program of the gospel. It is another thing for him to be perfected and endowed with the full blessings and powers which the plan of life and salvation make available to him. As man is perfected, these blessings and powers are given to him in the divine patriarchal order, and to this end he must receive all the rites and ordinances of the house of the Lord.

Because the full program of the kingdom of God could only be established by means of the temple, the ordinances of the house of the Lord were said to be the "foundation of Zion."[17] Without the temple, the kingdom could not be developed on earth beyond its primary stages. The Prophet therefore wrote by revelation to the Saints: "There is not a place found on earth that he [God] may come to and restore again that which was lost unto you, or which he hath taken away, even *the fulness of the priesthood.*"[18] Of the Nauvoo Temple, the Quorum of the Twelve wrote: "In this house, *all the ordinances will be made manifest,* and many things will be shown forth, which have been hid from generation to generation."[19] The Prophet thus explained: "The Temple of the Lord . . . will be so constructed as to enable all the functions of the Priesthood to be duly exercised."[20]

So important was the temple to the program of the gospel that the Prophet explained: "The Church is not fully organized, in its proper order, and cannot be, until the Temple is complete."[21] He urged the Saints to hasten the work on the Nauvoo Temple. "I am anxious that the brethren should have their endowments and receive the fullness of the Priesthood," he said. "Then the Kingdom will be established."[22] He intended "to organize the Church in its proper order" after the temple at Nauvoo had been completed.[23] Because of the place of the temple in the plan of salvation, Joseph Smith viewed the completion of the Lord's house at Nauvoo as an event "of the greatest importance to the Church and the world."[24]

Endowment of Zion with Glory Through Temple Ordinances

The ordinances of the gospel are channels through which divine truth and power can come to man. By receiving the higher ordinances of the house of the Lord and by establishing the system of society which is based upon them, the Saints can be sanctified and endowed with the glory of God. A revelation explained that these sacred rites and ordinances were given "for the beginning of the revelations and foundation of Zion, and for the glory, honor, and endowment of all her municipals."[25] Thereby the Saints are to be crowned "with honor, immortality, and eternal life [i.e., celestial glory]."[26] The Prophet referred to the temple as a house in which God could reveal "the glories of His kingdom." He declared that through the "perfect order" which is revealed in the temple, God sends "forth power, revelations, and glory."[27] For this reason Joseph Smith prayed as he dedicated the Kirtland Temple and looked forward to the programs which were to be carried out in that holy sanctuary:

. . . and now, Holy Father, we ask thee to assist us, thy

people, with thy grace, in calling our solemn assembly, that it may be done to thine honor and to thy divine acceptance;

And in a manner that we may be found worthy, in thy sight, *to secure a fulfillment of the promises which thou hast made unto us, thy people, in the revelations given unto us;*

That thy glory may rest down upon thy people, and upon this thy house, which we now dedicate to thee, that it may be sanctified and consecrated to be holy, and that *thy holy presence may be continually in this house;*

And that all people who shall enter upon the threshold of the Lord's house may *feel thy power,* and feel constrained to acknowledge that thou hast sanctified it, and that it is thy house, a place of thy holiness. . . .

And that this house may be a house of prayer, a house of fasting, a house of faith, *a house of glory* of God, even thy house. . . .

And we ask thee, Holy Father, that thy servants may go forth from this house *armed with thy power,* and that thy name may be upon them, and *thy glory round about them. . . .* [28]

Latter-day scriptures reaffirm the testimony of the Bible that upon every dwelling place of mount Zion in the last days, and upon her assemblies, "the Lord will create . . . a cloud and smoke by day, and the shining of a flaming fire by night."[29] In 1823, the angel Moroni stated that the latter-day Zion would spread abroad and the Saints would increase in spiritual truth and power until they were sanctified and received "an inheritance where the glory of God" rested upon them.[30] The Book of Mormon confirmed this promise. Speaking to the Nephites about the New Jerusalem, Jesus said: "The powers of heaven shall be in the midst of this people; yea, even I will be in the midst of you."[31] Revelations to Joseph Smith express the same view. Of the New Jerusalem, one said: "The glory of the Lord shall be there."[32] Concerning the temple that is to be built in the New Jerusalem, another revelation said: "Inasmuch as my people build a house unto me in the name of the Lord, and do not suffer any unclean thing to come into it, that it be not defiled, my glory shall rest upon it; yea, and my presence shall be there, for I will come into it, and all the pure in heart that shall come into it shall see God."[33]

Because Joseph Smith and his associates held that these blessings could be realized by administering the sacred rites and ordinances of the temple to the faithful and by establishing the society of Zion, which has its basis in the covenants of the temple, the Quorum of the Twelve at Nauvoo wrote: "God requires of His Saints to build Him a house wherein His servants may be instructed, and *endowed with power from on high.*"[34] In a personal letter, Brigham Young explained: "As he [God] established ancient Israel, so he will establish his people in the last days, and hath set them to build him a house *where his glory may be made manifest, and where he can show his power;* also where his servants may be endowed with knowledge and wisdom to teach his gospel among all nations of the earth."[35]

The Renewal of the Earth to Glory by Establishment of Temple-Centered Society

The Prophet taught that it will be by establishing this divine program that Christ will renew the earth to a paradisiacal state of glory in the millennium. Having developed His glory among the Saints to a significant degree, Jesus will appear in glory to destroy the wicked, and the great spiritual powers and blessings which have been developed among the Saints in Zion will then be extended throughout the earth.[36] Concerning this divine program and its objectives, the latter-day Seer said:

> Truly this is a day long to be remembered by the Saints of the last days,—*a day in which the God of heaven has begun to restore the ancient order of His kingdom* unto His servants and His people,—a day in which all things are concurring to bring about the completion of the fullness of the Gospel, a fullness of the dispensation of dispensations, even the fullness of times; *a day in which God has begun to make manifest and set in order in His Church those things which have been,* and those things which the ancient prophets and wise men desired to see but died without beholding them; a day in which those things begin to be made manifest, which have been hid from before the foundation of the world, and which Jehovah has promised should be made

known in His own due time unto His servants, *to prepare the earth for the return of His glory, even a celestial glory, and a kingdom of Priests and kings to God and the Lamb, forever, on Mount Zion,* and with him the hundred and forty and four thousand whom John the Revelator saw, all of which is to come to pass in the restitution of all things.[37]

The Kirtland Blessings And Endowment

Preparations for Endowment with Power

In the Kirtland Temple, Joseph Smith began to develop the divine program by which the Saints could be endowed with glory and by which the earth will eventually be renewed to a state of paradisiacal glory. The initial manifestations of divine power were referred to as "the *beginning* of the blessings which shall be poured out."[38] The Prophet thus exclaimed: "Hosanna, hosanna, hosanna to Almighty God, *that rays of light begin to burst forth upon us even now.*"[39] Having reminded the Saints that they were "called to hold the keys of the mysteries," he observed a few months after the Kirtland manifestations had transpired: "Some have tasted *a little of these things,* many of which *are to be poured down from heaven* upon the heads of babes; yea, upon the weak, obscure and despised ones of the earth."[40] The experience of the Saints at Kirtland was but a foretaste of greater things to come in the last days. The latter-day Seer therefore admonished them to institute a reformation in their lives, that they might become "as little children, without malice, guile or hypocrisy."[41] Only then could they receive the full spiritual powers which they anticipated.

Joseph Smith held that spiritual powers and blessings such as were received on the day of Pentecost, in New Testament times, and among the Saints at Kirtland, Ohio, were not manifest without cause or preparation. They came by developing faith in Christ among the people and by administering the appropriate ordinances of the Holy Priesthood to those who believed. The latter-day Seer explained that the ancient apostles tarried in Jerusalem after Christ's ascension in order to prepare for the spiritual endowment which they were given on the day of Pentecost. "Had they not work to do in Jerusalem?" he queried. "They did work, and prepared a people for the Pentecost."[42] As the new dispensation began in modern times, Joseph Smith also prepared the Elders to receive such a conferment of glory and power.

That the Saints might receive the initial manifestations of glory and power in this dispensation, they were instructed by revelation in January, 1831, to move to Ohio, with the promise: "And there you shall be endowed with power from on high." Three days later another revelation referred to the anticipated manifestation as "a blessing such as is not known among the children of men"—one that would "be poured forth" upon their heads.[43] With a similar note of anticipation, the Prophet promised the Twelve in 1835:

> . . . if we are faithful, and live by every word that proceeds forth from the mouth of God, I will venture to prophesy that we shall get a blessing that will be worth remembering, if we should live as long as John the Revelator; our blessings will be such as we have not realized before, nor received in this generation.[44]

In order to receive the promised spiritual blessings and powers, the Saints were commanded to build a temple at Kirtland. As they began this task, a revelation explained: "I gave unto you a commandment that you should build a house, in the which house I design to endow those whom I have chosen with power from on high; for this is the promise of the Father unto you; therefore I command you to tarry, even as mine apostles in Jerusalem."[45] Having stressed the need to construct this edifice, Oliver Cowdery wrote in behalf of some prominent brethren at Kirtland, nearly two years before the anticipated events occurred: "Within that house, God shall pour out his Spirit in great majesty and glory, and encircle his people with fire more gloriously and marvelously than at Pentecost."[46]

Like the disciples on the day of Pentecost, the Latter-day

Saints were "to be taught from on high." To this end a revelation instructed: "Sanctify yourselves and ye shall be endowed with power."[47] During the spring and summer of 1835, the Elders' School at Kirtland was closed and the members were sent out to preach the gospel "preparatory to the endowment" of power and glory.[48] Their work in the ministry would help them acquire faith and humility to obtain the blessing. When the school opened again that fall, Joseph Smith admonished the Elders to prepare for "the glorious endowment" of divine power that God had in store for the faithful.[49]

The Twelve were also encouraged to "prepare their hearts in all humility for an endowment with power from on high." This admonition was followed by a revelation reproving them for their weaknesses and declaring that they would have to humble themselves before God in order "to receive an endowment" of power.[50] The Prophet charged: "The endowment you are so anxious about, you cannot comprehend now, nor could Gabriel explain it to the understanding of your dark minds; but strive to be prepared in your hearts, be faithful in all things, that when we meet in the solemn assembly . . . [we may] be clean every whit."[51]

Higher Ordinances of Priesthood Administered

Even before the temple was finished and dedicated, Joseph Smith administered some of the higher ordinances of the priesthood which pertain to the house of the Lord to several of the brethren.[52] Through these ordinances they could receive greater spiritual powers and blessings than they could normally acquire through the gift of the Holy Ghost alone. The Prophet seems to have given these higher ordinances to the Elders before the temple was finished and dedicated so that they might be prepared to participate in the solemn assembly which was held in the Lord's house shortly after it was dedicated.[53] This was not the full temple ceremony which was later given to the Saints at Nauvoo, Illinois, but consisted, as Brigham

Young explained, of "some of the first, or introductory, or initiatory ordinances, preparatory to an endowment."[54] According to Erastus Snow, the number who received these blessings "in the house of the Lord in Kirtland was about three hundred and sixty."[55]

Dedication of Kirtland Temple

The dedicatory services for the temple were held March 27, 1836, at 9:00 A.M., with the meeting continuing until 4:00 P.M. that day. During the services mention was made repeatedly of the spiritual blessings and powers which the Saints could receive through the program of the temple. President Sidney Rigdon began the services by reading the 96th and 24th Psalms. "Sing unto the Lord, bless his name; shew forth his salvation from day to day," the Psalmist wrote in words that were particularly appropriate. "Declare his glory among the heathen, his wonders among all people." Again:

> Lift up your heads, O ye gates; and be ye lifted up, ye everlasting doors; and the King of glory shall come in. . . .
>
> Who is this King of glory? The Lord of hosts, he is the King of glory.[56]

The choir then sang a hymn concerning the coming of Christ in glory. After the invocation, the choir again sang:

> God is the only Lord,
> Our shield and our defense;
> With gifts His hands are stored;
> We draw our blessings thence.
> He will bestow on Jacob's race
> Peculiar grace, and glory too.[57]

The major address of the day was delivered by President Ridgon, who declared that the reason Jesus had not a place "to lay His head" during His earthly mission was because of the unbelief of the people "in present revelation." Elder Rigdon further remarked "that their unbelief in present revelation was the means of dividing that generation into the various sects and parties that existed."

Though they were "zealous worshipers according to outward forms," they denied the power and revelation of God. The same condemnation rested upon men in modern times. The speaker "admitted there were many houses, many sufficiently large, built for the worship of God, but not one except this, on the face of the whole earth, that was built by divine revelation; and were it not for this the dear Redeemer might, in this day of science, this day of intelligence, this day of religion, say to those who would follow Him: 'The foxes have holes, the birds of the air have nests, but the Son of Man hath not where to lay His head.'"[58]

So confident was the Prophet that the Saints would receive an endowment of glory and power from God that he dictated the dedicatory prayer by the Spirit of revelation and had it prepared beforehand in printed form. Therein the latter-day Seer prayed:

> Let the anointings of thy ministers be sealed upon them with power from on high.
>
> Let it be fulfilled upon them, as upon those on the day of Pentecost; let the gift of tongues be poured out upon thy people, even cloven tongues as of fire, and the interpretation thereof.
>
> And let thy house be filled, as with a rushing mighty wind, with thy glory.[59]

After the dedicatory prayer, the choir sang a new hymn which had been prepared for the occasion, written by William W. Phelps and entitled "The Spirit of God Like a Fire is Burning." The first three stanzas were particularly appropriate:

The Spirit of God like a fire is burning!
The latter-day glory begins to come forth;
The visions and blessings of old are returning,
And angels are coming to visit the earth.

The Lord is extending the Saints' understanding,
Restoring their judges and all as at first;
The knowledge and power of God are expanding;
The veil o'er the earth is beginning to burst.

We'll call in our solemn assemblies in Spirit,
To spread forth the kingdom of heaven abroad,
That we through our faith may begin to inherit
The visions and blessings and glories of God.[60]

During the dedicatory services, some divine manifestations occurred. "President Frederick G. Williams arose and testified that while President Rigdon was making his first prayer, an angel entered the window and took his seat between Father Smith and himself, and remained there during the prayer."[61] Heber C. Kimball later declared that both President Williams and Joseph Smith, Sr. "had a fair view of his person."[62] "David Whitmer also saw angels in the house."[63] As the meeting came to a close, the Prophet recorded: "President Brigham Young gave a short address in tongues, and David W. Patten interpreted, and gave a short exhortation in tongues himself, after which I blessed the congregation in the name of the Lord, and the assembly dispersed a little past four o'clock, having manifested the most quiet demeanor during the whole exercise."[64]

Endowment with Power

The evening of the dedication the Prophet met with the several quorums of the priesthood in the temple to instruct them in the procedure of the ordinances which were to be administered in the temple. He also "gave instructions in relation to the spirit of prophecy, and called upon the congregation to speak, and not to fear to prophesy." "Do not quench the Spirit," he admonished, "for the first one that opens his mouth shall receive the Spirit of prophecy." Whereupon, the Prophet reported:

> Brother George A. Smith arose and began to prophesy, when a noise was heard like the sound of a rushing mighty wind, which filled the Temple, and all the congregation simultaneously arose, being moved upon by an invisible power; many began to speak in tongues and prophesy; others saw glorious visions; and I beheld the Temple was filled with angels, which fact I declared to the congregation. The people of the neighborhood came running together (hearing an unusual sound within, and seeing a bright light like a pillar of fire resting upon the

Temple), and were astonished at what was taking place. This continued until the meeting closed at eleven P.M.[65]

In referring to this incident, George A. Smith declared that hundreds of brethren had participated in "a greater manifestation of the power of God than that described by Luke on the day of Pentecost." He reported: "There came a shock on the house like the sound of a mighty rushing wind, and almost every man in the house arose, and hundreds of them were speaking in tongues, prophesying or declaring visions, almost with one voice."[66] Levi Jackman, who was present, also wrote: "I believe that as great things were heard and felt and seen as there was on the day of Pentecost with the apostles."[67]

That this was not a radical burst of fanatical zeal was evident in the fact that the Prophet had complete control of the situation; and for all its dynamic elements, it was an intelligently organized and directed experience in which members of the priesthood were given as much of the plan and power of the gospel as they could then bear.[68] Having attended the meetings which were held in the temple during this period and noted that the Spirit was "as profusely poured out" as on the day of Pentecost, Benjamin Brown reported:

> Hundreds of Elders spoke in tongues, but many of them being young in the Church, and never having witnessed the manifestation of this gift before, felt a little alarmed. This caused the Prophet Joseph Smith to pray the Lord to withhold the Spirit. Joseph then instructed them on the nature of the gift of tongues, and the operation of the Spirit generally.
>
> We had a most glorious and never-to-be-forgotten time. Angels were seen by numbers present. . . .[69]

Several others spoke of these and related incidents. Heber C. Kimball, Jedediah M. Grant, Vinson Knight, John Tanner, and Joel H. Johnson reported participating in these "manifestations of the power of God."[70] Erastus Snow gave a more detailed description in which he declared that "the angels of the Lord appeared" to some and "cloven tongues like fire sat upon many" of the brethren, and that "they prophesied and spoke with tongues as the Spirit gave them utterance."[71] Orson Pratt recalled: "They were filled from the crown of their heads to the soles of their feet with the power and inspiration of the Holy Ghost, and uttered forth prophecies . . . which have been fulfilling from that day to the present."[72] Not having been a recipient of these manifestations at the dedicatory services, Milo Andrus approached the Prophet and was informed that to receive such blessings he must desire them with all his heart. He therefore fasted and prayed before partaking of the Lord's Supper in the solemn assembly. He later testified that as he partook of these holy emblems he "saw the Holy Ghost descend upon the heads of those present like cloven tongues of fire." Whereupon he exclaimed: "It is enough, O Father, I will bear a faithful testimony of it while I live."[73]

Divine manifestations similar to these occurred on several occasions. Vilate Kimball wrote: "It was a season of great rejoicing, indeed, to the saints, and great and marvelous were the manifestations and power in the Lord's house."[74] Eliza R. Snow reported that she "was present on the memorable event of the dedication of the temple, when the mighty power of God was displayed," then said: "After its dedication [the Saints] enjoyed many refreshing seasons in that holy sanctuary."[75] Having reported the ministry of angels and the manifestation of "cloven tongues of fire" in the temple, Heber C. Kimball said:

> This continued several days and was attended by the marvelous spirit of prophecy. Every man's mouth was full of prophesying, and for a number of days or weeks our time was spent in visiting from house to house, administering bread and wine, and pronouncing blessings upon each other to that degree, that from the external appearances one would have supposed that the last days had truly come, in which the Spirit of the Lord was poured out upon all flesh, as far as the Church was concerned, for the sons and daughters of Zion were full of prophesying. . . . During this time many great and marvelous visions were seen.[76]

Others reported the manifestation of God's glory at Kirtland. Having spoken of "an abiding holy heavenly influence" which pervaded the temple at this period, Eliza R. Snow said: "Not only were angels often seen within, but a pillar of light was several times seen resting down upon the roof."[77] Of one of these incidents, Prescindia Huntington said:

> In Kirtland, we enjoyed many very great blessings, and often saw the power of God manifested. On one occasion I saw angels clothed in white walking upon the temple. It was during one of our monthly fast meetings, when the saints were in the temple worshipping. A little girl came to my door and in wonder called me out, exclaiming, "The meeting is on the top of the meeting house!" I went to the door, and there I saw on the temple angels clothed in white covering the roof from end to end. They seemed to be walking to and fro; they appeared and disappeared. The third time they appeared and disappeared before I realized that they were not mortal men. Each time in a moment they vanished, and their reappearance was the same. This was in broad daylight, in the afternoon. A number of the children in Kirtland saw the same.
>
> When the brethren and sisters came home in the evening, they told of the power of God manifested in the temple that day, and of the prophesying and speaking in tongues. It was also said, in the interpretation of tongues, "That the angels were resting down upon the house."[78]

The enlightening spiritual powers which were manifested in the temple permeated the community of Kirtland so that "the gifts of the gospel" were abundantly expressed and "a general joy pervaded the hearts of the Saints."[79] Eliza R. Snow wrote:

> We had the gift of prophecy—the gift of tongues—the interpretation of tongues—visions and marvelous dreams were related—the singing of heavenly choirs was heard, and wonderful manifestations of the healing power, through the administrations of the Elders, were witnessed. The sick were healed—the deaf made to hear—the blind to see and the lame to walk, in very many instances. It was plainly manifest that a sacred and divine influence—a spiritual atmosphere pervaded that holy edifice.[80]

Solemn Assembly

Following the dedication of the temple, the first solemn assembly was held in this dispensation. Such assemblies are designed to be held in the temples of the Lord.[81] Their purpose is one of solemn worship so that by the exercise of great faith, by prayer, and by fasting, the Saints can draw near to God and receive a significant outpouring of the Holy Spirit with its divine gifts, power, and blessings. Therein appropriate admonition may also be given, according to the needs of the Church at the time.

The Prophet indicated that solemn assemblies were to be held regularly, according to the needs of the Saints and the worthiness of the Elders. He therefore prayed, asking God that those who were ordained to the priesthood might be prepared "to receive an endowment [of divine power] in Thy house, even according to Thine own order *from time to time,* as Thou seest them worthy to be called into Thy solemn assembly."[82]

Solemn assemblies are conducted according to a prescribed order. "We must have all things prepared, and call our solemn assembly as the Lord has commanded us, that we may be able to accomplish His great work, and it must be done in God's own way," Joseph Smith explained to the Twelve. "The house of the Lord must be prepared, and the solemn assembly called and organized in it, according to the order of the house of God."[83] In January, 1836, the Prophet met with other authorities of the Church to consider the solemn assembly and to draft rules and regulations to govern the house of the Lord.[84] Later that month, President Smith reported: "In the evening met the Presidency . . . and counseled on the subject of endowment, and the preparation for the solemn assembly, which is to be called when the house of the Lord is finished."[85] After instructing the priesthood on these matters, the Prophet again wrote: "Having set all the quorums in order, I returned to my house, being weary with continual anxiety and labor, in putting all the authorities in order, and in striving to purify them for the solemn assembly, according to the commandment of the Lord."[86]

On the evening of Sunday, March 27, 1836, the day the temple was dedicated, Joseph Smith met with the several quorums of the priesthood to instruct the brethren in the order of sacred ordinances which were to be performed in the temple the following Wednesday, in the solemn assembly.[87] While meeting in the temple the evening before the assembly was held, the Prophet and other presiding authorities were instructed to cleanse their bodies and partake of the sacrament that they might "be made holy" before God and "thereby be qualified to officiate" in the ordinances which were to be administered the next day. The Prophet reported: "The Holy Spirit rested down upon us, and we continued in the Lord's House all night, prophesying and giving glory to God."[88] At eight o'clock the next morning, the Presidency, the Twelve, the Seventies, the High Council, the Bishops and their entire quorums, the Elders and all the official members of the Kirtland Stake of Zion, amounting to about three hundred people, met in the temple and received one of the sacred ordinances of the priesthood. Joseph Smith reported: "The brethren began to prophesy upon each other's heads . . . and continued prophesying, and blessing, and sealing them with hosanna and amen, until nearly seven o'clock in the evening."[89]

Bread and wine were then brought in and the Prophet reported: "I observed that we had fasted all the day, and lest we faint, as the Savior did so shall we do on this occasion; we shall bless the bread, and give it to the Twelve, and they to the multitude."[90]

Having been in the temple during the preceding night and all of that day, the Presidency retired to their homes at nine P.M., leaving the meeting in the charge of the Twelve. Joseph Smith wrote:

> The brethren continued exhorting, prophesying, and speaking in tongues until five o'clock in the morning. The Savior made His appearance to some, while angels ministered to

others, and it was a Pentecost and an endowment indeed, long to be remembered, for the sound shall go forth from this place into all the world, and the occurrences of this day shall be handed down upon the pages of sacred history, to all generations; as the day of Pentecost, so shall this day be numbered and celebrated as a year of jubilee, and time of rejoicing to the Saints of the Most High God.[91]

Consummation of Basic Gospel Program

As the Prophet was about to leave the solemn assembly, he reported: "I . . . observed to the quorums, that I had now completed the organization of the Church, and we had passed through all the necessary ceremonies, that I had given them all the instruction they needed, and that they now were at liberty, after obtaining their licenses, to go forth and build up the Kingdom of God."[92] Apparently the administration of the ordinances which were then given in the temple, consummated the basic program of the gospel insofar as it could be established by the commission which Joseph Smith had received at that time. He had established the program of the preparatory gospel, by which those who expressed faith could come unto Christ and be justified before the bar of God by the power of His atonement, and the program of the everlasting gospel, by which the obedient could draw upon the truth and light of the Holy Spirit to be sanctified and to mature in the divine image of the Son of God. He had organized the several quorums, councils, and offices of the priesthood to facilitate the spread of the gospel, to manage the affairs of the Saints, and to establish the program of Zion.[93] Finally, in the temple at Kirtland the latter-day Seer had given the Saints those sacred ordinances by which they could stand clean of the sins of the world and be sealed by the Holy Priesthood. Shortly after the solemn assembly was held, other keys and rights of the priesthood were committed to Joseph Smith and Oliver Cowdery by which the divine patriarchal order could be organized upon the earth.[94] But that was a higher echelon of organization and of power. In the solemn assembly, the basic program of the gospel was consummated, which the Prophet had begun to develop six years earlier when the Church was organized.

Summary

Joseph Smith held that temples play an important role in the plan of the restored gospel, for therein the higher ordinances of the plan of life and salvation are administered. For this reason the program of the gospel cannot be complete without the temple. Through the higher covenants and ordinances of the gospel, and by building up the society of Zion which is based upon them, the Saints can acquire the glory of God to a significant degree. By building up the kingdom of God on this spiritual plane, the faithful can also contribute to the ultimate objective of renewing the earth to a state of paradisiacal glory.

As the Church moved from New York to Ohio early in 1831, the Saints were promised that there they would be endowed with power from on high, as "the beginning of the blessings"[95] which they could receive by establishing the kingdom of God on the earth in the last days. To this end they were required to build a temple at Kirtland. There the Prophet administered to the Saints the initial ordinances of the house of the Lord as they were then revealed. There they enjoyed a modern Pentecost as a foretaste of the blessings which will follow when the Spirit of God is poured out upon all flesh. There also the first solemn assembly in this dispensation was held. All these things are vital factors in the over-all program of establishing the millennial kingdom upon the earth.

Notes

1. HC, IV, p. 608.
2. D&C 124:28, 39, 40. Joseph Smith stated that the Nauvoo Temple would be a place "where instructions from the Most High will be received, and from this place go forth to distant lands."—HC, IV, p. 269.
3. D&C 124:38–39.
4. 2 Nephi 5:16.

5. See, for example, Jacob 1:17; 2:2; Mosiah 1:18; 2:1–7; 7:17; 11:10, 12; 19:5; Alma 10:2; 3 Nephi 11:1.

6. D&C 57:2–3.

7. D&C 36:8; 42:36. See also D&C 97:15–17.

8. D&C 88:119–120.

9. HC, V, p. 423.

10. *Ibid.*, pp. 423–424. Still again: "Why gather the people together in this place? For the same purpose that Jesus wanted to gather the Jews—to receive the ordinances, the blessings, and glories that God has in store for His Saints."—*Ibid.*, p. 427.

11. *Ibid.*, III, p. 380.

12. D&C 88:107.

13. D&C 76:95.

14. See chapter twelve in this volume.

15. HC, V, p. 424.

16. *Ibid.*, VI, p. 184, citing John 14:2. (The word "house" is italicized in the original.)

17. D&C 124:39.

18. D&C 124:28.

19. HC, IV, p. 449.

20. *Ibid.*, p. 269.

21. *Ibid.*, p. 603.

22. JD, XII, p. 49.

23. HC, IV, p. 604.

24. *Ibid.*, pp. 492–493.

25. D&C 124:39.

26. D&C 124:55.

27. HC, V, p. 423; IV, p. 208. The Prophet spoke of the temple as the place where the Saints could "receive the ordinances, the blessings, and glories that God" has in store for them.—*Ibid.*, V, p. 427.

28. D&C 109:10–13, 16, 22.

29. Isaiah 4:5.

30. MA, II (October, 1835), p. 199.

31. 3 Nephi 20:22; 21:25.

32. D&C 45:67.

33. D&C 97:15–16.

34. HC, IV, p. 449.

35. Letter of Brigham Young to C. Brown of Pensacola, Florida, written at Nauvoo, Illinois, August 27, 1845; in "Brigham Young Papers, 1843–1853," Church Historian's Library, Salt Lake City, Utah.

36. This point will be discussed in greater detail in volume IV of this series.

37. HC, IV, pp. 492–493. The plan and program of Zion as a temple-oriented society will be discussed in volume III of this study.

38. D&C 110:10.

39. HC, V, p. 362.

40. *Ibid.*, III, p. 296.

41. *Ibid.*

42. *Ibid.*, V, p. 259.

43. D&C 38:32; 39:15.

44. HC, II, p. 309.

45. D&C 95:8–9.

46. Letter of Oliver Cowdery to John F. Boynton at Saco, Maine, written May 6, 1834; Cowdery Collection, Huntington Library, San Marino, California; used by permission.

47. D&C 43:16.

48. HC, II, p. 218.

49. *Ibid.*, p. 301.

50. *Ibid.*, pp. 287, 300. See also p. 53.

51. *Ibid.*, p. 309. See also pp. 334, 339, 345, 364, 368, and 373.

52. During the Kirtland period, these blessings were given only to men. Since they were priesthood ordinances, they were confined to men who had been ordained to the priesthood. For example Benjamin F. Johnson wrote:

> I attended the dedication of the Temple and all subsequent meetings. I knew of the endowments received by the elders, and learned of the ministering of the angels at the time of their appearance in the Temple; but *as I had not yet received the Priesthood I did not receive the higher blessings.*—Johnson, *My Life's Review*, p. 23.

53. This conclusion is supported by the fact that before the second solemn assembly was held in the Kirtland Temple, in April, 1837, many of those who had been ordained to the priesthood, but who had not received these blessings, were given them "that all might be prepared" for the assembly.—HC, II, p. 475.

54. JD, II, p. 31.

55. The journal of Erastus Snow, pp. 5–6.

56. Psalm 96:2–3; 24:7, 10.

57. HC, II, pp. 412–413. The first hymn was written by Parley P. Pratt and the second by William W. Phelps.

58. *Ibid.*, pp. 414–415. See Matthew 8:18–20.

59. D&C 109:35–37. For evidence that the dedicatory prayer had been prepared in printed form, see JD, XI, p. 9.

60. MA, II (March, 1836), p. 280; HC, II, p. 426.

61. HC, II, p. 427; MA, II (March, 1836), p. 281.

62. Helen Mar Whitney, "Early Reminiscences," *Women's Exponent*, IX (February 1, 1881), p. 130. See also Orson F. Whitney, *Life of Heber C. Kimball* (Salt Lake City, 1945), p. 91.

63. HC, II, p. 427.

64. *Ibid.*, p. 428.

65. *Ibid.*

66. JD, II, p. 215; XI, p. 10.

67. "A Short Sketch of the Life of Levi Jackman—1797–1876," *Mormon Diaries*, XIV, No. 5, p. 17.

68. See JD, II, p. 215, where George A. Smith expressed this point.

69. *Testimonies For The Truth: A Record of Manifestations of the Power of God, Miraculous and Providential, Witnessed in The Travels and Experiences of Benjamin Brown* (Liverpool, England, 1853), pp. 10–11.

70. *Journal History*, March 27, 1836; *The Contributor*, IV, p. 242; Lola Belnap Coolbear, "Sketch of the Life of Vinson Knight," p. 4; John Tanner, "Sketch of an Elder's Life," *Scraps of Biography, Tenth Book* (Salt Lake City, 1883), p. 14; "Diary of Joel Hills Johnson, 1802–1882," I, p. 17. See also Wilford Woodruff, *Leaves From My Journal* (Salt Lake City, 1882), p. 21.

71. The journal of Erastus Snow, pp. 9–13. Of the ministry of angels at the Solemn Assembly, Heber C. Kimball said: "While these things [i.e., the ordinances then being administered] were being attended to, the beloved disciple John was seen in our midst by Joseph Smith, Jun., Oliver Cowdery and others."—Helen Mar Whitney, "Early Reminiscences," *Women's Exponent,* IX (February 1, 1881), p. 130.

72. JD, XVIII, pp. 131–132.

73. As related by the recipient and recorded in "Diaries of Charles L. Walker, 1833–1904," II, pp. 650–651. In his autobiography, Elder Andrus wrote "I was in Kirtland at the dedication of the Temple and the endowment of the Elders . . . I saw fire descend and rest on the heads of the Elders, and they spoke with tongues, and prophesied."—Milo Andrus, *Autobiographical Sketch,* pub. by his son, Milo Andrus, Jr., p. 4.

74. Tullidge, *op. cit.,* p. 110.

75. *Ibid.,* p. 65.

76. Whitney, *op. cit.,* p. 93.

77. Tullidge, *op. cit.,* p. 99.

78. *Ibid.,* p. 207.

79. Johnson, *My Life's Review,* p. 23.

80. Snow, *Biography and Family Record of Lorenzo Snow,* p. 11.

81. See D&C 124:39.

82. HC, II, p. 334. For the report of the second solemn assembly held in the Kirtland Temple, see *ibid.,* pp. 475–480.

83. *Ibid.,* pp 308–309.

84. *Ibid.,* pp. 364, 367.

85. *Ibid.,* p. 385.

86. *Ibid.,* p. 388.

87. *Ibid.,* p. 428.

88. *Ibid.,* p. 430.

89. *Ibid.,* pp. 430, 431.

90. *Ibid.,* p. 431.

91. *Ibid.,* pp. 432–433.

92. *Ibid.,* p. 432.

93. As the Prophet's work related to the organization of the Church, see *ibid.,* pp. 124, 308.

94. This subject will be discussed in chapter twelve.

95. D&C 110:10.

12

The Divine Patriarchal Order

> *Let all my saints . . . build a house to my name, for the Most High to dwell therein.*
>
> *For there is not a place found on earth that he may come to and restore again that which was lost unto you, or which he hath taken away, even the fulness of the priesthood.* —REVELATION TO JOSEPH SMITH.

The Lord through Joseph Smith made it clear that it is not enough for man to be born of water and of the Spirit and thereby become a son of Jesus Christ in eternal life. To realize the full purpose of his being, man must also become a father spiritually, under Christ, in the sense that he is an agent through whom the living attributes and powers of the Holy Spirit are developed in his children in the flesh. The gospel program requires those who become sons of Christ to be organized into a divine patriarchal order where each man is made a father spiritually over his children on earth. This is an important feature of the gospel plan. It is by the sacred rites, ordinances, and covenants which are administered in the temple that the Saints are organized into this divine family order and become fathers and mothers under Christ in developing the divine attributes and powers of eternal life in their children.

Restoration Of Keys Of Divine Patriarchal Order

Early Beginnings of Divine Patriarchal Order

Since the divine patriarchal order has its basis in the covenant of baptism by which those who are born into the kingdom of God become sons and daughters of Jesus Christ, it had its beginning in this dispensation in the ministry of John the Baptist to Joseph Smith and Oliver Cowdery, in May, 1829.[1] John's mission anciently was to go forth "in the spirit and power of Elias, *to turn the hearts of the fathers to the children, and the disobedient to the wisdom of the just; to make ready a people prepared for the Lord.*"[2] The Aaronic Priesthood was restored in modern times to fulfill the same purposes. Those who received it were to begin the work of building up the divine patriarchal order in preparation for the coming of Christ—the Father of all who acquire membership in the celestial family order.[3]

After having begun to teach the plan of birth into the kingdom of God in the new dispensation, Joseph Smith started, on January 21, 1836, to organize the divine patriarchal order as a sanctified system on earth. He began to administer the ordinance which was made the foundation of the temple rites through which the divine family order is organized, by giving the ordinance to his father, Joseph Smith, Sr., who had previously been ordained to be the Patriarch to the Church. In conjunction with the ordinance, Joseph Smith, Sr. was blessed by the First Presidency of the Church to be the Patriarch to the Church and to attend to all the duties that pertained to that office. The members of the First Presidency, beginning with the eldest, then received the ordinance under the hands of Patriarch Smith. When the Prophet received the sacred rite, the Patriarch sealed upon him "the blessings of Moses, to lead Israel in the latter days, even as Moses led him in days of old; also the blessings of Abraham, Isaac and Jacob."[4]

It is apparent that the above ordinance was patriarchal in nature, and that Joseph Smith received special rights and blessings which pertained to him alone as the presiding officer of the Dispensation of the Fulness of Times. Patriarch Smith, who had been ordained to the office of Patriarch to the Church on December 18, 1833, was empowered by the First Presidency to officiate in the patriarchal office in giving this ordinance to members of that presiding body. As an additional blessing, the Patriarch sealed upon the Prophet the blessings of Moses and of Abraham, Isaac and Jacob.[5] Though the full keys and powers of the divine patriarchal order were not given to the latter-day Seer until April 3, 1836, it appears that in the above ordinance he had sealed upon his head the basic powers of presidency over the family of Christ in this dispensation.[6]

The Prophet's position as the presiding figure in the divine patriarchal order in this dispensation is like that of Abraham in his. "As I said unto Abraham concerning the kindreds of the earth," a revelation declared, "even so I say unto my servant Joseph."[7] Abraham is a father in eternal life under Christ of all who are born into the kingdom of God during and after his day.[8] The latter-day Seer's appointment to a like position in his day and for suceeding generations was foreshadowed when Christ appeared to him in February, 1831, and instructed him to seal several individuals to eternal life. To them the Prophet said: "He [Christ] has given you all to me."[9] By the ordinance referred to above and by the appointments which he later received from Moses, Elias, and Elijah,[10] Joseph Smith was given the full right through the priesthood to be the father in eternal life under Christ of all who are born into the kingdom of God in this dispensation.

Coming of Moses, Elias, and Elijah

Only the initial ordinances of the divine patriarchal order were given to the Saints in the Kirtland Temple. Brigham Young explained that even though those "preparatory ordinances" were "accompanied by the ministration of angels, and the presence of the Lord Jesus

Christ, [they] were but a faint similitude of the ordinances of the House of the Lord in their fulness."[11] A few days after the solemn assembly was held in the Kirtland Temple, in March, 1836, the keys and powers by which the more complete program of the divine patriarchal order could be built up and perfected were given to Joseph Smith and Oliver Cowdery. With the restoration of these keys and powers, new ordinances which pertain to the divine family order were to be performed and new arrangements in church organization made. A higher echelon of divine organization, doctrine, and power was to be established.

The keys and powers of the higher program were restored on Sunday, April 3, 1836. After the administration of the Lord's Supper, Joseph Smith and Oliver Cowdery retired to the pulpit of the temple, the veils separating that place from the congregation having been lowered, and bowed themselves in solemn and silent prayer. They wrote that upon rising from prayer:

> The veil was taken from our minds, and the eyes of our understanding were opened.
>
> We saw the Lord standing upon the breastwork of the pulpit before us; and under his feet was a paved work of pure gold, in color like amber.
>
> His eyes were as a flame of fire; the hair of his head was white like the pure snow; his countenance shone above the brightness of the sun; and his voice was as the sound of the rushing of great waters, even the voice of Jehovah, saying:
>
> I am the first and the last; I am he who liveth, I am he who was slain; I am your advocate with the Father. . . .
>
> After this vision closed, the heavens were again opened unto us; and Moses appeared before us, and committed unto us the keys of the gathering of Israel from the four parts of the earth, and the leading of the ten tribes from the land of the north.
>
> After this, Elias appeared, and committed the dispensation of the gospel of Abraham, saying that in us and our seed all generations after us should be blessed.
>
> After this vision had closed, another great and glorious vision burst upon us; for Elijah the prophet, who was taken to heaven without tasting death, stood before us, and said:
>
> Behold, the time has fully come, which was spoken of by the

mouth of Malachi—testifying that he [Elijah] should be sent, before the great and dreadful day of the Lord come—

To turn the hearts of the fathers to the children, and the children to the fathers, lest the whole earth be smitten with a curse—

Therefore, the keys of this dispensation are committed into your hands; and by this ye may know that the great and dreadful day of the Lord is near, even at the doors.[12]

Visitation of Moses

The keys and conferrals which were given to Joseph Smith and Oliver Cowdery in the Kirtland Temple enabled them to accomplish several things in establishing the divine patriarchal order on the earth. The scattered remnants of ancient Israel were to be gathered in the latter days. As early as 1823, the angel Moroni informed Joseph Smith of the nature of this great work.[13] Among the gathered remnants, with others who would identify themselves in the same covenant, the divine patriarchal order was to be established. To this end Moses, who held the keys of the gathering and leading of Israel anciently, restored those keys to the earth in 1836.

Coming of Elias

Elias conferred upon Joseph Smith and Oliver Cowdery the same divine rights, privileges, and promises which God gave anciently to Abraham and his elect posterity in the flesh—his descendants through Isaac and Jacob.[14] These rights, privileges, and promises are those which pertain to the divine patriarchal order as it centered in Abraham and the patriarchs before him. In this conferral it was as though Elias said to the Prophet, "By this appointment you are a modern Abraham possessing that which God gave to the ancient patriarchs. In your day and for the generations of the earth to come, the rights, privileges, and promises which God gave to Abraham will center in you."

The divine patriarchal order, which has its basis in the

covenant of baptism, is brought to fruition in the new and everlasting covenant of marriage, in which the sons and daughters of Christ are made fathers and mothers spiritually over their children in the flesh and are given the promises which were conferred upon the Prophet and his associate by Elias. A revelation declared that by means of the new and everlasting covenant of marriage "Abraham received promises concerning his seed, and of the fruit of his loins."[15] It then said to Joseph Smith: "This promise is yours also, because ye are of Abraham."[16] The same general blessings are given to all who embrace the sacred covenant of eternal marriage.

Like all other promises which have their origin in the appointments which were made in the Grand Organizational Council before man was placed upon the earth, the promises which were given to Abraham's descendants through Isaac and Jacob were contingent upon their faith and their responsiveness to the Holy Spirit in mortality. These sacred rights and promises consisted of: (1) the promise that Abraham's descendants would be numerous and that they would continue in the world and out of the world (in the resurrection) without end;[17] (2) the right of his elect posterity to receive the articles and covenants of adoption by which they could become sons and daughters of Jesus Christ in the living attributes and powers of eternal life;[18] (3) the right of his elect descendants in the flesh to bear the priesthood of God;[19] (4) the right of his elect children to receive those sacred covenants and sealing powers of the priesthood which are administered in the house of the Lord by which they could be organized according to the divine patriarchal order and become fathers and mothers spiritually under Christ in the divine family order;[20] and (5) the right of his elect posterity, by complying with the above requisites, to be endowed with the glory and power of God.[21]

Two major responsibilities accompanied these blessings and promises: (1) the responsibility of building up the divine patriarchal order to be an ensign and a standard to the world, and thus preparing the Saints to be endowed with glory; and (2) the charge to preach the gospel to all other families of the earth, that by obedience to the plan of life and salvation responsive souls throughout the world might become sons and daughters of Christ and become part of the divine patriarchal order through adoption.

Appearance of Elijah

After Elias had committed a dispensation of appointment and promise to Joseph Smith and Oliver Cowdery, Elijah then revealed the priesthood and the sacred covenants by which the appointments and promises which were given by Elias could be administered to men in the latter days. In 1823, the angel Moroni quoted Malachi's prophecy to Joseph Smith concerning the coming of Elijah, and gave significant clarifications concerning the nature of the ancient prophet's latter-day ministration. Moroni's version states:

> Behold, I will *reveal* unto you the Priesthood, by the hand of Elijah the prophet, before the coming of the great and dreadful day of the Lord.
>
> And *he shall plant in the hearts of the children the promises made to the fathers,* and the hearts of the children shall turn to their fathers.
>
> If it were not so, the whole earth would be utterly wasted at his coming.[22]

Elijah came to *reveal* the priesthood.[23] To reveal is to make known or disclose, as something before unknown or unseen—to give knowledge or to divulge. Elijah thus revealed the use or function of the priesthood in a sphere of action theretofore unknown, and he committed the keys by which the priesthood could be used in this new sphere and by which it could perform the new ordinances.[24] In referring to this new usage, Brigham Young said: "There are keys to open up other ordinances which I will mention."[25] Elijah committed these keys to men on earth. Joseph Smith explained that God would "send Elijah *to seal the children to the fathers, and the fathers to the children.*"[26] This was a new way in which the sealing power of the priesthood was to function. Of the key to that power, Parley P. Pratt said: "This last key of the Priesthood is the most sacred of all, and pertains exclusively to the First Presidency of the Church, without whose sanction, and approval or authority, no sealing blessing shall be administered pertaining to things of the resurrection and the life to come."[27] By the keys of the priesthood which Elijah restored, the divine patriarchal order can be established on earth and extended to the faithful in past generations until all the righteous children of Adam are sealed together in one great patriarchal unit.[28]

Moroni also declared to Joseph Smith that Elijah would "plant in the hearts of the children the promises made to the fathers."[29] The fathers are the ancient patriarchs. And the promises which were made to the fathers are those promises which God gave to Abraham and other great patriarchs concerning their descendants in the flesh, which promises Elias conferred upon Joseph Smith and Oliver Cowdery in the Kirtland Temple. By the keys and functions of the priesthood which Elijah revealed, these promises may be planted in the hearts of the children—that is, actually given to the children—of the ancient patriarchs in the latter days. The difference between the conferrals which were made by Elias and Elijah, therefore, is that Elias committed a dispensation of appointment and promise, while Elijah revealed the glorious fact that the priesthood could be used to confer these appointments and promises upon the Saints, and he gave the keys and covenants of the priesthood by which this could be done.

Joseph Smith spoke on two occasions of the nature of the keys and powers of the priesthood which Elijah restored in the last days. He said:

> Elijah was the last Prophet that held the keys of the Priesthood, and who will, before the last dispensation, restore the authority and deliver the keys of the Priesthood, in order that all the ordinances may be attended to in righteousness. It is true that the Savior had authority and power to bestow this blessing; but the sons of Levi were too prejudiced. "And I will

send Elijah the Prophet before the great and terrible day of the Lord," etc., etc. Why send Elijah? Because he holds the key of the authority to administer in all the ordinances of the Priesthood; and without the authority is given, the ordinances could not be administered in righteousness.[30]

Again the Prophet said: "The spirit, power, and calling of Elijah is, that ye have power to hold the key of the revelations, ordinances, oracles, powers and endowments of the fulness of the Melchizedek Priesthood and of the kingdom of God on the earth; and to receive, obtain, and perform all the ordinances belonging to the kingdom of God, even unto the turning of the hearts of the fathers unto the children, and the hearts of the children unto the fathers, even those who are in heaven."[31]

This statement makes it plain that Elijah revealed the priesthood and committed the keys to build up the kingdom of God as a patriarchal structure, not merely as a church or as a social order. Thus, while Elias appointed Joseph Smith and Oliver Cowdery to the same rights, privileges, and promises which God gave to the ancient patriarchs, Elijah revealed the priesthood and committed the keys and covenants which were necessary in order to organize the kingdom of God as a divine family order and to seal upon the faithful the rights, privileges, and promises which Elias gave. The Prophet observed: "He [God] shall send Elijah the prophet, and *he shall reveal the covenants of the fathers in relation to the children, and the covenants of the children in relation to the fathers.*"[32] Again: "Elijah shall reveal *the covenants to seal the hearts of the fathers to the children, and the children to the fathers.*"[33]

Nature Of Divine Patriarchal Order

Antiquity of Divine Patriarchal Order

The Book of Abraham indicates that though the divine patriarchal order began on this sphere with Adam, it had its origin in heaven before the creation of the earth. "It came down from the fathers, from the beginning of time,"

Abraham wrote, "yea, even from the beginning, or *before the foundations of the earth.*"[34] This divine family order thus came down in eternity by generation to Adam, and from Adam it extended to the patriarchs of later times on this earth.

For men on this earth, the divine patriarchal order begins with the Father, Elohim—the Man of Holiness. Joseph Smith taught that this exalted being is not merely a creator in the sense that He is an organizer, but that He is our Father. He is the great head of human procreation—the Father of our organized spirits, directly, and of our physical bodies, indirectly, through Adam.[35] He is also the center of the living attributes and powers of eternal life, or glory. From Him, these divine attributes and powers are dispensed to man through Christ, with the keys, rights, and powers by which the divine patriarchal order can be established and perpetuated. The Prophet interpreted a certain figure in facsimile number two in the Book of Abraham as representing "God sitting upon his throne, revealing through the heavens the grand Key-words of the Priesthood."[36] Through these the divine patriarchal order is established among the righteous in the several worlds which God creates. Through Christ, this divine family order is designed to unite the saints of all ages on the earth into one great family under the Man of Holiness, each father receiving proper respect and recognition in each aspect of life within the over-all program.

Eternal Marriage the Basis of Divine Patriarchal Order

One of the glorious truths which was revealed to Joseph Smith was that the sacred relationships of marriage and of the home should continue both in time and in eternity, if the covenant of marriage is made and kept according to the law of God and sealed by the Holy Priesthood.[37] The new and everlasting covenant of marriage is the crowning covenant of the divine patriarchal order and the source from which all the rights, privileges, and blessings that are associated with that system flow.

Within the divine patriarchal order, wives are united with their husbands in the new and everlasting covenant of marriage, and children are secured to their parents in a sacred family order that is designed to continue forever. By organizing each family of the faithful into an eternal unit and by uniting each generation of the righteous to the succeeding generation, the divine patriarchal order can be built up and perpetuated in the earth.[38]

Organization of Divine Patriarchal Order in Temple

Joseph Smith taught that the ordinances of the house of the Lord are those by which the divine patriarchal order can be established on earth and perpetuated from generation to generation.[39] "Go to and finish the temple," he said as he spoke to the Saints of the Patriarchal Priesthood, "and God will fill it with power, and you will then receive more knowledge concerning this priesthood."[40]

When the Prophet began to administer the program of the temple, he explained that he then "set forth the order pertaining to the Ancient of Days."[41] The Ancient of Days is the oldest man, Adam,[42] and the order which pertains to the Ancient of Days is the divine patriarchal order over which Adam, or Michael,[43] presides, "under the counsel and direction of the Holy One, who is without beginning of days or end of life."[44] By means of the temple, that eternal family order was again to be established on earth among those who accepted the gospel in the last days.

Righteous Men Priests and Kings unto God

Within the divine patriarchal order, righteous men were to be made kings and priests (and their wives queens and priestesses) over their faithful descendants. Joseph Smith repeatedly made reference to these major objectives of the gospel program. Referring to biblical testimony of the millennial kingdom, he said: "John represents the sound which he heard from heaven, as giving thanks and glory to God, saying that the Lamb . . . had made them kings and priests unto God: and they should reign on the earth." "If the Saints are not to reign," the Prophet queried, "for what purpose are they crowned?"[45] As he spoke of the millennial kingdom to be established through the work of the latter-day dispensation, Joseph Smith referred to it as "a kingdom of Priests and kings to God and the Lamb, forever."[46] Of the purpose of the temple in organizing this patriarchal kingdom, he said:

> As soon as the Temple and baptismal font are prepared, we calculate to give the Elders of Israel . . . those last and most impressive ordinances, *without which we cannot obtain celestial thrones.* But there must be a holy place prepared for this purpose, . . . that men may receive their endowments and *be made kings and priests unto the most High God.*[47]

Righteous Men Fathers in Eternal Life

As a priest in the divine patriarchal order, each righteous man is a father over his children in the divine attributes and powers of eternal life. Having become a son of Jesus Christ by being born into the kingdom of God, each faithful man may grow up spiritually to become, in turn, a father under Christ within the divine patriarchal system. To this end, he must receive the sacred rites, ordinances, and covenants of the house of the Lord.

Ordinances are channels of divine mercy and power. Through the higher ordinances of the priesthood which are administered in the temple, a righteous man can acquire greater manifestations of divine truth and power than he can normally receive through the gift of the Holy Ghost alone. Joseph Smith spoke of the faithful receiving the "power of the Priesthood" through the ordinances of the temple.[48] "You need an endowment, brethren," he said, "in order that you may be prepared and able to overcome all things." Of the expressions of the spiritual power which they could acquire in the temple, he said: "The sick will be healed, the lame made to walk, the deaf to hear, and the blind to see, through your instrumentality."[49] For this reason, apparently, these rites and ordinances are referred to as the endowment ceremony, for thereby the

Saints can be endowed with power from God. With these greater channels of divine power open to him, a faithful man can become a father spiritually in the full sense that is possible within the divine patriarchal order.

One who is a father spiritually under Christ possesses the right and responsibility to confer the blessings and powers of the priesthood and of the gospel upon his children in the flesh. A man who receives all the blessings of the temple is not a father merely because he gives physical endowments to those who are tabernacled in the flesh as his children, but because he can also lawfully develop in them the divine attributes and powers of the Spirit which lead eventually to eternal life. This is a paternal requirement of the highest order. The Prophet may have had this general concept in mind when he suggested: "There are many teachers, but, perhaps, not many fathers."[50]

According to latter-day revelation, Adam was the first man on earth to be born into the kingdom of God and thus to become a son of Jesus Christ in eternal life.[51] He was also the first to receive the sacred covenants upon which the divine patriarchal order is built,[52] and in this way he was made a father spiritually over his righteous descendants in the flesh. Under Christ, he presides over the divine patriarchal order for this earth, as the great spiritual head in the eternal family of the righteous. But even though Adam is the great progenitor in physical life of all men on earth, only those who embrace the gospel and thereby acquire membership in the divine patriarchal order become his children in the living attributes and powers of eternal life.

Joseph Smith taught that Adam was called Michael because of his place in the divine patriarchal order. Having been born into the kingdom of God and having acquired the keys of the priesthood over his posterity in the flesh, with the right to dispense to them the spiritual blessings and powers that lead to eternal life, he was to stand as the father of both physical and divine endowments of life for his children to the latest generation. "He is Michael," the Prophet explained, *"because he was the first and father of all, not only by [physical] progeny, but the first to hold the spiritual blessings,* to whom was made known the plan of ordinances for the salvation of his posterity unto the end, and to whom Christ was first revealed, and *through whom Christ has been revealed from heaven, and will continue to be revealed from henceforth."*[53] This statement is in harmony with a revelation which declared: "[God] . . . hath appointed Michael your prince, and established his feet, and set him upon high, and *given unto him the keys of salvation under the counsel and direction of the Holy One,* who is without beginning of days or end of life."[54]

The name Michael means "Who is like God?" The Man of Holiness is the source of all the attributes and powers of life in the total plan of life and salvation—in spirit life, in physical life, and in eternal life. If the interrogation above is applied to Michael, or Adam, it may be said that he is like God in that through him the attributes and powers of both physical and eternal life are given to man.

Other patriarchs after Adam were given the same rights, powers, and privileges concerning their descendants. In addition, they were made fathers by adoption of those from all other families of the earth, during and after their day, who embraced the gospel and became sons and daughters in the celestial family of Jesus Christ. For this reason the Lord promised Abraham: " . . . as many as receive this Gospel *shall be called after thy name, and shall be accounted thy seed, and shall rise up and bless thee, as their father."*[55] This means that when the divine patriarchal order is perfected for this earth, those who embrace the gospel from all families of the earth will become the children of the patriarchs, in one great celestial family, through the sealing power of the priesthood.

That which was true of Adam and of other ancient patriarchs is also true in a general way of every man who embraces the gospel and receives all the sacred ordinances and covenants of the temple.

Divine Patriarchal Order Sealed

Joseph Smith taught that when the divine patriarchal order has been organized by means of the sacred covenants of the temple, the sealing power of the Melchizedek Priesthood can be used in behalf of those who are tried and proved, to make their calling and election sure to the sacred family relationships which exist in eternity within the divine patriarchal order. Through the sealing power of the priesthood, the faithful are made in actual fact priests and kings (and priestesses and queens) to God within the divine family order, with the promise guaranteed to them by the sealing power of the Holy Priesthood that they will reign with Christ in the millennial society and in eternity.[56] Those who are finally crowned receive a fulness of the priesthood. "For any person to have the fullness . . . he must be a king and a priest," Brigham Young explained. "A man may be anointed king and priest long before he receives his kingdom."[57] By the action of the sealing power, the divine plan of life and salvation is consummated so far as man's earth life is concerned, and the faithful are prepared to receive exaltation in the celestial kingdom of God.

Sealing of Children to Parents

The same basic principles which apply to marriage for time and eternity also hold true in the binding of children to their parents in a family unit for eternity. Concerning children, the Prophet said to the Saints: "In order for you to receive your children to yourselves you must have a promise—some ordinance; some blessing, in order to ascend above principalities."[58]

Children who are born within the covenant of eternal marriage are bound automatically to their parents according to the provisions of that covenant. But if children are not born within the new and everlasting covenant of marriage, they must be sealed to their parents by the power and authority of the Holy Priesthood if the family unit is to continue in eternity.

Interrelationship of Temple Ordinances

The Prophet implied that there is an interrelationship between the rites and ordinances of the temple similar to that of the first principles and ordinances of the gospel,[59] so that a person may have to receive all the rites and ordinances of the house of the Lord in order to have any of them prove efficacious in the final analysis. The latter-day Seer declared: "Those who will not receive all the ordinances [of the temple] will come short of the fullness of that [celestial] glory, *if they do not lose the whole of it.*"[60] In receiving the initial ordinance of the house of the Lord, a man is given the promise (based upon his faithfulness) of becoming a king and a priest in the kingdom of God. Thereafter the program of the temple is designed to bring man to realize that exalted station in eternity. There may be no halfway place at which he can stop. Should he fail to achieve the full objectives of that program, he may lose all of that which the temple has prepared him to receive.[61]

Divine Patriarchal Order Instituted

Basic Ordinance Given in Kirtland Temple

The basic ordinance of the program by which the divine patriarchal order was to be established was administered in the Kirtland Temple to many who had previously received the priesthood.[62] Orson Pratt explained, however, that this was not the full development of the endowment.[63] This was the same basic ordinance which the Prophet received as referred to in the beginning of this chapter,[64] except that he was given additional blessings by virtue of his position as head of the divine patriarchal order in this dispensation.

Introduction of Ordinances of Holy Endowment

In the months following the divine manifestations and conferrals which occurred in Kirtland, the Saints had little time to enjoy the temple they had built. With Americans in general they were caught in the financial collapse of 1837. The majority of the Saints left Kirtland under trying circumstances and spent a hectic period with other members of the Church who had settled in Missouri. Soon after this the Saints were driven from Missouri and were faced with the task of building another city and temple at Nauvoo, Illinois, beginning in 1839. Their second temple was designed as a holy sanctuary in which they could perform the higher rites, ordinances, and covenants by which they could be organized as families within the divine patriarchal order. However, Joseph Smith was prompted to have these blessings administered to some of the brethren and their wives before the Nauvoo Temple was finished. His decision to do so proved to be inspired, for he was killed several months before that structure was completed.

The Prophet began on May 4, 1842, to introduce among the Saints the more complete program of the house of the Lord. Reporting the activities of that day, he said:

> I spent the day in the upper part of the store, that is my private office . . . in council with General James Adams, of Springfield, Patriarch Hyrum Smith, Bishops Newel K. Whitney and George Miller, and President Brigham Young and Elders Heber C. Kimball and Willard Richards, instructing them in the principles and order of the Priesthood . . . setting forth the order pertaining to the Ancient of Days, and all those plans and principles by which any one is enabled to secure the fullness of those blessings which have been prepared for the Church of the First Born, and come up and abide in the presence of the Eloheim in the eternal worlds. In this council was instituted the ancient order of things for the first time in these last days. And the communications I made to this council were of things spiritual, and to be received only by the spiritual minded: and there was nothing made known to these men but what will be made known to all the Saints of the last days, so soon as they are prepared to receive, and a proper place is prepared to communicate them,

even to the weakest of the Saints; therefore let the Saints be diligent in building the Temple, and all houses which they have been, or shall hereafter be, commanded of God to build; and wait their time with patience in all meekness, faith, perseverance unto the end, knowing assuredly that all these things referred to in this council are always governed by the principle of revelation.[65]

This statement can be understood fully only by those who have received the ordinances of the house of the Lord and are thoroughly acquainted with the plan of life and salvation. The essential point is that in the temple the faithful are given sacred rites and covenants by which they are organized into a divine patriarchal order which on this earth centers in the Ancient of Days—the oldest man, Adam. This is the "ancient order of things," the rights, privileges, and promises of which were centered in later generations in Abraham, and in modern times in Joseph Smith.[66]

In the above statement, the Prophet also taught that by organizing themselves according to the divine patriarchal order, Latter-day Saints could secure the fulness of those blessings which pertain to the church of the Firstborn. Admission into that church requires that man make his calling and election sure to celestial glory, through righteousness and by the sealing power of the Holy Priesthood. And before he can secure a fulness of the blessings which pertain to the church of the Firstborn, he must receive all the ordinances of the house of the Lord and be sealed unto exaltation in the celestial kingdom of God.[67] In this way, man can come up in the resurrection to abide in "the presence of the Eloheim [i.e., the Gods] in the eternal worlds"[68] and be made one with them in the ever-increasing family order of eternity.

There were those other than the seven men listed above who received the higher ordinances of the priesthood in the upper floor of the Prophet's store before the temple was finished. On December 2, 1843, Joseph Smith reported that several brethren "received their endowments and further instructions in the Priesthood."[69]

Some women also received these sacred rites and ordinances together with their husbands. There is no ordinance or blessing of the priesthood given to the Saints in the temple which is not designed to be conferred upon women in association with their husbands. While addressing the Female Relief Society in April, 1842, Joseph Smith "spoke of delivering the keys of the Priesthood to the Church, and said that the faithful members of the Relief Society should receive them in connection with their husbands, that the Saints whose integrity had been tried and proved might know how to ask the Lord and receive an answer."[70]

Ebenezer Robinson, who served as an editor of the *Times and Seasons,* reported that women as well as men were given the endowment ordinances at Nauvoo.[71] Emma Smith apparently received them in 1843[72] and was instrumental in administering them to other women. In his journal, Heber C. Kimball wrote: "My wife Vilate and many females were received into the holy order."[73] Having reported a mission which George A. Smith performed in the East, Bathsheba W. Smith wrote: "Soon after my husband's return we were blessed by receiving our endowments and were sealed under the holy law of Celestial Marriage which was revealed July 12, 1843."[74] Many years later, in 1894, Wilford Woodruff commented that he and Bathsheba W. Smith were the only persons then living who received their blessings of the temple from the Prophet Joseph Smith.[75]

Joseph Smith apparently obtained many elements of the temple ceremony from the writings of Abraham which came into his possession in 1835. In his interpretation of facsimile number 2 in the Book of Abraham, the latter-day Seer wrote: "Is made to represent . . . the grand Key-words of the Holy Priesthood, as revealed to Adam in the Garden of Eden, as also to Seth, Noah, Melchizedek, Abraham, and all to whom the Priesthood was revealed."[76] Another part of the facsimile, he said: "Represents God sitting upon his throne, revealing through the heavens the grand

Key-words of the Priesthood."[77] Again, another part of the facsimile, "Contains writings that cannot be revealed unto the world; but it is to be had in the Holy Temple of God."[78]

The Prophet also obtained much information about the temple and its sacred rites and ordinances by direct revelation. Concerning the Nauvoo Temple, the Lord said:

> . . . verily I say unto you, let this house be built unto my name, that I may reveal mine ordinances therein unto my people;
>
> For I deign to *reveal* unto my church things which have been kept hid from before the foundation of the world, things that pertain to the dispensation of the fulness of times.
>
> *And I will show unto my servant Joseph all things pertaining to this house, and the priesthood thereof,* and the place whereon it shall be built.[79]

Having obtained a knowledge of the principles and ordinances of the temple program, the latter-day Seer proceeded to arrange them in their proper order. Brigham Young, who was intimately associated with the Prophet in this work, later said of the institution of the endowment ceremony at Nauvoo:

> We went into the large room over the store in Nauvoo, Joseph Smith divided up the room the best that he could, . . . gave us our instructions as we passed along from one department to another, . . . And after we had got through, Brother Joseph turned to me and said, "Brother Brigham, this is not arranged right, but we have done the best we could under the circumstances in which we are placed, and I want you to take this matter in hand *and organize and systematize all these ceremonies. . . .*" I did so and each time I got something more so that when we went through the Temple at Nauvoo I understood and knew how to place them there.[80]

The Prophet felt a sense of urgency in administering these sacred ordinances and instructions to others, and in conferring upon the Twelve a similar right to do so. "I know not why," he commented, "but for some reason I am constrained to hasten my preparations, and to confer upon the Twelve all the ordinances, keys, covenants, endowments, and sealing ordinances of the Priesthood, and so set before them a pattern in all things pertaining to the sanctuary and the endowment therein." Having done so he rejoiced exceedingly. "The Lord is about to lay the burden on your shoulders and let me rest awhile," he declared to the Twelve; "and if they kill me, the Kingdom of God will roll on, as I have now finished the work which was laid upon me, by committing to you all things for the building up of the kingdom according to the heavenly vision, and the pattern shown me from heaven."[81] John Taylor observed:

> Joseph Smith, before his death, was much exercised about the completion of the Temple in Nauvoo, and the administering of the ordinances therein. In his anxiety and for fear he should not live to see the Temple completed, he prepared a place over what was known as the brick store . . . where to a chosen few he administered those ordinances that we now have today associated with endowments, and that if anything should happen to him—which he evidently contemplated—he would feel that he had then fulfilled his mission, that he had conferred upon others all the keys given to him by the manifestations of the power of God.[82]

When the Nauvoo Temple was sufficiently completed and prepared, the sacred rites and ordinances which Joseph Smith administered to a limited number of people before his death were then given more generally to the Saints. In January, 1845, Brigham Young wrote to Wilford Woodruff of his intentions: "In all probability by next December we shall be giving the Saints their endowments."[83] In April, 1845, the Twelve wrote to Lyman Wight: "There is every prospect of getting on the roof [of the temple] and finishing some rooms by next autumn when we shall commence administering the ordinances of endowment according to the commandment."[84]

The ordinances of the endowment were administered for the first time in the Nauvoo Temple during the afternoon and evening of December 10, 1845.[85] In noting the activities of that day, Heber C. Kimball wrote in his journal that, while President Brigham Young made the final preparations of the celestial room for the endowment,

Mary Ann Young, Vilate Kimball, and Elizabeth Ann Whitney received the initial ordinance of the sacred ceremony in another part of the temple.[86]

Thereafter the endowment ceremony was administered to many of the Saints. To Wilford Woodruff, Brigham Young reported on December 17, 1845:

> We have now commenced the endowment in the attic story of the Lord's house. We are engaged night and day and have given the endowment to about 400 persons among whom is Sister Smoot who is much pleased at the fulfillment of your prophecy, "That she should go into the Lord's house."[87]

New and Everlasting Covenant of Marriage Instituted

As early as 1831, the Prophet spoke of some points of doctrine relating to the patriarchal order of marriage.[88] But how early he understood the full concept of marriage within that divine family order is not known. He included some features of the divine patriarchal order in marriage ceremonies which he performed before the coming of Elias and Elijah. While solemnizing the marriage of Newel Knight and Lydia Goldthwaite in November, 1835, he "remarked that marriage was an institution of heaven, instituted in the garden of Eden; that it was necessary it should be solemnized by the authority of the everlasting Priesthood." In the ceremony, he "pronounced upon them the blessings that the Lord conferred upon Adam and Eve in the garden of Eden, that is, to multiply and replenish the earth, with the addition of long life and prosperity."[89] In reporting the solemnizing of a marriage in January, 1836, which ceremony "was conducted after the order of heaven," Joseph Smith said: "I pronounced upon them the blessings of Abraham, Isaac, and Jacob, and such other blessings as the Lord put into my heart."[90]

Though these ceremonies included features of the concept of marriage within the divine patriarchal order, they lacked some of the most important elements of the more complete program which the Prophet later instituted, including the fact that when the marriage union is properly solemnized it will continue in the resurrection forever.[91] In referring to a period in the winter of 1840 when he was closely associated with the Prophet, Parley P. Pratt wrote:

> During these interviews he taught me many great and glorious principles concerning God and the heavenly order of eternity. It was at this time that I received from him the first idea of eternal family organization, and the eternal union of the sexes in those inexpressibly endearing relationships which none but the highly intellectual, the refined and pure in heart, know how to prize, and which are at the very foundation of everything worthy to be called happiness.
>
> Till then I had learned to esteem kindred affections and sympathies as appertaining solely to this transitory state, as something from which the heart must be entirely weaned, in order to be fitted for its heavenly state.
>
> It was Joseph Smith who taught me how to prize the endearing relationships of father and mother, husband and wife, of brother and sister, son and daughter.
>
> It was from him that I learned that the wife of my bosom might be secured to me for time and all eternity; and that the refined sympathies and affections which endeared us to each other emanated from the foundation of divine eternal love. It was from him that I learned that we might cultivate these affections, and grow and increase in the same to all eternity; while the result of our endless union would be an offspring as numerous as the stars of heaven, or the sands of the sea shore.
>
> It was from him that I learned the true dignity and destiny of a son of God, clothed with an eternal priesthood, as the patriarch and sovereign of his countless offspring. It was from him that I learned that the highest dignity of womanhood was, to stand as a queen and priestess to her husband, and to reign for ever and ever as the queen mother of her numerous and still increasing offspring.
>
> I had loved before, but I knew not why. But now I loved—with a pureness—an intensity of elevated, exalted feeling, which would lift my soul from the transitory things of this grovelling sphere and expand it as the ocean. I felt that God was my heavenly Father indeed; that Jesus was my brother, and that the wife of my bosom was an immortal, eternal companion; a kind ministering angel, given to me as a comfort, and a crown of glory for ever and ever. In short, I could now love with the spirit and with the understanding also.
>
> Yet, at that time, my dearly beloved brother, Joseph Smith,

had barely touched a single key; had merely lifted a corner of the veil and given me a single glance into eternity.[92]

Joseph Smith dictated the revelation setting forth the law governing the new and everlasting covenant of marriage on July 12, 1843.[93] The Lord instructed the Prophet that for a man to have claim upon his wife in eternity he must be given a binding promise to that effect by the Holy Priesthood. To exist forever, a contract such as that of marriage must be made according to the law of God, so that it is centered in a system of law which exists throughout eternity. Of the conditions of the law of the new and everlasting covenant of marriage, the revelation said: "All covenants, contracts, bonds, obligations, oaths, vows, performances, connections, associations, or expectations, that are not made and entered into and sealed by the Holy Spirit of promise, of him who is anointed, both as well for time and for all eternity, and that too most holy, by revelation and commandment through the medium of mine anointed, whom I have appointed on the earth to hold this power, . . . are of no efficacy, virtue, or force in and after the resurrection from the dead; for all contracts that are not made unto this end have an end when men are dead."[94]

That which God establishes is done according to His law and by His authority. The revelation explained:

> Behold, mine house is a house of order, saith the Lord God, and not a house of confusion.
>
> Will I accept an offering, saith the Lord, that is not made in my name?
>
> Or will I receive at your hands that which I have not appointed?
>
> And will I appoint unto you, saith the Lord, except it be by law, even as I and my Father ordained unto you, before the world was?
>
> I am the Lord thy God; and I give unto you this commandment—that no man shall come unto the Father but by me or by my word, which is my law, saith the Lord.[95]

The revelation then states that "everything that is in the world, whether it be ordained of men, by thrones, or principalities, or powers, or things of name, whatsoever they may be," that are not made by the law and authority of God "shall be thrown down, and shall not remain after men are dead, neither in nor after the resurrection." Only those things will remain which are of God. That which is not ordained by Him and His law will be "shaken and destroyed."[96] As these facts apply to the covenant of marriage, the revelation said: "Therefore, if a man marry him a wife in the world, and he marry her not by me nor by my word, and he covenant with her so long as he is in the world and she with him, their covenant and marriage are not of force when they are dead, and when they are out of the world; therefore they are not bound by any law when they are out of the world."[97]

The same principle holds true when, by mere human authority or by a usurpation of divine authority, a covenant is made for both time and eternity. Here the revelation states:

> . . . if a man marry a wife, and make a covenant with her for time and for all eternity, if that covenant is not by me or by my word, which is my law, and is not sealed by the Holy Spirit of promise, through him whom I have anointed and appointed unto this power, then it is not valid neither of force when they are out of the world, because they are not joined by me, saith the Lord, neither by my word; when they are out of the world it cannot be received there, because the angels and the gods are appointed there, by whom they cannot pass; they cannot, therefore, inherit my glory; for my house is a house of order, saith the Lord God.[98]

Within the gospel and under the authority of the Holy Priesthood, marriage is performed for time and for all eternity. The Lord said of the law which governs the new and everlasting covenant of marriage:

> . . . if a man marry a wife by my word, which is my law, and by the new and everlasting covenant, and it is sealed unto them by the Holy Spirit of promise, by him who is anointed, unto whom I have appointed this power and the keys of this priesthood; and [in addition] it shall be said unto them—Ye shall come forth in the first resurrection; and if it be after the first resurrection, in the next resurrection; and shall inherit thrones,

kingdoms, principalities, and powers, dominions, all heights and depths—then shall it be written in the Lamb's Book of Life, that he shall commit no murder whereby to shed innocent blood, . . . it shall be done unto them in all things whatsoever my servant hath put upon them, in time, and through all eternity; and shall be of full force when they are out of the world; and they shall pass by the angels, and the gods, which are set there, to their exaltation and glory in all things, as hath been sealed upon their heads, which glory shall be *a fullness* and *a continuation of the seeds* forever and ever.[99]

The word "fulness," italicized in the above quotation, means a fulness of the Father's glory. Concerning the new and everlasting covenant of marriage, God declared: "No one can reject this covenant and be permitted to enter into *my glory.*"[100] He then stated: "And as pertaining to the new and everlasting covenant, *it was instituted for the fulness of my glory;* and he that receiveth a fulness thereof must and shall abide the law."[101] To have "a continuation of the seeds forever and ever" is to have power to beget children after the resurrection forever.[102] Brigham Young explained: "When our spirits receive their bodies [in the resurrection], and through our faithfulness we are worthy to be crowned, we will then receive authority to produce *both spirit and body.*"[103] To the power of procreation which man now possesses will be added the power to beget spirit children. Like the Man of Holiness, the righteous who are exalted in celestial society will have power to organize spirit with its primal intelligence and stand as fathers and gods over their children in eternity. Their respective patriarchal kingdoms will then extend into eternity and they will be exalted in the divine patriarchal order of celestial society over their continually extending family. They will be fathers in all three basic stages in the over-all plan of life and salvation—spirit life, physical life and eternal life.[104]

These are the most distinctive features of the new and everlasting covenant of marriage. From the above explanation it can be seen that, like the apex of a pyramid, that sacred covenant fulfills and crowns all other covenants within the divine plan of life and salvation. The program which begins on earth with baptism is brought to fruition in eternity through the covenant of eternal marriage. Through that covenant those who become sons and daughters of Jesus Christ are given a fulness of the glory of God and are made fathers and mothers in eternal life over their children on this sphere and in eternity, within the divine patriarchal order. For this reason Joseph Smith taught that the ordinances of the temple were those by which man may "come up and abide in the presence of the Eloheim [i.e., the Gods] in the eternal worlds."[105] To abide in the presence of the Man of Holiness and other supreme beings like Him,[106] man must possess the same general powers and rights which they possess; he must be a father in the three basic stages of life which are mentioned in the paragraph above. A revelation declared: "Strait is the gate, and narrow the way that leadeth unto the exaltation and continuation of the lives, and few there be that find it, *because ye receive me not in the world neither do ye know me.*"[107] Christ then added:

> But if ye receive me in the world, then shall ye know me, and shall receive your exaltation; that where I am ye shall be also.
>
> This is eternal lives—to know the only wise and true God, and Jesus Christ, whom he hath sent. I am he. Receive ye, therefore, my law.[108]

Exaltation and Eternal Lives

The statements in the revelation quoted above use two terms to designate the state and power of those who enjoy an eternal marital union within the divine patriarchal order of celestial society: first, "exaltation"; and second, "eternal lives," with its synonym "the continuation of lives." The term "exaltation" comes from the word "exalt," which means to raise or elevate in position or rank—to give glory, to pay high honor, or to magnify. In the above statement, the term "exaltation" therefore means for man to be exalted to a place of power and authority within the divine patriarchal order of the celestial kingdom. Since this is a divine family order, he must be made a patriarch, a priest, and a king over an ever-increasing progeny in eternity in order to be exalted in celestial society. To be exalted, man must be endowed with a fulness of the glory of the Father in the resurrection, which is to have "eternal life,"[109] and to possess the power to beget children forever in the resurrection, which is to have "eternal lives"—a "continuation of lives," or a "continuation of the seeds forever and ever."[110] These three terms—"exaltation," "eternal life," and "eternal lives"—therefore are directly related in meaning, but they each denote a different aspect of the future state of the righteous within celestial society.

Summary

Joseph Smith taught that celestial society is patriarchal in its structure, and that all who are born into the kingdom of God must be organized by the covenants and powers of the priesthood into a divine patriarchal order under Christ, who is their Father in the living attributes and powers of eternal life. In the Kirtland Temple, important keys and promises were restored by which this divine patriarchal order could be established in the latter days. Moses committed the keys of the gathering of Israel and the leading of the ten tribes from the land of the north. With the gathering of Israel, the true patriarchal order of Israel (the divine patriarchal order) is to be established and perfected on earth. To this end Elias restored the special promises, rights, blessings, and privileges which God gave anciently to Abraham. And Elijah revealed the covenants and keys by which the divine patriarchal order can be organized among the living and can be extended back through past generations to the patriarchs of old.

The divine patriarchal order has its origin in eternity and came down by generation to Adam, and from Adam to the patriarchs in later ages. The new and everlasting covenant of marriage is the crowning covenant of the divine family order and the source from which all the rights, privileges, and blessings that are associated with that eternal system flow. The sacred rites and covenants of the temple are those by which the divine patriarchal order can be established on earth and perpetuated from generation to generation. Therein righteous men are made kings and priests (and women queens and priestesses) unto God over their posterity in the flesh and in eternity; and as priests, men are fathers in the living attributes and powers of the Holy Spirit. Having received the covenants of this divine system, the Saints were then required to make their calling and election sure to the promised blessings by receiving the sealing power of the Holy Priesthood.

Joseph Smith administered the basic ordinance of the divine patriarchal order to several men at Kirtland, Ohio, and at Nauvoo he began to administer the more complete program by which the divine order could be established among the Saints. He also dictated a revelation which set forth the law governing the new and everlasting covenant of marriage which is the crowning covenant of the divine family order. Only by means of this sacred covenant can the Saints acquire exaltation and eternal lives, with a fulness of glory, in the celestial kingdom of God.

Notes

1. See Volume I of this study, the section in chapter four entitled "The Aaronic Priesthood Restored."
2. Luke 1:17.
3. See HC, VI, p. 254, where Joseph Smith stresses this point.
4. *Ibid.,* II, pp. 379–380.
5. *Ibid.*
6. The place of Joseph Smith in the divine patriarchal order will be treated more fully in volume III of this study.
7. D&C 124:58. See also D&C 132:30–31.
8. See Abraham 2:10.
9. The journal and memoirs of Mary Elizabeth Rollins Lightner, pp. 2–3; *Young Woman's Journal,* XVI, pp. 556–557.
10. See the sections that follow in this chapter.
11. JD, II, p. 31.
12. D&C 110:1–4, 11–16; HC, II, pp. 434–436.
13. See HC, I, pp. 12–13; MA, I (April, 1835), pp. 109–112. Israel's right to the privileges and blessings of the divine patriarchal order will be discussed

in volume III of this work, and the subject of Israel's gathering will be treated in volume IV.

14. See Genesis 12:1–3; 17:1–9; 26:1–5; 28:1–4, 10–15. See also D&C 27:10; 86:8–11; 124:58; 132:30–31.

15. D&C 132:29–30.

16. D&C 132:31.

17. D&C 132:30.

18. Romans 9:4; HC, IV, pp. 359–360.

19. Abraham 2:9–11.

20. HC, IV, pp. 359–360.

21. Romans 9:4; HC, IV, pp. 359–360. This right comes as a natural blessing to those who fulfil all the requirements associated with points two and four in the above paragraph.

22. HC, I, p. 12; D&C 2; Smith 2:38–39.

23. In the sense that Elijah revealed new functions pertaining to the priesthood and committed the keys to perform them, his visitation resulted in a restoration of these things.

24. The basic power to seal or bind is inherent in the priesthood which was restored by Peter, James, and John, and the power was used before the coming of Elijah to seal the faithful to eternal life and thereby make their calling and election sure to celestial glory. See the section in chapter thirteen entitled "Manifestations Of Sealing Power."

25. JD, XVI, p. 165.

26. HC, VI, p. 251.

27. MS, V (March, 1845), p. 151.

28. The second phase of Elijah's mission will be discussed in chapters seventeen and eighteen.

29. HC, I, p. 12; D&C 2; Smith 2:38–39. Moroni also indicated that this would cause the hearts of the children to turn to their fathers. The turning of the hearts of the children to the fathers will be discussed in chapters seventeen and eighteen.

30. *Ibid.,* IV, p. 211.

31. *Ibid.,* VI, p. 251.

32. *Ibid.,* V, p. 530.

33. *Ibid.,* p. 555.

34. Abraham 1:3.

35. See Volume I of this study, the section in chapter seven entitled "Pre-earth Man a Spirit Child of God"; and also the section in chapter thirteen entitled "The Origin of Life on Earth."

36. Abraham, Facsimile 2, figure 7.

37. See D&C 132. The new and everlasting covenant of marriage is discussed in a later section of this chapter entitled "New and Everlasting Covenant of Marriage Instituted."

38. The divine patriarchal order must also be extended back through past generations to the ancient patriarchs, as discussed in chapters seventeen and eighteen.

39. See also the section in chapter eighteen entitled "Perfecting The Divine Patriarchal Order."

40. HC, V, p. 555.

41. *Ibid.,* pp. 1–2.

42. See *ibid.,* III, p. 386.
43. See D&C 128:21.
44. D&C 78:16.
45. HC, II, pp. 20–21. See Revelation 5.
46. *Ibid.,* IV, p. 493.
47. *Ibid.,* VI, p. 319. The divine program by which righteous men are made kings within the divine patriarchal order will be discussed in detail in volume III of this work.
48. *Ibid.*
49. *Ibid.,* II, p. 309.
50. *Ibid.,* III, p. 301.
51. Moses 6:52–68.
52. See Abraham, Facsimile No. 2, Figures 3, 7, and 8. For a discussion of the role of Adam in the gospel plan, see the section in chapter fifteen entitled "Adam's Place in the Gospel."
53. HC, IV, p. 207.
54. D&C 78:16.
55. Abraham 2:10.
56. The subject of making one's calling and election sure is discussed in chapters thirteen and fourteen.
57. HC, V, p. 527.
58. *Ibid.,* VI, p. 366.
59. See the section in chapter one entitled "Necessity of All the Principles and Ordinances."
60. HC, V, p. 424.
61. A possible exception to this may be that a person might fail to receive all the covenants of the temple, or not prove capable of carrying the great responsibilities which accompany all the covenants of the Lord's house, and yet be worthy and able to use in some degree the greater spiritual powers which are made available to man through the holy endowment (or through a part of the holy endowment) ordinance. Specific information from the Prophet on these technicalities, however, is not available.
62. Erastus Snow stated that about three hundred and sixty men were given this ordinance at Kirtland. See the the journal of Erastus Snow, pp. 5–6.
63. JD, XIX, p. 16.
64. See the section in this chapter entitled "Early Beginnings of Divine Patriarchal Order."
65. HC, V, pp. 1–2. On the following day, Joseph Smith wrote: "General Adams started for Springfield, and the remainder of the council of yesterday continued their meeting at the same place, and myself and brother Hyrum received in turn from the others, the same that I had communicated to them the day previous."—*Ibid.,* pp. 2–3.

In the evening of July 26, 1872, Brigham Young stated in the Ward Meeting house of the 14th Ward in Salt Lake City, Utah, that he was the only one alive of seven men to whom "the Prophet revealed the Endowments and Sealing."—The Diary of Charles L. Walker, under date.

In the meeting of May 4th, Joseph Smith may not have administered to them the full ordinances of the endowment ceremony. On May 26, 1843, he wrote in his journal: "At five P.M. I met in council in the upper room, with my brother Hyrum, Brigham Young, Heber C. Kimball, Willard Richards, Judge

James Adams, Bishop Newel K. Whitney and William Law, and gave them their endowments."—HC, V, p. 409. On the 28th, the Prophet again reported: "At five P.M. I met with Brother Hyrum, Brigham Young, Heber C. Kimball, Willard Richards, Newel K. Whitney, and James Adams, in the upper room to attend to ordinances and counseling."—*Ibid.*, p. 412. Finally he wrote on May 29:

> At nine A.M., I met in council with brother Hyrum, Brigham Young, Heber C. Kimball, Willard Richards, Newel K. Whitney, and James Adams.
>
> Singing, and prayer by Elder Brigham Young. Conversation, instruction and teaching concerning the things of God. Had a pleasant interview.—*Ibid.*, pp. 412–413.

Heber C. Kimball may have erred on the date when these ordinances were given, for he later noted in his journal:

> June, 1842 I was initiated into the ancient order . . . in company with nine others, viz: Joseph Smith, Hyrum Smith, Wm Law, Wm Marks, Judge Adams, Brigham Young, Willard Richards, George Miller, N. K. Whitney.—The journal of Heber C. Kimball, under date; original journal in church Historian's Library, Salt Lake City, Utah.

66. For the place of Joseph Smith in the divine patriarchal order, see D&C 124:58; 132:30–31.

67. For a discussion of the church of the Firstborn, see the section in chapter fourteen entitled "Right to Commune With Church of the Firstborn."

68. HC, V, pp. 1–2. For Joseph Smith's explanation that the term *Elohim* can mean "Gods," see Volume I of this study, the section in chapter five entitled "The Godhead."

69. *Ibid.*, VI, p. 98.

70. *Ibid.*, IV, p. 604.

71. *The Return,* II, p. 252.

72. Family Group Sheet of Joseph and Emma Smith, in the Utah Genealogical Society.

73. The journal of Heber C. Kimball, January, 1844.

74. Autobiography of Bathsheba W. Smith, unpublished manuscript in Church Historian's Library, Salt Lake City, Utah, under date of 1843. She added:

> I heard the Prophet Joseph charge the twelve with the duty and responsibility of administering the ordinances and endowments and of sealing for the living and [the] dead. I met many times with Brother Joseph, and others who had received their endowments, in company with my husband in an upper room dedicated for that purpose and prayed with them repeatedly in those meetings.—*Ibid.*

75. *The Young Woman's Journal,* August, 1894.

76. Figure No. 3.

77. Figure No. 7.

78. Figure No. 8.

79. D&C 124:40–43.

80. The diary of L. John Nuttall, February 7, 1877 (some punctuation added).

81. As reported by Parley P. Pratt, in MS, V (March, 1845), p. 151.

82. JD, XXV, p. 183. For statements by Orson Hyde and Wilford

Woodruff about the introduction of these rites and ordinances, see MS, V (March, 1845), pp. 104, 109; JD, XXI, p. 194.

83. Letter of Brigham Young to Wilford Woodruff, written at Nauvoo, Illinois, January 27, 1845; original letter in Church Historian's Library, in "Brigham Young Papers, 1843–1853."

84. Letter of the Twelve to Lyman Wight, written at Nauvoo, Illinois, April 17, 1845; original in Church Historian's Library, in "Brigham Young Papers, 1843–1853."

85. See HC, VII, pp. 541–544.

86. The journal of Heber C. Kimball, under date. Since some, if not all, of these women had previously been given the temple ordinances, they may have repeated them in the temple at this time or performed them vicariously for the dead.

87. Letter of Brigham Young to Wilford Woodruff, written at Nauvoo, Illinois, December 17, 1845; original in Church Historian's Library, Salt Lake City, Utah, in "Brigham Young Papers, 1843–1853."

88. These points concern the plurality of wives within that divine order and will be discussed in volume III of this study.

89. HC, II, p. 320.

90. *Ibid.,* p. 378.

91. The blessings of eternal increase and the full concept of the rights and promises which belong to the descendants of those whose parents and forefathers are united according to the new and everlasting covenant of marriage were also lacking. These features will be discussed more fully in volume III of this study.

92. *The Autobiography Of Parley Parker Pratt,* pp. 297–298.

93. The written statement of that revelation is in answer to a question the Prophet had asked the Lord many years earlier concerning the propriety of taking plural wives. It is not known if the written revelation conveys only the initial information which he received years earlier in answer to his question, or if it includes additional points of knowledge which may have been revealed later.

94. D&C 132:7.

95. D&C 132:8–12.

96. D&C 132:13–14.

97. D&C 132:15.

98. D&C 132:18.

99. D&C 132:19.

100. D&C 132:4.

101. D&C 132:6.

102. On this point the Prophet said:

> Except a man and his wife enter into an everlasting covenant and be married for eternity, while in this probation, by the power and authority of the Holy Priesthood, they will cease to increase when they die; that is, they will not have any children after the resurrection. But those who are married by the power and authority of the priesthood in this life, and continue without committing the sin against the Holy Ghost, will continue to increase and have children in the celestial glory.—HC, V, p. 391.

103. JD, XV, p. 137.

104. For a discussion of these basic stages of life, see Volume I of this study, the section in chapter eight entitled "The Way Of Life."

105. HC, V, p. 2. For Joseph Smith's explanation that the term *Elohim* means "Gods," see Volume I of this study, the section in chapter five entitled "The Godhead."

106. The subject of plurality of Gods will be treated in volume IV of this work.

107. D&C 132:22.

108. D&C 132:23–24.

109. See Volume I of this study, the section in chapter eight entitled "Eternal Life."

110. D&C 132:19, 22, 24.

13

The More Sure Word of Prophecy

I beseech you to go forward, go forward and make your calling and your election sure.—JOSEPH SMITH.

Joseph Smith reaffirmed and made clear the biblical doctrine that by growing in the truth and power of the gospel man can eventually receive a guarantee from God that he will receive specified blessings in the resurrection. In obtaining this guarantee, man makes his calling and election sure to those blessings. Brigham Young and Willard Richards explained that "the general principle of election" means "that God has chosen or elected certain individuals to certain blessings, or to the performance of certain works."[1] This the Lord does before man is tabernacled in the flesh on earth. These appointments, however, are contingent in nature. Before man can realize them in mortality, he must fulfil the requirements which God places upon him in his earthly state. But having done this and having developed sufficiently in the truth and power of the gospel, man can make sure his promise of the final reward of the gospel appointments in eternity. This is what it means for a person to make his calling and election sure.

In making his calling and election sure to celestial glory and power, man has the promise of eternal life sealed upon him by the power of the Holy Priesthood. For this reason that promise is called the more sure word of prophecy. It is a prophetic statement or word that is more sure than the pre-earth appointments which were made.[2] The Prophet explained: "The more sure word of prophecy means a man's knowing that he is sealed up unto eternal life, by revelation and the spirit of prophecy, through the power of the Holy Priesthood."[3] Of the relationship between making sure one's calling and election to eternal life and the more sure word of prophecy, he said: "I would exhort you to go on and continue to call upon God *until you make your calling and election sure for yourselves, by obtaining this more sure word of prophecy,* and wait patiently for the promise until you obtain it."[4]

Doctrine Of Making Man's Calling And Election Sure

Faithful Sealed to Eternal Life

The Prophet stressed that after man has embraced the gospel he should press forward in the divine plan of life and salvation until the Lord finally says to him, "Son, thou shalt be exalted."[5] This promise, sealed upon man by the power of the Holy Priesthood, is a guarantee that he will obtain eternal life in the resurrection. Because this is man's objective in the gospel, the latter-day Seer advised the Saints to gather their relatives to Nauvoo that they might "be *sealed* and saved."[6] The Book of Mormon also makes this the objective of the gospel. King Benjamin admonished his people: "I would that ye should be steadfast and immovable, always abounding in good works, *that Christ, the Lord God Omnipotent, may seal you his,* that you may be brought to heaven, that ye may have everlasting salvation and eternal life."[7]

Joseph Smith discussed this subject with the Saints in the October conference, in 1831. He stressed that "the order of the High Priesthood was, that they have power given them to seal up the Saints unto eternal life."[8] In other words, it is a basic purpose and design of the priesthood—an objective or end-result of its divine program—to seal the Saints to eternal life. In referring to those in a former dispensation who attained these blessings, the Prophet asked "what object" they had gained by achieving them. He then answered: "It was *the established order* of the kingdom of God."[9] Man cannot enter into the presence of God and receive the permanent endowments of His glory unless he has previously made sure his calling and election to those blessings. This is a fundamental requirement in the plan of life and salvation.[10]

There are several examples in latter-day scripture of individuals who obtained a guarantee from the Lord that they would receive eternal life. To Alma the elder the Lord said: "Thou art my servant; and I covenant with thee that thou shalt have eternal life."[11] Enos, another Nephite prophet, apparently received such a guarantee, for he wrote:

> . . . I soon go to the place of my rest, which is with my Redeemer; for *I know that in him I shall rest.* And I rejoice in the day when my mortal shall put on immortality, and shall stand before him; then shall I see his face with pleasure, and he will say unto me: Come unto me, ye blessed, *there is a place prepared for you in the mansions of my Father.*[12]

To the Twelve whom Jesus chose to administer the affairs of His church in the Western hemisphere after His resurrection, He promised: "After that ye are seventy and two years old ye shall come unto me in my kingdom; and with me ye shall find rest."[13] And as Moroni labored abridging the record of the Jaredites, he received from the Lord this assurance: "Thou hast been faithful; wherefore, thy garments shall be made clean. And because thou hast seen thy weakness thou shalt be made strong, even unto the sitting down in the place which I have prepared in the mansions of my Father."[14]

Power to Seal Inherent in the Melchizedek Priesthood

The power to seal or bind the edicts and promises of God so that they will afterwards be realized is inherent in the Melchizedek Priesthood and constitutes a basic power of that priesthood. The elders who were sent to teach the gospel to the world were given power "to *seal* both on earth and in heaven, the unbelieving and rebellious."[15] Of the action they could take in regard to the righteous, the Lord said in November, 1831: " . . . of as many as the Father shall bear record, *to you shall be given power to seal them up unto eternal life."*[16] These basic sealing powers were exercised on repeated occasions from the time the Church was organized in 1830, and the blessings which the Prophet taught would come to those who were sealed to eternal life were also manifested early in the dispensation.[17]

Right to Be Sealed Available to All Saints

Joseph Smith taught that the promise of eternal life, with the blessings which follow that guarantee, is open to every person who will embrace the gospel and apply its truths and powers in his life. Speaking of the doctrine of making man's calling and election sure, the Prophet observed: "This principle ought (in its proper place) to be taught, for God hath not revealed anything to Joseph, but what He will make known unto the Twelve, and even the least Saint may know all things as fast as he is able to bear them."[18] A revelation also referred to those who "are sealed by the Holy Spirit of promise" and declared that this blessing is given to "all those who are just and true."[19]

The Prophet stressed that in the final analysis salvation is an individual responsibility. Each person must apply the gospel in his life and mature in its divine blessings and powers until he makes his calling and election sure. "We have no claim in our eternal compact, in relation to eternal things, unless our actions and contracts and all things tend to this end," the latter-day Seer observed. "But after all this," he declared, "you have got to make your calling and election sure."[20] Having cited an injunction by the Apostle Peter for the saints in his day to achieve this objective in the gospel, Joseph Smith said: "If this injunction would lie largely on those to whom it was spoken, how much more those of the present generation!"[21]

Two Procedures for Making Calling and Election Sure

In general, there are two procedures by which man can acquire a guarantee that he will be given eternal life in the world to come. They both require that man follow the same general path, which is obedience to the requirements of the gospel. But they vary in the point of time when the individual may know with a surety that the gift of eternal life will be his in the resurrection. First, having received the gospel, a person may develop in its blessings and powers to the end of his mortal life. Those who do so have the promise, given as a guarantee, that they will receive eternal life in the resurrection. However, they have no guarantee that they will receive this blessing until they have passed through mortality. Second, having received the gospel, a person may apply its divine program in his life and mature in its blessings to the extent that the promise of eternal life, as an authoritative declaration, is sealed upon him by the power of the Holy Priesthood before he passes from mortality. In this event, he is given the guarantee of eternal life before his day of mortal probation is over. Joseph Smith explained that, having embraced the gospel, man must "continue to humble himself before God, hungering and thirsting after righteousness, and living by every word of God." The Lord will then say to him, "Son, thou shalt be exalted." The Prophet concluded: "When the Lord has thoroughly proved him, and finds that the man is determined to serve Him at all hazards, then the man will find his calling and his election made sure."[22]

Challenge of Enduring to the End

In referring to the first and more general way[23] by which the Saints can acquire a guarantee of eternal life in the resurrection, a revelation said: "If you keep my commandments and endure to the end you shall have eternal life."[24] This is the standard scriptural promise which is given to all who receive the gospel. In stressing this general approach to man's quest for eternal life, Nephi declared:

> . . . my beloved brethren, after ye have gotten into this straight and narrow path [by embracing the gospel], I would ask if all is done? Behold, I say unto you, Nay; for ye have not come thus far save it were by the word of Christ with unshaken faith in him, relying wholly upon the merits of him who is mighty to save.
>
> Wherefore, *ye must press forward with a steadfastness in Christ, having a perfect brightness of hope, and a love of God and of all men.* Wherefore, if ye shall *press forward, feasting upon the word of Christ, and endure to the end,* behold, thus saith the Father: Ye shall have eternal life.[25]

An illustration of this way of obtaining a guarantee of eternal life in the resurrection is found in the case of King Follett, a faithful elder who was killed at Nauvoo. Speaking to the friends and loved ones of Elder Follett, the Prophet said:

> I am authorized to say, by the authority of the Holy Ghost, that you have no occasion to fear; for he is gone to the home of the just. Don't mourn, don't weep. I know it by the testimony of the Holy Ghost that is within me.[26]

The task of enduring to the end is positive, rather than negative, in its nature, and it requires the man of faith to mature in the spiritual union which he has achieved with Christ through the gospel. A nonchalant approach will not do, for a revelation said of those who begin to traverse the path to eternal life but who fail to acquire celestial glory in the resurrection: "These are they who are not valiant in the testimony of Jesus; wherefore, they obtain not the crown over the kingdom of our God."[27]

Modern scriptures indicate that man must in several ways endure to the end. First, man must give himself without reservation to Christ and endure by fasting and prayer in that sacred relationship to the end of his mortal life. A Nephite prophet said:

> . . . my beloved brethren, I would that ye should come unto Christ, who is the Holy One of Israel, and partake of his salvation. Yea, come unto him, and *offer your whole souls as an offering unto him, and continue in fasting and prayer, and endure to the end;* and as the Lord liveth ye shall be saved.[28]

Second, a man must endure in his faith on Christ's name to the end. Joseph Smith wrote by revelation: "And we know that all men must repent and believe on the name of Jesus Christ, and worship the Father in his name, and *endure in faith on his name to the end,* or they cannot be saved in the kingdom of God."[29] It was for this purpose that priests and teachers were ordained among the Nephites, "to preach repentance and remission of sins through Jesus Christ, *by the endurance of faith on his name to the end.*"[30]

Third, man must endure in following the example of righteousness which Christ set to the end of his mortal probation. Nephi observed:

> . . . the voice of the Son came unto me, saying: He that is baptized in my name, to him will the Father give the Holy Ghost, like unto me; wherefore, *follow me, and do the things which ye have seen me do.*
>
> Wherefore, my beloved brethren, I know that if ye shall *follow the Son, with full purpose of heart, acting no hypocrisy and no deception before God, but with real intent,* repenting of your sins, witnessing unto the Father that ye are willing to take upon you the name of Christ, by baptism, . . . then cometh the baptism of fire and of the Holy Ghost. . . .
>
> And I heard a voice from the Father, saying: Yea, the words of my Beloved are true and faithful. He that endureth to the end, the same shall be saved.
>
> And now, my beloved brethren, I know by this that unless a man shall endure to the end, *in following the example of the Son of the living God,* he cannot be saved.[31]

The requirement to follow the example of Christ which Nephi stressed includes man's need to obtain a degree of the same divine power which Jesus obtained and manifested to others in His earthly ministry. This fact is plainly indicated in the above explanation by Nephi.

Fourth, man must endure to the end in keeping the

commandments of God. To his son Shiblon, Alma said: "As you have commenced in your youth to look to the Lord your God, even so I hope that you will *continue in keeping his commandments;* for blessed is he that endureth to the end."[32]

Fifth, a man must endure in Christ's mercy to the end. Having been forgiven in baptism, he must also retain a remission of sins through the power of the atonement and grow daily in the truth and power of the Spirit which are given to him through the mercy of Christ. Alma declared: "Whosoever repenteth shall find mercy; and he that findeth mercy and endureth to the end the same shall be saved."[33]

Finally, man must endure the afflictions and crosses of the world unto the end; and if necessary, he must do so even at the sacrifice of his life. "I have decreed in my heart, saith the Lord, that I will prove you in all things, whether you will abide in my covenant, even unto death, that you may be found worthy," a revelation declared. "For if ye will not abide in my covenant ye are not worthy of me."[34] Another revelation promised: "All they who suffer persecution for my name, and endure in faith, though they are called to lay down their lives for my sake yet shall they partake of all this glory"—the glory the righteous receive in the resurrection.[35] To Joseph Smith and Sidney Rigdon, the Lord said:

> Verily, verily, I say unto you, if they [those who refused to obey the gospel] reject my words, and this part of my gospel and ministry, blessed are ye, for they can do no more unto you than unto me.
>
> And even if they do unto you even as they have done unto me, blessed are ye, for you shall dwell with me in glory.[36]

Conditions Governing Those Who Make Their Calling and Election Sure

Joseph Smith held that when a man in mortality makes his calling and election sure to eternal life, he stands in a different relationship with God than he did before he received that guarantee. He has met the fundamental challenge of his mortal probation; he has developed spiritually so that he can return to the presence of God and claim the promises which are ordained for those who make their calling and election sure. Consequently he is under a greater responsibility to obey the law of God.

The promise of eternal life is given initially to man on a contingent basis through the covenant of baptism. But when he makes his calling and election sure to celestial glory, that promise is guaranteed to him—sealed, or made sure—providing he does not sin against the Holy Ghost and thereby become a son of perdition. Except for this possibility, he will receive in the resurrection the promise which was sealed upon him. To an associate who had received this guarantee, the Prophet explained:

> Your life is hid with Christ in God, and so are many others. *Nothing but the unpardonable sin can prevent you from inheriting eternal life for you are sealed up by the power of the Priesthood unto eternal life,* having taken the step necessary for that purpose.[37]

Joseph Smith referred again to this reservation in the sealing power of the priesthood as he discussed the subject of falling from grace. He said:

> The doctrine that the Presbyterians and Methodists have quarreled so much about—once in grace, always in grace, or falling away from grace, I will say a word about. They are both wrong. Truth takes a road between them both, for while the Presbyterian says "once in grace, you cannot fall;" the Methodist says: "You can have grace today, fall from it to-morrow, next day have grace again; and so follow on, changing continually." But the doctrine of the Scriptures and the spirit of Elijah would show them both false, and take a road between them both; for, according to the Scripture, if men have received the good word of God, and tasted of the powers of the world to come, if they shall fall away, it is impossible to renew them again, seeing they have crucified the Son of God afresh, and put Him to an open shame; so there is a possibility of falling away; you could not be renewed again, and the power of Elijah cannot seal against this sin, *for this is a reserve made in the seals and power of the Priesthood.*[38]

There is no reservation in the promise which is given

to those who make sure their calling and election to eternal life by enduring faithfully to the end of their mortal probation. "A man cannot commit the unpardonable sin after the dissolution of the body," Joseph Smith explained. "They must do it in this world."[39]

The fact that a man on earth is sealed to eternal life does not prevent him from committing sin or insure that he will not commit sin. He is, however, under a greater obligation to be virtuous and true than those who have not received the guarantee of eternal life. Since it is not possible for man to be totally sanctified and remain in mortality,[40] it follows that even after a person has made his calling and election sure to eternal life there will still be elements of mortal corruption in his flesh which will war against his desire for righteousness and exert an influence designed to lead him away from God. Man's day of probation is not over until he has been freed by death from the war with the flesh in its fallen state.[41] The question therefore may be asked, What obligation is man under to divine law when he makes sure his promise to celestial glory? Having spoken of the unpardonable sin in regard to those who make their calling and election sure, Joseph Smith added: "All other sins will be visited with judgment in the flesh, and the spirit being delivered to the buffetings of Satan until the day of the Lord Jesus."[42] It is not consistent with divine truth and mercy for the atonement of Christ to pay the debt of wilful sin after an individual has been sealed to eternal life. There is such a thing as man placing himself beyond the reach of Christ's mercy and forgiveness.

There is a difference between wilful sin and sin committed inadvertently as a result of the weaknesses of the flesh. It is in cases of wilful sin that those who make their calling and election sure are visited with judgments. Having sealed some brethren at Kirtland to eternal life in 1833, Joseph Smith warned that "if any of them should *sin wilfully* after they were thus cleansed, and sealed up unto eternal life, they should be given over unto the buffetings of Satan until the day of redemption."[43]

In March, 1832, the Prophet created an organization known as the "united order," which was to direct the economic affairs of the Saints under the law of consecration and stewardship.[44] Those who were chosen to direct this divine economic order had made their calling and election sure to eternal life[45] and were bound by covenant to administer the program of the order according to the spiritual and moral requirements of that higher standard or law. The Lord said by revelation:

> . . . a commandment I give unto you, to prepare and organize yourselves by a bond or everlasting covenant that cannot be broken.
>
> And he who breaketh it shall lose his office and standing in the church, *and shall be delivered over to the buffetings of Satan until the day of redemption.*[46]

Again the Lord directed:

> . . . it is expedient for my servants . . . [Newel K. Whitney, Sidney Rigdon, Joseph Smith, Oliver Cowdery, and Martin Harris] to be bound together by a bond and covenant that cannot be broken by transgression, *except judgment shall immediately follow,* in your several stewardships—
>
> To manage the affairs of the poor, and all things pertaining to the bishopric both in the land of Zion and in the land of [Kirtland]. . . .
>
> This order I have appointed to be an everlasting order unto you, and unto your successors, inasmuch as you sin not.
>
> And the soul that sins against this covenant, and hardeneth his heart against it, shall be dealt with according to the laws of my church, *and shall be delivered over to the buffetings of Satan until the day of redemption.*[47]

Two years later, after the Saints had passed through the turbulent experiences which occurred in Jackson county, Missouri, the Lord again spoke concerning the united order and those who were directing its affairs:

> Verily I say unto you, my friends, I give unto you counsel, and a commandment, concerning all the properties which belong to the order which I commanded to be organized and

established, to be a united order, and an everlasting order for the benefit of my church, and for the salvation of men until I come—

With promise immutable and unchangeable, that inasmuch as those whom I commanded were faithful they should be blessed with a multiplicity of blessings;

But inasmuch as they were not faithful they were nigh unto cursing.

Therefore, inasmuch as some of my servants have not kept the commandment, but have broken the covenant through covetousness, and with feigned words, I have cursed them with a very sore and grievous curse.

For I, the Lord, have decreed in my heart, that inasmuch as any man belonging to the order shall be found a transgressor, or, in other words, shall break the covenant with which ye are bound, *he shall be cursed in his life, and shall be trodden down by whom I will;*

For I, the Lord, am not to be mocked in these things—

And all this that the innocent among you may not be condemned with the unjust; and that the guilty among you may not escape; *because I, the Lord, have promised unto you a crown of glory at my right hand.*

Therefore, inasmuch as you are found transgressors, you cannot escape my wrath in your lives.

Inasmuch as ye are cut off for transgression, ye cannot escape the buffetings of Satan until the day of redemption.[48]

The statements of promise and of judgment in the revelations above can be understood only in light of the doctrines which are set forth in this chapter. Those who make their calling and election sure to celestial glory and power are under a greater responsibility to keep the commandments of God than others who have not obtained a guarantee of future blessings. Sidney Rigdon may be cited as a case in point. After the death of Joseph Smith, he sought unlawfully to lead the Church and finally came out in open opposition to the authority of the Twelve. Thereupon he was tried for his conduct, and at the conclusion of the trial William W. Phelps moved that he "be cut off from the church, and *delivered over to the buffetings of satan until he repent.*" After this proposal was discussed and voted upon by the assembled Saints, "President Young arose and *delivered Sidney Rigdon over to the buffetings of satan* in the name of the Lord, and all the people said, Amen."[49]

The same general conditions govern those who make their calling and election sure and are sealed in the marriage relationship for eternity. The law of eternal marriage contains both the basic principles of that law and the principles, promises, and regulations which pertain to those who make sure their calling and election to an eternal marital union.[50] Concerning those who are in the latter category, the revelation said: "Verily, verily, I say unto you, if a man marry a wife according to my word, and they are sealed by the Holy Spirit of promise, according to mine appointment [through the power of the Holy Priesthood], and he or she shall commit any sin or transgression of the new and everlasting covenant whatever, and all manner of blasphemies, and if they commit no murder wherein they shed innocent blood, yet they shall come forth in the first resurrection, and enter into their exaltation; but they shall be destroyed in the flesh, and shall be delivered unto the buffetings of Satan unto the day of redemption, saith the Lord God."[51]

The provisions set forth in this statement do not apply to those who are married in the temple for time and eternity on a contingent basis, but only to those in mortality who make their calling and election sure to this sacred relationship. Should they commit any transgression of the new and everlasting covenant of marriage, except the unpardonable sin wherein they commit murder by shedding innocent blood, they may still receive their exaltation in the resurrection. "I am yours in time and throughout all eternity," Vilate Kimball wrote to her husband after they received this guarantee. "This blessing has been sealed upon us, by the Holy Spirit of Promise; and cannot be broken only through transgression or committing a grosser crime than your heart or mine is capable of, that is murder."[52] But in case of lesser sins which are serious in their nature, the law of God would require those who have been sealed to exaltation to be "destroyed in the flesh, and [their spirits in the spirit world be] delivered unto the buffetings of Satan unto the day of redemption."[53] To be destroyed in the flesh means to be subject to capital punishment—to have one's life taken through the proper process and action of civil law within the kingdom of God.[54]

Manifestations Of Sealing Power

Sealing Blessings Given to Joseph Smith

It is not known when Joseph Smith was given the guarantee that he would receive eternal life, but evidence points to an early date. At a conference of the Church held October 25, 1831, he said: "Many of us have gone at the command of the Lord in defiance of everything evil, and obtained blessings unspeakable, in consequence of which *our names are sealed in the Lamb's book of life,* for the Lord has spoken it."[55] The Prophet was also one of a group of brethren to whom the Lord gave, or reaffirmed, the promise of eternal life in December, 1832.[56] An added feature of this promise as it applied to the Prophet was expressed in March, 1833, in a revelation which said of the keys of the priesthood which he held over the last dispensation of the gospel: "Verily I say unto you, the keys of this kingdom *shall never be taken from you,* while thou art in the world, neither in the world to come."[57]

Joseph Smith expressed the fact that his calling and election was made sure while in conversation with a friend about a woman who was following the ways of the world. "I would like to do something for her so she can be saved," the Prophet remarked with deep feeling and concern.

"Brother Joseph, how do you know you yourself will be saved?" his acquaintance inquired.

"I know I will," he replied. "I have the oath of God on it, and God cannot lie."[58]

Sealing Blessings Administered by Joseph Smith

The earliest recorded instance of a person in this dispensation receiving the guarantee that he would obtain eternal life in the resurrection seems to have been at the first conference of the Church, in June, 1830. "The Holy Ghost was poured out upon us in a miraculous manner," Joseph Smith reported—"many of our number prophesied, whilst others had the heavens opened to their view." Among the latter was Newel Knight of whom the Prophet said:

> A vision of the future burst upon him. . . . He saw heaven opened, and beheld the Lord Jesus Christ, seated at the right hand of the majesty on high, *and had it made plain to his understanding that the time would come when he would be admitted into His presence to enjoy His society for ever and ever.*[59]

Several Saints at Kirtland, Ohio, were sealed to eternal life early in February, 1831, shortly after the Prophet moved to that area from the state of New York. Of the gathering at which this action took place, one who was present said:

> After prayer and singing, Joseph began talking. He began very solemnly and very earnestly. Suddenly, his countenance changed and he stood mute; he seemed almost transfixed. He was looking ahead and his face outshone the candle which was on a shelf just behind him. I thought I could almost see the cheek bones. He looked as though a searchlight was inside his face. I never saw anything like it on earth. I could not take my eyes away from him. I shall remember him as he looked then as long as I live.
>
> After a short time he looked at us very solemnly, as if to pierce each heart, then said, "Brothers and Sisters, do you know who has been in your midst this night?"
>
> One of the Smith family said, "An angel of the Lord?"
>
> Joseph did not answer. Martin Harris was sitting at the Prophet's feet on a box. He slid to his knees, clasped his arms around the Prophet's knees and said, "I know, it was our Lord and Saviour, Jesus Christ."
>
> Joseph put his hand on Martin's head and answered, "Martin, God revealed that to you. Brothers and Sisters, the Saviour has been in your midst this night. I want you to remember it. He cast a veil over your eyes for you could not endure to look upon Him. You must be fed with milk and not meat. I want you to remember this as if it were the last thing that escaped my lips. He has given you all to me, and *commanded me*

to seal you up to Everlasting Life, that where he is there you may be also. And if you are tempted of Satan say, 'Get behind me Satan, *for my Salvation is secure.*'"[60]

All the members of the Colesville Branch—those Saints who had joined the Church under adverse circumstances in the area of Colesville, Broome county, New York—made their calling and election sure and were sealed to eternal life in 1831. This took place shortly after they and the Prophet arrived in the vicinity of Jackson county, Missouri, in the summer of that year.[61] In December the following year, a revelation declared to some early brethren at Kirtland:

> Verily, thus saith the Lord unto you who have assembled yourselves together. . . .
>
> The alms of your prayers have come up into the ears of the Lord of Sabaoth, and *are recorded in the book of the sanctified, even them of the celestial world.*
>
> Wherefore, I now send upon you another Comforter, even upon you my friends, that it may abide in your hearts, even the Holy Spirit of promise; which other Comforter is the same that I promised unto my disciples, as is recorded in the testimony of John.
>
> *This Comforter is the promise which I give unto you of eternal life, even the glory of the celestial kingdom. . . .*[62]

That month Joseph Smith gave blessings to his parents and to members of his father's family in which it appears that he gave some of them the promise of eternal life. To his mother, he said: "She shall have eternal life."[63] Of his father, he declared: "He shall also possess a mansion on high."[64] Of Hyrum, he promised: "He shall have eternal life."[65] And concerning William, he said: "He shall be saved unto the uttermost."[66]

There were others who received such blessings about this time. Speaking of the elders who attended a conference of the Church, in January, 1833, the Prophet reported: "By the power of the Holy Ghost I pronounced them all clean from the blood of this generation." In this action, they were "sealed up unto eternal life."[67]

It is reported that before some members of Zion's

Camp left Kirtland, in May, 1834, to go to the aid of their distressed brethren in Missouri, the Prophet sealed them to eternal life. They were promised that they would "come forth in the day of the Lord Jesus," but if they sinned "they would be delivered over to the buffeting of Satan for the destruction of the flesh." Apparently this blessing was later given to all members of the camp, for after all branches of that body had been united, a member of the camp reported: "We were called together again and were sealed up unto eternal life the same as in Kirtland."[68]

Sealing Blessings Administered by Elders

There were those other than the Prophet who exercised the basic sealing power of the priesthood at an early time in this dispensation. In November, 1831, a revelation declared to "the faithful elders" of the Church: "And of as many as the Father shall bear record, to you shall be given power to seal them up unto eternal life."[69] This they did. Having labored as a missionary in the vicinity of Benson, Vermont, from October 25, 1831, until the middle of January, 1832, Jared Carter said of a meeting which he held with the Saints in that area before he left them to continue his work elsewhere:

> While I, in the commencement of the meeting, was praying, *I was directed* to pray most earnestly that God would grant unto us *sealing grace.* After this I felt directed by the Spirit to declare unto the brethren that that day was *a sealing time* with them, as I had prayed in faith that they might be blessed. My communication to them caused some of the brethren to tremble, for this was something that they had never before experienced. But I exhorted them to call more earnestly on the Lord. We then began to pray, but the Spirit, as I viewed it in my mind, was not yet poured out; therefore, I again arose and devoted a few minutes to further exhortations, and then requested all the brethren and sisters to call upon the Lord with one accord. Accordingly, all of us lifted our voices to God, and while we were praying the Spirit rested down upon us. We then administered the Sacrament and it appeared to me that the Church of Christ in that locality was sealed up to the Lord, and it was likewise made plain to me that every one of us present should meet again in

Zion. I then felt as though I could leave them without fear, for I had a testimony that God would keep them.[70]

Orson Pratt wrote of his labors with Lyman Johnson in the area of Charleston, Vermont, in August, 1833:

> The 26th, in the forenoon the Church at Charleston, Vt., with some other brethren from other towns, met together and called upon the Lord; and the Lord heard their prayers and moved upon his servant Lyman [Johnson] by the power of the Holy Ghost to seal them up unto eternal life. And after this the brethren arose one by one and said that they knew that their names were sealed in the Lamb's Book of Life, and they all did bear this glorious testimony save two or three.[71]

Later, on September 8, 1833, Elders Johnson and Pratt sealed the members of the church at Bath, New Hampshire, to eternal life.[72]

In the spring of 1839, while Joseph Smith and others were unjustly confined in a Missouri dungeon, Heber C. Kimball struggled against great odds caring for the Saints and striving to free the brethren from their unjust confinement. "I felt very sorrowful and lonely," he related. "The following words came to my mind, and the Spirit said unto me, 'write,' which I did by taking a piece of paper and writing on my knee as follows: 'Verily I say unto my servant Heber, thou art my son, in whom I am well pleased; for thou art careful to hearken to my words, and not transgress my law, nor rebel against my servant Joseph Smith, for thou hast a respect to the words of mine anointed, even from the least to the greatest of them; *therefore thy name is written in heaven, no more to be blotted out for ever.*'"[73]

Sealing Blessings Administered by Patriarchs

The sealing power of the priesthood was also exercised at times under the authority of the Patriarchal Priesthood, in conjunction with the practice of giving patriarchal blessings to the Saints. A revelation stated that Hyrum Smith, as the Patriarch to the Church, was given the right "to hold the sealing blessings of my church, even the Holy

Spirit of promise, whereby ye are sealed up unto the day of redemption, that ye may not fall notwithstanding the hour of temptation that may come upon you."[74] In a patriarchal blessing given March 9, 1842, Patriarch Smith informed Heber C. Kimball that he had "attained the Holy Seal of promise as one that is chosen and sealed unto eternal life." Continuing, the patriarch said: "For this are you called and chosen and sealed, for the hand of God is with you to prosper you, and to save you and your house, even to the uttermost."[75]

That same day Patriarch Smith said in a blessing upon the head of Vilate Kimball, the wife of Elder Kimball:

> Beloved Sister: I lay my hands upon your head in the name of Jesus, and *seal you unto eternal life*—sealed here on earth and sealed in heaven, and *your name written in the Lamb's Book of Life never to be blotted out.*
>
> The same is mentioned and manifested to comfort your heart, and to be a comfort unto you henceforth all your days. It is even a promise according to the mind of the Spirit, and the Spirit shall bear record of the truth; the same is called the Second Comforter, not his presence, but his promise. *The same is as immutable as an oath by Himself,* because there is none greater, and there is no greater promise nor no greater blessing that can be given, and no greater riches, it being the riches of eternity, which are the greatest riches of all riches.[76]

Sealing Family Units Together

The program of the temple is designed to give the Saints the rites, ordinances, and covenants which are necessary for exaltation in the celestial kingdom without their making their calling and election sure to these blessings at the time they receive them. Thereafter they can then make their calling and election sure either by receiving the more sure word of prophecy while they yet live in mortality or by enduring faithful to the end of their earthly probation.[77]

When Joseph Smith introduced the divine patriarchal order and began to organize the Saints according to its eternal principles, the sealing power which Elijah revealed was manifested to make their calling and election sure to those sacred family relationships. God said to the Prophet: "I am the Lord thy God, and will be with thee even unto the end of the world, and through all eternity; for verily *I seal upon you your exaltation,* and prepare a throne for you in the kingdom of my Father, with Abraham your father." The Lord then added, as He spoke of the latter-day Seer: "I am with him, as I was with Abraham, thy father, *even unto his exaltation and glory.*"[78]

For a man to be sealed to exaltation in the celestial kingdom, he must make his calling and election sure to the blessings of eternal marriage in the resurrection. In referring to one who does so, a revelation said:

> . . . ye shall come forth in the first resurrection; and if it be after the first resurrection, in the next resurrection; and shall inherit thrones, kingdoms, principalities, and powers, dominions, all heights and depths—then shall it be written in the Lamb's Book of Life, that he shall commit no murder whereby to shed innocent blood, and if ye abide in my covenant, and commit no murder whereby to shed innocent blood, it shall be done unto them in all things whatsoever my servant hath put upon them, in time, and through all eternity; and shall be of full force when they are out of the world; and they shall pass by the angels, and the gods, which are set there, to their exaltation and glory in all things, as hath been sealed upon their heads, which glory shall be a fulness and a continuation of the seeds forever and ever.[79]

Joseph Smith once said to a close associate who had been sealed to exaltation within the divine patriarchal order:

> Nothing but the unpardonable sin can prevent you from inheriting eternal life for you are sealed up by the power of the Priesthood unto eternal life, having taken the step necessary for that purpose.
>
> Except a man and his wife enter into an everlasting covenant and be married for eternity, while in this probation, by the power and authority of the Holy Priesthood, they will cease to increase when they die; that is, they will not have any children after the resurrection. But those who are married by the power and authority of the priesthood in this life, and continue [maturing in the gospel] without committing the sin against the

Holy Ghost, will continue to increase and have children in the celestial glory.[80]

It is also designed that family units should be sealed together by the power and authority of the Holy Priesthood. Concerning the sealing power of the Holy Priesthood as it may be exercised in the organization of the divine patriarchal order, Joseph Smith said:

> Let us suppose a case. Suppose the great God who dwells in heaven should reveal himself to Father Cutler here, by the opening heavens, and tell him, I offer up a decree that whatsoever you seal on earth with your decree, I will seal it in heaven; you have the power then; *can it be taken off?* No. Then what you seal on earth, by the keys of Elijah, is sealed in heaven; and this is the power of Elijah. . . .
>
> Again: The doctrine or sealing power of Elijah is as follows:—If you have power to seal on earth and in heaven, then we should be wise. The first thing you do, go and seal on earth your sons and daughters unto yourself, and yourself unto your fathers in eternal glory, and go ahead, and not go back, but use a little wisdom, and seal all you can, and when you get to heaven tell your Father that what you seal on earth should be sealed in heaven, according to his promise. I will walk through the gate of heaven and claim what I seal, and those that follow me and my counsel.[81]

The Prophet taught the Saints that making their calling and election sure to the sacred family relationships of the new and everlasting covenant of marriage was a major goal which they could achieve through the program of the gospel. In referring to the work of establishing the divine patriarchal order on earth, he declared that "the spirit and power of Elijah is to come, . . . holding the keys of power, building the Temple [i.e., the divine patriarchal order which centers in the temple and of which the temple is a symbol] to the capstone, *placing the seals of the Melchizedek Priesthood upon the house of Israel,* and making all things ready." He stressed that "Elijah was to come and prepare the way and build up the [divine patriarchal] kingdom before the coming of the great day of the Lord."[82] Having spoken of the sealing power which Elijah revealed and commissioned man to use in modern times, the latter-day

Seer therefore admonished: "I would advise all the Saints to go to with their might and gather together all their living relatives to this place [Nauvoo], *that they may be sealed and saved.*"[83]

Explanations Of The More Sure Word Of Prophecy

Comments on Ancient Testimonies

Joseph Smith based his explanations of the doctrine of calling and election on the writings of the ancient apostles. Having noted that those ancient witnesses exhorted the faithful to achieve this objective, the Prophet observed: "This is the sealing power spoken of by Paul in other places."[84] The latter-day Seer then quoted the following from the writings of Paul:

> In whom [Christ] ye also trusted, that after ye heard the word of truth, the gospel of your salvation: in whom also *after that ye believed, ye were sealed with the holy Spirit of promise,*
>
> *Which is the earnest [i.e., the assurance or guarantee] of our inheritance until the redemption of the purchased possession,* unto the praise of his glory.[85]

The word "earnest" in this statement means an assurance of something which is to come—a binding pledge such as in the payment of earnest money, which is money paid in advance to bind a bargain or a covenant. The seal of the Holy Priesthood, which is attested to by the Holy Spirit, is the earnest, or guarantee, of the inheritance which the faithful will receive in eternity.

One of the best testimonies of this doctrine in the Bible was given by Peter, and to this Joseph Smith made reference on more than one occasion. Having enumerated many principles of spiritual growth which are required by the law of the gospel, Peter wrote:

> . . . if these things be in you, and abound, they make you that ye shall neither be barren nor unfruitful in the knowledge of our Lord Jesus Christ. . . .
>
> Wherefore . . . brethren, *give diligence to make your calling and election sure: for if ye do these things, ye shall never fall:*

For so an entrance shall be ministered unto you abundantly into the everlasting kingdom of our Lord and Saviour Jesus Christ.

Wherefore I will not be negligent to put you always in remembrance of these things, though ye know them, and be established in the present truth. . . .

We have not followed cunningly devised fables, when we made known unto you the power and coming of our Lord Jesus Christ, but were eye-witnesses of his majesty.

For we received from God the Father honour and glory, when there came such a voice to him from the excellent glory, This is my beloved Son, in whom I am well pleased.

And this voice which came from heaven we heard, when we were with him in the holy mount.

We have also a more sure word of prophecy; whereunto ye do well that ye take heed, as unto a light that shineth in a dark place, until the day dawn, and the day star arise in your hearts.[86]

In referring to Peter's statement, Joseph Smith said: "There are three grand secrets lying in this chapter, which no man can dig out, unless by the light of revelation, and which unlocks the whole chapter as the things that are written are only hints of things which existed in the prophet's mind, which are not written concerning eternal glory."[87] Peter's writings, which the Prophet considered to be penned in the "most sublime language of any of the apostles,"[88] were but allusions to the specific program by which man can make sure his calling and election to celestial glory and power.

According to Joseph Smith, the first grand secret revealed in Peter's writings was, "Knowledge is the power of salvation." Having cited the principles of spiritual growth which are enumerated in the law of the gospel and which Peter mentioned, the Prophet said:

If these things be in you, and abound, they make you that ye shall neither be barren nor unfruitful in the knowledge of our Lord Jesus Christ. . . . *What is the secret—the starting point?* . . . How did he obtain all things? *Through the knowledge of Him who hath called him. There could not anything be given, pertaining to life and godliness, without knowledge.*[89]

Again Joseph Smith explained:

Add to your faith knowledge, etc. *The principle of knowledge is*

> *the principle of salvation.* The principle can be comprehended by the faithful and diligent; and every one that does not obtain knowledge sufficient to be saved will be condemned. *The principle of salvation is given us through the knowledge of Jesus Christ.*
>
> Salvation is nothing more nor less than to triumph over all our enemies and put them under our feet. And when we have power to put all enemies under our feet in this world, and a knowledge to triumph over all evil spirits in the world to come, then we are saved, as in the case of Jesus, who was to reign until He had put all enemies under His feet, and the last enemy was death.[90]

In this statement, the Prophet spoke of that knowledge which man can obtain only through the gospel. "Knowledge through our Lord and Savior Jesus Christ is the grand key that unlocks the glories and mysteries of the kingdom of heaven," he stressed.[91] This included "a knowledge of the priesthood."[92] Though men of his day were "crying out against prophets, apostles, angels, revelations, prophesying and visions," the Prophet considered these things to be "the key that unlocks the heavens" and puts man in possession of "the glories of the celestial world."[93]

The second grand key in Peter's epistle was that the saints should make their "calling and election sure" to celestial glory and power. Having spoken of the plan of spiritual growth which is outlined in the gospel and having exhorted the saints to make their calling and election sure, Peter added: " . . . for if ye do these things, ye shall never fall: for so *an entrance shall be ministered unto you abundantly* into the everlasting kingdom of our Lord and Saviour Jesus Christ."[94] Those who make their calling and election sure find the gate to celestial glory opened wide, for they have a guarantee of eternal life.

Of the ancient Apostle's instructions, Joseph Smith said:

> He lays this injunction upon the people "to make your calling and election sure." He is emphatic upon this subject—after adding all this virtue, knowledge, etc., "Make your calling and election sure."[95]

Joseph Smith identified the third grand key in Peter's

statement as being a recognition of the fact that "it is one thing to be on the mount [of transfiguration] and hear the excellent voice [from heaven bear testimony that Jesus is the Son of God], &c., &c., and another to hear the voice declare to you, You have a part and a lot in that kingdom."[96] It is not enough for man to acquire a testimony that Jesus is the Son of God. Each person must make his calling and election sure and thereby acquire a personal guarantee that he will have a part hereafter with Christ in the kingdom of heaven. On this point the Prophet said:

> Now, there is some grand secret here, and keys to unlock the subject. Notwithstanding the apostle exhorts them to add to their faith virtue, knowledge, temperance, &c., yet he exhorts them to make their calling and election sure. And though they had heard an audible voice from heaven bearing testimony that Jesus was the Son of God, yet he says we have a more sure word of prophecy, whereunto ye do well that ye take heed as unto a light shining in a dark place. Now, *wherein could they have a more sure word of prophecy than to hear the voice of God saying, This is my beloved Son, &c.*
>
> Now for the secret and grand key, *Though they might hear the voice of God and know that Jesus was the Son of God, this would be no evidence that their election and calling was made sure, that they had part with Christ, and were joint heirs with Him.* They then would want that more sure word of prophecy, *that they were sealed in the heavens and have the promise of eternal life in the kingdom of God.*[97]

More Sure Word of Prophecy Based on Doctrine of Election in the Flesh

The doctrine that man can make his calling and election sure to blessings in the resurrection and thereby receive the more sure word of prophecy has its basis in the appointments which were made in the Grand Organizational Council before man was placed upon the earth.[98] Having referred to the power of the priesthood by which man's calling and election can be made sure, Joseph Smith said: "Here is the doctrine of election that the world has quarreled so much about; but they do not know anything about it."[99]

In the Grand Organizational Council, many spirits were appointed, or elected, to be born in the flesh in chosen lineages (such as those of Abraham and of the patriarchs before and after his day) where they would be natural heirs to the blessings, rights, privileges, and promises of the gospel or of the divine patriarchal order. Here the doctrine of election had its origin. But the actual realization of those blessings was made contingent upon each individual's faithfulness in mortality. Joseph Smith explained that the "unconditional election of individuals to eternal life" from before the foundation of the world was not taught by the ancient apostles. "God did elect or predestinate, that all those who would be saved, should be saved in Christ Jesus, and through obedience to the Gospel," the Prophet said; "but He passes over no man's sins, but visits them with correction, and *if his children will not repent of their sins He will discard them.*"[100]

There are two phases to the doctrine of election. The first, which has to do with the appointments that were made in the Grand Organizational Council, is the doctrine of election in the flesh. But the blessings which are associated with these appointments and promises should not end with mortality; they are designed to extend into eternity and find their full realization in the resurrection. Having embraced the gospel on earth and received the foreappointed blessings by covenant on a contingent basis, man may obtain a knowledge of that election by revelation in mortality and have it renewed in the flesh.[101] He must then make sure his right to the promised blessings in eternity. This is the second phase of the doctrine of election—the doctrine of making one's calling and election sure. This phase of the doctrine of election begins when man embraces the gospel on earth and receives the foreappointed blessings by covenant on a promissory basis. When he makes sure his calling and election to those blessings and appointments in eternity by getting them sealed upon him by the power and authority of the Holy Priesthood, that action consummates the total program except for the actual realization of the specified blessings and appointments in the resurrection.

Joseph Smith associated the two aspects of the doctrine of election in an address which he gave to the Saints at Nauvoo, but unfortunately his specific remarks were not recorded. After reporting his teachings on the sealing power of the Holy Priesthood, the summary record of his speech concludes: "The speaker continued to teach the *doctrine of election* and the *sealing powers* and principles, and spoke of the *doctrine of election with the seed of Abraham,* and the *sealing of blessings upon his posterity,* and *the sealing of the fathers and children,* according to the declarations of the prophets."[102] From this report it seems apparent that the Prophet correlated the promises which the Lord made to Abraham with the principles by which the divine patriarchal order is built up and the faithful are finally sealed together for eternity in the sacred family order.

Two aspects of the spirit of prophecy also operate in the above program. When men were foreordained in the Grand Organizational Council to receive the Holy Priesthood and its various offices and callings on earth, the spirit of prophecy was expressed in making those appointments. Joseph Smith therefore wrote that a man must be called of God "by prophecy" in order to receive an office in the ministry, which apparently means that he must be called as a result of a prophetic declaration which was made in the Grand Organizational Council.[103] But like the initial phase of the doctrine of election, the pre-earth prophecy was made on a contingent basis and was subject in its realization to the individual's faithfulness on earth. But when a person receives the gospel and makes his calling and election sure to the blessings and appointments of the priesthood, he may in this way obtain a guarantee of the promised blessing as *a more sure word* of prophecy.[104] This is an extension, or a further development, of the spirit of prophecy as it was expressed initially in the Council, for after a man makes his calling and election sure by being proved in his mortal state, he may then receive *a more sure* word of prophecy by which he can know that he will obtain the designated blessings in the resurrection. The more sure word of prophecy, therefore, is a prophetic word that is more sure than the prophetic word which was given to man in the pre-earth life and which pertained to his calling and election to privileges and appointments in the flesh.[105]

Doctrine Of Reprobation

Joseph Smith and other leading men among the Saints spoke of the doctrine of reprobation in conjunction with the doctrine of election.[106] The term "reprobation" comes from the word "reprobate," and it refers to one who is abandoned to sin and lost to all sense of duty and righteousness. Reprobation is the act of reprobating, or of being abandoned by God to a sinful course in life. In some respects, therefore, the doctrine of reprobation is the opposite of that of election.

The priesthood not only has power to seal the faithful to specific blessings in the resurrection but "to seal both on earth and in heaven, the unbelieving and rebellious."[107] Concerning this expression of the sealing power, Joseph Smith said:

> This spirit of Elijah was manifest in the days of the Apostles, in delivering certain ones to the buffetings of Satan, that they might be saved in the day of the Lord Jesus. They were sealed by the spirit of Elijah unto the damnation of hell until the day of the Lord, or revelation of Jesus Christ.[108]

The doctrine of reprobation rises out of the infinite knowledge of God, His power to discern the desires and dispositions of men, and His responsibility to execute justice and judgment upon recalcitrant souls. It is based in the principle of man's free agency and in no way violates that principle. When man turns his heart from righteousness so that his desires are set to do evil, the Lord may consign him to a judgment which is suited to his situation and desires. God may even foreknow when man will turn his heart wholly to wickedness and thereby use him to carry out a divine purpose. Such was the fact with Judas and Pharaoh. For this reason Moses was instructed to say to the latter in behalf of the Lord: "For this cause have *I raised thee up, for to shew in thee my power;* and that my name may be declared throughout all the earth."[109] Having quoted this statement in an article entitled "Election and Reprobation," Brigham Young and Willard Richards explained:

> God had promised to bring the house of Israel up out of the land of Egypt at his own appointed time; and with a mighty hand and an outstretched arm, and great terribleness (Deut. xxvi, 8.) He chose to do this thing that His power might be known and his name declared throughout all the earth, so that all nations might have the God of heaven in remembrance, and reverence his holy name; and to accomplish this it was needful that He should meet with opposition to give Him an opportunity to manifest His power; *therefore He raised up a man, even Pharaoh, who, He foreknew, would harden his heart against God of his own free will and choice,* and would withstand the Almighty in His attempt to deliver His chosen people, and that to the utmost of his ability; and he proved himself worthy of the choice, for he left no means unimproved which his wicked heart could devise to vex the sons of Abraham, and defeat the purposes of the Most High, which gave the God of Abraham an opportunity to magnify His name in the ears of the nations, and in sight of this wicked king, by many mighty signs and wonders, sometimes even to the convincing of the wicked king of his wickedness, and of the power of God, (Exod. viii: 28, etc.) and yet he would continue to rebel and hold the Israelites in bondage; and this is what it meant by God's hardening Pharaoh's heart. He manifested Himself in so many glorious and mighty ways, that Pharaoh could not resist the truth without becoming harder; so that at last, in his madness, to stay the people of God, he rushed his hosts into the Red Sea and they were covered with the floods.[110]

The consequences of reprobation are not limited to this mortal sphere. Joseph Smith spoke, for example, of Pharaoh's base desires and of the use God is making of him in the spirit world after death. The Prophet wrote:

> I preached this morning to a large congregation. The subject

matter of my discourse was drawn from 32nd and 33rd chapters of Ezekiel, wherein it was shown that old Pharaoh was comforted and greatly rejoiced that he was honored as a kind of a king devil over those uncircumcised nations that go down to hell for rejecting the word of the Lord, notwithstanding His mighty miracles, and fighting the Saints; the whole exhibited as a pattern to this generation, and the nations now rolling in splendor over the globe, if they do not repent, that they shall go down to the pit also and be rejoiced over, and ruled over by old Pharaoh, king - devil of mobocrats, miracle - rejecters, Saint - killers, hypocritical priests, and all other fit subjects to fester in their own infamy.[111]

Summary

Joseph Smith taught that it is possible for mortal man to make his calling and election sure to celestial glory and power in the resurrection and thereby obtain the more sure word of prophecy by which he may know that he is sealed unto eternal life. This is one of the major objectives of the gospel, and it is open to every person who will embrace the gospel and apply the program of salvation in his life. The Prophet therefore exhorted the Saints: "Oh! I beseech you to go forward, go forward and make your calling and your election sure; and if any man preach any other Gospel than that which I have preached, he shall be cursed."[112]

There are two ways by which man may achieve this objective. One is to endure faithful in the gospel to the end of this mortal probation. The other is to persist in applying the principles and powers of the gospel to such an extent that the guarantee of eternal life is given before mortal death, qualified by the fact that man can break the seal by committing the unpardonable sin.

Those who are sealed to eternal life stand in a more responsible relationship with God than those who have not achieved this objective. Should man sin wilfully after being sealed to eternal life, it is not consistent with divine truth and mercy for the atonement of Christ to pay the debt of such transgressions, and man himself must be responsible for satisfying the demands of divine justice. The law of God therefore requires that such individuals be delivered to the buffetings of Satan until the day of their redemption. Such provisions also apply to those who make their calling and election sure to the relationship of eternal marriage.

There are several examples of the sealing power of the priesthood being manifested in modern times, many of which took place early in this dispensation. Some instances occurred in the ministries of the Prophet and the Elders of the Church. The sealing power also was exercised by patriarchs. On several occasions, Joseph Smith spoke on the subject of making man's calling and election sure and drew support for his teachings from the writings of ancient prophets and apostles. This doctrine is based upon the doctrine of election in the flesh, and it assumes that those who were appointed in the Grand Organizational Council to receive gospel blessings and responsibilities in the flesh, subject to their faithfulness on earth, can here receive a guarantee that they will realize the fruition of these blessings and responsibilities in the resurrection. This guarantee is a more sure word of prophecy, whereas the initial calling which was made in the Grand Organization Council before man was placed upon the earth was contingent in nature.

The doctrine of reprobation is associated with that of election; and, like the doctrine of election, it has its basis in the free agency of man and the foreknowledge of God. When necessary, those holding the Holy Priesthood have power to seal up the rebellious to await the judgments of God. And in such cases, the Lord may use those individuals to carry out his divine purposes in the earth.

Notes

1. HC, IV, p. 258.

2. See the section in this chapter entitled "More Sure Word of Prophecy Based on Doctrine of Election in the Flesh." This term comes from 2 Peter 1:19. In some early editions of the Doctrine and Covenants (see D&C 131:5), it is referred to as "the more sure word of prophecy mentioned by Peter."

3. D&C 131:5. On another occasion, he explained that the more sure word of prophecy is "that they were sealed in the heavens and had the promise of eternal life in the kingdom of God." It is to have "this promise sealed unto them."—HC, V, p. 388.

4. HC, V, p. 389.

5. *Ibid.*, III, p. 380.

6. *Ibid.*, VI, p. 184.

7. Mosiah 5:15. An earlier chapter in this book has explained that "eternal" is one of the names of God and that it denotes the kind of life He has, which is to possess the living attributes and powers of celestial glory and to operate in universal space through the agency of that glory. It also explains that to acquire a fulness of glory in the resurrection man must enter into the new and everlasting covenant of marriage. (See Volume I of this study, the section in chapter eight entitled "Eternal Life.") To what, then, were the Saints sealed who made their calling and election sure before the covenant of eternal marriage was revealed?

Scripturally, the term "eternal life" is used with both a general and a restricted meaning. In a general sense, it applies to all who are redeemed from the fall of Adam in that they are brought back into the presence of God. A revelation explained that in the resurrection the righteous will be "raised in immortality unto eternal life," while the wicked will be raised unto "eternal damnation," because by failing to repent they "cannot be *redeemed from their spiritual fall.*" (D&C 29:43–44.) The Book of Mormon also uses the term "eternal life" to denote redemption to the presence of God. Speaking of those who would come forth from the grave at the time of Christ's resurrection, Abinadi said: "They are raised *to dwell with God* who has redeemed them; *thus they have eternal life* through Christ." Continuing, the Nephite Prophet explained:

> . . . they are they that have died before Christ came, in their ignorance, not having salvation declared unto them. And thus the Lord bringeth about the restoration of these; and *they have a part in the first resurrection, or have eternal life, being redeemed by the Lord.*
>
> And little children also have eternal life. (Mosiah 15:23–25.)

In the restricted sense, eternal life is defined as "the greatest of all the gifts of God" (D&C 14:7), which is to receive a fulness of celestial glory. Those who receive eternal life come to know God by being made like Him. Consequently, they become gods, or exalted beings, within the celestial kingdom of glory. (See HC, VI, p. 306.) To achieve this objective, they must faithfully comply with the requirements of the new and everlasting covenant of marriage. (See D&C 132: 4, 6, 19, 21.)

It may therefore be asked, to what future reward were the faithful sealed who were given the guarantee of eternal life before the new and everlasting covenant of marriage was revealed? Existing evidence suggests two possibilities: first, they could merely have been sealed to come forth in the resurrection to possess celestial glory, without the specific promise of exaltation within the divine patriarchal order. Second, they could have been given the guarantee that they would receive a fulness of celestial glory on the assumption that their faithfulness and spiritual maturity were such that they would embrace the further covenants upon which exaltation in celestial society is based, when those covenants and obligations were made known to them. Evidence indicates that those who received the initial seal were not exempt from the requirement to enter into the new and everlasting covenant of marriage and receive the seal of the priesthood on that sacred relationship.

8. *Journal History,* October 25, 1831. See also the *Far West Record,* Church Historian's Library, Salt Lake City, Utah, under date.

9. HC, VI, p. 51.

10. The full program of sealing the faithful to celestial relationships will be consummated at the beginning of the millennial era when the Lord "shall have sealed all things, unto the end of all things."—D&C 77:12.

11. Mosiah 26:20.

12. Enos 1:27.

13. 3 Nephi 28:3.

14. Ether 12:37.

15. D&C 1:8–9.

16. D&C 68:12.

17. It is sometimes supposed that there were no sealing powers associated with the priesthood in the present dispensation until Elijah ministered to Joseph Smith and Oliver Cowdery in 1836, but the writer feels that this conclusion cannot be supported in light of historical evidence or the actions and teachings of Joseph Smith. It is apparent that before the coming of Elijah, many of the Saints were sealed to eternal life and received the second Comforter.

18. HC, III, p. 380. The discourse from which this statement is taken was delivered first to the Twelve and later to the Saints in general. See *ibid.,* IV, p. 10.

19. D&C 76:53.

20. HC, V, p. 403.

21. *Ibid.*

22. *Ibid.,* III, p. 380.

23. That is, it is presently the more general way the Saints receive the promise of eternal life. But this may not always be the case once the kingdom of God is established on earth with its full program, blessings, and powers. See HC, III, p. 380 (in light of D&C 84:98 and Jeremiah 31:34), where Joseph Smith teaches that eventually every man remaining on earth will be raised to this spiritual standard.

24. D&C 14:7. See also D&C 6:13.

25. 2 Nephi 31:19–20. In conjunction with this challenge and promise, see the Prophet's discussion in HC, II, pp. 19–22.

26. HC, VI, p. 315.

27. D&C 76:79.

28. Omni 1:26.

29. D&C 20:29. See also D&C 20:25.

30. Moroni 3:3.

31. 2 Nephi 31:12–13, 15–16.

32. Alma 38:2.

33. Alma 32:13.

34. D&C 98:14–15.

35. D&C 101:35.

36. D&C 6:29–30.

37. HC, V, p. 391.

38. *Ibid.,* VI, pp. 252–253.

39. *Ibid.,* p. 314.

40. See Volume I of this work, the section in chapter seventeen entitled "The Perseverance of the Righteous in Mortality."

41. In the resurrection the body is raised to a state of incorruption, and in this sense the struggle with the flesh is not continued after the reunion of the spirit and the body.

42. HC, V, pp. 391–392.

43. *Ibid.,* I, pp. 323–324. See also JD, IX, p. 288, for a statement by Brigham Young on "wilful transgression."

44. The law of consecration and stewardship, as well as the united order, will be treated in volume III of this study.

45. Speaking of those who were made members of the united order, the revelation directing the Prophet to organize it said:

> The *kingdom is yours and the blessings thereof are yours, and the riches of eternity are yours. . . .*
>
> *For ye are the church of the Firstborn. . . .*—D&C 78:18, 21.

To be a member of the church of the Firstborn, a person must make his calling and election sure to eternal life. See the section in chapter fourteen entitled "Right to Commune with Church of the Firstborn."

46. D&C 78:11–12.

47. D&C 82:11–12, 20–21.

48. D&C 104:1–9.

49. HC, VII, pp. 268, 269.

50. See, for example, D&C 132:49, 57. This seems to be true also in respect to verse 19.

51. D&C 132:26.

52. Letter of Vilate Kimball to Heber C. Kimball, written at Nauvoo, June 8, 1843, and recorded in the journal of Heber C. Kimball, 1840–1845; original journal in Church Historian's Library, Salt Lake City, Utah.

53. D&C 132:26.

54. The Church has no power to deprive any person of life or property. Nor will it have such power when the millennial kingdom is fully established on earth. An official proclamation expressing the views of the Saints on such points states: "We do not believe that any religious society has authority to try men on the right of property or life, to take from them this world's goods, or to put them in jeopardy of either life or limb, or to inflict any physical punishment upon them."—D&C 134:10. When the full law and program of the kingdom of God are established, such matters will be handled by the government of God—the political organization within the kingdom which will maintain freedom and justice for all men.

55. *Far West Record,* under date, Church Historian's Library, Salt Lake City, Utah; found also in TPJS, p. 9.

56. D&C 88:1–4.

57. D&C 90:3. A revelation in February, 1831, seems to imply that he had not at that time been given the guarantee that he would hold these keys in eternity. See D&C 43:3–4. It should be kept in mind that this promise was in addition to the guarantee of eternal life.

58. The journal and memoirs of Mary Elizabeth Rollins Lightner, p. 7.

Though it is not known specifically when this conversation took place, evidence points to the Nauvoo period of the Church.

59. HC, I, p. 85. The record does not state if there was any action by the priesthood on earth at that time to make the promise official and binding by its power.

60. The journal and memoirs of Mary Elizabeth Rollins Lightner, pp. 2–3; *Young Woman's Journal,* XVI, pp. 556–557. In the above quotation, the writer has combined the statements made by Mrs. Lightner into one statement containing all the details of her report.

61. From an account of early historical events, written by Joseph Knight, Sr., Church Historian's Library Salt Lake City, Utah.

62. D&C 88:1–4.

63. HC, I, p. 466.

64. *Ibid.*

65. Manuscript report, December 18, 1833, Church Historian's Library, Salt Lake City, Utah; found also in TPJS, p. 41.

66. HC, I, p. 467.

67. *Ibid.,* p. 323.

68. The journal of Reuben McBride, Brigham Young University Library. The writer has corrected spelling and punctuation in this quote.

69. D&C 68:7, 12.

70. *Journal History,* September 27, 1831.

71. The journal of Orson Pratt, August 26, 1833.

72. *Ibid.,* under date.

73. Whitney, *op. cit.,* p. 253.

74. D&C 124:124. As a general rule, such promises are now given in patriarchal blessings on a contingent basis, subject to the person proving worthy to receive them.

75. Solomon P. Kimball, *Life of David P. Kimball,* pp. 125–127.

76. *Ibid.,* pp. 127–128.

77. This means that though a man and his bride may be married for time and all eternity by the authority and power of the priesthood, they are not actually "sealed" to that relationship until they have made their calling and election sure to exaltation in the celestial kingdom. To seal is to secure or bind—to fasten up or enclose securely. Technically speaking, only those are sealed who make their calling and election sure and are given the more sure word of prophecy.

Reference has been made in an earlier chapter to the Holy Spirit of promise. (See the section in chapter eight entitled "Justification by the Holy Spirit.") The Holy Ghost must ratify all ordinances and promises of the gospel. He therefore may ratify the initial marriage covenant, which is made on a contingent basis, subject in the realization of its blessings in eternity to the faithfulness of the contracting parties. But until a man and his wife have made their calling and election sure to an eternal union and this promise is ratified by the Holy Ghost, their union is not actually sealed in the true and full sense of the word.

78. D&C 132:49, 57.

79. D&C 132:19.

80. HC, V, p. 391.

81. *Ibid.,* VI, pp. 252, 253; MS, XXIII, pp. 102–103.

82. HC, VI, p. 254.
83. *Ibid.*, p. 184.
84. *Ibid.*, III. p. 379.
85. Ephesians 1:13–14, as cited in HC, III, pp. 379–380.
86. 2 Peter 1:8, 10–12, 16–19.
87. HC, V, pp. 401–402.
88. *Ibid.*, p. 392.
89. *Ibid.*, pp. 402–403.
90. *Ibid.*, pp. 387–388.
91. *Ibid.*, p. 389.
92. *Ibid.*, pp. 402–403.
93. *Ibid.*, p. 389.
94. 2 Peter 1:10–11.
95. HC, V. pp. 402–403.
96. *Ibid.*, p. 403.
97. *Ibid.*, p. 388.
98. See Volume I of this study, the section in chapter eleven entitled "The Grand Organizational Council."
99. HC, VI, p. 252.
100. *Ibid.*, IV, p. 360. As the Prophet indicates, some aspects of the doctrine of predestination are true. God predestines that man will be saved in and through Christ. There is no other name given whereby salvation can come to man. God also predestines that in salvation man must be conformed to the divine image of Christ. There is no other person in whom and through whom man can be glorified.
101. Parley P. Pratt said of Abraham: "When he had been sufficiently proved according to the flesh, the Lord manifested to him the election before exercised towards him in the eternal world. He then renewed that election and covenant, and blessed him, and his seed after him."—JD, I, pp. 258–259.
102. HC, V, pp. 530–531.
103. Articles of Faith No. 5. See Alma 13:3ff for an explanation of this doctrine. For a treatment of this subject in relation to the Grand Organizational Council, see Volume I of this study, the section in chapter eleven entitled "Men are Called of God by Prophecy."
104. See D&C 131:5.
105. As indicated in the preceding section of this chapter, this is not the only way the guarantee of eternal life is a more sure word, or something that is more sure in its nature than something else. Having cited Peter's admonition to the ancient saints to make their calling and election sure and thereby receive the more sure word of prophecy, Joseph Smith said: "Now, wherein could they have a more sure word of prophecy than to hear the voice of God saying, This is my beloved Son."—HC, V, p. 388. The Prophet then explained that it is one thing for a person to know that Jesus is the Son of God and another thing for him to know that in the resurrection he is guaranteed a place with Christ in the kingdom of heaven, and that the guarantee of eternal life is a more sure indication of what his state will be in the resurrection than for him to hear a voice from heaven bear testimony that Jesus is the Son of God. But the fact that the more sure word of prophecy is more sure than one thing does not prevent it from being more sure than another. As a *prophetic word,* it is more sure than the prophetic word which was given to those who were called

and elected in the pre-earth to receive specified blessings in the flesh. Apparently it was in this sense that the Apostle Peter used the term, for in his epistle he was writing to many who had not been on the mount and received the testimony of Christ which he then received. Yet he said, "*We* have also a more sure word of prophecy."—2 Peter 1:19.

106. See, for example, an article written by Brigham Young and Willard Richards entitled "Election and Reprobation," in HC, IV, pp. 256–266.

107. D&C 1:8.

108. HC, VI, p. 252.

109. Exodus 9:16.

110. HC, IV, pp. 263–264. Where the King James translation of the Bible says "the Lord hardened the heart of Pharaoh," Joseph Smith's Inspired Revision states that "Pharaoh hardened his heart." See Exodus 9:12; 10:1, 20, 27; 11:9–10; 14:4, 8, 17 in comparison with the equivalent verses in the Prophet's work.

111. HC, V, p. 22.

112. *Ibid.*, VI, p. 365.

14

The Second Comforter

I will pray the Father, and he shall give you another Comforter, that he may abide with you for ever.—JESUS.

Joseph Smith taught that within the program of the gospel there are two Comforters. "One is the Holy Ghost, the same as given on the day of Pentecost, and that all Saints receive after faith, repentance, and baptism," he explained. "The other Comforter spoken of is a subject of great interest," the Prophet continued, "and perhaps understood by few of this generation."[1] Concerning it, a revelation declared: "This Comforter is *the promise which I give unto you of eternal life,* even the glory of the celestial kingdom."[2]

Second Comforter Defined

Essentially the second Comforter is the promise, or guarantee, of eternal life which man receives when he makes his calling and election sure to celestial glory. This promise carries with it certain privileges, including the right (subject to the will of God) to enjoy in some degree the manifestations of celestial glory on earth and to commune personally with those who reside in the presence of God. Similar to the fact that the laying on of hands following baptism entitles man to the blessings of the Holy Ghost through the continued exercise of his faith, so does the guarantee of eternal life entitle the recipient to the personal ministry of Christ and other holy beings who reside in the presence of God.[3]

The doctrine of the second Comforter must be seen in the context of man making his calling and election sure. Hyrum Smith declared that the promise of eternal life which he sealed upon Vilate Kimball in a patriarchal blessing was "called the Second Comforter, *not his presence, but his promise.*"[4] He implied that there was a difference between the two aspects of the second Comforter, but that in a general way the promise of eternal life and the presence of Christ were both referred to as the second Comforter.

This view is reflected in a statement by the Prophet. In discussing the second Comforter, he first spoke of man making his calling and election sure. "After a person . . . receives the Holy Ghost, (by the laying on of hands), which is the first Comforter," he explained, "then let him continue to humble himself before God, hungering and thirsting after righteousness, and living by every word of God, and the Lord will soon say unto him, *Son thou shalt be exalted.*" This is the guarantee of eternal life. The Prophet continued: "When the Lord has thoroughly proved him, and finds that the man is determined to serve Him at all hazards, *then the man will find his calling and his election made sure, then it will be his privilege to receive the other Comforter,* which the Lord hath promised the Saints."[5]

From this statement it is apparent that the promise of eternal life normally precedes the manifestations which relate to the second Comforter. But having set the doctrine in its proper context, Joseph Smith seems to have referred to the second Comforter as being *both the promise of eternal life and the personal manifestation of Christ and other divine beings to the worthy recipient.* "Now what is this other Comforter?" he inquired. "It is no more nor less than the Lord Jesus Christ Himself; and this is the sum and substance of the whole matter; that when any man obtain this last Comforter [i.e., the promise of eternal life?], he will have the personage of Jesus Christ to attend him, or appear unto him from time to time, and even He will manifest the Father unto him, and they will take up their abode with him, and the visions of the heavens will be opened unto him, and the Lord will teach him face to face."[6]

According to the Prophet, Jesus promised the second Comforter to His disciples before He was crucified. Having referred to a person making his calling and election sure, the Prophet explained: "Then it will be his privilege to receive the other Comforter, which the Lord promised the Saints, as is recorded in the testimony of St. John, in the 14th chapter, from the 12th to the 27th verses."[7] In this statement, Jesus said:

> . . . I will pray the Father, and He shall give you *another Comforter,* that he may abide with you forever;
>
> Even *the Spirit of Truth;* whom the world cannot receive, because it seeth him not, neither knoweth him; but ye know him; for he dwelleth with you, and shall be in you.
>
> I will not leave you comfortless: *I will come to you. . . .*
>
> He that hath my commandments, and keepeth them, he it is that loveth me: and he that loveth me shall be loved of my Father, and *I will love him, and will manifest myself to him. . . .*
>
> If a man love me, he will keep my words: and my Father will love him, and *we will come unto him, and make our abode with him.*[8]

Two points in this statement are of special importance: First, Jesus associated the other Comforter directly with the Spirit of truth, which is the Holy Ghost. Joseph Smith made it clear that the Holy Ghost Himself is not the second Comforter, but that He ratifies and thereby binds the promise of eternal life upon faithful saints. The Prophet and others were given this same promise in a revelation: "Wherefore, I now send upon you *another Comforter,* even upon you my friends, that it [i.e., the other Comforter] may abide in your hearts, *even the Holy Spirit of promise; which other Comforter is the same that I promised unto my disciples, as is recorded in the testimony of John."*[9] Having identified this Comforter as that which Jesus promised to His disciples, the revelation then declared that that Comforter (i.e., the Holy Spirit of promise), which was to abide in their hearts, was "the promise . . . of eternal life, even the glory of the celestial kingdom."[10] *The other Comforter of which Christ spoke, therefore, was the divine promise or guarantee sealed in the hearts of the faithful by the revelation and power of the Holy Spirit that they would receive eternal life in the world to come, which is the glory of the celestial kingdom.* This is the more sure word of prophecy, which is for a man to know "that he is sealed up unto eternal life, *by revelation and the spirit of prophecy,* through the power of the Holy Priesthood."[11]

Second, Jesus stated that He would manifest Himself to those disciples who received the other Comforter, and that even the Father would reveal Himself unto them. Of Christ's promise as recorded in John 14:23, Joseph Smith wrote by revelation: "The appearing of the Father and the Son, in that verse, is a *personal appearance;* and the idea that the Father and the Son dwell in a man's heart is an old sectarian notion, and is false."[12] The promise of eternal life, which is sealed in the heart of man by the power of the Holy Ghost, therefore carries with it the privilege of receiving the personal manifestations of the Father and the Son.

The Prophet indicated that the blessings of the second Comforter are also given in the spirit world to those who make their calling and election sure to eternal life by enduring faithful in the gospel to the end of their mortal probation. In referring to faithful saints who passed away in his day, he said: "Those who have died in the faith are now in the celestial kingdom of God."[13] By this statement he did not mean that they were then resurrected, but that they dwelt in a state of celestial glory. He wrote in a revelation that "there are *two kinds* of beings in heaven," namely (1) resurrected beings having bodies of flesh and bones and (2) spirits "who are not resurrected *but inherit the same glory.*"[14] The latter group includes those who endure faithful in the gospel until mortal death. The corruption in the body which in mortality acts as a deterring force pushing man away from God is left behind as the spirit departs the physical tabernacle, and if the person has been faithful in his day of probation he then enters into a state of glory and is given the privilege of the second Comforter in the spirit world. Joseph Smith therefore taught that "the spirits of the just are exalted to a greater and more glorious work . . . in their departure to the world of spirits," and that there they are "enveloped in flaming fire" or glory.[15]

Blessings Of The Second Comforter

Right to Commune with the Father and the Son

Those who make their calling and election sure to celestial glory and in this way receive the second Comforter, or the promise of eternal life, may have the privilege of communing personally and openly with the Man of Holiness and His Son Jesus Christ. Revelations given through Joseph Smith refer to this promise in the gospel program. "The power and authority of the higher, or Melchizedek Priesthood, is to hold the keys of all the spiritual blessings of the church," one revelation explained—"to . . . have the heavens opened unto them, . . . and to enjoy the communion and presence of God the Father, and Jesus the mediator of the new covenant."[16] In referring to the blessings of the second Comforter, Joseph Smith also spoke repeatedly of the Saints communing personally with God the Father and his Son Jesus Christ.[17]

Right to Commune with Angels

Joseph Smith taught that those who make their calling and election sure have the privilege of communing with "an innumerable company of angels."[18] He observed that "Paul [the Apostle] speaks of the Church coming to an innumerable company of angels."[19] The Prophet also explained:

> The Kingdom of Heaven is like a grain of mustard seed. The

mustard seed is small, but brings forth a large tree, and the fowls lodge in the branches. *The fowls are the angels.* . . . We may come to an innumerable company of angels, have communion with and receive instruction from them. . . . Paul had these things, and we may have the fowls of heaven lodge in the branches, etc.[20]

The Aaronic Priesthood holds the keys of the ministry of angels.[21] But the right to commune with such beings is also extended to those who are sealed to eternal life.[22] It is possible that man does not need to achieve as great a degree of spiritual maturity to receive this privilege as he does to stand in the presence of God. A revelation to the Saints concerning their challenge to acquire the blessings of the second Comforter thus stated: "Ye are not able to abide the presence of God now, *neither the ministry of angels;* wherefore, continue in patience until ye are perfected."[23]

Angels are not a special creation of God separate from man, and they do not have wings.[24] They are holy men who held the priesthood during earth life and who thereafter continue to act in special callings to fulfil the will of God. Joseph Smith "explained the difference between an angel and a ministering spirit; the one a resurrected or translated body, with its spirit ministering to embodied spirits—the other a disembodied spirit, visiting and ministering [primarily] to disembodied spirits."[25] He spoke, for example, of the angel Moroni as being a resurrected personage.[26] Of the being who appeared to the Apostle John, he said: "The angel that appeared to John on the Isle of Patmos was a translated or resurrected body."[27] To illustrate the distinction between ministering spirits and angels, the Prophet explained:

> Jesus Christ became a ministering spirit (while His body was lying in the sepulchre) to the spirits in prison, to fulfill an important part of His mission, without which He could not have perfected His work, or entered into His rest. After His resurrection He appeared as an angel to His disciples.[28]

"Angels have advanced higher in knowledge and power than spirits," the latter-day Seer declared.[29] One reason for their ascendancy is that those who are resurrected are tabernacled in bodies of flesh and bones.[30] But even though "these men are in heaven," the Prophet explained that "their children are on the earth," and "their bowels yearn over us."[31] For this reason God sends resurrected beings down to earth as angels. This will be true particularly in the latter days. Joseph Smith said of the building up of Zion: "All these authoritative characters will come down and join hand in hand in bringing about this work." When the Saints are finally sanctified and all things are ready, the Prophet concluded: " . . . the Son of Man will descend, the Ancient of Days sit; we may [then] come to an innumerable company of angels, have communion with and receive instruction from them."[32] When a people have been prepared for the millennium, they will realize in great measure the blessings which are reserved for those who are sealed to eternal life.

Right to Commune with Spirits of Just Men Made Perfect

It is also the privilege of those who make their calling and election sure and thereby receive the second Comforter to commune with the spirits of just men made perfect. These are the disembodied spirits of those who have obtained and retained a state of justification on earth through the program of the gospel. They are the spirits of the justified who are made perfect by being endowed with glory as they enter the spirit world at mortal death. Hence they are designated as "the spirits of just men *made* perfect." Having acquired the promise of eternal life either by receiving the more sure word of prophecy on earth or by enduring in the gospel to the end of their mortal probation, they are privileged to dwell in the presence of God in the spirit world.[33] Of their ministry to those who make their calling and election sure, Joseph Smith said: "The spirits of just men are made ministering servants to those who are sealed unto life eternal, and it is through them that the sealing power comes down."[34]

On more than one occasion the Prophet referred to the

spirits of just men made perfect as being included among those celestial beings with whom the faithful may commune when they receive the second Comforter. Speaking of New Testament times, he said: "The Hebrew Church 'came unto *the spirits of just men made perfect,* and unto an innumerable company of angels, unto God the Father of all, and to Jesus Christ, the Mediator of the new covenant.'"[35] Again, in referring to the ultimate objectives of the gospel, he made reference to the Saints coming up to commune with "an innumerable company of angels, . . . *the spirits of just men made perfect,* and . . . Jesus the Mediator of the new covenant."[36]

Right to Commune with Church of the Firstborn

In a broader and more inclusive sense, the ministry of celestial beings to which man is entitled when he receives the promise of eternal life includes those who are members of the church of the Firstborn beyond the veil. A revelation explained that it is the purpose and design of the Melchizedek Priesthood to bring the Saints to the point of spiritual maturity and power which will enable them to "commune with . . . the church of the Firstborn."[37] "This is the state and place the ancient Saints arrived at when they had such glorious visions," Joseph Smith said—"Isaiah, Ezekiel, John upon the Isle of Patmos, St. Paul in the three heavens [manifestation], and all the Saints who held communion with the . . . Church of the First Born."[38]

The revelations and teachings of Joseph Smith indicate that the church of the Firstborn is the heavenly church of Christ and consists, essentially, of the sanctified saints in eternity who are endowed with the glory of the celestial kingdom. By being sealed to eternal life, the faithful on earth are also made members of the church of the Firstborn. A revelation therefore said of some brethren whose calling and election were made sure: "Ye are the church of the Firstborn, and he [Christ] will take you up in a cloud, and appoint every man his portion."[39] In the most inclusive sense, the membership of the church of the

Firstborn is comprised of those who have made their calling and election sure to eternal life, whether they live on earth, in the spirit world, or in a resurrected state. Because the Saints on earth who are sealed to eternal life become members of that church, they have a right by faith (subject to the will of God) to commune with the church of the Firstborn beyond the veil.

Latter-day Saint literature makes several references and allusions to the church of the Firstborn: First, a revelation equates this select body or inner church with the church of Enoch.[40] Enoch and his people matured in the program of the gospel until they made their calling and election sure and entered into the rest of the Lord,[41] endowed with His glory. Of them it was said: "The Lord came and dwelt with his people, and . . . the glory of the Lord . . . was upon his people."[42]

Second, as indicated above, the church of the Firstborn consists of those who overcome spiritual death and have a right to the glory and power of God. Referring to celestial glory, a revelation explained: " . . . *which glory is that of the church of the Firstborn,* even of God, the holiest of all, through Jesus Christ his Son."[43] Another revelation referred to the church of the Firstborn as those "who have received the fulness of the Father."[44] Again, Christ explained: "All those who are begotten through me *are partakers of the glory of the same* [i.e., of the Son of God], and *are the church of the Firstborn.*"[45] Birth into the kingdom of God opens the way to membership in the church of the Firstborn; but having been born again, man must be given the right to partake of the glory of Christ, by making his calling and election sure, in order to become a member of the inner church. The right to partake of the glory of the church of the Firstborn is given to those who receive the second Comforter.[46]

Third, to obtain a fulness of the blessings which pertain to the church of the Firstborn, man must acquire exaltation in celestial society—come forth to inherit the highest degree of celestial glory in the resurrection.[47] As

Joseph Smith instituted the sacred ordinances of the temple by which man may attain these blessing in eternity, he explained that those ordinances contained "all those plans and principles by which any one is enabled to secure *the fullness of those blessings which have been prepared for the Church of the First Born,* and come up and abide in the presence of the Eloheim [i.e., the Gods] in the eternal world."[48] In referring to those "who are the church of the Firstborn" and who acquire exaltation in that glorified body, a revelation said:

> They are they into whose hands the Father has given all things—
>
> They are they who are priests and kings, who have received of his fulness, and of his glory;
>
> And are priests of the Most High, after the order of Melchizedek, which was after the order of Enoch, which was after the order of the Only Begotten Son.
>
> Wherefore, as it is written, they are gods, even the sons of God—
>
> Wherefore, all things are theirs, whether life or death, or things present, or things to come, all are theirs and they are Christ's, and Christ is God's. . . .
>
> And they see as they are seen, and know as they are known, having received of his fulness and of his grace;
>
> And he makes them equal in power, and in might, and in dominion.[49]

Right to Commune with General Assembly

Joseph Smith associated the term "general assembly" directly with the church of the Firstborn and indicated that that divine assembly consists of a body of celestial beings with whom those who are sealed to eternal life may commune. He taught that the purpose of the Melchizedek Priesthood is to mature the Saints spiritually so that they can "commune with the *general assembly* and church of the Firstborn."[50] The Prophet therefore declared that those in ancient times who made their calling and election sure to celestial glory "held communion with the general assembly and Church of the First Born."[51]

To be more specific, early Latter-day Saint literature uses the term "general assembly" in two separate but related ways: first, as indicated above, it is used in conjunction with the term "the church of the Firstborn"; second, it refers to the official assembly of the church of the Firstborn, or that church in official assembly. The Prophet's Inspired Revision of the Bible makes the latter implication when it promises: "And *the general assembly of the church of the first-born* shall come down out of heaven, and possess the earth, and shall have place until the end come."[52]

The general assembly of The Church of Jesus Christ of Latter-day Saints consists of the several quorums of the priesthood and official members organized into a general priesthood assembly. When properly organized and conducted, the general assembly constitutes the highest body in authority in the Church. Therein is centered "the spiritual authority of the church."[53] If the general assembly of the church of the Firstborn were an equivalent body of the inner church of Christ, it would consist of the several quorums or units of the priesthood and the official members beyond the veil of that glorified body, organized into a great priesthood unit or assembly. It therefore would be the church of the Firstborn in official assembly; and it could also be referred to in conjunction with the church of the Firstborn, as is suggested in point one in the preceding paragraph. The second Comforter embraces the right to commune with that divine and authoritative body.

Right to Come to Mount Zion and Heavenly Jerusalem

Joseph Smith, like the Apostle Paul, used the terms "Mount Zion" and the "heavenly Jerusalem" to denote the abode of glorified beings with whom those saints who make their calling and election sure may commune. Speaking of the Hebrew Church in New Testament times, Paul said:

> . . . ye are come unto mount Sion, and unto the city of the

living God, the heavenly Jerusalem, and to an innumerable company of angels,

To the general assembly and church of the firstborn, which are written in heaven, and to God the Judge of all, and to the spirits of just men made perfect,

And to Jesus the meditator of the new covenant. . . .[54]

While writing on the same theme, Joseph Smith said:

A man may be saved, after the judgment, in the terrestrial kingdom, or in the telestial kingdom, but he can never see the celestial kingdom of God without being born of water and the Spirit. He may receive a glory like unto the moon [i.e., of which the light of the moon is typical], or a star [i.e., of which the light of the stars is typical], but *he can never come unto Mount Zion, and unto the city of the living God, the heavenly Jerusalem,* and to an innumerable company of angels; to the general assembly and Church of the First-born, which are written in heaven, and to God the judge of all, and to the spirits of just men made perfect, and to Jesus the Mediator of the new covenant, *unless he becomes as a little child, and is taught by the Spirit of God.*[55]

This statement, written in 1832, reveals the Prophet's view of the gospel at an early date: the ultimate objectives of the plan of life and salvation, and the way by which man must achieve them. The society of Zion which he sought to establish was to be built on a plane which would enable the Saints to make their calling and election sure to eternal life, for Mount Zion on earth was to be in direct communion with the eternal Mount Zion, and the New Jerusalem was to be in union spiritually with the heavenly Jerusalem.

Explanations Concerning The Second Comforter

Second Comforter Available to All Saints

The second Comforter with all its divine blessings is not limited to a given class or group of individuals. It is within the reach of all who will apply the program of life and salvation in their lives to the degree which is required to obtain it and its blessings. The Prophet is quoted in the preceding chapter as stating that every person who will pay the price of dedication can make his calling and election sure to eternal life.[56] It follows, therefore, that every person who will do this can receive the blessings of the second Comforter. On this point, a revelation stated emphatically: "Verily, thus saith the Lord: It shall come to pass that *every soul* who forsaketh his sins and cometh unto me, and calleth on my name, and obeyeth my voice, and keepeth my commandments, *shall see my face and know that I am.*"[57] To a group of women at Nauvoo, Joseph Smith said:

> If you live up to your privileges, the angels cannot be restrained from being your associates. Females, if they are pure and innocent, can come in the presence of God.[58]

Second Comforter the Result of True Faith

The Prophet constantly stressed in his teachings and through the scriptures which he gave to the world that the blessings which relate to the second Comforter are the ultimate products of man's faith in Jesus Christ. The brother of Jared is an illustration of this point. His faith was such that "he could no longer be kept without the veil."[59] To him, the pre-earth Christ said: "Because of thy faith thou hast seen that I shall take upon me flesh and blood; and never has man come before me with such exceeding faith as thou hast; for were it not so ye could not have seen my finger." The record then states: "The Lord showed himself unto him, and said: Because thou knowest these things ye are redeemed from the fall; therefore ye are brought back into my presence; therefore I show myself unto you."[60]

Joseph Smith taught that those who acquire true faith—like Enoch, the brother of Jared, and Moses—obtain power with God "to behold him face to face."[61] The latter-day Seer explained:

> All things were in subjection to the Former-day Saints, according as their faith was. By their faith they could obtain heavenly visions, the ministering of angels, have knowledge of

the spirits of just men made perfect, of the general assembly and church of the first born, whose names are written in heaven, of God the judge of all, of Jesus the Mediator of the new covenant, and become familiar with the third heavens, see and hear things which were not only unutterable, but were unlawful to utter.[62]

Obtaining Second Comforter a Major Objective of the Gospel

Joseph Smith repeatedly taught that as a product of true faith in Christ, the blessings of the second Comforter constitute a major objective of the gospel.[63] A revelation he received states that since the Melchizedek Priesthood administers the gospel and holds "the key of the knowledge of God," its purpose is to bring the Saints to the point of spiritual union with Christ which will enable them to receive the second Comforter.[64] Another revelation on this point explained: "The power and authority of the higher, or Melchizedek Priesthood, is to hold the keys of all the spiritual blessings of the church—to have the privilege of receiving *the mysteries of the kingdom of heaven, to have the heavens opened unto them, to commune with the general assembly and church of the Firstborn, and to enjoy the communion and presence of God the Father, and Jesus the mediator of the new covenant.*"[65]

To attain the celestial kingdom in the resurrection, man must receive the second Comforter, either in this life or in the spirit world after death.[66] A revelation stated that those who are "sealed by the Holy Spirit of promise" become celestial beings in the resurrection, and that they constitute the church of the Firstborn.[67] Speaking of this class of beings in the resurrection, the revelation stressed: "These are they *who have come* to an innumerable company of angels, to the general assembly and church of Enoch, and of the Firstborn."[68] It is noteworthy that the verb in this statement denotes completed action. These are they who *"have come,"* etc. Before the resurrection, they have matured in the gospel to the point of communing with beings who reside above the veil. Having met the challenge of returning to the presence of God, they therefore will inherit celestial glory in the resurrection.

Challenge to Obtain Second Comforter

Joseph Smith's experiences were not unique to him. True, he was a spiritual giant whose soul was refined and honed to a fine edge. Consequently he had a great capacity to commune with God. He said of his experience in receiving the blessings of the second Comforter: "The sound saluted *my ears*—'Ye are come unto Mount Zion, and unto the city of the living God, the heavenly Jerusalem, and to an innumerable company of angels, to the general assembly and church of the firstborn, which are written in heaven, and to God the Judge of all, and to the spirits of just men made perfect, and to Jesus the Mediator of the new covenant.'"[69] Again: "Paul saw the third heavens, and I more."[70] To a prominent individual in the East, he wrote: "I . . . have witnessed the visions of eternity, and beheld the glorious mansions of bliss. . . . I . . . have heard the voice of God, and communed with angels."[71] But having obtained the blessings of the second Comforter, the Prophet desired others to achieve them also. In a discourse in which he spoke repeatedly of these blessings, he concluded: "Let us seek for the glory of Abraham, Noah, Adam, the Apostles, who have communion with these things, and then we shall be among that number when Christ comes."[72]

The promise of the personal manifestation of Christ was given repeatedly to the Saints in revelations through Joseph Smith. In November, 1831, the Lord gave them such a promise and explained the change in nature which man must experience in order to achieve it:

> . . . inasmuch as you strip yourselves from jealousies and fears, and humble yourselves before me, for ye are not sufficiently humble, *the veil shall be rent and you shall see me and know that I am*—not with the carnal neither natural mind, but with the spiritual.
>
> For no man has seen God at any time in the flesh, except quickened by the Spirit of God.

> Neither can any natural man abide the presence of God, neither after the carnal mind.
>
> Ye are not able to abide the presence of God now, neither the ministering of angels; wherefore, continue in patience until ye are perfected.
>
> Let not your minds turn back; and when ye are worthy, in mine own due time, ye shall see and know that which was conferred upon you by the hands of my servant Joseph Smith, Jun.[73]

Along with the promise which this revelation held out to the Saints, two points were stressed: First, man cannot see God with the unregenerated natural mind, neither with the carnal mind, but only with the spiritual, for only when he is quickened by the Holy Spirit can he see God. To achieve a spiritual nature, one must put off the natural man by acquiring the transforming power of the Holy Spirit.[74] Being quickened sufficiently by the Spirit in this new state, man can then see God. Here the requirement to be born again is correlated with the greater challenge of receiving the blessings of the second Comforter.

Second, it is only by receiving the blessings of the second Comforter that man can realize fully that which he is given in the gospel. The Saints were not then able to abide the presence of God, or even the ministering of angels, but they were admonished to continue in patience until they were perfected enough to receive these blessings. Then they would know what had been conferred upon them through the instrumentality of Joseph Smith. When they finally stood in the presence of God and were made partakers of His glory, they would see the gospel in its true light—as a practical program leading man to the presence of God. They would then realize that which they had received through the Prophet.

In another statement in which the promise of the personal manifestation of Christ was given to the Saints early in this dispensation, the Lord said:

> Behold, that which you hear is as the voice of one crying in the wilderness—in the wilderness, because you cannot see him—my voice, because my voice is Spirit; my Spirit is truth; truth abideth and hath no end; and if it be in you it shall abound.

And if your eye be single to my glory, your whole bodies shall be filled with light [through the Holy Spirit], and there shall be no darkness in you; and that body which is filled with light comprehendeth all things.

Therefore, sanctify yourselves that your minds become single to God, *and the days will come that you shall see him; for he will unveil his face unto you,* and it shall be in his own time, and in his own way, and according to his own will.[75]

This revelation too stresses that man must become a recipient of the Holy Spirit and mature in its divine endowments until he can enter into the presence of God. To do this, man must bring his life into such union with the will of God—through faith and by personal discipline—that his eye will be single to the glory of God. Then his whole body will be filled with the light of the Spirit. Through this divine and intelligent agent, man may eventually comprehend all things, and by following this path he can enter into the presence of the Lord.

Early Successes in Obtaining Second Comforter

During the years before the Saints were endowed with power from on high at Kirtland, in 1836, the Prophet made a special effort to sanctify them and to develop in them the kind of faith and spiritual maturity which would enable them to behold Christ in His glory.[76] He expected the Savior to make a major appearance in the temple, and the Saints to behold Him in the solemn assembly which was held upon its completion. As early as January, 1833, Joseph Smith wrote to the presiding brethren among the Saints in Missouri of the first of these appearances: "The Lord commanded us, in Kirtland, to build a house of God, and . . . on conditions of our obedience He has promised us great things; yea, even a visit from the heavens to honor us with His own presence."[77] Several months before the solemn assembly was held at Kirtland, the Prophet promised the Saints: "All who are prepared, and are sufficiently pure to abide the presence of the Savior, will see Him in the solemn assembly."[78]

This promise was based upon the fact that before that

assembly would be held many of the brethren would be sealed to eternal life and thereby would have received the right to the blessings of the second Comforter.[79] These blessings were not given to all the Saints, but only to those God should "name out of all the official members."[80] In speaking of those to be chosen, a revelation said:

> There has been a day of calling, but the time has come for a day of choosing; and let those be chosen that are worthy.
>
> And it shall be manifest unto my servant, by the voice of the Spirit, those that are chosen; and they shall be sanctified.[81]

The next day Joseph Smith met in a council of High Priests, and some "individuals were called and chosen, as they were made manifest" to him by the "voice of the Spirit."[82] In following this procedure, the Prophet complied with the revelation which stated that only those of whom God bore record should be sealed to eternal life.[83]

When the Presidency of the Church and other officials received these sacred rites in January, 1836, the Prophet revealed the object he hoped to achieve: "As Paul said, so say I, let us come to visions and revelations."[84] In reporting the blessings of the second Comforter which these brethren then received, the latter-day Seer wrote:

> The heavens were opened upon us, and I beheld the celestial kingdom of God, and the glory thereof, whether in the body or out I cannot tell. I saw the transcendent beauty of the gate through which the heirs of that kingdom will enter, which was like unto circling flames of fire; also the blazing throne of God, whereon was seated the Father and the Son. I saw the beautiful streets of that kingdom, which had the appearance of being paved with gold. . . .[85]

After relating other things which he saw, the Prophet explained:

> Many of my brethren who received the ordinance with me saw glorious visions also. Angels ministered unto them as well as to myself, and the power of the Highest rested upon us, the house was filled with the glory of God, and we shouted Hosanna to God and the Lamb. My scribe also . . . saw, in a vision, the armies of heaven protecting the Saints in their return to Zion, and many things which I saw.[86]

After these manifestations were over, the Bishop of Kirtland with his counselors and the Bishop of Zion and his counselors received the sacred rite under the hands of Joseph Smith, Sr. It was then "confirmed by the Presidency, and the glories of heaven were unfolded to them also."[87] The High Councilors of Kirtland and Zion were then invited into the room and given the same blessings, whereupon the Prophet related:

> The visions of heaven were opened to them also. Some of them saw the face of the Savior, and others were ministered unto by holy angels, and the spirit of prophecy and revelation was poured out in mighty power; and loud hosannas, and glory to God in the highest, saluted the heavens, for we all communed with the heavenly host.[88]

The next day Joseph Smith and others attended a regular session of a Hebrew school at Kirtland. But instead of pursuing their studies, the brethren "spent the time in rehearsing to each other the glorious scenes that occurred on the preceding evening."[89] That evening the First Presidency met with the Council of the Twelve Apostles, the Presidency of the Seventy, and others to give them these sacred blessings. The latter-day Seer reported: "The heavens were opened and angels ministered unto us."[90]

These blessings were then given to the Presidency of the Seventy, and the Prophet stated: "The heavens were opened unto Elder Sylvester Smith, and he, leaping up, exclaimed: 'The horsemen of Israel and the chariots thereof.'"[91]

The latter-day Seer reported on the concluding portion of the meeting as follows:

> President Rigdon arose to conclude the services of the evening by invoking the blessing of heaven upon the Lord's anointed, which he did in an eloquent manner; the congregation shouted a long hosanna: the gift of tongues fell upon us in mighty power, angels mingled their voices with ours, while their presence was in our midst, and unceasing praises swelled our bosoms for the space of half-an-hour.[92]

Later, other quorums of the priesthood received these

blessings. Having instructed the quorum of High Priests and the quorum of Elders in the procedures they should follow, the Prophet went to organize and instruct the quorum of the Seventy. He reported:

> I found the Twelve Apostles assembled with this quorum, and I proceeded, with the quorum of the Presidency, to instruct them, and also the seven presidents of the Seventy Elders, to call upon God with up-lifted hands, to seal the blessings which had been promised to them. . . . As I organized this quorum, with the presidency in this room, President Sylvester Smith saw a pillar of fire rest down and abide upon the heads of the quorum, as we stood in the midst of the Twelve.
>
> When the Twelve and the seven presidents were through with their sealing prayer, I called upon President Sidney Rigdon to seal them with uplifted hands; and when he had done this, and cried hosanna, that all the congregation should join him, and shout hosanna to God and the Lamb, and glory to God in the highest. It was done so, and Elder Roger Orton saw a mighty angel riding upon a horse of fire, with a flaming sword in his hand, followed by five others, encircle the house, and protect the Saints, even the Lord's anointed, from the power of Satan and a host of evil spirits, which were striving to disturb the Saints.
>
> President William Smith, one of the Twelve, saw the heavens opened, and the Lord's host protecting the Lord's anointed.
>
> President Zebedee Coltrin, one of the seven presidents of the Seventy, saw the Savior extended before him, as upon the cross, and a little later, crowned with glory upon his head above the brightness of the sun.
>
> After these things were over, and a glorious vision, which I saw, had passed, I . . . returned to the room of the High Priests and Elders, and attended to the sealing of what they had done, with up-lifted hands.[93]

When the solemn assembly was held in the Kirtland Temple, in March, 1836,[94] similar blessings were given to many who were present. Throughout the day and until five o'clock the next morning the brethren "continued prophesying, and blessing, and sealing them with hosanna and amen."[95] Heber C. Kimball reported: "While these things were being attended to the beloved disciple John was seen in our midst by the Prophet Joseph, Oliver Cowdery and others."[96] The Prophet said: "The Savior made His appearance to some, while angels ministered to others, and it was a Pentecost and an endowment indeed long to be remembered." Because this was the beginning of the manifestation of God's glory among the Lord's people in the latter days, the Prophet stated that the report of these manifestations would be "handed down upon the pages of sacred history, to all generations" of the future.[97]

Purposes Of The Second Comforter

Basis for Giving World a Sure Testimony

God's testimony in the world is established on a sure foundation through the manifestations of the second Comforter. To establish faith in the world, God sends angels to commune with those who possess "strong faith and a firm mind in every form of godliness."[98] He also manifests Himself personally to such individuals. These men are then required to bear testimony through the power of the Holy Ghost concerning the work of God. Joseph Smith therefore taught that in past ages God has centered the keys of His work on earth in those who have been seers—men who have penetrated the veil and have been taught through the visions and revelations of God. Having spoken of the blessings of the second Comforter, he admonished:

> Wherefore, we again say, search the revelations of God; study the prophecies, and rejoice that God grants unto the world Seers and Prophets. They are they who saw the mysteries of godliness.[99]

The Prophet then referred to many things which the ancient oracles saw by which the testimony and knowledge of God were established in the world.

As a case in point, the latter-day Seer taught that this was the basis upon which the Apostles of Jesus were sent to testify to the world in their day. Christ concluded His last great commission to them with the promise: "Lo, I am with you alway, even unto the end of the world."[100] This promise, Joseph Smith made clear, was a reassurance that they would have the blessings of the second Comforter to attend them in their ministry. He said:

> He, the Lord, . . . [was] a priest forever, after the order of Melchizedek, and the anointed Son of God, from before the foundation of the world, and they [were] the begotten sons of Jesus through the gospel, to teach all nations—and lo I am with you always to the end of the world—that is—*by the other comforter which the world cannot receive*—for ye are witnesses—having the testimony of Jesus which is the spirit of prophecy.[101]

Means of Revealing Higher Knowledge

The Prophet taught that there is an important reason why all faithful saints should receive the blessings of the second Comforter. This reason is that man cannot be saved in ignorance of the divine truth which is communicated to him through the gospel. In referring to the purpose of Christ's ministry to those who make their calling and election sure, the latter-day Seer said: "The Lord will teach him face to face, and *he may have a perfect knowledge of the mysteries of the Kingdom of God.*"[102] Of communion with angels, he declared: "We may come to an innumerable company of angels, have communion with and *receive instructions from them.*"[103] For the same purpose the faithful may commune with the spirits of just men made perfect. "What would it profit us to come unto the spirits of the just men," Joseph Smith inquired, "but *to learn and come up to the standard of their knowledge?*"[104] Book learning and knowledge acquired by mere human experience alone will not suffice.[105] "The best way to obtain truth and wisdom is not to ask it from books, but to go to God in prayer, and obtain divine teaching," he explained.[106] "Could you gaze into heaven five minutes, you would know more than you would by reading all that ever was written on the subject."[107] Continuing, he stressed: "I assure the Saints that truth, in reference to these matters, can and may be known through the revelations of God in the way of His ordinances, and in answer to prayer."[108]

Joseph Smith held that the gospel is a system by which divine truth can be given to man, beginning with the principle of faith and the gift of the Holy Ghost and culminating with the sealing power by which faithful individuals can make their calling and election sure to celestial glory and acquire the blessings of the second Comforter. Speaking of divine truth, he said: "Knowledge of these things can only be obtained by experience *through the ordinances of God* set forth for that purpose."[109] According to Joseph Smith, the Apostle Peter understood the purpose of the gospel to be one of revealing divine truth to man. Having quoted from 1 Peter 1:3–5 and 2 Peter 1:1–3, the latter-day Seer said:

> These sayings put together show the apostle's views most clearly, so as to admit of no mistake in the mind of any individual. He says that all things that pertain to life and godliness were given unto them through the knowledge of God and our Saviour Jesus Christ. And if the question is asked, *how were they to obtain the knowledge of God?* (for there is a great difference between believing in God and knowing him—knowledge implies more than faith. And notice, that all things that pertain to life and godliness were given through the knowledge of God) the answer is given—*through faith they were to obtain this knowledge; and, having power by faith to obtain the knowledge of God, they could with it obtain all other things which pertain to life and godliness.*
>
> By these sayings of the apostle, we learn that it was by obtaining a knowledge of God that men got the knowledge of all things which pertain to life and godliness, and this knowledge was the effect of faith; so that all things which pertain to life and godliness are the effects of faith.[110]

In these statements, the Prophet taught that the truth which is given to man through the second Comforter is that which he must eventually receive in order to be saved.

Those things which man may learn through the second Comforter, which are difficult to convey by intellectual processes alone, include many precious truths concerning the divine nature of God. A revelation in May, 1833, assured the Saints that by achieving the blessings of the second Comforter they could understand their relationship in the Spirit to Jesus and His relationship in glory to the Father. The revelation said:

> Verily, thus saith the Lord: It shall come to pass that *every soul* who forsaketh his sins and cometh unto me, and calleth on my name, and obeyeth my voice, and keepeth my commandments, *shall see my face and know that I am;*
>
> *And that I am the true light that lighteth every man that cometh into the world;*
>
> *And that I am in the Father, and the Father in me, and the Father and I are one—*
>
> *The Father because he [i.e., Elohim] gave me of his fulness, and the Son because I was in the world and made flesh my tabernacle, and dwelt among the sons of men.*[111]

In a statement in which he enumerated many things which holy men in past ages have been taught through the second Comforter, Joseph Smith said:

> They . . . saw the mysteries of godliness; they saw the flood before it came; they saw angels ascending and descending upon a ladder that reached from earth to heaven; they saw the stone cut out of the mountain, which filled the whole earth; they saw the Son of Man come from the regions of bliss and dwell with men on earth; they saw the deliverer come out of Zion, and turn away ungodliness from Jacob; they saw the glory of the Lord when he showed the transfiguration of the earth on the mount; they saw every mountain laid low and every valley exalted when the Lord was taking vengeance upon the wicked; they saw truth spring out of the earth, and righteousness look down from heaven in the last days, before the Lord came the second time to gather his elect; they saw the end of wickedness on earth, and the Sabbath of creation crowned with peace; they saw the end of the glorious thousand years, when Satan was loosed for a little season; they saw the day of judgment when all men received according to their works, and they saw the heaven and the earth flee away to make room for the city of God, when the righteous receive an inheritance in eternity.[112]

The Prophet held that if holy men in past ages were taught and shown such things by obtaining the second Comforter, the Saints could receive similar blessings on the same principle. Having cited the examples above, he stressed:

Fellow sojourners upon earth, *it is your privilege to purify yourselves and come up to the same glory, and see for yourselves, and know for yourselves.* Ask, and it shall be given you; seek, and ye shall find; knock, and it shall be opened unto you.[113]

Many things which are taught to those who receive the second Comforter go beyond the knowledge which is contained in the written word of God, or that which God permits His prophets to write. Having recorded but a small fraction of the information which he and Sidney Rigdon were given in a heavenly vision concerning the destiny of the human family in eternity,[114] Joseph Smith said at the conclusion of the written report:

> But great and marvelous are the works of the Lord, and the mysteries of his kingdom which he showed unto us, which surpass all understanding in glory, and in might, and in dominion;
>
> Which he commanded us we should not write while we were yet in the Spirit, and are not lawful for man to utter;
>
> Neither is man capable to make them known, for *they are only to be seen and understood by the power of the Holy Spirit, which God bestows on those who love him, and purify themselves before him;*
>
> *To whom he grants this privilege of seeing and knowing for themselves.*[115]

As this statement indicates, some knowledge given to those who receive the second Comforter is so sacred that the recipients are forbidden to communicate it to others. For example, the Prophet said:

> The Hebrew Church [in New Testament times] "came unto the spirits of just men made perfect, and unto an innumerable company of angels, unto God the Father of all, and to Jesus Christ, the Mediator of the new covenant." What did they learn by coming to the spirits of just men made perfect? *Is it written? No. What they learned has not been and could not have been written.*[116]

According to Joseph Smith, the Apostle Paul received such knowledge. "Paul ascended into the third heavens," he explained, "and he could understand the three principal rounds of Jacob's ladder—the telestial, the terrestrial, and the celestial glories or kingdoms, *where Paul saw and heard things which were not lawful for him to utter.*"[117] Of his own experience, the latter-day Seer said: "I know a man that has been caught up to the third heavens, and can say, with Paul, that *we have seen and heard things that are not lawful to utter.*"[118]

Because many of the ancient saints obtained the blessings of the second Comforter through the application of true faith and obedience to the gospel, they were in a position to teach the world the things of God, though they were in humble circumstances and in many instances lacked worldly knowledge. Joseph Smith explained:

> This is the reason that the fisherman of Galilee could teach the world—because they sought by faith, and by faith obtained. And this is the reason that Paul counted all things but filth and dross—what he formerly called his gain he called his loss; yea, and he counted all things but loss for the excellency of the knowledge of Christ Jesus the Lord. Philippians iii. 7, 8, 9, and 10. Because he obtained the faith by which he could enjoy the knowledge of Christ Jesus the Lord, he had to suffer the loss of all things. This is the reason that the Former-day Saints knew more, and understood more, of heaven and of heavenly things than all others besides, because this information is the effect of faith—to be obtained by no other means.[119]

The knowledge which the ancient saints obtained of divine things was real and soul-stirring, so much so that the things of this world were swallowed up in a hope of immortal glory. The Prophet taught that the Latter-day Saints should acquire the same knowledge and reflect the same disposition.

Way to All Truth

By obtaining the blessings of the second Comforter, man can eventually acquire a fulness of the truth and light of the Father's glory. Having declared that if man's eye is single to the glory of God his body will be filled with light, or with the Spirit, a revelation to Joseph Smith promised: "That body which is filled with light comprehendeth all things."[120] It then declared: "Therefore, sanctify yourselves that your minds become single to God and the days will come that you shall see him; for he will unveil his face unto you."[121]

Jesus exemplified the way to all truth. Having defined truth as "knowledge of things as they are, and as they were, and as they are to come," Christ said in a revelation to the Prophet:

> The Spirit of truth is of God. I am the Spirit of truth, and John bore record of me, saying: *He received a fulness of truth, yea, even of all truth.*
>
> And no man receiveth a fulness unless he keepeth his commandments.
>
> *He that keepeth his commandments receiveth truth and light, until he is glorified in truth and knoweth all things.*[122]

Three major points either mentioned or implied in this statement must be understood if one is to catch the meaning of the Lord's explanation: First, Christ as a glorified being is inseparably associated with that divine substance or essence which is called the Spirit of truth. The Spirit of truth, known also as the Holy Spirit, centers in God and is given to man through Christ. Hence Jesus is said to be the Spirit of truth.[123] The Spirit of truth, which is the glory of God, emanates from the presence of God to fill the immensity of space; and as God's divine agent, it communicates to Him a knowledge of all things throughout His vast domain. When Jesus obtained a fulness of the glory of the Father, He received the full truth and power of that primary being. This is the central theme expressed in this revelation.[124]

Second, man must acquire a fulness of truth the same way Jesus did. Man thinks and acts only by the influence of a quickening and enlightening spiritual power which is given to him from God.[125] But the physical senses of man alone are limited in their ability to perceive and acquire truth. If man is to receive a fulness of truth he must receive in its fulness the living and enlightening power of that Spirit which constitutes the glory of God. Being filled with a fulness of that Spirit which is in and through all things, man may then know all things.[126]

Third, to obtain a fulness of glory, man must acquire truth and light through the principle of revelation, by expressing living faith in Christ and by obeying the law of God. The intellectual process alone can never bring man to achieve a fulness of truth. True faith includes but requires more than the expression of mental powers. In the expression of faith, the whole soul of man—both the powers of mind and body—reaches up to God in the quest for truth, and man is brought into a living spiritual union with Christ. Only when man has developed in this divine relationship until he is glorified in truth will he know all things. Being endowed with the full glory of God,—which is intelligence, or, in other words, light and truth[127]—he will then have a fulness of truth.

Because this is the goal of the plan of life and salvation, John Taylor explained: "The Gospel embraces principles that dive deeper, spread wider, and extend further than anything else that we can conceive."[128] According to Brigham Young, it also "incorporates every true principle there is in heaven and on earth" into its body of knowledge.[129] George Q. Cannon therefore said: "The Gospel embraces all truth, and there is no truth of any nature or name, whether it be scientific, or moral, or religious, that is not comprehended within the scope of the Gospel of Jesus Christ."[130]

Entering Into The Rest Of The Lord

Joseph Smith explained that those who make their calling and election sure to celestial glory thereby enter into the rest of the Lord. A revelation defined the term "rest" as "the fulness of his [God's] glory."[131] This is a state in which man is brought by the action of his faith into the presence of God and is given access to the glory and power of the Lord.[132] He also partakes significantly of the divine fruits, or attributes, of the Holy Spirit and is filled with that joy and peace which Christ alone can give to the human soul.

To enter into the Lord's rest, man must traverse the path of the gospel upward out of the world's state of spiritual darkness and death into the presence of God; he must acquire the blessings of the second Comforter. Concerning this divine state of rest and of man's need to prepare for it, the Prophet said:

> God has in reserve a time, or period appointed in His own bosom, when He will bring all His subjects, who have obeyed His voice and kept His commandments, *into His celestial rest.* This rest is of such perfection and glory that man has need of a preparation before he can, according to the laws of that kingdom, enter it and enjoy its blessings. This being the fact, God has given certain laws to the human family, which, if observed, are sufficient to prepare them to inherit this rest.[133]

The Prophet declared that it was "the order of the kingdom" which had been restored to earth through his instrumentality "to prepare men for the rest of the Lord."[134] According to the Book of Mormon, this is the objective of the Melchizedek Priesthood and its divine law. Alma taught that God had prepared this holy calling "from the foundation of the world for such as would not harden their hearts, . . . that they . . . might *enter into his rest.*"[135] Having stated that in earlier times those who received this priesthood and established its divine law in their midst thereby became "pure and spotless before God," Alma stressed: " . . . and there were many, exceeding great many, who were made pure and *entered into the rest of the Lord their God.*" To men in his day, he therefore said: "And now, my brethren, I would that ye should humble yourselves before God, and bring forth fruit meet for repentance, *that ye may also enter into that rest.*"[136]

Since man can make his calling and election sure to celestial glory either by acquiring the more sure word of prophecy or by enduring with living faith to the end of his mortal probation, it follows that he can enter into the rest of the Lord in either of these two ways. There have been those who entered into rest while still on earth.[137] But faithful saints who endure to the end of their mortal lives also have the promise of entering into the Lord's rest after they pass from this sphere.[138]

This challenge has confronted the people of God in every age. According to Joseph Smith's Inspired Revision of the Bible, the Lord declared to Moses that, having been given the opportunity, the ancient Israelites failed to "enter into my presence, *into my rest.*"[139] That volume also reports that the Apostle Paul explained Israel's failure and said to the Hebrew saints:

> . . . to whom sware he [God] that they should not *enter into his rest,* but to them that believed not?
>
> So we see that they could not enter in because of unbelief.
>
> Let us therefore fear, lest, a promise being left us of *entering into his rest,* any of you should seem to come short of it.
>
> For unto us *was the rest preached,* as well as unto them; but the word preached did not profit them, not being mixed with faith in them that heard it.
>
> For we who have believed *do enter into rest,* as he said, As I have sworn in my wrath, If they harden their hearts they shall not *enter into my rest;* also, I have sworn, If they will not harden their hearts, they shall *enter into my rest.*[140]

The Nephite prophets also took the failure of their Israelite fathers to heart and sought to prevent their people from coming under the same condemnation. "We labor diligently among our people, that we might persuade them to come unto Christ, and partake of the goodness of God," Jacob reported, "*that they might enter into his rest,* lest by any means he should swear in his wrath they should not enter in, as in the provocation in the days of temptation while the children of Israel were in the wilderness."[141] Alma also admonished his people to become righteous so that they could enter into a state of rest; and he warned them that by taking a contrary course, they could "not enter into the rest of the Lord."[142] When Jesus ministered to the Nephites after His resurrection, He reaffirmed these teachings. Speaking of the kingdom of the Father, He said: "No unclean thing can enter into his kingdom; therefore nothing entereth *into his rest* save it be those who have washed their garments in my blood, because of their faith, and the repentance of all their sins, and their faithfulness unto the end."[143] Because the gospel gives to man both the immediate and the post-mortal objective of entering into the presence of God, Mormon characterized those who achieve the first of these goals as "peaceful followers of Christ" who obtain sufficient hope to "enter into the rest of the Lord" on earth and continue therein until they can "rest with him in heaven."[144] Having received the blessings of the second Comforter on earth, they finally realize the full object of their faith in the resurrection.

In like manner, latter-day revelations mention the need for the Saints to meet the challenge of entering into the Lord's rest. To those who were called to initiate the last dispensation, the Lord said: "I speak unto you that are chosen in this thing, even as one, that you may enter into my rest."[145] A revelation on priesthood explained that this can only be achieved by man partaking of the "power of godliness" as it is manifested through the Melchizedek Priesthood and its ordinances.[146] And in speaking of the great culminating purposes of this dispensation, the Prophet referred to the time "when every man shall enter into his [God's] eternal presence and into his immortal rest."[147] When these purposes are accomplished, the work of perfecting the Saints will be complete, and all the righteous in eternity will be given the blessings of the second Comforter.

This was the reason the Saints sought to establish the society of Zion in Missouri. When they neglected to apply the principles that would enable them to enter into the Lord's rest, Joseph Smith warned: "I say to you (and what I say to you I say to all), hear the warning voice of God, lest Zion fall, and the Lord swear in His wrath the inhabitants of Zion shall not enter into His rest."[148] Unfortunately the Prophet's admonition was not sufficiently heeded, and the Saints have since been denied many of the blessings which the latter-day Seer had hoped they would realize.

Summary

Joseph Smith explained that within the program of the gospel there are two Comforters: the Holy Ghost and the divine promise, or guarantee, sealed in the hearts of the faithful by the Holy Spirit that they will receive eternal life in the world to come. The latter Comforter carries with it the right (subject to the will of God) to commune with Christ and the Father, an innumerable company of angels, the spirits of just men made perfect, the church of the Firstborn, and the general assembly of the church of the Firstborn. One who receives the second Comforter has the right to come to Mount Zion and the heavenly Jerusalem—the abode of glorified beings in eternity.

Man may obtain the guarantee of eternal life either by receiving the more sure word of prophecy in this life or by enduring faithful in the gospel to the end of his mortal probation. The first way entitles him to enjoy the blessings of the second Comforter in mortality. But in either case the faithful receive those blessings in the spirit world after mortality, for the spirits of the just dwell in the midst of celestial glory.

The second Comforter is available to all who embrace the gospel. The blessings associated with this Comforter are the final products of true faith in Jesus Christ, and receiving these blessings is a major object of the gospel plan. For these reasons, the Prophet challenged the Saints repeatedly to seek the blessings of the second Comforter. Several saints received the manifestations of the second Comforter early in this dispensation, particularly at Kirtland and in association with the Kirtland Temple.

By means of the second Comforter, a sure testimony of Christ is established in the world. The purpose of the second Comforter is also to reveal to the Saints the mysteries of God and to give them a greater knowledge of His eternal ways. In this way, the faithful can eventually acquire a knowledge of all truth. Since the design of the gospel is to bring fallen man into the presence of God, those who receive the second Comforter also enter into the rest of the Lord where they partake of that peace and joy which Christ alone can give to man.

Notes

1. HC, III, p. 380.
2. D&C 88:4.
3. Man can receive some blessings of the Holy Ghost before baptism, and in a similar way there are those who seem to have been given some of the blessings of the second Comforter before they made their calling and election sure to eternal life.
4. Kimball, *op. cit.*, pp. 127–128.
5. HC, III, p. 380.
6. *Ibid.*, p. 381.
7. *Ibid.*, p. 380.
8. John 14:16–18, 21, 23, cited in HC, III, p. 381.
9. D&C 88:3.
10. D&C 88:4.
11. D&C 131:5.
12. D&C 130:3. This statement should not be confused with the fact that the divine nature of God dwells within all things, which the Prophet taught to be a true doctrine.
13. HC, VI, p. 315.
14. D&C 129:1–3.
15. HC, VI, p. 52.
16. D&C 107:18–19. See also D&C 67:10; 76:67–69; 84:19–24; 93:1.
17. See HC, I, p. 283; III, p. 381; V, p. 530; VI, p. 51. See also D&C 130:3.
18. HC, I, p. 283.
19. *Ibid.*, III, p. 388. See also *ibid.*, VI, p. 51. For the statement by Paul, see Hebrews 12:23.
20. HC, III, p. 389.
21. See D&C 13.
22. This does not mean that angels minister only to those who hold the Aaronic Priesthood or are sealed to eternal life, but that those who have been ordained to that priesthood or those who have been sealed to eternal life have a right to their ministrations.
23. D&C 67:13.
24. HC, III, p. 392.
25. *Ibid.*, IV, p. 425. See also *ibid.*, III, p. 392; VI, p. 51.
26. See *ibid.*, III, p. 28.
27. *Ibid.*, IV, p. 425. That personage said to John: "I am thy fellowservant, and of thy brethren the prophets."—Revelation 22:9. See also Revelation 19:10.
28. HC, IV, p. 425.
29. *Ibid.* VI, p. 51.
30. See *ibid.*, III, p. 392; VI, p. 51.
31. *Ibid.*, III, p. 389.
32. *Ibid.*
33. See again the discussion of this point in the section in this chapter entitled "Second Comforter Defined."
34. HC, VI, p. 51.
35. *Ibid.*

36. *Ibid.,* I, p. 283. For another statement by the Prophet, see *ibid.,* V, p. 530.

37. D&C 107:18–19.

38. HC, III, p. 381.

39. D&C 78:21. See this statement in light of declarations in D&C 78:12, 21; 82:11, 21; 104:9–10. Both the righteous dead and the righteous living will be caught up to meet Christ when He comes in glory. The promise of being caught up in a cloud is therefore a general promise to the righteous and does not necessarily imply that it would be fulfilled while those concerned lived on the earth.

40. D&C 76:67.

41. See JD, III, p. 320.

42. Moses 7:16–17.

43. D&C 88:5.

44. D&C 76:71.

45. D&C 93:22.

46. See D&C 88:3–5.

47. See D&C 131:1–4, for reference to the three degrees within the celestial kingdom.

48. HC, V, p. 2. One might infer from this statement that the church of the Firstborn consists of the celestial church and that to obtain the full blessings of that church man must receive the higher ordinances of the gospel.

49. D&C 76:54–59, 94–95.

50. D&C 107:18–19.

51. HC, III, p. 381.

52. I. R., Genesis 9:23.

53. D&C 107:32. See also HC, II, p. 285.

54. Hebrews 12:22–24.

55. HC, I, p. 283. For another statement by the Prophet, see *ibid.,* V, p. 530.

56. See again *ibid.,* III, p. 380.

57. D&C 93:1.

58. HC, IV, p. 605.

59. Ether 12:21.

60. Ether 3:9, 13.

61. *Lectures on Faith,* No. 2.

62. *Ibid.,* No. 7.

63. See again the section in chapter one entitled "Man's Ultimate Goal in the Gospel."

64. D&C 84:19–22.

65. D&C 107:18–19. Various parts of this revelation have been quoted in past sections of this chapter.

66. The sealing action of the priesthood is the gateway to that kingdom. See 2 Nephi 31:17–20; Mosiah 5:15; D&C 76:51–63. It is said erroneously at times that baptism and the laying on of hands for the gift of the Holy Ghost constitute the gate to the celestial kingdom. But these ordinances are merely the gate *to the path* which leads to the celestial kingdom—not the gate into that kingdom. Baptism and the reception of the Holy Ghost are the gate into the earthly church of Jesus Christ, but the sealing power of the priesthood

constitutes the gate into the higher or inner church which is called the church of the Firstborn.

67. D&C 76:53–54.

68. D&C 76:67.

69. HC, V, p. 530.

70. *Ibid.,* p. 392.

71. *Ibid.,* VI, p. 78.

72. *Ibid.,* III, p. 392. For a treatment of Joseph Smith as a seer, see Hyrum L. Andrus, *Joseph Smith The Man And The Seer* (Salt Lake City; Deseret Book Co., 1960), chapter 5.

73. D&C 67:10–14.

74. See Mosiah 3:19: 27:25–26.

75. D&C 88:66–68.

76. See chapter eleven, the section entitled "Preparations for Endowment with Power."

77. HC, I, p. 316.

78. See, for example, *ibid.,* I, pp. 323–324; D&C 68:12.

79. See the section in chapter eleven entitled "Solemn Assembly."

80. HC, II, p. 309.

81. D&C 105:35–36.

82. HC, II, pp. 112–113.

83. See D&C 68:12.

84. HC, II, p. 380. For the Apostle Paul's statement, see 2 Corinthians 12:1.

85. HC, II, p. 380.

86. *Ibid.,* p. 381.

87. *Ibid.,* pp. 381–382.

88. *Ibid.,* p. 382.

89. *Ibid.*

90. *Ibid.,* pp. 382–383.

91. *Ibid.,* p. 383.

92. *Ibid.*

93. *Ibid.,* pp. 386–387.

94. See the section in chapter eleven entitled "Solemn Assembly."

95. HC, II, pp. 431, 432–433.

96. Whitney, *op cit.,* p. 92.

97. HC, II, pp. 432–433.

98. Moroni 7:30.

99. HC, I, p. 283.

100. Matthew 28:20.

101. TS, III (September 1, 1842), p. 905.

102. HC, III, p. 381.

103. *Ibid.,* p. 389.

104. *Ibid.,* V, p. 530.

105. In man's effort to acquire truth, the study of books has a place. A revelation explained: "And *as all have not faith,* seek ye diligently and teach one another words of wisdom; yea, seek ye out of the best books words of wisdom; seek learning, even *by study* and also *by faith."*—D&C 88:118. Because all men do not have the faith which is required to learn through the channel of revelation, the educational process must of necessity begin with the study of good

books. By seeking to learn through study and by faith, man may then come to the superior process for acquiring knowledge which the Prophet utilized and advocated.

106. HC, IV, p. 425.

107. *Ibid.,* VI, p. 50.

108. *Ibid.,* p. 51.

109. *Ibid.,* p. 50.

110. *Lectures on Faith,* No. 7.

111. D&C 93:1–4. For a discussion of Christ's relationship in glory with the Father and man's relationship in the Spirit with Christ, see chapters eight and nine in Volume I of this study.

112. HC, I, pp. 283–284.

113. *Ibid.,* p. 284.

114. Of this vision, Joseph Smith said: "I could explain a hundred fold more than I ever have of the glories of the kingdoms manifested to me in the vision, were I permitted, and were the people prepared to receive them."—*Ibid.,* V, p. 402.

115. D&C 76:114–117.

116. HC, VI, p. 51.

117. *Ibid.,* V, p. 402. See 2 Corinthians 12:1–4.

118. HC, V, p. 556. See also p. 392.

119. *Lectures on Faith,* No. 7.

120. D&C 88:66–67.

121. D&C 88:68.

122. D&C 93:24, 26–28.

123. See D&C 93:11.

124. See, for example, D&C 93:11–17.

125. See Volume I of this study, the section in chapter ten entitled "The Light of Life and Reason Within Man."

126. See D&C 50:24; 88:66–67.

127. D&C 93:36.

128. JD, XVI, pp. 369–370.

129. *Ibid.,* VII, p. 239. See also *ibid.,* III, p. 80; XIII, pp. 146, 255; XVI, p. 160, for other statements by Brigham Young.

130. *Ibid.,* XX, p. 287. See also *ibid.,* XIV, p. 57, for another statement by George Q. Cannon.

131. D&C 84:24.

132. See Volume I of this study, the section in chapter thirteen entitled "The Seventh Day One of Rest."

133. HC, II, p. 12.

134. *Ibid.,* p. 228.

135. Alma 13:5–6.

136. Alma 13:11–13.

137. Enoch and his people entered into the Lord's rest. See, for example, Moses 7:16–17; JD, III, p. 320. It is apparent that Melchizedek and his people also achieved this objective. See I. R., Genesis 14:34; Alma 13:6–16.

138. See, for example, Enos 1:27; Alma 13:29; 40:12; Moroni 10:34; D&C 59:2; 101:31; 121:32.

139. I. R., Exodus 34:2. See also D&C 84:24.

140. I. R., Hebrews 3:18–19; 4:1–3.

141. Jacob 1:7.

142. Alma 12:34–37; 13:12–16; 16:17.

143. 3 Nephi 27:19.

144. Moroni 7:3.

145. D&C 19:9. The Prophet wrote: "Our trust is in God, and we are determined, His grace assisting us, to maintain the cause and hold out faithful unto the end, that we may be crowned with crowns of celestial glory, and enter into the rest that is prepared for the children of God."—HC, I, p. 450.

146. D&C 84:19–24.

147. D&C 121:32.

148. HC, I, p. 316.

15

The Gospel from Adam to Israel

> *God . . . is the same yesterday, to-day, and forever; and the way is prepared for all men from the foundation of the world, if it so be that they repent and come unto him.*
>
> *For he that diligently seeketh shall find; and the mysteries of God shall be unfolded unto them, by the power of the Holy Ghost, as well in these times as in times of old, and as well in times of old as in times to come; wherefore, the course of the Lord is one eternal round.*—NEPHI.

One of the great truths which Joseph Smith made clear is that the gospel of Jesus Christ is an eternal system—that there is but one plan of life and salvation, and that the principles, ordinances, and laws of that plan have been unchanged from the beginning of the world. Biblical testimony regarding the full revelation of God to man in ancient times is lacking. But latter-day scriptures clarify that the gospel was given to Adam, and that it has been revealed to men on earth in varying degrees of fulness in successive dispensations since the earliest ages of the world. It is God's program of sanctifying fallen man by mercy and enlightening power to a condition that will allow him to return to the presence of the Lord and partake of immortal glory. In each dispensation, men have sought to achieve this great objective.

The Prophet and his associates held that this view of the plan of life and salvation is reasonable and consistent, and latter-day scriptures reflect this position. When

Alma's son Corianton questioned why the gospel of Jesus Christ should be known among men before the earthly ministry of the great Redeemer, his father replied:

> . . . is not a soul at this time as precious unto God as a soul will be at the time of his coming?
>
> Is it not as necessary that the plan of redemption should be made known unto this people as well as unto their children?
>
> Is it not as easy at this time for the Lord to send his angel to declare these glad tidings unto us as unto our children, or as after the time of his coming?[1]

Antiquity Of The Gospel

Gospel Plan Formulated in Heaven

Joseph Smith wrote repeatedly by revelation that the plan of life and salvation was formulated "before the foundation of the world."[2] He explained that an "everlasting covenant" was made between the three personages of the Godhead "before the organization of this earth, and relates to their dispensation of things to men on the earth"[3]—to their revelation of divine truth and power through the gospel to man. Again he said: "It appears that the great and glorious plan of His [God's] redemption was previously provided; the sacrifice prepared; the atonement wrought out in the mind and purpose of God, even in the person of the Son, through whom man was now to look for acceptance and through whose merits he was now taught that he alone could find redemption."[4] For this reason the Prophet concluded that if man is to attain salvation, he must be subject "to certain rules and principles which were fixed by an unalterable decree before the world was."[5] "The first step in [the] salvation of man is the laws of eternal and self-existing principles," he declared.[6] "The great thing for us to know is to comprehend what God did institute before the foundation of the world."[7]

"Ordinances instituted in the heavens before the foundation of the world, in the priesthood, for the salvation of men, are not to be altered or changed," the latter-day Seer declared. "All must be saved on the same principle."[8] He explained: "The gospel has always been the same; the ordinances to fulfill its requirements, the same, and the officers to officiate, the same; and the signs and fruits resulting from the promises, the same."[9] A revelation therefore stated that salvation in all ages of the world has been based upon the exercise of faith in Jesus Christ—"not only [for] those who believed after he came in the meridian of time, in the flesh, but [for] all those from the beginning, even as many as were before he came, who believed in the words of the holy prophets, who spake as they were inspired by the gift of the Holy Ghost, who truly testified of him in all things."[10] With this view of the gospel, the *Times and Seasons,* the official publication of the Church at Nauvoo, was dedicated to the proclamation of "the great plan of salvation which was devised in heaven from before the foundation of the world, as made known to the Saints of God, in former, as well as in latter days; and is like its Author, the same in all ages, and changeth not."[11]

A revelation stated specifically that baptism is "a new and everlasting covenant, even that which was from the beginning."[12] The Prophet explained that before Christ the people "were baptized in the name of Jesus Christ to come," and thereafter they were "baptized in the name of Jesus Christ, crucified, risen from the dead and ascended into heaven."[13] A revelation stated that the law of eternal marriage was also "instituted from before the foundation of the world."[14] The same was true of the law governing the plurality of wives. Here the revelation said: "I am the Lord thy God, and will give unto thee the law of my Holy Priesthood, as was ordained by me and my Father before the world was."[15] Writing generally of the laws of the gospel, Joseph Smith said: "There is a law, irrevocably decreed *in heaven before the foundations of this world,* upon which all blessings are predicated—and when we obtain any blessing from God, it is by obedience to that law upon which it is predicated."[16] Of the program of the temple, he also said: "The order of the house of God *has been, and ever will be, the same,* even after Christ comes; and after the termination of the thousand years it will be the same; and we shall finally enter into the celestial kingdom of God, and enjoy it forever."[17]

Man Had the Gospel in Ancient Times

Though little is known in secular history of man in ancient times, William W. Phelps wrote in behalf of the Church: "We have a right to say from facts revealed, that, before the flood, they knew more than the world will believe now: yes they had a knowledge of the mysteries of eternity, that have been hid from the eyes of wicked men for ages and generations; mysteries and glories which have been sought for by holy men, and seen by an eye of faith."[18] From the standpoint of biblical evidence, Joseph Smith considered it a fact "beyond the power of controversy" that God spoke to Adam and revealed the gospel to him and other early patriarchs. If it were not so, he inquired, "How did they begin to offer sacrifice to God in an acceptable manner?"[19] The Prophet pointed to the biblical statement that Abel received witness from God that he was righteous.[20] This being true, did not God speak to him? If so, would not God deliver the plan of redemption to Abel? "How could Abel offer a sacrifice and look forward with faith on the Son of God for a remission of his sins, and not understand the Gospel?" the latter-day Seer inquired. The offering of sacrifice could not be done in righteousness except by faith in something to come. Otherwise Cain's offering would have been equally acceptable. "And if Abel was taught of the coming of the Son of God," the Prophet reasoned, "was he not taught also of His ordinances?"[21]

Of the view that the gospel and its ordinances were not known till the days of John the Baptist, Joseph Smith said: "For our part we cannot believe that the ancients in all ages were so ignorant of the system of heaven as many suppose, since all that were ever saved, were saved through the power of this great plan of redemption, as much before the coming of Christ as since; if not, God has had different plans in operation (if we may so express it), to bring men back to dwell with Himself; and this we cannot believe." To support his position, the Prophet referred to Paul's declaration that the gospel was preached to Abraham (Galatians 3:8). This being true, in whose name was the gospel preached to Abraham? If not in the name of Christ, was it the gospel? "And if it was the Gospel, and that preached in the name of Christ, had it ordinances?" he asked. "If not, was it the Gospel?"[22]

Some may argue that there was no program of salvation before the coming of Christ except that which involved the law of sacrifice. But the Prophet pointed to the fact that Abraham offered sacrifices and also had the gospel preached to him. For this reason he knew of Christ, and Jesus could say to the Jews: "Your father Abraham rejoiced to see my day; and he saw it, and was glad (John 8:56)." Continuing, Joseph Smith said: "We find also, that when the Israelites came out of Egypt they had the Gospel preached to them, according to Paul in his letter to the Hebrews, which says: 'For unto us was the Gospel preached, as well as unto them: but the word preached did not profit them, not being mixed with faith in them that heard it (see Hebrews 4:2).'" Finally, the Prophet pointed to Paul's statement that the Law of Moses was "added because of transgression." To what was it added, if not to the gospel which the Israelites originally had preached unto them?[23]

Adam And The Gospel

Introduction of the Gospel into the World

The gospel was not revealed to Adam immediately after he fell from his paradisiacal state. He may have been given time to become conditioned to his fallen state, so that obedience to the gospel would be a challenge to him. He and Eve had had children, and their children had had children, before the gospel plan was made known.[24] But

God had given Adam and Eve commandments "that they should worship the Lord their God, and should offer the firstlings of their flocks, for an offering unto the Lord."[25] This they did without knowing the purpose of these instructions. A revelation to Joseph Smith explained:

> And after many days an angel of the Lord appeared unto Adam, saying: Why dost thou offer sacrifices unto the Lord? And Adam said unto him: I know not, save the Lord commanded me.
>
> And then the angel spake, saying: This thing is a similitude of the sacrifice of the Only Begotten of the Father, which is full of grace and truth.
>
> Wherefore, thou shalt do all that thou doest in the name of the Son, and thou shalt repent and call upon God in the name of the Son forevermore.
>
> And in that day the Holy Ghost fell upon Adam, which beareth record of the Father and the Son, saying: I am the Only Begotten of the Father from the beginning, henceforth and forever, that as thou hast fallen thou mayest be redeemed, and all mankind, even as many as will.[26]

Thus Adam was taught the purpose of the law of sacrifice and its relationship to the atoning sacrifice of Jesus Christ. It was a similitude of the great sacrifice of the Lamb of God, foreshadowing the central act by which salvation would be given to man. Adam was also taught the basic legal procedure by which man could approach God, which was to do all things in the name of the Son of God. The first man and his descendants were to repent and call upon God in the name of the Son forevermore.

Though Adam and Eve accepted this revelation with joy, their children registered a different response when they heard preached the message of redemption. The revelation to Joseph Smith continued:

> And Adam and Eve blessed the name of God, and they made all things known unto their sons and their daughters.
>
> And Satan came among them, saying: I am also a son of God; and he commanded them, saying: Believe it not; and they believed it not, and they loved Satan more than God. And men began from that time forth to be carnal, sensual, and devilish.

And the Lord God called upon men by the Holy Ghost everywhere and commanded them that they should repent;

And as many as believed in the Son, and repented of their sins, should be saved; and as many as believed not and repented not, should be damned; and the words went forth out of the mouth of God in a firm decree; wherefore they must be fulfilled.[27]

Adam was also taught the basic principles and ordinances of the gospel. God said: "If thou wilt turn unto me, and hearken unto my voice, and believe, and repent of all thy transgressions, and be baptized, even in water, in the name of mine Only Begotten, who is full of grace and truth, which is Jesus Christ, the only name which shall be given under heaven, whereby salvation shall come unto the children of men, ye shall receive the gift of the Holy Ghost, asking all things in his name, and whatsoever ye shall ask, it shall be given you."[28] Through the gift of the Holy Ghost, Adam could ask and receive all things which were expedient for him to receive to accomplish his mortal probation and return to the presence of God.[29] In this way, he could acquire again the divine truth and power which he had lost in the fall.

Having made the above statement, the Lord taught Adam that by subscribing to these initial principles and ordinances of the gospel, man could be born into the kingdom of heaven.[30] This was the basic message of the gospel in ancient times.[31]

To Adam were also revealed the higher ordinances of the gospel, by which he and his faithful descendants could be exalted in the celestial kingdom. In these sacred rites and ordinances, man is given "the grand Key-words of the Holy Priesthood" which the Prophet declared were given to Adam and the ancient patriarchs, and to "all to whom the Priesthood was revealed."[32]

Adam's Place in the Gospel

Joseph Smith taught that Adam occupies a significant place in the plan of salvation for this earth. He was the first to receive the gospel,[33] and "under the counsel and direction" of Jesus Christ he was given "the keys of salvation" over his posterity to all generations of time.[34] According to the Prophet, the Son of God holds "the keys of the universe";[35] but "under the direction of the Lord," Adam presides over all dispensations of gospel power and authority for man on earth.[36] Of Adam's position in the priesthood, the latter-day Seer said: "The Priesthood was first given to Adam; he obtained the First Presidency, and held the keys of it from generation to generation."[37] It is through Adam that "Christ has been revealed from heaven, and will continue to be revealed from henceforth."[38] Again Joseph Smith explained:

> The Priesthood is an everlasting principle, and existed with God from eternity, and will to eternity, without beginning of days or end of years. The keys have to be brought from heaven whenever the Gospel is sent. When they are revealed from heaven, it is by Adam's authority.[39]

"Adam holds the keys of the dispensation of the fullness of times," Joseph Smith continued; "i.e., the dispensation of all the times have been and will be revealed through him from the beginning to Christ, and from Christ to the end of all the dispensations that are to be revealed."[40] Speaking of angels who have been sent to reveal the gospel to man, the Prophet said: "These angels are under the direction of Michael or Adam, who acts under the direction of the Lord."[41]

Joseph Smith held that there were divine purposes for making the program of the gospel consistent from age to age. First, he observed that "there has been no change in the constitution of man since he fell."[42] Consequently the divine program by which man may be renewed spiritually in Christ must remain unchanged and be the same in every age. Second, he taught that it is the design of God that in the Dispensation of the Fulness of Times there should be a gathering in and a tying together of all things that have been revealed from the beginning—a union of all divine truth, power, rites, and ordinances in one final dispensation. To facilitate this great purpose, it was necessary for the program of the gospel to be consistent from the beginning. The Prophet explained:

> . . . the purpose [of God] in Himself in the winding up scene of the last dispensation is that all things pertaining to that dispensation should be conducted precisely in accordance with the preceding dispensations.
>
> And again, God purposed in Himself that there should not be an eternal fullness until every dispensation should be fulfilled and gathered together in one, and that all things whatsoever, that should be gathered together in one in those dispensations unto the same fullness and eternal glory, should be in Christ Jesus; *therefore He set the ordinances to be the same forever and ever, and set Adam to watch over them, to reveal them from heaven to man, or to send angels to reveal them.*[43]

Adam's Objectives in the Gospel

As stated in an earlier chapter,[44] Joseph Smith taught that even though Adam transgressed the law of Eden and was cast out of God's presence, "he was not deprived of the previous knowledge which he had of the existence of God."[45] Nor did he lose a knowledge of the glory which he had enjoyed during the earth's paradisiacal state. Think what this point meant in light of Adam's experience! Though he fell, Adam retained his knowledge of God and of the nature of life in his initial paradisiacal state. What, then, did it mean to Adam when God said: "As thou hast fallen *thou mayest be redeemed,* and all mankind, even as many as will"?[46] What was redemption to Adam but to be brought back, eventually, into the presence of God—to a state of glory similar to that from which he fell?

In God's statement to Adam the central purpose of the gospel was made known.[47] To Adam the gospel was the way by which he and his descendants could regain those living spiritual powers which had been withdrawn from the earth as a result of the transgression in Eden. Realizing very vividly what he had lost and what was meant by redemption from the fall, Adam exclaimed: "Blessed be the name of God, for because of my transgression my eyes are opened [to the knowledge of good and evil], and in this life I shall have joy, and *again in the flesh I shall see God.*"[48] Eve likewise rejoiced: "Were it not for our transgression we never should have . . . known . . . *the joy of our redemption, and the eternal life [i.e., immortal glory] which God giveth unto all the obedient.*"[49]

To call attention to the great objective of the gospel, Adam assembled the righteous of his descendants together in a valley called Adam-ondi-Ahman and blessed them before his death. "This is why Adam blessed his posterity," Joseph Smith explained; "he wanted to bring them into the presence of God."[50] Adam then realized his desire to a degree, for "the Lord appeared unto them."[51] But even this blessing was short of the ultimate purpose of the gospel, which was to bring all those of Adam's descendants who would obey its divine truths back into the presence of God and to endow them with celestial glory.

Other great patriarchs and prophets shared Adam's desire. Joseph Smith explained: "In the first ages of the world, . . . there were Eliases [i.e., teachers of the gospel] raised up who tried to restore these very glories, but did not obtain them." For example, in later ages "Moses sought to bring the children of Israel into the presence of God, through the power of the Priesthood, but he could not." But despite their failure, the Prophet declared: "They prophesied of a day when this glory would be revealed." That day would be in "the dispensation of the fullness of times, when God would gather together all things in one."[52] The ancient hope—the great objective of the gospel as Adam understood it—would then be realized.

Ministry Of Enoch

The Gospel as Taught by Enoch

Enoch had more success than other ancient patriarchs and prophets in achieving the ultimate goals of the gospel. His father, Jared, taught him "in all the ways of God";[53]

and as a responsive student, Enoch sought diligently to do the will of God until, as Joseph Smith observed, he obtained "faith in God, and power with him to behold him face to face."[54] Christ revealed Himself to Enoch in the office, power, and capacity of the Father[55] and showed many glorious things to the ancient patriarch, including the coming of the Son of Man to earth to make His infinite sacrifice. Enoch was also shown the building of the New Jerusalem in the last days in preparation for the millennial reign of Christ.[56] Having received the blessings of the second Comforter, Enoch was able to sanctify his people through the gospel so that they also entered into the presence of God.

As Enoch journeyed in the land, the Spirit of God descended upon him, and a voice from heaven instructed him to proclaim the gospel among the people.[57] "Behold my Spirit is upon you, wherefore all thy words will I justify," the Lord declared; "and the mountains shall flee before you, and the rivers shall turn from their course; and thou shalt abide in me, and I in you; therefore walk with me."[58] The gospel which he was to proclaim was a system of divine truth and power, and in his ministry he was to exemplify that central fact.

In teaching the gospel, Enoch spoke of the fallen nature of man and of his need to be born into the kingdom of God.[59] Thereby man could be sanctified from all sin, enjoy the words of eternal life in this world, and acquire eternal life—the living attributes and powers of celestial glory—in the world to come.[60] This was the plan of salvation for all men, through the atoning blood of Jesus Christ.[61] "Behold our father Adam taught these things," Enoch concluded, "and many have believed and become the sons of God, and many have believed not, and have perished in their sins, and are looking forth with fear, in torment, for the fiery indignation of the wrath of God to be poured out upon them."[62]

Zion of Enoch

Joseph Smith held that it is only when all aspects of life are gathered together in one under the law of Christ—in that union which is ideal in individualism[63]—that the glory of God can be manifested visibly and permanently among the Saints.[64] Enoch and his people demonstrated the correctness of this principle. By founding their whole society—their social, economic, and political institutions—upon the law of God they became a righteous people among whom the powers of the Spirit were greatly concentrated. The Lord came and dwelt in their midst, and it was said: "The fear of the Lord was upon all nations, *so great was the glory of the Lord, which was upon his people."* God blessed their land, and they prospered as a people. Under the law of Zion, "they were of one heart and one mind, and dwelt in righteousness; and there was no poor among them."[65]

In discussing the program which Enoch developed among his people, Joseph Smith treated it as "a divine philosophy" by whose application Enoch's "people and the city, and the foundations of the earth on which it stood, *had partaken of so much of the immortal elements [i.e., the Holy Spirit], bestowed upon them by God through the teachings of Enoch,* that it became philosophically impossible for them to remain any longer upon the earth." The contrast between the glory which was developed in Zion and the spiritual darkness of the world was too great for Enoch's city to remain longer upon the earth.[66] Consequently, by utilizing the divine power which they had acquired through the gospel, the people of Enoch's city were translated to a terrestrial state of glory.[67]

In a similar explanation, Brigham Young observed that Enoch had learned enough "from Adam [who still remembered the nature of life in his initial paradisiacal state] and his associates *to know how to handle the elements,"* so that eventually "he obtained power to take his portion of the earth and move out a little while, where he remains to this day."[68] To do this, however, Enoch and his people first had to "enter into their rest"—into the presence of God as heirs of His glory.[69] They developed in the plan of life and salvation until they made their calling and election sure to eternal life and were sealed by the power of the priesthood to those sacred family relationships by which they could be exalted in celestial society.[70] They then acquired the right by covenant to enter into the presence of God and partake of His glory. Having brought his people to this state of spiritual excellence, Enoch obtained "power to translate himself and his people, with the region they inhabited, their houses, gardens, fields, cattle, and all their possessions."[71]

Some interesting contrasts can be drawn between Enoch's civilization and that of modern man. Enoch placed emphasis upon regenerating man by establishing that divine system of principles, ordinances, and laws through which man can acquire the truth and power of God. Modern man, on the other hand, has placed primary emphasis upon material things external to himself which can be used to enhance his life in physical comforts and conveniences. The gospel plan does not suggest that man should discard material things or the methods of technical research, but that he should sanctify them and subordinate them to divine truth. This modern man has not done. And when compared with Enoch and his people, it appears that man now is so engrossed in the worship of transistors, computers, reactors, etc., and so committed to a materialistic philosophy of life, that he is almost oblivious to the greater truth that man himself is a divinely organized mechanism capable of being purified, refined, and matured in the acquisition of divine truth and power to the point that he can partake of the glory of God. In the exercise of divine power, greater miracles can be performed than those which are produced by modern man. Having entered into that new stage of life which the gospel makes possible, Enoch's people were able to establish true and lasting brotherhood in their society, solve the riddle of social justice, conquer disease, and hold in abeyance the forces of physical death. Modern scriptures also testify that Enoch and his people got out into space earlier and have stayed up longer than modern materialistic man.[72]

Joseph Smith believed in the exercise of divine power in the same way as did Enoch. The report of a discourse which he gave at Nauvoo states: "The speaker, before closing, called upon the assembly before him to humble themselves in faith before God, and in mighty prayer and fasting to call upon the name of the Lord, *until the elements were purified over our heads, and the earth sanctified under our feet, that the inhabitants of this city may escape the power of disease and pestilence,* and the destroyer that rideth upon the face of the earth, and that the Holy Spirit of God may rest upon this vast multitude."[73] Like Enoch, the Prophet sought to develop the blessings of the Spirit among the Saints as a means of eradicating disease and sanctifying the elements about them.

Joseph Smith taught that "translation is a power which belongs to this [Melchizedek] Priesthood."[74] But as in the case of Enoch and his people, man must achieve a given standard of spiritual excellence before he can exercise this power. That standard is set forth in the following statement from the Prophet's Inspired Revision of the Bible:

> . . . God having sworn unto Enoch and unto his seed with an oath by himself; that every one being ordained after this order and calling [of the Melchizedek Priesthood] should have power, by faith, to break mountains, to divide the seas, to dry up waters, to turn them out of their course;
>
> To put at defiance the armies of nations, to divide the earth, to break every band, to stand in the presence of God; to do all things according to his will, according to his command, subdue principalities and powers; and this by the will of the Son of God which was from before the foundation of the world.
>
> *And men having this faith, coming up unto this order of God, were translated and taken up unto heaven.*[75]

The central point of this statement is that the Melchizedek Priesthood in ancient times was a means of receiving divine truth and power, and a man of faith could perform marvelous works, do all things which accorded with the will of the Lord, and break every band that opposed his rise to a state of glory in the presence of God. Having realized these objectives by making sure his calling and election to celestial glory and entering into the rest of the Lord,[76] the man of faith could then receive the power to be translated.

The term "heaven" in the last line of the above quotation from the Inspired Revision means a state of glory. Of the order of life which is enjoyed by translated beings in such a state, Joseph Smith explained in greater detail:

> Many have supposed that the doctrine of translation was a doctrine whereby men were taken immediately into the presence of God, and into an eternal fullness [of celestial glory], but this is a mistaken idea. Their place of habitation is that of the terrestrial order, and a place prepared for such characters He held in reserve to be ministering angels unto many planets, and who as yet have not entered into so great a fullness [of glory] as those who are resurrected from the dead. . . . Translation obtains deliverance from the tortures and suffering of the body, but their existence will be prolonged as to the labors and toils of the ministry, before they can enter into so great a rest and glory.[77]

When the ancient city of Zion was translated, "Methuselah, the son of Enoch, was not taken, that the covenants of the Lord might be fulfilled which he made to Enoch; for he truly covenanted with Enoch that Noah should be of the fruit of his loins."[78] Following the translation of Enoch's city, the gospel continued to be taught to the people of the earth, with the mortal ministers assisted by heavenly messengers who bore "testimony of the Father and the Son." A revelation explained: "And the Holy Ghost fell on many, and they were caught up by the powers of heaven into Zion."[79] In this way the righteous were translated and joined Enoch and his people, leaving Methuselah, Lamech, and Noah, with the latter's sons, to proclaim the final testimony of the gospel to the inhabitants of the antediluvian world.

Ministry Of Noah

Noah's Place in the Gospel

Joseph Smith declared that under Christ, Noah stands next to Adam as the third greatest prophet to live on earth, measured by his place in history and the keys of the priesthood he received. "He was called of God to this office," the Prophet explained, "and was the father of all living in his day, and to him was given the dominion."[80] In Noah were centered the keys of the Holy, or Melchizedek, Priesthood,[81] as well as the keys of the patriarchal order of the priesthood,[82] for the earth during and after his day. Speaking of this subject in relation to Noah, Joseph Smith said: "We behold the keys of this Priesthood consisted in obtaining the voice of Jehovah that He talked with him [Noah] in a familiar and friendly manner, that He continued to him the keys, the covenants, the power and the glory, with which He blessed Adam at the beginning."[83]

The Gospel as Taught by Noah

Joseph Smith said of the program of the gospel in Noah's day: "Now taking it for granted that the scriptures say what they mean, and mean what they say, we have sufficient grounds to go on and [can] prove from the Bible that the gospel has always been the same; . . . therefore, as Noah was a preacher of righteousness he must have been baptized and ordained to the priesthood by the laying on of the hands, &c."[84] A revelation to the Prophet confirmed these conclusions: "And Noah and his sons hearkened unto the Lord, and gave heed, and they were called the sons of God."[85] To become a son of God, man must be born of water and of the Spirit.[86]

The above revelation also states: "The Lord ordained Noah after his own order, and commanded him that he should go forth and declare his Gospel unto the children of men, even as it was given unto Enoch."[87] Of his message, the revelation said: "Noah prophesied, and taught the things of God, even as it was in the beginning."[88] Noah said:

> Hearken, and give heed unto my words;
> Believe and repent of your sins and be baptized in the name of Jesus Christ, the Son of God, even as our fathers, and ye shall receive the Holy Ghost, that ye may have all things made manifest; and if ye do not this, the floods will come in upon you.[89]

Noah lived in a day when both the church and the world were in a state of decay. When he called the people to repent, many who were affiliated with the Church of Jesus Christ came to him and said: "Behold, we are the sons of God; have we not taken unto ourselves the daughters of men [i.e., nonmembers of the church]? And are we not eating and drinking, and marrying and giving in marriage? And our wives bear unto us children, and the same are mighty men, which are like unto men of old, men of great [worldly] renown." The revelation concludes: "And they hearkened not unto the words of Noah."[90] John Taylor explained: "One of the great evils that existed among the people was that the sons of God married the daughters of men: or, in other words, many who were connected with the Church mixed themselves up with those who were not; and thus their hearts were drawn away from God, and in the sight of God they were no better than those who rejected His servants; and consequently they perished with the disobedient and wicked."[91]

Among those who married outside the church were the granddaughters of Noah. In referring to Noah's sons, the above revelation said:

> And when these men began to multiply on the face of the earth, and daughters were born unto them, the sons of men saw that those daughters were fair, and they took them wives, even as they chose.
> And the Lord said unto Noah: The daughters of thy sons have sold themselves; for behold mine anger is kindled against the sons of men, for they will not hearken to my voice.[92]

Noah's task of preaching the gospel to a degenerate world was a difficult and perplexing one. Not content to disbelieve, men came out in open opposition to him and the work of God, even though Noah was a prophet, presiding patriarch, and king over the society of the antediluvian world[93] and should therefore have been respected and sustained in his mission. A revelation to Joseph Smith explained: "In those days there were giants on the earth, and they sought Noah to take away his life; but the Lord was with Noah, and the power of the Lord was upon him."[94] The Prophet is said to have taught: "As regards Noah, he was mobbed and broken up four times while building the ark."[95]

Though Noah's task was difficult, the Lord sustained him and honored him in the keys of the priesthood which he held. In the priesthood, man works in a covenant relationship with God. Having given a prophet the keys of the priesthood over the earth, the Lord respects the righteous interests and feelings of that prophet, and He does nothing in relation to man without first revealing His will to that prophet.[96] Man, on the other hand, must exert himself to help bring about God's righteous purposes. In a revelation which Wilford Woodruff received in 1880, the view was expressed that God requires His prophets, apostles, elders, and saints to inquire of Him and petition Him in righteousness in order to bring about the blessings which are to be poured out upon Zion in the last days, and in order to bring righteous judgments upon the wicked.[97] This principle, in respect to the latter type of action, operated in the ministry of Noah. When he preached the gospel and was rebuffed by the utter disbelief of corrupt and perverse men who sought his life, "It repented Noah, and his heart was pained that the Lord had made man on the earth, and it grieved him at the heart." Whereupon the Lord said: "I will destroy man whom I have created, from the face of the earth, both man and beast, and the creeping things, and the fowls of the air; for it repenteth Noah that I have created them, and that I have made them; and he hath called upon me; for they have sought his life."[98]

The Genesis text of the above statement states: "And it repented *the Lord* that he had made man on the earth, and it grieved him at his heart."[99] Joseph Smith corrected this passage to say, "It repented Noah. . . ."[100] That such a change was needful may be seen when it is asked: Is it logical that a divine being who possesses foreknowledge would find Himself in a situation that required repentance? Should the program to clothe organized spirits with physical bodies never have been put into operation because a generation of men totally abandoned themselves to wickedness? Did God err on this great issue of life so that He found it necessary to repent? If so, why did He people the earth again through Noah and his sons? Instead of God repenting, it is more consistent that Noah should repudiate man in the perverse stiuation in which he then saw him and justly desire that God had not created him.

Ministry Of Melchizedek

Revelations given to Joseph Smith make it clear that Melchizedek was a real person—not a mythical character or a man without a father.[101] He was a great High Priest in the system, or order, of the priesthood over which the Son of God presides. Of him Alma wrote: "Now, there were many before him, and also there were many afterwards, but none were greater; therefore, of him they have more particularly made mention."[102] Continuing, the Nephite prophet explained:

> Melchizedek . . . was . . . a high priest after this same order which I have spoken, who also took upon him the high priesthood forever.
>
> And it was this same Melchizedek to whom Abraham paid tithes; yea, even our father Abraham paid tithes of one-tenth part of all he possessed. . . .
>
> Now this Melchizedek was a king over the land of Salem; and his people had waxed strong in iniquity and abomination; yea, they had all gone astray; they were full of all manner of wickedness;
>
> But Melchizedek having exercised mighty faith, and

received the office of the high priesthood according to the holy order of God, did preach repentance unto his people. And behold, they did repent; and Melchizedek did establish peace in the land in his days; therefore he was called the prince of peace, for he was the king of Salem; and he did reign under his father.[103]

In addition to being a king over the land of Salem under the authority of the Holy Priesthood,[104] Melchizedek was the presiding High Priest of the church in his day. For this reason Abraham—a patriarch and therefore a subordinate to the great High Priest—paid tithes to Melchizedek. With such distinction did Melchizedek fill this office that the Holy Priesthood was named after him. "Before his day it was called *the Holy Priesthood, after the Order of the Son of God,*" Joseph Smith wrote by revelation. "But out of respect or reverence to the name of the Supreme Being, to avoid the too frequent repetition of his name, they, the church, in ancient days, called that priesthood after Melchizedek, or the Melchizedek Priesthood."[105]

It is possible that Melchizedek's knowledge of Christ included an understanding of the sacred emblems of His atoning sacrifice. Of a meeting of the great high priest with Abraham, Joseph Smith's Inspired Revision of Genesis states: "Melchizedek, king of Salem, brought forth bread and wine; and he break bread and blest it; and he blest the wine, he being the priest of the most high God, and he gave to Abram, and he blessed him, and said, Blessed Abram, thou art a man of the most high God, possessor of heaven and of earth."[106] "In this action of Melchizedek, in administering the bread and wine, by virtue of his priestly office," John Taylor queried, "is there not a representation of the body and blood of our Lord and Savior Jesus Christ, as also indicated by the Messiah Himself when He partook of the passover with His disciples?"[107]

After the city of Enoch was translated, holy men in later ages sought to establish the same order of society which Enoch developed, that a day of righteousness might come to the earth. But because of wickedness and abominations they did not realize their desire, and they confessed that "they were strangers and pilgrims on the earth."[108] Among those who possessed these desires were Melchizedek and his people. Having referred to the Holy Priesthood and the power which it possesses to translate righteous men, Joseph Smith's Inspired Revision of Genesis states:

> . . . now Melchizedek was a priest of this order; therefore he obtained peace in Salem, and was called the Prince of peace.
>
> And his people wrought righteousness, and obtained heaven, and sought for the city of Enoch which God had before taken, separating it from the earth, having reserved it unto the latter days, or the end of the world.[109]

This statement reveals the spiritual standard which Melchizedek and his people achieved. They wrought righteousness and "obtained heaven"—a state where they enjoyed the glory and power of God.[110] This means that as a people, they traversed the path from their fallen spiritual state in mortality to the presence of God; they made their calling and election sure to celestial glory and received the blessings of the second Comforter. Having achieved these things, they "sought for the city of Enoch which God had before taken." The above statement does not say expressly that they were translated, but it does indicate that the necessary requisites were met to receive that blessing.

In later ages, the righteous sought not only to emulate Enoch but also Melchizedek and his people. Having admonished his brethren to apply the gospel in their lives so that they could enter into the rest of the Lord, Alma said: "Yea, humble yourselves even as the people in the days of Melchizedek, who was also a high priest after this same order which I have spoken, who also took upon him the high priesthood forever."[111] Alma then stressed the purpose of the gospel, which was that the obedient "might enter into the rest of the Lord."[112]

Ministry Of Abraham

Though the faithful after the flood sought to establish the gospel order on earth, men in general began again to turn from the Lord. Abraham, who lived ten generations after Noah, wrote: "My fathers having turned from their righteousness, and from the holy commandments which the Lord their God had given unto them, unto the worshiping of the gods of the heathen, utterly refused to hearken to my voice." In their apostasy, "their hearts were set to do evil."[113] To the great patriarch, the Lord said: "My people have gone astray from my precepts, and have not kept mine ordinances, which I gave unto their fathers; and they have not observed mine anointing, and the burial, or baptism wherewith I commanded them; but have turned from the commandment, and taken unto themselves the washing of children, and the blood of sprinkling; and have said that the blood of the righteous Abel was shed for sins; and have not known wherein they are accountable before me."[114]

But despite this situation, Abraham grew in the gospel until he obtained the blessings of the second Comforter. When he was about to be sacrificed upon a heathen altar because of his righteousness, he cried unto the Lord. And as he was filled with "the vision of the Almighty," an angel of God[115] unloosed his bands and said: "Abraham, Abraham, behold, my name is Jehovah, and I have heard thee, and have come down to deliver thee, and to take thee away from thy father's house, and from all thy kinsfolk, into a strange land which thou knowest not of."[116] Later, the Lord appeared to Abraham and revealed the great promises that would be his within the divine patriarchal order.[117] By vision through the Urim and Thummim and by personal communion with God, Abraham was also shown Kolob and the great stellar system which that mighty sphere governs, the intelligences or spirits which God organized in the pre-earth state, the noble and great spirits whom God selected to be His rulers in the priesthood on earth, the Grand Council of the Gods where the plan was made to create and place life upon the earth, and the actual creation of the earth in seven days of Kolob's time.[118]

As a presiding figure in the divine patriarchal order in ancient times, Abraham had a major responsibility to teach the gospel. As stated earlier in this volume,[119] the children of the patriarchs were lawful heirs to the gospel. Thereby they could be adopted into the celestial family of Christ and become fathers and mothers spiritually under Him in that divine family order. This meant that the ancient patriarchs had the responsibility to teach their children the plan of birth into the kingdom of God, and to offer all families of the earth the gospel so that they too could be numbered among the children of Christ. Of the ancient patriarchs, a revelation said: "They were preachers of righteousness, and spake and prophesied, and called upon all men, everywhere, to repent; and faith was taught unto the children of men."[120] It is in this respect that an evangelist, who is a patriarch,[121] is one who is called to preach the gospel.

Like the patriarchs in earlier times, Abraham was given the responsibility of preaching the gospel, and this right and responsibility was appointed to his elect descendants in the flesh for all ages of time after his day. "As it was with Noah so shall it be with thee," the Lord said to him; "but through thy ministry my name shall be known in the earth forever."[122] This commission is directly related to God's promise that in Abraham all nations of the earth would be blessed. The Lord said: "I will bless thee above measure, and make thy name great among all nations, and thou shalt be a blessing unto thy seed after thee, *that in their hands they shall bear this ministry and Priesthood unto all nations.*"[123]

In fulfilling his obligation to teach the gospel, Abraham proclaimed its saving truths to the people in the land of Canaan — the land which God promised to give to him and his descendants when the latter were worthy to receive that inheritance. Of this commission, Abraham wrote:

> . . . I, Abraham, and Lot, my brother's son, prayed unto the Lord, and the Lord appeared unto me, and said unto me: Arise, and take Lot with thee; for I have purposed to take thee away out of Haran, and to make thee a minister to bear my name in a strange land which I will give unto thy seed after thee for an everlasting possession, when they hearken to my voice.[124]

Abraham had been preaching the gospel in the vicinity of Haran before he received this commission, for when he and Lot left that place they took "the souls" they had "won in Haran" and proceeded to the land of Canaan.[125]

The fact that Abraham taught the gospel to the Canaanites helps Latter-day Saints understand why God's judgments were later sent upon them when Israel came out of Egypt to occupy that land. In referring to the Canaanites, Nephi said: *"This people had rejected every word of God,* and they were ripe in iniquity; and the fulness of the wrath of God was upon them; and the Lord did curse the land against them, and bless it unto our fathers; yea, he did curse it against them unto their destruction, and he did bless it unto our fathers unto their obtaining power over it."[126] Like the people in the days of Noah, the Canaanites had rejected the gospel and had reached the point of corruption where mercy and forbearance could no longer have claim upon them, and the justice of God was finally expressed in wrath and condemnation against them.

Abraham also journeyed into Egypt as an ambassador of the Lord. In preparation for his mission among the Egyptians, God revealed many things to him concerning the cosmos and the eternal nature of man. "I show these things unto thee before ye go into Egypt," the Lord explained, "that ye may declare all these words."[127]

In the above missions, Abraham fulfilled the divine commission which he received to preach the gospel, and he set an example which all others who would truly become his children, spiritually as well as physically, must emulate.[128]

Summary

Joseph Smith taught that the divine plan of life and salvation is the embodiment of eternal truths and was formulated in heaven before the earth was created. It was first introduced on earth in the days of Adam, and it has been taught by all the great prophets in succeeding generations. For this earth, Adam holds the keys of the priesthood, through which the gospel is revealed, in all generations of time. Whenever angels have been sent to make known to man the truths and powers of the gospel, it has been by Adam's authority.

The gospel is the divine program by which fallen man may receive a remission of personal sins and be sanctified by eternal truth and power until he is able to dwell in the presence of God and be endowed with His glory. Having fallen from a paradisiacal state of glory, Adam endeavored to apply the gospel to the end that its objectives might be realized by himself and his faithful descendants. Enoch and his people were successful in achieving these objectives. They became a sanctified people with whom the Lord dwelt, and they were endowed to a great degree with the glory of God.

After Enoch and his people were translated, Noah was called to proclaim the final testimony of divine truth and power to the antediluvian world. Following the flood, there were those who sought to establish the same divine order of society as Enoch developed. Thereby Melchizedek and his people became sanctified and entered into the presence of the Lord. Meanwhile, Abraham was called to be a minister of God. Through him and his righteous descendants the Lord promised to make His name known in the earth forever. Abraham exemplified this divine commission by preaching the gospel extensively in his day and applying its principles in his life until he received the blessings of the second Comforter.

Notes

1. Alma 9:17–19.
2. D&C 124:33; 128:5, 8, 22; 130:20; 132:5, 11, 28, 63. See also Alma 22:13.
3. Joseph Smith Papers, 1839–1841, Church Historian's Library, Salt Lake City, Utah; found also in TPJS, p. 190.
4. HC, II, p. 15.
5. *Ibid.,* VI, pp. 50–51.
6. Joseph Smith Papers, *op. cit.;* found also in TPJS, p. 181.
7. HC, V, p. 529.
8. *Ibid.,* p. 423.
9. TS, III (September 1, 1842), p. 904.
10. D&C 20:25–26.
11. TS, I (November, 1839), p. 1. Brigham Young declared: "There is no evidence to be found in the Bible that the Gospel should be one thing in the days of the Israelites, another in the days of Christ and his apostles, and another in the 19th century, but, on the contrary, we are instructed that God is the same in every age, and that his plan of saving his children is the same."—JD, X, p. 324.
12. D&C 22:1.
13. TS, III (September 1, 1842), pp. 904–905.
14. D&C 132:5. See also verse 11.
15. D&C 132:28. See also verse 63. This law will be discussed in Volume III of this work.
16. D&C 130:20–21.
17. HC, II, p. 309.
18. EMS, I (May, 1833), pp. 93–94. See also JD, I, p. 235.
19. HC, IV, p. 208. See TS, III (September 1, 1842), pp. 904–905.
20. See Hebrews 11:4.
21. HC, II, pp. 15–16.
22. *Ibid.,* pp. 16–17.
23. *Ibid.* For the last reference by the Apostle Paul, see Galatians 3:19. As further evidence to support the Prophet's argument, the words of Paul to the Corinthians may be cited:

> Moreover, brethren, I would not that ye should be ignorant, how that all our fathers were under the cloud, and all passed through the sea; and were all baptized unto Moses in the cloud and in the sea; and did all eat the same spiritual meat; and did all drink the same spiritual drink: for they drank of that spiritual Rock that followed them: and that Rock was Christ.—1 Corinthians 10:1–5.

24. See Moses 5:2–3. William W. Phelps wrote: "It ought to be known, for it is published, that after Adam and Eve were driven out of the garden of Eden, they had many children, and the children went forth two and two and began to multiply and replenish the earth; yea, and all this too, before Adam had the gospel preached unto him or was baptized."—EMS, I (April, 1833), pp. 84–85.
25. Moses 5:5.
26. Moses 5:6–9.
27. Moses 5:12–15.

28. Moses 6:52.
29. See, for example, D&C 88:63–65; Mormon 9:21, 28.
30. Moses 6:53–68. See the section in chapter seven entitled "Enoch's Explanation of Rebirth."
31. See Moses 7:1.
32. Abraham, Facsimile No. 2.
33. HC, IV, p. 207.
34. D&C 78:16; HC, IV, p. 207.
35. HC, III, p. 387; D&C 76:22–24; 88:36–39, 51–61.
36. HC, III, pp. 387–388; IV, pp. 208–209.
37. *Ibid.,* III, p. 385.
38. *Ibid.,* IV, p. 207.
39. *Ibid.,* III, p. 386.
40. *Ibid.,* IV, pp. 207–208.
41. *Ibid.,* p. 208.
42. *Ibid.,* II, p. 17.
43. *Ibid.,* IV, p. 208.
44. See the section in chapter three entitled "Role of Testimony."
45. *Lectures on Faith,* No. 2.
46. Moses 5:9.
47. See the section in chapter one entitled "Objectives And Purposes Of The Gospel."
48. Moses 5:10.
49. Moses 5:11.
50. HC, III, p. 388.
51. D&C 107:54.
52. HC, III, p. 388. For a scriptural reference to the effort of Moses, see D&C 84:19–24.
53. Moses 6:21, 41.
54. *Lectures on Faith,* No. 2.
55. See Volume I of this study, the section in chapter nine entitled "Christ Speaks as the Father."
56. See Moses 6 and 7. For Joseph Smith's commentary on God's revelation to Enoch, see HC, II, pp. 260–261.
57. Moses 6:26–27.
58. Moses 6:34.
59. See the section in chapter seven entitled "Enoch's Explanation Of Rebirth."
60. Moses 6:59.
61. Moses 6:62.
62. Moses 7:1.
63. The elements of union and individualism among the Saints will be treated in volume III of this study.
64. Having spoken of ancient Eliases who tried unsuccessfully to restore the earth to a state of paradisiacal glory, Joseph Smith indicated that this objective would be achieved in the Dispensation of the Fulness of Times, when God would gather together all things in one. Only when this is done, he explained, will the Saints enjoy direct communion with celestial beings and the earth be renewed to a state of glory. See HC, III, pp. 388–389. This point will be discussed more fully in volumes III and IV of this study.

65. Moses 7:16–18.

66. Reported by Joseph Young, Sr. in his *History of the Organization of the Seventies, Also, A Brief Glance at Enoch and His City* (Salt Lake City, 1878), p. 11.

67. See HC, IV, pp 209–210.

68. JD, III p. 320. Of Enoch's relationship with Adam, William W. Phelps said:

Few persons are aware that Adam lived long enough, in the first days, to witness the gathering of the saints, by Enoch, as well as the building up of Zion. Adam lived to see, at least, seven generations of his children around him, multiplying and replenishing the earth. Adam fell asleep in the Lord only fifty seven years before Zion, even the city of Enoch, was taken up to the bosom of God.—EMS, I (April, 1833), pp. 84–85.

69. JD, III, p. 320. See D&C 84:24, where a revelation states that the term "rest" means to enter into the glory of the Lord. Joseph Smith also stated that Enoch and his people became "righteous enough to come into the presence of God, and walk with him."—TS, III (September 1, 1842), p. 905.

70. See chapter thirteen for a discussion of the subject of making man's calling and election sure.

71. JD, III, p. 320.

72. Concerning this last point, see Moses 7:21; D&C 45:11–12.

73. HC, IV, pp. 556–557.

74. *Ibid.,* pp. 209–210.

75. I. R., Genesis 14:30–32.

76. For a discussion of these points as they relate to the gospel, see chapter thirteen.

77. HC, IV, pp. 209–210. Evidence indicates that Joseph Smith received special revelation on the subject of translated beings, which evidently included a personal visitation from Enoch. For statements concerning the latter point, see D&C 128:21; JD, XX, pp. 174–175; XXI, pp. 65, 94. Of the Prophet's revelation on translated beings, Orson Pratt said:

> Joseph Smith inquired concerning their condition, whether they were subject to death during that period, and was informed . . . that [eventually] these personages have to pass through a change equivalent to that of death; notwithstanding their translation from the earth, a certain change has to be wrought upon them that is equivalent to death, and probably equivalent also to the resurrection of the dead. But before that change comes they minister in their office unto those of another order, that is the terrestrial order.—JD, XVII, p. 148.

Joseph Smith evidently possessed considerable information on translated beings as is apparent from comments which he made. After expressing himself on the subject of Enoch, he promised: "More shall be said of him and terrestrial bodies in another treatise." Again, as he concluded his remarks: "But we shall leave this subject and the subject of terrestrial bodies for another time, in order to treat upon them more fully."—HC, IV, pp. 209–210. The report of Joseph Young, Sr., seems to indicate that he may have fulfilled this promise, but that much of what he said was not recorded. See Young, *op. cit.,* pp. 9–13.

78. Moses 8:2.

79. Moses 7:27.

80. HC, III, p. 386.

81. D&C 84:15.
82. D&C 107:52; Abraham 1:2–3, 18–19.
83. HC, IV, p. 210.
84. TS, III (September 1, 1842), p. 904.
85. Moses 8:13.
86. See chapter seven for a discussion of the way by which man can become a son of God.
87. Moses 8:19.
88. Moses 8:16.
89. Moses 8:23–24.
90. Moses 8:20–21.
91. JD, XXVI, p. 90.
92. Moses 8:14–15.
93. For evidence of Noah's presiding position in the Melchizedek Priesthood by which he was the Lord's prophet on earth, see D&C 84:14–15. For evidence that he held the keys of the Patriarchal Priesthood in a family-oriented society, see D&C 107:40–52. For the fact that he reigned as a king in that system, see Abraham 1:25–26. The situation may have been such that all men may not have recognized his authority in these positions.
94. Moses 8:18.
95. Sayings of Joseph Smith, from those who heard him and later reported that which he said, in "Joseph Smith, Jr. Papers," Church Historian's Library, Salt Lake City, Utah. Once when the Prophet was in the shop of Dimick Huntington he talked of the history of the earth. According to Huntington, he said that while Noah was building the ark and preaching "the wicked people mobbed and drove him four times."—*Young Woman's Journal,* II, p. 467; The diary of Charles L. Walker, December 5, 1891.
96. See Amos 3:7.
97. This revelation was given to him while he dwelt in a shepherd's tent in Arizona Territory. A copy is in the Church Historian's Library, Salt Lake City, Utah.
98. Moses 8:25–26.
99. Genesis 6:6.
100. Moses 8:25–26.
101. The book of Hebrews implies that Melchizedek was "without father, without mother, without descent, having neither beginning of days, nor end of life."—Hebrews 7:3. But Joseph Smith's Inspired Revision of the Bible renders this passage as follows: "For this Melchizedek was ordained a priest after the order of the Son of God, *which order* was without father, without mother, without descent, having neither beginning of days, nor end of life."—I. R., Hebrews 7:3.
102. Alma 13:19. John Taylor stated that Shem, the son of Noah, was Melchizedek. See TS, V (December 15, 1844), p. 746. There is also a Jewish tradition which affirms this identity of Melchizedek. See, for example, *The Book of Jasher* 16:11–12. In discussing this issue, students of Joseph Smith's thought refer to a revelation which states: "Abraham received the priesthood from Melchizedek, who received it *through the lineage of his fathers,* even *till* Noah."—D&C 84:14. Depending upon the meaning of the word "till," this statement may suggest that there were "fathers" between Melchizedek and Noah. If so, Shem could not have been Melchizedek. However, Webster's

New International Unabridged Dictionary gives the following as one of the definitions of "till": " . . . during the whole time from the starting point up to; *up or down* to [a specified time]." Taking this definition of the word "till" into consideration, it may be that the above statement should be understood to mean, "Abraham received the priesthood from Melchizedek, who received it through the lineage of his fathers, even [from Adam] till Noah." This view is supported by the next statement in the revelation which reads: "And from Noah *till* Enoch, through the lineage of *their* fathers [i.e., the fathers of both Enoch and Noah]."—D&C 84:15. If this interpretation is correct, it is possible that Shem could have been Melchizedek. The writer is indebted to Dr. Ellis T. Rasmussen of the Brigham Young University and Thomas G. Truitt of the Church Historian's Library for supplying arguments which support the latter interpretation.

103. Alma 13:14–15, 17–18.

104. Joseph Smith taught that the order, or system, of priesthood which Melchizedek received contains the office of king as well as priest. See TPJS, p. 318; HC, V, pp. 517–518. The political rights of the Melchizedek Priesthood will be discussed in volume III of this study.

105. D&C 107:3–4. (Italics in the original.)

106. I. R., Genesis 14:17–18.

107. Taylor, *op. cit.*, p. 83.

108. D&C 45:12–13.

109. I R., Genesis 14:33–34.

110. See, for example, D&C 129:1, 3, where the word "heaven" is used to denote a state of glory.

111. Alma 13:14.

112. Alma 13:16. See also Alma 13:6, 11–13.

113. Abraham 1:5–6.

114. I. R., Genesis 17:4–7.

115. Abraham 1:15; 2:13.

116. Abraham 1:16. For a discussion of the fact that angels speak by and in the name of Christ, see volume I of this study, the section in chapter nine entitled "Christ Speaks as the Father."

117. Abraham 2:6–13.

118. Abraham 3, 4, 5.

119. See the section in chapter twelve entitled "Coming of Elias."

120. Moses 6:23.

121. See D&C 107:39, HC, III, p. 381.

122. Abraham 1:19.

123. Abraham 2:9. The divine patriarchal order under Abraham will be discussed in volume III of this study.

124. Abraham 2:6.

125. Abraham 2:15.

126. 1 Nephi 17:33–35.

127. Abraham 3:15.

128. Jesus challenged the Jews of His day: "If ye were Abraham's children, ye would do the works of Abraham."—John 8:39.

16

The Gospel from Israel to Modern Times

Some, when they had heard, did provoke: howbeit not all that came out of Egypt by Moses.

But . . . to whom sware he that they should not enter into his rest, but to them that believed not? . . .

Let us therefore fear, lest, a promise being left us of entering into his rest, any of you should seem to come short of it.

For unto us was the gospel preached, as well as unto them: but the word preached did not profit them, not being mixed with faith in them that heard it.

For we which have believed do enter into rest.—PAUL.

Revelations to Joseph Smith teach that many people from the time of Moses to the present day had the gospel, and that some applied its divine program until they obtained the blessings of the second Comforter. The Prophet also made clear the nature of the revelation which was given to Israel through Moses and its relationship to the earthly ministry of Christ and His apostles. The objectives of the gospel in those dispensations are plainly revealed, and the apostasy which took place from the Church of Jesus Christ in New Testament times is made apparent. Modern revelations also set forth the ultimate purpose of the Dispensation of the Fulness of Times, which is to renew the earth through the power of the gospel and establish it again in a state of paradisiacal glory.

Israel The Chosen People

Spiritual Foundations of Israel

Though there were others who endeavored to develop the principles and powers of the gospel on earth after the flood, the Lord eventually centered the rights of the priesthood by promise in the descendants of Abraham, through Isaac and Jacob, who is Israel. In this way, God sought to develop a righteous people through whom He could establish and sustain His law in the earth. To Abraham, the Lord said of the priesthood: "I give unto thee a promise that this right shall continue in thee, and in thy seed after thee (that is to say, the literal seed, or the seed of the body) shall all the families of the earth be blessed, even with the blessings of the Gospel, which are the blessings of salvation, even of life eternal."[1] Like Abraham and the great patriarchs before him, members of the chosen family were expected to be "preachers of righteousness."[2]

Jacob, the father of Israel, persisted in the plan of the gospel until he received the blessings of the second Comforter. Joseph Smith referred to him as one who "saw the mysteries of godliness" when he beheld "angels ascending and descending upon a ladder that reached from earth to heaven."[3] According to the Prophet, "the three principal rounds of Jacob's ladder" represented the kingdoms of glory which man will inherit in the resurrection.[4] To Jacob was also revealed the future of his descendants to the latter days.[5] With Abraham and Isaac his fathers, Jacob stands as a foremost figure in the patriarchal kingdom of Jehovah after the flood and in all generations to follow.

Desire of God for Israel

As God's chosen people, Israel was expected to seek for and achieve the same spiritual blessings and powers which the righteous in former ages had enjoyed. When Moses led the Israelites out of Egypt, he sought to develop them in spiritual excellence and power to be like the people of Enoch, so that they could be endowed with glory and enter into the presence of God. Having explained that it is only through the Melchizedek Priesthood and its sacred ordinances that "the power of godliness is manifest" and that without receiving "the power of godliness . . . no man can see the face of God, even the Father, and live," a revelation to Joseph Smith stated: "Now this Moses plainly taught to the children of Israel in the wilderness, and *sought diligently to sanctify his people that they might behold the face of God.*" He wanted them to enter into the Lord's rest, "which rest is the fulness of his glory."[6]

In commenting upon this statement, George Q. Cannon explained that without the enlightening and regenerating power which may be obtained through the Melchizedek Priesthood and its sacred ordinances, there are limits to which a people can go in their effort to attain the presence of God:

> They cannot attain to the fullness of the glory of God the Eternal Father, without the presence of the Melchisedek Priesthood. . . .
>
> Without this Priesthood, without its ordinances, without its powers, [or] without its gifts, "no man can see the face of God, even the Father, and live." Therefore it is essential that, if a people should be exalted unto the presence of God, they should have this Melchisedek or greater Priesthood, and the ordinances thereof, by the means of which they are to be prepared, or they shall be prepared to enter into the presence of God the Father, and endure His presence.[7]

Ministry of Moses

Israel had been in Egypt many years before the time of Moses. Joseph, the favored son of the patriarch Jacob, was sold by his brothers into Egyptian slavery. But he rose to great spiritual and political heights as the Pharaoh's prime minister, and through his influence the Israelites settled in Egypt. Later, however, there arose another Pharaoh who "knew not Joseph,"[8] and the chosen people of the Lord were placed in a state of servitude and bondage.

By obtaining the blessings of the second Comforter, the Patriarch Joseph was shown many important things concerning the future of Israel. "Joseph truly saw our day," Lehi declared as he spoke of the revelations of God to the earlier patriarch.[9] Among other things, the Patriarch Joseph learned that Moses would be raised up to lead the children of Jacob out of Egypt. To the ancient Joseph, God said: "Moses . . . I have said I would raise up unto you, to deliver my people, O house of Israel, . . . out of the land of Egypt."[10] The patriarch later said:

> . . . I am sure of the promise of Moses; for the Lord hath said unto me, I will preserve thy seed forever.
>
> And the Lord hath said: I will raise up a Moses; and I will give power unto him in a rod; and I will give judgment unto him in writing. Yet I will not loose his tongue, that he shall speak much, for I will not make him mighty in speaking. But I will write unto him my law, by the finger of mine own hand; and I will make a spokesman for him.[11]

Revelations to Joseph Smith indicate that before Moses went to deliver Israel from Egypt he had attained the blessings of the second Comforter by complying with the program of the gospel; he had traversed the path of faith upward into the presence of God.[12] He was "caught up into an exceedingly high mountain," and there he "saw God" and talked with Him.[13] This great theophany occurred some time after the episode of the burning bush[14] and before Moses went to deliver Israel from Egypt.[15] On that occasion, the Lord showed Moses the earth, even all of it, so that "there was not a particle of it which he did not behold, discerning it by the Spirit of God." Moses also saw all the inhabitants of the earth. In addition, God explained to him that He had created "worlds without number," that the "first man of all men" thereon He had called Adam, and that as one earth had passed away with its atmospheric heavens, another had been formed, so that there is no end to His works nor to His words. Finally, the Lord stated that the great purpose of His work in creating these many spheres, and the way by which He continually acquires glory, is "to bring to pass the immortality and eternal life of man."[16]

With this great revelation of God's works and purposes to sustain him, Moses went to Egypt, where the Lord had prepared the way beforehand to magnify His name in the earth, to develop faith in the Israelites, and to bring judgments upon the Egyptians for their wickedness. In referring to His divine purposes, God said to Pharaoh through Moses: "For this cause have I raised thee up, for to shew in thee my power; and that my name may be declared throughout all the earth."[17] It was necessary, therefore, that God "meet with opposition to give Him an opportunity to manifest His power," Brigham Young and Willard Richards wrote; "therefore He raised up a man, even Pharaoh, who, He foreknew, would harden his heart against God of his own free will and choice, and would withstand the Almighty in His attempt to deliver His chosen people."[18]

To such a degree was the power of God revealed through Moses in the plagues which were brought upon Egypt that the proud and defiant Pharaoh was finally willing to release 600,000 men, with their women, children, cattle, etc., from serving him and his people as slaves.[19] "Moreover the man Moses was very great in the land of Egypt, in the sight of Pharaoh's servants, and in the sight of the people."[20] But more important than this, the Israelites came to esteem Moses to the extent that they were willing to follow him into the desert. After they had crossed the Red Sea through another remarkable display of God's power, and the Egyptian army, which pursued them when Pharaoh again hardened his heart, had perished in the water, the record states: "And Israel saw that great work which the Lord did upon the Egyptians; and the people feared the Lord, and believed the Lord, and his servant."[21]

The Lord also manifested His glory visibly to Israel so that the Israelites had ample opportunity to acquire a hope for that glory. As they left Egypt, "the Lord went before them by day in a pillar of a cloud, to lead them the way; and by night in a pillar of fire, to give them light; to go by day and night."[22] When Pharaoh pursued Israel with his army, "the angel of God, which went before the camp of Israel, removed and went behind them; and the pillar of the cloud went from before their face, and stood behind them; and it came between the camp of the Egyptians and the camp of Israel; and it was a cloud and darkness to the Egyptians, but it gave light by night to the Israelites, so that the one came not near the other all the night."[23]

Joseph Smith made it clear that the initial principles and ordinances of the gospel were given to Israel as they tarried on the shore of the Red Sea. The Apostle Paul stated that they "were all baptized unto Moses in the cloud [i.e., the glory, or Spirit, of God] and in the sea." Thus they were born of water and of the Spirit. Continuing, Paul explained: " . . . and [they] did all eat the same spiritual meat; and did all drink the same spiritual drink: for they drank of that spiritual Rock that followed them: and that Rock was Christ."[24] In commenting upon this statement, the Prophet said: "Aaron was baptized in the cloud and in the sea, together with all Israel, as is related by the Apostle in Corinthians."[25] Again the latter-day Seer said:

> Paul told about Moses' proceedings; spoke of the children of Israel being baptized.—(I Cor. x:1–4). He knew this, and that all the ordinances and blessings were in the [Israelite] Church.[26]

Three months after the Israelites left Egypt they arrived at Mount Sinai. Moses then began the task of sanctifying the people and establishing them upon the law of God on a grand scale, with the Lord personally directing the program. "If ye will obey my voice indeed, and keep my covenant, then ye shall be a peculiar treasure unto me above all people," God explained, " . . . and ye shall be unto me a kingdom of priests, and an holy nation."[27] They were to become like the people of Enoch. "He designed to lead them forward under the guidance of the everlasting Priesthood," George Q. Cannon stressed, " . . . until they should behold the face of their God and see Him for themselves."[28]

In preparing Israel for these great blessings, the Lord instructed Moses: "Go unto the people, and sanctify them to day and to morrow, and let them wash their clothes, and be ready against the third day: for the third day the Lord will come down in the sight of all the people upon mount Sinai."[29] On this great occasion, the Israelites were also to be given the sacred laws and ordinances which would take them into the presence of God, endowed with His glory.

When the time came for God to reveal Himself and His law to Israel, the record states:

> . . . there were thunders and lightnings, and a thick cloud upon the mount, and the voice of the trumpet exceeding loud; so that all the people that was in the camp trembled.
>
> And Moses brought forth the people out of the camp to meet with God; and they stood at the nether part of the mount.
>
> And mount Sinai was altogether on a smoke, *because the Lord descended upon it in fire:* and the smoke thereof ascended as the smoke of a furnace, and the whole mount quaked greatly.
>
> And when the voice of the trumpet sounded long, and waxed louder and louder, Moses spake, and God answered him by a voice.
>
> And the Lord came down upon mount Sinai, on the top of the mount: and the Lord called Moses up to the top of the mount; and Moses went up.[30]

When Israel beheld God's glory on Mount Sinai, they also heard the voice of the Lord speak to them.[31] But the living word, conveyed by the penetrating and regenerating power of the Spirit or glory of God,[32] was more than they could bear. They said to Moses: "Speak thou with us, and we will hear: but let not God speak with us, lest we die."[33] Moses later recounted Israel's response to the voice of God:

> . . . when ye heard the voice out of the midst of the darkness, (for the mountain did burn with fire,) that ye came near unto me, even all the heads of your tribes, and your elders;
>
> And ye said, Behold, the Lord our God hath shewed us his

glory and his greatness, and we have heard his voice out of the midst of the fire: we have seen this day that God doth talk with man, and he liveth.

Now therefore why should we die? for this great fire will consume us: if we hear the voice of the Lord our God any more, then we shall die. . . .

Go thou near, and hear all that the Lord our God shall say: and speak thou unto us all that the Lord our God shall speak unto thee; and we will hear it, and do it.[34]

The Israelites were not prepared at this time to enter into the presence of the Lord, for they had not yet received the laws and ordinances by which they could be sanctified to that extent.[35] Their response to the voice of the Lord, therefore, was consistent with their state. Yet their expressions to Moses were lacking in faith and in a hope for the glory of God. George Q. Cannon explained:

They hardened their hearts and could not endure the presence of the Lord. "Go thou, Moses, and speak to God," said the children of Israel, "and then tell us what God has to say: be thou mouthpiece, be thou God to us; we will be content with this, the face of God is too terrible for us. We desire not to enter into His presence. We shall be content to have thee give to us the word of God." These were, in effect, their words, and their actions corresponded to these words. As Paul says, "Which voice (the voice of God) they had heard entreated that the word should not be spoken to them any more, for they could not endure that which was commanded." Moses stood between them and God. They could not endure the presence of God. They hardened their hearts against it.[36]

Joseph Smith expressed an eternal principle when he said: "The moment we revolt at anything which comes from God, the devil takes power."[37] This was true of Israel. Amid the display of glory on Mount Sinai, God revealed the law of Zion to Moses. "The sight of the glory of the Lord was like devouring fire on the top of the mount in the eyes of the children of Israel," the record states. "And Moses went into the midst of the cloud . . . and . . . was in the mount forty days and forty nights."[38] But when the people saw that Moses delayed to return from the mount, they persuaded Aaron to make a golden calf, which they began to worship in idolatrous fashion.[39] Their lack of faith and their failure to respond with a hope for the glory of God turned into spiritual rebellion. They turned from sacred spiritual insight to carnal and sensual practices.

When the Lord saw Israel engaged in idolatry, He was about to destroy the people; but Moses pleaded in their behalf. With mercy, the Lord responded, as recorded in Joseph Smith's Inspired Revision of the Bible: "If they will repent of the evil which they have done, I will spare them, and turn away my fierce wrath; but, behold, thou shalt execute judgment upon all that will not repent of this evil this day."[40]

After Moses had carried out these instructions, God again spoke to him. "If I have found grace in thy sight," Israel's leader then pleaded, "shew me now thy way, that I may know thee." Moses also desired the Lord to still accept Israel as His people and to let His presence—His glory and power—go with them. "For wherein shall it be known here that I and thy people have found grace in thy sight?" he reasoned. "Is it not in that thou goest with us?"[41]

Since the object of the gospel is to bring man into the presence of God, Moses desired to learn more about God's glory. "I beseech thee," he exclaimed to the Lord, "show me thy glory." God then said: "I will make all my goodness [i.e., glory] pass before thee." But, He qualified:

> Thou canst not see my face at this time, lest mine anger be kindled against thee also, and I destroy thee, and thy people; for there shall no man among them see me at this time, and live, for they are exceeding sinful. And no sinful man hath at any time, neither shall there be any sinful man at any time, that shall see my face and live.
>
> And the Lord said, Behold, thou shalt stand upon a rock, and I will prepare a place by me for thee.
>
> And it shall come to pass, while my glory passeth by, that I will put thee in a cleft of a rock, and cover thee with my hand while I pass by.
>
> And I will take away mine hand, and thou shalt see my back parts, but my face shall not be seen, as at other times; for I am angry with my people Israel.[42]

This incident illustrates the degree of purity of the holy powers of life which are centered in God and revealed as His glory. It also makes known the state of perfection to which man must attain, eventually, in order to dwell with God. Neither the natural man nor the carnal man can abide the glory of God.[43] When God manifested all His glory, or goodness, even Moses could not endure it, but was permitted to see only the back parts of God and the glory which shone therefrom. Previously God had explained to him: "No man can behold all my glory, and afterwards remain in the flesh on the earth."[44] The Lord therefore took the precautions which are mentioned above. In this way, Moses could get a better idea of the greatness of God's glory without being exposed directly to the full power and purity of God's divine nature.

Moses was privileged to continue with the Lord and learn of His glory, but Israel's rebellion at Sinai cost her much. Even though the Lord had promised Moses that His presence would continue to go before the camp of Israel, the people were deprived of the means of entering into the presence of God and of partaking of His glory. They could still be spectators, but they could not partake of the glory which they saw. When Moses came down from the mount and saw the people engaged in idolatry and all its attendant evils, he broke the tablets of stone on which God had written the law by which the people could be sanctified and enter into the presence of the Lord. Thus Israel never actually heard that higher law. Joseph Smith observed: "The law revealed to Moses in Horeb never was revealed to the children of Israel as a nation."[45] When Moses later received a second set of tablets from God, the law which they contained varied significantly from that which he had initially received. In reporting the giving of the second set of tablets, Joseph Smith's Inspired Revision of the Bible states:

> And the Lord said unto Moses, Hew thee two other tables of stone, like unto the first, and I will write upon them also, the words of the law, according as they were written at the first on

the tables which thou brakest; *but it shall not be according to the first, for I will take away the priesthood out of their midst; therefore my holy order, and the ordinances thereof, shall not go before them; for my presence shall not go up in their midst, lest I destroy them.*

But I will give unto them the law as at the first, but it shall be after the law of a carnal commandment; for I have sworn in my wrath, that they shall not enter into my presence, into my rest, in the days of their pilgrimage.[46]

This statement indicates that only through the Holy Priesthood, its sacred ordinances, and the order or system of society that can be built thereon, could Israel have been endowed with the glory of God.[47] Had they possessed the Holy Priesthood and built up the sacred order of society that can be established upon the covenants of that priesthood, they could have had the presence of God in their midst, not merely out front leading the camp of Israel. But since they were unworthy of entering into God's presence, or into His rest, the Lord took away the means by which they could achieve this glorious privilege. "They hardened their hearts and could not endure his presence," a revelation to Joseph Smith explained; "therefore, the Lord in his wrath, for his anger was kindled against them, swore that they should not enter into his rest while in the wilderness, which rest is the fulness of his glory."[48] Later, when the divine decree was fully carried out, the Lord "took Moses out of their midst, and the Holy Priesthood also; and the lesser [i.e., Aaronic] priesthood continued, which priesthood holdeth the key of the ministering of angels and the preparatory gospel."[49] "All priesthood is Melchizedek, but there are different portions or degrees of it," Joseph Smith stated. "That portion which brought Moses to speak with God face to face was taken away; but that which brought the ministering angels remained."[50]

Lesser Law of Moses

In speaking of the desire of ancient prophets and patriarchs to build up a system by which their people could attain the glory and power of God, Joseph Smith said: "Moses sought to bring the children of Israel into the presence of God, through the power of the Priesthood, but he could not."[51] Israel's rebellion was again expressed in the events associated with the giving of the second set of tablets upon which God wrote the lesser law, by which the children of Jacob were finally governed. Having been with God again for forty days and nights, Moses assimilated so much glory that when he came down from the mount "the skin of his face shone" so that the Israelites feared to come near him until he veiled his face.[52] Here again they expressed their desire to get away from the presence of the Lord. Because of the hardness of their hearts, they rejected the higher spiritual truths and powers of the everlasting gospel; and in later generations when the law of Moses was read, the veil was still upon their hearts.[53]

Joseph Smith explained the nature of Israel's rebellion and the consequences which followed it. "When God offers a blessing or knowledge to a man, and he refuses to receive it, he will be damned," he said. "The Israelites prayed that God would speak to Moses and not to them; in consequence of which he cursed them with a carnal law."[54] That law proved to be more compatible with their nature and lack of faith. It issued strict injunctions governing personal conduct and elaborated the law of sacrifice into a variety of rituals which centered attention upon the atoning sacrifice which Christ would make. For this reason, the law of carnal commandments was considered a schoolmaster to bring the people to Christ.[55]

The Israelites were also taught of Christ in other ways. When fiery serpents were sent among them for their rebellion, Moses was instructed to make a brazen serpent and place it upon a pole with the promise that all who looked upon it would be healed.[56] According to Alma, this was a "type" or symbol of Christ. But though "many did look and live," he added: "Few understood the meaning of those things, and this because of the hardness of their hearts." There were also "many who were so hardened that they would not look, therefore they perished."[57]

The program which Israel was finally given through

Moses was two-fold in nature. First, it gave the people the preparatory gospel, which consisted of the first three principles and ordinances of the gospel;[58] the decalogue, or ten commandments, as the divine law of conduct governing those who received these principles and ordinances; and the law of carnal commandments. In stressing that this law was part of the greater program of the preparatory gospel, Joseph Smith cited the statement of the Apostle Paul that the law "was *added* because of transgression";[59] he then queried: "What, we ask, was this law *added* to, if it was not added to the [Preparatory] Gospel?"[60] Since the Israelites were finally given only the preparatory gospel, it seems apparent that the right to receive the Holy Ghost, as it was given to them on the shore of the Red Sea, was rescinded.

The power of the Holy Ghost was manifested in some measure in the ministry of the Aaronic Priesthood and in that of its appendage the Levitical Priesthood. Joseph Smith taught that "the Holy Ghost is God's messenger" to minister in all channels of the priesthood.[61] The power of the priesthood is the authoritative expression of the power of the Holy Ghost.[62] But though the priests and Levites in ancient Israel could enjoy the power of the Holy Ghost and utilize its influence in their official priesthood acts, they did not necessarily possess the gift of the Holy Ghost, nor did they have authority by the Aaronic Priesthood to bestow that precious gift upon others.

The lesser law contained a negative element, also. "The law was given under Aaron for the purpose of pouring out judgments and destructions," Joseph Smith explained.[63] The Israelites were heirs in the flesh to the full program of the gospel by which they could have established Zion on earth as a sanctified society, which would have enabled them to partake of the glory of God. But they refused to do this. Consequently, the judgments of God were associated with the lesser law which they received. The Prophet declared: "God cursed the children of Israel because they would not receive the . . . law [of the Melchizedek Priesthood] from Moses."[64]

Second, the divine program gave Israel the benefit of the ministry of special prophets who held the Melchizedek Priesthood and thereby directed the religious, social, economic, and political functions of Israel. Joseph Smith explained that "all the prophets [of ancient Israel] had the Melchizedek Priesthood, and were ordained by God himself."[65] Elijah was the last of Israel's prophets to hold "authority to administer in all the ordinances of the [Melchizedek] Priesthood."[66] Many of these prophets, if not all, received the blessings of the second Comforter. In this respect, Joseph Smith made special mention of Isaiah, Ezekiel,[67] and Daniel.[68] Since a person must make his calling and election sure before he can be translated,[69] it is apparent that Elijah also obtained such blessings. But it is not known to what extent the prophets of Israel were permitted to administer the higher ordinances of the gospel to the children of Israel. Though David was a king and received some priesthood rights and powers, the Prophet remarked that he did not obtain the fulness of the Holy Priesthood.[70]

But Israel did not sustain the spiritual requirements of the lesser law. Nor did the people see clearly the intent of that law to bring them to Christ. Instead, the Jews permitted the law of Moses to become an end within itself, with emphasis upon the letter rather than upon the Spirit. Priestcraft and hypocrisy eventually prevailed in Jerusalem. Yet there were some who looked in faith for the coming of the Messiah to fulfil the inspired teachings and prophecies relating to His mission on earth.

Law Of God Among Nephites

Higher Gospel Law Among Nephites

The Lord's dealings with the Nephites indicate that when the people of God were worthy to receive the higher blessings of the gospel, they were not denied them. Being a more righteous branch of Israel, the Nephites were given the gift of the Holy Ghost[71] and the higher order of gospel law and ordinances which pertains to the Melchizedek Priesthood. In speaking of the blessings of the second Comforter which he received, Lehi said: "The Lord hath redeemed my soul from hell; *I have beheld his glory,* and I am encircled about eternally in the arms of his love."[72] Nephi testified of seeing Christ[73] and said: "Wherefore, my soul delighteth to prophesy concerning him, for I have seen his day, and my heart doth magnify his holy name."[74] Of some of the blessings which he received by obtaining the second Comforter, Nephi said:

> My voice have I sent up on high; and angels came down and ministered unto me.
>
> And upon the wings of his Spirit hath my body been carried away upon exceeding high mountains. And mine eyes have beheld great things; yea, even too great for man; therefore I was bidden that I should not write them.[75]

Jacob also obtained the second Comforter. In speaking of Jesus, Nephi said: "My brother, Jacob, also has seen him as I have seen him."[76] To Jacob, Lehi therefore said: "I know that thou art redeemed, because of the righteousness of thy Redeemer; for thou hast beheld that in the fulness of time he cometh to bring salvation unto men. And thou hast beheld in thy youth his glory."[77]

Because the program of the gospel which the Nephites had was designed to bring them to realize the blessings of the second Comforter, Jacob wrote: "We labor diligently among our people, that we might persuade them to come unto Christ, and partake of the goodness of God, *that they might enter into his rest,* lest by any means he should swear in his wrath they should not enter in, as in the provocation in the days of temptation while the children of Israel were in the wilderness."[78] King Benjamin admonished his people to be steadfast and immovable in righteousness, that they might be sealed unto eternal life.[79] And having shown that in earlier ages "there were many, exceeding great many, who were made pure and entered into the rest of the Lord their God" by establishing the divine order which has its basis in the law and covenants of the Melchizedek Priesthood, Alma said to members of the church in his day: "And now, my brethren, I would that ye should humble yourselves before God, and bring forth fruit meet for repentance, *that ye may also enter into that rest.*"[80]

Law of Moses Among Nephites

The Book of Mormon has much to say about the purpose and intent of the law which Moses gave to Israel. Being Israelites, the Nephites observed "to keep the judgments, and the statutes, and the commandments of the Lord in all things according to the law of Moses."[81] Yet they understood that the law of carnal commandments was given because "the Lord God saw that his people were a stiffnecked people,"[82] and that its intent was to lead men to Christ. Centuries before Christ, Nephi wrote: "Behold, my soul delighteth in proving unto my people the truth of the coming of Christ; for, for this end hath the law of Moses been given, and all things which have been given of God from the beginning of the world, unto man, are the typifying of him."[83] Alma also held that "the law of Moses was a type" of Christ's sacrifice.[84] To Abinadi it was "a shadow of those things which are to come." For this reason, he taught that salvation came not by the law of Moses, but "through Christ the Lord, who is the very Eternal Father."[85] "Were it not for the atonement, which God himself shall make for the sins and iniquities of his people," he concluded, " . . . they must unavoidably perish, notwithstanding the law of Moses."[86] Nevertheless, Alma explained, "the law of Moses did serve to strengthen their faith in Christ; and thus they did retain a hope through faith, unto eternal salvation, relying upon the spirit of prophecy, which spake of those things to come."[87] A classic statement concerning the relationship of the law of Moses to Christ was made by Jacob, who, having referred to the hope of the prophets in the glory of Christ, said:

> Behold, they believed in Christ and worshiped the Father in his name, and also we worship the Father in his name. And for this intent we keep the law of Moses, it pointing our souls to him; and for this cause it is sanctified unto us for righteousness, even as it was accounted unto Abraham in the wilderness to be obedient unto the commands of God in offering up his son Isaac, which is a similitude of God and his Only Begotten Son.
>
> Wherefore, we search the prophets, and we have many revelations and the spirit of prophecy; and having all these witnesses we obtain a hope, and our faith becometh unshaken, insomuch that we truly can command in the name of Jesus and the very trees obey us, or the mountains, or the waves of the sea.[88]

Like other Israelite prophets, the Nephite oracles were ordained to the Melchizedek Priesthood. But because the Nephites were a more righteous branch of Israel than the Jews, the prophets on the Western hemisphere taught their people a fuller program of the gospel, and they testified of the enlivening and regenerating spiritual powers which could be acquired through Christ. The following statement from Nephi illustrates their position on the law of Moses and the gospel:

> . . . notwithstanding we believe in Christ, we keep the law of Moses, and look forward with steadfastness unto Christ, until the law shall be fulfilled.
>
> For, for this end was the law given; wherefore the law hath become dead unto us, and we are made alive in Christ because of our faith; yet we keep the law because of the commandments.
>
> And we talk of Christ, we rejoice in Christ, we preach of Christ, we prophesy of Christ, and we write according to our prophecies, that our children may know to what source they may look for a remission of their sins.
>
> Wherefore, we speak concerning the law that our children may know the deadness of the law; and they, by knowing the deadness of the law, may look forward unto that life which is in Christ, and know for what end the law was given. And after the law is fulfilled in Christ, that they need not harden their hearts against him when the law ought to be done away.[89]

When Jesus appeared among the Nephites after His

resurrection, He confirmed the teachings of their prophets concerning the law of Moses. Having given them the law of the gospel to supersede that law which Moses gave, and having charged them to be the salt of the earth and a light to the world, He said:

> Think not that I am come to destroy the law or the prophets. I am not come to destroy but to fulfil;
>
> For verily I say unto you, one jot nor one tittle hath not passed away from the law, but in me it hath all been fulfilled. . . .
>
> Therefore those things which were of old time, which were under the law, in me are all fulfilled.
>
> Old things are done away, and all things have become new.[90]

But even after Jesus had made these statements, there were some "who marveled, and wondered what he would [do] concerning the law of Moses; for they understood not the saying that old things had passed away and that all things had become new." The Lord therefore explained in greater detail:

> Marvel not that I said unto you that old things had passed away, and that all things had become new.
>
> Behold, I say unto you that the law is fulfilled that was given unto Moses.
>
> Behold, I am he that gave the law, and I am he who covenanted with my people Israel; therefore, the law in me is fulfilled, for I have come to fulfil the law; therefore it hath an end.
>
> Behold, I do not destroy the prophets, for as many as have not been fulfilled in me, verily I say unto you, shall all be fulfilled.
>
> And because I said unto you that old things have passed away, I do not destroy that which hath been spoken concerning things which are to come.
>
> For behold, the covenant which I have made with my people is not all fulfilled; but the law which was given unto Moses hath an end in me.
>
> Behold, I am the law, and the light. Look unto me, and endure to the end, and ye shall live; for unto him that endureth to the end will I give eternal life.
>
> Behold, I have given unto you the commandments; therefore keep my commandments. And this is the law and the prophets, for they truly testified of me.[91]

Ministry Of John The Baptist

Joseph Smith threw light upon many important aspects of the ministry of John the Baptist. John's birth preceded that of Christ's by but a few months. The Prophet explained:

> When Herod's edict went forth to destroy the young children [in his effort to kill Jesus], John was about six months older than Jesus, and came under this hellish edict, and Zacharias caused his mother to take him into the mountains, where he was raised on locusts and wild honey. When his father refused to disclose his hiding place, and being the officiating high priest at the Temple that year, was slain by Herod's order, between the porch and the altar, as Jesus said.[92]

According to Joseph Smith, the kingdom of God had its beginning in New Testament times with John. "Where there is a prophet, a priest, or a righteous man unto whom God gives His oracles, there is the kingdom of God," the latter-day Seer stated. He said of John: "There was a legal administrator, and those that were baptized were subjects for a king; and also the laws and oracles of God were there; therefore the kingdom of God was there; for no man could have better authority to administer than John; and our Savior submitted to that authority Himself, by being baptized by John; therefore the kingdom of God was set up on the earth, even in those days of John."[93]

A revelation stated that John was filled "with the Holy Ghost from his mother's womb." It also explained: "He was baptized while he was yet in his childhood, and was ordained by the angel of God at the time he was eight days old unto this power, to overthrow the kingdom of the Jews, and to make straight the way of the Lord before the face of his people, to prepare them for the coming of the Lord, in whose hand is given all power."[94]

Joseph Smith taught that John was given "the keys of the Aaronic Priesthood,"[95] which constitute the right to direct the functions of that priesthood on earth. The Prophet said: "He had his authority from God, and the oracles of God were with him, and the kingdom of God for a season seemed to rest with John alone."[96] This meant that he was placed in a presiding position over those who held the Aaronic Priesthood in Palestine, and in this way he had power to overthrow the kingdom of the Jews. The latter-day Seer explained:

> John, at that time [at the baptism of Jesus], was the only legal administrator in the affairs of the kingdom there was then on the earth, and holding the keys of power. The Jews had to obey his instructions or be damned, by their own law; and Christ Himself fulfilled all righteousness in becoming obedient to the law which he had given to Moses on the mount, and thereby magnified it and made it honorable, instead of destroying it. The son of Zacharias wrested the keys, the kingdom, the power, the glory from the Jews, by the holy anointing and decree of heaven.[97]

Jesus stated that "among those that are born of women" there was not a greater prophet than John the Baptist.[98] Joseph Smith gave three reasons why this was true. Of the first reason, the Prophet said:

> He [John] was entrusted with a divine mission of preparing the way before the face of the Lord. Whoever had such a trust committed to him before or since? No man.[99]

The latter-day Seer declared of the second reason:

> He was entrusted with the important mission, and it was required at his hands, to baptize the Son of Man. Whoever had the honor of doing that? Whoever had so great a privilege and glory? Whoever led the Son of God into the waters of baptism, and had the privilege of beholding the Holy Ghost descend in the form of a dove, or rather in the *sign* of the dove, in witness of that administration?[100]

The third reason was that John was given power to terminate, or bring to an end, the kingdom of the Jews as has been explained earlier in this section. "These three reasons," Joseph Smith concluded, "constitute him the greatest prophet born of a woman."[101]

Though the identity of the recipient in the following statement is not fully clear, it appears that John the

Baptist was given one of the most important revelations known to man concerning the divine nature of God,[102] as a manifestation of the blessings of the second Comforter.[103] "John saw and bore record of the fulness of my glory," Jesus stated in a revelation to Joseph Smith. "And he bore record, saying: I saw his glory, that he was in the beginning, before the world was; therefore, in the beginning the Word was, for he was the Word, even the messenger of salvation—the light and the Redeemer of the world; the Spirit of truth, who came into the world, because the world was made by him, and in him was the life of men and the light of men."[104] Having testified further that the worlds were made by Christ, as well as all men and all things, John continued:

> I, John, bear record that I beheld his glory, as the glory of the Only Begotten of the Father, full of grace and truth, even the Spirit of truth, which came and dwelt in the flesh, and dwelt among us.
>
> And I, John, saw that he received not of the fulness at the first, but received grace for grace;
>
> And he received not of the fulness at first, but continued from grace to grace, until he received a fulness;
>
> And thus he was called the Son of God, because he received not of the fulness at the first.
>
> And I, John, bear record, and lo, the heavens were opened, and the Holy Ghost descended upon him in the form of a dove, and sat upon him, and there came a voice out of heaven saying: This is my beloved Son.
>
> And I, John, bear record that he received a fulness of the glory of the Father;
>
> And he received all power, both in heaven and on earth, and the glory of the Father was with him, for he dwelt in him.[105]

This divine manifestation and testimony is sufficient to establish John the Baptist as one of the greatest prophets. Apparently his testimony was the basis of the testimonies of other gospel writers in New Testament times.[106] In his brief but effectual ministry, John made straight the path before the Lord of life by declaring the preparatory gospel and by directing the attention of the people to the great Redeemer whose purpose was to reveal the higher ordinances and sanctifying power which Israel, under Moses, had rejected. John declared: "I indeed baptize you before he cometh, that when he cometh he may baptize you with the Holy Ghost and fire."[107]

Ministry Of Christ And His Apostles

Establishment of Melchizedek Priesthood

As the great High Priest of the Holy Melchizedek Priesthood,[108] Jesus established the authority, power, and keys of that divine order again upon the earth. "He built up the Kingdom," Joseph Smith explained, "chose apostles, and ordained them to the Melchizedek Priesthood, giving them power to administer in the ordinances of the Gospel."[109] Thereby, according to George Q. Cannon, there was a "restoration of the Priesthood in its fullness, that Melchizedek Priesthood which Moses held, and through which he exercised such mighty power among the children of Israel."[110] The writer of the epistle to the Hebrews noted the change which was then made in the priesthood, from the lower order which was given to the sons of Aaron and the tribe of Levi to the higher system after the order of Melchizedek, and the goal that was made possible by that change:

> If therefore *perfection* were by the Levitical priesthood, (for under it the people received the law,) what further need was there that another priest should rise after the order of Melchisedec, and not be called after the order of Aaron?
>
> *For the priesthood being changed, there is made of necessity a change also of the law.*[111]

This statement makes it clear that man can achieve perfection only by the aid of the blessings and power of the Melchizedek Priesthood, and that when Christ established that order of the priesthood on earth there was of necessity a change in the law which the people of God were required to obey. Jesus gave the higher law in the Sermon on the Mount.[112] Having done so and having declared that old things were done away so that all things had become new, the Master admonished His disciples to become perfect.[113] By the new program which He gave, that goal was made possible.

With the ancient authority and power again made available to man, Jesus and His Apostles tried to achieve the same goals which Moses sought to realize. George Q. Cannon explained: "It was God's design—if the people would have submitted to it, if they would have received the message that He sent unto them through John [the Baptist] and afterwards through His beloved Son—to have restored the Kingdom even to Israel, and *to have built up the Kingdom in great power and glory upon the earth.*"[114]

Christian System

Joseph Smith taught: "Although there are two priesthoods, yet *the Melchizedek Priesthood comprehends the Aaronic or Levitical Priesthood,* and is the grand head, and holds the . . . keys of the Kingdom of God in all ages of the world, . . . and *is the channel through which all knowledge, doctrine, the plan of salvation, and every important matter is revealed from heaven.*"[115] Though the law of carnal commandments which the Aaronic Priesthood had administered from the time of Moses was done away after the crucifixion of Christ, the latter-day Seer made it clear that the lesser priesthood was retained in the New Testament Church and placed under the direction of the Apostleship, thus continuing the program of the preparatory gospel after the coming of Christ.[116] In this way, all the avenues of mercy and sanctifying power of the preparatory gospel and the everlasting gospel were opened to man.

Latter-day Saint spokesmen stressed that, according to plain declarations which are found in the New Testament, the Christian system which Jesus established was designed to be perpetuated without change in its major offices and functions to succeeding generations. They cited the statements of the Apostle Paul that when Christ ascended up on high He "gave gifts unto men." Paul said of these divine gifts and of their intended purposes and continuance in the Church of Jesus Christ:

> . . . he gave some, apostles; and some, prophets; and some, evangelists; and some, pastors and teachers;
>
> *For the perfecting of the saints, for the work of the ministry, for the edifying of the body of Christ:*
>
> *Till we all come in the unity of the faith, and of the knowledge of the Son of God, unto a perfect man, unto the measure of the stature of the fulness of Christ:*
>
> That we henceforth be no more children, tossed to and fro, and carried about with every wind of doctrine, by the sleight of men, and cunning craftiness, whereby they lie in wait to deceive;
>
> But speaking the truth in love, *may grow up into him in all things,* which is the head, even Christ:
>
> From whom the whole body fitly joined together and compacted by that which every joint supplieth, according to the effectual working in the measure of every part, maketh increase of the body unto the edifying of itself in love.[117]

Joseph Smith and his associates also cited the Apostle Paul to show that the Church of Jesus Christ in New Testament times was analogous to a living body, and that one organ (i.e., office, calling, or divine gift) could not say to another, "I have no need of thee." Paul declared that even the less honorable and uncomely parts of the body of Christ were important. Those who believed in Christ were "baptized into one body" and were "all made to drink into one spirit." Consequently there was to be "no schism in the body."[118] Concluding his analysis of the body of Christ, Paul wrote of some of its leading offices and gifts:

> . . . God hath set some in the church, first apostles, secondarily prophets, thirdly teachers, after that miracles, then gifts of healing, helps, governments, diversities of tongues.
>
> Are all apostles? are all prophets? are all teachers? are all workers of miracles?
>
> Have all the gift of healing? do all speak with tongues? do all interpret?
>
> But covet earnestly the best gifts. . . .[119]

This was the Church of Jesus Christ with its divine gifts and offices. In baptism (which was performed by immersion for the remission of sins),[120] repentant believers "put on Christ,"[121] being "*planted* together in the likeness of his death" with the hope that they would "be also in the likeness of his resurrection."[122] Those who were baptized were given the gift of the Holy Ghost.[123] Of this divine gift, Peter declared: "The promise [of the gift of the Holy Ghost] is unto you, and to your children, and to all that are afar off, even as many as the Lord our God shall call."[124] There would be no exceptions. That precious gift would be given to them by the laying on of hands.[125]

Joseph Smith wrote to a newspaper editor that Christ sought to establish the new covenant which God, through Jeremiah, had declared He would make with His people.[126] By means of this new covenant, the Lord promised to put His "law in their inward parts, and write it in their hearts."[127] Because the enlightening and regenerating power of the Holy Spirit was to be manifested through the new covenant, the Apostle Paul wrote that each recipient of it would become an epistle of Christ, "written not with ink, but with the Spirit of the living God; not in tables of stone, but in the fleshly tables of the heart." This was the "new testament" which Christ established; it was an abiding principle of revelation and power to every worthy saint, rather than a written letter only.[128]

By the regenerating power of the everlasting gospel, many in New Testament times developed spiritually until they made their calling and election sure and received the blessings of the second Comforter. Jesus promised this Comforter to the eleven apostles.[129] Paul reminded the Ephesian saints that they "were sealed with the Holy Spirit of promise."[130] And Peter declared: "We have also a more sure word of prophecy."[131] Joseph Smith wrote that by the blessings of the second Comforter Peter, James, and John "saw the glory of the Lord when he showed the transfiguration of the earth on the mount."[132] The Prophet also indicated that John was given other manifestations in the realm of the second Comforter in the great apocalypse which he received on the Isle of Patmos.[133] The latter-day Seer explained that, by acquiring similar privileges, the

Hebrew church came "to an innumerable company of angels—to God the Judge of all—the spirits of just men made perfect; to Jesus the Mediator of the new covenant."[134] In this way they were taught things which were so sacred that they could not be written.[135]

Paul contrasted the glory that could be revealed through the gospel with that which had been manifested to Israel when the lesser law was given to them by Moses. The manifestation of glory and power on that occasion was such "that the children of Israel could not steadfastly behold the face of Moses for the glory of his countenance." But this glory could be eclipsed by the greater glory which was made available through Christ, the Apostle declared. "For if the ministration of condemnation be glory," he explained, "much more doth the ministration of righteousness exceed in glory."[136] The people of Enoch's city, for example, received more glory than that which shone from Moses when he came from the mount. Because it was the central purpose of the gospel to develop in man the divine nature of God, Paul wrote: "We all, with open face beholding as in a glass the glory of the Lord, are changed into the same [divine or glorified] image from glory to glory, even as by the Spirit of the Lord."[137]

The Gospel Among The Gentiles

When Israel rejected her God and crucified Him, she was broken off; no longer was she accorded the privileges which she had enjoyed as God's chosen people. Though the Israelites were heirs in the flesh to the priesthood and the blessings of the gospel, Joseph Smith said of God's dealings with His elect people: "He passes over no man's sins, but visits them with correction, and if His children will not repent of their sins He will discard them."[138] For the time, at least, Israel was discarded as a people.[139] Orson Pratt explained:

> After Israel lost the kingdom, they had no more power nor auhority which God recognized: their priesthood which could once bless and curse with authority, became powerless. Their

ministrations were as useless as those of heathen priests; their forms and ceremonies were as lifeless and ineffectual as those of Paganism. God had forsaken the nation, by withdrawing the kingdom with all its supernatural fruits; [and in this state] eighteen long centuries of terrible midnight darkness have rolled over the heads of that devoted apostate race.[140]

After Israel was broken off, the gospel was given to the gentiles. Joseph Smith explained: "The Jews, as a nation, having departed from the law of God and the Gospel of the Lord, prepared the way for transferring it to the Gentiles."[141] Again he said: "After this chosen family had rejected Christ and His proposals, the heralds of salvation said to them, 'Lo we turn unto the Gentiles'; and the Gentiles received the covenant, and were grafted in from whence the chosen family were broken off."[142] Orson Pratt explained: "The Gentiles, as soon as they received it [the gospel], began to have visions, dreams, prophecies, revelations, angels, tongues, interpretation of tongues, healings, miracles, and, in short, all the fruits of the kingdom that Israel enjoyed in the days of their righteousness."[143]

Universal Apostasy

"But the Gentiles have not continued in the goodness of God," Joseph Smith declared, "but have departed from the faith that was once delivered to the Saints, and have broken the covenant in which their fathers were established (see Isaiah 24:5); and have become high-minded, and have not feared."[144] To illustrate this important point, the Prophet said:

Christ said to His disciples (Mark 16:17, 18), that these signs should follow them that believed:—"In my name shall they cast out devils, they shall speak with new tongues; they shall take up serpents; and if they drink any deadly thing, it shall not hurt them; they shall lay hands on the sick, and they shall recover"; and also, in connection with this, read 1st Corinthians, 12th chapter. By the foregoing testimonies we may look at the Christian world and see *the apostasy there has been from the apostolic platform;* and who can look at this and not exclaim, in the language of Isaiah, "The earth also is defiled under the inhabitants thereof; because they have transgressed the laws, changed the ordinances, and broken the everlasting covenant?"[145]

Following the example of the Prophet, leading authorities among the Latter-day Saints repeatedly cited biblical prophecies and evidence which confirm that the gentiles had departed from the Christian system, with its divine gifts and powers, which was given to them.[146] The Apostle Paul wrote prophetically of a great "falling away" which would occur from the divine system which Christ and the Apostles endeavored to establish. The "man of sin" would then be "revealed," he declared, "the son of perdition; who opposeth and exalteth himself above all that is called God, or that is worshipped; so that he as God sitteth in the temple of God, showing himself that he is God."[147] Men would "heap to themselves teachers, having itching ears," he declared. "And they shall turn their ears from the truth, and shall be turned into fables."[148] The Apostle Peter also warned that there would come "false teachers." "And," he said, "many shall follow their pernicious ways; by reason of whom the way of truth shall be evil spoken of."[149] In summarizing biblical declarations of the universal apostasy from the true Christian system, Orson Pratt wrote:

> The great apostasy of the Christian Church commenced in the first century, while there were yet inspired apostles and prophets in their midst; hence Paul, just previous to his martyrdom, enumerates a great number who had "made shipwreck of their faith," and "turned aside unto vain jangling;" teaching "that the resurrection was already past," giving "heed to fables and endless genealogies," "doting about questions and strifes of words, whereof came envyings, railings, evil surmisings, perverse disputings of men of corrupt minds, and destitute of the truth, supposing that gain is godliness." This apostasy had become so general that Paul declares to Timothy, "that all they which are in Asia be turned away from me;" and again, he says, "At my first answer, no man stood with me, but all men forsook me;" he further states, that "there are many unruly and vain talkers and deceivers, teaching things which they ought not, for filthy lucre's sake." These apostates, no doubt, pretended to be very righteous; for, says the Apostle, "they profess that they know

God, but in works they deny him, being abominable and disobedient, and unto every good work reprobate." Near the close of the first century, the apostasy had become so universal, that only seven churches throughout all Asia, Africa, and Europe, were considered worthy of being either reproved or blessed by the voice of revelation [which was given to John on the Isle of Patmos]; and even these seven were so corrupted by the doctrine of the Nicolaitanes, and of Balaam, by the fornications and adulteries of Jezebel, and by losing their "first love," and becoming "neither cold nor hot," that the Almighty considered them, with a very few exceptions, as "dead," and threatened to "spew them out of his mouth"—to cast them "into great tribulation," and "kill their children with death"—to "fight against them with the sword of His mouth"—and to "remove the candlestick" or Church, "out of its place."[150]

Modern scriptures make repeated reference to the universal apostasy which took place from the system which Jesus and the apostles established. A revelation which explained Christ's parable of the wheat and the tares said: "Behold, verily I say, the field was the world, and the [ancient] apostles were the sowers of the seed; and after they have fallen asleep the great persecutor of the church, the apostate, the whore, even Babylon, that maketh all nations drink of her cup, in whose hearts the enemy, even Satan, sitteth to reign—behold he soweth the tares; wherefore, the tares choke the wheat and drive the church into the wilderness."[151] Thus the true church of Christ, with its divine gifts, ordinances, and powers, was taken from among men.

In vision, Nephi was shown this period of apostasy. He saw "the foundation of a great and abominable church" which displaced the true Christian Church. Of the foreign system which perverted "the right ways of the Lord," the ancient seer said:

> . . . I saw among the nations of the Gentiles the foundation of a great church.
>
> And the angel said unto me: Behold the foundation of a church which is most abominable above all other churches, which slayeth the saints of God, yea, and tortureth them and bindeth them down, and yoketh them with a yoke of iron, and bringeth them down into captivity.

And it came to pass that I beheld this great and abominable church; and I saw the devil that he was the foundation of it.

And I also saw gold, and silver, and silks, and scarlets, and fine-twined linen, and all manner of precious clothing; and I saw many harlots.

And the angel spake unto me, saying: Behold the gold, and the silver, and the silks, and the scarlets, and the fine-twined linen, and the precious clothing, and the harlots, are the desires of this great and abominable church.

And also for the praise of the world do they destroy the saints of God, and bring them down into captivity.[152]

Owing to the perversion of the true Christian system and because of deficiencies in the scriptural writings which the gentiles in later ages would possess, Nephi beheld that "an exceeding great many" would stumble, and Satan would have "great power over them."[153] While the gentiles were in this condition, many churches would be built up among them. Nephi wrote of the religious scene which would ensue:

. . . the Gentiles are lifted up in the pride of their eyes, and have stumbled, because of the greatness of their stumbling block, that they have built up many churches; nevertheless, they put down the power and miracles of God, and preach up unto themselves their own wisdom and their own learning, that they may get gain and grind upon the face of the poor.

And there are many churches built up which cause envyings, and strifes, and malice.[154]

Again the ancient seer said, as he wrote of the churches which would be built up in the latter days:

. . . it shall come to pass in that day that the churches which are built up, and not unto the Lord, when the one shall say unto the other: Behold, I, I am the Lord's; and the others shall say: I, I am the Lord's; and thus shall every one say that hath built up churches, and not unto the Lord—

And they shall contend one with another; and their priests shall contend one with another, and they shall teach with their learning, and *deny the Holy Ghost, which giveth utterance.*

And they deny the power of God, the Holy One of Israel; and they say unto the people: Hearken unto us, and hear ye our precept; for behold there is no God today, for the Lord and the

Redeemer hath done his work, and he hath given his power unto men;

Behold, hearken ye unto my precept; if they shall say there is a miracle wrought by the hand of the Lord, believe it not; for this day he is not a God of miracles; he hath done his work.

Yea, and there shall be many which shall say: Eat, drink, and be merry, for tomorrow we die; and it shall be well with us.

And there shall also be many which shall say: Eat, drink, and be merry; nevertheless, fear God—he will justify in committing a little sin; yea, lie a little, take advantage of one because of his words, dig a pit for thy neighbor; there is no harm in this; and do all these things, for tomorrow we die; and if it so be that we are guilty, God will beat us with a few stripes, and at last we shall be saved in the kingdom of God.

Yea, and there shall be many which shall teach after this manner, false and vain and foolish doctrines, and shall be puffed up in their hearts, and shall seek deep to hide their counsels from the Lord; and their works shall be in the dark.

And the blood of the saints shall cry from the ground against them.

Yea, they have all gone out of the way; they have become corrupted.

Because of pride, and because of false teachers, and false doctrine, their churches have become corrupted, and their churches are lifted up; because of pride they are puffed up.

They rob the poor because of their fine sanctuaries; they rob the poor because of their fine clothing; and they persecute the meek and the poor in heart, because in their pride they are puffed up.

They wear stiff necks and high heads; yea, and because of pride, and wickedness, and abominations, and whoredoms, they have all gone astray save it be a few, who are the humble followers of Christ; nevertheless, they are led, that in many instances they do err because they are taught by the precepts of men.[155]

Dispensation Of The Fulness Of Times

State of Modern Christianity

The Dispensation of the Fulness of Times was introduced with an official statement by the glorified Christ to Joseph Smith in the spring of 1820 concerning the state of modern Christianity. Having asked the Lord which of all the churches of his day was right and which one he should join, the Prophet was told: "I must join none of them, for they were all wrong, and the personage who addressed me said that all their creeds were an abomination in His sight: that those professors were all corrupt; that 'they draw near to me with their lips, but their hearts are far from me; *they teach for doctrines the commandments of men: having a form of godliness, but they deny the power thereof.*'"[156]

Though the Book of Mormon recognizes and denounces the state of modern Christianity, it centers attention upon the work of the Lord in the last days and upon God's desire to bring man to embrace the fulness of the gospel. Having shown Nephi the apostate condition of Christianity in the latter days, an angel explained:

> . . . the Lord God [will not] suffer that the Gentiles shall forever remain in that awful state of blindness, which thou beholdest they are in, because of the plain and most precious parts of the gospel of the Lamb which have been kept back by that abominable church, whose formation thou hast seen.
>
> Wherefore saith the Lamb of God: I will be merciful unto the Gentiles . . . in that day, insomuch that I will bring forth unto them, in mine own power, much of my gospel, which shall be plain and precious, saith the Lamb.[157]

Nephi beheld that, to fulfil this promise, "other books" containing scriptural writings would come forth "by the power of the Lamb" in the last days. The angel explained: "These last records, which thou hast seen among the Gentiles, shall establish the truth of the first, which are of the twelve apostles of the Lamb, and shall make known the plain and precious things which have been taken away from them; and shall make known to all kindreds, tongues, and people, that the Lamb of God is the Son of the Eternal Father, and the Savior of the world; and that all men must come unto him, or they cannot be saved."[158] In this way, a great program would be launched in the last day. Speaking of it, the Lord said: "Forasmuch as this people draw near unto me with their mouth, and with their lips do honor me, but have removed their hearts far from me, and their fear towards me is taught by the precepts of men—therefore, I will proceed to do a marvelous work among this people, yea, a marvelous work and a wonder, for the wisdom of their wise and learned shall perish and the understanding of their prudent shall be hid."[159]

Ministry of Joseph Smith

The restoration of the pure Christian system upon the earth in its fulness required that many heavenly messengers minister to Joseph Smith. After the Prophet's glorious vision of the Father and the Son in the spring of 1820, the angel Moroni became his director in the revelation and translation of the Book of Mormon, and Joseph Smith received many visitations from him during the course of that work.[160] Before the time the Prophet received the gold plates from which the Nephite scripture was translated, other former prophets of the Nephite civilization also ministered to him, including such individuals as Nephi, Alma, and Mormon.[161] After he received the Nephite record, and until the time of his death in 1844, the latter-day Seer was a constant recipient of the blessings and ministrations which are related to the second Comforter. Few men have ever realized the higher blessings of the gospel to the degree that he received them.

In ushering in the Dispensation of the Fulness of Times, the Lord committed to Joseph Smith all the keys and powers of the Holy Priesthood which had been given to prophets of God since the days of Adam. Having referred to heavenly manifestations to himself by Moroni, Michael (i.e., Adam), and Peter, James, and John, the latter-day Seer summarized: "And the voice of Michael, the archangel; the voice of Gabriel, and of Raphael, and of divers angels, from Michael or Adam down to the present time, all declaring their dispensation, their rights, their keys, their honors, their majesty and glory, and the power of their priesthood; giving line upon line, precept upon precept; here a little, and there a little; giving us consolation by holding forth that which is to come, confirming our hope!"[162] Of the ministrations which Joseph Smith received, John Taylor later said:

> Although the Church was so few in number the principles and purposes of God were developed fully to the vision of his [Joseph Smith's] mind, and he gazed [by heavenly vision] upon the things that are to transpire in the latter-days associated with the dispensation that he was called upon by the Amighty to introduce. He learned by communication from the heavens, from time to time, of the great events that should transpire in the latter days. He understood things that were past, and comprehended the various dispensations and the designs of those dispensations. He not only had the principles developed, but he was conversant with the parties who officiated as the leading men of those dispensations, and from a number of them he received authority and keys and priesthood and power for the carrying out of the great purposes of the Lord in the last days, who were sent and commissioned specially by the Almighty to confer upon him those keys and this authority, and hence he introduced what was spoken of by all the prophets since the world was; the dispensation in which we live which differs from all other dispensations in that it is the dispensation of the fulness of times, embracing all other dispensations, all other powers, all other keys and all other privileges and immunities that ever existed upon the face of the earth.[163]

Though Joseph Smith was "a feeble youth, inexperienced, [and] without a knowledge of the learning of the day," John Taylor explained that "God put him in possession of that kind of intelligence, and what may be termed a scientific knowledge of all things pertaining to this earth, and the heavens, . . . which was altogether ahead of all the intelligence that existed in the world." Thus equipped, the Prophet began to introduce the great latter-day dispensation "by following the education he had received from the Almighty, by teaching the principles of life and salvation, the principles of the everlasting Gospel, by conferring upon others that priesthood which had been conferred upon him, *and by organizing a state of things that was after the pattern of the heavens, that was calculated to live and grow and increase, that had the principle of life and vitality within itself, and that was calculated to draw together the honest in heart and assimilate them in their ideas and views and feelings and faith, and empower them to operate with him and with the Lord and with the holy priesthood that had existed in former ages."*[164]

The Prophet was informed that as the work of the latter-day dispensation developed in its onward course, the great purposes of God concerning the earth and its inhabitants in the latter days would be fulfilled. Having spoken of the establishment of the new dispensation in 1823, the angel Moroni said: " . . . it will increase the more [it is] opposed, and spread farther and farther, increasing in knowledge till they [the Saints] shall be sanctified and receive an inheritance where the glory of God shall rest upon them."[165] When this takes place, the angel continued, God's purposes in regard to the scattered remnants of His ancient covenant people, Israel, will be fulfilled.[166] They will come to Zion and be "crowned with glory—that is, be given the higher sealing powers of the priesthood by which they can acquire glory—"by the hands of the servants of the Lord."[167] "When this is fulfilled will be brought to pass the saying of the prophet," Moroni explained—"'And the Redeemer shall come to Zion, and unto them that turn from transgression in Jacob, saith the Lord.'"[168]

Joseph Smith taught that the Saints can establish Zion in her glory by building up that holy order of society which is founded upon the covenants of the Melchizedek Priesthood.[169] When this is accomplished, he declared, "The Son of Man will descend, the Ancient of Days sit; we may [then] come to an innumerable company of angels, have communion with and receive instruction from them."[170] The ancient objective of the gospel—that which Adam sought to achieve through the divine plan of life and salvation—will then be realized by Christ coming in glory to destroy the wicked and renew the earth to a paradisiacal state somewhat like that which it enjoyed before Adam fell.

Summary

Through Israel as a chosen people, God endeavored to establish His law in the earth, by giving them the gospel, sanctifying them through its divine truth and power, and bringing them into His presence as He did the people of Enoch in earlier times. Moses, having received the blessings of the second Comforter, sought diligently to raise Israel to the standard of spiritual maturity that would qualify them to enter into the presence of God and partake of His glory. To this end, the power and glory of God were manifested to the Israelites as they came out of Egypt. But when they beheld God's glory and heard His voice, they failed to express a true hope for that glory. Evidencing a lack of faith, they finally rejected the divine offer and turned to idolatry. Consequently they were given a lesser law than that which God originally delivered to Moses. The lesser law retained the preparatory gospel and the decalogue, but added the law of carnal commandments instead of the higher order of the everlasting gospel, which pertains to the Melchizedek Priesthood. Except for the fact that all the prophets of Israel were given the Melchizedek Priesthood, the Israelites as a people were left with only the Aaronic Priesthood which administered the lesser law. It was the purpose of the lesser law to bring Israel to Christ.

Jesus restored the higher order of the priesthood which had been taken from Israel with Moses, and He centered that system in the holy apostleship. In this way, Christ gave His disciples the higher law and the greater spiritual powers by which they could be sanctified and endowed with celestial glory. But because of apostasy, that divine system with its apostles, prophets, and spiritual gifts was not perpetuated. Instead, a religious system foreign to the New Testament Church developed under the name of Christianity, and in later ages a babel of churches arose, each claiming to teach and administer the gospel of Christ.

The personal appearance of the Father and the Son to Joseph Smith introduced the Dispensation of the Fulness of Times. Thereafter other heavenly beings ministered to the Prophet until all the keys, powers, and authority which were committed to ancient prophets for the salvation of man had been restored to the earth in modern times. Through this heavenly system, Zion was to be established and the earth renewed eventually to a paradisiacal state of glory.

Notes

1. Abraham 2:11.
2. Moses 6:23.
3. HC, I, p. 283. See Genesis 28:10–22.
4. HC, V, p. 402.
5. See Alma 46:24–26; 3 Nephi 10:17; 20:22.
6. D&C 84:19–24.
7. JD, XXV, p. 292.
8. Exodus 1:8; Acts 7:18.
9. 2 Nephi 3:5.
10. 2 Nephi 3:9–10.
11. 2 Nephi 3:16–17. In light of the promised redemption of Israel from Egypt, the following passage is of interest: "And Moses took the bones of Joseph with him: for he had straitly sworn the children of Israel, saying, *God will surely visit you;* and ye shall carry up my bones away hence with you."—Exodus 13:19.
12. Moses' vision recorded in Moses 1 is such an experience. Moses had received the Melchizedek Priesthood from his father-in-law Jethro. See D&C 84:6. Since this priesthood administers the gospel and holds the key to the knowledge of God (see D&C 84:19), Moses obviously had the gospel.
13. Moses 1:1–2.
14. After the Lord had made an initial appearance to Moses, He withdrew and Satan came desiring Moses to worship him. But the man of God refused and explained: "[God] . . . gave me commandment *when he called unto me out of the burning bush,* saying: Call upon God in the name of mine Only Begotten, and worship me."—Moses 1:17. The episode of the burning bush was a past incident in the life of Moses.
15. When Satan had been dispatched (see the footnote above), Moses again called upon the Lord. He then heard a voice saying: "Blessed art thou, Moses, for I, the Almighty, have chosen thee, and *thou shalt be made stronger than many waters; for they shall obey thy command as if thou wert God.*" Continuing, the Lord said: "And lo, I am with thee, even unto the end of thy days; for *thou shalt deliver my people from bondage,* even Israel my chosen."—Moses 1:25–26. Such incidents as the dividing of the Red Sea and the delivering of Israel from Egypt were still in the future for Moses.
16. Moses 1.
17. Exodus 9:16.
18. HC, IV, p. 263. See again the section in chapter thirteen entitled "Doctrine Of Reprobation."

19. See I. R., Exodus 12:37.
20. Exodus 11:3.
21. Exodus 14:31.
22. Exodus 13:21.
23. Exodus 14:19–20.
24. 1 Corinthians 10:1–4.
25. TS, III (September 1, 1842), p. 904.
26. HC, III, p. 389.
27. Exodus 19:5–6.
28. JD, XXV, p. 291.
29. Exodus 19:10–11.
30. Exodus 19:16–20.
31. See Exodus 20:19, 22; Deuteronomy 4:36; 5:22, 25.
32. For example, when Jesus appeared among the Nephites after His resurrection, He was introduced by the voice of God out of heaven, which "did pierce them that did hear to the center, insomuch that there was no part of their frame that it did not cause to quake; yea, it did pierce them to the very soul, and did cause their hearts to burn."—3 Nephi 11:3.
33. Exodus 20:19.
34. Deuteronomy 5:23–27.
35. This point will be discussed later in the chapter.
36. JD, XXV, p. 293. See also D&C 84:24.
37. Joseph Smith Papers, 1839–1841, Church Historian's Library, Salt Lake City, Utah; found also in TPJS, p. 181.
38. Exodus 24:17–18.
39. Exodus 32.
40. I. R., Exodus 32:14.
41. Exodus 33:16.
42. I. R., Exodus 33:18–23. It seems from this statement that Moses' relationship to the Israelites as their leader placed him in the eyes of God under some restrictions which arose from the sinfulness of his people.
43. See D&C 67:10–12.
44. Moses 1:5.
45. HC, V, p. 555. Horeb is another name for Sinai. This statement implies that the law which is recorded in Exodus 20 to 31 is not all that Moses received at that time.
46. I. R., Exodus 34:1–2. See also I. R., Deuteronomy 10:2.
47. This sacred system, with its law and program, will be discussed in volume III of this work.
48. D&C 84:24.
49. D&C 84:25–26. For a discussion of the preparatory gospel, see the section in chapter one entitled "Preparatory Gospel Compared with Everlasting Gospel."
50. Manuscript statement by Joseph Smith, January 5, 1841, Church Historian's Library, Salt Lake City, Utah; found also in TPJS, pp. 180–181.
51. HC, III, p. 388.
52. Exodus 34:28–35.
53. See 2 Corinthians 3:13–15.
54. HC, V, p. 555.
55. Alma 25:15–16; Galatians 3:24.

56. Numbers 21:5–9.
57. Alma 33:19–20.
58. Faith in the Lord Jesus Christ, the doctrine of repentance, and baptism by immersion for the remission of sins.
59. Galatians 3:19.
60. HC, II, p. 17.
61. *Ibid.*, V, p. 555.
62. See Volume I of this study, the section in chapter ten entitled "The Power of the Priesthood."
63. HC, V, p. 554.
64. *Ibid.*, p. 555.
65. Manuscript statement by Joseph Smith, January 5, 1841, Church Historian's Library, Salt Lake City, Utah; found also in TPJS, p. 181.
66. HC, IV, p. 211.
67. *Ibid.*, III, p. 381.
68. *Ibid.*, V, p. 65.
69. See I. R., Genesis 14:30–32; JD, III, p. 320.
70. See HC, VI, p. 253.
71. See 1 Nephi 10:17; 2 Nephi 31:12, 18; Jacob 6:8–9; Alma 9:21.
72. 2 Nephi 1:15.
73. 2 Nephi 11:2.
74. 2 Nephi 25:13. See 1 Nephi 11:13–34.
75. 2 Nephi 4:24–25.
76. 2 Nephi 11:3.
77. 2 Nephi 2:3–4.
78. Jacob 1:7.
79. Mosiah 5:15.
80. Alma 13:12–13. See also Alma 12:34–37; 13:6, 16; 57:36.
81. 2 Nephi 5:10.
82. Mosiah 3:14.
83. 2 Nephi 11:4.
84. Alma 25:15.
85. Mosiah 16:14–15.
86. Mosiah 13:28.
87. Alma 25:16. An antagonist to the Nephite faith accused them of converting "the law of Moses into the worship of a being which ye say shall come many hundred years hence."—Jacob 7:7.
88. Jacob 4:5–6.
89. 2 Nephi 25:24–27. See also Jarom 1:11.
90. 3 Nephi 12:17–18, 46–47.
91. 3 Nephi 15:2–10.
92. TS, III (September 1, 1842), p. 902. For a report on the edict of Herod, see Matthew 2:16. For the statement of Jesus concerning Zacharias, see Matthew 23:25.
93. HC, V, p. 258.
94. D&C 84:27–28.
95. Manuscript report of Joseph Smith's teachings, July 23, 1843, Church Historian's Library, Salt Lake City, Utah; found also in TPJS, p. 319; HC, V, pp. 257, 258.
96. HC, V, p. 257.

97. *Ibid.*, p. 261. Again the Prophet commented: "John having the power took the Kingdom by authority."—Manuscript report of Joseph Smith's teachings, July 23, 1843, *op. cit.*

98. Matthew 11:11; Luke 7:28.

99. HC, V, p. 260.

100. *Ibid.*, pp. 260–261. (Italics in the original.)

101. *Ibid.*, p. 261.

102. See D&C 93:6–18. There is reason to question which John received this revelation—John the Baptist or John the Apostle. In the introductory note of the present edition of the Doctrine and Covenants, James E. Talmage identifies the person mentioned as John the Apostle. But the revelation implies that it may have been John the Baptist. He testified of Jesus: "I, John, bear record, and lo, the heavens were opened, and the Holy Ghost descended upon him in the form of a dove, and sat upon him, and there came a voice out of heaven saying: This is my beloved Son."—D&C 93:15. Joseph Smith's Inspired Revision of the Bible confirms the fact that John the Baptist "saw . . . the heavens opened" when the Holy Ghost descended on this occasion. See I. R., Matthew 3:45 in conjunction with Matthew 3:16. Since this event took place before John the Apostle became a disciple of Jesus (see Matthew 4:21–22), the person who gave the above testimony was undoubtedly John the Baptist, unless John the Apostle, who was a disciple of John the Baptist, was present as an observer of the baptism of Jesus and received a like vision at that time. However, both Orson Pratt and John Taylor identify John the Baptist as the person giving the testimony which is recorded in Doctrine and Covenants 93. See *Deseret Evening News*, II (March 9, 1878), No. 90; Taylor, *Mediation And Atonement* (Salt Lake City, 1950), p. 55.

103. This is the context in which the report of John's testimony is set. See D&C 93:1 ff.

104. D&C 93:6–9.

105. D&C 93:11–17. For a treatment of the important ideas in this statement, see Volume I of this study, the section in chapter eight entitled "Christ As The Son Of God."

106. This seems to be true particularly of John the Apostle, who may have utilized the testimony of John the Baptist in beginning his account of Jesus. See John 1.

107. I. R., Matthew 3:38.

108. See Hebrews 5:6; 6:20.

109. Manuscript report of a discourse by Joseph Smith, July 23, 1843, Church Historian's Library, Salt Lake City, Utah; found also in TPJS, p. 318.

110. JD, XXV, p. 291–292.

111. Hebrews 7:11–12. See the verses which follow this statement in Hebrews for evidence that the gospel writer was applying these words specifically to Christ and the change which He instituted.

112. For a discussion of this subject, see chapter ten.

113. Matthew 5:48; 3 Nephi 12:48.

114. JD, XXV, p. 292.

115. HC, IV, p. 207.

116. Joseph Smith used the example of Philip's ministry in Samaria to illustrate the continuation of the functions of the Aaronic Priesthood in the New Testament Church.—*Ibid.*, VI, pp. 249–250. See Acts 8, where it is

apparent that Philip had authority to baptize but not to confer the gift of the Holy Ghost. The writer of the epistle to the Hebrews also distinguished between the lesser and the higher priesthood and implied that they were both in the New Testament Church. See Hebrews 5:4–5.

117. Ephesians 4:8, 11–16. For statements by the Prophet and others citing this declaration by Paul, see HC, V, pp. 28–29; JD, XIV, p. 53; XVI, p. 373.

118. Corinthians 12:1–26.

119. 1 Corinthians 12:28–31. For statements by the Prophet and others, see HC, I, p. 454; IV, p. 609; V. pp. 27–29; JD, XIV, p. 53; XVII, p. 310.

120. For the purpose and mode of baptism, see Mark 1:4; Luke 3:3; Acts 2:38; 22:16; Romans 6:3–5; Colossians 2:12. The English verb "to baptize" derives from the Greek *baptizo* and means to dip or immerse.

121. Galatians 3:27.

122. Romans 6:3–5. See also Matthew 3:16; Mark 1:5, 9, 10; John 3:23; Acts 8:38–39.

123. Acts 2:37–38; 8:14–20; 9:31; 10:44–48; 11:15; 19:1–6. See also Matthew 3:11; Mark 3:11; Luke 12:11; 24:49; John 14:16–17, 26; 15:26; 16:7–14; 20:21; Acts 1:5.

124. Acts 2:37–39.

125. Acts 8:12–18; 19:1–6.

126. HC, I, p. 313.

127. Jeremiah 31:31. This promise was given specifically to the house of Israel (the northern kingdom) and the house of Judah (the southern kingdom), and after Israel's latter-day restoration it will have its full consummation in relation to the gathered remnants. See HC, I, pp. 312–316.

128. 2 Corinthians 3:1–6.

129. John 14:16–23; HC, III, pp. 379–381; D&C 88:3–4.

130. Ephesians 1:13–14; HC, III, pp. 379–380.

131. 2 Peter 1:19; HC, V, pp. 387–389, 401–403.

132. HC, I, p. 283. See also Matthew 17:1–8; Mark 9:2–8; Luke 9:28–36; 2 Peter 1:16–18; D&C 63:20–21.

133. HC, III, p. 381. See also *ibid.*, I, pp. 283–284.

134. *Ibid.*, III, p. 388. See Hebrews 12:23.

135. See HC, VI, p. 51.

136. 2 Corinthians 3:7–9.

137. 2 Corinthians 3:18.

138. HC, IV, p. 360.

139. God's covenant with the ancient patriarchs is that He will remember their posterity in the latter days and bring them again to be His elect people. This part of the divine program will be discussed in volume IV of this study.

140. From a treatise on "The Universal Apostasy," written by Orson Pratt, Liverpool, England, January 1, 1851.

141. HC, V, p. 257.

142. *Ibid.*, I, p. 313. See Acts 13:46.

143. Pratt, *op. cit.*

144. HC, I, pp. 313–314. See also *ibid.*, V, p. 424.

145. *Ibid.*, I, p. 314. The last biblical reference cited by the Prophet is found in Isaiah 24:5.

146. See, for example, JD, VII, pp. 212–213; VIII, p. 262; XII, p. 64–71,

246–247; XIV, pp. 52, 293–294; XVI, pp. 74, 344–350; XVIII, pp. 44, 170–179; XIX, pp. 352–353; XXI, p. 251; XXIV, pp. 83–93, 185, 204–212, 340, 370–371; XXV, pp. 206–207, 332.

147. 2 Thessalonians 2:1–5.

148. 2 Timothy 4:3.

149. 2 Peter 2:1–2.

150. Pratt, *op. cit.*

151. D&C 86:2–3.

152. 1 Nephi 13:4–9.

153. 2 Nephi 13:29.

154. 2 Nephi 26:20–21.

155. 2 Nephi 28:3–14.

156. HC, I, p. 6; Smith 2:19.

157. 1 Nephi 13:32–33, 34.

158. 1 Nephi 13:39–40.

159. 2 Nephi 27:25–26.

160. For a discussion of this subject, see Hyrum L. Andrus, *Joseph Smith the Man and the Seer* (Deseret Book Co., Salt Lake City, Utah), pp. 69–77.

161. See *ibid.,* pp. 80–81.

162. D&C 128:21.

163. JD, XX, pp. 174–175. Both John Taylor and his brother William Taylor asserted that Joseph Smith was as well acquainted with such personalities as the Father, Jesus, Adam, Seth, Enoch, Abraham, Isaac, Jacob, the apostles in Palestine, and the apostles who ministered to the Nephites, as they and their associates were with each other. See JD, XXI, pp. 65, 94; *Young Woman's Journal,* XVII, p. 548. For a discussion of this subject, see Andrus, *op. cit.,* chapter four.

164. JD, XX, p. 175.

165. MA, II (October, 1835), p. 199.

166. *Ibid.*

167. D&C 133:32.

168. MA, II (October, 1835), p. 199.

169. This holy order of society will be discussed in volume III of this study.

170. HC, III, p. 389.

17

The Doctrine of Salvation for the Dead

For for this cause was the gospel preached also to them that are dead, that they might be judged according to men in the flesh, but live according to God in the spirit.—PETER.

"The great designs of God in relation to the salvation of the human family, are very little understood by the professedly wise and intelligent generation in which we live," Joseph Smith charged. Men of his day understood very little "concerning the plan of salvation, the requisitions of the Almighty, the necessary preparations for heaven, the state and condition of departed spirits, and the happiness or misery that is consequent upon the practice of righteousness and iniquity."[1] This was true particularly when it came to man's understanding of the divine program by which God designs to save those who do not hear the true gospel of Jesus Christ on earth or are not privileged to embrace it in mortality. According to the Prophet, the Saints have a vital role to play in this phase of the divine plan of life and salvation.

Basic Views On Doctrine Of Salvation For Dead

Mercy and Compassion of God

"Our heavenly Father is more liberal in His views, and boundless in His mercies and blessings, than we are ready to believe or receive," the Prophet observed.[2] Man's views concerning the mercy and justice of God are often colored by his personal prejudices and biases. Joseph Smith explained:

> The Mussulman condemns the heathen, the Jew, and the Christian, and the whole world of mankind that reject his Koran, as infidels, and consigns the whole of them to perdition. The Jew believes that the whole world that rejects his faith and are not circumcised, are Gentile dogs, and will be damned. The heathen is equally as tenacious about his principles, and the Christian consigns all to perdition who cannot bow to his creed, and submit to his *ipse dixit.*[3]

Continuing, he said:

> But while one portion of the human race is judging and condemning the other without mercy, the Great Parent of the universe looks upon the whole of the human family with a fatherly care and parental regard; He views them as His offspring, and without any of those contracted feelings that influence the children of men, causes "His sun to rise on the evil and on the good, and sendeth rain on the just and on the unjust." He holds the reins of judgment in His hands; He is a wise Lawgiver, and will judge all men, not according to the narrow, contracted notions of men, but, "according to the deeds done in the body whether they be good or evil," or whether these deeds were done in England, America, Spain, Turkey, or India. He will judge them, "not according to what they have not, but according to what they have," those who have lived without law, will be judged without law, and those who have a law, will be judged by that law. We need not doubt the wisdom and intelligence of the Great Jehovah; He will award judgment or mercy to all nations according to their several deserts, their means of obtaining intelligence, the laws by which they are governed, the facilities afforded them of obtaining correct information, and His inscrutable designs in relation to the human family; and when the designs of God shall be made manifest, and the curtain of

futurity be withdrawn, we shall all of us eventually have to confess that the Judge of all the earth has done right.[4]

Death and Man's Eternal Destiny

"It is an opinion which is generally received, that the destiny of man is irretrievably fixed at his death, and that he is made either eternally happy, or eternally miserable," the latter-day Seer observed; "that if a man dies without a knowledge of God, he must be eternally damned, without any mitigation of his punishment, alleviation of his pain, or the most latent hope of a deliverance while endless ages shall roll along." But "however orthodox this principle may be," he continued, "we shall find that it is at variance with the testimony of Holy Writ."[5] The Prophet then cited several biblical statements to support his claim:

> Our Savior says, that all manner of sin and blasphemy shall be forgiven men wherewith they shall blaspheme; but the blasphemy against the Holy Ghost shall not be forgiven, neither in this world, nor in the world to come [Matthew 12:31], evidently showing that there are sins which may be forgiven in the world to come, although the sin of blasphemy [against the Holy Ghost] cannot be forgiven. Peter, also, in speaking concerning our Savior, says, that "He went and preached unto the spirits in prison, which sometimes were disobedient, when once the long suffering of God waited in the days of Noah," (I Peter iii:19, 20). Here then we have an account of our Savior preaching to the spirits in prison, to spirits that had been imprisoned from the days of Noah; and what did He preach to them? That they were to stay there? Certainly not! Let His own declaration testify. "He hath sent me to heal the broken hearted, to preach deliverance to the captives, and recovering of sight to the blind, to set at liberty them that are bruised." (Luke iv:18.) Isaiah has it—"To bring out the prisoners from the prison, and them that sit in darkness from the prison house." (Isaiah xlii:7.) It is very evident from this that He not only went to preach to them, but to deliver, or bring them out of the prison house.[6]

Having set forth the arguments above, Joseph Smith gave a practical illustration to show how absurd is the view that man's eternal destiny must be set at death. He said:

I will suppose a case which is not extraordinary: Two men, who have been equally wicked, who have neglected religion, are both of them taken sick at the same time; one of them has the good fortune to be visited by a praying man, and he gets converted a few minutes before he dies; the other sends for three different praying men, a tailor, a shoemaker, and a tinman; the tinman has a handle to solder to a can, the tailor has a buttonhole to work on some coat that he needed in a hurry, and the shoemaker has a patch to put on somebody's boot; they none of them can go in time, the man dies, and goes to hell: one of these is exalted to Abraham's bosom, he sits down in the presence of God and enjoys eternal, uninterrupted happiness, while the other, equally as good as he, sinks to eternal damnation, irretrievable misery and hopeless depair, because a man had a boot to mend, the buttonhole of a coat to work, or a handle to solder on to a saucepan.[7]

Again he illustrated:

Suppose the case of two men, brothers, equally intelligent, learned, virtuous and lovely, walking in uprightness and in all good conscience, so far as they have been able to discern duty from the muddy stream of tradition, or from the blotted page of the book of nature.

One dies and is buried, having never heard the Gospel of reconciliation; to the other the message of salvation is sent, he hears and embraces it, and is made the heir of eternal glory. Shall the one become the partaker of glory and the other be consigned to hopeless perdition? Is there no chance for his escape?[8]

The Prophet held that such views which would consign to perdition a man who did not hear the gospel on earth were "worse than atheism." "The truth shall break down and dash in pieces all such bigoted Pharisaism," he declared; "the sects shall be sifted, the honest in heart brought out, and their priests left in the midst of their corruption."[9] The latter-day Seer had little respect for the contracted views of many religious teachers. "The idea that some men form of the justice, judgment, and mercy of God, is too foolish for an intelligent man to think of," he stated. "The plans of Jehovah are not so unjust, the statements of holy writ so visionary, nor the plan of salvation for the human family so incompatible with common sense."[10] Continuing, he reasoned:

If human laws award to each man his deserts, and punish all delinquents according to their several crimes, surely the Lord will not be more cruel than man, for He is a wise legislator, and His laws are more equitable, His enactments more just, and His decisions more perfect than those of man; and as man judges his fellow man by law, and punishes him according to the penalty of the law, so does [the] God of heaven judge "according to the deeds done in the body." To say that the heathens would be damned because they did not believe the Gospel would be preposterous, and to say that the Jews would all be damned that do not believe in Jesus would be equally absurd; for "how can they believe on him of whom they have not heard, and how can they hear without a preacher, and how can he preach except he be sent;" [Romans 10:14–15] consequently neither Jew nor heathen can be culpable for rejecting the conflicting opinions of sectarianism, nor for rejecting any testimony but that which is sent of God, for as the preacher cannot preach except he be sent, so the hearer cannot believe without he hear a "sent" preacher, and cannot be condemned for what he has not heard, and being without law, will have to be judged without law.[11]

Hearing the Gospel after Death

According to Joseph Smith, the organized spirit of man "existed before the body, can exist in the body; and will exist separate from the body, when the body will be mouldering in the dust; and will in the resurrection be again united with it."[12] On the basis of this fundamental proposition, he taught:

> There is never a time when the spirit [of man] is too old to approach God. All are within the reach of pardoning mercy, who have not committed the unpardonable sin, which hath no forgiveness, neither in this world, nor in the world to come. There is a way to release the spirits of the dead; that is by the power and authority of the Priesthood—by binding and loosing on earth.[13]

At the time of the resurrection all men will be redeemed to a degree of glory which accords with their ability to live the law of God, except those who sin against the Holy Ghost.[14] This means that a great work is done in the spirit world after death to teach the plan of life and salvation to those who reside in that sphere. Joseph Smith also held that the Saints on earth have a vital work to perform in redeeming to celestial glory those in the spirit world who will obey celestial law. Concerning the general nature of this work and the lengths to which it must ultimately extend, he said:

> I have a declaration to make as to the provisions which God hath made to suit the conditions of man—made from before the foundation of the world. What has Jesus said? All sin, and all blasphemies, and every transgression, except one, that man can be guilty of, may be forgiven; and there is a salvation for all men, either in this world or the world to come, who have not committed the unpardonable sin, there being a provision either in this world or the world of spirits. Hence God hath made a provision that every spirit in the eternal world can be ferreted out and saved unless he has committed that unpardonable sin which cannot be remitted to him either in this world or the world of spirits. God has wrought out a salvation for all men, unless they have committed a certain sin; and every man who has a friend in the eternal world can save him, unless he has committed the unpardonable sin. And so you can see how far you can be a savior.[15]

God's Covenant in Behalf of Dead

The Prophet's statement above indicates that God made provisions for the salvation of the dead "before the foundation of the world."[16] These provisions were made according to His foreknowledge. Having spoken of the foreknowledge of God—that "the past, the present, and the future were and are, with Him, one eternal 'now'"—Joseph Smith said: "He was acquainted with the situation of all nations and with their destiny; He ordered all things according to the council of His own will; *He knows the situation of both the living and the dead, and has made ample provision for their redemption, according to their several circumstances, and the law of the kingdom of God, whether in this world, or in the world to come.*"[17]

When the plan of life and salvation was presented in the pre-earth councils, Jesus promised to redeem those who would come to earth but not have in mortality the opportunity to receive that plan; they would be given a state of glory and power which they prepared themselves to enjoy in the resurrection. This redemption Christ would accomplish according to the principles of mercy, justice, truth, and equity. Since the Saints on earth were to be involved in some vital aspects of this great work, Joseph Smith spoke of the Dispensation of the Fulness of Times as being a dispensation in relation to the dead which was designed "to meet the promises made by Jesus Christ before the foundation of the world for the salvation of man."[18] The latter-day Seer therefore declared: "The salvation of Jesus Christ was wrought out for all men, in order to triumph over the devil; for *if it did not catch him in one place, it would in another;* for he stood up as a Savior."[19]

Justice and Mercy of God

Ultimately the living and the dead have equal opportunity to achieve salvation. Some of the Saints had inquired: "What has become of our fathers? Will they be damned for not obeying the Gospel, when they never heard it?" To these questions the Prophet replied: "Certainly not. But they will possess the same privilege that we here enjoy, through the medium of the everlasting Priesthood, which not only administers on earth, but also in heaven."[20] Indeed, the divine plan for saving the dead "presents the Gospel of Christ in probably a more enlarged scale than some have imagined."[21]

If the plan of the gospel were not sufficiently comprehensive to extend the blessings of salvation to all men according to the principles of truth, justice, and mercy, God would be lacking in these essential attributes. But since the divine program is designed to save all men who will hearken to its message, Joseph Smith said of the plan of salvation for the dead: "This doctrine presents in a clear light the wisdom and mercy of God in preparing an ordinance for the salvation of the dead."[22] "A view of these things," he explained, "reconciles the Scriptures of truth, justifies the ways of God to man, places the human family upon an equal footing, and harmonizes with every principle of righteousness, justice and truth."[23] Again he observed:

This doctrine appears glorious, inasmuch as it exhibits the greatness of divine compassion and benevolence in the extent of the plan of human salvation.

This glorious truth is well calculated to enlarge the understanding, and to sustain the soul under troubles, difficulties and distress.[24]

Having written of the great purposes of the gospel in redeeming the dead and uniting the righteous of all ages together in Christ, the Prophet could exclaim:

Now, what do we hear in the gospel which we have received? A voice of gladness! *A voice of mercy from heaven;* and a voice of truth out of the earth; *glad tidings for the dead;* a voice of gladness *for the living and the dead;* glad tidings of great joy.[25]

Doctrine Of Baptism For Dead

Basic Principles of Baptism for Dead

"There is baptism, &c., for those to exercise who are alive," Joseph Smith explained, "and baptism for the dead who die without the knowledge of the Gospel."[26] Of the latter baptism, he said: "The Saints have the privilege of being baptized for those of their relatives who are dead, whom they believe would have embraced the Gospel, if they had been privileged with hearing it, and who have received the Gospel in the spirit, through the instrumentality of those who have been commissioned to preach to them while in prison."[27] Again:

Every man that has been baptized and belongs to the kingdom has a right to be baptized for those who have gone before; and as soon as the law of the Gospel is obeyed here by their friends who act as proxy for them, the Lord has administrators there to set them free. A man may act as proxy for his own relatives; the ordinances of the Gospel which were laid out before the foundations of the world have thus been fulfilled by them, and we may be baptized for those whom we have much friendship for; but it must be revealed to the man of God, lest we should run too far.[28]

Biblical Evidence of Baptism for Dead

Joseph Smith asserted that "the Bible supported the doctrine" of salvation for the dead and that "this doctrine was the burden of the scriptures."[29] In a letter to the Twelve, he said of baptism for the dead: "Aside from knowledge independent of the Bible, I would say that it was certainly practiced by the ancient churches; and St. Paul endeavors to prove the doctrine of the resurrection from the same, and says, 'Else what shall they do which are baptized for the dead, if the dead rise not at all? why are they then baptized for the dead?'"[30] After quoting this statement by the Apostle Paul, George Q. Cannon explained in greater detail:

> Among other arguments which he brought forth to convince the Corinthians that there was such a thing as resurrection he appeals to the fact there was such a doctrine as baptism for the dead in the Church and practiced by the former day Saints, and to enforce the doctrine he uses the words I have read, one of the most powerful arguments that he could adduce in favor of the resurrection. How useless it would be for men and women to be baptized for the dead, if the dead rise not at all; but the dead do rise, and the Saints are baptized for them. I might paraphrase his words and reason upon them in this way. The dead are baptized, for we are baptized for them, and they do rise or else all our labor would be in vain in going forth and being baptized for them.[31]

"If there is one word of the Lord that supports the doctrine of baptism for the dead," the Prophet declared, "it is enough to establish it as a true doctrine."[32] He said:

> The doctrine of baptism for the dead is clearly shown in the New Testament; and if the doctrine is not good, then throw the New Testament away; but if it is the word of God, then let the doctrine be acknowledged; and it was the reason why Jesus said unto the Jews, "How oft would I have gathered thy children together, even as a hen gathereth her chickens under her wings,

and ye would not!"—that they might attend to the ordinances of baptism for the dead as well as other ordinances of the priesthood, and receive revelations from heaven, and be perfected in the things of the kingdom of God—but they would not. This was the case on the day of Pentecost: those blessings were poured out on the disciples on that occasion. God ordained that He would save the dead, and would do it by gathering His people together.[33]

Baptism for Dead and Rights of Priesthood

The doctrine of salvation for the dead, including baptism for the dead, must be seen in light of the rights and powers which belong to the priesthood. "If we can, by the authority of the Priesthood of the Son of God, baptize a man in the name of the Father, of the Son, and of the Holy Ghost, for the remission of sins," Joseph Smith reasoned, "it is just as much our privilege to act as an agent, and be baptized for the remission of sins for and in behalf of our dead kindred, who have not heard the Gospel or the fulness of it."[34] The priesthood is not limited in its authority to performing ordinances which are binding only on the earth in mortality. Orson Pratt explained:

> The authority committed into the hands of the servants of God, in all dispensations of the Gospel, is the power to bind on the earth, and it is bound in heaven,—to seal on the earth and it is sealed in heaven,—to loose on the earth, and it is loosed in the heavens; and whosesoever sins they remit here on the earth, they are to be remitted in the heavens; and whosesoever sins they retain here upon the earth, they are retained against those individuals in the heavens. This is the authority of the servants of God in all dispensations of the Gospel from the earliest ages of the world until the present time.[35]

In speaking of the power of the priesthood in relation to the ordinance of baptism for the dead, Joseph Smith said:

> The nature of this ordinance consists in the power of the priesthood, by the revelation of Jesus Christ, wherein it is granted that whatsoever you bind on earth shall be bound in

heaven, and whatsoever you loose on earth shall be loosed in heaven. . . .

It may seem to some to be a very bold doctrine that we talk of—a power which records or binds on earth and binds in heaven. Nevertheless, in all ages of the world, whenever the Lord has given a dispensation of the priesthood to any man by actual revelation, or any set of men, this power has always been given. Hence, whatsoever those men did in authority, in the name of the Lord, and did it truly and faithfully, and kept a proper and faithful record of the same, it became a law on earth and in heaven, and could not be annulled, according to the decrees of the great Jehovah. This is a faithful saying. Who can hear it?[36]

Orson Pratt explained how the sealing power which Elijah commissioned Joseph Smith to use operates in behalf of the dead. Having first referred to the power to organize and seal all things pertaining to the divine patriarchal order, on earth and in heaven, he said:

Therefore, when by that authority the servants and handmaids of the Lord go forth and are baptized for those that are dead, it is recorded and sealed on the earth. The administrator who officiates for and in behalf of the dead does it by authority. . . . This is recorded in the sacred records kept on the earth; and the recording angel who takes cognizance of the ordinances on the earth makes a record of the same in heaven.[37]

Vicarious Nature of Gospel Plan

In referring to saving the dead, the Prophet stressed that "it was *the truth, not men,* that saved them; but men, by actively engaging in rites of salvation substitutionally [i.e., vicariously] become instrumental in bringing multitudes of their kindred into the kingdom of God."[38] Performance of an ordinance alone will not do. "You might as well go and be baptized for a devil as for a man who will not receive the Gospel in the spirit world," Heber C. Kimball stressed.[39] But properly understood and expressed, the doctrine of salvation for the dead rests upon a vicarious principle. This is true in the case of the atonement of Jesus Christ, and it is also true in the doctrine of salvation for the dead. Orson Pratt explained:

> How could you have atoned for yourselves? If it had not been for the agency of another being that acted for you and in your behalf, you must have perished eternally. . . . We could not have helped ourselves. Hence, the Son of God came forth and made an atonement, not for himself, but for and in behalf and in the name of his younger brethren, that they, through his blood, and through certain conditions of the Gospel, might receive forgiveness of their sins. One of these conditions is baptism: but spirits [who have departed this life without hearing the true gospel] are placed in a condition where they cannot receive this ordinance. And now, why not somebody have authority to go and administer [vicariously] for them and in their behalf? Not only Jesus has acted in behalf of the children of men, but it pertains to the same Priesthood and Apostleship, wherever it is placed, to act for and in behalf of the children of men. . . .
>
> Just so, the dead could not help themselves without messengers being sent to them in their prison-houses, and without persons in the flesh being authorized to receive Gospel ordinances for them and in their behalf.[40]

After referring to the vicarious nature of the atonement of Christ, George Q. Cannon also said:

> In like manner, Malachi says, in speaking of the Prophet Elijah coming before the great and terrible day of the Lord: "The hearts of the fathers shall be turned to the children." What for? Because the children can act vicariously for them; "and the hearts of the children shall be turned to the fathers," because the children will feel after their fathers; they will search for their genealogies, and learn of their ancestors, and they will go forth and perform ordinances in the flesh for their dead, which the dead can not perform for themselves, and act vicariously for them.[41]

Introduction Of Doctrine Of Salvation For Dead

Before the Prophet taught the doctrine of salvation for the dead, he had been asked the question many times: "What is the condition of the dead, those that lived and died without the Gospel?"[42] Upon receiving the restored gospel, hundreds of people were led to exclaim: "Oh, that my father, mother, brother, sister, husband, wife, children, grandfather or grandmother had heard this doctrine as the Elders teach it! How gladly they would have embraced it!"[43] For these and other reasons Joseph Smith was prompted to inquire of the Lord concerning the fate of the dead. "It was a matter of inquiry with him," Brigham Young explained. "He considered this question not only for himself, but for the brethren and the Church."[44]

Apparently the details of the plan of salvation for the dead were not revealed to the Prophet all at once. In January, 1836, he received a revelation which said: "All who have died without a knowledge of the Gospel, who would have received it if they had been permitted to tarry, shall be heirs of the celestial kingdom of God."[45] In May, 1838, the question was asked, "If the Mormon doctrine is true, what has become of all those who died since the days of the Apostles?" To this inquiry, the latter-day Seer wrote: "All those who have not had an opportunity of hearing the Gospel, and being administered unto by an inspired man in the flesh, must have it hereafter, before they can be finally judged."[46]

These early statements are of a general nature and do not disclose the details of the plan of salvation for the dead. Apparently the initial revelation on these points was given to Joseph Smith in the year 1840.[47] In a letter to the Twelve, he said of baptism for the dead: "I first mentioned the doctrine in public when preaching the funeral sermon of Brother Seymour Brunson."[48] Colonel Brunson died in the Prophet's home August 10, 1840, and his funeral services were held on August 15th.

Simon Baker was present at the funeral of Colonel Brunson and later said of the Prophet's address:

> He read the greater part of the 15th Chap. of [1] Cor[inthians] and remarked that the Gospel of Jesus Christ brought glad tidings of great joy, and then remarked that he saw a widow in that congregation that had a son who died without being baptized, and this widow [had read] . . . the sayings of Jesus, "Except a man be born of water and of the Spirit he cannot enter the kingdom of heaven," and that not one jot nor tittle of

the Saviour's words should pass away, but all should be fulfilled. He then said that this widow should have glad tidings in that thing. He also said the Apostle [Paul] was talking to a people who understood baptism for the dead, for it was practiced among them. He went on to say that people could now act for their friends who had departed this life, and that the plan of salvation was calculated to save all who were willing to obey the requirements of the law of God.[49]

Regulations Governing Baptism For Dead

Performance of Ordinances According to Strict Order

The Lord's house being one of order, all things must be done for the salvation of the dead according to the law which God has given. Speaking of the ordinance of baptism for the dead, in April, 1845, Brigham Young said: "In order that this ordinance of God may be valid, and recognized by Him, it must not be performed in a haphazard way, but with a thorough knowledge of the true manner of its performance, that the purpose to be answered and the object to be gained may be secured."[50] Letters written by the Prophet before his death verify this statement.[51]

Baptism for Dead in Temples

The Prophet stated that there must be "a place built expressly for . . . men to be baptized for their dead."[52] "In regard to the law of the Priesthood," he explained, "There should be a place where all nations shall come up from time to time to receive their endowments; and the Lord has said this shall be the place for the baptisms for the dead."[53] In other words, the ordinance of baptism for the dead should be performed in temples. "One of the ordinances of the house of the Lord is baptism for the dead," the latter-day Seer declared. "God decreed before the foundation of the world that that ordinance should be administered in a font prepared for that purpose in the house of the Lord."[54] A revelation declared that such sanctuaries were to be built "in Zion and in her stakes, and in Jerusalem."[55]

When the doctrine of baptism for the dead was first revealed to the Church, baptisms were performed for a time in the Mississippi river. But this was a temporary practice, and a revelation to Joseph Smith explained:

> . . . a baptismal font there is not upon the earth, that they, my saints, may be baptized for those who are dead—
>
> For this ordinance belongeth to my house, and cannot be acceptable to me, only in the days of your poverty, wherein ye are not able to build a house unto me.
>
> But I command you, all ye my saints, to build a house unto me; and I grant unto you a sufficient time to build a house unto me; and during this time your baptisms shall be acceptable unto me. . . .
>
> But verily I say unto you, that after you have had sufficient time to build a house to me, wherein the ordinance of baptizing for the dead belongeth, and for which the same was instituted from before the foundation of the world, your baptisms for your dead cannot be acceptable unto me.[56]

Orson Pratt explained that a practical reason for centering the ordinance of baptism for the dead in the temple is that "the house of God is a house of order, the kingdom of God is a kingdom of order, and everything must be conducted with order, and with power and authority, so that when it is sealed on earth it is sealed in the heavens, that the records on earth and in heaven may agree—that the Priesthood on earth and in heaven may agree—that they may be one."[57]

Symbolism in Baptism for Dead

Baptism for the dead should also be performed in the house of the Lord so that the symbolism which is related to that ordinance can properly be expressed. The Prophet explained that baptism in water is made "to answer the likeness of the dead, that one principle might accord with the other." "To be immersed in the water and come forth out of the water," he continued, "is in the likeness of the resurrection of the dead in coming forth out of their graves." But in the case of baptism for the dead there should be an added symbolism. "Consequently," he observed, "the baptismal font was instituted as a similitude of the grave, and was commanded to be in a place underneath where the living are wont to assemble, to show forth the living and the dead, and that all things may have their likeness, and that they may accord one with another—that which is earthly conforming to that which is heavenly."[58]

Recording of Baptisms for Dead

The law governing the administration of baptisms for the dead required that a recorder be present to record the ordinance, and that witnesses observe it. Writing by revelation, Joseph Smith instructed: "When any of you are baptized for your dead, let there be a recorder, and let him be eye-witness of your baptisms; let him hear with his ears, that he may testify of a truth, saith the Lord."[59] Again he wrote: "Let him [the recorder] be very particular and precise in taking the whole proceedings, certifying in his record that he saw with his eyes, and heard with his ears, giving the date, and names, and so forth, and the history of the whole transaction; naming also some three individuals that are present, if there be any present, who can at any time when called upon certify to the same, that in the mouth of two or three witnesses every word may be established."[60]

The Prophet admitted that this order of things was "very particular," but explained: "Let me tell you that it is only to answer the will of God, by conforming to the ordinance and preparation that the Lord ordained and prepared before the foundation of the world, for the salvation of the dead who should die without a knowledge of the gospel."[61] For authoritative acts to be binding on earth and in heaven they must be recorded properly. Otherwise the power to seal on earth and have the given action binding in heaven cannot be exercised in righteousness. The latter-day Seer therefore instructed the Saints: "Whatsoever you record on earth shall be recorded in heaven, and whatsoever you do not record on earth shall not be recorded in heaven."[62] The requirement to record official acts therefore is inseparably associated with a given ordinance and must be complied with if that ordinance is to be binding in heaven.

The previous quotation implies that the recording on earth of baptisms for the dead results in a corresponding action in heaven. Earthly records therefore are necessary, the Prophet explained to the Saints, "that in all your recordings it may be recorded in heaven; whatsoever you bind on earth, may be bound in heaven; whatsoever you loose on earth may be loosed in heaven."[63]

Out of these two records—the earthly and the heavenly—the dead will be judged. Joseph Smith explained: "John the Revelator was contemplating this very subject in relation to the dead, when he declared, as you will find recorded in Revelation 20:12—'And I saw the dead, small and great, stand before God; and *the books* were opened; and *another book* was opened, which is the book of life; and the dead were judged out of those things which were written in the books, according to their works.'"[64] First, John saw that certain books were opened; then he stated that another book was opened, which is the book of life. Of the first records, Joseph Smith said: "The books spoken of must be the books which contain the record of their works, and refer to the records which are kept on the earth."[65] He then explained to the Saints: "Out of the books shall your dead be judged, according to their own works, whether they themselves have attended to the ordinance in their own *propria persona,* or by the means of their own agents, according to the ordinance which God has prepared for their salvation from before the foundation of the world, according to the records which they have kept concerning their dead."[66] Concerning the second record which John saw, the Prophet said: "The book which was the book of life is the record which is kept in heaven."[67] In referring to the judgment in light of these two sets of records, Orson Pratt said:

> The sacred books kept in the archives of eternity are to be opened in the great judgment day, and compared with the records kept on the earth; and then, if it is found that things have been done by the authority and commandment of the Most High, in relation to the dead, and the same things are found to be recorded both on earth and in heaven, such sacred books will be opened and read before the assembled universe in the day of judgment, and will be sanctioned by Him who sits on the throne and deals out justice and mercy to all of his creation.[68]

Joseph Smith also placed the keeping of records in context with the doctrine that there is a series of major councils, some past and some to be held in the future, by which the inhabitants of the earth are organized in preparation for their eternal existence in the resurrection.[69] It is important that accurate and authentic records be kept of all transactions by which the divine patriarchal order is built up among the living and the dead, that such records may be presented in a final Grand Council where all things pertaining to the divine family order will be checked before the righteous are prepared for eternity. The Prophet said:

> All persons baptized for the dead must have a recorder present, that he may be an eyewitness to record and testify of the truth and validity of his record. *It will be necessary, in the Grand Council, that these things be testified to by competent witnesses.* Therefore let the recording and witnessing of baptisms for the dead be carefully attended to from this time forth. If there is any lack, it may be at the expense of our friends; they may not come forth.[70]

Administration Of Higher Ordinances For Dead

Because the plan of the gospel does not end with the obedient being born into the kingdom of God as sons and daughters of Jesus Christ, those who receive the ordinances of rebirth vicariously must also be given the rites and ordinances of the temple which are necessary to become fathers and mothers spiritually under Christ in the divine patriarchal order. And their children must be sealed to them within the celestial order. For these reasons, Joseph Smith explained: "It is not only necessary that you should be baptized for your dead, but you will have to go through all the ordinances for them, the same as you have gone through to save yourselves."[71] This meant that the Saints would have to receive "all the ordinances, baptisms, confirmations, . . . ordinations and sealing powers upon their heads, in behalf of all their progenitors who are dead."[72] Again the Prophet said: "Every man who wishes to save his father, mother, brothers, sisters and friends, must go through all the ordinances for each one of them separately, the same as for himself, from baptism to ordination, . . . and receive all the keys and powers of the Priesthood, the same as for himself."[73] Orson Pratt reasoned:

> If baptism for the dead is true, every other divine ordinance is equally true and necessary for the dead, for one is just as consistent as the other. The laying on of hands in confirmation upon a person that is living here in the flesh, for and in behalf of those who are in their graves, is just as consistent as baptism for the dead.
>
> Again, if our fathers and mothers, grandfathers and grandmothers, have died without being married by divine authority, the same authority that would cause a people to act for the dead in relation to baptism, would cause them to act for and in behalf of the dead in relation to their marriage ceremonies too. Such a plan gives them all a chance.[74]

Summary

Joseph Smith affirmed that men in his day knew very little about the plan of life and salvation, particularly as it relates to those who have not had the opportunity to hear and embrace the gospel in mortality. God is more liberal in His views than man may suppose. He treats all men with justice, mercy, and equity. His work of saving man does not terminate when man passes from mortality.

Contrary conclusions are not scriptural and are worse than atheism. Man may learn the gospel after death, and all men will attain a degree of salvation commensurate with their worthiness, except those who rebel wilfully against truth and refuse to repent. Before the earth was created, God made provision for the salvation of all men. If the plan of life and salvation did not reach a person in mortality, it would be extended to him in the spirit world after death. In these provisions the justice and mercy of God are revealed and reconciled.

The Prophet made it clear that there is a baptism for men who are alive and a baptism for the dead who die without the knowledge of the gospel. This doctrine is supported by biblical evidence and is based upon the right and power of the priesthood to perform acts authoritatively on earth and have them sealed or loosed in heaven according to its decree. Here, as in the atonement, the plan of salvation rests upon a vicarious principle.

The doctrine of baptism for the dead was first taught by the Prophet at the funeral services of Colonel Seymour Brunson, August 15, 1840. He later made it clear that such ordinances should be performed according to a strict order in temples built for that purpose. The dead will be judged according to these records as well as those which are kept in heaven. The same general principles hold true in regard to the higher ordinances of the gospel by which the divine patriarchal order is organized and perpetuated in eternity.

Notes

1. HC, IV, p. 595.
2. *Ibid.,* V, p. 136.
3. *Ibid.,* IV, p. 595.
4. *Ibid.,* pp. 595–596.
5. *Ibid.,* p. 596.
6. *Ibid.,* pp. 596–597. On the extent of Christ's forgiveness, Joseph Smith said on another occasion: "All sins shall be forgiven, except the sin against the Holy Ghost; for Jesus will save all except the sons of perdition."—*Ibid.,* VI, p. 314.
7. *Ibid.,* IV, pp. 597–598. This statement should not be construed to mean that the Prophet condoned death-bed repentance. He said:

> We should take warning and not wait for the death-bed to repent. . . .

It is the will of God that man should repent and serve Him in health, and in the strength and power of his mind, in order to secure his blessings, and not wait until he is called to die.—*Ibid.*, p. 554.

8. *Ibid.*, pp. 425–426.
9. *Ibid.*, p. 426.
10. *Ibid.*, pp. 597, 598.
11. *Ibid.*, p. 598.
12. *Ibid.*, p. 575.
13. *Ibid.*, p. 425.
14. The Prophet's teachings on this subject will be treated in volume IV of this work.
15. HC, VI, pp. 313–314.
16. *Ibid.*
17. *Ibid.*, IV, p. 597.
18. *Ibid.*, VI, p. 313.
19. *Ibid.*, p. 314.
20. *Ibid.*, IV, p. 598.
21. *Ibid.*, p. 231.
22. *Ibid.*, p. 426.
23. *Ibid.*, p. 599.
24. *Ibid.*, p. 425.
25. D&C 128:19. The breadth of divine mercy which is expressed in the plan of salvation as it pertains to the dead was spoken of by other prominent Latter-day Saints. Orson Pratt declared: "It is the most charitable doctrine that was ever preached to the nations of the earth."—JD, VII, p. 88. George Q. Cannon said: "To my mind there is something godlike in the Gospel of salvation. I can see beauty, and the power of God in it. I understand from this that there is a plan of salvation capable of saving all men."—*Ibid.*, XIV, p. 319.
26. HC, VI, p. 365. In support of this statement, it may be noted that the Apostle Paul lists "the doctrine of *baptisms*" as well as the "laying on of hands" for the gift of the Holy Ghost in his delineation of the first principles and ordinances of the gospel. See Hebrews 6:1–2.
27. *Ibid.*, IV, p. 231.
28. *Ibid.*, VI, pp. 365–366.
29. *Ibid.*, IV, pp. 426, 569.
30. *Ibid.*, p. 231.
31. JD, XIV, p. 318. For similar commentaries by Orson Pratt, see *ibid.*, VII, p. 82; XVIII, p. 52.
32. HC, IV, p. 569.
33. *Ibid.*, V, p. 425.
34. *Ibid.*, IV, p. 569.
35. JD, VII, p. 83. See, for example, Matthew 16:19; 18:18.
36. D&C 128:8, 9.
37. JD, VII, pp. 83–84.
38. HC, IV, p. 425.
39. JD, V, p. 90.
40. *Ibid.*, VII, p. 85.
41. *Ibid.*, XIV, p. 318. For Malachi's prophecy, see Malachi 4:5–6.
42. JD, XVI, p. 165.
43. *Ibid.*, XIV, p. 317.

44. *Ibid.,* XVI, p. 165.
45. HC, II, p. 380.
46. *Ibid.,* III, p. 29.
47. Brigham Young placed the date at "about the year 1840–41."—JD, XVI, p. 165.
48. HC, IV, p. 231.
49. *Journal History,* August 15, 1840. The widow to whom the Prophet referred was Jane Harper Neymon. She later reported that after Joseph Smith introduced this subject, he said: "I have laid the subject of baptism for the dead before you. You may receive or reject it as you choose." Sister Neymon then went and was baptized by Harvey Olmstead for her son Cyrus Livingston Neymon. Vienna Jaques witnessed the ordinance by riding into the river on horseback to get close enough to hear the ceremony. When the form of the ceremony was related to the Prophet, he sanctioned it as being correct.—See *ibid.*

When the ordinance of baptism for the dead was first revealed, men were permitted to be baptized for women and women for men. But this was later changed so that men could be baptized only for men and women only for women, that a given individual might continue and perform all the required ordinances for a deceased person. For explanations by Wilford Woodruff, Brigham Young, and Orson Pratt, see JD, V, pp. 84–85, XVI, pp. 165–166, 335.
50. Discourse of Brigham Young at Nauvoo, April 6, 1845; handwritten copy of the address in "Brigham Young, Addresses, 1843–1845," Church Historian's Library, Salt Lake City, Utah.
51. See D&C 127, 128.
52. HC, VI, p. 319.
53. *Ibid.,* p. 365.
54. *Ibid.,* V, p. 424.
55. D&C 124:36.
56. D&C 124:29–31, 33.
57. JD, VII, p. 86.
58. D&C 128:12–13.
59. D&C 127:6.
60. D&C 128:3. See also HC, V, p. 141.
61. D&C 128:5.
62. D&C 128:8.
63. D&C 127:7.
64. D&C 128:6.
65. D&C 128:7.
66. D&C 128:8.
67. D&C 128:7.
68. JD, VII, p. 84. For another statement by Elder Pratt, see *ibid.,* XVI, pp. 259–260.
69. See Volume I of this study, the section in chapter eleven entitled "The Grand Organizational Council."
70. HC, V, p. 141.
71. *Ibid.,* VI, p. 365.
72. *Ibid.,* p. 184.
73. *Ibid.,* p. 319. See also *ibid.,* V, p. 425.
74. JD, XVIII, p. 53. See also *ibid.,* XVI, p. 259, for another statement by Orson Pratt.

18

Saviors on Mount Zion

And saviours shall come up on mount Zion to judge the mount of Esau; and the kingdom shall be the Lord's. —OBADIAH.

Joseph Smith stated that "it is no more incredible that God should *save* the dead, than that he should *raise* the dead."[1] But in the work of saving the human family, much had to be done. The gospel had to be taught in the spirit world after mortal death, the ordinances of the plan of life and salvation had to be administered on earth vicariously for the dead, and those who became sons and daughters of Jesus Christ in all ages of time had to be organized into one great family under the Son of God, their celestial Father. The Prophet taught that by helping to accomplish this work the Saints would become "saviors on mount Zion." They would do something for the dead which was important to their salvation and which the dead could not do for themselves.

Divine Plan For Saving Dead

Gospel Program in Spirit World

"The spirits in the eternal world are like the spirits [which are embodied] in this world," Joseph Smith explained.[2] "They now exist in a place where they converse together the same as we do on the earth."[3] Again he stated:

> In this world, mankind are naturally selfish, ambitious and striving to excel one above another; yet some are willing to build up others as well as themselves. So in the other world there are a variety of spirits.[4]

The spirits of the dead, whether righteous or wicked, go to the spirit world after mortality with the same basic dispositions which they manifested on earth. The Prophet explained:

> There has been much said about the word hell, and the sectarian world have preached much about it, describing it to be a burning lake of fire and brimstone. But what is hell? It is [a] . . . modern term, and is taken from hades. . . .
>
> Hades, the Greek, or Sheol, the Hebrew, these two significations mean a world of spirits. Hades, Sheol, paradise, spirits in prison, are all one: it is a world of spirits.
>
> The righteous and the wicked all go to the same world of spirits until the resurrection.[5]

In making this statement, the Prophet meant that the differences which exist among spirits in the spirit world are those which pertain to *state* and not *place.* The wicked suffer a withdrawal of the Spirit of God which results in their being in a state of spiritual darkness or hell,[6] according to the degree of their depravity. But the righteous are endowed with the Spirit or glory of God to a great degree,[7] and they congregate together in places where they enjoy the blessings of the priesthood and the gospel.

Righteous spirits minister in the authority and power of the priesthood to those in the spirit world who will receive the truth and light of the gospel. Joseph Smith taught that "the keys of power and knowledge" are with the spirits of the just.[8] All who do not hear the gospel on earth, therefore, are privileged to hear it "in the spirit, through the instrumentality of those who have been commissioned to preach to them while in [spirit] prison."[9]

To support these points, Joseph Smith cited the Apostle Peter's statement that Jesus "went and preached unto the spirits in prison, which sometimes were disobedient, when once the long-suffering of God waited in the days of Noah."[10] "Here then we have an account of our Savior preaching to the spirits in prison," the Prophet explained, "to spirits that had been imprisoned from the days of Noah."[11] In this function, "Jesus Christ became a ministering spirit (while His body was lying in the sepulchre) to the spirits in prison, to fulfill an important part of His mission, without which He could not have perfected His work, or entered into His rest."[12] The Prophet said on another occasion:

> There has been much said by modern divines about the words of Jesus (when on the cross) to the thief, saying, "This day shalt thou be with me in paradise." King James' translators make it out to say paradise. But what is paradise? It is a modern word: it does not answer at all to the original word that Jesus made use of. Find the original of the word paradise. You may as easily find a needle in a haymow. Here is a chance for battle, ye learned men. There is nothing in the original word in Greek from which this was taken that signifies paradise; but it was—This day thou shalt be with me in the world of spirits: then I will teach you all about it and answer your inquiries. And Peter says he went and preached to the world of spirits (spirits in prison, I Peter, 3rd chap. 19th verse), so that they who would receive it could have it answered by proxy by those who live on the earth, etc.[13]

Joseph F. Smith, nephew of the Prophet and later President of the Church, was shown in vision the ministry of Christ to the spirit world. He beheld that Jesus ministered personally only to the righteous who awaited with great joy and anticipation His coming to the spirit world. "But unto the wicked he did not go, and among the ungodly and the unrepentant who had defiled themselves while in the flesh, his voice was not raised, neither did the rebellious who rejected the testimonies and the warnings of the ancient prophets behold his presence, nor look upon his face." Instead, from among the righteous, Christ "organized his forces and appointed messengers, clothed with power and authority, and commissioned them to go forth and carry the light of the gospel to them that were in darkness, even to all the spirits of men." In this way, the gospel was preached to the dead.[14]

There are three classes of beings who need the ministry of the priesthood in the spirit world in order to achieve a degree of salvation: (1) those who never had the opportunity to hear the gospel in mortality but who would have received it had they been given that privilege; (2) those who failed in the ages before mortality to prepare themselves to obey a celestial law and who therefore come to earth as heathen nations, where they live without that law, die without it, and are redeemed without it;[15] and (3) those who hear the gospel on earth and reject it while in the flesh, but who later are called to repentance in the spirit world and receive a degree of salvation according to their ability to live the laws of life. The last-named group may be divided into two general classes: (1) those who reject the gospel on earth but repent after suffering the judgments of God in spirit prison,[16] and (2) those who are thrust "down to hell and suffer the wrath of Almighty God, until the fulness of times [after the millennium], when Christ shall have subdued all enemies under his feet, and shall have perfected his work."[17]

When those who would receive the gospel come to mortality under circumstances which do not give them the opportunity to hear its inspired message, because of the apostasy, wickedness, or false traditions of their fathers, they are still candidates for celestial glory. By revelation to Joseph Smith, the Lord said:

> All who have died without a knowledge of this Gospel, who would have received it if they had been permitted to tarry, shall be heirs of the celestial kingdom of God; also all that shall die henceforth without a knowledge of it, who would have received it with all their hearts, shall be heirs of that kingdom, for I, the Lord, will judge all men according to their works, according to the desire of their hearts.[18]

Concerning the basis upon which salvation is given to this class of spirits, Orson Pratt said:

> Those spirits of our fathers whose bodies are in their graves

> can repent, for they have not lost their agency; they can believe in Jesus Christ, for that is an act of the mind: they can reform from every evil, because they are agents; for it is the spirit that can do good or evil. That same being, called the spirit, can repent in the eternal worlds as well as here; it can believe in Jesus Christ and in his atonement in the eternal worlds as well as here: and if the Gospel is preached to them there, they can receive it there, so far as the acts of the mind are concerned; but they could not receive baptism there, for that is an ordinance pertaining to the body: it is an outward ordinance—an ordinance instituted particularly for those that are in the flesh.[19]

Except for obeying the outward ordinances of the gospel, those who are in the spirit world may therefore do all that is necessary to accept and apply the principles of the plan of life and salvation in their lives.

Little has been revealed concerning the program of salvation which is given to those who die and are redeemed without celestial law. Joseph Smith referred to them as "the heathen of ages *that never had hope.*"[20] They are destined to come forth in the first resurrection after Christ has appeared in glory and ushered in the millennium. That which they receive will be "tolerable" for them; it will coincide with their ability to live the laws of God and to enjoy the blessings of salvation.[21] But in general their place in eternity will be the terrestrial kingdom of glory.[22] Aside from bringing about the resurrection and glorification of this class of beings, it is not known specifically how the priesthood ministers in the spirit world to facilitate their salvation. Presumably they must be taught concerning Christ and the requirements of terrestrial salvation.

As has been indicated, the program of preaching glad tidings of salvation in the spirit world also extends to those who hear the gospel on earth but reject it while in the flesh. The spirits of those who perished in the flood in Noah's day are an example of this group. They were born into a corrupt social order which had been built up in earlier ages by the wickedness of their fathers. Nevertheless, the gospel was preached to them, and they rejected it. Concerning them, the Lord said to Enoch:

> . . . they are without affection, and they hate their own blood; and the fire of mine indignation is kindled against them; and in my hot displeasure will I send in the floods upon them, for my fierce anger is kindled against them. . . .
>
> But behold, *their sins shall be upon the heads of their fathers;* Satan shall be their father, and misery shall be their doom; and the whole heavens shall weep over them, even all the workmanship of mine hands; wherefore should not the heavens weep, seeing these shall suffer?
>
> But behold, these which thine eyes are upon shall perish in the floods; and behold, I will shut them up; a prison have I prepared for them.
>
> And that which I have chosen [i.e., Christ] hath plead before my face. Wherefore, *he suffereth for their sins, inasmuch as they will repent in the day that my Chosen shall return unto me* [after making the atonement], and until that day they shall be in torment.[23]

Not being fully responsible for their sins, those who perished in the flood were consigned to prison in the spirit world, while their fathers who built up the corrupt social order in antediluvian times were sent to hell.[24] Enoch was shown the state of these two classes of men at the time of Christ's resurrection. Having first noted that the righteous from the days of Adam to Christ were resurrected with the Master, the record of Enoch's vision states: "And as many of the spirits as were in prison came forth, and stood on the right hand of God; and the remainder [i.e., those who had been consigned to hell] were reserved in chains of darkness until the judgment of the great day."[25]

The report of Enoch's vision does not indicate specifically what is meant by the statement that the spirits in prison "came forth."[26] They apparently came forth from spirit prison, but it is not clear whether or not they were then resurrected. Nor is it known what program they were required to obey in order to be redeemed. Their final state in the resurrection will be the terrestrial kingdom of glory.[27] Of such characters and others, Joseph Smith wrote: "A man may be saved, after the judgment, in the terrestrial kingdom, or in the telestial kingdom, but he can never see the celestial kingdom of God without being born of water and the Spirit."[28] Apparently the ordinances of baptism and the laying on of hands for the gift of the Holy Ghost are not necessary for redemption to any kingdom but the celestial. Repentance and some degree of faith in Jesus Christ, however, are necessary for redemption to the terrestrial kingdom.[29]

A fate similar to that which befell those who perished in the flood awaits the wicked in the last days. On this point, Joseph Smith quoted Isaiah's prophecy concerning the judgments which will be meted out when Christ comes to "punish the host of the high ones that are on high, and the kings of the earth upon the earth." Of the wicked at that time, Isaiah said: "They shall be gathered together, as prisoners are gathered in the pit, and shall be shut up in the prison, *and after many days shall they be visited.*" "As the antediluvians had their day of visitation," the Prophet concluded, "so will those characters referred to by Isaiah, have their time of visitation and deliverance, after having been many days in prison."[30]

As Enoch's vision indicates, the wicked who wilfully pervert the ways of the Lord and are thrust down to hell do not receive the program of salvation by which they can be redeemed "until the judgment of the great day,"[31] which will be after the millennium. Their place in eternity will be the telestial kingdom of glory.[32] Little has been revealed concerning the principles of salvation which they will have to embrace, aside from the principle of repentance. A revelation states that these are they who receive not "the gospel, neither the testimony of Jesus, neither the prophets, neither the everlasting covenant."[33] They will be required to repent, however, and in doing so they will receive a forgiveness of sins.[34] A revelation also said of them: "These all shall bow the knee, and every tongue shall confess to him who sits upon the throne forever and ever; for they shall be judged according to their works, and every man shall receive according to his own works, his own dominion, in the mansions which are prepared."[35]

Thus the plan of salvation will eventually be proclaimed to all who dwell in the spirit world; and after the unrighteous have suffered the judgments of God, all who repent will be redeemed to a state of glory according to the degree of truth they are willing to receive and are able to apply.[36] Joseph Smith explained:

> So long as a man will not give heed to the commandments, he must abide without salvation. . . . But when he consents to obey the Gospel, whether here or in the world of spirits, he is saved.
>
> A man is his own tormentor and his own condemner. . . . All will suffer until they obey Christ.[37]

By refusing to obey the gospel, man fails to prepare himself to live a higher law and achieve a greater glory in the resurrection. He is therefore his own condemner. In failing to repent, man also subjects himself to the judgments of God on earth and in the spirit world.

Need of Earthly Ordinances

Man's existence on earth does not end at mortal death. This earth is his home; the righteous will dwell upon it again after they and the earth have been glorified.[38] Joseph Smith taught that the divine principles and ordinances of the gospel which lead man to life and light in the presence of God are revealed to him "in view of no eternal dissolution of the body, or tabernacle."[39] As earthly ordinances, they pertain to his existence on this sphere now and in eternity. They therefore must be performed on the earth by the authority which has been given to man on this sphere. All those who attain residence on the earth in its celestial state must officially enter the divine patriarchal order (which consists of the celestial family of Christ) by subscribing to the articles of adoption by which they become sons and daughters of the Master, and they must be organized and sealed in their respective places within the divine family order by receiving the higher ordinances and covenants which are administered in the house of the Lord. The Prophet explained:

The Lord has an established law in relation to the matter: there must be a particular spot for the salvation of our dead. I verily believe there will be a place, and hence men who want to save their dead can come and bring their families, do their work by being baptized and attending to the other ordinances for their dead, and then may go back again to live and wait till they go to receive their reward.[40]

Perfecting The Divine Patriarchal Order

Divine Patriarchal Order in Past Generations

The Prophet held that the coming of Elijah made it possible for the Saints to organize themselves according to the divine patriarchal order and to extend that sanctified family order to past generations, thereby uniting the righteous of the whole human family into one divine system under Christ. Concerning Malachi's prophecy that Elijah would be sent in the latter days, Joseph Smith said: "The Bible says, 'I will send you Elijah the Prophet before the coming of the great and dreadful day of the Lord; and he shall turn the heart of the fathers to the children, and the heart of the children to the fathers, lest I come and smite the earth with a curse.'"[41] The latter-day Seer then commented: "Now, the word *turn* here should be translated bind, or *seal.*"[42] Thus the children were to be sealed to the fathers by the coming of Elijah. In stressing that the sealing of children to worthy parents was to extend to past generations, he said:

Was this [action of sealing children to parents] merely confined to the living, to settle difficulties with families on earth? By no means. It was a far greater work. Elijah! what would you do if you were here? Would you confine your work to the living alone? No; I would refer you to the Scriptures, where the subject is manifest: that is, without us, they could not be made perfect, nor we without them; the fathers without the children, nor the children without the fathers.

I wish you to understand this subject, for it is important; and if you receive it, this is the spirit of Elijah, *that we redeem our dead, and connect ourselves with our fathers which are in heaven,* and seal up our dead to come forth in the first resurrection; and here we want the power of Elijah *to seal those who dwell on earth to those who dwell in heaven.* This is the power of Elijah and the keys to the [patriarchal] kingdom of Jehovah.[43]

Gathering of All Things Together in Christ

The kingdom of Christ is patriarchal in nature. And it is designed to gather together in Jesus, both on earth and in heaven,[44] all those who become the sons and daughters of the Master by baptism. To this end, those who embrace the gospel must be organized into a sanctified family order and sealed to their worthy parents and forebears in all past generations, until every worthy descendant of Adam is established in the celestial family under Christ. For this reason Elijah was to come. Joseph Smith said: "He shall send Elijah, the Prophet, &c., and restore [i.e., gather together] all things in Christ."[45] Again he explained:

> The hearts of the children of men will have to be turned to the fathers and the fathers to the children, living or dead, to prepare them for the coming of the Son of Man. If Elijah did not come, the whole earth would be smitten.[46]

The angel Moroni referred to the work of perfecting the divine patriarchal order through the program of the latter-day dispensation when he quoted with significant clarifying phrases Malachi's prophecy concerning the coming of Elijah. The heavenly messenger declared that by the priesthood which Elijah would reveal, the promises which God gave to the ancient patriarchs or fathers (those promises which were related to the divine patriarchal order in past ages) would be planted in the hearts of the children—given to the obedient of their children in the latter days. Of the results which would follow this action, Moroni said: " . . . and the hearts of the children shall turn to their fathers. If it were not so, the whole earth would be utterly wasted at his [Christ's] coming."[47]

The fact that the hearts of the children would turn to their fathers implies that, after the coming of Elijah, many people would seek for knowledge concerning their ancestors. Interest in genealogical research would spring up in the hearts of men, particularly among the Latter-day Saints. "If Elijah the Prophet is to be sent before the great and dreadful day of the Lord to turn the hearts of the children to the fathers," Orson Pratt reasoned, "you may be assured that we shall learn something about the genealogy of those fathers."[48] Of the interest in genealogical research which began to develop after Elijah came, Elder Pratt said:

> A great many have wondered why so many people in the eastern, southern and middle States have been stirred up for a number of years past in searching out their ancestors. Now the Lord does a great many things unknown to the people, and this is one of them. The people do not know why they are interested in their ancestry, but they are wrought upon by some invisible operation, and they feel very anxious to know about their progenitors.[49]

Malachi's prophecy, when viewed in light of the divine patriarchal order and the need to extend the blessings of that system to past generations, implies that temples would be built and a great work inaugurated to administer the ordinances thereof in behalf of the dead. For this reason Joseph Smith associated baptism for the dead with the work of establishing the "ancient order of things" upon the earth. He wrote: "As the great purposes of God are hastening to their accomplishment, and the things spoken of in the prophets are fulfilling, as the kingdom of God is established on the earth, and the ancient order of things restored, the Lord has manifested to us this day and privilege, and we are commanded to be baptized for our dead."[50] He might have added that the Saints were also instructed to perform the higher ordinances of the gospel in behalf of the dead.

It is because the gospel plan has the objective of uniting the faithful of all ages in Christ, which will be realized for the righteous of past ages as the millennial kingdom of Christ is ushered in,[51] that the latter-day dispensation of the gospel is called the Dispensation of the Fulness of Times. Joseph Smith taught that through the coming of Elijah, God would "restore all things in Christ." Largely as a result of

Elijah's mission, he said, "the dispensation of the fullness of times will bring to light the things that have been revealed in all former dispensations; also other things that have not been before revealed."[52] Having quoted Malachi's prophecy of the coming of Elijah, Joseph Smith continued:

> It is sufficient to know, in this case, that the earth will be smitten with a curse unless there is a welding link of some kind or other between the fathers and the children, upon some subject or other—and behold what is that subject? It is the baptism for the dead. For we without them cannot be made perfect; neither can they without us be made perfect. Neither can they nor we be made perfect without those who have died in the gospel also; *for it is necessary in the ushering in of the dispensation of the fulness of times, which dispensation is now beginning to usher in, that a whole and complete and perfect union, and welding together of dispensations, and keys, and powers, and glories should take place, and be revealed from the days of Adam even to the present time.* And not only this, but those things which never have been revealed from the foundation of the world, but have been kept hid from the wise and prudent, shall be revealed unto babes and sucklings in this, the dispensation of the fulness of times.[53]

This is a work unlike that which has been accomplished in any previous dispensation; no other dispensation of the gospel has been commissioned to fulfil such a mission. "It is true they were gathered from time to time in the heavens," Orson Pratt observed, "to wait there for the time when all the righteous of this globe should be gathered into one vast assembly—the fathers with the children, and the children with the fathers."[54] But the work of consummating the great task and of perfecting the divine patriarchal order for all ages was reserved for the saints in the last days. Joseph Smith explained that for this reason "it is necessary that the sealing power should be in our hands to seal our children and our dead for the fulness of the dispensation of times."[55]

Interdependence of Man

Joseph Smith taught that salvation is not solely an individual matter. The faithful are saved and exalted only in family units, and only as they become united by the sealing powers of the priesthood with the righteous of Adam's children in all generations of the earth. "It is necessary that those who are going before and those who come after us should have salvation in common with us," the Prophet explained; "and thus hath God made it obligatory upon men." For this reason, he continued: "God said, 'I will send you Elijah the prophet before the coming of the great and dreadful day of the Lord: and he shall turn the heart of the fathers to the children, and the heart of the children to their fathers, lest I come and smite the earth with a curse.'"[56]

The interdependence of individuals within the human family is evidenced upon every hand, both in the immediate family circle and in society at large, so much so that it assumes the position of a law of nature. "No man is an island; no man stands alone," either in life or in salvation. Even trials and afflictions, though not experienced personally by all, may teach man the meaning of tribulations and the value of opposition. When by expressing pure love man achieves true empathy (not merely sympathy) with the afflicted and distressed, he not only may observe but may share measurably in the refining benefits of their experiences. The same is true of the benefits that come from the joyous experiences of others. The man who lives outside himself in true love of others thereby achieves a perception of life and its meaning which more contracted souls never acquire. He learns vicariously. By pure love he is knit to humanity in a union which adds depth and meaning to his soul. He becomes a man of sorrow, and he is acquainted with grief. Yet peace and joy predominate in his heart. Through human experience he acquires qualities which are divine.

God's program for saving the dead is founded upon an expanded expression of the principle of man's interdependence. Joseph Smith called the cementing or binding force within this great program the spirit of Elijah, which is the divine spirit or power which binds the heart of man in the gospel to the home, to the family, and to humanity at large within the divine patriarchal order. By this spirit, the sons and daughters of Jesus in all ages of time are united together, thus restoring "all things in Christ."[57]

According to the Prophet and his associates, it was necessary for the hearts of the fathers to turn to their children on earth in three ways in order for the divine patriarchal order of the earth to be established and perfected. Concerning the first way, Joseph Smith said: "We cannot be perfect without the fathers, &c. *We must have revelation from them.*"[58] By revelation from the fathers, the great and eternal plan of life and salvation was revealed again to men on earth, expressed in and through the divine patriarchal order.

Second, by the ministrations of the ancient patriarchs and prophets, the priesthood was restored to earth with its divine keys and powers. "Had it not been for the fathers that are dead, where would have been the Priesthood?" Orson Pratt inquired. "Is there any possible way by which the people calling themselves Latter-day Saints could have been benefited by the authority and Priesthood of heaven, unless it were through our fathers who were sent from heaven, holding the authority and conferring it upon the children, that they might officiate in behalf of those who died without the knowledge of the Gospel?"[59]

Third, the Prophet taught that, as agents beyond the veil, the fathers are to participate in the great work of gathering their children into the divine patriarchal order in the last days. In referring to the ancient patriarchs and prophets, he said:

> These men are in heaven, but their children are on the earth. Their bowels yearn over us. . . . *All these authoritative characters will come down and join hand in hand in bringing about this work.*
>
> The Kingdom of Heaven is like a grain of mustard seed. The mustard seed is small, but brings forth a large tree, and the fowls lodge in the branches. *The fowls are the angels.* Thus angels come down, combine together *to gather their children,* and gather them.

We cannot be made perfect without them, nor they without us.[60]

There are three ways in which the hearts of the children must turn to their fathers in order for the divine patriarchal order of the earth to be built up and perfected: First, the children on earth must help seek out and gather into the gospel from the nations and peoples of the earth the latter-day descendants of the fathers. In his preparatory work, the spirit of Elias, which is the spirit of the gospel or of the divine patriarchal order, is made manifest to bring the obedient to the eternal family of Jesus Christ.

Second, the children must seek out the genealogies of their fathers so that the necessary information may be known and used for performing the ordinance of baptism for the dead and for organizing and sealing family units together within the divine patriarchal order.

Third, the children must build temples and officiate in them for and in behalf of their dead kindred, in all the rites and ordinances of the gospel which are necessary to extend the divine patriarchal order to past generations, with all its blessings, rights, and powers.

The Prophet spoke repeatedly of the responsibility of the Saints to their worthy ancestors. On one occasion he said:

> I will open your eyes in relation to your dead. All things whatsoever God in his infinite wisdom has seen fit and proper to reveal to us, while we are dwelling in mortality, in regard to our mortal bodies, are revealed to us in the abstract, and independent of affinity of this mortal tabernacle, but are revealed to our spirits precisely as though we had no bodies at all; and those revelations which will save our spirits will save our bodies. God reveals them to us in view of no eternal dissolution of the body, or tabernacle. Hence the responsibility, the awful responsibility, that rests upon us in relation to our dead; for all the spirits who have not obeyed the Gospel in the flesh must either obey it in the spirit or be damned.[61]

At another time Joseph Smith spoke of the need to perfect the divine patriarchal order of the earth by the Saints performing the higher ordinances of the gospel in behalf of the worthy dead and connecting themselves to the ancient patriarchs. "We cannot be made perfect without them," he declared, "nor they without us."[62] He therefore stressed: "The greatest responsibility in this world that God has laid upon us is to seek after our dead. The apostle says, 'They without us cannot be made perfect.'"[63] "This doctrine was the burden of the scriptures," he declared on another occasion. "Those Saints who neglect it in behalf of their deceased relatives, do it at the peril of their own salvation."[64] Having explained that Jesus sought to gather the Jews in His day "that they might attend to the ordinance of baptism for the dead as well as other ordinances of the priesthood, and . . . be perfected in the things of the kingdom of God,"[65] the Prophet said:

> Hence it was that so great a responsibility rested upon the generation in which our Savior lived, for, says he, "That upon you may come all the righteous blood shed upon the earth, from the blood of righteous Abel unto the blood of Zacharias, son of Barachias, whom ye slew between the temple and the altar. Verily I say unto you, all these things shall come upon this generation." (Matthew xxiii:35, 36.) Hence *as they possessed greater privileges than any other generation, not only pertaining to themselves, but to their dead, their sin was greater, as they not only neglected their own salvation but that of their progenitors, and hence their blood was required at their hands.*[66]

Need for Revelation to Perfect the Divine Patriarchal Order

Joseph Smith taught that all things which pertain to the establishment of the divine patriarchal order must be "governed by the principle of revelation,"[67] and that man's endeavor to acquire such blessings "without law, without revelation, without commandment" can only lead to "everlasting regret."[68] Particularly in the final stages of the work of perfecting the divine patriarchal order, revelation may be necessary to supply missing genealogies and to instruct the earthly officiators in the work which is to be accomplished. Orson Pratt said:

> We shall learn by the spirit of revelation whom to be

baptized for, and whom to officiate for in the holy ordinances of the Gospel. Herein is the necessity of revelation. Take away revelation from this great dispensation of the fulness of times, and I would not give you much for the mission of Elijah, or for the dispensation itself. Take away that great principle that always characterized all other dispensations, and you throw us into uncertainty on tens of thousands of important subjects.[69]

As Zion is built and the Saints are sanctified, many of them will receive the blessings of the second Comforter. The glory of God will eventually rest upon Zion and Jesus will mingle among the sanctified in Zion.[70] In that period of time, which will precede Christ's coming in glory in the clouds of heaven, the divine patriarchal order will be perfected in preparation for the millennial reign.[71] Joseph Smith wrote by revelation that in the period after the opening of the seventh seal and before the coming of Christ in glory, God will "complete the salvation of man, and judge all things, and shall redeem all things, except that which he hath not put into his power, when he shall have *sealed all things, unto the end of all things.*"[72] Speaking of the operation of the spirit of revelation in this great work, Orson Pratt first referred to the principle of revelation in ancient days, then said:

> So it will be in relation to the revelations of genealogies of the Saints of the living God. If they are to feel after their fathers that are dead, and redeem them by the holy ordinance of baptism, they will not go to work in the dark. . . . There will be an order in the house of God; there will be a Moses there, or, in other words, a man holding the keys and authority of these things.
>
> Moses was the great Prophet in Israel. . . . Says the Lord, . . . I will talk to him face to face, and the similitude of the Lord shall he behold. So in the dispensation of the latter days, a Moses will stand in the congregation filled with the Holy Ghost, and the spirit of revelation will be upon him, to receive instruction from the heavens in regard to the fathers and the dispensation over which he presides.[73]

According to Orson Pratt, genealogical information will also be revealed through the Urim and Thummim and by the ministry of angels. Having referred to the fact that

God deigns to reveal hidden things to the Saints in the last days, he said:

Among these hidden things that are to be revealed are the books of genealogy, tracing individuals and nations among all people, back to ancient times.

It may be inquired—"How can all this be done?" We answer, by the Urim and Thummim, which the Lord God has ordained to be used in the midst of his holy house, in his Temple. . . . When that instrument is restored to the house of God, to the Temple of the Most High, our ancestry, that is, the ancestry of all the faithful in the church of Jesus Christ of Latter-day Saints will be made manifest. Not all at once, but by degrees. Just as fast as we are able to administer for them, so will the Lord God make manifest, by the manifestation of holy angels in his house, and by the Urim and Thummim, those names that are necessary, of our ancient kindred and friends, that they may be traced back to the time when the Priesthood was on the earth in ancient times.[74]

Becoming Saviors Upon Mount Zion

Joseph Smith taught that those who extend the divine patriarchal order back through past ages, by administering the ordinances of the gospel vicariously in behalf of the dead, become saviors upon Mount Zion and fulfil the words of Obadiah, who said as he spoke "of the glory of the latter day: 'And saviors shall come up on mount Zion to judge the remnant of Esau, and the kingdom shall be the Lord's.'"[75]

According to this interpretation, Obadiah was speaking of Zion in the latter days. "Upon mount Zion shall be deliverance, and there shall be holiness," the ancient prophet wrote, "and the house of Jacob [i.e., the tribes of Israel] shall possess their possessions." Obadiah stated that "the house of Jacob shall be a fire, and the house of Joseph a flame," which may refer to the glory that will come upon Israel. Meanwhile judgments will be poured out upon the foes of Israel, including the house of Esau. Saviors will come up on Mount Zion to judge the house of Esau, by determining their worthiness to receive the saving ordinances of the gospel by which they may enter the divine patriarchal order and be exalted with the sanctified in eternity. All this will take place in that day when "the kingdom shall be the Lord's."[76]

Joseph Smith "presented baptism for the dead as the only way that men can appear as saviors on Mount Zion."[77] A savior is one who saves, or is instrumental in saving, another person. Having cited Obadiah's prophecy, George Q. Cannon explained: "There shall be saviors in the last days, acting in a lesser capacity, it is true, but still somewhat in the capacity of our Lord and Savior Jesus Christ, for their dead."[78] After inquiring how the Saints were to become saviors on Mount Zion, the Prophet said:

> By building their temples, erecting their baptismal fonts, and going forth and receiving all the ordinances, baptisms, confirmations, . . . ordinations and sealing powers upon their heads, in behalf of all their progenitors who are dead, and redeem them that they may come forth in the first resurrection and be exalted to thrones of glory with them; and herein is the chain that binds the hearts of the fathers to the children, and the children to the fathers, which fulfills the mission of Elijah.[79]

Summary

The Prophet reasoned that it is no more incredible for God to *save* the dead than it is for Him to *raise* the dead in the resurrection. To this end, the gospel is taught in the spirit world. There, righteous spirits empowered with the priesthood teach the divine truths of salvation to others, according to the ability and willingness of the recipients to receive them. Jesus initiated this work among the dead after His death on the cross, to which the Apostle Peter testified.

There are three general classes of beings who need the ministry of the priesthood in the spirit world in order to achieve a degree of salvation: First, there are those who never heard the gospel on earth but who would have received it had they had the opportunity. To these the gospel is taught in the spirit world, and for these the ordinances of the gospel are performed vicariously on earth. Second, there are those who failed in the ages before mortality to prepare themselves to be able to obey celestial law on earth and in eternity. They live on earth, die, and in general are redeemed to terrestrial glory without celestial law, and that which they receive will be "tolerable" for them.[80] It is not known what degree of truth they are required to receive in order to attain terrestrial salvation or what ordinances, if any, they must obey. Third, there are those who reject the gospel on earth but are later called to repentance in the spirit world after they have suffered the judgments of God. This class of spirits consists of two groups: First, there are those who are confined in spirit prison after death. Generally speaking, these spirits repent when the message of redemption is given to them in the spirit world,[81] and they are redeemed to terrestrial glory in the resurrection.[82] Second, there are spirits who are thrust down to hell in the spirit world for their iniquities. These are redeemed to a telestial glory in the last resurrection and judgment.[83]

By performing the ordinances of celestial redemption and exaltation in behalf of the worthy dead, the Saints can establish the divine patriarchal order among the righteous of past generations and eventually perfect the celestial family of Christ for this earth. They can gather together all things in Christ, both on earth and in heaven. In this divine program, the hearts of the fathers turn to their children on earth and the hearts of the children turn to their fathers who have passed away, as foretold by Malachi. The righteous, therefore, are dependent upon each other for ultimate salvation. The Prophet taught that the Saints were in need of revelation from the fathers. From the fathers they received the priesthood and its keys, and the fathers are to join in the work of gathering and redeeming their children in the last days. In turn, the Saints must do those things which are required to perfect the divine patriarchal order which the fathers cannot do for themselves. For this reason, Joseph Smith stressed repeatedly the responsibility which the Saints have in regard to their fathers. In many aspects of this work, they must receive revelation from heaven to guide them in their labors. But in doing the necessary work for the dead, the Saints become saviors upon mount Zion.

END VOLUME II

Notes

1. HC, IV, p. 425. (Italics in the original.)
2. *Ibid.*, V, p. 403.
3. *Ibid.*, VI, p. 311.
4. *Ibid.*, V, p. 388.
5. *Ibid.*, p. 425.
6. See Alma 34:35; 40:11–14.
7. D&C 129:1–3; HC, V, p. 315; Alma 40:11–14.
8. HC, VI, p. 51.
9. *Ibid.*, IV, p. 231. See also *ibid.*, VI, p. 365.
10. *Ibid.*, IV, p. 596, citing 1 Peter 3:19–20.
11. *Ibid.*, IV, p. 596.
12. *Ibid.*, p. 425.
13. *Ibid.*, V, p. 424–425. One should not infer from this statement that Jesus' native tongue was Greek; the Prophet was referring to the early translation of Christ's words into Greek.
14. *The Improvement Era*, XXII (December, 1918), pp. 166–170.
15. In general, this class of beings will be redeemed to terrestrial glory. See D&C 45:54; 76:72. The degrees of glory will be discussed in volume IV of this work.
16. D&C 76:73–74. This group is redeemed to terrestrial glory.
17. D&C 76:106. This group is redeemed only to telestial glory.
18. HC, II, p. 380.
19. JD, VII, pp. 82–83.
20. TS, IV (February 1, 1843), pp. 82–83.
21. D&C 45:54.
22. D&C 76:72.
23. Moses 7:33, 37–39.
24. For statements concerning God's judgment upon persons of the latter class, see D&C 76:103–106; Revelation 21:8.
25. Moses 7:57. The term "great day" means the final judgment after the millennium. See D&C 76:106–107.
26. Moses 7:57.
27. See D&C 76:73–74.
28. HC, I, p. 283.
29. Consider, for example, two points: First, it is said of those who are redeemed to terrestrial glory that they "receive not the testimony of Jesus in the flesh, but afterwards received it."—D&C 76:74. Second, Jesus saves man from, not in, his sins. See Alma 11:36–37.

30. HC, IV, pp. 596–597, citing Isaiah 24:20–22. Referring to the same prophecy, Orson Pratt said:

> You see, from these passages, that in the last days many of those kings and high ones who will not place themselves in a position to receive the Gospel, and who die ignorant of its principles, will be gathered together as prisoners in the pit, and be shut up for many days, with a fearful looking for the judgment of the great day. They will not know what is coming—what will befall them, like all prisoners guilty of crime. But after many days they shall be visited by the servants of God, as Jesus visited the antediluvians with a message: the door of their prison will be thrown open, after they have been sufficiently long confined; and if they repent, they can be redeemed; but if they will not repent, they will be taken from thence and cast into outer darkness.—JD, VII, p. 87.

31. Moses 7:57.

32. See D&C 76:81–90, 98–112.

33. D&C 76:82, 101.

34. It is here that all manner of sin will eventually be forgiven except the sin against the Holy Ghost. See Matthew 12:31.

35. D&C 76:110–111.

36. It appears that those who sin against the Holy Ghost become so darkened in mind that they will not repent even when they are subjected to the judgments of God in the spirit world. Consequently, they will be resurrected but will not be redeemed to a kingdom of glory.

37. HC, VI, p. 314.

38. D&C 88:15–20.

39. HC, VI, p. 312.

40. *Ibid.*, p. 319.

41. *Ibid.*, p. 183, citing Malachi 4:5–6.

42. HC, VI, p. 184. (Italics in the original.)

43. *Ibid.*, pp. 251–252.

44. See Ephesians 1:9–10.

45. HC, IV, p. 426.

46. *Ibid.*, III, p. 390.

47. D&C 2:2–3.

48. JD, VII, p. 86.

49. *Ibid.*, XVIII, p. 53.

50. HC, IV, p. 599.

51. A revelation refers to the early stages of the millennial era as being a time when God will "complete the salvation of man, and judge all things, and shall redeem all things, except that which he hath not put into his power, *when he shall have sealed all things, unto the end of all things.*"—D&C 77:12.

52. HC, IV, p. 426.

53. D&C 128:18.

54. JD, VII, p. 82.

55. HC, VI, p. 313.

56. *Ibid.*, citing Malachi 4:5–6.

57. HC, IV, p. 426.

58. *Ibid.*, VI, p. 252.

59. JD, VII, p. 81.

60. HC, III, p. 389.

61. *Ibid.*, VI, pp. 312–313. Brigham Young reported: "Joseph Smith said, the Lord whispers to the spirit in the tabernacle the same as though it were out of it. That is correct and true."—JD, IX, p. 287.

62. HC, III, p. 389.

63. *Ibid.*, VI, p. 313, citing Hebrews 11:37–40.

64. *Ibid.*, IV, p. 426.

65. *Ibid.*, V, p. 425.

66. *Ibid.*, IV, p. 599.

67. *Ibid.*, V, p. 2.

68. *Ibid.*, p. 135.

69. JD, VII, p. 86.

70. See for example 3 Nephi 20:22; 21:25; D&C 45:67; 97:15–16.

71. This subject will be discussed in greater detail in volume IV of this work.

72. D&C 77:12–13.

73. JD, VII, p. 87.

74. *Ibid.*, XVI, pp. 260–261.

75. HC, IV, p. 599, citing Obadiah 1:17–21.

76. Obadiah 1:17–21.

77. HC, IV, p. 425.

78. JD, XIV, pp. 318–319.

79. HC, VI, p. 184.

80. D&C 45:54; 76:72.

81. See Moses 7:37–39.

82. See D&C 76:73–74.

83. Moses 7:57; D&C 76:81–90, 98–112.

Index